BIRTH OF THE
BRAVEST

BIRTH OF THE
BRAVEST

A HISTORY OF THE

NEW YORK FIRE DEPARTMENT

from 1609 to 1887

A. E. COSTELLO

A TOM DOHERTY ASSOCIATES BOOK

NEW YORK

BIRTH OF THE BRAVEST

First published in 1887 by A. E. Costello. This is a substantially abridged version of *Our Firemen: A History of the New York Fire Departments.*

Book design by Mark Abrams

This book is printed on acid-free paper.

A Forge Book
Published by Tom Doherty Associates, LLC
175 Fifth Avenue
New York, NY 10010

www.tor.com

Forge® is a registered trademark of Tom Doherty Associates, LLC.

ISBN 0-765-30582-8

First Edition: September 2002

Printed in the United States of America

0 9 8 7 6 5 4 3 2 1

This Book is dedicated to Our Firemen.

If Prometheus was worthy of the wrath of Heaven for kindling the first fire upon earth, how ought all the gods honor the men who make it their professional business to put it out.
—John G. Saxe

CONTENTS

8   Contents

BIRTH OF THE
BRAVEST

CHAPTER I

GENESIS OF FIRE EXTINGUISHING

*1609–1664.—Manhattan Island as seen by the Discoverer, Henry Hudson.—
"A Rugged Fragment of Creation."—Primitive Fire Apparatus.—Quaint
Customs.—Dutch Architecture.—First Fire Ordinance (1648).—Fire Wardens
and Surveyors of Buildings.—The Reign of the Knickerbockers.*

In considering the history of the Fire Departments of New York City some
degree of attention must necessarily be given to a variety of subjects calculated
to illustrate the growth and rapid development of the city. And what a wonderful
story that is! What a bewildering panorama it reveals! What changes have to be
noted, what pregnant events dwelt upon, and what a wonderful tale of progress
is to be unfolded! What alterations, moreover, have occurred in the locality now
occupied by the city of New York since the ship of the discoverer first entered
its quiet waters, or even since the burgomasters and schepens of New Amsterdam
surrendered the infant metropolis to its English captors. The cluster of trading
houses and rude huts of those days has expanded into the first city of the United
States and the third largest in the world, containing over one million and a half
of inhabitants, and untold wealth. But marvelous as is this material progress, it
is not a whit more so than the story of the New York firemen. This gallant
band of citizens has been and still continues to be, the protectors and defenders
of the city in all its varied stages—from infancy to manhood. Such changes as
have been effected from time to time in the organization of the departments
have been brought about to conform to pressing public requirements and to
keep pace with the times. Hence it became necessary, at successive periods, to
pass a number of municipal ordinances regulating the force and defining their
duty. These ordinances contain a pretty comprehensive history of the doings and
operations of the firemen of our city.

It is also a noteworthy circumstance that the New World, even in its youth,
should have shown its parent how best to guard against the dreadful ravages of
fire, and how most scientifically to fight the flames which had been the terror
of the Old World.

Europe, with its ages of civilization, and with all its inventive talent, had conceived nothing like the New York Fire Departments. No transatlantic city could show so devoted a band of men as our old volunteers; and to-day our new Department stands unrivaled for efficiency. The fame of the Paid Department has crossed the seas. One of the first sights which visitors to our shores are anxious to see is a fire engine house. An exhibition drill is to them something to be remembered in after years. But the volunteers were the pioneers of the glory of the Fire Department of New York. It is not too much to say that they built up the present admirable system. They, at least, largely and directly contributed to the perfection of its organization.

Our early firemen were drawn from all ranks in life—the greater part from the most influential classes. Each man felt he had a stake in the city, and readily volunteered his services. Many of them were individually the makers of our history. As a body, they have written one of the most remarkable pages in the history of the country. A volume devoted to these gallant fellows ought, therefore, to be a very interesting one.

As we have already intimated, we cannot touch a single company of the fire department, or the briefest period of the annals of that company, without finding ourselves face to face with some interesting bit of the history of New York. The histories of New York are all excellent in their way, but not one, we presume to say, has dealt with its people as this history does. We have walked into the people's houses, so to speak, and have become intimate with them as no ordinary historian, who views men and manners afar off, has yet thought of doing. The result of our industry, of our new departure, appears in every page. The Fire Department is co-existent with the first Dutch settlement. It makes us acquainted with the British colonists; it carries us into revolutionary times; we are borne along in the telling of its story to those piping times of peace when the only enemy that menaced the Empire City was the fire fiend or the importation of disease; it brings us up to the stirring political times that for thirty years preceded the rebellion, and then it launches us into those years, red with the blood of contending brothers, and wherein those gallant firemen have played a conspicuous part. The experience of the firemen has been of use to the architect and the merchant. Nearly every improvement in the way of building has been the suggestion of men who have seen the evil effects of old methods and styles. They have given a fillip to the inventiveness of the practical engineer, and have helped to improve, in various ways, the useful arts. Thus, it will be seen, that no one who is ambitious to write a true history of the Fire Department can fail of writing a history of New York City, with all that the name implies.

What, then, would Henry Hudson, the intrepid navigator, when he landed on these shores, have thought of such a story, had the enchanted wand of some wizard transformed the primeval beauties of Manhattan Island into the panoramic picture which it presents to-day, with its vast population, its commercial enterprises, and teeming business life. Surely, the adventurous skipper of the "Vlie-boat" or "Half Moon" would have thought it impossible that in the period of two and three-quarters of a century such a metamorphosis could have taken place. Well may we believe that he lingered with enthusiastic delight along the picturesque shores of the harbor and the bay, the magnificence of the scenery being such as to cause him rapturously to exclaim, "It is as beautiful a land as the foot of man can tread upon!"

The site of New York originally presented only a wild and rough aspect, covered with a thick forest, its beach broken and sandy, or rocky and full of inlets forming marshes. These irregularities of surface rendered it all the more undesirable for building purposes. The early colonists made but little effort to overcome or remove those rude obstacles of nature in the path of civilized life.

"A more forbidding spot of earth," remarks a local historian, "on which to erect a great city has seldom been seen than was presented in the original ground plan of the city of New York; and in rearing a city on such a foundation the builders have combined the arts of the stonecutters of ancient Petraea and the amphibious labors of the founders of Venice and St. Petersburg."

Sudden acclivities and projecting crags were originally intermingled with ponds and marshes. In some parts the tide penetrated nearly to the middle of the island; and in others were fresh water ponds, elevated considerably above tide-water. Midway between the Hudson and East Rivers was a pond of fresh water, which was discharged by a brook running southeastwardly to the East River, through a vast swamp or estuary—the tract now reaching from Pearl Street on the west to Catharine Street on the east, and extending up nearly to Chatham Street. To the west of this swamp was another of less extent, separated from the former by a ridge, upon which Pearl Street runs. This, in after years, was long known as Beekman's swamp. To the west of the fresh pond was a valley of wet land reaching down to the Hudson, and ending in a marsh, a region now traversed by Canal Street. Beyond this belt of fresh water and marshes, that almost insulated the part below them, there lay to the northeastward a fine tract of arable land and extensive meadows, the southeastern angle of which was known for many years as Corlaer's Hook, so called after an early proprietor. Farther up, on the eastern side, the land was more broken and rocky, swelling into eminences, with intervening swamps and morasses. The west side of the island was less varied in its natural features. The shore of the Hudson for a distance of three or four miles was low, and intersected by bays and estuaries.

As seen by the early navigators, this rugged fragment of creation was clothed in its primeval forests. The land thus discovered was not altogether an uninhabited waste. Scattered and enfeebled bands of the great family of the Mohegans were found along the banks of the Hudson. In character, habits, and pursuits, the human tenants of these wilds were but one remove from their irrational associates of the wilderness.

Adrian Block and his companions, whose ship was destroyed by fire, suffered great hardships on the island in the winter of 1613. They erected four huts near the southern point of the island, or about the present site of No. 39 Broadway. These were the first human habitations constructed by Europeans on the island of Manhattan.

Ten years later, the dwellers, who had increased in numbers, built themselves huts, and, for the common protection, constructed a fort, which they made in the form of a regular square, with four bastions. Those who could not find room within the fort built houses under the walls, and they formed the first street. This they called Hoogh Straat, now Pearl Street. Presently rude cottages began to cluster about the block house, and in good time the incipient metropolis assumed the title of New Amsterdam, while the whole territory of Hudson's River was called New Netherland. During the directorship of Peter Minuet (1624–33) the whole island of Manhattan was purchased from the Indians for a sum about equal to twenty-four dollars. As the rigorous winter season demanded a plentiful supply of fuel, the dry and inflammable nature of the huts—for houses they can scarcely be called—often gave rise to very destructive and alarming conflagrations. As early as the year 1628, it is recorded that some of the property of the colonists had been destroyed by fire. The experience of this, their first fire, was not lost upon them, for we find that in this year, "the making of brick, lime, and potash, was now begun, and grist and saw mills were built."

"On this island of Manhattan," says the Rev. Isaac Jogues, "and in its environs, there may well be four or five hundred men of different sects and nations; the Director-General told me that there were persons of eighteen different languages; they are settled here and there on the river, above and below, as the beauty and conveniences of the spot invited each to settle; some mechanics, however, who ply their trades, are ranged under the fort; all the others were exposed to the incursions of the natives, who, in the year 1643, while I was there, actually killed some two score Hollanders, and burnt many houses and barns full of wheat."

After the conclusion, on the part of the authorities, to build a city tavern, in the year 1642, its site was selected close to the shore, south of the road to the ferry. The building was of considerable dimensions and cost; and this place was chosen for its situation, as giving a good appearance to the town from the harbor. The building was erected near high water mark, on the present northwest corner of Pearl Street and Coenties Alley. After the organization of the city magistracy, in 1653, this building was ceded to the city for the purpose of a city hall, and was used as such until the year 1699. Its principal use was for the sittings of the burgomasters and schepens, and for the prison. The chamber occupied for the sitting of the magistrates was on the southeast corner of the second story, the prison chamber being in the rear, on the other side of the house, facing a yard which extended to "Hoogh Straat" (Pearl Street). Upon the roof was a cupola, in which was hung a bell, in the year 1656, which was rung for the assembling of the magistrates, and also on occasions of the publication of proclamations, the proclamations being read in front of the hall.

More permanent and substantial improvements were inaugurated by Governor Stuyvesant. He had been director of the company's colony at Curaçoa, where he lost a leg in an unsuccessful attack on the Portuguese island of Saint Martin. Being obliged to return to Holland for surgical aid, the directors, in recognition of his "Roman courage," sent him to New Netherland as "redresser-general" of all abuses. He arrived in New Amsterdam in the middle of May, 1647, and found the colony in a "low condition." The aspect of city affairs was certainly not attractive. Fences were straggling, the public ways crooked, and many of the houses, which were chiefly built of wood and thatched with straw, encroached on the lines of the streets.

To remedy these defects stringent ordinances were passed, and "surveyors of buildings" were appointed (July 25, 1647) to regulate the erection of new houses "within or around the city of New Amsterdam." Citizens were obliged to see to the sweeping of their chimneys, while the abolishment of wooden chimneys and thatched roofs was decreed.

These are the names of the surveyors of buildings: His Excellency, Lubert van Duicklargen, the Equipage-master; Paulus Leendersen Vandiegrist, and the Secretary, Cornelis Van Teinhoven. These officials were "authorized and empowered to condemn all improprieties and disorder in buildings, fences, palisades, posts, and rails." Persons designing to build, plant, or settle, within or about the city of New Amsterdam, were warned, "that nothing shall be done or undertaken without the knowledge, consent, and examination of the aforesaid surveyors of buildings, in the penalty of twenty-five carolus guilders; and also of having whatever they may have put up removed."

Fires were of frequent occurrence. The inflammable materials of which the houses were composed, and the insufficient means of extinguishing the flames, led to great anxiety and insecurity, and a corresponding vigilance, or what was deemed vigilance, in the prevention of fire. As the houses of the New Amsterdamers were mostly confined to the southern point of the island, the settlement was well supplied with water with which to do battle in case of emergency. Besides being within easy reach of the waters of the bay, the East and the North Rivers, a stream "deep enough for market boats" to ascend flowed in from the bay through the center of the present Broad Street as far as Exchange Place. Also, there was generally to be found a well or cistern in the garden of each house. But this abundant supply of water was about as practical a factor in the extinguishment of fire as were the "oceans of water" to the thirsty mariners, who, nevertheless, had "not a drop to drink." This paradox will be understood when it is stated that it was a difficult matter for the so-called firemen of this primitive era to utilize these natural sources of supply, and still more difficult of accomplishment to transport the water in sufficient quantities to the scene of the conflagration. The water had to be carried by hand, and "in such emergencies," remarks the Hon. Charles P. Daly, "we may imagine the scene of confusion that must have ensued when tubs, pails, or other means of carrying water, had to be hastily improvised to stay the progress of a fire."

This state of affairs was not destined to last long. It was the first period of fire organization. Other and more potent methods were, however, soon to be inaugurated. In order to introduce these methods the city fathers of those days, after due deliberation, and as a result of their combined official wisdom, signed the doom of wooden chimneys and thatched roofs, while four fire wardens were appointed to enforce the ordinance. This was the first step in the right direction; other plans were under consideration, and their adoption followed in good time. But as it took a very long while to set the wheels of Dutch official machinery in motion, reforms of every kind were slow and uncertain, and the easygoing burghers were content with one progressive measure at a time. Hence it came to pass that the year 1648 was a memorable one in the annals of New Amsterdam, for it was then that the first fire ordinance was passed. Houses, or log cabins, had been run up with an entire disregard to the alarming possibilities of the ravages of fire. These rude dwellings were, it would seem, specially constructed with a view to their speedily becoming a prey to the devouring element. Wooden chimneys and thatched roofs were certainly not designed to stay the fury of the flames. These naturally inflammable materials were subjected to a double process of seasoning, namely, to heat within and the rays of the sun without. Hence, a spark ignited them and a flame destroyed. It was in this year, then (1648), that a system of fire police was first established, the immediate cause of which was the happening of fires in two places. The preamble to this ordinance declares that "it had come to the knowledge of his excellency, the Director-General, that certain careless persons were in the habit of neglecting to clean their chimneys by sweeping, and of paying no attention to their fires, whereby lately fires have occurred in two houses." Mention is made of the fact that the danger of fire is greater as the number of houses increases, particularly as the majority of the houses were built of wood and covered with reeds, while some of the houses, it is pointed out, had wooden chimneys, "which is very dangerous." Therefore it is declared to be advisable and highly necessary to look closely into the matter.

From this time forth it is ordered no wooden or platted chimneys shall be permitted to be built in any houses between the Fort and the Fresh Water, but that those already standing shall be suffered to remain during the good pleasure of the fire wardens. To the end that the foregoing may be duly observed, the following persons were appointed fire wardens: From the Council, the Commissary Adrian Keyser; and from the Commonalty, Thomas Hall, Martin Krieger, and George Woolsey. They, in their turn, it is stipulated, shall visit all the houses in the city, between the Fort and the Fresh Water, and shall inspect the chimneys whether they be kept clean by sweeping, and as often as any shall be discovered to be foul they shall condemn them, and the owners shall immediately, without any gainsaying, pay the fine of three guilders for each chimney thus condemned—to be appropriated to the maintenance of fire ladders, hooks, and buckets, which shall be provided and procured the first opportunity. And in case the houses of any person shall be burned, or be on fire, either through his own negligence or his own fire, he shall be mulcted in the penalty of twenty-five guilders, to be appropriated as aforesaid.

The appointment of these fire wardens may be regarded as the initiatory effort to establish a system of protection against fire. They are the first fire functionaries, and as such it is interesting to learn something about them beyond their names. Martin Krieger was the proprietor of a famous tavern opposite the Bowling Green. At a later period, when the city was incorporated and a municipal government formed, he was a member of Governor Stuyvesant's council, and from this time until the capture of the city by the British he filled many important offices. Thomas Hall was an Englishman. Having been captured by the Dutch and paroled, he took up his residence among his friendly captors, and in time became a man of wealth, filling many public offices. He owned a large farm in the vicinity of Spruce and Beekman Streets. This farm in later years passed into the hands of William Beekman, the ancestor of the Beekman family. Adrian Keyser was officially connected with the Dutch West India Company, by whom the New Netherlands was founded. He was afterwards a member of the Executive Council. George Woolsey, like Thomas Hall, was an Englishman. He came out as the agent of Isaac Allerton, a leading Dutch trader. The descendants of these men are to this day honored residents of this city.

A survey of the town was begun in 1654 and completed in 1656. The city was then laid down on a map and confirmed by law, "to remain, from that time forward, without alteration." Streets were also laid out, some of which were crooked enough. The city then contained by enumeration, "one hundred and twenty houses, with extensive garden lots," and one thousand inhabitants. One of the first acts of the city authorities, after the incorporation of New Amsterdam, was the framing and passage of an order similar to the one promulgated in 1648. From this it is inferred that but little attention was paid to the previous proclamation, and as a consequence several fires had occurred, "and further dangers are apprehended." Then the ordinance decrees that it is incumbent on the fire officials "to perform their duties as fire wardens according to the custom of our

Fatherland," and names the following as such fire wardens: Hendrick Hendrick-son Kip, Govert Loockerman and Christian Barents, "who are hereby authorized to visit all the houses and chimnies within the city jurisdiction."

In 1657 the progress of the city became so marked that it was thought appropriate to give to its thoroughfares the names of streets, which was accordingly done, and they are enumerated as follows:

T' Marckvelt (the Marketfield), De Heere Straat (the principal street), De Hoogh Straat (the High Street), De Waal (the Wall), T' Water (the Water), De Perel Straat (the Pearl Street), aghter de Perel Straat (behind the Pearl Street), De Brouwer Straat (the Brewer Street), De Winckel Straat (the Shop Street), De Heere Graft (the principal canal), De Prince Graft (the Beaver Canal), T' Marck-velt Steegre (the Marketfield Path), De Smits Valley (the Smith's Valley).

The Dutch burghers did not stop here. They had put their hand to the plow and were not going to turn back. In addition to the foregoing measures for the common safety in case of fire, a rattle-watch of eight men was established. The duties appertaining to this watch were imposed upon each of the citizens by turn. Streets were for the first time paved with stone. There were no sewers, and the pavement extended to the width of only ten feet from the front of the houses, the center of the street being left bare for the more easy absorption of the water.

The inauguration of these reforms must have transformed the budding city, from a condition which Governor Stuyvesant on his arrival had designated as "low," into one of comparative order and shapeliness. The hog-pens, and other offensive structures, must have also disappeared from the public thoroughfares, while, no doubt, a more substantial order of buildings had taken the place of the houses which were "built of wood and covered with reeds and had wooden chimneys," for we find the Director-General in a proclamation enlarging upon "the beauties of a well-regulated city, with good dwelling houses and spacious gardens;" and also glowingly dwelling upon "the blessed augmentation of the population and trade of the city."

Towards the latter part of the year 1657 the need of regular leather fire buckets was much felt. None existed in the colony, and the thought of manufacturing them themselves was too visionary and impracticable to be entertained just then. As the Fatherland was depended upon to furnish nearly all the artificial necessaries of life, it was decided to send to Holland for the buckets, as specified in the following resolution:

> *Whereas*, in all well-regulated cities it is customary that fire buckets, ladders, and hooks are in readiness at the corners of the streets and in public houses, for time of need; which is the more necessary in this city on account of the small number of stone houses and the many wooden houses here;

therefore, the Director-General and Councillors do authorize the Burgo-masters and Schepens of this city, either personally or through their trea-surer, to demand immediately for every house, whether small or great, one beaver or eight guilders in sewant; and to procure from fatherland, out of the sum collected in this manner, two hundred and fifty leathern fire buck-ets, and also to have made some fire ladders and fire hooks; and to maintain this establishment, they may yearly demand for every chimney one guilder.

This tax was promptly collected by the city authorities, but the much coveted fire buckets were still beyond the reach of the city fathers. The resolution, quoted above, looking to the mother country for their procurement, was reconsidered, as it would take a long time before they could have reached this country. So, after waiting some months, it was decided to invoke the aid of the city shoe-makers. But the shoemakers of those primitive days lacked confidence in their ability to perform the task assigned them. Four out of the seven Knights of St. Crispin responded to the call to meet the city fathers in solemn and serious conclave. The date of the meeting was the first of August, 1658. The views of each shoemaker were solicited. The first declined "the arduous undertaking;" the second declared he had no material; the third, more enterprising, proposed to contract to make one hundred buckets for the consideration of six guilders and two stuyvers each (about two dollars and fifty cents), and the fourth, after much persuasion, consented to make the remaining fifty upon the same terms.

These are the terms agreed upon:

Remout Remoutzen agrees to make the said buckets all out of tanned leather, and to do all that is necessary to finish them in the completest manner for the price of six guilders two stuyvers each (about two dollars and fifty cents each), half sewant, half beavers, a fourth part of the half beavers to be "passable," three-fourths whole beavers: on these conditions he is to make one hundred buckets, which he promises to do between this and All-Saints' Day. Adrian Van Lair, on the same terms, to make fifty buckets.

But Rome was not built in a day, and at the end of six months from the date of the above agreement, that is to say, on the twentieth of January, following, the one hundred and fifty leather fire buckets were delivered at the Stadt House, where fifty of the number were deposited. The remainder were divided in lots and placed at the residences of nine of the principal inhabitants, namely:

Numbers 1 to 50, in the City Hall; 51 to 62, in Daniel Litschoe's tavern (present Pearl Street, near Wall); 63 to 74, in the house of Abraham Verplanck, in the Smith's Valley, (Pearl Street, near Fulton); 75 to 86, in the house of

Joannes Pietersen Vanbruggh (Hanover Square); 87 to 98, in the house of Burgomaster Paulus Leendenen Vandiegrist, (Broadway, opposite Exchange Place); 99 to 110, at the house of the Sheriff (or Schout) Nicasius de Se'le, (southeast corner Broad Street and Exchange Place); 111 to 122, at the house of Pieter Wolfersen Van Couwenhoven, (northwest corner Whitehall and Pearl Streets); at the house of Jan Jansen, Jr., ten; at the house of Hendrick Hendrickson Kip, Sen., ten, (Bridge, between Whitehall and Broad Streets); at the house of Jacobus Backer, ten, (Broad, between Stone and South William Streets).

The burning of a small loghouse on a bluff overlooking the bay, where Castle Garden now stands, led to the establishment of the first fire company in 1658. This organization, disrespectfully dubbed the "Prowlers," consisted of eight men, furnished with two hundred and fifty buckets, hooks, and small ladders, and each of its members was expected to walk the street from nine o'clock at night until morning drum-beat, watching for fire while the town slumbered.

This company was organized by ambitious young men, and was known also as the "rattle-watch." It was soon increased to fifty members, and did duty from nine P.M. until sunrise, all the citizens who could be roused from their beds assisting in case of fire. One of the first fire buckets is still preserved by James Van Amburgh, of Westchester County, whose ancestor was one of these early firemen. The first serious fire had occurred the year before, in 1657, when Sam Baxter's house caught fire—from a blazing log which rolled out of the fireplace during the night—and was completely consumed. It was regarded as the handsomest dwelling in the settlement of the early Dutch, and its destruction gave the needed impetus for the organization of a fire company.

Even the veteran firemen who still survive would laugh if they would read the manner in which those early fire laddies undertook to provide against conflagrations. One of the rules was that each citizen of New Amsterdam was required to fill three buckets with water after sunset, and place them on his doorstep for the use of the fire patrol in case of need. Another Dutch ordinance directed that ten buckets should be filled with water at the town pump, "wen ye sun do go down," and these were to be left in a rack provided for that purpose, so that the members of the "rattle-watch" could readily lay their hands upon them "if ye fyer does go further yan ye efforts of ye men and call for water."

When the fire was extinguished, the buckets of the citizens that had been used were thrown in a great heap on the common, and the town-crier, mounting a barrel, shouted lustily for each bucket proprietor to come and claim his own. As the stirring nasal cry,

"Hear ye! O! I pray ye,
Lord masters claim your buckets,"

penetrated to the suburbs of the town, boys ran from all directions, and fought savagely on the grass at the crier's feet, to see who should carry home the buckets belonging to rich men, knowing that the reward would be a cake or a glass of wine, or a small coin.

The prevention of fire was a subject which caused much anxiety and unremitting attention. To see that the ordinances were carried out, frequent examinations were made of the chimneys and houses. These precautions caused much annoyance to the order-loving Dutch matrons, who, doubtless, regarded such visits as an intrusion. The worthy fire functionaries found their zeal but ill-requited. They were often insulted and abused, but they bore it all with true Dutch fortitude, until their female persecutors called them "chimney sweeps." This was the crowning indignity, and not to be borne. Retaliatory measures were adopted. The *goede vrouws* were summoned before the magistrates and fined for their discourteous conduct. This, it seems, did not mend matters, for the office of fire warden fell into disuse, and the ordinance became a dead letter.

Public wells at this time were found to be no less a public than a private necessity, equally indispensable in time of peril by fire as in the preservation of the public health. The first public well was dug in front of the fort in 1658. This well afforded an abundant supply of spring water, and "it became the great resort of the inhabitants during the remaining period of the Dutch occupation." The public wells were situated in the middle of the streets, and the water was passed from them in buckets through long rows of citizens to the scene of fire. Water was raised from these wells by the old Egyptian method of a balance pole and bucket, a mode still familiar in country parts. So far as drinking purposes were concerned, the water so obtained was very bad.

Dwellings of a more costly character than had previously been known were soon to be erected. In 1657, Peter Cornelisen Vanderveen built a fine house on the present Pearl Street. The year following, Governor Stuyvesant erected a large house in the vicinity of the present Whitehall Street, the name of which street it is alleged has been derived from the white hall of the Dutch governor. Others followed, and the demand thus occasioned induced the establishment of a brick-yard in the year 1659, by De Graff and Hogeboom, and brick buildings after this period became the fashion with all who could afford the additional expense. Compared with more recent times, those dwellings must be considered as extremely inexpensive. A house and lot of the value of one thousand dollars of our present currency would then have been of the first class; they rarely exceeded eight hundred dollars. Rents varied from twenty-five dollars to one hundred dollars.

About the year 1656 several merchants had erected stone edifices, and schools had been established. The houses put up in the earliest period were usually one story high, with roofs of straw and chimneys of wood. These were succeeded by houses of brick and tile—the gable end usually to the street; apparently by a succession of steps from the line where the roofs commenced, the wall on the street, from each side tapering to the top at the center, in a point where often was a weathercock. And frequently on the street front, in iron figures, was designated the year in which the house was built. The street door was divided crosswise in the middle, the upper half having a large brass or iron knocker on it. A porch or "stoop" was at the front, on which the street door opened; and on each side was a bench, on which, in pleasant weather, some of the family were wont to sit and pass their leisure hours, often in company with a friend or neighbor. An alley on one side made a passageway to the rear part of the building, where was the family kitchen with its huge fireplace. The plan of the town at that period was substantially the same as is now found in the same locality. The water line, however, has been carried out far beyond its original place. The fort was located just below the present Bowling Green. From the fort a broad, straight roadway, led back towards the cultivated boweries farther up the island. This was from the beginning the principal street of the town, though not a favorite one for residences on account of its distance from the water. The Dutch called it "De Heere Straat," or Main Street. The English changed its name to Broadway.

The Dutch, in imitation of what was done in Holland, built dykes in Broad Street, as far up as the City Hall. The city was enclosed with a wall or palisades from Trinity Church across Wall Street to the East River.

Like most other Dutch villages of former times, the town of New Amsterdam was not wanting in its supply of windmills. These machines played an important part in those days, when there was no water power convenient. The windmill adjoining the fort, and standing upon the present State Street, was the first of its kind erected by the Dutch. Another windmill occupied the eminence on Broadway, between the present Liberty and Cortlandt Streets. Farther eastward on the heights along the East River shore was another windmill, opposite the ferry landing from Long Island. Another stood upon the south part of the present City Hall Park. Yet another was erected on the North River shore, below the present St. Paul's Church. "These, and several others," says Valentine, "erected from time to time, on prominent points of the landscape, were distinguishing features of the Dutch city of New Amsterdam." The first windmill in Broadway, near Cortlandt Street having decayed, it was ordered in 1662 that there be another erected on the same ground, "outside of the city land-port (gate) on the Company's farm."

The vicinity of Chatham Street, south of Pearl Street, was, in its natural condition, very high ground, and was called Catimut's Hill. It had also at times the names of Windmill Hill and Fresh Water Hill. In 1662 a windmill was erected in this vicinity—west of the present Chatham Street and a little north of Duane Street. This mill was in existence for over half a century. An old windmill, erected, it is supposed, at a very early date on the Bayard estate, stood on the easterly side of Elizabeth Street, midway between the present Canal and Hester Streets. It was still standing for some years after the revolutionary war, the last relic, it is supposed, of that kind of structure in this city.

The British seized the Dutch possessions of New Netherland in 1664. This marked a transformation in the municipal affairs of the city government. But those Batavian pioneers have bequeathed to the city many of their noblest characteristics, which have descended to the present day.

CHAPTER II

PRIMITIVE FIRE APPLIANCES

1664–1731.—The British Take Possession of New Netherland.—Establishment of a "Burger Wagt."—Inadequate Supply of Fire Buckets and Hooks and Ladders.—Action of Governor Dongan and his Council.—Adoption of Means for the Extinguishment of Fires.—Pavement of Streets.—Appointment of Fire Wardens.— "Throw out Your Buckets."—The City at the Commencement of the Seventeenth Century.

When Governor Nicolls wrested the province from the Dutch, he, in a letter written in 1665, to the Duke of York, said: "Such is the mean condition of this town (New York) that not one soldier to this day has lain in sheets, or upon any other bed than straw." This, however, did not prejudice him to the extent that he could not appreciate the natural advantages of the place. "The best of all his majesty's towns in America," is what he says upon entering it. This is what he predicts of the city: "Within five years the staple of America will be drawn hither, of which the brethren of Boston are very sensible."

During the military rule of Governor Colve, who held the city for one year, everything partook of a military character. Then the Dutch mayor, at the head of the city militia, held his daily parades before the City Hall (Stadt Huys); and every evening, at sunset, he received from the principal guard of the fort, called the "hoofd wagt," the keys of the city, and thereupon proceeded with a guard of six to lock the city gates; then to place a "burger wagt," a citizen guard, as night watches at assigned places. They also went the rounds at sunrise to open the gates, and to restore the keys to the officer of the fort.

On the thirtieth of January, 1674, there was a meeting of civic officials in regard to fire matters. There were present Captain Knyff, on behalf of the Honorable Governor; Anthony De Mill, schout; Johannes De Peyster, Johannes Van Brough, and Aegidius Luyck, burgomasters; William Beekman, Jeronimus Ebbingh, Jacob Kipp, Lourens Van der Speigill, and Guilame Ver Planck, schepens. At this meeting the fire wardens presented a written report of the number of fire buckets and other implements "found by them to be provided." They made a demand for an additional supply of the implements, "requesting that this court will be pleased to order that such fire hooks and ladders as are necessary may be made."

When the city came permanently under British dominion by the peace of 1674, its former exclusive Knickerbocker character began gradually to wear off. At that time almost all the houses presented their gabled ends to the street, and all the most important public buildings, such as "Stuyvesant Huys" on the water edge, at present Moore and Front Streets, and the Stadt Huys or City Hall, on Pearl Street, at the head of Coenties Slip, were then set on the foreground, to be more readily seen from the river. The chief part of the town lay along the East River (called "Salt River" in early days), and descending from the high ridge of ground along the line of Broadway. A great artificial dock for vessels existed between "Stuyvesant Huys" and the bridge over "the canal," where it debouched on the present Broad Street.

As already intimated, New York was in primitive days the "city of hills." Thus, at the extreme south end of Broadway, where the ancient fort formerly stood, was a mound, quite as elevated as the present general level of the street in front of Trinity Church, and thence regularly declining from along that street to "the beach" on the North River. The hills were sometimes precipitous, as from Beekman's and Peck's Hills, in the neighborhood of Pearl Street and Beekman and Ferry Streets, and from the Middle Dutch Church on Nassau Street down to Maiden Lane. Between many of the hills flowed in several invasions of water, such as "the canal," so called to gratify Dutch recollections, which was an inroad of water up Broad Street. Up Maiden Lane flowed another inroad through Smith's marsh or valley. A little beyond Peck's Slip existed a low water course, which in high tide ran quite up to the Collect, and thence, joining with Lispenard's swamp on the North River side, produced a union of waters quite across the city, converting it occasionally into an island. This accounts for the lowness of Pearl Street where it traverses Chatham Street. There they had to use boats occasionally to cross foot passengers over from either side of the high rising ground.

The importance of taking precautions against the happening of conflagrations was recognized in many ways, as is evidenced by the ordinances framed and the measures adopted from time to time. On the sixteenth of February, 1676, all persons having any of the city's ladders, buckets or hooks, in their custody, were called upon to immediately deliver them to the mayor. It was also ordered that wells be dug, as follows: "One in the street over against the house of Fowliff Johnson's, the butcher; another in the broadway against Mr. Vandicke's; another in the street over against Derrick Smith's; another in the street over against the house of John Cavildore; another in the yard or rear of the Cytie Hall; another in the street over against Cornelius Van Borsum's." On the twenty-eighth of February there was published a list of persons that had "noe chimneys, or not fitt to keepe fire in," and an order was issued by the mayor and aldermen calling upon these delinquents to cause suitable chimneys to be built without delay. In

January of the following year John Dooly and John Vorrickson Meyer were appointed to inspect all the chimneys and fire hearths in the city, and on the fifteenth of March, 1683, a law was enacted empowering the appointment of viewers and searchers (fire wardens) of chimneys and fire hearths, to report to the mayor and aldermen, who could impose a fine not exceeding twenty shillings for each default; prohibiting the laying of straw, hay, or other combustible matter in their dwelling houses, or places adjoining the same, "but at a distance from their houses and the streets; and providing for hooks, ladders, and buckets, to be kept in convenient places;" and, further that "if any person should suffer his chimney to be on fire he should pay the sum of fifteen shillings."

On the ninth of September following, the mayor, aldermen, and commonalty of the city, petitioned the governor to confirm unto them the several ancient customs, privileges, and immunities granted by the former governor of the province, Col. Richard Nicolls, 1665, who incorporated the inhabitants of the city, New Harlem, and all others inhabiting the island of Manhattan, as a body politic and corporate under the government of a Mayor, Aldermen, and Sheriff, etc.

In responding to the petition of the corporation of the ninth of September, Governor Dongan and his council, at a meeting held on December 6, stipulated that the city should "appoint one, or more if necessary, to look after the chimneys for the preventing of fire, and that all houses keep one or more leather buckets."

A public chimney-sweep was appointed for the city (1685), who was to cry his approach through the public streets, and who probably originated the whoop peculiar to his vocation. His rates were fixed by law at a shilling and eighteen-pence per chimney, according to the height of the house.

Great damage seems to have been done by fire in January, 1686. The Common Council, at a meeting held on February 28 of that year, referred to the absence of means for the extinguishment of fires, and it was ordered that every inhabitant whose dwelling house had two chimneys should provide one bucket, and for more than two chimneys, two buckets; that all brewers possess five buckets apiece, and all bakers three, said buckets to be provided before September twenty-fifth ensuing, under a penalty for neglect of five shillings for each bucket. Five years later, on the twenty-fifth of November, 1691, this order was re-enacted. But there were added the stipulations that the buckets should be provided by the occupants, and the cost thereof allowed them by the landlord out of the rent, and "every man to marke the bucketts with the letters of his land-lord's name, upon forfeiture of six shillings, for the use of the citty, to be paid by the tenant on default," etc. The mayor was empowered to acquit "poore people" of the penalty.

At the same time, Derrick Vandenburgh, John Rose, Snert Olphite, and Gar-rett Rose were appointed to "goe round the towne and view each fireplace and chimney, that they be sufficient and clean swept," with the penalty of three shillings and sixpence to each inhabitant for each defect.

Chief among the substantial indications of progress was the completion in 1693 of the Garden Street Church. It was built in the midst of a beautiful garden, "a great distance up town," fronting a narrow lane called Garden Alley, which afterwards became Garden Street, and is now Exchange Place. This year Wall Street was first paved to the width of ten feet, in front of the houses facing the wall.

A fire occurred in that part of the town called the "Fly" in February, 1692, at which several buckets were lost. Complaints reached the mayor that people of thievish propensities had appropriated them, whereupon His Honor issued an order directing the crier to give notice round the city that the stolen buckets be taken to the mayor immediately so that they might be restored to their owners. Other appliances besides buckets had been thought of. Two years before the fire in the "Fly," five "brant masters" (fire wardens) had been appointed on January 4, 1690. These fire wardens were: Peter Adolf, Derck van der Brincke, Derck ten Eyk, Jacob Borlen, and Tobeyas Stoutenburgh, and it had been ordered that five ladders be made and provided for service at fires, with sufficient hooks therefor.

In 1693, it was ordered "that every inhabitant in the streets hereinafter mentioned, shall, before the first of August next, cause to be paved, with pebble stones, so much of said street as shall front their respective premises." Thence follows the designation of the streets to be paved, eight in number. The crude condition of the city in respect to its streets may also be inferred from an order made in this year, that "the poisonous and stinking weeds before everyone's door be forthwith plucked up." The above system of paving continued for many years, and it is believed that, up to the time of the Revolution, the "kennel" ran through the centers of the streets, and if sidewalks existed, they were the voluntary work of the adjacent owners. No regulations are to be found in the public ordinances concerning either their construction or repair.

After the revolutionary war, the subject of city improvements was under a commissioner, instead of a committee of the Common Council. Gerard Bancker was the first street commissioner.

Additional precautions were now taken against occurrences of fires. In 1697, the aldermen and assistant-aldermen were authorized to appoint two persons as fire wardens in every ward. The penalty of three shillings was imposed for the neglect to remedy defective flues and hearths—one-half to the city and one-half to the wardens—and if a chimney should take fire after notice had been given to clean it, the occupant was mulcted in the sum of forty shillings. This is the first record of a paid Fire Department in the city of New York. The system had advanced beyond the limits of "viewers" and "overseers," and had reached a

point where something like an organization was effected, and arrangements completed for paying, fining, and discharging the men, who were obliged to view
the chimneys and hearths once a week. In short, a more prompt and systematic
performance of duty was required.

The practice of having every house supplied with fire buckets now became
general, and was continued long after the introduction of fire engines. The manner in which an alarm of fire was given in the night time is graphically told by
the Hon. Charles P. Daly: "If a fire broke out at night," he says, "the watchman
gave the alarm with his rattle, and knocked at the doors of the houses, with the
cry, 'Throw out your buckets!' the alarm being further spread by the ringing of
the bell at the fort and by the bells in the steeples of the different churches.
When the inmates of a house were aroused, the first act was to throw out the
buckets in the street, which were of sole leather, holding about three gallons,
and were also hung in the passage close to the street door. They were picked
up by those who were hastening to the fire, it being the general custom for
nearly every householder to hurry to the fire—whether by day or by night—
and render his assistance. As soon as possible two lines were formed from the
fire to the nearest well or pump, and when they gave out, the line was carried
to the next one or to the river. The one line passed up the full buckets, and the
empty ones were passed down the other line. No one was permitted to break
through those lines, and if any one attempted to do so, and would not fall in
and lend a helping hand, a bucket of water or several were instantly thrown over
him. Each bucket was marked with the name or number of the owner, and,
when the fire was over, they were all collected together and taken in a cart,
belonging to the city, to the City Hall. A bellman then went round to announce
that the buckets were ready for delivery, when each householder sent for his
bucket, and, when recovered, hung it up in the allotted place, ready for the next
emergency."

During this period (1697) a night watch was established, composed of "four
good and honest inhabitants of the city, whose duty it shall be to watch in the
night time, from the hour of nine in the evening till break of day, until the
twenty-fifth of March next; and to go round the city, each hour of the night,
with a bell, and there to proclaim the season of the weather and the hour of the
night."

The erection of the City Hall in Wall Street, at the head of Broad (in 1700),
was the great event which established Wall Street as the central point of interest
for leading business and professional men. The City Hall was supported upon
brick arches over the sidewalk, under which pedestrians could pass from street
to street in all directions. One of the rooms on the first floor was at a later day
appropriated for the reception of the first two fire engines in New York, imported from London.

Four able-bodied men were appointed watch and bellmen for the city in 1702, from November 1 to April 1 following. They were to go, every hour in the night, through the several streets, publishing the time of the night; to apprehend disturbers of the peace, etc., and to see that no damage be done by fires. A lantern, bell, and hour-glass were provided for them by the city.

The Common Council, on the sixth of November, 1703, ordered that the aldermen of each ward should command the respective constables therein to make a house to house inspection, to ascertain whether the number of fire buckets required by law were kept on hand, and to present the delinquents for prosecution.

New and more stringent regulations were now passed in respect to fires: the fire wardens were directed to keep strict watch of all hearths and chimneys within the city, and to see that the fire buckets were hung up in their right places throughout the wards, and two hooks and eight ladders were purchased at the public expense for the use of the fire department.

This system prevailed, with slight modifications, until the introduction of the hand engines from London.

A law for the better prevention of fire was published at the City Hall on November 18, 1731. After the customary ringing of three bells, and a proclamation had been made for silence, it provided for the appointing of "viewers of chimneys and hearths," to make monthly inspections; the fine of three shillings for neglecting the directions of the fire wardens, re-enacting the fine of forty shillings for chimneys on fire, and establishing a like fine for "viewers" who should refuse to serve, and a fine of six shillings for neglect of duty; providing for the obtainment of hooks, ladders and buckets, and fire engines, to be kept in convenient places; for leather buckets to be kept in every house; a penalty for not possessing the required number of buckets, and a fine for detaining other men's buckets.

CHAPTER III

THE FIRST HAND ENGINES

*1731–1782.—Introduction of Machines from London.—Newsham's Engine.—
Formation of the First Fire Companies.—Who the Original Fire Laddies
Were.—Location of Stations.—How the Department Force Increased.—Terms
of Service.—Privileges and Exemptions.—Act of Incorporation.*

The year 1731 was the beginning of a memorable epoch in the history of New York and its famous Fire Department. Then came into use the new hand fire engines. Then was laid the foundation of that gallant, emulous, and self-sacrificing body of volunteers, the record of whose deeds will read to posterity like an old romance. Just as the chronicles of the doughty Crusaders touch the hearts of the youth of to-day, so will the history of the achievements of the old volunteer companies of the Empire City fire the bosoms of generations to come. This year saw the nucleus of a fine body of athletic men, ever ready to risk life and limb for the public weal. Soon were to be identified with those primitive engines, names that will live forever in our history, such as the Harpers, the Macys, the Townsends, the Goelets, William H. Appleton, Zophar Mills, George T. Hope, Marshall O. Roberts, and James Kelly. It was the beginning of the era of the clattering machine, with its rushing, shouting, bold and dashing attendants, as ready to fight their fellows for the place of honor in the hour of danger as the devouring flames themselves.

On the sixth of May, 1731, the city authorities passed the following resolution:

> *Resolved*, With all convenient speed to procure two complete fire engines, with suctions and materials thereto belonging, for the public service; that the sizes thereof be of the fourth and sixth sizes of Mr. Newsham's fire engines, and that Mr. Mayor, Alderman Cruger, Alderman Rutgers, and Alderman Roosevelt, or any of them, be a committee to agree with some proper merchant or merchants to send to London for the same by the first conveniency, and report upon what terms the said fire engines, etc., will be delivered to this corporation.

The committee named reported at a meeting of the Common Council, held on June 12, 1731, that they had proposed to Messrs. Stephen De Lancey and John Moore, merchants, to send for two fire engines to London, by the ship *Beaver*, of Mr. Newsham's new invention of the fourth and sixth sizes, with suctions, leathern pipes, and caps, and other materials; and that those gentlemen had undertaken to purchase and deliver them to the corporation at an advance of one hundred and twenty percent on the foot of the invoice (exclusive of insurance and commissions), and that the money should be paid for the same within nine months after the delivery of the same.

Towards the close of November of 1731 the good ship *Beaver* was sighted off port, and on December 1st workmen commenced to fit up "a convenient room" in the new City Hall for securing the fire engines, and on the fourteenth, the engines being in the meanwhile landed and "secured," a committee was appointed to have them cleaned and the leathers oiled and put into boxes ready for immediate use.

"The importation by the city of these fire engines," says the Hon. Charles P. Daly in his valuable treatise on "The Origin and History of the New York Fire Department," was an incident of no ordinary importance. There was no subject upon which at that time the inhabitants of the city felt a deeper interest than the most effectual means of extinguishing fires, for the loss of property by conflagration was a calamity to which the city from its first settlement had been particularly exposed."

These engines were designated as No. 1 and No. 2. They were located in separate sheds, in the rear of the City Hall, No. 1 on the east side of the building, and No. 2 on the west side, facing King Street, now Nassau.

The aldermen and the assistant aldermen were in charge of the apparatus in those days, and they were called overseers. The mayor and aldermen took charge at fires, the public at large being compelled to do fire duty. No one over twenty-one years of age was exempt, and for a refusal to do duty they were liable to a fine of one pound or five dollars.

When the two engines were received by the city from London, they were a great curiosity, the people being fully as much interested as in the days when silver coinages were brought out.

Peter Rutger, a brewer and an assistant alderman of the North Ward, was the first man that ever had charge of a fire engine on Manhattan Island, and John Roosevelt, a merchant, was the second.

In 1677 the city contained three hundred and sixty-eight houses; in 1693 the number was five hundred and ninety-four; in 1696 it was put down at seven hundred and fifty; and when the two fire engines arrived from London, the population of the city was eight thousand six hundred and twenty-eight, and the number of houses was about one thousand two hundred.

Up to this time, as has been shown, the only means of extinguishing fire was the carrying of water in buckets and the use of ladders and fire hooks. These primitive appliances, however, were more effective instruments as fire apparatus than might be inferred in view of the vast and ingenious mechanical appliances and machinery in use at the present day. Architecture had not then, as now, taken the same ambitious flight. The buildings originally were chiefly of one story, and few houses exceeded two stories. The first three story house put up in the city was erected in the year 1696, in Pearl Street, opposite Cedar Street, and was built by a member of the Depeyster family.

Mr. Newsham advertised his engines in the following terms:

Richard Newsham, of Cloth Fair, London, engineer, makes the most substantial and convenient engines for quenching fires, which carries *continual streams* with great force. He hath play'd several of them before his majesty and the nobility at St. James, with so general an approbation that the largest was at the same time ordered for the use of that royal palace. The largest engine will go through a passage about three foot wide, in complete working order, without taking off or putting on anything; and may be worked with ten men in the said passage. One man can quickly and with ease move the largest size about in the compass it stands in and is to be played without rocking, upon any uneven ground, with hands and feet or feet only, which cannot be paralleled by any other sort whatsoever. There is conveniency for twenty men to apply their full strength, and yet reserve both ends of the cistern clear from incumbrance, that others, at the same time, may be pouring in the water which drains through large copper strainers. The staves that are fixed through leavers, along the sides of the engine, for the men to work by, though very light, as alternate motions with quick returns require; yet will not spring and lose time the least; but the staves of such engines as are wrought at the ends of the cistern, will spring or break if they be of such length as is necessary for a large engine when considerable power is applied; and cannot be fixed fast, because they must at all times be taken out before the engine can go through a passage. The playing two streams at once, do neither issue a greater quantity of water, nor, is it new, or so useful, there having been of the like sort at the steel-yard, and other places, thirty or forty years, and the water being divided, the distance and force are accordingly lessened thereby. ★ ★ ★ As to the treddles on which men work with their feet, there is no method so powerful, with the like velocity or quickness, and more natural safe for the men. Great attempts have been made to exceed, but none yet could equal this sort; the fifth size of which hath played above the grasshopper upon the Royal Exchange, which is upward of *fifty-five yards high*, and this in the presence of many thousand spectators.

Those with suction feed themselves with water from a canal, pond, well, etc., or out of their own cisterns, by the turn of a cock, without interrupting the stream ★ ★ ★ and play off large quantities of water to a great distance, either from the engine or a leather pipe or pipes of any length required. ★ ★ ★ The five large sizes go upon wheels, well boxed with brass, fitted to strong iron axles, and the other is to be carried like a chair.

It appears, nevertheless, that Newsham had produced nothing new, as all the potent properties of his engine had been for a long time previously known. The superiority of his machine consisted simply in the ingenious mechanical adaptation of familiar principles. In form it resembled the machine in use when engines were worked by hand.

The practical usefulness of the new engines was soon tested, as appears from the following paragraph in the Boston *Weekly News Letter* of January 6, 1732, under the head of "News from New York:"

Last night, about twelve o'clock, a fire broke out in a joiner's house in this city. It began in the garret, where the people were all asleep, and burnt violently; but by the aid of the two fire engines, which came from London in the ship *Beaver*, the fire was extinguished after having burnt down the house and damaged the next.

Some person, little apprehending, as it may be supposed, that it would descend as a memorial to our day, made an accompanying rough pen and ink sketch of one of these engines, which, though rude and badly drawn, is sufficient to indicate its structure and the manner in which it was worked. This engine, with slight modifications, continued in use down to 1832, and long afterwards, in this city.

The experience of the fire of the seventh of December, referred to above, had doubtless pointed out the necessity of putting the engines in charge of some competent and skillful person, and, accordingly, on the twenty-first of January following, the mayor and four aldermen were appointed a committee to employ workmen to put them in good order, and to engage persons by the year to keep them in repair and to work them when necessary. Anthony Lamb was accordingly appointed overseer, or, as the office was afterwards called, chief engineer, at a salary of twelve dollars a year, and he and the persons employed by the year under him may be said to have been the first regularly organized Fire Department. The sheds fitted up for these two engines in the rear of the City Hall would not seem to have been sufficiently commodious, and, accordingly, in

1736, the corporation ordered a convenient house to be built "contiguous to the watch house in Broad Street, for their security and well keeping." This building, the first engine house in the city, was in the middle of Broad Street, half way between Wall Street and Exchange Place. The watch house stood at the head of Broad Street, and immediately behind it, in the middle of the street, this engine house was built. Lamb held the office of chief engineer until 1736, when he was succeeded by Jacob Turk, a gunsmith, who appears to have been a man of considerable mechanical skill and ingenuity.

Fire engines were built and for sale in this city six years after their first introduction, as will be seen by the following advertisement from the *New York Gazette*, May 9, 1737:

> A Fire-engine, that will deliver two hogsheads of water in a minute, in a continual stream, is to be sold by William Lindsay, the maker thereof. Enquire at Fighting Cocks, next door to the Exchange Coffee-house, New York.

The engines were being constantly changed from one ward to another, to please the aldermen. If an alderman or an assistant could get an engine located in his ward, it was a big thing, and the friends of the alderman would freely build a house to put it in.

Several attempts were made to build engines after those brought over from London, but most all failed who attempted it. One Bartholomew Weldern built two, neither one of which would work. The price allowed for building an engine in those days was fifty pounds.

Thomas Lote was the first man that ever built an engine in this country that was used. It was known as No. 3, and on its completion was located adjoining "Kalch-Hook Pond." A full description of the company will be found on another page.

In December, 1737, the General Assembly of the colony passed an act enabling the corporation to appoint not more than forty-two able, discreet, sober men, as firemen; an equal number to be appointed out of the six wards on the south side of Fresh Water. An enumeration of the trades of twenty-eight will be interesting, and is as follows: blacksmiths, 4; blockmaker, 1; cutter, 1; gunsmiths, 2; carpenters, 5; bricklayers, 2; ropemaker, 1; carmen, 2; coopers, 4; bakers, 2; cordwainers, 4.

The Volunteer Fire Department, so established, lasted for one hundred and twenty-seven years. A high compliment, and one that no doubt was deserved, was paid to the city's firemen in the preamble to this act, in these words: "The inhabitants of the city of New York of all degrees, have very justly acquired the reputation of being singularly and remarkably famous for their dilligence and services in cases of fires," and it was, doubtless, this fact that led to the institution of the voluntary system. This act recites, furthermore, that the firemen "have, at very great charge and expense, supplied themselves, and are provided with two fire engines and various sorts of poles, hooks, iron chains, ropes, ladders and several other tools and instruments, for the extinguishment of fires. They were to manage and care for the fire apparatus," to be "called the firemen of the city of New York," and be ready for service "by night as well as by day." To "compel and oblige them" to be "diligent, industrious and vigilant," the Common Council were empowered to remove any of them and put others in their place, and, as an inducement to fill up the ranks, the firemen so appointed were "freed, exempted and privileged from the several offices of constable and surveyor of the highways, and of and from the being put into or serving upon any juries or inquest, and of and from being compellable to serve in the militia, or any of the independent companies of or in the said city, or any or either of them, except in cases of invasion, or other imminent danger." It was ordained likewise that the firemen enjoy the privileges given by the act of Assembly, on condition of their subjecting themselves to certain cited rules and regulations, of which these are an abstract:

Upon notice of the happening of a fire, they are to take the engines and assist in its extinguishment, and afterwards to wash the engines and preserve them in good order.

If absent from a fire without reasonable cause, to forfeit twelve shillings.

Once in each month to exercise the engines, so as to keep them in good order.

For any neglect of his duty, a fireman might be removed.

Forfeitures were to be recovered before the Mayor, Recorder, or any Alderman.

Thirty-five was the number of firemen chosen. These firemen served without salary.

The following year (1739) the corporation selected five firemen from each ward, or thirty in all, and passed an ordinance for their regulation or government.

Upon the breaking out of any fire within the city, "all sheriffs, under or deputy sheriffs, high constables, petty constables, and marshals" (upon notice thereof), were required to immediately repair to the scene of the conflagration, and with their rods, staves, and other badges of authority, aid and assist in extinguishing the said fires, and cause people to work to extinguish the flames. A part of their duty also was to protect property from the depredations of thieves, and to help the inhabitants to remove and secure their household goods. Thus was formed the first fire company in the city of New York.

Jacob Turk became the head of this new organization, and continued in the office for twenty-five years. Among other things, he introduced the well-known leather cap worn by the firemen to the present day. Turk was succeeded by Jacob Stoutenburgh, a gunsmith, and was one of the thirty firemen originally appointed in 1738. He continued to be the chief engineer down to the Revolution. When he was appointed in 1761, the city had largely increased in population and territory, and, in consequence, the force in the following year was augmented to two assistants and sixty men. After the breaking out of the Revolution, it was converted into a military organization consisting of two battalions, commanded by Stoutenburgh, and was composed of one adjutant, one captain, five lieutenants, and one hundred and thirty-four men. It retired, necessarily, as a part of the military, with the retreat of the American army from the city in 1776, and the extent of the ravages of the dreadful conflagration which followed immediately after the entrance of the British troops was mainly owing to the want of firemen in the city.

The governor's house in the fort, on the eighteenth of March, 1741, was discovered to be on fire, and notwithstanding the efforts of the Fire Department—then but recently organized, and having the benefit of one or two fire engines—that edifice, together with the chapel erected about fifty years previously, and all the other buildings in the fort, were entirely consumed. The conflagration was at this time attributed to the carelessness of a plumber who had left fire in a gutter between the house and the chapel, and it was so reported by the governor to the legislature. A week after, the chimney of Captain Warren's house, near the fort, took fire, but the flames were soon extinguished with little damage. A few days after, a fire broke out in the storehouse of Mr. Van Zandt, which was attributed to the carelessness of a smoker. Three days later, the hay in a cow stable near the house of Mr. Quick was discovered to be on fire. The alarm was given, and the flames were soon suppressed. While returning to their homes, a fifth alarm called the firemen to the house of Mr. Thompson, where it was said fire had been placed in a kitchen loft where a negro usually slept. The next day coals were discovered under the stables of John Murray in Broadway. The following morning, a fire broke out in the house of Sergeant Burns, opposite the fort; and a few hours after, the roof of Mr. Hilton's house, near the Fly Market, was discovered to be on fire. Both were extinguished without much damage, but the rapid recurrence of so many fires alarmed the inhabitants, and a rumor was soon circulated that the negroes had plotted to burn the city. The magistrates met the same afternoon to consult about the matter, and while they were still in session another fire broke out in the roof of Colonel Philipse's storehouse. The alarm became universal; the negroes were seized indiscriminately and thrown into prison. People and magistrates were alike panic-stricken. The Common Council assembled and offered a reward of one hundred pounds and a full pardon to any conspirator who would reveal his knowledge of the plot with the names of the incendiaries. From the eleventh of May to the twenty-ninth of August, one hundred and fifty-four negroes were committed to prison, fourteen of whom were burnt at the stake, eighteen hanged, seventy-one transported, and the rest pardoned or discharged for the want of sufficient evidence. In the same time, twenty-four whites were committed to prison, four of whom were executed.

On December 1, 1741, fourteen additional firemen were appointed.

In this year also a committee of the Common Council was appointed "to inspect the ladders, hooks, etc., and to cause one hundred leather buckets to be made."

The number of houses in the city, in the year 1744, was as hereby particularized:

The west side of Broadway to the river	129
The east side of Broadway, with the west side of Broad Street	232
The east side of Broad Street, with the west side of William Street	324
The east side of William Street, with the west side of Pearl Street	242
The east side of Pearl Street to the East River	214
Total	1,141

Professor Kahn, who visited this city in 1748, thus describes it: "Most of the houses are built of bricks, and are generally strong and neat, and several stories high; some have, according to the old architecture, turned the gable end towards the street but the new houses are altered in this respect. Many of the houses have a balcony on the roof, on which the people sit in the evenings in the summer time; and from thence they have a pleasant view of a great part of the town, and likewise of part of the adjacent water and of the opposite shore. The roofs are commonly covered with tiles or shingles, the latter of which are made of the white fir tree, which grows higher up in the country. The inhabitants are of opinion that a roof made of these shingles is as durable as one made of white cedar. The walls of the houses are whitewashed within, and I did not anywhere see hangings, with which the people in this country seem in general to be little acquainted. The walls are quite covered with all sorts of drawings and pictures in small frames. On each side of the chimney they usually have a sort of alcove, and the wall under the window is wainscotted, with benches near the window. The alcoves, as well as all of the woodwork, are painted with a bluish-gray color."

"The streets do not run so straight," he further adds, "as those of Philadelphia, and have sometimes considerable bendings; however, they are very spacious and well-built, and most of them are paved, excepting in high places, where it has been found useless. In the chief streets there are trees planted, which, in summer, give them a fine appearance, and, during the excessive heat at that time, afford a cooling shade. I found it extremely pleasant to walk in the town, for it seemed quite like a garden. The trees, which are planted for this purpose, are chiefly of two kinds; the water beech is the most numerous, and gives an agreeable shade in summer by its large and numerous leaves. The locust tree is likewise frequent; its fine leaves, and the odoriferous scent which exhales from its flowers, make it very proper for being planted in the streets, near the houses, and in gardens. There are likewise lime trees and elms in these walks, but they are not, by far, so fragrant as the others. One seldom meets with trees of the same sort adjoining each other, they being in general placed alternately. Besides numbers of birds of all kinds which make these trees their abode, there are likewise a kind of frog, which frequents them in great numbers during the summer. They are very clamorous in the evening, and in the nights (especially when the days have been hot and a rain is expected), and in a manner drown the singing of the birds. They frequently make such a noise that it is difficult for a person to make himself heard."

It was decided, in February, 1749, to build an engine house in Hanover Square, and to procure one hundred new fire buckets. Three years later, in May, the watch prison was designated a house for a fire engine, and six small speaking trumpets were purchased.

On February 23, 1753, a fire broke out in the new Free School House, kept by Mr. Joseph Hildreth, clerk of Trinity Church, which entirely destroyed the building. The steeple of Trinity Church was set on fire several times from the flying coals, but the fire was happily extinguished and the steeple preserved. The whole loss sustained was set down at two thousand pounds.

Peter Clopper was allowed three pounds for building an engine house, "on a vacant lot called Rutgers' Walk, in the east ward of the city." Engine Company No. 26, it is believed, occupied the site of this building in after years in Rutgers Street.

In addition to the law for the better preventing of fire which was ordained on the eighth of November, 1756, an ordinance was passed in November, 1757, decreeing that no person should have, keep or put any hay or straw in barracks or piles in his yard or garden, or in any other place, to the southward of Fresh Water, except in close buildings erected for the purpose; and that no person should have, keep, or put any hay or straw in any house, stable or building within the same limits, that should be within ten feet of any chimney, hearth, or fireplace, or place for keeping ashes, under the penalty of twenty shillings for every offense, one-half of which should be recovered for the church wardens for the use of the poor of the city, and the other half for the person who should prosecute the complaint. The new barracks adjacent to the workhouse being unprotected, a fire engine and fifty buckets were sent there. In order to provide additional and more powerful fire engines, it was decided at a meeting of the Common Council, held on June 20, that the remainder of the money acquired by the sale of the city's fire-arms to General Abercrombie, be sent to England for the purchase there of one large fire engine, one small one, and two hand engines, with some buckets, etc.

In July, Jacob Stoutenburgh was appointed overseer of the fire engines and appurtenances, agreeing to take care of them and keep them in good order for the sum of thirty pounds per year. The following year Mr. Stoutenburgh was known as the engineer of the department, having as assistants Samuel Bell and Jasper Ten Brook. The working force consisted of twelve men for each of the six wards.

No attempt was made to light the streets by public authority until the year 1762, excepting a temporary ordinance in the latter part of the previous century, requiring the occupants of every tenth house to hang out a lantern upon a pole. An act of Assembly was passed in the above year giving the corporation authority to provide means for lighting the city. In the same year the first posts and lamps were purchased. In 1770 a contract was made with J. Stoutenburgh for supplying oil and lighting the city lamps, for the sum of seven hundred and sixty dollars. In 1774 the city employed sixteen lamplighters. This system of lighting the city remained substantially the same until the contract with the New York Gaslight Company, in 1823, by which certain parts of the city were to be lighted with gas.

Nicholas De Reimer was appointed foreman in the East Ward, on January 4, 1765, in the place of David Hansen, deceased; and Nathan Fish was appointed a foreman in the place of David Scott, who had removed to Albany.

On October 14, John Silvester was appointed a fireman in the place of Andrew Gotier, the then assistant foreman in the Dock Ward.

In 1767 it was directed that all the roofs in the city should be covered with slate or tiles. For some years, however, tiles alone were used, the first building roofed with slate being, it is said, the City Hotel, in Broadway, erected about 1794.

The number of firemen in the city had been increased by February 1, 1769, to one hundred and thirty.

The law prescribing a penalty for permitting chimneys to take fire through neglect to keep them clean became practically obsolete because of the unwillingness of neighbors to turn informers and help to prosecute for violations of it. It was therefore deemed necessary in November, 1771, to appoint Johannis Myer to perform that disagreeable but necessary service; and the penalties were to be devoted to a firemen's fund for the purchase of material required by them in the prosecution of their duties. The engineer in this year, for "maintaining" ten engines and for his own salary, drew the sum of thirty-three pounds and six shillings. The following year a third assistant engineer was appointed, and three additional engines were purchased.

Five acres on Broadway were purchased during the year 1773, and buildings erected at a cost of about eighteen thousand dollars, for the New York Hospital. Before their completion their interior was burned out by an accidental fire, and the work thus retarded for a considerable time.

"The Provost House," at the Battery, wherein dwelt Governor Tryon, was consumed by fire at midnight on December 17 of this year. The family escaped with difficulty. The governor's daughter leaped from the second story window, and her maid, Elizabeth Garrett, afraid to follow her, was burned to death. Greater mischief would have been wrought but for the snow on the adjacent buildings.

Christopher Colles, in 1774, had partly constructed a reservoir in Broadway, near Pearl Street, the completion of which was stopped by the Revolutionary war.

Isaac Bangs, a New England trooper of 1776, thus describes the New York of that period: "I spent most of the day in viewing the city, which is more extensive than I imagined. It is nearly as populous as the town of Boston. The public edifices are more numerous, yet not in general so magnificent as those of Boston. ★ ★ ★ On the southwest part of the town, which is a point between the two rivers, is a very strong and costly fort, built by the king's troops. Outside the fort, at the edge of the water, was a battery, erected at a vast expense to the king, of hewn stone, being about ten feet high, and having the inside filled up to form an inclined plane, sloping inwardly down to a wall one and a half feet high. Over this the cannon were to play. But as so low a wall would not be a sufficient cover for the men, our people were busily employed in making a turf wall upon the stone wall, and when we arrived, had almost finished as complete a battery as ever I saw. From the above-mentioned fort, a spacious street, running east-northeast in a straight line, reached without the town above a mile. In this, near the fort, is the equestrian statue of George III." Lieutenant Bangs refers to the "new" water works, and says that the well water is very bad and unwholesome, "so that the inhabitants prefer to buy water for making coffee, out of carts employed in carrying it around the city." One Sunday he dropped into a church, but could not understand a word of the service because it was all in Dutch. On another Sunday, this observant soldier says: "In the forenoon I attended public worship at the Congregational meeting; was very much disappointed with the preaching. The parson had invited a chaplain of the army to do his work for him, who performed it miserably. Being tired of such nonsense as I heard in the forenoon, I tried the Church of England in the afternoon. But the satisfaction I received from the substance of an excellent sermon was greatly abated by the pedantic behaviour of the priest, the irreverent conduct of the people, and the foolish parade of ceremonies. I am determined next Sunday (unless I find better entertainment) to attend worship with the Dutch priest, whom I heard last week, choosing rather to worship where I understand nothing than to hear and see such folly."

On the fifteenth of September, 1776 (soon after the disastrous battle on Long Island), the British troops took possession of the city, and in their train were refugees from all sections. Later, traders and speculators came in hordes by every transport fleet from Great Britain, and a large business sprung up in the purchase and sale of army supplies, but the city itself found no profit in this abnormal traffic. The streets and buildings were allowed to go to decay, with the exception of temporary repairs for sanitary reasons, and the glories of the once thriving city were but a story of the past.

Up to 1776 there were but seven engines and two bucket and ladders, or trucks, although there were building at the time one for No. 8. During the early part of this year the whole force of the Fire Department, consisting of a little over one hundred and seventy, formed themselves into a home guard, with Jacob Stoutenburgh as chief, but virtually under command of General Washington.

Two terrible conflagrations added to the measure of distress and ruin. Hardly had the British troops taken possession, ere (on the twenty-first of September, 1776,) a disastrous fire, breaking out in a small wooden house on the wharf near Whitehall, occupied by dissolute characters, spread to the northward, and consumed the entire city westward of Broadway to the very northernmost limit. In this terrible calamity, which owed its extent to the desertion of the city and the terror of the few remaining inhabitants, four hundred and ninety-three houses were destroyed, including old Trinity and the Lutheran Church. Another destructive fire broke out on Cruger's wharf on the third of August, 1778, and burned about fifty-four houses.

The cause of so many houses being burned was attributed to the military taking the directions of the fire from the firemen. The commander-in-chief, to whom complaint was made by the citizens, gave general orders that in future no military man should interfere with any fire that might happen within the city.

The following is a list of the number of houses burned (1778): Col. Wm. Bayard, six houses and stores; Messrs. John and Henry Cruger, six houses; Gerardus Duyckinck, seven houses; Peter Mesier, two dwelling houses; David Provost, four houses and two pulled down; Capt. Thomas Brown, four houses; Mr. Varick, one house; estate of Andrew Meyer, one house.

Several of the inhabitants were restrained from going out to assist at night from a fear that they might be arrested as suspicious persons. In fact, several decent citizens were sent to the provost guard for examination, and some had to stay there two or three days until their "loyalty" could be made out. In one case, even a good loyalist, sometimes inclined "to taste a drop too much," was, by misapprehension of his character and in the excitement of the moment, hung up on a sign-post at the corner of Cherry and Roosevelt Streets.

These fires occurred while the British held possession of the city, and excited a fear at the time that the "American Rebels" had purposed to oust them by their own sacrifices, like another Moscow. It was, however, established that they were the result of accident and not of design.

After the great fire of 1776, Major-General Jas. Robertson issued the following proclamation:

> *Whereas*, There is ground to believe that the Rebels, not satisfied with the Destruction of Part of the City, entertain Designs of burning the Rest. And it is thought that a Watch to inspect all the Parts of the City to apprehend Incendiaries and to stifle Fires before they rise to a dangerous Height might be a necessary and proper means to prevent such a calamity. Many of the principal inhabitants have applied to me to form such a Watch and have all offered to watch in person, etc.

The Revolution caused an abrupt break in the municipal history. The meetings of the Mayor's Court of Quarter Sessions and the Common Council ceased after July 4, 1776. On the occupation of the city by the British they were not resumed; but, the city being placed under martial law, military courts of police took their place. When, after this seven years' blank, the forms of municipal government were restored, it was under the constitution of the State of New York adopted in 1777.

The mayor and superintendent-general, in 1778, made proclamation to the citizens that John Norris, at the corner house, near the Main Guard, and David Henry Mallows, near the Tea Water Pump, had the care of the chimney-sweeps, and that on a note in writing being left at either of their houses, a sweep would be sent to the place designated. A fine of five pounds, previously established, it was declared, would be punctually exacted from every inhabitant whose chimney should take fire through neglect. Each chimney should be swept once in every four weeks. Similarly, notice was given that John Roome was appointed to examine the stoves put up in the city, and the places allotted by the inhabitants to keep their ashes in. The inhabitants were reminded that "the injudicious method of firing stoves, and keeping ashes, having often endangered this city, it is expected that the citizens will punctually attend to such directions as Mr.

Roome may judge necessary, in order to prevent the calamity of fire, which is equally to be dreaded by every inhabitant."

On June 14, 1780, by permission of the commandant, a scheme was devised and put in operation for the purpose of procuring an additional number of fire buckets for the use of the city. The prizes offered ranged from one thousand dollars to eight dollars. There were one thousand five hundred and two prizes, four thousand four hundred and ninety-eight blanks, and six thousand tickets at four dollars each, representing twenty-four thousand dollars, subject to a deduction of fifteen per cent. This scheme, when launched, was backed up with this admonition: "Depending on the liberality of those who wish to promote the common good, as well as to secure their own private interest, a large number of buckets are already contracted for and will soon be completed. As the safety of every individual is, in this measure, blended with public utility, it is not doubted but the same laudable spirit which on many former occasions has readily exerted itself, will again step forth for the speedy accomplishment of so necessary a purpose."

A number of citizens formed themselves into companies, in January of 1781, calling themselves by the names of the Friendly Union, Hand-in-Hand, and Heart-in-Hand Fire Companies. Their object was to undertake every service in their power, in case of fire, by removing and securing the effects of such of their fellow citizens whose situation, at such time, should require their attention. In order to be distinguished, they wore round hats with black brims and white crowns. They were exempted from handling buckets, or assisting in working the engines.

The troops in garrison were found to be derelict in the matter of complying with the order for cleaning of chimneys, and it was requested that in future the officers quartered in this city once in every month "will send to this office (barracks office, Maiden Lane) for an order for the sweeping of their chimneys."

The whole increase of the city during the century of English domination did not exceed twenty thousand, an increase which seems at the present day vastly disproportionate to the commercial and agricultural advantages of the city and province. But this surprise will decrease when the jealous and narrow-minded restrictions thrown around the colony are considered. As early as 1705 Governor Cornbury, writing from New York to his official superiors in England, expresses himself in these terms: "I hope I may be pardoned if I declare my opinion to be that all these coloneys, which are but twigs belonging to the main tree (England), ought to be kept entirely dependent upon and subservient to England, and that can never be if they are suffered to go on in the notions they have, that as they are Englishmen, so they may set up the same manufactures here as people may do in England."

The Department (up to 1776) consisted as follows:

Engine Company No. 1—Location, rear of City Hall.

Engine Company No. 2—Rear of City Hall,

Engine Company No. 3—At Kalch-Hook Pond.

Engine Company No. 4—Broadway and a lane leading down to Jansen's windmill, midway between Little Queen and Fair Streets.

Engine Company No. 5—On "Smit Valley," now Pearl Street.

Engine Company No. 6—Crown Street, near King, now Nassau.

Engine Company No. 7—Duke Street, leading down to Terry, now Stone.

Engine Company No. 8—At the Tar Pits, foot of now Maiden Lane.

Truck Company No. 2—Fair, near King Street.

Truck Company No. 2—S. E. of the Battery, adjoining the Basin.

During the war the Department was completely demoralized, but two engines having survived. Most of the members were killed, and when the British evacuated the city only one of the engines left would work.

CHAPTER IV

BEGINNING OF A NEW ERA

1783–1797.—The British Evacuate the City.— "Henceforth New York was to Move on her Marvelous Career."—Address of the Firemen to Governor Clinton.—Formation of a new Fire Organization.—The Fresh Water Pond.— New Companies Organized.—Fire Buckets and Their Uses.—Location of Engine Houses.

On the twenty-fourth of March 1783, Robert R. Livingston, the Secretary of Foreign Affairs, notified General Washington, then at West Point, of the agreeable intelligence of a general peace, and on the ninth of April following, at twelve o'clock, peace was proclaimed from the steps of the City Hall by the town major. On the twenty-fifth day of November the American army, under the command of Major-General Henry Knox, marched from Harlem to the Bowery Lane, where they remained until one o'clock, when, the British posts being withdrawn, the American column marched in and took possession of the city. The new era began upon this day; henceforth New York was to move on her marvelous career. In a few years she appears, reorganized, rebuilt, with new architecture, new institutions, *facile princeps*, the imperial city of the continent. The compact part of the city extended to Chambers Street on the north and to Catharine Street on the east. Fort George stood on the north end of the Battery, and barracks for soldiers on the south end. The upper barracks were in the park, on Chambers Street. The prison, new prison, and house of correction were in the park, the latter where now stands the City Hall. The fresh water pond on Centre Street was in part surrounded by hills. The hospital building stood near Broadway and Duane Street. A line of fortifications extended from the high grounds on the east part of the city to Bunker Hill, near Grand Street, between the Bowery and Broadway, and westward across Broadway to another eminence; fortifications were also erected farther west of Broadway, near the river, on a line with Fourteenth Street. All beyond was cleared fields.

In the lower parts of the city there was little to be seen but heaps of ruins. By far the greatest part of the buildings were composed of wood and covered with shingles, bricks and stones being very little used. Washington and West Streets were not in existence, and the project of making new grounds by encroachments on the rivers had been scarcely thought of. In a secluded spot, in the present Reade Street, near Broadway, was a burying ground for people of color, in the neighborhood of which there was scarcely to be found a single house; and immediately to the northward stretched fields and meadows, which extended far and wide. Very few streets were paved, and the workmanship of these few was performed in such a manner as would now be deemed very awkward; one gutter running through the center, which was the lowest part of the street, and the elevation on both sides being towards the houses. Of banks and insurances offices there was not one in the city. At the commencement of the Revolutionary War there were nineteen places of public worship; but at its close there were only nine. Trinity and the old Lutheran Church were consumed by the great fire, November 21, 1776, and the other churches, as well as the college, were used by the British as barracks, jails, hospitals, and riding schools.

The Bank of New York was the first banking institution established in this city, commencing operations in 1784, although not chartered until 1791, the banking house being located on the corner of Wall and William Streets. It was followed by the Manhattan Company, incorporated in 1799, located at No. 23 Wall Street; by the Merchants' Bank, incorporated in 1805, located at 25 Wall Street; by the United States Bank, located at 38 Wall Street, about 1805; by the Mechanics' Bank, incorporated in 1810, located at 16 Wall Street. These were the pioneer banking institutions, which were soon after rapidly increased in number.

Insurance companies were in existence in this city still earlier than banks. "We believe," says Valentine, "the first institution of the kind after the Revolutionary War was called the Mutual Assurance Company. We find that in 1815 there were already thirteen insurance companies established in Wall Street."

The principal event which settled the character of Wall Street as the center of interest in the city, and which brought about it the leading men of business and professional life, was the erection of the old City Hall, opposite Broad Street, in 1700; which building became afterwards the Capitol of the United States, and the site of which is still used for public purposes, thus perpetuating the influence of the original selection of that site down to the present day. The City Hall remained in use for the objects for which it was erected about a century. After the Revolutionary War this building received additional historic interest as the first place of meeting of the Congress of 1789, and the inauguration of George Washington as president.

Shortly after the British troops had taken their final departure, this manly missive (a *fac-simile* of the original) was penned:

To His Excellency George Clinton Esq.
Governor of the State of New york in Ameri=
.ca &c.ᵃ   May it please your Excellency

As the Change of Government
has now taken place on the Arrival of your Excellency
in this City — We the Fire Engineers of the Several Fire
Engines, and Companies belonging to the same, beg leave
to lay before your Excellency, the State and Condition
of the Fire Engines &c.ⁿ — as also of the several Companies
and Number of Men now belonging to the same.

We further beg leave to represent to your Excellency
That the Fire Engines with the other emplements belong=
.ing, were before the late Fire all in good Condition, and
the Companies under good Order and Regulations: And
as there are at present a Number of Fire Buckets ---
wanting, and Also Some Necessary to be done (Occasioned
by the late Fire) to the several apparatus belonging to
the Engines, which require immediate dispatch. not
knowing how soon they may be wanted — We think it
Our duty, and therefore take this early Opportunity to
represent this matter to your Excellency, as the safety

and preservation of this Metropolis at Times depend greatly in keeping the Engines in good Order.

We now beg leave to inform your Excellency, that we held a Commission Jointly and Severally, under the late Governor Robertson, and are happy to say we always gain'd applause from the Citizens for Our good Conduct in the Alarming time of Fire in this City — Should it please your Excellency to Continue us in this office under your Administration we will always Act with such Conduct, as we make no Doubt will, when Called upon in Time of Fire gain the applause of your Excellency, as well as in the late Fire we have of the Citizens. — — We

Remain with Great Respect

Your Excellency's Most Obed.t &

Most Hum.ble Serv.ts

John Balthaser Dash.

George Stanton

Francis Dominick

Jeronemus Alstyne

New York 27th November 1783.

A List of the Names of the Foremen and Common men, belonging to the several Fire Engines, with the Members of the Same, —

Engine —

		Men
N.	Jacob Boelen, Foreman — — — —	12
2.	John Burt Syng — — — Do — — — —	12
3.	John C. Cuntzius — — — Do — — — —	16
4.	John Post — — — — — Do — — — —	13
5.	Daniel Penlyck — — — Do — — —	22
6	Nicholas Carmer — — — Do — — —	21
7.	Ahasuerus Turk — — Do — — — —	24
8	Henry Riker — — — — Do — — — —	23
9.	Charles Doughty — — — Do — — —	16
10	Isaac Meade — — — Do — — —	22
11	Christopher Henniges — Do — — —	16
12	John B. Dash Jun. — Do — — —	12
13	Richard Deane — — Do — —	12
14	Benjamin Birdsall — Do — — —	10

Men belonging to
Ladders and hooks }—

No. 1	Daniel Cotheng	Foreman —	12
2.	William Wright — Do — — —		10

253

What was recognized as the upper extremity of Broadway in 1784, and the utmost limit of the city pavement, was the site of St. Paul's Chapel. The fields were open to the north as far as a line ranging eastwardly from Warren Street, where the prospect was bounded by those more useful than agreeable objects, the bridewell, the poorhouse, the gaol, and the gallows. Towards the west, however, there was nothing to obstruct the view of the North River but two low houses at the corner of Vesey Street and the college building. The "fields," as the area comprised in the park was then called, were neither enclosed nor planted. The streets leading from Broadway to the river had been laid out as high as Warren Street, yet they were but partially built upon, and, for the most part, with houses of an inferior description. None above Dey Street had been regulated and paved; nor had the ridge, commencing near the Battery and extending the length of the island, been dug through as far even as Cortlandt Street. Great Dock Street, or that part of Pearl between Whitehall and Coenties Slip, with the other streets in the neighborhood in the immediate vicinity of Fort George, within which the Colonial Government House was situate, had long been considered the court end of the town. But, even before the Revolution, Wall Street was regarded as a rival seat of fashion, to which it established an exclusive claim, and maintained it until superseded by Park Place (or Robinson Street). Little Dock Street, now merged in Water Street, and that part of the original Water Street which lay adjacent to the Albany pier, were occupied by the river trade; while the remainder of Water Street, and such parts of Front Street as had already been recovered from the river, formed the emporium of foreign commerce. This, indeed, was the case as far up as the Coffee House Slip, and gradually extended to Maiden Lane, at the foot of which was the *Vly* market and the Brooklyn ferry; whilst at the head of it stood the Oswego Market, fronting on Broadway. Above, on the East River, as far as Dover Street, the wharves were chiefly occupied by down-easters with their cargoes of notions, or by Long Islanders with their more substantial freights of oysters, clams, and fine white sand. Beyond Dover Street, the shipyards commenced, extending at first no farther than to the "New," or, as it is now called, "Pike" Slip. Crossing from Dover to Great Queen (since Pearl) Street, and following the latter beyond its intersection with Chatham Street, and along that part of Pearl then called Magazine Street, the *"Kolch,"* or "Fresh Water Pond" was reached; whence, through the "Tea Water Pump," in Chatham Street, the city was supplied with water for domestic use, distributed to the inhabitants by means of carts surmounted by casks. Nor was this the only use made of the "Collect," as it was called in English. Its southern and eastern banks were lined with furnaces, potteries, breweries, tanneries, ropewalks, and other manufactories, all drawing their supplies of water from the pond.

Numerous fire buckets had disappeared from time to time—expropriated or irremediably damaged. So great had the deficiency thus created become, by the commencement of 1784, that the Common Council appointed a committee to ascertain the number wanting, and to make contracts for new buckets.

The first regular organization of the Fire Department of the city of New York appears to have been effected on the fifteenth of February, 1786, when it was ordered by the Common Council that a roster of persons be appointed firemen, during the pleasure of the Board.

In May, 1785, a fire engine was purchased of Richard Deane for the sum of forty pounds sterling. In July of that year the French church was burnt. In October, as "the season in which fires most frequently happen was approaching," the law for the better preventing of fire was published in the newspapers of the city, so that no one could plead ignorance.

Although no effort appears to have been made by State laws prior to 1787 to organize any force of men specially charged with the extinguishment of fires in this city, it is worthy of note that two previous enactments had been made looking toward the prevention of fires, one in 1785, and the other the following year. The first of these laws was aimed at "the pernicious practice of firing guns, pistols, rockets, squibs, and other fireworks, on the eve of the last day of December, and the first and second days of January," and provided for a fine of forty shillings for the offense of firing off any gun, etc., within a quarter of a mile of any building on the days named. In the event of the fine not being paid, then the offender went to jail, "there to remain without bail or mainprize for the space of one month."

The other, passed in 1786, was directed against "the storing of pitch, tar, turpentine, resin, linseed oil, or shingles," as well as against the firing off of guns, pistols, etc. It prohibited the storing of any of the substances named in any place "south of fresh water in said city," under a penalty of ten pounds. But any ship chandler was allowed to have "near his door in the open street" not to exceed twenty barrels at any one time, "in order the more readily to supply the merchant ships, and others who may have occasion for small quantities of such commodities." Any person discharging any firearms or fireworks "on any lane, street, or ally, garden, or other enclosure, or in any other place where persons usually walk "south of fresh water," was liable to a penalty of twenty shillings, or to be imprisoned for ten days. If the offender were a slave, it was provided that he was to be "publickly whipped on the naked back as many times as the justice shall prescribe, not exceeding thirty-nine."

On March 15, 1787, the first act regulating the keeping and storing of gunpowder was passed. By this law, any gunpowder in greater quantity than twenty-eight pounds, found by any fireman outside of the powder magazine and within one mile of the City Hall, was forfeited to the use of such fireman, without the formality of any legal process whatever.

On November 1, 1780, the Hand-in-Hand Fire Company was organized. Certain rules and regulations were at various times agreed on, and adopted at a meeting held at the Coffee House on November 20, 1788. "The utility of associations for the purpose of averting as much as possible the ruinous consequences which may occasionally happen by fire," the preamble recites, "induced a number of individuals to form themselves into select companies, with the laudable view of affording their particular aid to each other, and to the community at large." Under this impression the society was formed. Among the articles of association was one requiring that each member should provide himself with two bags, consisting of three-and-a-half yards raven's duck (with proper strings), marked with the owner's name at length, and "H. H.," the initials of the company; also with a round hat, the crown to be painted white, and thereon the letters "H. H.," painted black, as large as the crown would permit; of which hat should be considered as the badge of distinction of the company in case of fire. Another article provided that there should be a watchword given by the president or vice-president, in order to prevent deception from intruders at the removal of effects in case of fire; and the watchword was to be demanded by one of the members, who should be placed as sentinel at the house or store in danger.

The earliest state law providing for the protection of the city from the ravages of fire, and upon which is founded all subsequent legislation relating to the appointment and equipment of firemen, is that passed on March 19, 1787, entitled "an act for the better extinguishment of fires in the city of New York." By that act, the Common Council was authorized and required to appoint "a sufficient number of strong, able, discreet, honest, and sober men, willing to accept, not exceeding three hundred in number of the inhabitants, being freeholders or freemen of said city, to have the care, management, working and using the fire engines and the other tools and instruments, now provided or hereafter to be provided for extinguishing fires, ★ ★ ★ which persons shall be called The Firemen of the City of New York; and who, with the engineers of the same city are hereby required and enjoined to be ready at all times, as well by night as by day, to manage, work and use all the same fire engines, and other of the tools and instruments aforesaid."

The firemen so appointed were made subject to such rules as the Common Council might prescribe "for the frequent exercising, trying and using of the same fire engines, tools, and other instruments."

It was decided in February, 1788, to remove the engine located in Nassau Street to a house to be erected on the ground belonging to the Reformed Protestant Dutch Congregation adjoining the North Church.

The meddlesome and often obstructive character of the help given to the firemen by boys and excitable young men, which caused so much trouble and anxiety in later times to the controllers of the Department, seems to have developed itself as early as 1789, for it is recorded as a decree of the august and reverend fathers of the city, that after the twelfth of August of that year no person under the age of thirty years should be appointed to the office of a fireman. But that law proved to be a decided drawback instead of a benefit to the Department, and it was therefore repealed in the following November.

The fire engines of the smallest size were used to approach nearest to the fire, and were, therefore, best adapted for the "leaders" to convey water through windows and narrow passes. When the "leaders" were used, none but firemen were willing to support them, and "it was attended by a general wetting by the water which gushes out of the seams." The foreman of these engines petitioned the Common Council for an assignment of ten men to each company, and their petition was acceded to in March, 1790.

A project was conceived about the year 1789 for converting the Fresh Water Pond, and the grounds adjacent, to the embellishment of the city. A company was formed with that view, and a plan drawn, laying out a park, embracing the great and lesser Collect, and extending from the north side of Reade Street to the present site of Grand Street, so as to include the eminence called "Bunker's Hill." The "Little Collect" commenced at the foot of the hill, on the north side of Reade Street, and was divided from the principal pond by a mound or knoll, through which Pearl Street was carried. On this knoll stood the "Old Powder House," from which the street leading to it from Broadway, now part of Pearl Street, derived its name of Magazine Street.

The plan for the conversion of the Collect, as stated, fell through, principally because the supposition of the city's ever extending so far out upon the island was thought by capitalists too visionary to be acted on. Another project, of a more utilitarian character, was subsequently entertained, namely, to connect the Collect with both rivers, thus converting it into a dock, with wharves and warehouses surrounding its margin. But such were the limited views generally prevalent at that day in regard to the probable increase of the city in size, business, wealth, and population, it was believed the dock would never be wanted.

Between 1787 and 1790 the streets leading from Broadway to Hudson River, from Cortlandt Street upward to the hospital, were regulated, and some of them paved. On the west side, Broadway was paved as far out as Warren Street, and large and substantial brick houses were gradually making their appearance. Greenwich Street, in which the most conspicuous object was the Bear Market, now superseded by the more extensive erection dignified with the name of Washington Market, was prolonged, by leveling high grounds extending northward from the foot of Warren Street, where stood Vauxhall House and Garden, once the seat of Sir Peter Warren. In this year the first sidewalks in the city were laid on the west side of Broadway, from Vesey to Murray Streets, and opposite for the same distance along the bride-well fence. These were narrow pavements of brick and stone, scarcely wide enough to permit two persons to walk abreast.

On March 24, 1791, the Legislature passed a law prohibiting the erection of wooden buildings of three or more stories below what is now Canal Street. All buildings to be erected within this space should be constructed of stone or brick, and should be covered, "except the flat roof thereof," with slate or tile. But such flat roof "may be composed of board or shingles, provided it does not exceed two-fifths of the space of the roof, and be surrounded by a substantial balcony or balustrade." An exception is made to the roofing of existing buildings, and also in favor of buildings erected on ground "not capable of sustaining a foundation, upon which a stone or brick structure can be sustained." This latter exception authorizes the erection of wooden buildings on such grounds within the limits named, after the filing of a favorable report of the majority of five disinterested persons appointed by the mayor to examine the condition of the ground in question.

A revised law for preventing and extinguishing fires was passed on November 10, 1791, which, among other provisions, called for the appointment of fire wardens in the respective wards of the city.

As marks of distinction at fires, and insignia of official position, it was decreed by the same law that the wardens should wear caps and carry certain wands and trumpets. And it was further ordered that all fines recovered as penalties for violations of the fire laws should be paid to the engineer, and by him appropriated as the fire marshal should direct.

In this year belong the earliest extant records of any fire company in the city, namely, those of Engine No. 13, which began in the month of November; also, the first written report known to have been made of the doings of the Fire Department proper, was made on the fourth of this month. The meeting was held in the house of Jacob Brouwer, in Nassau Street. The minutes of this meeting inform us that "engineers, firemen, and representatives" attended, but that the engineers and foremen were the only "representatives" present.

The Fire Department, on the twentieth of December, 1791, held a meeting of representatives of their organization, authorized by their different companies, and framed a constitution, for the purpose of establishing a fund for the relief of unfortunate firemen whose misfortune was occasioned while doing duty as firemen. This constitution reads as follows:

ARTICLE I. A fund, which shall be called The Fire Department Fund, shall be established with the moneys arising from chimney fires, certificates, and donations, and with such other moneys as may hereafter be agreed on by such fire companies as have already agreed or may hereafter agree to fund the same.

ARTICLE II. The Fire Department shall be represented as follows, viz.: The engineers to send one; a company composed of eighteen men or upwards to have two, and under eighteen, one representative; and such company to choose them on or before the first day of June in every year.

ARTICLE III. There shall be annually chosen, by ballot, by the representatives, out of their own body, a President and Vice-President, and out of the whole body of Firemen, at their first meeting, nine Trustees, a Treasurer and Secretary, which Treasurer shall give security to the Trustees for the faithful performance of his trust.

ARTICLE IV. The Trustees shall class themselves in three classes, viz., Nos. 1, 2, and 3. No. 1 shall go out the first year, No. 2 the second, and No. 3 the third year, and the representatives shall choose three new Trustees annually, at a meeting which shall be called by the President, or, in his absence, by the Vice-President, on the first Monday of July in every year, and as much oftener as any five representatives may require it.

ARTICLE V. The Trustees shall have the sole disposal of the moneys in the funds, which shall be for the relief of such disabled Firemen, or their families, as may be interested in this fund, and who may, in the opinion of a majority of the Trustees, be worthy of assistance.

ART. VI. At a meeting of the representatives, they shall have a right to inquire into the application of the funds, and, in case of a misapplication, or malconduct of any member, they shall have a right to call them to account, and, if found guilty of a breach of trust, shall be displaced, and a new Trustee or Treasurer elected.

In the month of December of this year, Nathaniel Hawkhurst, and some others in the vicinity of Burling Slip and Queen Street, proposed to the Corporation to purchase at their own expense a fire engine, and a proper place for its reception, if the Board would appoint them firemen. The proposal was accepted. In the same month, upon the representation of Foreman Kerley and the firemen of the engine located in Cherry Street, that it was too small for the service required of it, steps were taken to procure one of proper size, the Cherry Street engine to be removed to the almshouse. On the eighteenth of April, 1792, a fire engine, lately imported from London, was purchased from John W. Thompson for ninety pounds sterling.

The organization of the Fire Department up to January, 1792, consisted exclusively of engineers and foremen. The firemen, who were excluded, felt that they had a right to be represented, and they succeeded in carrying their point. By this change each company consisting of eighteen men were entitled to send two representatives, and each company consisting of less than this number was entitled to send one representative. Instead of all the engineers being members

of the organization, only one of them was admitted to membership. The following were elected officers: John Stagg, president; Ahasuerus Turk, vice-president;
William J. Elsworth, treasurer; Abraham Franklin, secretary.

The old Kennedy House (the Washington Hotel of later times) was located
at No. 1 Broadway. This building was an object of great historic interest. It was,
during the Revolution, occupied successively by Cornwallis, Clinton, Howe,
and Washington, and here André commenced his correspondence with Arnold.
The house was erected in 1760, by Hon. Captain Kennedy, afterwards Earl of
Cassilis. The great fires in 1776 and 1778 occurred while the British held possession of the city. This building was pulled down by Cyrus W. Field, who built
a more pretentious structure on its site.

The authorities went into the business of manufacturing their own engines—
or, rather, experimenting therein—in 1792, and had the satisfaction of receiving
a report in June of that year from Engineer Ellsworth, to the effect that the
engine had been successfully finished. It was deposited "in the rear of Mr. Mesier's lot, south of Cortlandt Street," under the direction of the aldermen and
assistant aldermen of the Fourth Ward.

About the same time the small engine at the almshouse was removed to the
Seventh Ward, to be located as the aldermen of that ward and the assistant
aldermen of the Sixth Ward should determine. This was the origination of Engine Company No. 19.

The manner of obtaining water at fires was principally by raising it in hand
buckets from the slips, which the inhabitants considered a most disagreeable duty.
The experiment of a copper pump for drawing water out of the river was suggested in the Council in July, 1792, and provoked a heated debate on the utility
of the measure, etc. It was agreed to, and the engineer was ordered to superintend
its construction.

The pump was completed by January, 1793, and deposited in the engine
house at the rear of the City Hall, and Richard Kip, and his father, James Kip,
were charged with the management of it.

In January, 1793, upon the representation of Engineer Ellsworth, that, on
account of the increase in the number of engines and firemen, an additional
engineer had become necessary, the Common Council appointed Ahasuerus
Turk an engineer.

The fire engine house in Greenwich Street was removed in July, to the Hay
Scales, in front of the basin at Thames and Little Queen Streets.

Owing to the heavy fall of snow during the month of December, sleds were
built for conveying Engines No. 17, 18, and 19, to fires, and two additional men
were added to Engine Company No. 19, who, because of their "remote situation
from the body of the city, found it difficult to transport their engine."

In 1793 the Common Council embodied all its rules for the conduct of the

Fire Department in a single ordinance. This ordinance is too valuable and too quaint a document not to be given nearly *verbatim:*

> "That the inhabitant and owner of every house in this city having less than three fireplaces shall provide one Leather Bucket; and having three fireplaces and under six, two; and having six fireplaces and under nine, four; and having nine Fire-Places and upwards, six; and of every Brew-House, Distilling and Sugar House, nine Buckets; and of every Bake House four Buckets, each of which Buckets ★ ★ ★ shall be sufficient to contain at least two Gallons and an half of Water, and shall be marked with at least the initial letters of the Landlord's Name, and shall be hung in the entry or near the Front Door ★ ★ ★ ready to be used for extinguishing fires, when there shall be occasion. The buckets to be got at the expense of the owner of the house, the tenant having the right to deduct the cost of the same from his rent. Penalty, six shillings for each bucket not provided.
>
> So many Firemen shall from time to time be appointed in each of the Wards of this city as the Common Council shall deem proper, and shall be called Fire Wardens, whose Duty it shall be, immediately on the cry of fire, to repair to the place where it shall be, and to direct the inhabitants in forming themselves into Ranks for handing the Buckets to supply the Fire Engines with Water, in such places and in such manner as they may think will best answer the purpose, under the direction of the Mayor, Recorder, and Aldermen, if present.

This ordinance further provides that the mayor, recorder, aldermen and assistants shall carry at fires "a white wand, at least five feet in length, with a gilded flame at the top; and each of the fire wardens shall wear upon those occasions a cap with the city arms painted on the front, and the crown painted white, and carry in his hand ★ ★ ★ a speaking trumpet painted white."

This ordinance also provides that when a fire occurs the watchman shall give notice to the fire wardens, whose names and addresses are required to be hung up in the watchhouse. "And it is enjoined on the inhabitants to place a lighted candle at the front window of their respective houses, in order that the people shall pass through the streets with greater safety." The men are also required at least once a month to exercise with their engines, etc., and to wash, clean, and examine them, under a penalty of six shillings; and for every failure to attend at the fire, and for leaving his engine while at a fire, and for failure to do his duty at a fire, a fine of twelve shillings is imposed, and to be removed from office as fireman. The chief engineer is required to see that all buckets are collected after fires, and carried to the City Hall, "and placed upon the pavement there under the Hall, so that the citizens may know where to find them."

The fire wardens are required to examine the houses and buildings in their respective wards, and to see that "they be properly furnished with buckets;" and also to examine fireplaces, chimneys, outhouses, and buildings, stoves and pipes thereof, and give notice of any danger or deficiency to the mayor or recorder, who can impose a fine of ten shillings, if he feels so disposed. Stoves could be erected without the approval of the fire wardens, but subject to a fine of twenty shillings.

The need of street numbers had been for some time rendered apparent by the increasing growth of the city, and, in 1793, the corporation appointed a committee to prepare and report a feasible system. This was done, and the proposed method, beginning at the next house in every street terminating at either of the rivers, at the intersection of the main street next the river, and numbering all houses below these intersecting streets, beginning with No. 1, looking upward in all the main streets and downward in all the slips, and so on to the end of the street or slip, was adopted by the corporation.

In 1793 the Fire Department consisted of twenty engines, two hook and ladder companies, twenty-two foremen, thirteen assistants, and three hundred and eighteen men.

About the year 1794 the fire engines were of a very inferior quality; and no water was to be had except from wooden-handle pumps. By a law of the corporation, every owner of a dwelling was obliged to procure a fire-bucket for every fireplace in the house or back kitchen. These buckets held three gallons, and were made of sole leather. They were hung in the passage, near the front door, and when the bell rang for fire the watchmen, firemen, and boys, while running to the fire, sang out, "Throw out your buckets." These were picked up by the first to come along. Two lines were formed, from the fire to the nearest pump; when the pump gave out the lines were carried to the nearest river; one line passed down the empty, the other passed up the full buckets. It was seldom that any person attempted to break through these lines. As we have said elsewhere he would be roughly handled if he tried it. The firemen expected every good citizen to give them aid.

Up to 1795 private citizens had furnished the fire-buckets. This plan did not prove satisfactory. As an improvement, each engine house was furnished with two poles, of sufficient length to carry twelve buckets each. These poles were carried on the shoulders of firemen when going to fires, as may be seen represented in engravings on old firemen's certificates. The general rule that prevailed was, that the first fireman to reach the engine house after an alarm of fire should have a right to the pipe, and take it with him to the fire; that the next four firemen to arrive should bear away the bucket-poles; and that the rest of the company should run off with the engine, "bawling out and demanding the aid of citizens as they proceeded on."

The small engine and house in Gold Street were removed in May, 1795, to the neighborhood of the hospital; and it was ordered that a new house be erected in Gold Street for an engine about to be purchased. Orders were also given for the erection of an engine house in the vicinity of that existing in Maiden Lane, which had become unfit for use, and had to be removed from Mr. Rutger's lot, on which it stood.

An amendment to the building laws was recommended in February, 1795, that no building, excepting those of stone or brick, and covered with slate or tile, should be of any greater height from the level of the ground to the lower part of the roof than twenty-eight feet, and that the pitch of the roof should not exceed ten inches per foot.

A fire engine was located adjacent to the Methodist Church, in the Seventh Ward, in June of this year. In October, an ordinance was passed compelling the Tea Water men to supply the engines with water in case of fire.

The Fresh Pond, or, as the Dutch designated it, *Kolch*, which name had been corrupted into the "Collect," was the scene of one of the most interesting events that the world ever saw. That was nothing less than the original experiment in steam navigation. Here, in 1795, was exhibited by John Stevens, of Hoboken, a boat with a screw propeller driven by a steam engine. The next year another experiment was made in the same place by John Fitch, the real inventor of steam navigation, with a ship's yawl, into which he had placed a rude steam engine of his own construction, with paddle-wheels at the sides of the boat. These experiments, with Fitch's invention, were made in the presence and under the inspection of Chancellor Livingston, and Stevens, and Roosevelt, and doubtless afforded many of the facts and suggestions through which Fulton made the art available for useful purposes.

Five men were added to each Hook and Ladder Company in November, 1796.

On December 9, about one o'clock, a destructive fire broke out near the center of Murray's Wharf, Coffee House Slip, which, notwithstanding the exertions of all the engines, and a vast concourse of the citizens, could not be got under until it terminated at the Fly Market, and having consumed nearly fifty buildings, the property of a number of citizens, some of whom, in consequence, were reduced from affluence to indigence.

The location of engine houses in 1796 was as follows:

No. 1 Engine House, opposite Groshan's brewhouse, Barley Street.
No. 2 Engine House, near the new Methodist Church.
No. 3 Engine House, Nassau Street, opposite City Hall.
No. 4 Engine House, fronting the Playhouse, John Street.
No. 5 Engine House.

No. 6 Engine House, at the College Wall, Murray Street.
No. 7 Engine House, Cliff Street, by the Church Wall.
No. 8 Engine House, adjoining the Gaol yard.
No. 9 Engine House, Whitehall Street, near the Government House.
No. 10 Engine House, top of Catharine Street, in Chatham Street.
No. 11 Engine House, Hanover Square.
No. 12 Engine House, at the junction of Pearl and Cherry Streets.
No. 13 Engine House, near Ferry Stairs, Fish Market.
No. 14 Engine House.
No. 15 Engine House, in Nassau Street, opposite the Federal Hall.
No. 16 Engine House, in Liberty Street, near the New Dutch Church.
No. 17 Engine House, near the New Slip.
No. 18 Engine House, on the Hill, John Street near Pearl Street.
No. 19 Engine House, Hester Street, near Bowery Lane.
No. 20 Engine House, Greenwich Street, at the new Albany Pier.
No. 21 Engine House, adjoining the burial ground of the Baptist Church, Gold
  Street.
No. 22 Engine House, George Street.

A new engine was purchased in January, 1797, for Engine Company No. 1, and the membership raised to twenty. At the same time the petition of Peter Curtenius and others for a fire engine in Greenwich Street, between Reade and Lispenard Streets, was granted.

John Halsey represented to the Common Council in February, 1797, that he would undertake to import from Hamburg two fire engines, with long hose, to convey water from the river into the interior of the city, of superior quality, and on cheaper terms than similar machines could be manufactured in this country. The Council gave Mr. Halsey encouragement, and appointed a committee to communicate with him.

CHAPTER V

IMPROVEMENT IN FIRE
EXTINGUISHING METHODS

*1798–1811.—Act of Incorporation (1798).—Formation of Fire Insurance
Companies.—Additional Fire Engines.—Description of the City about the
Close of the Eighteenth Century.—Rapid Extension of New York.—Great
Fire of 1804.—Fire Plugs.—Another Destructive Conflagration (1811).*

The act of March 19, 1787, limited the number of firemen to three hundred,
to be nominated and appointed by the Mayor and Common Council, and
they were by its provisions enjoined to be ready at all times, as well by night as
by day, to manage, control, and use the fire engines to be provided, and were
exempt from service as constables, jurors, and militiamen, and placed generally
under the regulation of the city government. In 1792 the number was increased
to four hundred and fifty. On the twentieth of March, 1798, however, upon a
petition of the firemen praying to be incorporated, the more effectually to enable
them to provide adequate funds for the relief of disabled and injured firemen,
and for the purpose of extinguishing fires, they were incorporated under the
name of the Fire Department of the City of New York.

The members of the Department and their successors were accordingly rendered capable of suing and being sued "in all courts and places whatsoever, in
all matters of actions, suits, complaints, causes and matters whatsoever, and that
they and their successors may have a common seal, and may change and alter
the same at their pleasure."

By this act, the firemen belonging to any of the engines of the city of New
York were declared to be and to continue as such until the year 1818 a body
politic, by the name of the "Fire Department of the City of New York." They
and their successors were declared capable of purchasing, holding, and conveying
any estate, real or personal, for the use of the said corporation, not to exceed
the sum of twenty thousand dollars. The said representatives, on the second
Monday of December in every year, elected by ballot, out of their own body,
a president and vice-president, and out of the whole body of firemen, three
trustees, a treasurer, secretary, and collector.

The trustees were divided into three classes; the first class to go out of office the first year; the second, the second year; and the third, the third year. These trustees managed the affairs and disposed of the funds of the corporation according to the by-laws, rules, and regulations.

The funds of the corporation were obtained from chimney fines, certificates, donations, etc.

The incorporation of the Fire Department appears to have acted as a signal for the formation of fire insurance corporations. That arm of the commerce of our great city, now grown so powerful and far-reaching, holding within its sweep untold millions of capital, was represented at this period, so far as the statutes of this state indicate, only by two companies, known as "The United Insurance Company" and "The Mutual Assurance Company."

The latter company was incorporated in 1798, March 23, on the mutual plan, and among its incorporators are to be found names familiar to all insurance men, many of which will be found intimately associated with the history and progress of life, as well as fire insurance in this city. They embrace such names as Thomas Pearsall, Nicholas Gouverneur, Abraham Varick, Wynant Van Zandt, Samuel Franklin, John Thompson, Robert Lenox, Gulian Verplank, Samuel Bowne, and Leonard Bleecker.

The first intimation in the municipal records of the Fire Department, of trouble arising from personal disagreements among members of a company, is given in the proceedings of the Board of Aldermen dated February 12, 1798. Therein it is set forth that the foreman and other members of Engine Company No. 7 complained against Jacob Tablie, one of their number, for rude and improper conduct, for refusing to observe the rules and regulations of the company, and disturbing the harmony thereof. The Board heard Mr. Tablie in his own defense, and concluded that the best interests of the company and the department demanded his removal, which was immediately effected, and John Drake was appointed in his stead.

A new fire engine was "imported" from Philadelphia in February, 1798, and placed in charge of Engine Company No. 15, stationed at the City Hall, and their old engine was packed off to the Seventh Ward.

Two fire engines arrived from Hamburg in the spring of 1799, and measures were taken for the erection of a house for them in the yard of the almshouse.

The jail bell of the old bridewell possessed a peculiar sound, known from all others. "I remember," writes an old New Yorker, "its sounding for a break-out by the prisoners, about the year 1800. Old Peter Lorillard, the tobacconist, was shot by a prisoner whom he tried to arrest. It was some months before he recovered." The shooting caused quite a sensation at the time.

About the year 1800 New York fairly overleaped the boundaries that seemed for a while to confine it. A line of low grounds and watercourses extended quite across the island, from the great swamp on the East River, through the Fresh

Water Pond and Lispenard's meadows, to the Hudson, cutting off the city from the high ground beyond. For a long time the only public highway over this low ground was the Boston road (now called the Bowery), which passed over a bridge near the head of Roosevelt Street. Recently a passage had been made on the shore of the Hudson, pretty nearly answering to the present Greenwich Street. But the growth of the city naturally caused it to expand beyond its former limits, and with the beginning of the nineteenth century the city began its progress "up-town."

About this time St. Paul's steeple was on fire, and was saved by a sailor climbing up the steeple. The great tea-water pump in Chatham Street was, when an emergency arose, utilized to extinguish the flames. Hundreds of water carts supplied housekeepers with this pure water, and as the fire occurred on a Sunday, all these water carts were employed in taking water to St. Paul's and the fire engines.

In January, 1800, the small Engine No. 21 was removed from the engine house in Gold Street, near the Baptist Meeting House, to the house in Greenwich Street, near the Industry Furnace, in the place of the old Engine No. 1, which had been removed to Engine House of No. 23, in Broadway, near the Hospital.

On the thirteenth of this month Uzziah Coddington, attached to Engine Company No. 14, was appointed a fire warden. On the twenty-seventh of the same month, Nicholas Van Antwerp, of Engine Company No. 11, was promoted to the position of an engineer.

Thomas Howell imported two fire engines from London in December, which the Corporation purchased from him for the sum of four thousand dollars. At a conference between the engineer and a committee of the Common Council, held in the same month, the following disposition of the new engines and alteration of some of the old ones was agreed upon:

The large engine (imported) was placed in the corner of the yard of the City Hall, and an engine house built adjoining the house of Mr. Verplank. It was numbered 3, and allowed a complement of twenty-four firemen. The other lately imported engine was placed in the jail-yard in the house where No. 8 lay, receiving that number, and being allowed twenty men. Old No. 8 was removed to the Furnace at the North River, and numbered 1, and its company increased to thirteen men. Engine No. 3 was removed to the Hospital, and numbered 23, to replace the engine sent to Poughkeepsie—No. 1—then at the Hospital, being out of order and useless. Engine No. 21, then at the Furnace, was returned to its original stand in Gold Street, near the Baptist Meeting House. The company of the old Engine No. 3, consisting of ten men, was put in charge of the new engine in the yard of the City Hall, and its strength increased to twenty-four men. The company belonging to Engine No. 8, consisting of thirteen men, was placed in charge of the new engine in the jail-yard, and the force increased to twenty men.

In addition to the foregoing, the Council committee recommended that a new engine house be built at the head of the Common Sewer, at Burling Slip, near Pearl Street, for Engine No. 18, and with respect to the floating engine, that a boat be immediately procured for it, and placed in one of the most central slips on the East River, with a force of thirty able-bodied men. Protests were subsequently presented against this location for the engine house, and it was decided that a more eligible site would be at Beekman's Slip, directly in the rear of a fountain erected by the Manhattan Company for supplying shipping with water. As these changes and assignments called for the employment of an additional number of fifty-one men, which would increase the firemen to a greater number than the law allowed, it was decided to apply to the legislature to increase the number of firemen to six hundred.

The Fire Department consisted of a single engineer, who received his appointment from the Common Council, and who was invested with absolute control over the companies, engines, and all else that pertained to the organization; a number of fire wardens, commissioned by the same authority to inspect buildings, chimneys, etc., and to keep order at fires; and several voluntary companies under the direction of a foreman, assistant, and clerk of their own choosing. A few engine houses had been built; the greater part of the hooks and ladders, buckets, etc., were deposited for safe keeping in the City Hall. Several of these pioneer companies retained their organization up to the time of the disbandment of the volunteer system.

At this time, the city, though the metropolis of the western world, was a mere village in comparison with the city of to-day. The city proper was bounded on Broadway by Anthony, on the North River by Harrison, and on the East River by Rutger Streets; and even within these limits the houses were scattering, and surrounded by large gardens and vacant lots; Broadway ended at Astor Place, where a pole fence, stretching across the road, formed the southern boundary of the Randall Farm, afterwards the endowment of the Sailors' Snug Harbor.

In November, 1802, the engine house in Hanover Square was removed to the Old Slip. On the twenty-ninth of the month the engine house of No. 4 in Nassau Street, between John and Fair Streets, was removed to the public ground near the office of the Kine-pock Institution.

According to the report of the fire wardens of the Third Ward there were, in March, 1803, one thousand three hundred and thirty-eight fire buckets, and a deficiency of six hundred and fifty-two. The inhabitants of that ward were opposed to throwing out or carrying their buckets to a fire; and so frequent had become the loss of buckets at fires, and on account of the impediments which existed in getting payment for those lost from the corporation, that many of the

Third Warders were in a revolt against the system, and declared they would not lend their buckets at all. In May one thousand fire buckets were ordered by the corporation for the use of the firemen. Engine No. 23 was destroyed at a fire which occurred in this month.

One of those terrible fires which were wont to ravage the city periodically before the introduction of fire-proof buildings and the existence of an efficient fire department, broke out on the eighteenth of December, 1804, in a grocery in Front Street, and raged with fury for several hours, burning the old Coffee House, on the corner of Pearl and Wall Streets, the scene of so many patriotic gatherings in the days of the Revolution, with many other of the old landmarks of the city. Forty stores and dwellings were destroyed by the fire, which was supposed to have been the work of an incendiary. The loss of property was estimated at two million dollars.

Even so early as this year the necessity of settling a regular plan of streets, for a distance of eight miles in length, and the width of the island, was anticipated by the legislature, and a plan was established by law comprehending in its features the cutting down of mountains and the filling up of valleys to a regular and uniform grade over all that extent.

In December the number of fire wardens in each ward was increased to six.

In 1805 another fire ordinance was passed, which is in many respects similar to that of 1793. It is more comprehensive, however, and the fines imposed are in U.S. currency.

It provides, in addition to the other, substantially as follows: The firemen of the city to consist of one chief, and as many other "engineers, fire wardens, hook and ladder men, and other firemen," as may be appointed by the mayor, etc., as firemen, and be distinguished by the said appellations.

The chief is to have control of the firemen, subject to the Common Council, and the engineers shall take proper measures for having the several engines "placed, filled and worked," at fires. He is also to have charge of the repairs of engines, and to see that they are kept in good working order.

It changes the distinguishing badges, etc., to be worn by fire officials at fires, as follows:

In order that the members of the Common Council, Engineers and Fire Wardens, may be more readily distinguished at Fires, the Mayor, Recorder, Aldermen, and Assistants, shall each have on those occasions a white wand of at least five feet in length, with a gilded flame at the top, and each of the engineers shall have a leather cap painted white, with a gilt front thereto, and an Engine painted thereon, and have a good speaking Trumpet painted black; and each of the Fire Wardens shall wear a like cap with the City arms painted on the front and the Crown painted black, and have also a speaking Trumpet, painted white. And the names and places of abode of the members of the Common Council, Engineers and Fire Wardens, shall from time to time be fixed up in writing in the Watch Houses by the Aldermen respectively in whose Ward the Watch House shall be. ★ ★ ★ And, moreover, it shall be the duty of every Watchman, upon the breaking out of fire at or near his Watch Station, to alarm the citizens by the crying of fire, and mentioning the street where it shall be on his way to the nearest Watch Station, "so that the citizens and firemen generally be made acquainted where and in what Street to repair."

But if a chimney takes fire after the watch is set, the watchman is enjoined to prevent the ringing of any bell, so that the firemen and citizens be not unnecessarily alarmed.

The former provision as to the placing of a lighted candle in the front window, is renewed here, and reappears in all ordinances down to the year 1860.

The hook and ladder men shall be divided into companies, which shall each choose a foreman, assistant, and clerk, out of their own number. They are required, under penalty of one dollar and fifty cents, in case of fire, to bring the necessary hooks and ladders to the scene of the fire, and to use the same, under the direction of the members of the Common Council and engineers, and after the fire is extinguished, to return them to where they are usually deposited. The capacity of the fire buckets is increased to two–and–a–half gallons.

The firemen (other than engineers, fire wardens, and hook and ladder men), shall be divided into companies, one to be assigned to each of the fire engines belonging, or that may hereafter belong, to the city, and each company shall choose a foreman, assistant, and clerk out of their number.

It became apparent in 1805 that the means employed for the extinguishment of fire required, and were susceptible of, much improvement. The increasing extent of the city and its population enhanced the possibilities of frequent and dangerous fires, at the same time that it supplied the means and indicated the propriety of putting the Fire Department upon a more effective and systematic footing. The utility of the floating engine had been fully established. But as it could not always be moved in due season to the place where it was wanted, it was proposed to procure another of the same kind. For a similar reason, and also because at some seasons the ice or other causes might wholly prevent the floating engines from being moved, it was recommended that two engines of like power be procured and placed on wheels, for service within the city. These latter were not intended as substitutes for the floating engines, but it was thought that four engines of the power specified were not more than could be usefully and profitably employed on many occasions. Certain of the engines then in use—Nos. 2, 5, 6, and 16—were both too small and greatly out of repair, and it was decided to sell them, and that in future uniformity in size and power in engines be attended to throughout the department. The screws of the leaders were of different sizes, which led occasionally to trouble at critical moments. Uniformity in that respect, too, was to be observed regarding engines of similar power, and every common engine should have at least four leaders of forty feet each.

In May, 1805, it was decided to build a new engine house in the Seventh Ward on a site offered by Smith Place in Rivington Street, between Third and Fourth Streets, and the chief engineer was ordered to furnish one of the best of the small engines for the company to be established there. On the thirteenth of the month the engine house in the City Hall yard was extended so as to admit of the reception of the engine then stationed in Nassau Street on ground belonging to the Presbyterian Church. The chief engineer was authorized, in September, to station fire engines at Greenwich Street, and form a new company. Divie Bethune, Jeremiah F. Randolph, Hector Scott, Peter H. Wendover, and Samuel L. Page, Jr., were appointed fire wardens of the Eighth Ward. Engine No. 13, situated at the Fly Market, was given a new location at the head of Burling Slip, in December. In the spring of the following year a new fire engine house was erected on the ground of the New Dutch Church in Liberty Street.

The streets were swept twice a week by the inhabitants, each opposite his own house; and for the collection of garbage a bell-cart came round daily in each street. The city was lit by lamps, with oil. Wood was the principal article of fuel, and hickory was deemed the best. The chimneys were swept by small negro boys, whose street cries in the morning drew forth many a denunciation from those whose slumbers were thus disturbed. With the break of day did the streets ring with their cries of "Sweep, ho! sweep, ho! from the bottom to the top, without a ladder or a rope, sweep, ho!" to a chorus or cry, in which often were added dulcet sounds of real harmony.

In 1807 there was a number of the old Dutch houses still standing, with their gable ends to the street, and the date of their erection in iron figures placed in the wall in front. Several of these stood in Broad, William, Garden, and Pearl Streets; two stood at the head of Coenties Slip, west side, near Pearl. The dates generally were from 1696, 1697, 1701, and 1702, showing that the city was pretty much confined to the near proximity of the old Dutch Church in Garden Street, built in 1693, and below Wall Street. Every one of these buildings has long since disappeared.

The city, at the time in question, contained about sixty thousand inhabitants. A large majority of the residents dwelt below Cortlandt Street and Maiden Lane. A sparse population then occupied that portion of the island which lay above the site of the New York Hospital on Broadway, and the grounds stretching northerly, now covered with magnificent buildings, were then graced with the sycamore, the elm, the oak, the chestnut, the wild cherry, the peach, the pear, and the plum tree, and further ornamented with gardens appropriated to horti-cultural products, with here and there the artichoke, the tulip, and the sunflower. Where now stand the Astor Library, the Mercantile Library, the Academy of Music, the Cooper Institute, and the Bible House, old Dutch gardens were abundant, cultivated with something of the artistic regularity of the Hollanders, luxuriating in the sweet marjoram, the mint, the thyme, the currant, and the gooseberry. Avenues, squares, and leading roads had not yet been laid out, and the street regulations in paving and sidewalks had reached but little above the City Hall Park, and in the Bowery only within the precincts of Bayard Street. The present City Hall was in a state of erection, and so circumscribed, at that time, was the idea of the city's progress, that the Board of Supervisors, by a slender majority, after a serious discussion, for economy's sake, decided that the postern part of the Hall should be composed of red stone, "inasmuch as it was not likely to attract much notice from the scattered inhabitants who might reside above Chambers Street."

Fire plugs were first introduced in 1807, the first plug being put down at the corner of William and Liberty Streets. The chief engineer approved of it so highly that he recommended that each block in the city be similarly supplied.

In June of this year a petition of residents in the vicinity of Corlears Hook for a fire engine was acceded to, and old No. 1, which had been superseded at the Methodist Meeting House by a larger engine, was sent there.

The full strength of the Fire Department was eight hundred and sixty-nine men, as compared with seven hundred and sixty-one in the previous year (1806). It was made up of seven engineers, forty-eight fire wardens, seven hundred and seventy-eight fire engine men, and thirty-six hook and ladder men. The number of fire engine companies was thirty-four, of which Nos. 28 and 33 were the smallest, having only ten men each, and Nos. 25, 3, and 8 were the largest, having forty, thirty-two, and thirty men respectively. The floating engine was in charge of forty men. There were only two hook and ladder companies. In November the strength of Engine Company No. 25 was raised to fifty. Two years after, in December, the full strength of the department was nine hundred and fifty-five men, of whom seven were engineers, fifty-five fire wardens, eight hundred and forty-seven fire engine men, and forty-six hook and ladder men— an increase of twenty-eight men over the previous year (1808).

An ordinance, passed January 11, 1808, provides that the Fire Department shall consist of "a chief engineer, and as many other engineers, fire wardens, fire engine men, hose men, and ladder men," as may be appointed by the Common Council. It gives absolute control in case of fire to the chief engineer over men and machines. The chief engineer must make examination of all apparatus, etc., at least once in six months, and report the same, with list of force, to the Common Council, to be published. He had charge of repairs, and was required when a fire was over to send all private fire buckets found in the vicinity to the City Hall for identification. The provisions are substantially as in the 1805 ordinance, with the exception of some additions and alterations which it is not necessary to notice.

A hook and ladder company, consisting of ten men, was established in the village of Greenwich in the summer of 1809.

The expenses incurred by the city for supplies to the Fire Department for the eight years ending 1809 amounted to forty-three thousand eight hundred and eighty-eight dollars, and it was suggested that, inasmuch as the fire insurance companies were greatly benefitted by the existing organization of the Fire Department, they should be called upon to defray some proportion of the expense.

The engine house standing on the burial ground of the congregation of the First Presbyterian Church, was donated to the church society by the city in May, 1809.

An attempt was made on the evening of the thirtieth of November, 1809, to set fire to the range of wooden buildings in Front Street, between Crane Wharf and Beekman Slip, by placing a coal of fire in some damp powder, and laying the same in a pile of staves at the rear of the store, No. 203 Front Street. The mayor, DeWitt Clinton, issued a proclamation, offering three hundred dollars reward for information which would lead to the discovery of the incendiaries.

The population of the city in 1810 was over ninety-six thousand; having added thirty-six thousand in ten years, and increased nearly threefold in twenty years. The city had extended with unprecedented rapidity, and, at the time mentioned, it covered more than four times the area that it embraced twenty years before. Broadway had been opened through to the Bowery, and on either side streets had been laid out as far up as Amity and Great Jones Streets. To the east of the Bowery, the streets running eastward were laid out as high up as North (Houston) Street, which had been fixed as the permanent boundary of the city; and crossing these, the present streets were laid out as far east as Norfolk Street.

The city was again devastated by a terrible conflagration (May 19, 1811), which broke out about nine o'clock on Sunday morning, near the northwest corner of Duane and Chatham Streets. The steeple of the Brick Church, and the cupola of the jail caught fire.

CHAPTER VI

ADOPTION OF A PLAN
FOR THE FUTURE CITY

1811–1822.—Two Sailors and a Prisoner Distinguish Themselves.—Laying of the Corner Stone of the City Hall.—Extension of Fire Limits.—Enactment of Laws for the More Effectual Prevention of Fires.—Duties of Firemen.—The Use of Fire Buckets Superseded by Hose.

O ne of the most important events of this period (1811) was the adoption of a plan for the future city, to which we owe the parallel streets and broad avenues of the upper part of the island, which contrast so strong with the narrow streets and crooked lanes of the down-town locality. The plan was due to Simeon Dewitt, Gouverneur Morris, John Rutherford, and S. Guel, who had been appointed by the legislature in 1801, as commissioners lay out and survey the whole island to Kingsbridge into streets and avenues. By the proposed plan, the streets beginning with the first on the east side of the Bowery above Houston Street, numbered upward to the extreme end of the island. These were intersected by twelve avenues, numbering westward from First Avenue—the continuation of Allen Street—to Twelfth Avenue upon the shores of the North River. As avenues were afterwards laid out to the eastward of the former, they were designated by the names of the letters of the alphabet A, B, C, and D. By this plan, the island was laid out with admirable regularity, while the squares and triangles which were formed by the junction of those time-honored thoroughfares which could not be removed, were converted into public parks for the adornment of the city. The despised Potter's Field became the beautiful Washington Square; the Bowery and Broadway met amicably in Union Square; Madison Square was formed from the union of the Old and the Middle Roads; the great salt meadow on the eastern side of the city was drained, and Tompkins Square, with hundreds of city lots, sprung up from its depths; valleys were filled up, hills were leveled, and art seemed destined to surmount the difficulties of nature, and to make every inch of New York island habitable ground.

On the nineteenth of May, of this year, the Brick Presbyterian Church took fire, and two seamen distinguished themselves in an especial manner, and at the imminent hazard of their lives, by ascending the steeple of the church which was on fire, and, by their exertions, arresting the progress of the flames until the leader of one of the engines could be brought to play upon it. The cupola of the jail became ignited from flying embers, and a debtor imprisoned therein proved so exceedingly active in helping to extinguish the flames that the Common Council directed their clerk to procure the issuance of a warrant in his favor for sixty dollars, thus restoring him to liberty and fame.

The corner stone of the City Hall was laid September 26, 1803. It was completed in 1812 at an expense of five hundred and thirty-eight thousand seven hundred and thirty-four dollars.

Fire bugs again made their appearance in January, 1811, when they burnt down the ropewalk of Peter Schermerhorn, on Orchard Street, and the mayor offered one thousand dollars reward for their apprehension.

The principal difficulty in extinguishing fires was to procure a sufficient supply of water. In the central part of the city the pumps and cisterns, which were principally relied on, became soon exhausted, and before a line composed of engines and leaders could be formed to the rivers, the fires too often had gained considerable headway. To remedy this defect, it was suggested in June, 1811, that two reservoirs of stone, sufficient to contain two hundred hogshead of water each, be built and located at or near each wing of the City Hall, to be supplied from the roof thereof, and the water to be used for no other purpose than the extinguishment of fires. It was recommended also that the different religious societies in the city be requested to cause to be built a reservoir adjacent to their respective places of worship, to be supplied with water from such places of worship, the water to be used only at fires.

Thomas Brown, chief engineer, resigned his office on November 11, on account of ill health. On the eighteenth of the month the foremen of thirty-six fire engines petitioned the Common Council to appoint Thomas Franklin as chief engineer, and the prayer of the petitioners was granted. Among the appointments made on the twenty-seventh of this month were: Peter Simons, silversmith, 275 Pearl Street, to Hook and Ladder No. 3, vice Simeon Fawcett, resigned; Mordecai Homan, merchant, 97 Fair Street, to Engine Company No. 3, vice Charles I. Field; William Pulis, butcher, Mott Street, to Engine Company No. 15, vice Walter Whitehead. A patent for a newly invented fire engine, more powerful in its operations and less expensive in its construction than the existing engines, was granted to Richard Crosby by the United States in the latter part of this year; and the Common Council authorized him, in January, 1812, to construct such an engine for the use of the city.

The frequent fires occurring in the fall of 1811 from no cause that could be reasonably ascribed, left no room to doubt that incendiaries were at their villainous work, and the mayor of the city again offered a reward of three hundred dollars for the apprehension and conviction of the offenders.

The fire wardens in December communicated to the Common Council that as the use of hose had in a great measure superseded the use of fire buckets, the ordinance requiring owners and occupants of houses to furnish buckets, should, in their opinion, be repealed, and also an application should be made to the legislature for an extension of the limits within which wooden buildings should not be erected.

In the following month the Council committee reported upon that communication that, notwithstanding the advantages arising from the use of leaders, cases might arise in the interior of the city when, by a speedy collection of buckets, the fire might be extinguished ere the line by engines and leaders could be formed, and consequently it would be imprudent to discontinue the ordinance as requested. The number of buckets required to be kept, might, however, be reduced by one-third, to lighten the burden on the citizens.

The condition of affairs in the city during the summer of 1812, whilst the national government was prosecuting the war against Great Britain, had become most critical. There were fears of commotions and riots fomented by evil disposed people, which, if allowed to pass unnoticed, might lead to serious and alarming consequences. At this juncture (July, 1812), the members of Engine Companies Nos. 39, 36, and 8, volunteered their services to the chief magistrate, to assist in quelling any riot or disturbance that might arise, reserving to themselves, however, the privilege of being commanded by their own officers, without the interference of any military officer whatever.

An act for the more effectual prevention of fires was passed April 9, 1813. This act made it obligatory that dwelling houses, storehouses, and other buildings, thereafter to be erected within the following boundaries, should be made and constructed of stone or brick, with party or fire walls, rising at least six inches above the roof, "and shall be covered, except the flat roof thereof, with tile or slate, or other safe materials, against fire, and not with board or shingles," within that part of the city to the northward of the point of the Battery, and a line beginning upon the East River, opposite Montgomery Street, thence through Montgomery Street to Cherry Street, thence down Cherry Street to Roosevelt, through Roosevelt to Chatham, down Chatham to Chambers Street, through Chambers Street to Broadway, up Broadway to Canal Street, thence, commencing again at Chambers Street and running to Hudson's river, including also the lots of ground on the northerly and easterly sides of the said streets through which the above-mentioned line runs, and including, also, the lots of ground fronting on both sides of Broadway, between Chambers and Canal Streets.

The above designated portion of the city also constituted "the Watch and Lamp District."

Section 66 declared it to be unlawful to store gunpowder, "except in the public magazine at the Fresh Water," and then only in certain designated quantities. Other sections prohibited the storage of sulphur, hemp, and flax, except in certain specified quantities, "in any one place in the city of New York, to the southward of the Fresh Water, nor to the southward of Rutgers Slip, under the penalty of twenty-five dollars." Pitch, tar, turpentine, rosin, spirits of turpentine, linseed oil, or shingles, were similarly quarantined.

The mayor, aldermen, and commonalty, were re-invested with the power "to appoint (as often as it shall be necessary) a sufficient number of strong, able, discreet, honest and sober men, ★ ★ ★ being freeholders of the city, to have the care, management, working, and using of the fire engines, and the other tools and instruments ★ ★ ★ for extinguishing of fires within the said city," which persons are to be called the firemen of the city of New York. During their continuance in that office, and no longer, they shall be exempted from serving in the office of constable, and from being impaneled or returned upon any juries or inquests, and of and from militia duty, "except in cases of invasion or other imminent danger."

Upon the breaking out of any fire within the city, the law required the sheriffs, deputy sheriffs, constables, and marshals, upon notice thereof, to repair immediately to the scene of the fire, with their rods, staves, and other badges of authority, and aid and assist in the extinguishing of the said fire, and cause the firemen in attendance to work; to prevent any goods or household furniture from being stolen; to seize all persons found stealing or pilfering; and to give their utmost assistance in removing and securing goods and furniture. They were subordinate to the mayor, recorder and aldermen, or any of them.

In case of fire, the mayor, or, in his absence, the recorder, with the consent and concurrence of any two of the aldermen, might order buildings to be pulled down.

The Common Council was authorized to pass ordinances for the extinguishment and prevention of fires; and also to regulate the keeping, carting, conveying, or transporting of gunpowder, or any other combustible or other dangerous material, within the bounds of the city; also to regulate the use of lights and candles in livery and other stables; to remove or prevent the construction of any fireplace, hearth, chimney, stove, oven, boiler, kettle, or apparatus, used in any manufactory or business, which might be dangerous in causing or promoting fires.

From the proceedings of the Common Council (November 29, 1813), it appears that the chief engineer (Thomas Franklin) proposed an amendment to the law, establishing a uniformity in the caps of firemen, which was agreed to, and the law directed to be amended accordingly.

On the tenth of January, 1814, the chief engineer reported that during the preceding year the sum of one thousand and ninety-two dollars and twenty cents had been received and collected from fines, which were applied to the relief of disabled firemen and their families, and for educating about seventy of their children. On the above date it was resolved that the staves of office to be carried at fires by members of the Common Council be similarly constructed with those lately made, (viz., with a gilded flame at the top), "and that the justices of the police and the superintendent of repairs be furnished with staves, to be used on like occasions."

The estimated value of the property belonging to the Fire Department at the close of 1814 was as follows:

15 brick buildings	$5,250.00
32 wood buildings	4,800.00
2 lots of ground	1,600.00
41 engines	26,200.00
Floating engine and boat	1,400.00
4 old engines not in use	750.00
13,085 feet leather hose	8,548.00
1,000 fire buckets	1,500.00
4 trucks, 15 ladders, and 20 fire hooks, etc.	1,200.00
Signal lanterns, torches, axes, etc.	150.00
Drag ropes	70.00
Stoves and pipes	150.00
Hose wagon	175.00
1 copper pump	30.00
20 loads nut wood	90.00
Total	$51,913.00

The extension of the city and the opening of new streets, though greatly checked, was not wholly suspended by the prostration of business consequent upon the unsettled condition of public affairs.

Immediately after the plan of the upper part of the city was definitely arranged, the Third Avenue was ordered to be opened and regulated from Stuyvesant Street to Harlem River, and a few years later a part of First Avenue was also brought into use. Several of the old streets in the lower part of the city were widened, straightened, and extended.

Soon after the return of peace (War of 1812), Broadway, above Canal Street, and Spring and Broome Streets, began to be occupied with buildings, and that portion of the city advanced rapidly in improvements and population.

But the greatest public work of this kind undertaken during this period was the opening of Canal Street. An immense canal was opened from the Collect to the Hudson River, by which a vast extent of low grounds was drained, and the pond itself almost annihilated. Over this canal was thrown an arch of substantial mason work, upon which was built one of the most spacious and elegant thoroughfares in the city, the whole of which cost about one hundred and fifty thousand dollars.

The firemen having determined to apply to the legislature to enact a law granting them certain privileges, and the renewal of their charter, deemed it expedient to place in the hands of the representatives the following calculations, showing the principles on which their petition was founded:

From this record it appears that there were in

1795, 5 fires and 9 alarms.			1805, 13 fires and 6 alarms			
1796, 6 " 6 "	Averaging		1806, 23 " 6 "	Averaging		
1797, 10 " 9 "	$13\frac{3}{5}$ per		1807, 21 " 10 "	$31\frac{2}{5}$ per		
1798, 6 " 5 "	annum.		1808, 23 " 14 "	annum.		
1799, 6 " 6 "			1809, 16 " 25 "			
1800, 9 9			1810, 25 19			
1801, 11 " 6 "	Averaging		1811, 26 " 27 "	Averaging		
1802, 10 " 7 "	$19\frac{3}{5}$ per		1812, 20 " 23 "	$55\frac{2}{5}$ per		
1803, 9 " 8 "	annum.		1813, 37 " 39 "	annum.		
1804, 16 " 13 "			1814, 29 " 32 "			

By this it appears that their duty had increased in a four-fold proportion in the space of twenty years. From actual calculation on the average of the preceding five years, there was an increase of two hundred and seventy-five hours actual duty per annum, or two hundred and seventy-five days in ten years, allowing ten hours for a day.

The amount of the Fire Department Fund, December 1, 1814, was ten thousand six hundred and twenty-two dollars and thirty-eight cents; the amount of moneys paid the previous year for the relief of indigent firemen, their widows, and the schooling of their children, was one thousand five hundred and eighty-six dollars and twenty-five cents.

The recommendation of the Common Council to the several religious congregations of the city to build cisterns at their respective churches, heretofore recorded, was entirely ignored, although it was a measure that would redound to the safety of the churches as well as of the adjacent property. The corporation had within the years from 1810 to 1814 displayed great interest in the organization and system of the Fire Department, procuring the best attainable apparatus; but its efforts were still handicapped by the lack of a sufficient supply of water. It was, therefore, decided in February, 1814, to apply to the legislature for an act empowering the corporation to build cisterns when and where it seemed advantageous to do so.

During this year five engines of six and one-half inch caliber and the necessary appurtenances, also a new truck for the Hook and Ladder Company at Greenwich, were purchased. The old Engines Nos. 20 and 23 were sold, the former for four hundred dollars cash, and the latter to the Pleasant Valley Manufacturing Company for six hundred dollars at six months.

On April 11, 1815, there was passed "an act for the more effectual prevention of fires in the city of New York." This extended the fire limits from "a line, beginning at the North River, at a place called Dekleyne's Ferry, a little to the northward of the state prison to the road commonly called the Sandy Hill Road, to the northward of the Potter's Field and the house of William Neilson, to the Bowery, to a street commonly called Stuyvesant Street, to the East River."

The Common Council adopted a resolution (March 25, 1816), on the petition of a number of carpenters and others, suspending the duties of the fire wardens under the ordinance prohibiting the storing and seasoning of lumber on premises within the fire limits, the enforcement of which, it was alleged, would inure to the loss and inconvenience of those tradesmen. But a fire occurred in November in Water Street, which was much intensified and caused much damage by reason of the burning of a quantity of lumber, stored in the immediate vicinity, which caught fire. The Common Council soon after repealed the resolution of the twenty-fifth of March.

The Fire Department (April 12, 1816) was continued as a body corporate and politic, in fact and in name, until the first day of May, 1838, "with all the rights, powers, and privileges, and subject to all the provisions, restrictions, limitations, and conditions mentioned and contained in the act entitled, 'An act to incorporate the Firemen of the city of New York.'"

The fire engine companies kept importuning the corporation for an increase in their membership, and it was, in consequence, found necessary in August, 1816, to make a regulation that all companies having engines of six and one-half inch caliber should have twenty-six men, and those that had a greater number be reduced to conform thereto, except the companies in the out wards, as to the strength of which the chief engineer should determine.

At a fire in John and Water Streets in December, Isaac Skaats, George Herrick, and John Talman had their limbs broken, incapacitating them from further duty. In April, 1817, the Common Council ordered that the sum of three hundred dollars be distributed among them.

These fires and a fire in Mott Street at about the same time, were of incendiary origin, and Jacob Hays, one of the city marshals, was mainly instrumental in bringing the miscreants to justice, for which service he was awarded a sum of three hundred dollars.

The number of engineers was increased, on December 23, 1816, from eight to ten.

The first hydrant ever used in New York was located in front of the dwelling house of Mr. George B. Smith, of Engine Company No. 12, in Frankfort Street, in the year 1817. This was the origin of the hydrant system in this city.

Any fireman, while in the performance of his duty as such, who should so maim or injure himself as to render him thereafter unable to perform the duties of a fireman, or who should have so maimed himself since the fifth of the preceding May (Act, February 28, 1817), was entitled to the benefit of the law passed the twelfth of April, 1816, fixing the time of service of firemen at ten years.

The leading features of the ordinance, passed May 5, 1817, are as follows:

The Fire Department to consist of a chief engineer, who shall have an annual salary of eight hundred dollars, payable quarterly, and as many other engineers, fire enginemen, hosemen, and hook and ladder men, as may from time to time be appointed by the Common Council. The chief engineer had the sole and absolute control and command over all the engineers and other persons of the Fire Department. It was his duty to examine— twice in every year—into the condition and number of the fire engines, fire buckets, and other fire apparatus, and fire engine houses belonging to the corporation, and report the same—once a year—to the Common Council, together with the names of all the members of the Fire Department, and the respective associations to which they belong; to cause all the private fire buckets which may remain after any fire is extinguished, to be collected and conveyed as soon as possible to the City Hall, to be there deposited, in order that the citizens may know where to find them; to report in writing all accidents by fire that may happen in the city, with the causes thereof, as well as can be ascertained, and the number and description of the buildings destroyed or injured, together with the names of the owners and occupants, to the city inspector, who shall keep a faithful register of the same. As many of the freeholders, or firemen, of the city, as the Common Council may deem proper, shall, from time to time, be appointed in each of the wards, to be denominated fire wardens; each of whom to be assigned and attached by the mayor to such company of firemen, having charge of a fire engine, as he shall think proper, and shall report himself to the chief, or other engineer, at every fire. The fire wardens of each ward to form a separate company, and each company to choose out of their own number a foreman and clerk, to make rules, regulating the time and manner of conducting their elections, etc. It was the duty of the said fire wardens, immediately on the alarm of fire, to repair to the place where it may be, and aid and assist in procuring supplies of water to the fire engines to which they are respectively assigned; and to such other fire engines as the chief engineer or other engineer may direct them to attend; to prevent the hose from being trodden on; and to keep all idle and suspected persons at a proper distance from the fire, and from the vicinity. Other duties were also imposed on the fire wardens, namely: twice a year, in the months of June and December, and as much oftener as they should think proper, to examine the dwelling houses and other buildings in their respective wards, to see that they are properly furnished with fire buckets; to examine the fireplaces, hearths, chimneys, stoves, and pipes thereto, ovens, boilers, kettles, or apparatus which, in their opinion, may be dangerous in causing or promoting fires, and the places where ashes may be deposited; ★ ★ ★ to enter into and examine all buildings, livery and other stables, hay boats or vessels, and places where any gunpowder, hemp, flax, tow, hay, rushes, fire wood, boards, shingles, shavings, or other combustible materials, may be lodged; ★ ★ ★ to make report whether any, and what cases of violations of the laws of this state, prohibiting the construction of wooden buildings within certain limits, etc.

The duties of firemen are thus defined:

As often as any fire shall break out in the said city, to repair immediately upon the alarm thereof, to their respective engines, hose wagons, hooks and ladders, and convey them to or near the place where such fire shall happen, and there, in conformity with the directions given by the chief engineer or other engineers, shall work and manage said engines, or apparatus and implements, with all their skill and power; and when the fire is extinguished, shall not remove therefrom but by the direction of an engineer; when they shall return their respective hose wagons, hooks and ladders, engines and apparatus, well washed and cleaned, to their several places of deposit. ★ ★ ★ The penalty for neglect of duty was as follows: for neglect to wash and clean the fire engines at stipulated times, for every default, one dollar; for neglect to attend at any fire, or leave his fire engine or other apparatus while at any fire, without permission, or shall neglect to perform his duty on such occasion, without reasonable excuse, for every default, three dollars; and if any fireman shall neglect to do his duty as such, in attending at fires, or in working, exercising, managing, trying, or using the said fire engine, or other implements, or apparatus for extinguishing fires, every such person shall, besides the fines and penalties aforesaid, be removed and displaced from his station.

The ordinance further recites:

In order that the members of the Common Council, engineers, and fire wardens may be readily distinguished at fires, the mayor, recorder, aldermen, and assistants, shall severally bear, on those occasions, a wand with a gilded flame on the top; and each of the engineers shall wear a leathern cap, painted white, with a gilded front thereto, and a fire engine emblazoned thereon, and shall also carry a speaking trumpet, painted black, with the words "Chief Engineer," "Engineer No. 1," etc., as the case may be, in white, which shall also be painted on their caps respectively; and each of the fire wardens shall wear a hat, the brim black, the crown painted white, with the city arms blazoned on the front, and shall also carry a speaking trumpet, painted white, with the word "Warden," in black painted thereon.

The firemen, when on duty, shall wear leathern caps, in the form heretofore used; and the said caps (except those worn by the Floating Engine Fire Company) shall be painted and distinguished in the manner following, viz.: the foremen of each of the fire engine companies (except the Floating Engine Company) shall wear a cap, painted black, with a white frontispiece, and the word "Foreman," with the initials of his name and the number of his engine painted thereon in black; and the firemen of the said fire engine companies (except as above excepted) shall wear a cap, painted black, with the initials of their names and the number of the engines to which they belong painted in the front thereof, in white. The foreman of each of the hook and ladder companies shall wear a cap, painted black, with a white frontispiece, and the word "Foreman," and the initials of his name, and the number of the company to which he belongs, and a hook and ladder painted thereon, in black; and the members of the said hook and ladder companies shall wear a cap, painted black, with the initials of their names, and number of the company to which they belong, with a hook and ladder painted in the front thereof in white. And the foreman of each of the fire hose companies shall wear a cap, painted black, with a white frontispiece, and the word "Foreman," and the initials of his name, and the number of the company to which he belongs, and a coil of hose painted thereon, in black; and the members of the said fire hose companies shall wear caps, painted black, with the initials of their names and the number of the company to which they belong, with a coil of hose painted thereon, in white. And the assistants to each respective company shall wear caps, painted in the same manner as that of the foreman of the company, with the word "Assistant" in lieu of the word "Foreman."

The ordinance also provided that the names and places of abode of the members of the Common Council, engineers, fire wardens, and foremen of their respective companies, and bell ringers, annually, in the month of December, should be printed and set up in the several watch houses in the city, by the city inspector; and whenever fire should happen in the night, the watchmen should give notice to each of the members of the Common Council, engineers, fire wardens, foremen, and bell ringers within their respective watch districts. Moreover, it was the duty of every watchman upon the breaking out of any fire to alarm the citizens by crying "Fire," and mentioning the street where it may be, so that the firemen and citizens may thereby be generally directed where to repair. In case, however, that a chimney only should be on fire—either by day or night—the fire bell at the City Hall, and the bells of the several churches shall not be rung; but only on occasions where a building shall be proclaimed to be on fire. And it is enjoined on the occupants to place a lighted candle at the windows of their respective buildings, when fire may happen at night, in order that citizens may pass along the streets with the greater safety.

Constables and marshals were also, on an alarm of fire, to repair to the place of such fire, with their staves of office, and to attend and obey such orders as might be given them by the mayor, recorder, or any of the aldermen or assistant aldermen.

Owners or occupants of every dwelling house, having less than three fire places shall provide one leathern bucket; and having three fireplaces and less than six, two leathern buckets, and having six fireplaces and less than nine, four leathern buckets; and having nine fireplaces and upwards, six leathern buckets, to be marked with at least the initial letters of the owner's name with the number of the house to which it belongs, and the name of the street in which such house is situate. Every brewhouse, distillery, sugarhouse, soap and candle manufactory and ship chandlery store, to provide nine leathern buckets, every bakehouse and air furnace to provide six, over and above the buckets provided for their respective dwelling houses. Each of these buckets to contain two gallons and a half of water, and to be suspended in some convenient place, ready to be delivered and used for extinguishing fires, when any should occur. Such buckets, moreover, to be furnished and provided at the expense of the inhabitant or occupant of said premises.

And if such inhabitant or occupant be a tenant, the price of such leathern bucket shall be allowed and deducted out of the rent, unless there be a special agreement between the parties to the contrary. "It shall nevertheless be optional," the ordinance declares furthermore, with any owner of a dwelling house, as aforesaid, to surrender and deliver over to the mayor, aldermen and commonalty such number of leathern buckets not exceeding one-half of the whole number such dwelling house is required to have; which buckets, when surrendered and delivered over to whomsoever the Common Council shall direct, shall become public buckets; and shall be deposited in such suitable place or places, in each ward, as they shall direct, and for which the owner of every such dwelling house, thereafter, from so many leathern buckets as shall be so surrendered and delivered over, and the same shall also be registered in a book, to be kept for the purpose, by the city inspector."

With some of the church congregations it was made the express duty for the sextons to ring the bells at an alarm of fire, and with others it was an implied duty. At the fire on December 19, 1818, only a few of the bells were rung, and in consequence a large proportion of the firemen were not alarmed.

This fact was taken cognizance of by the Common Council, who convened a meeting of church officers, whereat it was arranged that no such neglect of duty should occur thereafter, and, to facilitate matters, it was made the duty of the watchmen at the cry of fire immediately to alarm the sextons.

The propriety of taxing the fire insurance companies of the city for the whole or a proportion of the expense annually incurred for the Department was discussed in the Common Council in December, 1818, and the Committee on Applications to the Legislature were directed to inquire into its expediency.

On the twenty-seventh of December, 1819, the Committee on the Fire Department reported that the fire buckets were rapidly being superseded by the use of hose, and, on their recommendation, the use of fire buckets at fires was dispensed with.

Very soon every new engine was furnished with suctions, and the old machines were altered so as to use them. There was also an active and increasing demand for an additional supply of hose and hose carriages. The latter, at this time, consisted of a reel placed on the axle of two cartwheels, and was the invention of foreman David J. Hubbs. It was either attached to the engine by tail hooks, or drawn by two members of the company. "Hubbs' Baby," as the simple contrivance was called, was the origin of the hose companies.

According to the Comptroller's report for the year 1819 the amount expended for building engine houses in Fayette and Rose Streets, and at Greenwich, for ground and buildings, and building a house on Beaver Street, was twenty-one thousand and ninety-six dollars, and on account of engines to A. W. Hardenbrook, five thousand and ninety-six dollars and seventeen cents.

The floating engine had practically been in disuse during the year 1818, lying aground most of the time in her slip at the foot of Roosevelt Street. In the summer of 1819 it was taken to the Corporation Yard on Leonard Street, and there set up as a supply engine for extinguishing fires in that part of the city. A company was formed to manage it, called Supply Engine Company No. 1. This company was stationed over a large well of water in the Public Yard, from which she was never moved, and, consequently, never used only when the fire happened in the immediate neighborhood. The duties of the company, therefore, were much less arduous than those of other firemen, except the fire wardens. The Common Council, in view of these facts, decided in January, 1829, that no person should be eligible for membership in that company who had not borne the burden of the day by doing more active duty a few years previous, and, accordingly, fixed the necessary qualification for membership therein at a five years' service in the Department. But this action was repealed in February, 1830, for various reasons, among which were, that the term of service of firemen had been reduced from ten to seven years, and that during the existence of the restriction there had not been a single application for membership.

In conformity with an act passed in April, 1820, the fire wardens of the city were clothed with authority, in June of that year, to discharge the duties of health wardens, and were placed under the control of the Board of Health.

The value of the estate vested in the Fire Department as public property in 1820 was seventy-two thousand seven hundred and eighty-nine dollars.

The Common Council, on December 26, 1820, reduced the salary of the chief engineer, which had been eight hundred dollars, to five hundred dollars per annum. This ordinance also adopted the main features of the ordinance of May 5, 1817, and ordained that "no person shall be elected a fireman until he shall have attained the age of twenty-one years.'

On the tenth of June, 1822, the Common Council ordained that whenever the office of any of the engineers of the Fire Department shall become vacant, it shall be the duty of the engineers of that Department to nominate five persons from among the foremen as suitable persons to supply such vacancy, and to give notice thereof to the foremen of the fire companies, and to require them to meet at such time and place as the said engineers shall appoint; and that the said engineers and firemen shall then and there, or at such other time and place as they may appoint by joint ballot, designate from the persons so nominated the person whom they may wish to fill such vacancy; and that no person shall be considered as so designated who shall not receive a majority of all the votes which shall be given.

CHAPTER VII

GROWTH OF THE CITY
AND THE DEPARTMENT

1822–1835.—An Epoch in the City of New York.—The Yellow Fever Epidemic.—Enactment of New Building Laws.—The City Increasing with Unprecedented Rapidity.—The Services of Volunteers Dispensed With.— Location of Engine Houses.—Praise for the Fire Department.—Public Cisterns.—Insufficient Supply of Water.—Formation of a Hydrant Company.

The year 1822 forms an epoch in the municipal history of New York. The yellow fever, which had so often spread suffering and death among the inhabitants, made its last eccentric visit to our city in the autumn of that year. The people of the lower wards fled at its approach; the banker closed his doors, the merchant packed his goods, and churches no longer echoed the words of Divine truth. Hundreds of citizens fled the city altogether. But a few days elapsed from the first alarm, and business had found a refuge and a resting place. What was then the village of Greenwich, and is now the Ninth Ward of the city, suddenly became the center of trade and commerce. At a little distance from the spot where the larger merchants had made their temporary homes, ran a secluded country lane called Southampton Road. Trees that were ancient even in the time of the Revolution spread a grateful shade in the sultry days of summer. A convenient nook by the side of this quiet lane was chosen by a considerable number of Scotch weavers who had fled from the pestilence. This new home they called Paisley Place. Seventeenth Street, from Sixth to Seventh Avenue, is now the site of the spot where the Scotch weavers once hummed their native airs and sent the shuttle flying. It formed part of the great Warren estate. Admiral Warren, who died in Ireland in 1752, was an adopted citizen of New York, and had exercised considerable influence in the affairs of the colonial government. He had been knighted for his services in the royal navy while in command of a fleet on this station. The admiral married a daughter of Stephen De Lancey, an eminent New York city merchant. In the square now formed by Bleecker, Fourth, Perry, and Charles Streets, stood the Warren mansion, and through its illuminated courts flashed far and wide the splendors of its gaiety and fashion, renowned in the city, and on the trim lawns and terraces around the building often trod the feet of beauty. For forty years previous to 1867 the homestead was owned by Abraham Van Nest, a prominent merchant. A considerable portion of the Warren estate, including the little Paisley nook, passed into the possession of the Astor family.

The strength of the Department in June, 1822, was one thousand two hundred and sixty-nine men, including engineers and fire wardens; forty-six engines, including two at the new almshouse; four hook and ladder trucks; one hose wagon, with ten thousand two hundred and forty-five feet of hose in good order (including six hundred feet at the new almshouse); one thousand two hundred and ten feet of hose ordinary; and eight hundred and eighty feet bad; two hundred and sixty-eight fire buckets, seventeen ladders, twenty-three hooks, one machine for throwing down chimneys, and one copper pump. In February, 1821, old Engine No. 3 was sold for six hundred and forty dollars, and a new one purchased for seven hundred and fifty dollars; in June, old No. 25 was sold for three hundred dollars exclusive of hose, and a new one purchased at a cost of eight hundred and eight dollars; in October, old No. 5 was sold to A. W. Hardenbrook for five hundred dollars; in November, old No. 9 was sold for six hundred dollars. During 1822 (up to June) three new engines, Nos. 5, 9, and 28, were built at the corporation yard under the direction of Jacob Roome, superintendent of repairs, at a cost of five hundred and ninety-six dollars each, at least one hundred and fifty-four dollars apiece lower than the corporation had theretofore paid for engines of a similar size, and in point of workmanship and in other respects far superior (it was claimed) to any other belonging to the corporation.

A building law was enacted by the legislature, April 12, 1822, looking to the more substantial construction of new buildings, and the imposition of penalties for any infraction of the same. Yet another act was passed the following year (April 9, 1823) of a similar nature, requiring that certain buildings should be fireproof. Other laws, of like scope and tendency, were passed at various subsequent dates.

So eager were young men to put on the red shirt and the helmet of the fireman and be recognized as such, that it was only by the most rigid supervision and discrimination they were prevented from being enrolled in the companies, and the law was on all occasions strictly enforced. But in the winter of 1822–23 a great deficiency of firemen was experienced, and a memorial was presented by the Fire Department to the corporation praying for an amendment of the law so as to permit young men between the ages of eighteen and twenty-one to be chosen as firemen. But inasmuch as the law passed April 9, 1813, prescribed that none but freeholders and freemen were eligible, the Council decided that they had not power to do as requested.

For the six years preceding 1823 the cash expenses of the corporation for engines and apparatus, including the ground purchases and the engine houses erected, amounted to seventy-nine thousand nine hundred and ninety-six dollars and ninety-four cents, averaging thirteen thousand three hundred and thirty-two dollars per annum. The value of the estate vested in that species of public property was estimated in 1820 at seventy-two thousand seven hundred and eighty-nine dollars.

The number of engine companies (including hook and ladder companies) in January, 1823, was forty-seven, to which one thousand two hundred and fifteen men, all told, were attached, all of whom, when they should have served ten years from 1816, were to be exempted from serving as jurors, and all military duty thereafter. These facts suggested the question whether the existing number of engines was not more than was needed, and whether some of them could not be dispensed with, in view of the fact that the sum of nine thousand five hundred and sixty-six dollars was asked for in the annual estimate for departmental expenses for 1823 for the Fire Department. At that period no city in the Union incurred fire department expenses in anyway proportioned to the city of New York. In Philadelphia the engines and apparatus were furnished by individuals, and the privilege of exemption from jury and military duty were considered a sufficient remuneration, the City Council only appropriating about two thousand dollars towards the necessary repairs. The same economical system was pursued in the other cities throughout the United States. Mayor Allen, calling the attention of the Common Council to this matter, said that while they were drawing upon the property of the citizens in taxes so large an amount for fire purposes, and at the same time compelling them to perform nearly double duty as jurors in consequence of the exemption granted the firemen, it was no more than reasonable that the benefit to be derived in a public point of view should be commensurate with the sacrifice. Before the establishment of fire insurance companies in New York, the benefits derived from the Fire Department were perhaps equal to the expenditure. But it was very questionable then, when almost every species of property liable to be destroyed or injured by fire was insured against loss, whether any material public benefit was derived. The subject was of sufficient importance to the Common Council to cause an inquiry to be instituted whether the finances could not be relieved by a reduction of the expenses for the Fire Department. On the thirteenth of January the Common Council decided to apply to the legislature for authority to assess and levy annually a tax on fire insurance companies to be applied towards defraying the expenses of the Fire Department.

In conformity with the presentation of the condition of the finances by Mayor Allen, and his suggestion that retrenchment be introduced, if possible, the chief engineer, in July, 1823, reported that retrenchment was practicable only in the matter of hose, substituting hemp hose for leather, which was only half the price.

The strength of the Fire Department in June, 1823, was one thousand two hundred and eighty-four men, all told; forty-six engines, including two at the new almshouse; four hook and ladder trucks, one hose wagon, and eleven thousand five hundred and seventy-five feet of hose, good, bad, and indifferent; two hundred and eighty-five fire buckets, sixteen ladders, twenty-three hooks, one machine for pulling down chimneys, and one copper pump.

The engine houses were located as follows:

Engine.
1. Duane Street Market.
2. Eldridge, near Division Street.
3. Beaver, near Broad Street.
4. Ann Street, North Dutch Church.
5. Fulton Street, North Dutch Church.
6. College Yard, Murray Street.
7. Rose, near Frankfort Street.
8. Chambers, near Cross Street.
9. Marketfield, near Broad Street.
10. Fifth Street, near Second Avenue.
11. Old Slip.
12. Rose, near Frankfort Street.
13. Fulton Street, Fireman's Hall.
14. Vesey Street, near Church.
15. Christie, near Bayard Street.
16. Corporation Yard, Leonard Street.
17. Roosevelt, near Cherry Street.
18. Fulton Street, Fireman's Hall.
19. Eldridge Street, near Division.
20. Cedar, near Washington Street.
21. Fireman's Hall, Fulton Street.
22. Hester, near Orchard Street.
23. Hospital Yard, Anthony Street.
24. Prince and Wooster Streets, Watch House.
25. Tryon Row.
26. Madison, near Rutgers Street.
27. Watts, near Greenwich Street.
28. Mercer Street, near Prince.
29. Christopher and Hudson Streets.

Engine.
30. Christie, near Stanton Street.
31. Leonard, near Church Street.
32. Hester, near Orchard Street.
33. Cherry Street, near Corlears Hook.
34. Christopher and Hudson Streets.
35. Harlem Village.
36. Spring Street Church, near Varick Street.
37. Christie, near Stanton Street.
38. Bloomingdale Road, House of Refuge.
39. Vesey and Church Streets.
40. Mulberry, near Broome Streets.
41. Delancey and Attorney Street.
42. Foot of Roosevelt Street.
43. Manhattanville.
44. Columbia, near Stanton Street.
45. Yorkville.
46. Rose Hill.
47. Tenth Street, near Avenue D.
48. Fitz Roy Road, near Nineteenth Street.

H. and L.
1. Beaver, near Broad Street.
2. Tryon Row.
3. Christopher and Hudson Streets.
4. Eldridge Street, Watch House.
5. Delancey and Attorney Streets.
6. Mercer, near Prince Street.

Hose.
1. Tryon Row.

Besides the regularly appointed firemen, there were attached to each company a number of self-constituted firemen, who were known as "volunteers." Their services, it appears, were not appreciated by the Common Council, and on the twenty-first of June, 1824, a resolution was approved, and directed as a circular to each company, ordering them to dispense with the services of these men, and, in case of their non-compliance, to send the engine, hook and ladder, or hose cart, as the case might be, to the Corporation Yard, and report the company to the Common Council.

In June, 1824, the condition of the Fire Department called forth great praise from a special committee of the Common Council, who made a tour of inspection, and declared that it was not surpassed by any other in the United States. The volunteer boys, who assumed the dress and authority of firemen attached to companies, were the source of much annoyance, by causing false alarms of fire, whereby the members were constantly harassed and fatigued, and the machines injured to a great degree.

At this time the city was increasing with unprecedented rapidity. From actual enumeration, it appeared that in the year 1824 more than sixteen hundred new houses were erected, nearly all of them brick or stone. The price of real estate was also greatly increased. The erection of churches and other public edifices had become so frequent an occurrence as to forbid notice of each particular case. On the west side of the island the city proper was verging, nearly to Greenwich Village, which was also expanding into a large and well-built suburban ward. Eastward from the Bowery a settlement was springing up quite beyond the compact part of the city. In the middle portion, on both sides of Broadway, were many half rural residences of retired merchants and men of wealth. The old Potter's Field was becoming an obstacle to the city's progress in that vicinity, and it was accordingly determined to level and grade it, to be kept as a public promenade—the present Washington Square.

According to the report of Chief Engineer Jameson Cox, the condition of the Department in June, 1825, was:—Forty engines in good order, four indifferent, and two ordinary; four hook and ladder trucks and one hose wagon, ten thousand five hundred and seventy-four feet of hose, two hundred and twenty-eight fire buckets, eighteen ladders, and twenty-three hooks. With companies complete, the force would number one thousand three hundred and nineteen men, all told, but there were two hundred and thirty-one vacancies. During the year engine houses had been built for Companies Nos. 10, 19, and 33.

The Committee on the Fire Department reported on the twentieth of June on the subject of constructing public cisterns, and recommended a resolution, which was adopted, that the street commissioner be directed to prepare ordinances for the construction of ten public cisterns, the same to be used on the occasion of fire by the Fire Department. Subsequently, on the nineteenth of December, 1825, ordinances were passed for the construction of five additional cisterns. On the twenty-third of the same month, the Committee on the Fire Department were instructed to inquire into the expediency of filling all the public cisterns with water forthwith, and the fire companies were requested to volunteer their services to carry the above into effect.

A resolution was referred to the Committee on the Fire Department, in conjunction with the chief engineer, to mature a report to the Board of some more energetic and efficient plan to protect the firemen when on duty at fires from the encroachments of the surrounding populace. On the thirtieth of January, 1826, the committee reported the following resolution, which was adopted:

> *Resolved*, That his honor, the mayor, be requested to address a circular to each of the foremen of the several companies of fire wardens, calling their attention to that section of the law pointing out their duties at fires, and that each of them would enforce the same on the members of their companies, and that the penalties which may hereafter be incurred by the constables and marshals of the city for not attending fires, be enforced.

On the second of January, 1827, seven additional cisterns were ordered by the Common Council, and eighteen on the twenty-fifth of August, 1828.

The firemen of the city were an incorporated body, under the name and title of the Fire Department of the City of New York, and had certain emoluments allowed them, which they appropriated to charitable purposes, such as giving pensions to widows of deceased firemen, making donations to indigent disabled firemen, and furnishing necessary clothing to children of firemen, so as to enable them to attend the public schools. Each company appointed annually two of their number to represent them in the Fire Department, and such representatives, when assembled, appointed out of the body of firemen in the city a Board of Trustees, who were intrusted with the funds, and at whose discretion widows were put on the pension list, and donations were made. In consequence of severe and heavy losses which the Department had sustained in 1826 by several moneyed institutions in the city, the Board of Trustees had come to the conclusion that they would be under the necessity of suspending the pensions and donations, unless they received assistance from their fellow-citizens. In January, 1827, the Common Council, recognizing the close connection between the interests of the firemen and the Corporation, decided that it was proper and judicious to extend a helping hand, and directed the comptroller to issue his warrant for one thousand dollars in favor of the treasurer of the Fire Department Fund. Two years after another one thousand dollars was donated, because the frequency of fires in the fall of 1829, and the consequent increasing demand on the treasury of the Fire Department Fund from disabled and sick firemen, had left the treasury in December of that year almost exhausted. As many as eighty-eight widows, and a large number of orphan children, had to be provided for in that year.

At a fire at the Vauxhall Garden in August, 1828, one of the engine companies, and several members of other companies, refused to perform service, and a rumor prevailed throughout the city that the firemen as a body had refused to obey orders, which caused general alarm among the inhabitants. Upon investigation, it was found that the demoralization was very limited, and measures were taken to keep up the efficiency of the force.

"Firemen's Hall," in Fulton Street, had accommodations for four engines. The placing of so many machines in one immediate vicinity had been found to be prejudicial to the services of the Department, and in some instances to be a nuisance to the neighborhood. These facts, superadded to the necessity of providing engines for the upper part of the city by taking from the lower part those that could well be spared and were poorly supplied with men, had gradually caused the reduction of the number of engines there until, in February, 1829, only one was left, and the removal of that, too, had been decided on. The corporation concluded that the ground occupied for Fireman's Hall being no longer needed, they would sell it by auction, which was done on April 1.

In June, 1829, there were in the Department forty-eight engines, five hook and ladder trucks, with twenty-six ladders and twenty-nine hooks, and one thousand four hundred and thirty-two men with full companies, but only eight hundred and sixty-nine in actual service, there being five hundred and sixty-three vacancies.

Engine No. 28 was located on corporation ground on Mercer Street, and the council had directed that Hook and Ladder No. 6 should also be stationed there. It was therefore decided, in August, 1829, to erect a two-story brick building on the lot, in which, besides housing these companies, a ward court could be accommodated and the meetings of the Fire Department be held. Hence the origin of the present Firemen's Hall.

Although the natural advantages of New York in other respects were not excelled, nor perhaps equalled, by any city in the world, yet it had to be admitted that the supply of water for household purposes and for the extinguishment of fires was, in 1829, very meager. Various schemes had been adopted for the purpose of bringing water into the city, but none had as yet complied with the main object of their charters, so far as the public was concerned, and it was found that similar incorporations of private individuals, whether they proposed at their commencement to furnish pure and wholesome water or pure and first quality gas, had an eye only to the profits of their incorporations, and the public suffered under their monopolies.

The water pipes of the Manhattan Company extended to such parts of the city as they deemed advisable to put them in on the score of profit, and the upper part of the city, although not possessed of good water, had it, however, of a quality superior to that supplied by the Manhattan Company, and, therefore, the residents were unwilling generally to take the Manhattan water. The result was that all that part of the city lying above Grand Street, on Broadway, or Pearl Street on the east side of the city, did not have the use of the Manhattan water for the purpose of extinguishing fires. It became necessary, therefore, for the corporation to obtain a supply of water for that purpose to the upper part of the city.

The breadth of the island at Grand Street was then reckoned about two miles, and this did not materially differ as high up as Fourteenth Street. The extreme distance between those points was, consequently, one mile, and to bring water from either river at the extreme distance would require twenty-six engines, and thus the whole engine establishment could not form two lines. The furnishing water by engines from the rivers was not only too limited a mode to be at all relied on for that section of the city, but was also too laborious on the firemen.

Another mode of supply was by cisterns, which was in operation at this period to a limited extent. The corporation had forty public cisterns, at a cost of twenty-four thousand dollars, which usually contained one hundred hogsheads. To provide for the section of the city between Fourteenth and Grand Streets on Broadway, and Fourteenth and Pearl Streets on Chatham, by cisterns, would require the construction of at least sixty additional cisterns, on the scale of a cistern for each one thousand square feet, which, at an expense of six hundred dollars each, would call for an expenditure of thirty-six thousand dollars.

In March, 1829, the corporation decided to lay down two lines of iron pipes for the security against fire of the section of the city before described, one line of tubes to run from Fourteenth Street through the Bowery, to its termination at Chatham Street, and a line of tubes from Fourteenth Street through Broadway to Canal Street, connecting with a reservoir containing two thousand hogsheads (or as much as twenty cisterns) on Fourteenth Street.

The Committee on the Fire Department reported on the sixteenth of November, 1829, that, although they had excavated only fifty feet in depth at Thirteenth Street, yet the quantity of water would be sufficient to fill the reservoir and pipes, as it was estimated that seventy hogsheads of water were issued in a day; that the cast-iron tank was received from Philadelphia, and that the same should be inclosed with a brick or wooden building—the cost of the former being estimated at three thousand five hundred dollars, and of the latter two thousand dollars. Which report was agreed to.

A fireman should have experienced five years' service before he was eligible for appointment as a warden. In consequence of the reduction of the term of service of firemen from ten to seven years, the wardens encountered no small difficulty in procuring the aid of such competent persons as were willing to do the duty of wardens for the short space of time—two years—during which they were eligible for office. The ordinance affecting this matter was therefore amended in November, 1830, reducing the term of service for eligibility from five to three years.

The legislature, on April 16, 1831, extended the charter of the firemen of the city of New York, passed March 20, 1798, to the year 1860. The corporation was likewise empowered to purchase, hold, and convey any estate, real or personal, for the use and objects for which the said corporation was instituted, "but such real or personal estate shall not exceed the sum of fifty thousand dollars."

This act was amended March 25, 1851, by which the said corporation could hold and convey any estate, real and personal, for the use already mentioned, but not to exceed the sum of one hundred thousand dollars.

An important state law, relative to the prevention of fires in the city of New York, was enacted on the twentieth of April, 1830. This law was quite lengthy, containing forty-two sections. Reference can be made only to its general features. Party walls, the law declared, shall be constructed of stone or brick; outside party walls shall not be less than eight inches thick, except flues of chimneys; party or end walls shall rise and be extended to the roof, and so far through the same as to meet and be joined to the slate, tile, or other covering thereof, by a layer of mortar or cement; beams and other timbers in the party walls shall be separated from each other, at least four inches, by brick or mortar; all hearths shall be supported with arches of stone or brick. No timber shall be used in the front or rear of any building within such fire limits, where stone is now commonly used; every building within the fire limits, which may hereafter be damaged by fire, to an amount equal to the two-thirds of the whole value thereof, after the lapse of at least fifteen years from the time of its first erection, shall be repaired or built according to the provisions of this act; no wooden shed exceeding twelve feet in height at the peak shall be erected within the fire limits.

A large part of the act is devoted to the regulation of the keeping and storage of gunpowder.

A law, forming a hydrant company, was passed by the Common Council on July 16, 1831. This company consisted of a foreman, assistant, a clerk, and twenty men, who were firemen and hydrant men. It was their duty, on an alarm of fire, to proceed to the hydrants, and see to the water being properly let out, that the hydrants were not injured, that they were properly secured and put in order after the fire was extinguished; and also to see that the stopcocks were kept in order; and generally to attend to the engines being supplied with water from the reservoir; to report all injuries and defects which they might discover in any part of the works, to the chief engineer. The caps of said company were painted black, and had the words "Hydrant Company" on the frontispiece thereof.

A Fire and Building Department was created and organized by a law passed and approved in October, 1831. It was composed of three "discreet and proper persons," known as the Commissioners of the Fire and Building Department, and the commissioners were respectively designated a superintendent of buildings, chief engineer, and commissioner of the Fire Department.

The duty of the superintendent of buildings required him to advertise for estimates for all public buildings which might thereafter be erected under the authority of the Common Council, for all repairs to public buildings then in use, etc.

It was the duty of the chief engineer to report the names of persons who may be designated by the engineers and foremen as suitable persons to be appointed by the Common Council to fill vacancies in fire companies; in all cases of fire to have the sole and absolute command and control over all engines and members of the Fire Department; to direct the other engineers to take proper measures that the fire engines were suitably arranged and duly worked; to examine, once in every month, into the condition and number of the fire engines, and buckets, and other fire apparatus, and fire engine houses; and report the same to the Common Council twice in every year; and whenever any of the engines and apparatus should require to be repaired or new ones built, the chief engineer should personally inspect the building of the same; to report in writing all accidents by fire, with the probable causes thereof, etc.

Further, the commissioners should give their personal attention and supervision to the laying down of all such water pipes as the Common Council may direct, take charge of the reservoir and water establishment in Thirteenth Street, see that the hydrants were in order, etc.

The commissioners were obliged to give bonds in the sum of five thousand dollars, besides being sworn, for the faithful performance of their duties.

Pursuant to the organizing of the new Department, the enlargement of the house of Fire Engine Company No. 10, the erection of a two-story brick house on the lot corner of Delancey and Attorney Streets for the accommodation of a fire engine, hook and ladder company, and hose truck, the building of a hose house in Wooster Street, near Houston Street, the procuring of four thousand feet of hose, and the construction of a new engine for Company No. 11, were undertaken immediately.

In March, 1832, the fire limits were extended so as to include all that part of the city beginning on West Street, one hundred feet northerly from Spring Street, and running thence northerly along West Street to Bank Street, thence easterly through Bank Street to Greenwich Lane, thence southerly through Greenwich Lane to the east side of Sixth Avenue at a point northerly one hundred feet from Eighth Street, thence westerly along Sixth Avenue to a line distant southerly one hundred feet from Amity Lane, thence easterly and parallel with Amity Street to a line distant westerly one hundred feet from Greene Street, thence southerly and parallel with Greene Street to a line distant one hundred feet northerly from Spring Street, and thence westerly and parallel with Spring to West Street, at the place of beginning.

Also beginning at the Bowery, one hundred feet northerly from Rivington Street, and running thence northerly along the Bowery to a line distant southerly one hundred feet from North Street, thence easterly and parallel with North Street to Orchard Street, thence southerly along Orchard Street to a line distant one hundred feet northerly to Rivington Street, and thence westerly and parallel with Rivington Street, to the Bowery at the place of beginning.

The city in 1832 embraced a population of one hundred and eighty thousand souls, a collection of about thirty thousand houses, a tonnage of three hundred thousand four hundred tons, exclusive of ten thousand five hundred tons of steamboats, and an assessed value of property, including thirty-seven millions of personal estate, of one hundred and fourteen millions of dollars. Her lighted and paved streets, lined with houses, extended to Thirteenth Street on the North River, to the dry dock on the East River side, and to Thirteenth Street on "the Broadway and Bowery Streets." All the modern streets were straight and wide, graduated to easy ascents and descents; and where formerly very narrow lanes existed, or crowded edifices occurred, they had either cut off the encroaching fronts of houses, as in William Street and Maiden Lane, or cut through solid masses of houses, as in opening Beekman and Fulton Streets. The bounds of the city had been widened both on the North and East Rivers by building up whole streets of houses at and beyond Greenwich Street on the western side, and at and from Pearl Street on the eastern side.

The proviso in the law forming a hydrant company approved July 16, 1831, was repealed in May, 1832, and thenceforth it was ordained that no individual could be eligible for appointment as hydrant man unless he had served as a fireman for at least three years.

Although *quasi* officers of the municipality, it was charged that certain firemen frequently exhibited as much indifference to the injunctions of the authorities as might be looked for only from the lawless class. Hence, in July, 1832, it became necessary to promulgate a law ordaining that any fireman found guilty of an offense against the ordinances of the Common Council, and having thereby resigned or been expelled, should not be eligible to an appointment to any office of trust, in any company, nor reappointed a firemen in any case.

Also, it was not uncommon for the foreman or engineer of an engine company to hire out the engine, and to lend it, on his own responsibility, which was subversive of all semblance of discipline, and impaired the efficiency of the particular company. Consequently, a provision was incorporated in the law of July, 1832, that no fire engine should be let out for hire, or lent, in any case, without permission from the alderman or assistant alderman of the ward wherein it was wanted to be used, and the chief engineer, in default thereof, and the fireman so offending, would be removed from the Fire Department.

During the prevalence of the epidemic of cholera in 1832 the working force of the Department was much weakened by reason of sickness and death. Very often not enough men, nor even supernumeraries, boys and youths who loved to linger in the shadow of the engine house and be permitted to mingle with the hardy fire fighters, could be mustered to drag the engine to the scene of the conflagration. Horses had to be brought into requisition, as is attested by the fact that in November, 1832, the comptroller was authorized to pay the bill of James Gulick for eight hundred and sixty-three dollars and seventy-five cents, for horses "to drag the engines and hook and ladder trucks to the fires during the late epidemic."

The custom was in those days, upon the outbreak of fire, to ring the church bells as well as the fire bells, and when the fire happened during the night, the watchman in his tower should ring the alarm, and hang out of the window of the cupola a pole with a lantern on the end pointing in the direction of the fire, so that the firemen and citizens could readily know the whereabouts of the fire. Further, the watchmen (the police) were obliged to call out the street or between what streets the fire was located. The laws of the municipality regarding these observances were inflexible, delinquency on the part of the bellringers or the watchmen being visited with severe penalties.

The cost of supporting the Fire Department by the city varied considerably. In 1830 it amounted to twenty-two thousand nine hundred and sixty-two dollars. The actual number of fires that happened in that year were one hundred and nineteen; false alarms, one hundred and twenty-five; and the loss of property, one hundred and fifty-seven thousand one hundred and thirty-five dollars. In 1831 the expenses of the Department amounted to twelve thousand nine hundred and eighty-four dollars.

Careful calculations showed that although it cost in 1832 only eighteen thousand dollars to maintain the Fire Department, the individual firemen were taxed in their services two hundred and eighty-four thousand five hundred dollars annually. It is true their labors were rendered voluntarily, and they had an equivalent, but it did not render it less imperative on the city authorities, as the common guardians of this great community, to diminish the labors and personal exposures and risks of that meritorious, skillful and patriotic class of citizens.

The melancholy tidings of the death of the illustrious La Fayette, the friend and companion of Washington, the adopted son of America, the brave and faithful defender of liberty in both hemispheres, reached New York on June 19, 1834, just one month after his demise in Paris. Suitable honors were of course to be paid to the memory of this splendid character by the municipal authorities, and, in these days, no civic parade would be complete without the participation and presence of the members of the Fire Department in the usual and formal manner, a meeting was called whereat the following preamble and resolution were adopted, and programme for the parade agreed to:—

Whereas, we have learned of the death of General La Fayette, the tried patriot, the firm and devoted friend of America and her free institutions; he, who forsook the blandishments and ease of a luxurious court, who gave his fortune and risked his life for the independence of our happy Republic, therefore,

Resolved, That we, the firemen of the city of New York, will unite with our fellow-citizens on Thursday, the twenty-sixth instant, in paying such tribute of respect as the eminent virtues and patriotic services of one of America's dearest sons demand of a grateful and affectionate people.

The exempt firemen also attended in a body.

The Department assembled at Hospital Green, and the line was formed under the direction of the Grand Marshal, James Gulick, assisted by his aids, in the following order:

First, Fire Department Banner.

Second, Grand Marshal and two Aids.

Third, President, Vice-president, Trustees, Treasurer, Secretary, and Collector of the Fire Department.

Fifth, Exempt Firemen.

Sixth, The banners and implements equally distributed through the line, under the direction of the different marshals. The Brooklyn and Williamsburg firemen in the center.

After the ceremonies, the procession reorganized and proceeded up Greenwich Street to Canal, through Canal to Broadway, up Broadway to Grand Street, through Grand Street to East Broadway, down East Broadway to Chatham Square.

The alleged improper and riotous conduct of the members of several companies of the Department, and the congregating of idle and dissolute persons in the engine houses, had been for several months the subject of complaint from residents in the vicinity of engine houses. Boys and young men, too, obtained very ready access to the engines, and made it a matter of amusement to raise an alarm of fire as an excuse or cover to get the engines out and have a run. Evidently the engine companies could prevent these scenes. But in cases of fire the companies desired some assistance from these boys and young men, which induced them to countenance the assemblages. The Common Council investigated the complaints, and in October, 1834, reported that the members of some of the companies could not be depended upon to prevent the engine houses being entered and frequented by persons other than those belonging to the Fire Department, and suggested the enactment of a law providing a remedy.

That a prompt alarm of fire might be given, a watchman was stationed at all times in the cupola of the City Hall. The law so providing was approved by the mayor, April 1, 1835. The chief engineer, by and with the consent of the mayor, was empowered to appoint a competent number of persons to perform the duty of such watchmen, day and night, subject severally to removal by the chief engineer. These bellringers, nevertheless, were amenable at all times during the night to the rules and regulations of the Watch Department. On the occurrence of any fire, the City Hall bell should be rung by the watchman on duty in the cupola, and the ringing thereof maintained during the continuance of the fire. Notice of the locality of the fire was given by ringing said bell in a manner prescribed by directions given by the committee on fire and water and the chief engineer, and by hanging out a light in the direction of the fire. For neglect of any of the duties required by this law, the penalty imposed was removal from office by the chief engineer or captains of the watch.

Upon the happening of any fire, the several watchhouses and market bells were rung, and also all other alarm bells, and the same was done whenever any one alarm bell should ring, and the ringing thereof continued until the city bell had stopped.

It will be seen from these facts that the Fire Department kept pace with the growth of the city. The people were quick to recognize the importance of keeping up, both in numbers and efficiency, a body of men so necessary to the welfare of the growing metropolis. Year by year, nay, almost month by month, additions to the Department were made, and alterations effected to improve it. The enactment of the new building laws was a great help to the firemen, and its enforcement gave them a great advantage over their natural enemy—an advantage which prior to this they did not possess.

It will also be noted how eager the firemen were to maintain an *esprit de corps*. Before the period we are just concluding efforts had been made to diminish the number of the hangers-on of the Department. As the city grew these parasites increased, and the difficulty was all the greater to keep them off. We have shown how persistently and honorably the firemen endeavored to abate this nuisance. They could not wholly dispense with the services of outsiders, but those whom they did employ they took care should be of the best quality attainable.

It was only natural in the period we have just discussed that the Department should complain of the insufficiency of water. That was not a matter that could be attended to until science had a greater play than she experienced in those days. Indeed up to the present there has been a constant cry that New York has not all the water she needs. In the past as in the present the firemen did the very best they could to utilize what was at their disposal for the benefit of the city.

CHAPTER VIII

FEUDS AND THEIR SUPPRESSION

*1835–1842.—Frequency of Fires.—Element of Rowdyism in the Department.—
Bitter Feuds between Companies.—The Importance of the Services of the Fire
Department Universally Admitted.—A Proposition to Elect and Appoint Five
Fire Commissioners.—Efforts to Suppress "Volunteers."*

Mayor Lawrence, in September, 1835, called the attention of the Common
Council to the frequency of fires, and particularly the one in Fulton, Ann,
and Nassau Streets, and also the fire in Water Street and Maiden Lane, by which
a large amount of property was destroyed and lives lost. He expressed the belief
that these were the work of incendiaries, and he suggested the propriety of
offering a reward for such information as should lead to the detection and conviction of the criminals. The Council empowered him to do so in his discretion,
and, accordingly, a proclamation for five hundred dollars was issued.

Not more than a fortnight after the issuance of this proclamation another large
fire broke out in Franklin and Chapel (now College Place) Streets, earning every
mark of being of incendiary origin, and another reward of five hundred dollars
was offered.

Then followed the terrible conflagration of December 16, which destroyed
in one night twenty million dollars' worth of property, and dislodged more than
six hundred mercantile firms. By that calamity the extensive resources and irrepressible energies of the citizens were developed, and it forms a proud record
for the pages of history that not a single mercantile failure resulted therefrom,
and many of the heavy sufferers were among the most active in aiding the
widows, orphans, and infirm persons reduced to poverty and dependence.

The element of rowdyism in the Fire Department hitherto referred to as being
so pronounced that the citizens begged for the interference of the authorities,
again manifested itself at a fire which occurred on the night of January 1, 1836,
when Alderman Purdy, representing the Tenth Ward, was set upon and mer-
cilessly beaten by members of Engine Company No. 10, who were also accused
of abandoning their engine on that occasion. For the latter offense, nine officers
and members were expelled from the Department, and ten were suspended for

not complying with the requisitions to appear before a committee of the Common Council and testify in reference to the assault on Alderman Purdy.

With the opening of the spring of 1836, the number of fires in the city had increased to an alarming extent, and a proportionate increase in the number of firemen had become necessary. This increase was not attainable, by reason of the citizens being deterred from becoming firemen in consequence of the arduous and toilsome duties which the members of the Fire Department were incessantly called upon to perform. As the increase was absolutely necessary for the safety of the city, it became a duty incumbent on the authorities to encourage citizens to join the Fire Department by lessening, as far as possible, the labors of the firemen, as well as removing such impediments to their exertions as existed.

Among those impediments, that caused by young men—who appeared at fires in the garb of firemen—was especially prominent. The engineers had no control over them, and their insubordination, utter lawlessness, and the confusion they created, proved a continual source of annoyance and serious hindrance both to the engineers and the regular firemen, a great majority of whom would gladly dispense with their precarious assistance if by so doing they could be freed from all suspicion of participating in riots created by these boys, and which, instead of being assigned to their true cause, were attributed to the members of the Fire Department.

To accomplish these two purposes, it was determined to appoint four persons to each fire engine and hose company, and two persons to each hook and ladder company, to take care of the apparatus and assist generally, and making it the duty of all members of the Department to prevent persons not belonging to the Department, especially boys, from entering any house or handling any apparatus belonging to the Department, said appointees not to be considered as firemen, and to be paid at the rate of one hundred and fifty dollars per annum.

The Third Ward Hose Company, whose origin was traceable to the conflagration of December, 1835, tendered its services to the corporation in March, 1836, which were accepted, and they were recognized as a volunteer fire company, attached to, but not a part of, the Fire Department.

From the report of the chief engineer, John Ryker, Jr:, it appears that the condition of the Fire Department on October 3, 1836, was:

Forty-nine engine companies,

Six hook and ladder companies,

Nine hose companies,

with an active available force of nine hundred and thirty-seven men.

Half a century ago it was an honor to be an alderman or an assistant. They were elected by their fellow-citizens for their integrity and ability, and as a consequence, were entrusted and invested with privileges and functions of a magisterial nature. Hence it came about that, next to the mayor of the city, they were, perhaps, among civic functionaries, the most important. That was their status as concerns fires, for to them (as the law prescribed) the marshals and constables, repairing immediately on the alarm of fire with their staves of office to the scene of the fire, should report and should conform to such orders as might be given them by the mayor, the alderman and assistant of the ward, or by any one of the aldermen, for the preservation of the public peace, and the removal of all idle and suspected persons or others not actually or usefully employed in aiding the extinguishment of such fire, or in the preservation of property in the vicinity thereof, and if any marshal or constable should not attend at such fire or should neglect so to report himself, or to obey any orders that were given him, he should, unless he had a reasonable excuse, to be determined by the mayor, forfeit and pay five dollars for each offense.

Two persons were appointed to each fire engine and hose company (ordinance May 10, 1836), and two persons to each hook and ladder company within the lamp and watch district, their duty consisting of keeping all the apparatus of the companies in complete order and ready for immediate use; upon every alarm of fire they repaired forthwith to the house of the engine, hose, or hook and ladder company to which they were attached, and assisted the members in conveying the engine, carriage, or truck to the fire, and there assisted the company in getting the engine to work, or the hose ready for immediate action, under the direction of the officers of the company to which they belonged; and during the time such engine or hose carriage was employed at a fire, the two persons named in the ordinance took charge of the hose, and prevented any persons from treading on, or otherwise injuring the same. They also assisted the members, when the engine or hose carriage was discharged from duty, after the putting out of a fire, in taking up the hose and other apparatus, and assisted in conveying them, together with the engine or hose carriage, etc., to the house appropriated for it, and there washed and dried the hose, and cleaned and put in complete order all the apparatus, so as to be ready for immediate use, taking care, however, in no case to meddle with the works of an engine.

Those persons, similarly appointed and attached to a hook and ladder company, preserved the truck and apparatus belonging to their company from injury during the fire; assisted the members in raising or moving ladders and hooks, and rendered assistance, after the fire, in getting the apparatus to the house, etc.

"Among the novelties of New York," it was remarked by an observant writer (1837) "there is nothing perhaps which strikes a stranger with more surprise than the frequency of fires. There is scarcely a day from January to July, and from July to January, when there is not an alarm—a cry of fire— and a ringing of bells. But a single alarm, for each day in the year, would be too low an average. To say the bells are rung and the firemen called out five hundred times in the three hundred and sixty-five days, would not exceed the truth.

"Strangers are very often alarmed," continues the same writer, "as well as surprised, at the frequent cries of fires in this city, and fancy from the hideous outcry of the boys and the rueful jangling of the bells, that the fire is close to, if not within their very lodgings; and that New York is, every day, on the verge of a general conflagration. To this alarm, the bells very much, perhaps needlessly, contribute. As soon as an alarm of fire is given they fall to ringing in all quarters with great zeal and force; and some of them continue their clamor for a considerable time after the danger is past, or after the alarm is ascertained to be a false one. The first in the field, the most vigorous in action, and the last to quit, is the bell of the Middle Dutch Church. Who the ringer of that bell is we do not know; but this we will aver, that he labors with a zeal and perseverance that are quite astounding. We fancy he, now and then, gets up in his sleep to exercise his vocation. At any rate, whether asleep or awake, he seems to have a remarkable fondness for pulling at the end of a rope."

Severe and bitter quarrels were often the result of placing two engine companies under the same roof. This was illustrated by the perpetual and bitter feuds between Companies Nos. 34 and 29 and Hook and Ladder Company No. 3, whose houses, on the corner of Hudson and Christopher Streets, adjoined and were connected. The residents of the Ninth Ward, in the immediate vicinity, were much disturbed by the disorderly conduct of the members of these companies, regular and volunteer, and they memorialized the Common Council for an abatement of the annoyance by the removal of the engine companies. An investigation was made on the part of the Council, and so well established was the fact that gross scenes of outrage and abuse had often been perpetrated that the corporation took possession of the engines and placed them in the public yard until other locations for them should be determined on. The hook and ladder company was completely exonerated by the investigation, being declared to be a well regulated, efficient, and valuable company. The upshot of the matter was that the house corner of Hudson and Christopher Streets was sold, and the bellicose engine companies were located respectively on Morton and Bank Streets.

In May, 1838, the laws and ordinances relating to fires and the Fire Department were amended and modified so that the Department should consist of a chief engineer, nine assistant engineers, a water purveyor, and as many fire wardens, fire engine men, hosemen, and hook and ladder men as might from time to time be appointed by the Common Council. The chief engineer should be nominated by the engineers, foremen, and assistant foremen; and the assistant engineers by the foremen and assistant foremen of the fire companies, respectively, to the Common Council for appointment, and should hold their offices during the pleasure of the Common Council.

The salary of the chief engineer was fixed at twelve hundred dollars per year.

The water purveyor should be appointed by, and hold office during the pleasure of the Common Council, at a salary of one thousand dollars per year, take charge of the public reservoirs and establishments of water for the extinguishment of fires.

The engineers, foremen, and assistant foremen, should meet on the first Tuesday in June annually for the purpose of nominating a suitable person for chief engineer.

So many of the freeholders or freemen as the Common Council deemed proper should from time to time be appointed in each of the wards of the city, denominated fire wardens, assigned and attached by the mayor to such company of firemen as he should think proper, the fire wardens of each ward forming a separate company.

The names and places of abode of the members of the Common Council, engineers, fire wardens, and firemen of the respective companies, and bell ringers, were annually, in the month of June, printed and set up in the several watch-houses by the city inspector, and whenever any fire happened in the night, the watch gave notice to them within their respective watch districts.

Mayor Aaron Clark, in his annual message, referring to the Fire Department, said that their importance was universally admitted. They were to be congratulated, he said, upon their efficiency and usefulness, and the general harmony then prevailing among the companies composing the department, consisting, as it did, of a numerous body of citizens engaged in various pursuits and businesses, and voluntarily associated for the preservation of property and life from the ravages of conflagration, it had become identified with the safety and the happiness of the citizens. For intrepidity, skill, and firmness of purpose "in the summer's heat and the winter's cold," their firemen were unsurpassed by those of any country.

In July, 1838, the insurance companies urged upon the authorities the passage of an ordinance for the appointment of commissioners to investigate the causes of fires. The Common Council responded with a law to appoint three persons at a salary of one thousand dollars each per annum, who should attend at all fires, and immediately thereafter investigate the cause thereof, and file a report of the evidence taken and the result of their investigation.

The ordinance was to go into effect on the first of August, 1838, provided that the sum of four thousand dollars had been previously paid into the city treasury by one or more of the insurance companies, for the purpose of defraying the expenses incurred by the commission, which latter should continue in force so long as one or more of the companies should on or before June 1 in each year pay a similar amount.

The city in 1838 was divided into five districts, which were pointed out by the bell as follows:

First District—one stroke of the bell.

Second District—two strokes of the bell.

Third District—three strokes of the bell.

Fourth District—four strokes of the bell.

Fifth District—a continual ringing.

The First District was comprehended by a line from the foot of Murray Street to the City Hall, and in a line from the northwest corner of the City Hall parallel with the North River, to Twenty-first Street.

The Second District was bounded by the latter line, and a straight line from the City Hall to Third Avenue at Twenty-first Street.

The Third District was bounded by the latter, and a line from the City Hall to the East River above the dry dock.

The Fourth District was bounded by the latter, and comprehended all the space between that and the East River, as far down as Frankfort Street.

The Fifth District was all that part of the city below Frankfort and Murray Streets.

The encouraging and well-deserved compliment paid the Fire Department by Mayor Clark in 1838 was echoed in 1839 by Mayor Isaac L. Varian, who said, in addressing the municipal legislature, that it deserved their fostering care. During the past year the amount of property destroyed by fire was small, compared with former years. The introduction of water for the purpose of extinguishing fires through pipes and hydrants had afforded additional facilities to the firemen, and on the plan the pipes were being laid, a farther extension of them was deemed advisable, and contracts were made for the supply of six thousand five hundred water pipes.

A proposition was submitted to the legislature in June, 1840, without any application on the part of the Common Council, in regard to the Fire Department of this city, which was adopted by one branch of that body, but in the other was not acted on, and did not become a law. This proposition was to deprive the Common Council of all control over the Department, and place it in the hands of persons who were not in any way responsible to the public authorities, while it left the whole expenses of the Department to be paid from the treasury. Such a measure was not acceptable to the Common Council; and instead of removing the difficulties which had in former years operated injuriously against the Department, would have added, the Council claimed, new ones of a more serious character.

Since 1836 the introduction of political feelings and views into the general management of the Fire Department had materially affected its usefulness and tended much to produce the evils which the law above referred to was designed to remedy.

It was directed by the Common Council, March 11, 1840, that a cupola and alarm bell be placed on Center Market, and that the expense thereof be paid out of the general appropriation for the Fire Department, and that the superintendent of buildings and repairs, under the direction of the joint committee on fire water, contract for the same.

It was decreed also that a watchman should, at all times, be stationed at the cupola of the City Hall, reservoir, Center, Essex, and Jefferson Markets, for the purpose of giving an alarm whenever a fire occurred. The fire and water committee, by and with the consent of the mayor, appointed a competent number of persons to perform such duty by day and night, who were severally removable by the committee. These men were paid for their services, at the rate of two dollars per day, on their bills being certified by the chairman of the fire and water committee.

In the winter of 1841 it was sought to still further amend and modify the laws respecting the Fire Department. The firemen were to be appointed by and under the control, supervision, etc., of five commissioners, elected and appointed by the representatives of the New York Fire Department, holding office for five years, at one thousand dollars each per annum, to be known as "The Commissioners of the Fire Department of the City of New York," and no person should be appointed as a commissioner who had not served at least five years as a fireman. The commissioners should have power to appoint a chief engineer and seven assistant engineers, subject to removal at any time by said commissioners. They should have power to appoint the firemen, and to purchase all apparatus; to appoint on the recommendation of the alderman and assistant alderman of each ward, five persons to each ward, to be denominated "Fire Policemen;" to appoint two persons as cleaners; and to regulate and fix the salaries of chief and assistant engineers, the fire policemen, and the cleaners.

The salary of the chief engineer, it may be observed here, varied considerably. In 1819 it was $800 a year; in 1820, $500; in 1834, $1,000; in 1838, $1,200; in 1839, $500; in 1841, $1,000; in 1844, $1,500; in 1848, $2,000; in 1855, $3,000, and from 1857 to 1865, $5,000. Long before 1841 the chief engineer was the appointee of the Common Council, then he became the annual choice of the engineers, foreman and assistant foreman. In 1842 an ordinance was passed by which the chief engineer was nominated by the firemen, appointed by the Common Council and served until a majority of the firemen desired a new election. At various times there were heated arguments as to the best method of appointing or electing a chief engineer. The citizens showed their interest in the Department by joining in these discussions through the press. The opinion of the majority prevailed that that important officer should be the selection of the whole Department, and so we find that in 1853 a law was passed fixing his election by the firemen, who balloted for him every three years.

The regular firemen continued to be much harassed by so-called volunteer associations, their good name tarnished, and their efforts often frustrated. The Common Council again (November 10, 1841) denounced these volunteer associations and the practice of permitting them to assume the garb of firemen, and to mingle in the duties thereof. This, the ordinance declared, was not only in direct and open violation of the ordinances of the Common Council, but was calculated, in its results, to demoralize the character of youth, and bring reproach upon the Department, by the riotous and disorderly conduct in which these young men were so often engaged. Hence, the officers and members of each company were ordered forthwith to disband all associations of volunteers, and upon no occasion to suffer or permit them to have access to the public property; and all magistrates, watchmen, and police officers, were requested to prevent the congregating of all boys around or in the vicinity of the engine, hose, and hook and ladder houses, to the end that members of the Fire Department might be recognized as such, and be held responsible for all deviation from the path of duty, and the requirements of the ordinances of the Common Council.

Fire companies were interdicted from removing their apparatus out of the district in which the same was located, below Fourteenth Street, in case of fire, or an alarm of fire, under the penalty of being subject to expulsion or suspension from the Fire Department, unless they should be permitted to do so by the chief or both assistant engineers.

The fire districts were laid out as follows:

The First Fire District shall embrace all that part of the city lying north of a line from the foot of North Moore Street to the Halls of Justice, and west of a line running from the Halls of Justice, through Lafayette and Irving Places.

The Second Fire District shall embrace all that part of the city lying east of the first district, and north of a line running from the Halls of Justice to the foot of Roosevelt Street.

The Third Fire District shall embrace all that part of the city lying south of the first and second districts.

Engine Companies Nos. 22, 38, 42 (June 22, 1842), consisted of sixty men each, and all other engine companies of thirty men each; hose companies with four-wheeled hose carriages, of twenty-five men each; hose companies with two-wheeled hose carriages, eighteen men each; and hydrant companies, of fifteen men each; and the chief engineer was directed not to allow the above-named companies to exceed the number of men specified.

Engine Company No. 9 thereafter should be known as Hose Company No. 35; Engine Company No. 47 as Hose Company No. 34; Engine Company No.

17 as Hose Company No. 37; Third Ward Hose Company as Hose Company No. 27; Fifth District Hose Company as Hose Company No. 28; Hose Company No. 44 as Hose Company No. 29; Hose Company No. 43 as Hose Company No. 31; Hose Company No. 42 as Hose Company No. 32; making the number and locations of the fire apparatus as follows:

ENGINE COMPANIES.—THEIR NUMBERS AND LOCATIONS.

No. 1, Clinton Square, foot of Duane Street.

No. 2, Eldridge, near Division.

No. 3, Orange, near Prince.

No. 4, North Dutch Church, near Ann Street.

No. 5, North Dutch Church, near Ann Street.

No. 6, Reade Street, near West Broadway.

No. 7, Rose Street, near Frankfort Street.

No. 8, Ludlow, near Broome Street.

No. 9, Disbanded.

No. 10, Third Street, near Bowery.

No. 11, Wooster, near Prince Street.

No. 12, William, near Duane Street.

No. 13, Duane, near William Street.

No. 14, Corner of Vesey and Church Streets.

No. 15, Christie, near Walker Street.

No. 16, Disbanded.

No. 17, Disbanded.

No. 18, Amity, near Sixth Avenue.

No. 19, Elizabeth, near Grand Street.

No. 20, Cedar, near Greenwich Street.

No. 21, Lumber, near Cedar Street.

No. 22, Chambers, near Centre Street.

No. 23, Anthony, near Broadway.

No. 24, Seventeenth Street, near Ninth Avenue.

No. 25, Twenty-third Street, near Fifth Avenue.

No. 26, Madison, near Rutgers Street.

No. 27, Watts, near Greenwich Street.

No. 28, Disbanded.

No. 29, Horatio Street, near Ninth Avenue.

No. 30, Disbanded.

No. 31, West Broadway, near Beach Street.

No. 32, Hester, near Allen Street.

No. 33, Gouverneur, near Henry Street.

No. 34, Christopher, near Hudson Street.

No. 35, Harlem.

No. 36, Varick, near Vandam Street.

No. 37, Delancey, near Allen Street.

No. 38, Nassau, near Ann Street.

No. 39, Doyers, near Chatham Square.

No. 40, Mulberry, near Broome Street.

No. 41, Corner Delancey and Attorney Streets.

No. 42, Beaver, near William Street.

No. 43, Manhattanville.

No. 44, Houston, near Lewis Street.

No. 45, Yorkville, Third Avenue.

No. 46, Twenty-fifth Street, near
     Bull's Head.
No. 47, Disbanded.
No. 48, Thirteenth Street, near Sixth
     Avenue.

No. 49, Harlem.
No. 50, Bloomingdale Road, Har-
     senville.

HOSE COMPANIES.

No. 1, 4-wheeled, Duane, near William Street.
No. 2, 2 " William, near Duane Street.
No. 3, 2 " Centre, near Hester Street.
No. 4, 2 " Attorney, near Delancey Street.
No. 5, 4 " Mercer, near Prince Street.
No. 6, 4 " Gouverneur, near Henry Street.
No. 7, 2 " Christie, near Stanton Street.
No. 8, 4 " Cedar, near Nassau Street.
No. 9, 4 " Mulberry, near Broome Street.
No. 10, 2 " Roosevelt, near Cherry Street.
No. 11, 2 " Jefferson Market, Sixth Avenue.
No. 12, 4 " Seventeenth Street, near Ninth Avenue.
No. 13, 2 " Eldridge, near Division Street.
No. 14, 2 " Elizabeth, near Bayard Street.
No. 15, 2 " Essex Market, near Grand Street.
No. 16, 2 " Beaver, near Broad Street.

No. 17, 4-wheeled, Fifth Street, near Second Avenue.
No. 18, 2 " Franklin Market, Old Slip.
No. 19, 2 " Cortlandt Alley, near Canal Street.
No. 20, 2 " John, near Dutch Street.
No. 21, 2 " Henry, near Catharine Street
No. 22, 2 " Hester, near Allen Street.
No. 23, 2 " Charles, near Hudson Street.
No. 24, 2 " Renwick, near Spring Street.
No. 25, 2 " Leonard Street, near Broadway.
No. 26, 2 " Monroe, near Jefferson Street.
No. 27, 2 " Corner of Vesey and Church Streets.
No. 28, 2 " Chambers, near Centre Street.
No. 29, 2 " Willett, near Rivington Street.
No. 30, 2 " Bowery, near Thirteenth Street.
No. 31, 2 " Willett, near Rivington Street.
No. 32, 2 " Third Street, near Bowery.

No. 33, 2-wheeled, Sullivan, near Prince Street.

No. 34, 2 " Tenth Street, near Avenue D.

No. 35, 2 " Mercer, near Bleecker Street.

No. 36, 2-wheeled Henry, near Catharine Street.

No. 37, 2 " Monroe Market.

No. 38, 2 " Amity Street, near Sixth Avenue.

HYDRANT COMPANIES.

No. 1, John A. Blackledge, Foreman.

No. 2, Allen R. Jollie, Foreman.

No. 3, Daniel Coger, Foreman.

HOOK AND LADDER COMPANIES.

No. 1, Beaver, near Broad Street.

No. 2, Chambers, near Centre Street.

No. 4, Eldridge, near Walker Street.

No. 5, Corner Delancey and Attorney Streets.

No. 6, Mercer, near Prince Street.

No. 7, Harlem.

No. 8, Disbanded.

No. 9, Disbanded.

No. 10, Third Avenue, Yorkville.

Fire wardens to the number of six were stationed in each of the First, Second, Third, Fourth, Fifth, Sixth, Seventh, Eighth, Ninth, Tenth, Eleventh, Twelfth, Thirteenth, Fourteenth, Fifteenth, Sixteenth, and Seventeenth Wards.

The Common Council, on September 7, 1842, by ordinance, established the offices of a chief engineer, a superintendent of the aqueduct works, a water purveyor, and a register of rents, to hold their respective offices during the pleasure of the Common Council, unless sooner removed for cause by the Croton Aqueduct Board, with the concurrence of the Joint Croton Aqueduct Committee. The chief engineer, under the direction of the Croton Aqueduct Board, had the general executive care and superintendence of the Croton Aqueduct Works.

The superintendent and water purveyor had the care of laying down all the distributing pipes, hydrants, and stop-cocks, under the direction of the chief engineer and Croton Aqueduct Board; examined into, and reported to the Croton Aqueduct Board all applications for water, and generally did all such duty assigned to them; they attended all fires, provided against all unnecessary waste of water, and saw that all hydrants were closed at the termination of each conflagration.

The salary of the chief engineer was increased to one thousand five hundred dollars per annum.

CHAPTER IX

INTRODUCTION OF THE CROTON SERVICE

1842–1853.—Much Rioting among the Companies.—Condition of the Department.—The City Divided into Three Fire Districts.—The Morse Magnetic Telegraph.—Erection of a Water Tower.—The Hague Street Disaster.—Chief Carson's Charges.

The introduction of the Croton water into the city called for a thorough reorganization of the Department. That worthy and patriotic class of citizens would no longer be required to perform the laborious duty of dragging their engines for miles; and the services of the boys who congregated about the engine houses for the purpose of assisting to convey the engines to the fires would no longer be required. The period had now arrived—the summer of 1842—when the city authorities could with perfect ease, and with proper regard for the laborious exertions of the Fire Department, prevent boys and young men, not members of the Department, interfering in any manner with, or performing the duties of, firemen. When these excrescences should be lopped off from the Department, the high character and worth of the members proper would be at once appreciated, and the people would bear witness to their services and usefulness.

Serious and disgraceful fights and riots had occurred in the autumn of 1843 between different fire companies, principally originating with low and violent characters whose respective companies had been disbanded and broken up by the corporation, and who attached themselves to others on occasions of fires, to create fights and disorder, thus degrading the character and impairing the usefulness and discipline of the Fire Department. In order to prevent the repetition of such outrages, and effectually protect the respectable and well-disposed, the chief engineer, C. V. Anderson, solicited the Common Council for the establishment of a fire police, consisting of not less than twenty men, who should assemble at each fire to protect property and to suppress tumult.

The Common Council had no power to create such a body, and, therefore, a memorial to the legislature was prepared for authority to do so.

The condition of the Fire Department in August, 1843, was: thirty-seven engines in good order, two in indifferent order, and two rebuilding; thirty-eight hose carriages in good order, and one rebuilding; eight hook and ladder trucks, with forty-seven ladders and fifty-one hooks, and forty-eight thousand nine hundred feet of hose. There were then in the Department thirty-nine engine companies, forty hose companies, eight hook and ladder companies, and three hydrant companies, and one thousand six hundred and sixty-one men.

In March, 1843, in consequence of certain serious disturbances in the Department, the disbandment of certain companies, and among others of Engine Company No. 34, was recommended. The evidence concerning the fights between Engine Companies No. 34 and 27 substantiated the allegations of frequent and violent attacks, while not a solitary complaint had been made to the competent authorities, both companies having "preferred to fight it out to calling on the Common Council for protection." Engine Company No. 34 was disbanded, their apparatus returned to the public yard, and their house given to Hose Company No. 40. In May of that year No. 34 was reinstated.

In August, 1844, there were in the Department thirty-nine engines in good order, and one in indifferent order; thirty-eight hose carriages in good order, one indifferent, and two building; eight hook and ladder trucks, with forty-six ladders and forty-nine hooks; thirty-one thousand eight hundred and fifty feet of good hose, and six thousand two hundred and fifty feet of hose in ordinary, making in the whole thirty-eight thousand one hundred feet of hose; forty-one engine companies (one of which performed duty with a hose carriage), forty-one hose companies, eight hook and ladder companies, and one hydrant company; one thousand five hundred and eighty-one men.

In May, 1845, there were thirty-nine engines, thirty-eight hose companies, seven hook and ladder companies, and two hydrant companies. Thirty-three of the engines were located below Twenty-eighth Street, and of those thirty were six and one-half inch cylinder engines, one ten inch, and two nine inch cylinder engines.

The introduction of the Croton water, while it had added vastly to the ability of the Department to answer the ends of its organization, had likewise suggested various improvements. Hose carts had been multiplied, and had proved to be in many cases advantageous substitutes for the fire engine. From the lightness of their construction, they could be run with much greater facility to points where they were suddenly required, and being able from the hydrants to throw water to the elevation of ordinary buildings, they were found to equal in efficiency for the extinguishment of fires the class of engines principally used before the introduction of the water, and then constituting in numbers the bulk of the engine force.

During the year ending August 1, 1845, there were three hundred and fifty alarms of fire, two hundred and sixty of which called for the employment of the Department and its apparatus, and ninety arose from trivial causes. The amount of property destroyed during the same period (excluding the fire on July 19 in New and Broad Streets) was four hundred and seventy-four thousand eight hundred and thirty dollars. In the months of May and June alone there were sixty-seven actual fires.

The following is a return of the engine, hose, hook and ladder, and hydrant companies; their apparatus, places of deposit, condition, etc., together with the names of the engineers and foremen, on September 22, 1845:

ENGINE COMPANIES.

No. of Engine.	When Built.	Condition.	Foremen's Names.	Place of Deposit.
1	1827	Good.	Stephen T. Hoyt.	Clinton Square, foot of Duane Street.
5	1822	Good.	Hiran Arents.	40 Ann Street.
6	1839	Good.	H. C. Flander.	106 Reade Street.
7	1815	Condemned.	Alex. D. Renton.	6 Third Street.
8	1800	Good.	James Tyler.	91 Ludlow Street.
9	1824	Good.	Wm. M. Guest.	Corner 48th Street and 8th Avenue.
10	1824	Good.	John J. Terhune.	27th Street, near 10th Avenue.
11	1833	Good.	Abraham B. Purdy.	118 Wooster Street.
12	1828	Good.	John Gildersleeve.	74 Delancey Street.
13	1829	Good.	Danl. S. Weeks.	5 Duane Street.
14	1832	Good.	Hy. B. Venn.	Corner Church and Vesey.
15	1831	Good.	Nichls. T. Wilson.	49 Christie Street.
16	1825	Good.		152 20th Street.
18	1825	Good.	Peter A. Banta.	132 Amity Street.
19	1824	Condemned.	M. Eichells.	199 Christie.
20	1826	Good.	Horace F. Deen.	126 Cedar.
21	1835	Good.	Charles Daly.	5 Temple.
22	1840	Good.	Garrett B. Lane.	36 Chambers.
23	1833	Good.	Geo. McKinley.	Anthony (Worth), near Broadway.
24	1818	Good.	A. Lanson J. Brown.	255 17th Street.
25	1818	Good.	Arthur Gillender.	Bloomingdale Road and 24th Street.
29	1824	Good.	Thomas Lawrence.	14 Amos Street.
31	1823	Good.	Wm. H. Whitehead.	West Broadway, near Beach Street.
32	1838	Good.	Thos. Cooper.	101 Hester Street.

No. of Engine.	When Built.	Condition.	Foremen's Names.	Place of Deposit.
34	1823	Good.	David Broderick.	Christopher, near Hudson Street.
35	1827	Good.	Robt. Crawford.	121st Street, near 3d Avenue.
36	1836	Good.	John D. Brower.	Varick, near Vandam.
38	1842	Good.	John W. Schenck.	Ann, near Nassau.
41	1829	Good.	Joseph Hyde.	Corner Delancey and Attorney Streets.
42	1842	Good.	Hy. J. Mabbett.	88 Nassau Street.
43	1827	Good.	Danl. F. Tiemann.	Manhattanville.
44	1828	Good.	Isaac Sellick.	2d Street, near Lewis.
45	1837	Good.	Wm. Fulmer.	3d Avenue, Yorkville.
46	1835	Good.	Chas. H. Smith.	349 3d Avenue.
48	1827	Good.	Robt. Sutters.	152 20th Street.
49	1826	Good.	Epenetus Doughty.	126th Street (Harlem).
50	1840	Good.	Wm. Holmes.	Harsenville (Bloomingdale Road).

HOOK AND LADDER COMPANIES.

No. of Engine.	When Built.	Condition.	Foremen's Names.	Place of Deposit.
1	1843	Good Order.	Wm. H. Geib.	34 Chambers Street.
2	1839	Good Order.	Theodore R. De Forrest.	24 Beaver Street.
3	1840	Good Order.	No Company.	Horatio, near Ninth Avenue.
4	1845	Good Order.	Henry Morris.	Eldridge, near Walker Street.
5	1844	Good Order.	Wm. S. Lacour.	Corner Delancey and Attorney Streets.
6	1838	Good Order.	James M. Murray.	Mercer Street (Firemen's Hall).
7	1837	Good Order.	Johnson Gillen.	126th Street.
10	1839	Good Order.	Wm. Ackerman.	3d Avenue, corner 85th Street.

HOSE COMPANIES.

1	1834	Good.	Wm. H. Heath.	5 Duane Street.
2	1838	Good.	James Hudson.	262 William Street.
3	1838	Good.	James Elkins.	202 Centre Street.
4	1845	Good.	D. M. Smith.	Corner Delancey and Attorney Streets.

No. of Engine.	When Built.	Condition.	Foremen's Names.	Place of Deposit.
5	1835	Good.	Reuben B. Mount.	Mercer Street (Firemen's Hall).
6	1845	Good.	Addison B. Wight.	Gouverneur Street, near East Broadway.
8	1836	Good.	John W. Moore.	74 Cedar.
9	——	Building.	Hy. S. Mansfield.	174 Mulberry Street.
10	1838	Good.	John P. Hopkins.	111 Roosevelt Street.
11	1835	Good.	John W. Stinman.	14 Amos Street.
12	1837	Good.	Lewis Carpenter.	244 17th Street.
13	1844	Good.	John H. Blake.	Mangin, near Delancey Street.
14	1845	Good.	Hy. A. Burr.	2 Elizabeth Street.
15	1837	Good.	George Baker.	1 Eldridge Street.
16	1838	Rebuilding.	G. Callender.	24 Beaver Street.
17	1836	Good.	James Graydon.	40 5th Street.
18	1838	Good.	Thos. Minniette.	Franklin Market (Old Slip).
19	1838	Good.	Philip Lawrence.	Cortlandt Alley, near Canal Street.
20	1838	Good.	Genest M. Ottignon.	Ann Street, near Nassau Street.
21	1838	Good.	Franklin Waterbury.	Henry, near Catharine Street.
22	1838	Good.	Richd. H. Welch.	101 Hester.
23	1840	Good.	Wm. Cooper.	Horatio, near Ninth Avenue.
24	1839	Good.	Saml. Freer.	Spring Street near Greenwich Street.
25	1845	Good.	James E. Fountain.	Anthony, near B'way.
26	1840	Good.	Joseph Casilear.	166 Monroe Street.
27	1836	Good.	Peter L. Seely.	Corner Church and Vesey.
28	1844	Good.	Nathan Lane.	32 Chambers Street.
29	1841	Good.	Rodman E. Field.	77 Willett Street.
31	1841	Good.	Theodore Tucker.	5 Walnut Street.
32	1842	Good.	James L. Haight.	6 3d Street.
33	1841	Good.	Hy. Colgrove.	Sullivan, near Prince.
34	1842	Good.	Jerh. Simonson.	10th Street, near Dry Dock.
35	1840	Good.	Wm. M. Cahoone.	199 Mercer Street.
36	1840	Good.	Francis B. O'Connor.	Henry, near Market Street.
38	1843	Good.	John Gillelan.	132 Amity.
39	1838	Good.	Wm. J. Thompson.	349 3d Avenue.
40	1843	Good.	John A. Cregier.	168 Barrow Street.
41	1843	Good.	Robt. Zabriskie.	67 Watts Street.

HYDRANT COMPANIES.

| 1 | — | —— | Thos. Nichols. |
| 2 | — | —— | Chas. H. Clayton. |

From the foregoing report it will be seen that the Department was possessed of thirty-five engines in good order, and two condemned; thirty-six hose carriages in good order, and two rebuilding; eight hook and ladder trucks, with forty-four ladders and forty-eight hooks; thirty-seven thousand two hundred feet of hose in good order, and two thousand five hundred feet of hose in ordinary, making in the whole thirty-nine thousand seven hundred feet of hose; thirty-seven engine companies, thirty-eight hose companies, seven hook and ladder companies, and two hydrant companies; one thousand five hundred and sixty-seven men.

About 1852 the Common Council adopted an ordinance dividing the city into three fire districts, and confining the apparatus and labors of the firemen to the district in which their apparatus were located. The object of the ordinance was to lessen the duties of the firemen, and to prevent the great destruction of the apparatus which was caused by their being uselessly dragged over the city at every alarm of fire. In consequence, however, of the imperfect alarms of fire, it was considered unsafe to enforce strictly the ordinance.

It was generally conceded that ten thousand dollars per annum was a low estimate of the expense of repairs to the fire apparatus.

During the year ending August 1, 1846, there had been two hundred and fifty-eight fires and one hundred and thirty-nine false alarms of fire. Many of the fires had no doubt been extinguished before the alarm had reached the nearest bell station, yet, in consequence of there being no means afforded of notifying the bell-ringers of the extinguishment of the fire, or that the alarm was a false one, the bells were rung, and the firemen called unnecessarily from their business or their rest, thereby causing a loss of time and money to them and the apparatus dragged for miles over the city, creating a useless expense to the city. The Common Council, in November, 1846, in view of these facts authorized the introduction of Morse's magnetic telegraph into the Department.

Action was also taken in the matter at a meeting of the engineers and foremen held December 1, 1846, at which Mr. James L. Miller, of the engineers, offered the following:

> *Resolved*, That a committee of five be appointed from this body to urge upon the members of the Common Council the propriety of adopting the plan recommended by the chief engineer, in relation to the magnetic telegraph for the use of the Fire Department.

The resolution was unanimously adopted.

The number of fires was increasing every succeeding year, and occurring, as many of them did, under very suspicious circumstances, it appeared necessary that their origin should be investigated. During the night of the second of May, 1846, within about six hours, ten fires occurred, all of which, except one (the *True Sun* building), commenced in stables, and were no doubt the work of design. Nothing but the extraordinary exertions of the firemen prevented several serious conflagrations.

Successive acts of the legislature had reduced the term of service of firemen until, on November 16, 1847, a law went into effect making the period of servitude five years.

The various engine, hose, and hook and ladder companies, were granted the use of the Croton water, on paying the expenses of the introduction.

During the years 1847–8, the fire districts were laid out as follows:

First District.—The First Fire District shall embrace all that part of the city lying north of a line from the foot of North Moore Street to the Halls of Justice, and west of a line running from the Halls of Justice through Lafayette and Irving Places.

Second District.—The Second Fire District shall embrace all that part of the city lying east of the First District, and north of a line running from the Halls of Justice to the foot of Roosevelt Street.

Third District.—The Third Fire District shall embrace all that part of the city lying south of the First and Second Districts.

For the purpose of guiding the firemen more correctly to the fire, the districts are subdivided, and the district bells will be rung as follows. First District, first section, one stroke; First District, second section, two strokes; Second District, first section, three strokes; Second District, second section, four strokes; Third District, first section, five strokes; Third District, second section, six strokes.

For assistance, the signal will be the continual ringing of all district bells, except that on the City Hall, which will always ring the section in which the fire is raging.

Permission was granted (December 2, 1847) to Hugh Downing and Royal E. House to construct a line of telegraph, by setting posts in the ground, and extending from Fort Washington to the Bloomingdale Road, thence along said road to Sixth Avenue, to the fire station at Jefferson Market, thence to the fire stations at Centre and Essex Markets, thence to the City Hall, to the Merchants' Exchange. This permission was coupled with a proviso that Downing and House should put up the necessary wire and apparatus, and keep the same in order, and give the free and perpetual use of the invention for communicating alarms of fire from the City Hall to the different fire stations, and instruct the different bellringers in the use of said invention, and commence and continue the communication themselves, until the bellringers were instructed, in consideration of which they received from the city the sum of five hundred dollars.

The salary of the chief engineer was increased to two thousand dollars July 8, 1848.

The resignation of C. V. Anderson, chief engineer of the Fire Department, on November 22, 1848, was accepted, to take effect from the time a successor was appointed.

Alfred Carson was appointed to the vacancy of chief engineer of the Fire Department on December 7, 1848, and Clark Vanderbilt appointed an assistant engineer in place of Alfred Carson, promoted.

The fire limits (Act March 7, 1849) were extended so as to embrace all of the city situate to the southward of a line drawn one hundred feet north of Thirty-second Street, extending from east to Hudson River. All dwelling houses, stores, storehouses, and all other buildings, after the passage of this act, to be built or erected within the fire limits, "shall be made and constructed of stone or brick, or other fire-proof materials, and shall be constructed with party or outside walls."

The Act (section 28) further provides:

"The duties and powers that were by law conferred upon the fire wardens * * * prior to the passage of an act entitled 'An Act for the Establishment and Regulation of the Police of the City of New York,' passed May 4, 1844, as well as the duties and powers of fire wardens conferred upon the police by the said act, and by the act to amend the same, passed May 13, 1846, are hereby conferred upon the assistant engineers of the Fire Department, and upon their successors in office."

The duties appertaining to assistant engineers are detailed at length. Their compensation, the act declared, should be fixed by the Common Council, but should not exceed the sum of five hundred dollars per annum.

An office, denominated the Department of "Repairs and Supplies," was created by the legislature April 2, 1849, "which shall have cognizance of all repairs and supplies of and for roads and avenues, public pavements, repairs to public buildings, to fire engines and apparatus of the Fire Department, and the chief officer thereof shall be called the commissioner of repairs and supplies. There shall be four bureaus or branches in this department, and the chief officers shall be respectively denominated the 'superintendent of roads,' 'superintendent of repairs to public buildings,' 'superintendent of pavements,' and 'chief engineer of the Fire Department.'"

The salary of the water register in the Croton Aqueduct Department, July 21, 1849, was fixed at one thousand five hundred dollars per annum; the salary of the deputy water register at one thousand dollars; and the salary of the water purveyor, in the Bureau of Pipes and Sewers, was placed at one thousand five hundred dollars per annum. In October following the assistant engineers of the Fire Department, for the performance of the duties of fire wardens, were paid five hundred dollars per annum each.

In the summer of 1849 the condition of the Fire Department was such as to merit the confidence of the authorities and of the community at large. For efficiency it had never been excelled, and the promptness, zeal and fidelity with which the members discharged their arduous and self-imposed duties drew forth the warmest encomiums from those in authority. The force at that time consisted of about one thousand six hundred men, three first-class engines, six second-class engines, twenty-four small engines, nine hook and ladder trucks, eighteen four-wheeled hose carriages, twenty-five two-wheeled hose carriages, and fifty thousand feet of hose. The city was divided into three districts, the lower one containing the greatest amount of valuable property, covering comparatively a small space of ground, while the limit of the other districts was bounded only by the extent of the island. That imposed upon the firemen in the upper districts an unusual and oppressive amount of labor, and it was consequently proposed, as being in accord with the best interests and the desires of the citizens residing in the upper part of the city, to form a new district, comprising all that part of the city north of Twenty-second Street.

A water tower was erected in this year on the rear of lots on the north side of Twenty-second Street, between First and Second Avenues, and a bell weighing eight thousand pounds placed therein.

A most appalling disaster occurred on the morning of February 4, 1850. A steam boiler exploded in a large building, 5 and 7 Hague Street, completely demolishing it, and burying beneath its ruins one hundred and twenty persons, of whom sixty-four were killed and forty-eight wounded. The Fire Department rendered invaluable service in rescuing the imperilled people and in saving adjoining property from destruction by the fire which ensued, for which services they were the recipients of the sincere thanks of the Common Council. Details of this awful calamity will be found elsewhere in this book.

The Board of Fire Wardens organized, in compliance with the laws for the more effectual prevention of fires, passed March 29, 1850, were sworn in on April 30, 1850. They were divided into three classes by lot, drawn by the president of the Fire Department, Zophar Mills, as follows;

Class One, to serve for the term of one year.
Class Two, to serve for the term of two years.
Class Three, to serve for the term of three years.
Their organization was completed on May 7, 1850.
The whole number of complaints of violations of the laws, made to the Board

during the year ending April 1, 1851, amounted to six hundred and fifty-one. The number of old and dangerous buildings examined and reported to the chief engineer of the Fire Department as being exceedingly dangerous in case a fire should occur in either of them, forty-four. The quantity of gunpowder seized and delivered to the trustees of the Fire Department was one hundred and fifty-seven kegs and twenty cases, containing fifty canisters each.

Although the disreputable element in the Fire Department had been gradually growing less for some years, owing to the judicious and unrelenting weeding-out process in operation, still even at this date (the Fall of 1850), there were disagreeable and emphatic evidences of the existence of a rowdy crowd, upon whom a writ of ejectment should be served. At a fire in Gansevoort Street on the afternoon of August 7, Engine Company No. 34 detached the hose of Hose Company No. 35. At a fire in University Place on August 14, Engine Company No. 4 hindered Hose Company No. 35 from attaching to a hydrant, and William Story, of No. 4, made a personal assault on the foreman of the hose company. Hose Company No. 16 assaulted Engine Company No. 19, and injured their apparatus whilst they were going to a fire on the morning of August 16. Hose Company No. 13 was accused of several attacks on Hose Company No. 6; Hose Company No. 14 was reported for attacking Hose Company No. 26, and in-juring their apparatus. Of these complaints the charge of Engine Company No. 19, implicating Hose Company No. 16, was the most serious, disclosing circum-stances of the most aggravating character, and showing the premeditated nature of one of the most dastardly outrages that had ever disgraced the Fire Depart-ment. The apparatus of both companies were nearly new, having been in use only a short time. The carriage of No. 16 had been accidentally run into, upset and much damaged by the engine on August 14. Two evenings thereafter, as Engine Company No. 19 was proceeding up Third Avenue to an alarm of fire—doubtless raised for the express purpose—they were assailed by a large party of rowdies, several of their members seriously injured and driven from their engine, which was then wantonly upset and considerably damaged. Owing to threats made by persons connected with No. 16 there were good reasons for believing that the outrage had been perpetrated by them. Complaints were also made against Engine Company No. 16 by Engine Companies Nos. 24 and 34. An investigation resulted in the disbandment of No. 16, and the Common Council expressed their determination to arrest the spirit of rowdyism which seemed to be spreading in the Department, and which had so great a tendency to impair its character and efficiency.

A new fire district was formed January 5, 1850, and included all that portion of the city north of a line drawn through the center of Twenty-second Street, from the East to the North River. An additional assistant engineer was also elected.

The act of March 29, 1850, restored the office of fire warden, which had been abolished by the act of May 7, 1844, and declared, "that such fire wardens shall be twelve in number, and shall be selected from firemen of the city of New York, exempted by law from duty, at the time of such selection, whether then in active duty or not, and shall be appointed by the Common Council upon the nomination of the representatives of the Fire Department, by a majority of the votes cast by them for that purpose."

The fire wardens were divided into three classes (four in each class), by lot, to be drawn by the president of the Fire Department, or in case of his absence, by the vice-president, or by one of the trustees, at a time and place to be notified to said fire wardens. The classes were respectively numbered One, Two, and Three, according to the term of service of each. Class One served one year, Class Two served two years, Class Three served three years, and until their successors were appointed.

Their duties were defined substantially as follows: they were to inquire and examine into any and every violation of any of the provisions of the acts previously passed for the prevention of fires in the city of New York; to give, or cause to be given, a notice, in writing, signed by at least one of them, to the owner and builder respectively, of any such dwelling house, store, storehouse, building, ashhole, ashhouse, wooden shed, wooden building, or frame building, which should, after the passage of the act, be erected, altered, or enlarged. It was their duty also to report to the chief engineer the location of and particular circumstances attending any building constructed, or in the course of construction, deemed unsafe; also to report all cases where goods were improperly stored in any building, so as to hazard the lives of firemen, or where any building should from any cause have become unsafe. They should attend all fires in the fire districts respectively to which they were allotted, and to wear at such fires the usual fire cap, with the words "Fire Warden," and the number of such district, conspicuously painted thereon, in white, on a black ground. Their compensation, as fixed by the Common Council, was two hundred and fifty dollars per annum each.

This act also abolished the office of assistant engineer.

Chief engineer Alfred Carson, on September 30, 1850, submitted his yearly report to the Common Council, in compliance with the requirements of law. This report was charged with dynamite, and few of the leading city officials escaped unscathed, as its contents were scattered broadcast, hitting right and left, and sparing none. Members of the Common Council, police justices, aldermen, ward politicians, prominent firemen, and police captains, were fiercely and ruthlessly assailed. Chief Carson, to do him justice, seemed at least to have the courage of his convictions, but his discretion and judgment cannot be commended. That there were abuses, and very serious ones, in the Department, which called for remedial measures, none will deny. Many of these abuses struck at the very root of all semblance of authority and discipline in the Department, but they were the inherited development of a long number of years of misgovernment and mismanagement. No one man or official was responsible, nor could the evils complained of by Chief Carson be remedied by the most enthusiastic reformer or powerful official effort, except by the most revolutionary method. In fact, these abuses had grown up gradually, until they had become firmly rooted in the system and become a part, and a controlling part, of it. Firemen had inherited prejudices and resentments, and had come to regard themselves as possessed of exceptional privileges, and a large portion of the community, by their acquiescence or active support, helped to confirm them in this belief. The times, generally, viewed from the better ordered standpoint of the present day, were sadly out of joint. There seemed to be less regard for the law, and the administrators of justice often dispensed it with a very partial hand. Ward politics dominated the bench, and moulded all public action. It was a time when mob rule was a power in the city. We had then no police force worthy of the name, and the rougher element had no wholesome terror of the law, for even if arraigned for trial the rough who had committed himself was sure to find sympathy for his misdeeds among the politicians who controlled primary elections, a class from which were recruited the police justices, and even higher judicial dignitaries. These police justices, it may be noted, had had for a long time previously control of the police force, and they held their tenure of office more by protecting the turbulent element than by enforcing the laws and protecting law-abiding citizens. The firemen were a powerful and representative body of men. In pluck and daring we may not look upon their like again. They were both feared and respected. They could extinguish the political ambition of the most popular citizen as readily as they could put out the light of a blazing tar barrel. Their influence was far-reaching, and whenever they saw fit to indulge in a family jar, it was, as a rule, considered the safer course to let them severely alone and settle their difficulties among themselves.

Therefore, Chief Carson proved to be a reformer in a non-reforming age. No one wanted his reforming nostrums, or cared a straw about his charges, recommendations, or complaints. He was whistling against the wind, and was voted a crank. If Mr. Carson, it was argued, didn't like things as he found them, why did he accept office? The Department was no better or worse than it had been under his predecessor, who was a man of sterling integrity and strict official honor; but the intrepid—if bumptious—firemen found nothing to complain of; then why should Chief Carson? The chief's focal point of observation was sadly at variance with that of his colleagues and official superiors. There was a wide divergence in their views on these matters.

Mr. Carson's indictment was voluminous, and contained any number of counts. He found fault, for instance, with the method of appointing the fire-ringers from the police force, complained of their "gross neglect," their "utter irresponsibility," to the chief engineer, and suggested that the appointing power and control of these functionaries be taken out of the hands of the mayor and chief of police. He cited aggravated cases of neglect of duty of those fireringers, "which change and neglect," says the report, "not only shamefully jeopardizes property worth millions of dollars, but cause the firemen much unnecessary labor, through false alarms at the towers, and often lulling a whole district in a false security by striking the bells wrong, and giving no alarm when fire actually exists." The delay in the repair of the engine and hose houses was another source of unhappiness to the troubled soul of the censorious chief. The superintendent of public buildings, who had charge of such matters, came in for his share of the general fault finding, and Mr. Carson, as a remedy, petitioned for a transfer of the repairs and alterations of the different engine, hose, and hook and ladder houses, to the chief engineer.

Another evil against which the official soul of Chief Carson was up in arms, and against which he inveighed in the most emphatic and forcible terms, was "the outrageous spirit of rowdyism of certain clubs of desperate fighting men, called 'Short Boys,' 'Old Maid's Boys,' 'Rock Boys,' etc., organized after the mode of the clubs of London and Paris, whose members were shot down like dogs by the firemen of the latter city, and finally suppressed, as were the clubs in London some years since by the city authorities." Chief Carson was especially vehement in his references to the conduct of these "clubs." "These clubs," he repeats, "make deliberate and bloody attacks on our firemen while going to and returning from fires, destroying the apparatus, and often, by stratagem, putting certain companies in collision with each other, individual members against each other, and creating in every way endless broil and confusion in the Department. ★ ★ ★ I have had many of these villains," the chief goes on to say, "arrested for upsetting our engines, cutting the hose, beating our firemen almost to death, etc., but they were no sooner in prison than the captains of police, the aldermen, and judges of police, would discharge them, to commit fresh attacks on the firemen the following night, and while reeking with a terrible revenge for their arrest and temporary confinement." Some of these "club" men Chief Carson dubs "brutal looking monsters." ★ ★ ★ "The Old Maid's Boys," continues the chief, growing vehement, "a fearful and most deadly club, seized Hose No. 14, ran up alongside of Hose No. 26, attacked the firemen, upset the carriage, etc., doing considerable injury to the carriage. But why," he asks, desperately, "re-count these daily and daring outrages, when these bloodthirsty creatures are thus encouraged and liberated by aldermen, on whose conscientious watchfulness and unsullied integrity the people rely for the incarceration and severe punishment of these abandoned and heartless fiends."

The remainder of this bulky report is mainly taken up with the troubles existing among certain inharmonious bodies of fire laddies. From this it appears that William M. Tweed, the one time boss, and then foreman of Engine Company No. 6, was expelled for leading in an attack on Hose Company No. 31, and his company suspended for three months. The Common Council, however, to the deep disgust of Chief Carson, failed to ratify this sentence, and Mr. Tweed was let off with a suspension of three months. These Chief Carson calls "revolting facts."

There were in the Department twenty-five engines in good order, three in ordinary condition, and six building; thirty-two hose carriages in good order, thirteen indifferent, and two building; six hook and ladder trucks in good order, two indifferent, and one building; with forty-five ladders and seventy-four hooks; forty-five thousand three hundred feet of hose in good order, and nine thousand six hundred and fifty feet in ordinary condition, making in all fifty-five thousand nine hundred and fifty feet of hose; also thirty-four engine companies, forty-seven hose companies, nine hook and ladder companies, and one thousand eight hundred and ninety-eight men.

During the year ending August 1, 1850, there had been two hundred and eighty-nine fires, by which the loss or damage to buildings amounted to two hundred and seventy-eight thousand seven hundred and twenty-five dollars, including fourteen thousand dollars by the explosion in Hague Street, and in stock, furniture, etc., to one million sixteen thousand three hundred and sixty-eight dollars, including seventy thousand dollars by the explosion in the Hague Street fire. There had been one hundred and ninety-two alarms.

By ordinance of November 25, 1850, the city was divided into eight fire districts. The First District comprised all that part of the city lying north of Twenty-second Street and east of Sixth Avenue; the Second District comprised all that part of the city lying north of Twenty-second Street and west of Sixth Avenue; the Third District comprised all that part of the city bounded and contained as follows: Beginning at the foot of North Moore Street on the North River, and extending easterly in a straight line to the corner of Leonard and Church Streets, thence northerly in a straight line to the corner of Eighth Avenue and Twenty-second Street, thence westerly along Twenty-second Street to the North River, thence southerly along the North River to the place of beginning. The Fourth District was bounded as follows: Beginning at the corner of Leonard and Church Streets, running thence northerly in a straight line to the corner of Eighth Avenue and Twenty-second Street, thence easterly along Twenty-second Street to Lexington Avenue, thence southerly in a straight line to the corner of Elm and Leonard Streets, and thence westerly in a straight line to the corner of Church and Leonard Streets. The Fifth District was bounded as follows: Commencing at the corner of Elm and Leonard Streets, and running thence northerly in a straight line to the corner of Lexington Avenue and Twenty-second Street, thence easterly along Twenty-second Street to the East River, thence southerly and along the East River to Fourteenth Street, thence southwesterly in a straight line to the corner of Leonard and Orange Streets, thence westerly in a straight line to the place of beginning. The Sixth District: Beginning at the corner of Leonard and Orange Streets, and running thence easterly in a straight line to the foot of Market Street, on the East River, thence along the East River to Four-teenth Street, thence southwesterly in a straight line to the place of beginning. The Seventh District: Beginning at the foot of Market Street on the East River, and running thence westerly in a straight line to the corner of Leonard and Elm Streets, thence southerly along a straight line, intersecting Wall Street at the junction of Nassau, Wall, and Broad Streets, and continuing through the Battery to the North River. The Eighth District: Beginning at the foot of North Moore Street, on the North River, and running thence easterly in a straight line to the corner of Leonard and Elm Streets, thence southerly along a straight line, inter-secting Wall Street at the junction of Nassau, Wall, and Broad Streets, and con-tinuing through the Battery to the North River.

In case of fire in the First District, the signal shall be one stroke from the alarm bells; in the Second District, two strokes; in the Third District, three strokes; in the Fourth District, four strokes; Fifth District, five strokes; Sixth District, six strokes; Seventh District, seven strokes; Eighth District, eight strokes.

On the twenty-fifth of January, 1851, a resolution was approved by the mayor, directing the commissioner of repairs and supplies to contract with Richard H. Bull for the immediate completion of the telegraph wire and apparatus to all the fire alarm stations in the city, and the sum of six hundred dollars was appropriated to pay for the same.

By the act of July 11, 1851, the heads of departments, except the Croton Aqueduct Board, were elected every three years. The heads of departments nom-inated, and by and with the consent of the Board of Aldermen, appointed the heads of bureaus in their several departments, except the chamberlain, the re-ceiver of taxes, and the chief engineer of the Fire Department. The chief of the Fire Department "shall be elected in the same manner as is now or may hereafter be prescribed by law."

The strength of the Department on August 1, 1851, was twenty-six engines in good order, three ordinary, four building, and one rebuilding; forty-one hose carriages in good order, two ordinary, and six building; six hook and ladder trucks in good order, and two ordinary; forty ladders, and eighty-five hooks; forty-three thousand three hundred feet of hose in good order, fifteen thousand two hundred feet ordinary; thirty-four engine companies, forty-nine hose com-panies, eight hook and ladder companies, and three hydrant companies. There were two thousand two hundred and eleven men in the Department; if the companies were full there would have been two thousand eight hundred and eighty-eight men.

During the year ending August 1, 1851, there had been three hundred and nineteen fires, by which the loss on buildings amounted to one hundred and fifty-nine thousand four hundred and fifty-five dollars, and on wares five hundred and forty-eight thousand and twenty-three dollars, making the loss by fire seven hundred and seven thousand four hundred and seventy-eight dollars. There had been two hundred and thirty-eight alarms. These facts show an increase of thirty fires and forty-six alarms over the preceding year, but, at the same time, a decrease of five hundred and eighty-seven thousand six hundred and twenty-five dollars in the destruction of property.

The fire companies in the northern section of the city had long suffered great inconvenience for the want of a proper alarm. For their relief an iron tower was built on Thirty-third Street. A lot was procured for the erection of an iron tower in Spring Street, near Varick, which was much needed. The tower on Centre Street was much dilapidated and insecure, with a bell weighing only four thousand pounds. During a high wind, or an alarm, the tower would vibrate in a very noticeable manner. Its demolition was recommended, and a new tower to be put up on the lot where Engine No. 9 was located on Marion Street. The Jefferson Market bell tower was destroyed by fire on the twenty-ninth of July, and an iron tower was erected in its stead.

The connection of the bell towers with Fire Headquarters by telegraph was completed in the summer of 1851. Instantly the effectiveness of the connections was recognized, as the firemen were saved much unnecessary labor by the prevention of the numerous false alarms which had theretofore misled them.

The report of Chief Engineer Alfred Carson in this connection is worth recording.

"The entire (telegraphic) apparatus," says Mr. Carson, "is necessarily of very delicate construction, and must be used with great care by the bellringers, or it at once becomes utterly inoperative. And it grieves me to inform you (the Common Council) that the telegraphic apparatus is often seriously injured, either by the bellringers themselves, or by some of the numerous friends who unceasingly visit them, who often use it without occasion, simply to gratify their curiosity, thereby misleading and creating general confusion at the bell towers throughout the city, and, of course, throughout the Department."

The fire limits of the city, in the winter of 1851, were extended from Thirty-second Street to Fifty-second Street.

In January, 1854, Engine Companies Nos. 1, 2, 4, 5, 6, 7, 8, 9, 11, 12, 13,

14, 15, 16, 17, 18, 19, 20, 21, 22, 23, 24, 25, 26, 28, 29, 30, 31, 32, 33, 34, 35, 38, 41, 42, 43, 44, 46, 48, and 49, Hose Companies Nos. 1, 2, 3, 4, 5, 6, 7, 8, 9, 10, 11, 12, 13, 14, 15, 16, 17, 18, 19, 20, 21, 22, 23, 24, 25, 26, 27, 28, 29, 31, 33, 34, 35, 36, 37, 38, 39, 40, 41, 42, 43, 44, 45, 46, 47, 48, 49, 50, 51, 52, 53, and 54, Hook and Ladder Companies Nos. 1, 2, 3, 4, 5, 6, 7, 8, 9, and 11, were in possession of houses in good condition. The houses of Engine Companies Nos. 10 and 45, Hose Company No. 30, and of Hook and Ladder Company No. 10 were in a dilapidated condition, but yet occupied by them. The apparatus of all the companies were in good order, except those of Engines Nos. 20 and 36. Engine Companies Nos. 3, 27, 36, 37, and 40; Hose Companies Nos. 32, 55, and 56, and Hook and Ladder Companies Nos. 12 and 13 had no locations, except that Engines Nos. 36 and 37, and Hose Companies Nos. 55 and 56 were doing duty from temporary houses. Engine Company No. 39 occupied a temporary house, but a building was in process of erection for them in Thirty-first Street, near Seventh Avenue, and the engine in use by No. 9 was to be appropriated to their use.

It was made the duty of the policemen on duty, whenever an alarm of fire had been raised during the night, to give notice thereof to the several firemen residing within their respective beats, at their places of residence, who, in accordance with the fire regulations, ought to turn out on occasion of such alarm. Each fireman was required to deliver to the captain of police for the district in which he resided a statement of his name and place of residence, and the captains should furnish the several policemen under their charge with the names and residences of firemen residing within the respective beats of such policemen.

All third class engines were allowed in future ten additional men, so as to make their full complement forty.

The chief of police was authorized and required (Act, April 16, 1852) to make an investigation into the origin of every fire occurring in the city, and for that purpose he was invested with the same powers and jurisdiction as were possessed by the police justices.

At any alarm of fire it was the duty of the captains of police (Act, April 13, 1853) nearest the scene of conflagration forthwith to proceed to the same, with the reserve corps of their command, to be diligent in preserving order and in protecting property. The chief of police should also repair to the scene of the fire, and, with the assistance of the police force, use every exertion to save and protect property, and remove or cause to be removed, all idle and suspicious persons from the vicinity of the fire.

The hydrant companies were decreed to be of very little service, and it was believed that they might be dispensed with without detriment to the Department.

During the year 1853 several extremely violent fights took place between fire companies. Pistols and other dangerous weapons had been brought into requisition, and the apparatus upset and nearly destroyed. The worst of these encounters were between Engine Companies Nos. 6, 18, and 44, and Hose Companies Nos. 16 and 17. Yet no punishment had been inflicted, although the facts had been duly reported to the Common Council, who, instead of investigating the circumstances, allowed the matter to lie for several months, and then directed the chief engineer to return the apparatus which he had taken from them. If these acts of insubordination had received proper attention, and the persons who were found guilty of any serious offense were expelled forthwith, disbanding the companies to which they were attached, and transferring the unoffending members to other companies, the number of companies would have been reduced (for which the authorities had been clamoring), and the Department would have got rid of the persons who were bringing reproach upon it.

In July, 1853, the chief engineer, in compliance with a resolution of the Common Council, reported that he was quite satisfied of the great utility of the fire-alarm telegraph system introduced by Mr. Robinson, and he counseled the purchase of it. He had seen the immense advantages of it in regulating the striking of the several bells, as by means of it the alarms were always correctly transmitted, and at the same moment, from the station first discovering a fire to each and every one of the other stations. The apparatus could therefore be taken with greater dispatch to the vicinity of fires, and the labor of the firemen and the wear of the apparatus were materially lessened.

In the reports of the chief engineer for the years 1851, 1852, and 1853, the official action and integrity of the Common Council were brought into question, and the chief engineer indulged in epithets towards the members couched in language so unbecoming his position and so gross as to induce the belief that designing men were using him as a medium for venting their spleen upon the authorities. That was more than the aldermanic soul could endure, and Mr. Carson's decapitation was contemplated.

Soon petitions began to roll into the aldermanic chambers from various engine and hose companies, asking for the removal of Chief Carson. The Board of Aldermen, therefore, felt called upon to take action, and they passed a resolution at a meeting held on September 15, 1853, designed to ingloriously put an end to the career of the chief. This was referred to the Board of Assistant Aldermen for their concurrence, by whom it was shelved, and it never again saw the light of day.

By an act of the legislature, passed July 18, 1853, the salaries of the fire wardens were fixed at five hundred dollars per annum, instead of two hundred and fifty dollars, which they were in receipt of theretofore.

In December, 1853, the sum of twenty-four thousand eight hundred and eleven dollars was appropriated for a new building for the use of the Fire Department, to be called "Firemen's Hall," located in Mercer Street, between Prince and Houston Streets, of which more is said elsewhere.

The following table shows the population of New York City for a number of years:

Year.	Population.	Year.	Population.	Year.	Population.
1674	3,000	1746	11,717	1820	123,706
1678	3,430	1756	13,040	1825	166,000
1703	4,436	1771	21,863	1830	203,007
1712	5,840	1786	23,614	1835	270,089
1723	7,243	1790	33,131	1840	312,710
1731	8,622	1800	60,489	1845	371,223
1737	10,664	1810	95,519	1850	515,394

CHAPTER X

ABOLISHMENT OF
THE VOLUNTEERS

1854–1865—Creation of the Board of Fire Department Commissioners.—Peter Cooper's Plan.—How Abuses had Crept in.—Charges in the Newspapers.—Investigations Held.—Location of Companies.—Burning of the Cupola of the City Hall.—Exit the Old Volunteers.

In 1854 the Fire Department of New York was composed of nearly four thousand citizens, who devoted their time and exertions to the public service without any reward except the satisfaction derived from the faithful discharge of their duty as citizens. It was conceded that that branch of the civil service possessed the capacity for government in itself at least equal to that of the citizen soldiery who were left in the free and full management and control of their own internal affairs. Besides it was seen that the system of administering the affairs of the Fire Department through the Common Council was burdensome to the latter body, interfering with its more legitimate business, and had operated in experience unfairly and injuriously to the Department, greatly impairing its efficiency. An ordinance was therefore introduced creating a "Board of Fire Department Commissioners," composed of three persons from each of the eight sections of the fire districts, and three from that portion of the city known as the Twelfth Ward, two from each district being exempt firemen, and the third one of the active firemen of the city. The chief engineer should be an *ex officio* member of the board and all its committees.

The venerable Peter Cooper gave some attention to the prevention and extinguishment of fires, and communicated with the Common Council in that respect, February, 1854. The plan and principle which he advocated were designed to make the performance of fire duty a dollar-and-cent interest to some three-quarters of all the officers in the employ of the city government. He recommended the placing a boiler-iron tank, thirty feet in height, on the top of the existing reservoir on Murray Hill. That tank was to be filled, and kept full of water, by a small steam engine. Further, he proposed that the City Hall should be raised an additional story and covered with an iron tank that would hold some ten feet of water, the outside of the tank to be made to represent a cornice around the building. With that greater head and supply of water always at command and ready for connection with the street mains, the moment a signal was given from any police station it was apparent that all the hydrants could be made efficient to raise water over the tops of the highest houses in the city. Also he would cause to be placed in every street, at convenient distances, a small cart containing some three hundred feet of hose. These carts should be so light that one man could draw them to the nearest hydrant to the fire, and bring water on the fire in the shortest possible time. With that arrangement he proposed to make it the interest of every man in the police to watch incendiaries and thieves, and to use every possible effort to extinguish fires as soon as they had occurred.

Mr. Cooper had presented a similar programme twelve years previously.

In the spring of 1854 there were but one first-class engine in the Department, No. 38, nine and one-half inch cylinder; four second-class, Nos. 14, 21, 22, and 42; and three third-class, Nos. 5, 13, and 20. Nos. 14, 21, and 42 were each eight and one-half inch cylinder; No. 22, eight inch; Nos. 13, 7, 5, and 20, each six and one-half inches. The complement of men allowed to each company was as follows:

Engine No. 38 (first-class Philadelphia style), nine and one-half inch cylinder, sixty men; No. 22 (second-class piano), eight inch cylinder, fifty men; No. 42 (second-class piano), eight and one-half inch cylinder, fifty men; No. 14 (second-class Philadelphia), eight and one-half inch cylinder, seventy men; No. 21 (second-class Philadelphia), eight and one-half inch cylinder, seventy men; No. 5 (third-class New York style), six and one-half inch cylinder, forty men; No. 13 (third-class New York improved), seven inch cylinder, forty men; No. 20 (third-class New York improved), six and one-half inch cylinder, forty men.

The chief engineer was elected, every three years, by the members of the Fire Department, by ballot. The election for this office took place on the first Tuesday after the first Monday in February, 1854, and thereafter every succeeding three years.

The chief engineer was ordered not to receive any annual returns from companies but such as had conformed to section first of the ordinance, passed June 22, 1842, relative to the Fire Department, as follows: "The Fire Department of the city of New York shall consist of a chief engineer, assistant engineers, fire-enginemen, hose men, hook and ladder and hydrant men, who shall be citizens of the United States, of the age of twenty-one years and upwards;" and in future to receive no return of members to fill the vacancies in companies unless the foreman and secretary had made affidavit that such persons were citizens of the United States, and twenty-one years of age and upwards.

The Common Council instructed the mayor to appoint three persons to act as bellringers at each of the different alarm districts, such persons to be selected from among the exempt firemen. The bellringers, so appointed, received as remuneration for their services the sum of five hundred dollars each per annum, and were subject to removal by the mayor for misdemeanor or negligence of duty.

As foreshadowed by the action of the Board of Aldermen in their attempt to dismiss Carson, Chief Engineer, from office, and notwithstanding that numerous petitions from fire companies had requested such action, seemingly justifying it, there was yet a dormant feeling of dissatisfaction which manifested itself only after the inauguration of the new Council in 1854. In February of that year a committee of representatives of the Fire Department, Carlisle Norwood, D. Milliken, and Henry W. Belcher, presented a petition to the new Board, setting forth that during the preceding three or four years serious and gross abuses had crept into the Department by which not only its morals had been impaired, but its efficiency and discipline had been destroyed. The great majority of the firemen were of every vocation, the merchant, mechanic, artisan, from the professional and laboring classes; and that majority in point of character and respectability would challenge comparison with any other institution in the country. Their aim was to discharge the self-imposed duty with fidelity, and to elevate the character of their body; but to accomplish that they should be sustained by the authorities. That support had not been accorded for the preceding few years; for owing to a personal difficulty between the head of the Department and the municipal government, the latter had by every means in their power set at defiance the authority of the former, disregarded his recommendations, and thus given every encouragement to the riotous and disorderly to carry out their infamous and wicked designs without restraint. The result was that the Department which should have been the pride and the boast of the city had become a byword and reproach; charges of a heinous nature were freely made against some of its members through the public prints, which want of power on the part of the Department prevented them from investigating.

In connection with this matter a special meeting of the representatives of the Fire Department was held in Firemen's Hall on February 13, 1854, at which resolutions were adopted, stating that among the causes which had mainly brought about the deplorable condition of the Department had been prominently the flagrant conduct of the city government, which, instead of endeavoring to preserve the discipline and character of the Department, had done all in their power to destroy them by the indiscriminate creation of firemen, the restoration to membership of men expelled for bad conduct, the encouragement and license given to the riotous and disorderly by their neglect to punish them when brought before them; in a word, by the wholesale abuse of their authority to gratify personal ends and political purposes.

On the fourth of May, 1854, it was stated in a daily newspaper in regard to the Broadway catastrophe, that the chief engineer testified that within his knowledge a gang of men, wearing the garb of firemen, attended fires for the purpose of stealing; that he had known members of the Fire Department to be caught thieving; that in one case of a member expelled for stealing at a fire the Common Council had reinstated him; that a member, then foreman of an engine company, had been thus expelled and reinstated; that sometimes persons had attended fires dressed as firemen though not members of the Department; and that, in his judgment, more than one-half the fires that had occurred were the work of incendiaries.

The Common Council requested the chief engineer to inform them whether he had been correctly reported. He replied, on May 15, 1854, that if the evidence had been fully and correctly reported their inquiry would have been unnecessary. His reference to the reinstatement of persons expelled for stealing applied to the Common Council of 1853 and not to that of 1854. Attempts had been made to establish the fact that some of the persons killed were in the building for the purpose of stealing instead of extinguishing the fire, and that clothing recognized by the proprietors of the store as belonging to their stock was found upon some of the bodies. That was published far and wide, and made the occasion of severe comments on the Fire Department. The evidence adduced, however, showed that no clothing whatever from the establishment was found upon any of the bodies, except such as was placed under and upon them by their comrades after rescuing them from the ruins, in order that they might be carried to the hospital as comfortably as possible.

The following complement of men was allowed the different engine, hose, and hook and ladder companies, viz.: First class engines, sixty men; second class engines, fifty men; third class engines, forty men; hose companies, twenty-five men; hook and ladder companies, forty men. Hydrant companies to remain the same as previously.

The strength of the Department in September, 1854, consisted of thirty-three engines in good order, seven ordinary, and eight building; forty-three hose carriages in good order, seven ordinary, and six building; nine hook and ladder trucks in good order, two ordinary, and one building. The trucks were supplied with all necessary implements. There were in use forty thousand six hundred and fifty feet of good hose, and fifteen thousand eight hundred feet ordinary; forty-eight engine companies, fifty-seven hose companies, fourteen hook and ladder companies, and four hydrant companies; two thousand nine hundred and fifty-five men. If all the companies were full, there would have been four thousand four hundred and eighty men.

During the year ending September, 1854, there had been three hundred and eighty-five fires, with a loss on buildings of eight hundred and twenty-seven thousand and twelve dollars, and on wares two million and seventy-three thousand two hundred and seventy-two dollars. There had been two hundred and twenty-one additional alarms, mostly caused by burning chimneys, spirit-gas explosions, etc., while for the residue no real cause could be ascertained. The loss was large compared with former years. Doubtless one-half the fires were the result of incendiarism, and one-quarter of carelessness.

Captain Ditchett, of the Fourth Ward police, proposed for the better prevention of personal injury and loss of life, and of interference with the firemen while on duty at a fire, that policemen be stationed with flags by day and lighted signals at night at proper distances on the streets leading to fires, and all persons passing, or who persisted in remaining within, the lines, should be arrested, unless they had business there. To adopt that plan it would be necessary to procure a badge for the Department, to be worn by members at fires when not in fire dress; and a law should be passed making it a penal offense for any person to wear the badge, or other insignia of the Department, except firemen, which would act as a salutary check on rowdies and thieves prowling about fires, and enable the firemen to discharge their duties more effectively.

Following are the locations of company quarters for the years 1854–5:

LOCATION OF ENGINE COMPANIES, ETC.

Name.	No.	Location.
Hudson,	1,	West Forty-seventh Street, near Eighth Avenue.
Excelsior,	2,	21 Henry Street.
Broderick,	3,	(No location.)
Niagara,	4,	Mercer, near Amity Street.
Protection,	5,	61 Ann Street.
Americus,	6,	Henry, near Gouverneur Street.
Lexington,	7,	East Twenty-fifth Street, near Second Avenue.
Manhattan,	8,	71 Ludlow Street.
United States,	9,	47 Marion Street.
Water Witch,	10,	West Twenty-seventh Street, near Tenth Avenue.
Oceanus,	11,	Wooster, near Prince Street.
Knickerbocker,	12,	East Fiftieth Street, near Third Avenue.
Eagle,	13,	5 Duane Street.
Columbian,	14,	Church, near Vesey Street.
Peterson,	15,	49 Christie Street.
Croton,	16,	165 West Twentieth Street.
East River,	17,	Mangin, near Delancey Street.
Atlantic,	18,	Thirteenth Street, near Avenue C.
Lafayette,	19,	199 Christie Street.
Washington,	20,	3 Temple Street.

Name.	No.	Location.
Fulton,	21,	Anthony Street, near Broadway.
Protector,	22,	Chambers, corner Centre Street.
Waverley,	23,	223 Twelfth Street.
Jackson,	24,	West Seventeenth Street, near Ninth Avenue.
Cataract,	25,	Broadway, near East Twenty-sixth Street.
Jefferson,	26,	6 Third Street.
Fort Washington,	27,	Carmansville.
Pacific,	28,	Fourth Avenue, corner East Twenty-seventh Street.
Guardian,	29,	14 Amos Street.
Tompkins,	30,	East Twenty-second Street, near Second Avenue.
Hope,	31,	West Broadway, near Beach Street.
Bunker Hill,	32,	101 Hester Street.
Black Joke,	33,	Fifty-eighth Street, near Broadway.
Howard,	34,	Christopher, near Hudson Street.
Columbus,	35,	Third Ave., near One Hundred and Twenty-first St.
Equitable,	36,	Broadway, corner Sixty-ninth Street.
Tradesmen,	37,	Fifty-ninth Street, near Third Avenue.
Southwark,	38,	28 Ann Street.
Lady Washington,	40,	Crosby, near Broome Street.
Clinton,	41,	Attorney, corner Delancey Street.
Empire,	42,	2 Murray Street.
Manhattan,	43,	Manhattanville.
Live Oak,	44,	Houston, near Cannon Street.
Aurora,	45,	Eighty-fifth Street, corner Third Avenue.
Relief,	46,	Third Avenue, near East Twenty-sixth Street.
	47,	Yorkville.
Mazeppa,	48,	West Twenty-fourth Street, near Seventh Avenue.
Pocahontas,	49,	One Hundred and Twenty-sixth Street, Harlem.

HOSE COMPANIES.

Name.	No.	Location.
Eagler,	1,	Madison, near Pike Street.
Knickerbocker,	2,	5 Duane Street.
Independence,	3,	211 Hester Street.
Marion,	4,	Attorney, near Delancey Street.
New York,	5,	Fireman's Hall, Mercer Street.

Name.	No.	Location.
Croton,	6,	23½ Gouverneur Street.
Ringgold,	7,	East Thirteenth Street, near Fourth Avenue.
City,	8,	75 Cedar Street.
Columbian,	9,	174 Mulberry Street.
Liberty,	10,	Dover, near Pearl Street.
Gulick,	11,	14 Amos Street.
Washington,	12,	51 Horatio Street.
Jackson,	13,	Mangin, near Delancey Street.
Atlantic,	14,	19 Elizabeth Street.
Fulton,	15,	1½ Eldridge Street.
Tompkins,	16,	Houston, corner First Street.
Clinton,	17,	40 Fifth Street.
Franklin,	18,	28 Beaver Street.
American,	19,	52 Greene Street.
Humane,	20,	30 Ann Street.
Hudson,	21,	Foot of Duane Street.
Phenix,	22,	101 Hester Street.
Perry,	23,	51 Horatio Street.
National,	24,	315 Spring Street.
United States,	25,	Anthony Street, near Broadway.
Rutgers,	26,	Norfolk, near Division Street.
Neptune,	27,	106 Reade Street.
Pearl,	28,	Chambers, corner Centre Street.
Continental,	29,	77 Willett Street.
Laurel,	30,	West Twenty-seventh Street, near Tenth Avenue.
Putnam,	31,	5 Jackson Street.
Index,	32,	West Forty-eighth Street, near Eighth Avenue.
Warren,	33,	Sullivan, near Prince Street.
Star,	34,	Tenth Street, near Dry Dock.
Fifteenth Ward,	35,	199 Mercer Street.
Oceana,	36,	205 Madison Street.
Madison,	37,	Broadway, near East Twenty-sixth Street.
Amity,	38,	132 Amity Street.
Metropolitan,	39,	Third Avenue, near East Twenty-sixth Street.
Empire,	40,	142 Barrow Street.
Alert,	41,	67 Watts Street.
Mazeppa,	42,	West Thirty-fourth Street, near Tenth Avenue.
Pioneer,	43,	One Hundred and Twenty-third St., cor. Third Ave.

Name.	No.	Location.
Washington Irving,	44,	West Thirty-first Street, near Seventh Avenue.
Red Jacket,	45,	East Thirty-third Street, near Third Avenue.
America,	46,	83 Nassau Street.
Howard,	47,	Fourth Street, near Avenue D.
Americus,	48,	Eighty-fifth Street, corner Third Avenue.
Lady Washington,	49,	126 Cedar Street.
Corlies,	50,	10½ Mott Street.
Relief,	51,	East Fiftieth Street, near Third Avenue.
Undine,	52,	Harlem.
Naiad,	53,	179 Church Street.
Eureka,	54,	153 Franklin Street.
	55,	52 Amos Street.
	56,	140 Varick Street.

HOOK AND LADDER COMPANIES.

	No.	Location.
Mutual,	1,	Chambers, corner Centre Street.
Chelsea,	2,	West Twenty-fourth Street, near Seventh Avenue.
Phenix,	3,	132 Amity Street.
Eagle,	4,	20½ Eldridge Street.
Union,	5,	91 Ludlow Street.
Lafayette,	6,	Firemen's Hall, Mercer Street.
Mechanics,	7,	Harlem.
Empire,	8,	West Forty-eighth Street, corner Eighth Avenue.
America,	9,	East Twenty-ninth Street, near Second Avenue.
Narragansett,	10,	Eighty-fifth Street, near Third Avenue.
Knickerbocker,	11,	153 Franklin Street.
Friendship,	12,	East Thirteenth Street, near Fourth Avenue.

HYDRANT COMPANIES.

No. 1, Seventh and Eighth Districts.   No. 3, Third and Fourth Districts.

No. 2, Fifth and Sixth Districts.   No. 4, Fifth and Sixth Districts.

FIRE DISTRICTS.

First District.—All that part of the city lying north of Twenty-second Street, and east of the Sixth Avenue.

Second District.—All that part of the city lying north of Twenty-second Street, and west of the Sixth Avenue.

Third District.—Beginning at the foot of North Moore Street, North River, and extending easterly in a straight line to between Church Street and Broadway in Leonard Street, thence northerly in a straight line to the corner of Eighth Avenue and Twenty-second Street, thence westerly along Twenty-second Street to the North River.

Fourth District.—Beginning in Leonard Street, between Church Street and Broadway, running thence northerly in a straight line to the corner of Eighth Avenue and Twenty-second Street, thence easterly along Twenty-second Street to Lexington Avenue, thence southerly in a straight line to between Broadway and Elm Street, in Leonard Street, and thence westerly in a straight line to Leonard Street, between Church Street and Broadway.

Fifth District.—Commencing in Leonard Street, between Elm Street and Broadway, and running thence northerly in a straight line to the corner of Lexington Avenue and Twenty-second Street, thence easterly along Twenty-second Street to the East River, thence southerly and along the East River to Fourteenth Street, thence southwesterly in a straight line to the corner of Leonard and Orange (Baxter) Streets, thence westerly in a straight line to the place of beginning.

Sixth District.—Beginning at the corner of Leonard and Baxter Streets, and running thence easterly in a straight line to the foot of Market Street, East River, thence along East River to Fourteenth Street, thence southwesterly in a straight line to the place of beginning.

Seventh District.—Beginning at the foot of Market Street, East River, and running thence westerly in a straight line to Leonard Street, between Broadway and Elm Street, thence southerly along a straight line intersecting Wall Street at the junction of Nassau, Wall, and Broad Streets, and continuing through the Battery to North River.

Eighth District.—Beginning at the foot of North Moore Street, North River, and running thence easterly in a straight line to Leonard Street, between Broadway and Elm Street, thence southerly along a straight line intersecting with Wall Street at junction of Nassau, Wall, and Broad Streets, and continue through the Battery to North River.

In case of fire, the signals from the alarm bells were as follows: First District, one stroke; Second District, two strokes; Third District, three strokes; Fourth District, four strokes; Fifth District, five strokes; Sixth District, six strokes; Seventh District, seven strokes; Eighth District, eight strokes.

For assistance, the signal consisted of the continual ringing of the City Hall and all district bells.

The state legislature enacted a law, March 29, 1855, by which five commissioners were elected by the Fire Department, and to be known as "The Commissioners of the New York Fire Department." The commissioners so elected drew for the term of their respective offices, say, one for the term of five years;

one for the term of three years; one for the term of two years; and one for the term of one year; "and, annually thereafter, there shall be elected one commissioner to hold his office for the term of five years."

No person was eligible as such commissioner unless, at the time of election, he was an exempt fireman, and had ceased to be a member of the Fire Department, for at least three years prior to said election. Their duty consisted in inquiring into all applications for the organization of volunteer fire companies; no volunteer fire companies could be organized unless approved by said commissioners; unless—in case of disagreement by the commissioners—a three-fourths vote of all the members should overrule the decision of the commissioners.

The Corporation of the Fire Department, by act of the legislature, April 3, 1855, were permitted to hold real and personal estate, but not to exceed the sum of one hundred and fifty thousand dollars.

Members of the Fire Department (ordinance June 14, 1855) were required, when on duty as firemen, to wear the leathern cap as previously in use, or a badge. The badge was made of Prince's metal, bearing the words "New York Fire Department," each badge bearing a distinct number, in raised figures thereon, of white metal. The badge worn by exempt firemen was composed of white metal, with the figures thereon of Prince's metal, but in all other respects similar to the badge used by the active members of the Department. Said badges were struck from separate dies and numbered as the commissioners of the Fire Department might direct.

This ordinance made it the duty of the police, when a fire occurred, to form a line, at least two hundred feet distant from the said fire, on either side thereof; and under no circumstances should they permit any person to pass said line, unless said person should wear the uniform or badge of the Fire Department, the uniform of the insurance patrol, or be a member of the Common Council, a member of the Police Department, or an owner or resident of property within the prescribed lines.

The salary of the chief engineer was increased to the sum of three thousand dollars per annum.

The fire limits were extended to a line south of Forty-second Street, from the East to the Hudson River, on the fourteenth of April, 1856. This act required that buildings erected or to be erected within the fire limits should have front and rear walls, and side walls on both sides, whether such side walls be outside or party walls; and these outside and party walls of every such dwelling house, store, storehouse, or other building, should be constructed of stone, brick, or iron, and started and built upon foundations of stone or brick.

In August, 1856, the state of the Department had never been so encouraging or its working more perfect, and that too while laboring under many disadvantages. The Department consisted of fourteen engineers, one thousand six hundred and forty-four engine men, one thousand one hundred and twenty-eight hose men, three hundred and sixty-six hook and ladder men, and thirty-three hydrant men, amounting to a total of three thousand and eighty-five men, an increase of four hundred and fifty-four over the roll of 1855. These were divided into forty-six engine companies, fifty-eight hose companies, fourteen hook and ladder companies, and four hydrant companies. There were thirty-five engines in good condition, five ordinary, five building, and one rebuilding; forty-nine hose carriages in good condition, six ordinary, two building, and one rebuilding; twelve hook and ladder trucks in good condition, and two building. There was a total of sixty-eight thousand seven hundred and fifty feet of hose in use.

The loss by fires during the year ending July 31, 1856, was six hundred and thirty-two thousand and thirty dollars, being a decrease of five hundred and thirty-five thousand and eighty-nine dollars from 1855.

The rowdies had for a long time remained quiet, and it was hoped that the Department would not again be molested by them. But of late three attacks had been made. In one case Engine Company No. 41 were proceeding at great speed to a fire, when they were set upon by these miscreants with clubs, slungshots, and stones. Several members of the Department were knocked down, one of whom was run over by the engine and was seriously injured. Another, Hose Company No. 15, were attacked while attending to their duty, the men driven away, and the carriage upset in the street. The third was an attack on the engine house of Company No. 32 by a gang of rowdies. It was useless to look to the police justices for redress, for it was well known they dared not grant it, the political influences of the gangs being so great.

An ordinance to reorganize the Fire Department was introduced in July, 1856. It provided among other things for one chief engineer, eighteen assistants, and as many fire engine men, hook and ladder men, and hose men as were then or might thereafter be appointed by the Common Council in accordance with the provisions of "An act for the better regulation of the firemen in the city of New York," passed March 29, 1855. The chief and his assistants should severally be elected by the firemen by ballot. The first election for chief engineer should take place on the first Tuesday after the first Monday in February, 1857, and thereafter every three years; and the first election for assistant engineers on the first Tuesday after the first Monday in June, 1857. The chief engineer should at the time of his election be a fireman who had served the full term prescribed by law; should receive a yearly salary of three thousand dollars. Each of the assistants should be a fireman who had served three years, and should be an actual resident of the district in which he was nominated, and for which he was elected.

No fireman, while under suspension for any violations of the provisions of the ordinance, should be permitted to wear a fire cap bearing the frontispiece of the company to which he was attached nor allowed to vote, nor permitted to frequent the house occupied by his company, or take part in any of the meetings of said company.

At the quarterly meeting of the Board of Engineers and Firemen, held on September 4, 1856, it was decided that the number of men at that time allowed to the different fire companies, namely, first-class engines, sixty men; second class, fifty men; third class, forty men; hose companies, twenty-five men; and hook and ladder companies, forty men, was sufficient to perform the necessary duties of the respective companies, and that any further addition to companies by the Common Council would be prejudicial to the best interests of the Fire Department.

This action was deemed necessary because of a resolution adopted by the Board of Councilmen to increase the force of Hose Company No. 9 five men, on the face of the remonstrance and protest of the chief engineer of the Department. The Board of Aldermen concurred in the action of their legislative brethren, and filed away the communication of the fire chief for future action on the calends of February.

Harry Howard, of No. 108 Leonard Street, was elected chief engineer on February 3, 1857.

In January, 1858, the Fire Department was composed of fifty-two engine companies, sixty-two hose companies, fifteen hook and ladder companies, and four hydrant companies, with a force of over two thousand men. The estimate for that year for apparatus, and their repairs, etc., was sixty thousand dollars, and fifty thousand dollars for expenditures for buildings and repairs to them, salaries, and lighting the engine and other houses. The real estate and houses on leased ground belonging to the corporation, in use by the Department, were valued at three hundred thousand dollars, and the apparatus at seventy-five thousand dollars, the interest on which, at six per cent., would amount annually to twenty-two thousand five hundred dollars, making the total yearly cost of protecting the city against fires, independent of the use of the water and hydrants, about one hundred and thirty-two thousand five hundred dollars.

The voluntary service of the members of the Department frequently bestowed at the hazard, and often the sacrifice, of their lives, had given them a strong claim to the good will of the Common Council and of the citizens generally.

The introduction of steam fire engines into the Department had been the subject of consideration for the preceding two years, and an appropriation was made in 1857 of nineteen thousand five hundred dollars for the purpose of testing the experiment. But no definite steps had as yet been taken toward purchasing any apparatus of that description.

On the fourteenth of April, 1858, an act was passed by the legislature extending and continuing in force until the first of May, 1880, unless sooner altered, modified, or repealed, the act incorporating the firemen of the city of

New York, passed March 20, 1798, and all acts and parts of acts relating to said incorporation.

In February, 1858, one year after the selection of Chief Howard, the Department consisted of fourteen engineers, one thousand eight hundred and fifty members of engine companies, one thousand two hundred and fifty-seven members of hose companies, and four hundred and fifty two members of hook and ladder companies; making a total of three thousand five hundred and fifty-nine men, an increase of four hundred and seventy-four over the number on the rolls one year before. These were divided into forty-eight engine companies, sixty hose companies, and fifteen hook and ladder companies. There were forty-nine engines in good condition, nine ordinary, and two rebuilding; forty-three hose carriages in good condition, sixteen ordinary; eleven hook and ladder trucks in good condition, and four ordinary; twenty-seven hose tenders in good condition, seven ordinary, and fifteen building. There were in use thirty-three thousand four hundred feet of hose in good order, thirty-seven thousand four hundred and fifty feet in ordinary condition, and ten thousand four hundred feet in very bad condition.

There was a large decrease in the amount of losses by fire during 1857 as compared with 1856. Total number of fires for the year ending July 31, 1856, three hundred and fifty-four; alarms, one hundred and nine; total loss by fire six hundred and thirty-two thousand and thirty dollars. Total number of fires from February 17, 1857, to February 17, 1858, three hundred and twenty-two; alarms, one hundred and ninety-eight; total loss by fire, four hundred and twenty-eight thousand two hundred and sixty-six dollars.

All hook and ladder companies (ordinance January 7, 1857) were allowed ten additional men; all the hose companies, thirty men; all first class engines, seventy men; second class engines, sixty men; and third class, fifty men.

The Street Department superintended the making of, repairing, and lighting the public roads and avenues; constructing, repairing, and lighting the public buildings; repairing wells and pumps; supplying the public rooms and offices of the corporation, the court rooms, the police station houses, the engine, hose, and hook and ladder houses; and the public markets, with fuel, stationery, printing, and all other things necessary therefor; constructing and repairing fire engines, hose carts, hooks and ladders, hose, and other machines and apparatus for the use of the Fire Department. There were two bureaus in the Street Department, namely, a bureau for the building and repairing of wharves and piers, called the Bureau of Wharves; a bureau for constructing and repairing the public buildings, and repairing of wells and pumps; for the supplying of the public rooms and offices of the corporation, the court rooms, the police station houses, the engine, hose, and hook and ladder houses, and public markets, with fuel, stationery, printing, and all other things necessary therefor, called the "Bureau of

Repairs and Supplies;" a bureau for repairing fire engines and fire apparatus, under the direction of the chief engineer.

While proceeding to a fire in July, 1857, Chief Engineer Harry Howard was attacked with paralysis, the consequence of severe fire duty which he had previously performed.

An ordinance for the better regulation of the Fire Department went into operation on March 29, 1858. It became the duty of firemen to prevent boys or disorderly characters from congregating in or about the place of deposit of the various apparatus, and not to allow the said place of deposit to be used for any other purposes than those directly connected with the performance of their duty as firemen. No persons other than members and exempt members of the company, or of the Fire Department, in good standing, were allowed to sleep in any engine, hose, or hook and ladder house; the street doors should not be kept open, except while persons were passing in and out, or while any necessary repairs or cleaning were being performed. Good order should be preserved in and about the houses occupied by their respective companies. In going to or returning from a fire, the drag-rope was the proper place for the firemen, except the officers in command. These should prevent all boys and noisy improper persons from taking hold of the rope. On no account should a person, other than a member of the company, or a member or exempt member of the Fire Department, known to at least two of the members of the company present, be allowed to manage or have any control of the tongue or tiller of any apparatus in going to or returning from a fire. The officers and members of each and every company, when returning with their apparatus from a fire, or alarm of fire, were warned against any racing of their company with any other company, and cautioned to abstain from any conduct that would be likely to cause a breach of the peace, or reflect discredit on the Fire Department. Also it should be their duty to use all endeavors to cultivate good feeling among the members.

On the morning of August 18, 1858, a fire broke out in the City Hall. It was generally supposed that the fire was caused either from the burning candles, used in the windows of the City Hall for the illumination on the night preceding, on the occasion of the celebration of the completion of the first Atlantic telegraph cable, or from the fireworks discharged from the roof, the remains of which retained fire, and lodged in some unperceived place on the roof, or in some of the attics of the building, and suddenly burst forth into flames. The testimony taken at an investigation clearly established the fact that the fire originated from the remains of the fireworks and the empty boxes and cases used for them which were left on the roof.

A short time after the discovery of the fire the cupola became enveloped in flames. The fire then descended through the roof to the attic rooms, and soon to the governor's room. The valuable paintings, however, in the latter room, had been previously removed with great care, so that none of them were destroyed, or even injured, except one slightly damaged in taking it down. The flames were subdued at two o'clock A.M., after destroying the cupola, the greater part of the dome, the roof and the attic rooms in the front part of the hall, and considerably injuring and defacing the governor's room. The bell-cupola was also damaged, but the heavy frame work remained sufficiently strong to sustain the bell. The loss was estimated at fifty thousand dollars. No public written documents or records deposited in the several offices in the building were destroyed or injured. There were, however, in one of the attic rooms a large number of printed proceedings of the Common Council of each Board thereof, together with some other books, which were nearly all destroyed, or so much damaged as to be almost worthless. Duplicate copies of all those printed books were, however, in the City Library room, uninjured. The noble exertions of the Fire Department succeeded in saving both wings of the Hall from fire, and for the skill and success with which the members battled the flames, they received the thanks of the Common Council and the benedictions of the people at large.

The working organization of the Fire Department in February, 1859, consisted of fourteen engineers; one thousand nine hundred and twenty-two members of engine companies; one thousand two hundred and sixty-two members of hose companies; and five hundred and two members of hook and ladder companies; a total of three thousand seven hundred men, an increase of one hundred and forty-one over the previous year. The number of men allowed to each company were to first class engine companies, seventy men; second class, sixty men; third class, fifty men; hook and ladder, fifty men; and hose, thirty men. The amount of loss by fire showed an increase over 1858.

The Department had been much agitated on the subject of steam fire engines, and the merits of the innovation on hand power had been freely commented upon not only in the Department, but by all classes of citizens. The Common Council had for the use of the city two large steam fire engines from Messrs. Lee & Larned, patentees. Those engines had been completed and experimental exhibitions of their powers had been given at different times. They had also been put in practical operation on two occasions, namely, at the fire in Duane Street on the evening of January 17, 1859, and at the fire in South Street on January 24. But these tests failed to satisfy the members of the Department of the value of the steam fire engines, who stated that the expectations hoped from their introduction had not been in any manner realized.

In the light of present experience the following comment of the chief engineer, in this connection, is strange and interesting reading.

The steam engines then owned by the city, said the Chief, were large in size and powerful in action, and if permitted to discharge water at every fire would entail more damage by that element than the one it was sought to subdue. The propriety of their introduction into general use was questionable in his judgment, though their services might be rendered effective on extraordinary occasions when the Department might be called on to do extra or laborious duty. In that respect they might prove an addition as an auxiliary branch of the Department; but to be relied upon as the effectual weapon of defense against fire, he was disposed to question their capability and quickness in operation. The city of New York was protected by a Volunteer Fire Department unequaled in the world, and on their promptitude in responding to the call of duty the community relied for protection against the ravages of fire.

During the summer months of 1859 several fires had occurred in the upper portion of the city evidently the work of evil-disposed persons. The Common Council, therefore, authorized the mayor to offer a reward of one thousand dollars for the detection and conviction of the offenders.

The several fire insurance companies doing business in the city made a proposition to the city government to furnish and present a steam fire engine to the corporation. This proposition was accepted on the eighth of February, 1859.

John Decker succeeded Harry Howard as chief engineer of the Department in February, 1860. The working force then consisted of fourteen engineers, two thousand two hundred and thirty-four members of engine companies, one thousand four hundred and eleven members of hose companies, five hundred and eighty-two members of hook and ladder companies, making a total of four thousand two hundred and twenty-seven men, an increase of five hundred and twenty-seven over the force for 1859. These were divided into fifty engine companies, fifty-six hose companies, and seventeen hook and ladder companies.

Chief Decker, as well as his predecessor, took up the controversy on the subject of steam fire engines for the Department, condemning their use. He said that at large fires they were serviceable auxiliaries to the hand engines, but they could never take the place of the hand apparatus, as eight fires out of every ten that occurred were brought under subjection by the quickness of operation of the hand engines, so that there was no necessity for placing the steamers to work.

A resolution was introduced in the Board of Aldermen at the meeting held on January 10, 1861, directing that the legislature be memorialized for the passage of an act transferring the entire government of the Fire Department from the mayor, aldermen, and commonalty of the city of New York to the Board of Fire Commissioners, reserving only to the mayor, etc., the control, supervision, and ownership of the real estate, buildings and apparatus of the Department. The proposition was lost by a vote of six to eleven.

It had been represented to the Board of Aldermen that the Commissioners of the Fire Department had neglected and refused to report to the Common Council for approval their proceedings in the investigation of charges against members of the Department, with their decision thereon, claiming and insisting under authority of the laws creating the Board of Commissioners, passed March 29, 1855, as amended by the act of March 2, 1861, that their decisions were final and conclusive.

The Common Council regarded such claim as being derogatory of their authority and repugnant to the spirit of the laws, which provided an appeal from the decisions of all tribunals of inferior and limited jurisdiction, and decided to take steps to establish its falsity.

There was a force of four thousand and forty men in the Department in June, 1861. The total number of fires for the year ending May 31, 1861, was four hundred and three, and the total loss one million three hundred and forty-seven thousand two hundred and ninety-seven dollars, one-third of which was lost at one fire in Warren Street, in November, 1860. The following companies had been provided and were doing duty with steam fire engines: Nos. 2, 6, 7, 8, 26, 38, 42, 46, 47, and Exempt Engine and Hose Company No. 57. In addition to those, the Common Council had authorized the providing of steam engines for Companies Nos. 5, 21, 33, and Hose Company No. 52, making a total of sixteen steamers, which was considered a sufficient number for any ordinary emergency.

Never since the organization of the Fire Department had that institution been in a more thriving condition, nor had its prospects presented a fairer aspect than in 1862. During the year the general conduct of the members had been exceptionally good, the causes of complaint being fewer than in any preceding year, and the several companies appearing to vie with each other in their endeavors to uphold before the whole community the long-established, generally good reputation of the organization. The working force consisted of three thousand eight hundred and fourteen men, a decrease of four hundred and thirteen from 1861. The total number of fires for the year was three hundred and eleven, and the total loss one million four hundred and twenty-eight thousand five hundred and eighty-four dollars.

A large fire occurred in January, 1862, at the corner of Fulton and Pearl Streets. Owing chiefly to the large quantities of oils stored in two of the buildings, the fire spread with such fearful rapidity that it was only by the most extraordinary exertions on the part of the firemen that the city was saved from a conflagration second only to those of 1835 and 1845.

On a requisition made upon him by the Secretary of War, Mayor Opdyke dispatched to Fortress Monroe, in Virginia, on April 17, the two powerful hand engines built for and used by Engine Companies Nos. 16 and 31. Assistant Engineer John Baulch, together with two members from each company, proceeded to Fortress Monroe with the apparatus, and were employed to take charge of them.

The gross expenditure for the Department for the year 1862 amounted to three hundred and eighty thousand five hundred and twelve dollars and fifty-six cents; for the year 1861 it amounted to three hundred and thirty-seven thousand eight hundred and ninety-one dollars and seventy-eight cents, showing an increase for 1862 of forty-two thousand six hundred and twenty dollars and seventy-eight cents. Much of this expenditure was incurred for fire machines and apparatus, including a number of steam engines.

At a meeting of the representatives of the New York Fire Department, held on May 12, 1863, John J. Gorman was elected fire commissioner for the ensuing five years.

During the year 1862–'63 the loss by fire amounted to one million one hundred and ninety-one thousand nine hundred and twenty-two dollars. The number of fires was two hundred and sixty-eight.

The working force of the Department at the close of the year 1863–64 numbered three thousand nine hundred and sixty men, a decrease of two hundred and sixty-two from the previous year. The total loss amounted to two million nine hundred and thirty-five thousand and fifty-four dollars. The increase in loss was principally due to the numerous fires that occurred during the riots of 1863, the amount for July alone footing up one million one hundred and twenty-five thousand and sixty-eight dollars.

Intimation was given early in the year 1865 of the change that was so soon to take place in the constitution of the Fire Department. Certainly no city in the world possessed a more complete fire organization in the number of engines, the effectiveness of the steam machines, the copious supply of water, or the gallant army of volunteers directing these means for the preservation of property. The generosity and public spirit of the firemen could not be more highly appreciated, and nothing could efface the glorious records of their previous history, so full of instances of heroic daring and unselfish toil. Many of its friends, however, were of the opinion that the system so admirably adapted to a small city was not suited to a metropolis, and that economy, as well as the new machinery, demanded a change.

On March 30, 1865, the legislature passed an act creating a "Metropolitan Fire Department." On the thirty-first of March Chief Engineer Decker sent a communication to the Common Council requesting instructions in relation thereto. As some time would necessarily elapse before the new system could be properly and efficiently placed in a position to meet all that would be required therefrom in respect to the full protection of the lives and property of the citizens—the substitution of a paid system in place of the Volunteer organization—and as much suffering, and perhaps loss of life, might ensue in case of a disastrous conflagration unless the volunteer organization were continued in service, the Common Council urged upon the officers and members of the Department the public necessity of their still continuing their previous energetic and humane efforts in arresting on all occasions as theretofore the progress of the devouring element, thereby not only preventing thousands of helpless women and children from being rendered homeless and destitute, but wreathing around the memory of the volunteer organization of the New York Fire Department a record of fame and usefulness of which both themselves and their children in after time might well be proud.

The four commissioners appointed under the act organized on May 2. Immediately the attorney general of the state in his official capacity and on behalf of the people, sued out an injunction, enjoining them from taking possession of the city's property, also a writ of *quo warranto*, compelling them to show by what warrant they held their office as fire commissioners (the attorney general believing that the said "Metropolitan Fire Law" was unconstitutional).

The matter was tried in the Supreme Court, and finally carried to the Court of Appeals at Albany. That court on the twenty-second of June deciding the law constitutional, the commissioners took possession of the Department immediately.

Whatever the abuse that was heaped upon the volunteer firemen by those who desired to abolish the system from whatever motive, or whatever the danger that threatened them in the performance of their duty, the firemen, it must be said, were at all times ready and willing to assist to the utmost extent of their ability in preserving the lives and property of their fellow-citizens, and were deserving of unqualified praise for their self-sacrificing actions.

The Department was almost unanimously opposed to any change, and so powerful and unanswerable were their arguments before the committee of the assembly that their friends asserted the use of money (said to be fifty thousand dollars) by the insurance companies alone secured the passage of the act.

While the bill was pending before the legislature its advocates abused the members of the Volunteer Department unstintedly; but notwithstanding that shameful course the firemen did not desert the people, although it was freely asserted that the moment the bill would pass the legislature, they would cease to perform their duty. But the firemen disappointed their enemies, and kept on performing their duty as faithfully and cheerfully as they ever had done, until they were honorably discharged.

"The changes that have occurred," says an old resident and intelligent chronicler of the times, writing in 1862, "within my memory in the city at large, almost defy my own belief. The scenes of a moving panorama scarcely pass with greater rapidity before the vision. It is far from an easy task to recall the objects of local interest which have so suddenly disappeared. Time, and the inexorable demands of commerce and population and progress, are sweeping away all the landmarks associated with the traditions and memories of a past generation."

According to the last official report of the chief engineer of the Volunteer Fire Department, June 30, 1865, the working force consisted of three thousand four hundred and twenty-one men.

CHAPTER XI

STORIES OF THE COMPANIES

*Racing Rivals.—A Tragedy in the Tombs.—The Tea-water Pump.—
Celebrated Combats and Champions.—The "Battle of the Boots."—The Big
Bowery Fight.—Old. "Mose."—Chivalry of the Firemen.—Foraging for a
Supper.—Hard Work at the Fires.*

The way they used to do things in the Forties is told by an old fireman of
Hook and Ladder No. 4. "I joined Hook and Ladder No. 4," he said to
the writer, "in the spring of 1845. She was called the 'Screamer,' and we were
as proud of her as some of the survivors are now (1886) of their certificates on
their walls. I was a youngster then, and used to lay awake at nights fearful lest I
should miss an alarm. We used to have fine times at the station house. On fine
nights we used to sit around the door and sing. I was mighty fond of music, and
was so taken with Big McCollum's singing that I joined Truck 4 just to hear
him. That was in 1860. She was known officially as Eagle Hook and Ladder
No. 4, and lay in Eldridge Street, near Canal. Just above us in Christie Street
was Peterson Engine Company No. 31, and we had many a muss with that
company. We got up a song on them once like this:

> The silver hook and ladder,
>   The pretty, golden Four,
> To make Thirty-one the madder,
>   Wash the paint from off her door.

"The youngsters in the street used to take sides, and when one crowd met
another and heard this song sung, a fight was sure to result. One night there was
a row in front of our house, and our foreman, Jack Halligan, thinking the lads
had done each other enough damage took the hose and washed them off the
street. At that time there was another big rivalry going on between Americus,
nicknamed 'Big Six,' of which Bill Tweed was a member, and Engine Company
No. 41, called the 'White Ghost.' They were always looking for each other at
a fire, and washing each other. Well, Big Six got an assistant secretary, and a

'White Ghost' boy heard of it. At the next meeting of his company he got up and said:

" 'Mr. Chairman, I move we have an assistant sec. I don't know what an assistant sec. is, but No. 41 has got one, an' I'm hanged if we ought to let them pukes lay over us.'

"All the other fellows thought just as he did, so they voted themselves an 'assistant sec.,' without in the world knowing what he was to do. They also got up a song which ran something like this:

> Number Six has come on deck
> With a new assistant sec.,
>> Do ye mind?
> He's as dirty as its water,
> Tho' he thinks himself a snorter,
> But he really hadn't oughter,
>> Do ye mind?

"Oh, the races we used to have with the boys of No. 31! Either company first at the brow of Chatham Hill, where Chatham Square is now, would wait for the other, and then there would be a tight race down the hill to the fire. It made a good deal of bad blood. Some time in 1861 a fire broke out one night in the lower part of the old Eighth District. We went down the hill with all the boys hanging on to the ladders, except two at the tongue and one at the tiller. Engine No. 31 was right behind us. She crowded us mighty tight, and when she saw her chance at Mulberry Street, she jumped into us and upset the truck in the gutter. We lay all over the street, as if knocked over in battle, and the others went right on with yells of derision. Our truck was wrecked. But we got our revenge, when they came back, and many of them went home with broken jaws and sore heads. Next Sunday there was an alarm from the Seventh District. We had fixed up the old engine, and we had her to the top of the hill in a jiffy. Thirty-one met us, but we left them behind. When they arrived they turned the hose on us, and we had to sail right in and take it away from them, and washed three or four of them across the street. We fought all the way back, and 'laid out' several men before we got to Eldridge Street. Then the populace took a hand in, and for about four hours there was the biggest riot seen before the war. Bricks and stones were going around without owners, and half-a-dozen shots were fired. One fellow held his revolver in his coat-tail pocket, and fired her off at random. The police arrested five firemen and several runners, but through political influence they were never brought to trial."

In early days, before the introduction of the telegraphic system, notice was given of a fire by the ringing of bells. In 1835 it was ordered that a watchman be stationed constantly in the cupola of the City Hall to give the alarm. The bell was rung during the continuance of the fire, the locality of the blaze being indicated by ringing the bell in a prescribed manner, and by hanging out at night a light in the direction of the fire, and by day a flag. The watchhouses and markets had bells which were utilized for the same purpose, and the churches also rang their bells. Then watchmen were stationed in the cupolas of the Halls of Justice, the Reservoir, and Center, Essex, and Jefferson Markets, and received one dollar and seventy-five cents a day. In 1842 the city was divided into districts, and each district into sections, and a certain number of strokes for each section indicated the location of the fire. Each bell had its peculiar tone which a fireman soon learned, and could tell at once where the conflagration was. In 1844 the watchmen were legislated out of office, and three exempt firemen, appointed by the mayor, acted as ringers in each district. Their salary was six hundred dollars a year, increased in 1864 to one thousand dollars. At various times the regular bell towers were located at the City Hall, Essex Market, Center Market (afterwards Marion Street), Washington Market, Macdougal Street, Jefferson Market, Union Market, Twenty-second Street and First Avenue, Thirty-third Street, Fifty-first Street, Mount Morris, Yorkville, the Post office, and the Tombs.

Connected with the last-named cupola is a dramatic story, which we have referred to in a chapter on fires of the old Department. Alderman Clarkson Crolius, of the Sixth Ward had long urged the desirability of a bell tower on the Tombs prison for fire alarm purposes. At last, in 1842, he succeeded, and in November of that year it was completed save for a few finishing touches. The finishing touches, however, were not given, for on the eighteenth the cupola and a part of the roof were destroyed by fire, and the building threatened. The rumor that the fire was started for the purpose of rescuing John C. Colt, who was to have been executed on that day, was unfounded. Mr. Crolius made a thorough investigation and wrote a long report to the Common Council. On the previous day the alderman had inspected the tower. The watchman's room was built of pitch pine, and was to have been lined with tin. Alderman Crolius warned the watchman not to light a fire till the tin had been put in. But his warning was disregarded. The man made a roaring fire which, in the early hours of the morning of the eighteenth, ignited the woodwork and destroyed the structure. While the fire was blazing and the engines rattling outside, Colt, within his cell, took his own life and cheated the gallows.

Colt was a bright young man, well-connected and with numerous friends. By profession he was a teacher of bookkeeping. He was born at Hartford, Connecticut, where his father possessed a manufactory of silks and woollens. His brother was the renowned Samuel Colt, the inventor of the revolver, who had a checkered career. John got into financial difficulties in this city and had to borrow money. One of his creditors was Samuel Adams, who dunned his debtor.

Colt was then living at No. 11 Elizabeth Street, a house owned by James R. Mount's father-in-law. One day Adams went to John Colt's office and annoyed him. They quarrelled, blows were struck, and the hot-headed Colt struck his adversary on the temple with a stone pitcher. The blow was instantly fatal, and Adams fell dead. Colt rushed out, thoroughly alarmed by his rash act, and walked about in a terrible state of excitement. No one had seen the deed. The thought struck him that he could quietly get rid of the body and save his reputation. He packed the body in a barrel and had it conveyed at night to the ship Kalamazoo, lying at the foot of Market Street, but the contents of the barrel were discovered, and this secret means of getting rid of the corpse told against him and helped to convict him of wilful murder. On the night previous to the day set for his execution he was visited by Alderman Crolius and Sheriff Monmouth B. Hart, who was a friend of his. Colt had had a love intrigue, and the woman with whom he had been living was young, handsome, and of respectable family. He asked that he be allowed to be united in marriage with her. She was then in the warden's room, for she had been a constant visitor during the young man's imprisonment. Colt's request was granted. At twelve, midnight, the Rev. Dr. Lampson arrived, and the ceremony was performed. Upon its conclusion the convict prayed that he might be left alone for a few minutes with his wife. It was done, and then, so it was supposed, the devoted but unfortunate girl passed him a dirk knife which was to save him from the disgrace of a hangman's halter. Colt concealed the weapon in the waste pipe of the closet. The parting with his wife was an agonizing one. Each knew that by the act of the other they would never meet again alive in this world. Next morning, when the excitement of the fire had subsided, and his cell door was opened, young Colt was found dead, reclining on a settee, with the dirk knife in his bosom. About an inch of the blade had penetrated his heart. A few days before he had asked for and been given a work on anatomy, presumably to learn how most easily and effectively he could compass his own death. The knife was given by Mr. Crolius to Chief of Police Matsell. Two or three days previously his brother Samuel had exploded an invention of his, a torpedo, in the North River, and this circumstance gave rise to the rumor that he had been concerned in the conflagration to effect John's rescue. But it was untrue.

Chowder parties were often given by the companies, and these were notable events for the district. A large number of guests would be invited, and, of course, the big wigs. Lots of fun was to be had at these gatherings. After the eating and drinking dancing was indulged in, not the modern waltz, with its ungainly and vulgar variations, nor even the regulation square dance, but the good old-fashioned gymnastic exercise known as the step-dance. The accompaniment was often a banjo, sometimes a fiddle, and sometimes a flute, but whatever the music the enthusiasm of the dancers and the enjoyment of the spectators were always the same—superlative. Then, again, songs were sung and amusing stories told—stories about fires and firemen—but speeches were tabooed. Even in those slow-going days (slow in comparison with our own) people thought life was too short to indulge in or listen to the "long talk." Nearly ten years ago an old fire laddie, John Rogers, of Hose Company No. 39, gave his reminiscences in a pamphlet, and in reference to these parties said:

"About once a week we would procure a chowder pot, and with a halibut's head and 'fixin's' get up a chowder as was a chowder, the wherewith to pay for the same being collected by one of the boys going round with the hat. We did not eat the chowder in the dark, but had the engine house lighted on chowder nights with candles purchased at a neighboring grocery. Many of the boys lived near by, and these furnished from their homes plates and spoons sufficient to go round, and I venture to assert that no game supper with brilliantly lighted halls and music was ever enjoyed more than our chowder."

The engine house was their sanctuary—their loved sanctuary—and no priest could have a greater regard for his than the firemen for theirs. The inducement must have been exceedingly strong to get the boys away from it. All the amusement they wanted they could get there. Indeed, in those times their wants were few and their indulgences moderate. They did not even aspire to three cent cigars, one or two cents furnishing a weed satisfactory to their tastes. "One of the boys," says an old timer, "induced us one night to go a short distance from the engine house to a raffle for a stove with dance accompaniment, but we did not feel at home. I remember if there were some good looking girls present we could enjoy ourselves better in the old engine house in the dark a good deal. 'Our house' was not quite so large or so well appointed as the engine houses of the present day, being, I should say, about 30 by 14 feet, our engine, 10 by 4; standing in the center. We had no gas in the house, and, in fact, no lights whatever at our gatherings, being allowed so much oil a month from the Corporation yard, barely sufficient to supply our torches and signal lanterns while going to and at a fire, consequently we could use none in the engine house, except in setting things to rights after a fire, and at our monthly meetings. When gathered o' nights in the dark knowing each other by the voice we would talk on the passing topics of the day until we had talked out, when some of the boys would call for a song. Dick Flannigan, a fine singer, and still living, was generally called upon first, and would respond to the call with 'Red Robin,' 'The Angel's Whisper,' or some other popular ballad of the day, when it would be his 'call,' with a response immediately from the member called upon, and so, in free-and-easy fashion, without light and without beer, so much in vogue to-day, we passed away the evenings when no loud alarm rang out to call us forth to stay the flames. What with our score of singers and yarn spinners (many of the latter had learned to spin yarns on shipboard), the hours passed pleasantly and innocently, albeit rough (and ready) mechanics, with little worldly polish. Not infrequently were these sittings interrupted by shaking at the door and the cry of 'Turn out, here! fire! fire!' when all would start to their feet on the instant, the doors be flung open, the rope paid out, and forth we would dash in the direction of the fire, our 'souls in arms and eager for the fray.' "

But these routine amusements were broken in upon by the grand chowder parties, as we have said. Among the companies who were famous, in those later days of the Volunteers, for these suppers, were Hose Companies Nos. 33, 36, and 38, and Engine Companies Nos. 42 and 44. Even under the new regime the old boys kept up the old practice of giving Saturday night "chowders," especially the Warren Hose Company No. 33, which had merged into the Warren Association. There were times, however, when the firemen yearned for something a trifle more toothsome than chowder, and would go a little way out of the straight moral path to obtain it. A story is told of Hose Company No. 60 (M. T. Brennan). The editor of the old *Leader*, John Clancy, was for many years its foreman; he was the only journalist in the old department who ever held that rank. On one occasion No. 60 decided to treat themselves to a banquet. They went to the tremendous expense of buying a bushel of oysters, and clapped them in the kettle on the stove in the engine house, then in Elm Street. Martin J. Keese, who was once foreman of the company and later custodian of the City Hall, happened to drop in, viewed the preparations for the feast, and then thoughtfully informed the boys he had seen two magnificent chickens hanging out of the window of one of the members.

"What!" cried Clancy, "one of our boys with chickens, and we not invited! Let us have them here and then invite the churlish fellow."

At once a delegation was sent out to bring in the fowl. Keese tenderly unhooked the chickens while his companions saw that he was not interfered with in the transfer, and the triumphant party returned, and put in the chickens with the oysters. The delicious odor that floated out on a gentle breeze brought heads to many a window and water to many a mouth. Right opposite the engine house lived a Mrs. Hogan, who was attracted by the aroma.

"Arrah, boys," said the old lady, "what in the name of goodness have yez there? It's like a hevenly drame."

"It's a pot of elegant soup," said the genial John, and filling a bowl with the mixture he took it over to the good dame.

When he returned he heard a yell from Mrs. Hogan. "Oh! bad 'cess to yez, ye bastes, yez have cooked the chickens widout takin' out the enthrails. Och! I'm poizened."

A shout of laughter from the engine house caused Mrs. Hogan to use more rhetoric than she had intended.

But supper-parties and dancing-parties were not the only amusements indulged in by the fire-laddies. Some of them were addicted to that form of amusement which modern slang calls "mashing." To be sure, there is no reason why a fireman should not have an innocent flirtation as well as other citizens. Among the unfortunate flirtations was this one: A well-known actress, remarkable for her pretty face, was staying with a married friend in a cross-town street. She was in the habit of writing in one of the back rooms, and right opposite the window at which she sat was the abode of a young fireman. He had straw-colored whiskers, a sad-looking eye, and a flat face, but he thought himself handsome. Day after day he used to stare out of window at the handsome actress, till she came to regard him as a curiosity. Mistaking her glances, he felt emboldened to waft her kisses, and blushed while he did it. Then he made inquiries among the servants, and learned that the front room was occupied by Mrs. Smith. Upon this he squared his elbow and wrote a missive full of respectful love and devotion to Mrs. Smith. Unfortunately, Mr. Smith, who was a man of an extremely jealous disposition, found the letter on the hall-stand, opened it, and turned pale with rage when he read the allusion to the supposed flirtation. He caused one of his work-girls to write an answer. The young fireman responded, more love-missives passed to and fro, and at last an appointment was made. Mr. Smith was convinced his wife was false, and determined to destroy her lover before her face. The interview was held, and its uproarious character attracted the attention of the actress. She rushed in, found the wife dissolving in tears, her husband accusing her while flourishing a revolver, and the young man in a corner stupefied by the reception he met with. An explanation followed, laughter took the place of tears, and the machine runner raced off quicker than ever he did to a fire.

The engine was, so to speak, the apple of the eye of the old fireman. Once a fireman was seen to publicly hug and kiss his engine, after she had got the best of a rival company's engine. Again, a fire laddie, who would not have shed a tear for any trouble of his own, cried like a child when his machine was "washed." The public took an amazing interest in Fire Department matters. The "mysterious disappearance" of the picture on the back of Engine No. 14, about 1850, kept the whole city talking for days. She was a "crack" little engine and a great favorite. Harry Venn and Peter Ottignon (the Jolly Butcher), two of the most popular firemen of the city, had been foremen of her. When Ottignon was foreman the boys had the engine painted regardless of expense. The "engine artist" of the time was Quidor, who put what was regarded as a fine painting on her back, representing a handsome Indian and his squaw. One day, however, they got into a fight with another company, and as a punishment their engine was sent to the corporation yard—the greatest disgrace that could befall a company. The boys were naturally very downcast, but before the corporation truck had arrived to take away the "beauty," the painting was removed from her back, and hidden in a cellar. The lads were resolved to have some memento of her. When the Fire and Water Committee, however, found out what was done, they were indignant, and set detectives to work to look for that Indian and his squaw, and the daily newspapers were full of the accounts of the search. Only a few of the men were in the secret. In time No. 14 was reinstated in her old house, and then suddenly and mysteriously one bright morning the missing back was found attached to the engine. In the meantime the Indian and his squaw had traveled six thousand miles. This is how it happened: One of the old members of the company was Jim Lyons, who afterwards became a mate on board of one of the Havre Line of packets. The back was taken to his boarding house one night, and next day Lyons sailed for France, and, when he returned, brought back the engine plate with him.

This pretty little engine once had a terrific struggle at a fire with No. 34 (Old Howard). It was one of the most exciting contests known in the old Department, and is thus graphically described by an eyewitness, John D. Brower, one of the "vets," who subsequently went to San Francisco: "A fire had occurred in 'Mack-erelville.' No. 34 had come from Christopher and Hudson Streets, and had secured a good position for drawing water from a pond in the vicinity, her suctions running out about level with the box of the engine. There were several other short liners at work, passing the water from a pond nearer the fire, but as it threatened to be a big fire before it got through, and the 'Rovers' knew they had a good thing, No. 34 remained at its original place. Pretty soon the engines from away down-town arrived, and among them No. 14 from Vesey Street. When hailed by No. 34 to take their water, the boys cried 'Yes, yes,' for it was considered as showing a mean spirit or the white feather to refuse an offer of that kind. So after dragging her over several little hills and valleys, 14's boys turned her round to 34's butt, and made ready to take her water. No. 34 had already been working slowly, 'charging the hose,' as they called it, and when No. 14 gave the word in went the butt, and to work they went in good earnest, and the drumming of the engines in that line was music to the ear of the fireman, and tended to hurry him on to the scene of the fight, or the fun, when blocks away. It was a damp, drizzly night, with a cold wind from the east, but there were men surrounding those two engines, the pride of the Department, stripped to the buff, and working as they never could or never would work at anything else. There were around No. 14 Pete Ottignon, foreman at that time; Harry B. Venn, who had just resigned the position; Phil Jonas, Johnny Baum, Jim John-ston, Alf Chancellor, Boss Talliant, Dick Logan, Sam Baisley, Alex. Dunscombe, John Decker (a volunteer at that time), and others, cheering, working, and striv-ing, as though their lives were at stake to prevent one drop of water from running over 14's box. The first encounter lasted nearly ten minutes—a long time if a watch was held over men working as they were, when the order ' 'vast playing' came down the line, an order which was quite welcome to No. 14, but not quite so welcome to No. 34; for when the butt was taken out the water was found to be up to the bend. Then the friends of 34 became deeply concerned as to the duration of the fire; 14 was also by no means a disinterested party as to its continuance; in fact 14 would have hailed with joy about that time the order 'to take up,' and those of 34 would prefer seeing another cowshed or an old stable go rather than miss this glorious opportunity at one of the most energetic and efficient companies in the old Department. Then came a lot of 'chin,' criticisms, and opinions, as to whether 14 could or could not take the water, and in justice to her brave fellows it must be stated that it was thought at the time that the soft ground she stood on, made worse by the water from 34's butt every time it was taken out, helped in a great measure to bring on the misfortune that at last befell her; for while she stood fairly up so that the men could get at their work, she rattled the water out after it got to the bend as fast as it came in, making it rather lively for the engine ahead. But no quarter was given or taken in such matters; 'Up to the bend' did not frighten anybody. Those little engines could not get a good hold of the water until it was about there, but when it rose above that particular place, then look out for squalls. And in justice, too, to 'Old Howard' and her heroes, it was acknowledged that her butt on this occasion was not one to be trifled with. Drawing the water as she did with a level suction, it came from her butt almost as solid as a board, and to those not acquainted with the qualities of those little engines, it would seem almost impossible for one of them to throw the stream 34 showed that night, or for one of them to take it as long as 14 did."

By this time the position of the engines was breezed around, and the friends of both came hastening to their aid, until quite a crowd had assembled around both the contestants.

"At length the word came again for water, and all went to work with a will. They stood in rows three or four deep, and as fast as a man would drop off the brakes he would pass to the rear, and another would instantly take his place. When next the order ' 'vast playing' came down the line, the water was a trifle lower, and it was barely perceptible, but it gave encouragement to 14's crowd for the time, and delayed the hopes of those at the engine behind her, who were inwardly wishing for the fire to last a while longer. By this time 14 had settled in the soft ground almost up to her hubs, and therefore made much harder work of it. However, 34 was in pretty much the same condition, so it was also as fair for one as the other. The word again came, and never did the fire laddies work with better spirit and energy than they did that night. They worked with a will known only to those who have been placed in the like 'hole.' The water began to rise—slowly, to be sure, but it was rising. Then it was a sight to see the brave fellows of 14 and her 'crowd' exert themselves in order to keep her free. Harry

Venn, towering like a chief among heroes, stood on the rope-reel waving his trumpet over those at work on the brakes, and cheering them on by all sorts of endearing appeals. It soon became evident, however, from the dull heavy sound of the brakes, that it was as Johnston said, 'beginning to look dusty;' the water was rising, she was nearly full. Then a cheer around 34 told of confidence restored on her side. And then both sides stopped again, when the word was passed up the line, 'three-quarters full.' The hair on Logan's head stood straight out now, and Baum, Dozey, Baisley, Johnston, and Jones were all more or less grouty. Anything but a 'wash' for them. Venn looked distrustingly at the settled condition of the engine in the ground, examined the chains, and surveyed the scene like a man who felt that at any rate he was doing his best. All this time 34 had kept on working moderately, to keep the hose well charged, and when the word again came, at the first stroke of 14 in went the butt. This 'round' was of long duration, and, despite the heroic efforts of those willing hands to save her, the water gradually rose. One would have expected to see the brakes fly, as they did, that they would tear the little engine to pieces. Just so with 34. They were hammering the wood with a will, while a long drawn cheer from the crowd around her told those at the brakes they were not striving in vain, and made the cold, damp night air ring with life and animation. And when the word was passed down 'She's up to the rabbits,' followed soon after by the two single words, to delight or dismay, as the case might be, the firemen of long ago, 'She's over!' one would have thought that a Malakoff or a Gibraltar had been successfully stormed that night at Mackerelville.

"But there she stood, plucky little 14, when the order came to 'take up' full and dripping over. Her 'boys' had done their best, and there was no fault to find with the engine, yet she had received a stain upon her fair fame that would follow her for years, or until such time as the doubtful favor might be returned, if ever there was a possibility.

"Yes, there stood 14, pretty as a picture, even in her defeat, just out from the painter's, with a finely polished surface of black, ornamented and striped in gold, her silver-plated work shining with care, her burnished levers glistening in the torchlight, while her members and volunteers, and in fact the whole crowd around her appeared like men who had not been invited to take anything for a week. All old firemen know how galling it was in such cases to let water out by the way of the tail screw that they failed to pass over the leader bow. All the vets have been there. But so particularly hard did the result of this encounter at Mackerelville grate on the feelings of the members of 14 that the very next afternoon they sent a delegation to 14's house, with a request to measure her cylinders. Of course it was granted, and they were found to be like all others, except 38 and 42, in the department, just six and a half. It had been a fair and square tussle, engine to engine, fireman to fireman, pluck had been the same on both sides, but the luck was this time all on 34's."

The John Rogers already referred to has given reminiscences of rivalry in the old days. "The machine I 'run' with and thought the world of," said Rogers, " 'laid' east of the Bowery, near Division Street, and was of the little 'goose-neck' pattern, with six-inch chambers, and capable, with our crew at the brakes, of 'taking the water' of any neighboring engine and no favors asked. The sounding and inspiriting calls consequent upon forming a line in those days many yet remember. To me the grandest and most exciting affair that could be improvised was the various engines working in line at a fire when the flames were aggressive. I can see the line now, hear the stentorian shouts of the foreman, the uproar of voices generally, the pounding of the rapidly moving brakes, and other noises incident to a fire. A fire breaks out in Beekman Street, above Cliff. The bells sound the alarm; out rolls the engine, and down they go, the first making for the dock, where they are wheeled about, the wheels against the string-piece of the dock. Two men jump to each side of the engine, unbuckle the suctions (of sole leather, the baskets of brass) and screw them to the tail of the engine. By the time this is done, the 'butt' is unbuckled and the hose reeled off by two or three members, who start with it up street, dragging its length (two hundred feet) not slowly along by any means, the man first at the engine house and the first man at the tongue being entitled to hold the butt into the engine which is to take the water from the one on the dock, a rule with all companies.

"By the time these movements were effected another engine would come thundering down street, the foreman in charge of the first shouting at the top of his voice, 'Take our water, boys?' 'Yes,' would be the reply in most cases, when round would go that engine in position to 'take our water,' its hose reeled off and carried farther up the street to connect with the next engine coming along, and so on until the line was formed from the dock to the fire. The line formed and all being in readiness for the work in hand, the foreman of the engine on the fire (the one nearest the latter) would give the command to his company: 'Play away!' which was repeated all down the line to the engine 'at suction' on the dock, when the most enlivening and exciting scenes would be witnessed. Necessarily the suction engine had the longest stroke, from the fact that she had to draw the water before forcing it through her four lengths of hose, the two operations requiring great pressure upon the brakes. With the order to 'Play away!' the man holding the butt of the suction engine, assisted by two others who 'lightened up the hose,' would begin to brace his muscles and make ready for the coming of the rushing water. The force of water was immense as the stream poured into the receiving engine shortly after the commands of the foreman, 'Stand by your brakes, men!' 'Put in the butt' (to the holder of the latter), and play away, men!'

"The old-timer recollects well the music (enlivening to his ears) that followed these commands, and the young men of the present day can imagine how exciting it was to see twenty partially stripped men (ten on a side) manning the brakes of a short-stroke engine and dashing her down at the rate of sixty or seventy strokes a minute, some with their hair floating about their faces at every stroke, while that of others was confined by closely fitting skullcaps of red or striped flannel. Then upon the front of the engine the foreman would jump, and through his trumpet; or without the mouthpiece, shout to his men such stimulating cries as these: 'Every one of you, now, will you work?' 'Work her lively, lads!' 'You don't half work!' 'Now you've got her!' 'Stave her sides in!' 'Say you will, now!' and so on, his body swaying to the motion of the brakes, and he giving up only when his voice was gone, when some strong-bodied and loud-voiced member would relieve him. The men who worked at the brakes were now tired out, and were in turn relieved in a minute or minute and a half, that being as long as a man could work on the brakes in that position, the labor being so violent and exhausting. But there were plenty on each side the engine ready to fall in when the exhausted ones fell out, and an expert thing it was to fall in and catch the arm of the brake, between which and the box of the engine many a finger has been crushed, maiming many a fire-laddie for life. I could go on talking about 'playing in line' for hours—how one engine would 'nigger' another by getting eight or ten strokes ahead before the water from the butt could be discharged, how the man holding the butt would get knocked down for not taking it out of the engine he was supplying soon enough to please other parties. I could dwell on the 'boiling,' 'slopping,' and final 'washing,' and how the discomfited company of the washed engine would, in many cases, go in for a free fight in order to vent their mortification in not being able to play the water out as fast as the rear engine had played it in, resulting in a 'wash.' "

There were many fights, and hot ones, too, in the old department, but they grew out of a natural emulation and were not lacking in a certain rugged element of chivalry which promoted manhood, though somewhat at the expense of public order. The murderous revolver and assassin-like disposition which now mark its use were unknown in those days. The combats were fair hand-to-hand fights between man and man, and he who resorted to any other weapon than those which nature supplied was accounted a ruffian or a coward.

But when big fires happened all individual bickerings were sunk in a unanimous resolve to do their duty. This was notable in the great fire of 1811, which began on a Sunday, when all the firemen fraternized. Some unknown writer contributed to the papers across the ocean an original poem on what he called "The Clasped Hands of the Fire Brigade." The first stanza read:

They came from the altar to face the flame,
   From prayer to fight with fire;
And the flame which burns but never binds
   Was a bond to draw them nigher.

On Sunday morning, July 26, 1846, a big fight occurred in Broadway between the runners of several fire companies. The companies involved were Engine Companies Nos. 1, 6, 23, 31, and 36. The fight lasted a considerable time, and many of the combatants received more than they bargained for in their desire to have some fun. Subsequently, Andrew McCarty and Jeremiah Haley, of No. 1, and Alexander McDonald and Daniel Davenport, of No. 5, were expelled. On August 5, all the companies concerned were disbanded by order of the Common Council. In view of the magnitude of the combat, the aldermen considered they could not overlook the affair. The battle had raged all the way to Canal and Hudson Streets, and attracted an immense crowd of citizens. After the disbandment, there was not a single fire company left in the Fifth Ward. Benjamin J. Evans, who first began to run with No. 31 in 1843, became its assistant foreman, and subsequently joined Hose Company No. 5, on November 16, 1850, has given the writer the following particulars of this big fight:

"We were called out from our quarters in West Broadway on a still alarm, our foreman singing out, 'Come, pull away, boys, for West Broadway's alive!' As we were returning home, opposite the Park, we met Engine No. 6, and she commenced to bark. Then along came Equitable, and she thought she would help No. 6, but found that she was in a mighty pretty fix herself. No. 5, just then turned up near Ann Street, and the 'Short Boys' cry greeting their ears, they said, 'Let us go and help old 31, and make the Short Boys feel sick.' Chief Engineer Anderson was standing at the time on the Astor House steps. No. 6, which then lay in Reade Street, began to 'bear' at us, and a fight resulted. In the midst of it, No. 1 Engine, which lay at the foot of Duane Street, appeared and sided with No. 6. Then Engine 23, of Leonard Street, turned up and sailed in with us. No. 36 followed quickly, taking Six's side. Pipes, axes, and any weapon handy, were used in the fight. It was a terrific fight, and lasted a long while. At last, Anderson succeeded in putting a stop to it, and made us go down Canal Street instead of through Chambers, so as to avoid our foes. Foreman Jack Whitehead and Assistant Foreman Bill Whitehead were tremendous big men, whom nobody cared to tackle single-handed. Before the fight No. 5 sent their engine home in charge of a few men, and this precaution saved them from being disbanded."

Evans, one afternoon, while assistant foreman of No. 31, was with Engine No. 5, and got into a "muss" with No. 11 in Eighth Avenue. No. 11 "wiped the street" with him and his chums, and at last the men of No. 5 made off and Evans was left with only Uzziah Wenman to stand by him. After 31 was disbanded he joined 14 Hose, and subsequently he organized new 31. Evans went to the war with the Twelfth Regiment, N.Y., in April, 1861, and was taken prisoner at Harper's Ferry. His was the first regiment in Washington on May 24, 1861. Evans crossed the Long Bridge at Washington, and saw the rebel flag flying on the Marshal House about four in the morning. About five o'clock word was brought that Ellsworth was shot at Alexandria. After the war he went back to No. 31. Mr. Evans is now fifty-six years old, and connected with the Fire Department in Jersey City.

A single combat was the result of the rivalry between Engine Companies Nos. 30 and 44 ("Old Turk"). No. 30 lay in Christie Street, and Jack Teal was the foreman. Jim Jerolomon was the giant of No. 44, standing six feet four in height. In Chief Gulick's time No. 44 lay in Houston Street, near Lewis, and Bob Penny was foreman. On a Saturday afternoon a fire broke out in Milton Smith's stables, at Avenue D and Sixth Street. No. 44 was the first to reach the fire, and took suction from the foot of Sixth Street. No. 37 engine, which lay in Delancey Street, was friendly to No. 44, and was on her way to the fire, when Penny ran down to Union Market and told No. 37 to go to Fifth Street, the object of this being to make No. 30 take No. 44's water and get washed. Soon No. 30 came in, and Penny asked Teal, who commanded No. 30, to take 44's water. Teal replied, in a sarcastic manner: "Take yer water? Ye-e-s; why wouldn't we take it?" No. 30 got into line, and 44 butted into her. The butcher boys of Christie Street were good men, and held their own for a time, but when Penny got the stout lads from the shipyards on the brake of Old Turk nothing could equal them, and in fifteen minutes No. 30 was boiling over. Penny asked Gulick to send an engine to take 44's water. "Can't 30 take it?" asked the chief. Penny replied that a dozen Thirties couldn't take it. Gulick then ordered No. 30 away, and as Jerolomon took the butt out of 30 he squirted the water over "Thirty's fellers." Teal, who was a much smaller man, then struck Jerolomon, and a fight was the result. The next day Teal and Jerolomon met in Yorkville and fought. On the third round Teal claimed that Jerolomon was biting him, and on removing his shirt the print of teeth was found on his shoulder. The combat was then broken up. Teal was a joiner, and considered one of the best fighters of the time. Jerolomon was at another time a member of No. 17 engine, when she lay in Jackson Street, then Walnut.

In the year 1824 James P. Allaire, of the old firm of Allaire Bros., was foreman of "Black Joke" Engine Company No. 33. The name was given her in honor of an Albany sloop which distinguished herself in the war of 1812. She was painted a "nigger" black on the body, and had a gold stripe running all the way around. In 1832 her headquarters were in Gouverneur, between Henry and

Madison Streets, and Malachi Fallon was her foreman. She had on her ropes about forty men, nearly all of them being fighters. The company was known as a fighting one and "a pretty hard crowd." Fallon, after leaving No. 33, became chief of police of San Francisco, California. In 1842 James Burbridge was her foreman, and among the runners were two gigantic negroes, one named John Arno alias "Black Jack," and the other was called "Black Joe." Those darkeys made themselves very serviceable around the engine house, and felt themselves highly honored in being asked to do anything. They were not, however, allowed to bunk in the engine house. In the summer of 1842 No. 33 had a severe fight with No. 5 Truck and Hose Company No. 4. There had been a fire in Monroe, near Gouverneur Street, and these two companies combined to "lick" No. 33. And a terrible thrashing they gave 33, the fight lasting almost an hour; bloody heads, broken noses, black eyes, and torn clothes being plentiful. The fight originated in a supposition that while at work at the fire the men of No. 33 "splashed" water over the men of Nos. 4 and 5 while they were playing on the ruins. No. 33 denied that they had done so, but insisted upon having a fight, and they got it. In 1843 No. 33 was disbanded, but was reorganized in 1844, with ex-Alderman Peter Masterson as its foreman.

In 1832 No. 33 got into a difficulty with Engine Company No. 11. A fire occurred in Pearl Street, near Maiden Lane. No. 11 was taking water from the dock and supplied No. 33. Both companies were noted for their strength. No. 11 tried to "wash" No. 33, and failed after working all night. When daylight broke, the boys, tired out, went to breakfast, and then the runners or hangers-on of the engines took their places to keep up the supply of water. These "irregulars" were animated with the same sentiments that characterized the great men they were permitted to follow, and again it was sought to get No. 33 over, but in vain. Then No. 11 charged No. 33 with "niggering." This meant only working at intervals and compelling the supply engine to take out its butt. Hot words followed, and it was decided to settle the matter by a fight. As a rule champions were selected for the companies, and the rule was observed on this occasion. The engines were deserted, a ring was formed, and at it the gladiators went. In the midst of the fun the gigantic Gulick appeared upon the scene. He was the Chief Engineer. He settled the contest immediately. A blow from his fist was like a kick from a horse. He sailed right in and scattered the ring and the fighters in a minute.

No chief had ever so great a hold upon the firemen as James Gulick had. We refer in the chapter upon fires to the refusal of the men to work after the great fire of December, 1835, when the Common Council deposed him from office. Here is another instance of the affection the boys had for him. It was in the beginning of the same year, January 4, that a fire broke out in Centre Street, adjoining the works of the New York Gas Company, which destroyed two houses. Against the gable end of one of the burning buildings a large number of barrels of resin were piled. The firemen worked diligently to save these by rolling them into the street, and the night being intensely cold, some one kindled a small fire in the street with a part of the contents of a broken barrel, which the workmen employed by the gas company attempted to extinguish. They were warned by the firemen to desist, and a big, heavy fellow, who insisted upon putting out the fire, was shoved away. Thereupon a large number of his friends attacked the few firemen around the fire. Other firemen flew to the assistance of their comrades, and a regular fight ensued. The laddies conquered. Gulick heard of the affair, and, hastening to the scene, exclaimed: "What does all this shameful conduct mean at this moment?" One of the workmen flew at him and struck him from behind over the head with an iron bar. His fire-cap, however, protected him from serious injury. Turning upon his assailant the powerful Chief pursued him across the ruins of the fallen wall, and threw him down upon the bricks. Immediately some thirty or forty workmen surrounded Gulick. Then the cry was raised, "Men, stand by your Chief!" and in a twinkling the assailants were quickly routed and took refuge in the gas-house at the corner of Centre and Hester Streets. Gulick, by almost superhuman efforts, got into the gas-house first to prevent the excited firemen from entering. Amid volleys of coal-buckets he called upon the rioters inside to behave themselves and they should be protected. He was replied to by being rushed at with a red-hot poker; but, fortunately, his trumpet was under his arm, with its large bowl in front of him, through which the hot poker passed. He jumped from the stoop crying in stentorian tones: "Now, men, surround the house; don't let one of them escape!" They were all, or nearly all, arrested and locked up after receiving a sound drubbing. The firemen got very excited, and it seemed that a big riot would ensue. They rushed into the gas-house and attempted to destroy the machinery, and a dreadful explosion was imminent. But the Chief's firmness prevailed, and in a short time he quieted the men and restored peace.

One of the most famous fights of the old fire laddies goes by the name of "The Battle of the Boots." It is not a dignified name for a battle, still the conflict was a very heroic and very bloody one. There are several still living who participated in the affair. It took place in the summer of 1842, and was the result of an old feud between engine companies Nos. 27 and 34, and came off after extinguishing the fire in the New House furniture store, the shop attached to which is in Van Renwyck Street, which runs from Spring to Canal Street. That street is now called Renwick Street. Both companies were composed of smart men, both had made good records, and their rivalry was warm. The brave and unfortunate Dave Broderick was then foreman of No. 34. John J. Mount, as already stated above, was one of the volunteers of No. 27. Mount was one of the gay and festive Butt Enders, an association around Clinton Market, at the foot of Spring Street, who used to run with No. 27. Previous to this fire in Van Renwyck Street No. 27 was caught shorthanded and at a disadvantage by their opponents, and sustained a defeat. Although they laughed at it, and indeed seemed to regard it as a good joke, this severe check was brooded over by No. 27, and they determined soon to get even with their opponents. All the volunteers went up and joined the roll of No. 27 and then looked out for the "enemy." No. 27 ran to several fires without coming in contact with No. 34 until this fire in Van Renwyck Street occurred. No. 27 was early on hand, took the dock, gave water to their hated rivals, who in turn gave their water to some other engine. All the boys worked magnificently. Their first duty was to the public—to put out the fire—and no private interests were supposed to interfere with this.

About ten o'clock at night the fire was got under, and all the engines took up their hose. For some time No. 27's plan of battle had been arranged by Ely Hazelton, their "boss" warrior, the Napoleon and Achilles of the company. The signal for the fight was to be the word "boots," and when that was given every man was to "sail right in." Well, the ropes were lined inside and out, and No. 27 had all their friends around. When they got near Hudson Street they were almost abreast of No. 34. No. 34 was about to turn the corner, but three parts of No. 27's rope stretched across the way. Now was the moment; now had the hour of revenge arrived.

"Boots!" thundered the muscular and stentorian Hazelton.

Down went the ropes, up went the avenging hands of the lads of No. 27, and in a twinkling they were pummeling their opponents. Blows were rained with stunning force and bewildering rapidity, while the exchanges were few and far between. But the rush of No. 27 was like the fall of a mountain torrent reinforced by the 'whelming flood of a winter's storm, and the unfortunate boys of No. 34 were overpowered and swept away. The foreman and assistants in those days used to walk in rear of the engine. Foreman Broderick was far in the rear when the battle began, and, scarcely realizing what had happened, was marching up Hudson Street, near Spring, when he received a gentle hint of what was going on. One of the young fellows of No. 27 noticed the redoubtable Dave coming along. The temptation was too great, and he let fly at Broderick, who, as the old chroniclers of the tournaments say, "bit the dust." Dave's hat fell off and was lost to him. It became the trophy of No. 27. The boys of No. 34 rallied, but their opponents were this time determined to conquer or die, and full of enthusiasm charged *en masse* on No. 27 and drove them up the street. In the struggle Mount was struck in the stomach by the stave of a barrel and badly gashed. No. 34 was already whipped when its foreman and assistants put a stop to the further progress of the fight.

Broderick's fire cap was picked up, and carried in triumph by No. 27 to their engine house in Desbrosses Street, where it was placed on the flagstaff, and remained on exhibition all next day. The headquarters of this company was at Joe Orr's saloon, at the corner of Desbrosses and Greenwich Streets. Broderick called there on the afternoon following the fight, accompanied by Mike Walsh, Johnny Ketcham, and several other members of his company to negotiate for the return of his official headgear. Hazelton and some of his chums were there. The peace propositions did not proceed satisfactorily; indeed they resulted in a row. Walsh had his fingers broken, Broderick was run out of the place, and his aid-de-camps scattered. Dave was pursued into Washington Street, and he ran for safety into the restaurant kept by Budd. Mount saw his flight, and noticed the infuriated crowd that chased him. He at once stepped in between the pursued and pursuers, and arrested further hostilities. "You ought to be ashamed of your-selves," said he, "so many of you to attack one man. Let him have fair play." The temper of the crowd cooled, they acknowledged the justness of the rebuke, and allowed the young fireman to have his way. Mount then escorted Broderick to the latter's place, at the corner of Commerce and Hudson Streets, and was warmly thanked for his generous interposition.

Hazelton, the fighter, subsequently came to an untimely end. He gave himself up to drink, and all efforts to reform him were in vain. In 1850 he went on a spree, and one night he took an awl, put the point to his head, and drove it into his brain with a mallet. He died almost instantly.

Nearly the entire time of the Common Council was taken up in settling the disputes between Broderick's company (No. 34) and No. 27. They were always bitter enemies, and never lost an occasion to quarrel. Generally the battle ground was near Sweeney's Hotel, and not a meeting of the Council passed without the friends of both companies being present in force, carrying bludgeons, sticks, hooks, and every kind of fighting implements, as evidence for and against one another—trying to prove which was the aggressive party.

No. 40 ("Lady Washington") housed in Mulberry Street, near Grand. Her foreman and assistant foreman were Joseph Primrose and John Carlin, brother of William Carlin, who subsequently owned and kept the hotel on Fourteenth Street, opposite Macy's. Among the most conspicuous of her fighting men were: Mose Humphreys, a type setter (afterwards the prototype already referred to of Chanfrau's Mose in a "Glance at New York"), who died in the Sandwich Islands, where he had married a native woman, and reared a large family of young natives; and Jim Jeroloman, a shipbuilder, six feet four inches tall, who wore earrings, and who challenged "Yankee" Sullivan to a prize fight, but was easily beaten.

There were several other popular fire companies more or less in sympathy and in aggressive alliance with one or other of the above companies. Among these were No. 44 ("Live Oak") at the foot of Houston Street; No. 30 ("The

Tompkins"), of which Tom Hyer was a member; No. 34, at Christopher Street and Hudson, of which Dave Broderick was foreman, and Bill Poole—the only man who ever beat John Morrissey—was a member; and No. 33, afterwards "Big Six," of which William M. Tweed and Malachi Fallon were then only modest privates. Its foreman was Sam Purdy, who afterwards became the first lieutenant-governor of California. Purdy's father was the rider of Eclipse in his junior race on the Long Island course with Henry.

Between Nos. 15 and 40 an ill-feeling had been for a long while brewing. Both companies when running to down-town fires used frequently to meet in Chatham Street, and fright the town from its propriety with angry wranglings, or with excited shouts as they would "buck" the pavements, one on either side of the street, and engage in a furious contest of speed in their rival efforts to be first at the fire. On this remarkable occasion, however—it was a bright summer Sunday—the two companies, after several hours of arduous duty at a fire in South Street, near Wall, turned homeward about the same time, and passed up Pearl Street together, in dangerous proximity to each other. The ropes of both sides were—as usual on Sundays—fully manned. Probably five hundred men confronted each other on either side. It had been rumored early in the day that No. 40 intended to attack No. 15, and destroy its boasted invincibility. The presence in the ranks of the former, of several noted fighters from 34 and 44, lent color to this report, and the hostile companies were followed by an army of expectant lookers-on and partisans.

The two wheeled into Chatham Street together, No. 15 leading. No. 15 turned eastward on its usual way homeward, via the Bowery. No. 40 should have taken the westward course down Chatham Street to its house on Mulberry Street, but instead of doing so, followed its rival until the broad space of Chatham Square was reached. Here the two companies came abreast, and the satirical chaffing which up to this had marked their antagonism swelled into a chorus of mutual taunts and menaces. So they continued, until the Bowery was reached. At the head of 15's rope was "Country" McCluskey, confronted by the formidable Jim Jeroloman at the head of 40. At the rear of the line Hen Chanfrau was opposed by Mose Humphreys. Both sides were by this time ripe for conflict.

The two foremen, Colladay, on the part of No. 15, and Carlin, on the part of No. 40, passed rapidly up and down their respective lines, ostensibly endeavoring to preserve the peace, but in reality stimulating the courage and exciting the pride of their partisans. "Now, boys, no fighting," said Colladay, audibly, adding in an undertone, "but if they will have it, give it 'em good!" "Be quiet, men," said Carlin, loudly; then in a lower tone, "till they begin, then go in!" The vociferations of the opposing companies grew meanwhile louder and more threatening, until at last words being exhausted, both sides began to "peel" for the conflict which was felt to be inevitable. Jeroloman took out his earrings and put them in his pocket.

Passing from Chatham Square into the Bowery, the opposing companies, which up to that point had moved side by side, surrounded by a dense crowd, were, by the narrowing limits of the latter street, forced into collision. That proved the signal for the fray. The lines of each were extended nearly an entire block. The instant McCluskey and Jeroloman came within striking distance of each other, they dropped their respective ropes and became fiercely engaged. The shock of battle rolled down the line, and quicker than it takes to write the words, one thousand sturdy, stalwart fellows were fiercely grappling each other in a hand-to-hand fight. The din was frightful; louder than the furious exclamations that filled the air could be heard the resounding blows. The fighters were so thick that there was scarcely room for one to fall. Combatants who, so to say, felt themselves knocked down, were upheld by the pressure of the surrounding throng, and those who were unlucky enough to find mother earth were nearly trampled to death by the feet of friend and foe before they could escape. The leaders on both sides did their very best to maintain their reputation for courage and personal prowess. McCluskey, after a hot and desperate struggle, thrashed Jeroloman, Freeland triumphed over a noted fighter of No. 40, known as "Orange County," and other champions of No. 15 were making it all right.

The most conspicuous opponents at the other end of the line were Hen Chanfrau and Mose Humphreys. Both were pure-blooded Americans and men of noted bravery. At the crisis of their little difficulty, when victory appeared somewhat uncertain on whose gladiatorial arm to perch, a handsome bright-eyed lad of twelve years ran quickly out of Alvord's hat store, in which he had acted as clerk, and nimbly mounting an awning-post, shouted down to one of the combatants, who had just then pressed his antagonist backward over the tongue of 40's engine, and was pounding him very industriously, "Give it to him, Hen; Julia is looking at you from the window! Don't choke him; give him a chance to holler enough!" This nimble and encouraging youngster was Frank Chanfrau; and Mose Humphreys, who presently chorussed Frank's advice with a hearty acknowledgment of defeat, was to suggest to the then comedian in embryo a type of character which won him a double fortune and an enduring fame.

The fight lasted about thirty minutes. It resulted in the total defeat of No. 40, who abandoned their apparatus and fled precipitately. The victorious 15, determined to humiliate their antagonists in the most bitter manner known to the volunteer firemen of that day, seized the captured engine—which was beautifully painted in white and gold—dragged it to a pump, and deluged it with water. They held possession of it for hours, but finally released it to John Carlin. They, however, refused to permit any of "40's fellows" to enter their bailiwick, and the latter were made to suffer the additional mortification of seeing their beloved

"Lady Washington" drawn home from the scene of their defeat at the tail of a cart. This notable battle terminated hostilities between 15 and 40.

William H. Philp, a well-known artist and a whilom fireman, has many pleasant reminiscences to recall. One is the serenade and the torchlight procession in honor of Jenny Lind. During her first visit to this country she had given the proceeds of one of her concerts to the Firemen's Widow and Orphans Fund. In recognition of her generosity the firemen subscribed for the purchase of a copy of Audubon's Book on Birds, a very rare and costly work, and this was presented to her by a committee of firemen at the Irving House, corner of Broadway and Chambers Street. It was a beautiful night, and the whole department turned out with bands of music and torches. Broadway was crowded. Halting in front of the hotel the committee entered and made the presentation. Then Jenny Lind appeared on the balcony and bowed her acknowledgments many times, deafening cheers following each bow, torchlights waving and bands playing.

Mr. Philp went on the famous excursion to Philadelphia in 1852, where the Department was received by the municipal authorities, and the firemen shown about the city and most hospitably entertained. Mr. Philp thinks that it was about this period that the New York Fire Department reached the greatest epoch of its glory; there was an *esprit du corps* in the Department and a manly zeal in the discharge of duty not surpassed at any later period. It was witnessing the feats of the firemen at the Hague street explosion that inspired Mr. Philp with a desire to become a fireman, and he always took an active part with his company during the three years that he served. He was present at the Pearl Street fire in 1850; at the fire in the drug store of McKesson & Robbins, where a number of the firemen were injured by the spattering of vitriol from broken carboys; at the Jennings clothing store fire, opposite City Hall Park, and at the burning of the *Great Republic*, the largest sailing vessel then afloat.

The most trying fire ever attended by Mr. Philp was that in Broadway, between Grand and Howard streets, in the winter of 1853. It was a bitter cold night; the water froze in sheets on the firemen's backs while their faces were exposed to the heat of the fire. Many were totally benumbed, and one or two firemen were killed by falling walls. Mr. Philp declares that he endured nothing throughout the war of the Rebellion equal to his suffering on that memorable night. He is a member of the Volunteer Firemen's Association.

CHAPTER XII

MEMORABLE INCIDENTS

Running on the Sidewalks.—Attacked by Rowdies.—Concealing a Hydrant.— The Bunking Rooms.—Heroism of an Old Fire Laddie.—A Gallant Rescue.— Target Companies.—Knights of the Round Table.—Frank Clark, of "Old Turk."—A Fireman Becomes a Monk.

The weekly papers had published in 1854 articles reflecting upon the Department, and particularly referring to the rowdies who were permitted to run with the engines. On the twenth-fourth of January a special meeting was held at Fireman's Hall by the Board of Engineers and Foremen, and a committee was appointed to investigate the charges. The committee consisted of John Lynes, Hose Company No. 9; Noah L. Farnham, Hook and Ladder Company No. 1; John D. Dixon, Hose Company No. 54; Julian Botts, Engine Company No. 38; and William Tappan, Engine Company No. 7. The alleged rowdyism was shown to be due to the irresponsible runners who tacked themselves on to the companies.

The firemen at all times naturally took the shortest cut to a fire and the easiest road. The easiest was the sidewalk, which they used to clear like a flash of lightning. It was alleged that there was danger in this, and that it interfered with the liberty of the citizen. Nevertheless the boys thought it much better to run smoothly over the sidewalk than to bump along over the cobblestones. On May 20, 1853, the Common Council took the matter in hand. Alderman Smith proposed a resolution, notifying the engine companies that they would be dissolved if known to run on the sidewalk. In reference to this the *Fireman's Journal*, edited by Mr. Anthony B. Child, said on the following day:

"If Alderman Smith's resolution becomes a law we hope more attention will be paid by the authorities to the condition of the streets. In some of our principal thoroughfares it is almost impossible to drag an apparatus in the street. Not only is there severe labor requisite for such an act, but there is also the risk of the apparatus breaking down and danger to the men. If our streets were kept in a passable condition the firemen would not be obliged to take the walk. The firemen have to complain, not only of the deep ruts in the streets, but the manner in which they are lumbered up for building and railway purposes, thus giving the firemen but one resource—either to take the walk, or turn back and go six or seven blocks out of their way."

Through the death of a man the Grand Jury took notice of the infraction of the ordinance.

Sometimes the firemen were exceedingly annoyed by gangs of ruffians. About twelve o'clock on Thursday night, October 15, 1860, the Twenty-second Street bell started an alarm in the Third District. Engine Company No. 19 rolled out their machine and took the usual route, through Christie Street to Second Avenue, and then started up-town. Most of its members lay in the direction of Grand, Hester, and Walker Streets at that time. Those who rolled out the engine generally had to take her all the way up to the fire alone, with the exception of such slight help as they picked up on the way. On this occasion there were only six persons in the house when the alarm was given, but they were augmented by three or four strangers. As they neared the corner of Nineteenth Street a hundred ruffians or more saluted them with a volley of heavy stones, brickbats, etc., knocking down and injuring severely two of the members and one of the strangers. The rest were assaulted with clubs, sticks, etc., and were forced to leave their engine. The blackguards upset the engine, broke her tongue, smashed the large silver eagle on the top of the machine, and left her. One of the firemen had his nose broken.

No. 19 was always friendly with other companies, and her friends determined to stand by her in this emergency. One night the fire bell was set going, and several companies lay in wait in the vicinity in which No. 19 had encountered the ruffians, and through which she would come now. The gang, however, seemed to be apprehensive, and was afraid to come out. A gentleman who wrote about the outrage said:

"Now if these gentlemen (the gang) wish to have a pleasant evening's sport let them try the same game when she (No. 19) is coming from a Fourth or Fifth District fire. The companies are determined to take the law into their own hands. If they find these gentlemen they will give them the punishment they deserve."

Foreman J. J. Tindale, in reference to this letter, wrote that his company had no fighters in it, deprecated retaliation, but hinted pretty strongly that his men were able to take care of themselves.

At the great fire in New Street in 1845 the "innocence" of a fireman, or else the churlishness of a tradesman nearly caused loss of life. A fireman, named Sullivan, went into a grocery, kept by a German on the corner of Beaver and Pearl Streets, and had some refreshment. He told the storekeeper to charge the refreshments to his company, but the German, not relishing the idea, seized a large cheese knife, and striking Sullivan with it, laid open all one side of the fireman's head, inflicting almost a mortal wound. His comrades heard of the affair, and about forty of them hastened full of indignation to the spot. They utterly demolished the store, and were nearly killing the German, when the police arrived and rescued the tradesman.

One of the companies that felt extremely proud of itself and its engine was Hose No. 9. It could fairly lay claim to the title of a "crack" company. No. 9 was known as the "Silver Nine," because of the silver mountings of its carriage. Among her best known foremen were Harry Mansfield. Silver Nine lay in Mulberry Street near Broome. It was customary with all the companies, upon getting their machines back after repairs or redecorating, to give a grand feast. On one occasion the Silver Nine came back resplendent from the repair shop, and the boys did the honors in grander style than ever. Towards the close of the feast they became somewhat boastful, and declared that no company in the world could pass them. Some of its rivals—for no good company was ever without a rival—heard the boast, and resolved to "take the shine" out of Silver Nine. This company was the first to introduce bells on its hose carriage, and was, in consequence, looked upon as foppish.

A compact was entered into between No. 19 Hose (of which Uzziah Wenman was a member), Nos. 38, 15, and 3 Hose, to play a trick upon the boastful Silver Nine. It was determined that they should pass her four times in one night, and so forever dethrone her from her proud pre-eminence. A sham fire was to be started up-town about two o'clock on a Sunday morning. No. 9 would start out, the four companies in the conspiracy would lie in wait for her at certain points of the route, and each pass her in succession as she came along.

Hose 38 was to set fire to a lot of tar barrels about the corner of Seventeenth Street and Sixth Avenue, and then the hose companies were to be with their men all ready and waiting for Hose No. 9 to come along. As each company would keep its men fresh for the race, while, of course, the members of No. 9 Hose would be running all the time, it was calculated that each one of the four companies, fresh, would be able to pass No. 9, exhausted.

In the earlier part of Saturday evening the rope of No. 9 was laid out on the sidewalk ready for instant use, when a real fire broke out about nine o'clock at the foot of Market Street. This fire was no sooner put out than another occurred about eleven o'clock in Elm Street. It happened that at each of these fires Silver Nine was passed by other companies. The boys were more put out than the fire, and they were chafing at their defeat, when the sham fire was started up-town.

Silver Nine dashed out, hoping to be the first this time, but, alas, the plot was too well laid, and she was passed by each of the companies in the conspiracy according to arrangement. This was six times in one night she was passed, and such a series of defeats was almost unprecedented in the Department. The glory of Silver Nine was gone forever, and she never boasted more.

It must be said for No. 9 that she did not resort that night to any of the customary tricks to avoid being passed. Sometimes when a company saw itself on the eve of being outrun its foreman would shout, "Round to, and go back for more men!" or "Stop, and fix that wheel!" and in these cases there was no race. Occasionally, in trying to pass each other, engine or hose companies would be driven into piles of bricks, or holes, and men and machines would be injured. Companies used to hide behind walls, or piles of bricks, until rival companies came along, and would then rush out. This was a direct violation of the law, and was a common occurrence.

Once an engine company saw itself in danger of being passed in Dominick Street by a hose company, and it ran the latter upon a pile of bricks. The hose company, however, again came gamely up to the scratch, and in Varick Street was nearly passing its rival, but the men of the latter cut the straps that held up its arms, which fell among the men on the rope of the hose company, endangering their lives. Conduct like this every one condemned as cowardly and unworthy.

Many a fight has occurred for the possession of a hydrant. If a hose company arrived early at a fire it might possibly get a stream on from its own hose. But the engineers did not care for this, as they considered it ineffective; they desired the more solid and telling stream from an engine, and not infrequently would order its hose company to back out of the line and give its water to an engine. On one occasion a very funny, but, withal, fierce, fight took place for the possession of a hydrant. The survivors often laughed over it. Hose No. 14 was a popular company, and Henry A. Burr was foreman of it, and W. W. Corlies assistant foreman. One dark night there was a fire up-town, where the streets were then poorly paved and worse lighted—in fact, not lighted at all in some places. In one of these dark spots, not far from the fire, Burr, as the company dashed along, saw the outline looming up of a big hydrant. He instantly made for the hydrant, but found another man clutching at it also, a member of a rival company that had come along. Burr and the other fellow contended for that hydrant in the darkness; then, finding the fight going against him, Burr called for his men, who came. Then the other chap called out for his men, who came, and a fierce struggle took place in the dark for the supremacy and the hydrant. The fight was terminated in a curious way. One of the men, who was smoking while the rest were squabbling, lit a match at the end of his cigar and looked at the object for whose possession they were fighting all around him. Then he burst into a loud laugh, and no wonder; for what they thought was a hydrant wasn't a hydrant at all. It was only a buried cannon, with half of it sticking out of the ground. This discovery ended the fight.

A volunteer, belonging to No. 14 Engine, conceived what he thought a magnificent idea to become solid with the company. A new district had been opened up, and the firemen were not very well acquainted with it. But the volunteer, in rambling through the locality, noted a fire plug, and impressed its position on his memory. One night a fire occurred in this section, and the volunteer made a dash for the plug. He saw an old barrel near, clapped it over the plug, and sat on it. He began to smoke and assumed as graceful and careless an attitude as though he were an accomplished actor. An opposition company, dashing up and finding no hydrant, caused the volunteer to smile and chuckle. He was thinking of how proud No. 14 would be of him when they came along. He would then off with the barrel and reveal his treasure. But he didn't get the chance. Another company coming along saw the man on the barrel, and something about him made them suspicious. Perhaps he seemed too lazy and indifferent on the barrel. They rolled him off his seat, lifted up the barrel, and discovered the hidden hydrant. Alas, for that zealous runner and genius! He did not consort with No. 14 for a long time after. It was weeks before he was able to run, and more weeks before he could sit even on a chair. As for hydrants he never again sat on one.

The rivalry of the companies to get first to a fire originated the bunking system. The first companies to adopt its practice were the old rivals, Engines Nos. 5 and 14. The late Mayor Tiemann fought against the system because, he said, it would cause the ruin of many a young man. The Engine Companies Nos. 12 and 21 began bunking. Ex-Mayor Wickham, Charles E. Gildersleeve, and Andrew C. Schenck, of Hook and Ladder Company No. 1, organized a bunk room in order that the company when going to fires might not be outstripped by Hook and Ladder Company No. 4. "Andy" Schenck, to be near the tiller of the truck—which was the post of honor—threw the floor carpet upon the ladders, and slept on it. The instant an alarm was sounded, he slid down and seized the tiller. Mr. Wickham took for his pillow the lowest of the steps leading to the room above. When the company moved into its new house, each member contributed twenty-five dollars towards furnishing it. Engine Company No. 33 made friends with the sexton of All Saints' Episcopal Church (afterwards turned into a machine shop) in Grand Street near Pitt, the members lying in the pews, and using the ends of the cushions for bolsters. This was very nice and very comfortable, but 'ere long they were turned out and then hired the second story of a house in Scammel Street, one hundred and fifty feet from their engine house, and paid for it themselves. Some of the bunk rooms were remarkably orderly: no talking, for instance, was allowed in No. 38's after ten P.M. No. 36 would not permit card playing under penalty of fine or expulsion, or allow any drunken person to be brought to the house under the same penalties. When the city built engine houses the men were furnished with comfortable quarters.

When the new Department came into existence they used the old houses, but as improvements were made in the machines, and steamers became general, the houses were altered to suit the new order of things, or more suitable ones were built.

One of the most remarkable acts of heroism known to the annals of the old Fire Department, says Mr. John A. Cregier, was done by James R. Mount. On March 17, 1852, a fire broke out in a paint and paper hanging store at 89½ Bowery, cutting off the retreat of men, women, and children, who lodged in the third story. When Mount's company, No. 14 Hose, of which he was foreman, arrived, they found the inmates in a perilous position. Heartrending cries for help came from the windows. At one window a woman held a child, and was about to throw it into the street, when Foreman Mount cried out to her not to do it, and that he would go up to her. The gallant fireman started, but found his task no easy one. Under the stairs had been stored cans of paint, varnish, and oil. The stairs were partly burned through, and the flames and smoke were almost impassable. Fireman Joseph Skillman, who was afterwards killed at the Coffee Mills fire in Fulton Street, endeavored to dissuade his foreman from going up the stairs. "You will never come out alive," said Skillman. But Mount felt it to be his duty, and could not be deterred. Wrapping his coat around his head he dashed through flame and smoke up the stairs. At the top of the first flight he met a girl. She was too dazed and frightened to let Mount assist her, and she fainted. The foreman picked her up and cried out to Skillman that he would throw her down. He did so, and Skillman caught the insensible girl at the foot of the stairs. The devoted fireman then mounted to the next flight of stairs, at the head of which he found a man lying in what Mount first thought was a state of insensibility. The fireman put his hand down and felt him. The man was dead. There was no time to waste, so the gallant man started up the third flight. At the top he found another dead man in his night clothes. This man had, on the first alarm, got out, but had returned to secure forty-nine dollars in gold that he had left in his room. Next day the money was found clutched in his hand. His treasure was dearer to him than his life, and in foolishly striving to regain the former he sacrificed the latter.

Mount passed towards the front room through smoke so dense that he could almost shove it away with his hand. He opened the door, went in, closing the door after him, and found two women, two children, and two men, in a terrible state of excitement. Mrs. Muller was the woman who wanted to throw her child into the street. Mount calmed the frantic mother, and told them all to remain quiet for a few minutes, when he would return. Tying his coat about his head, he went back by the stairs, which were now almost burned away, passing on the landings the bodies of the dead men. He reached the street more dead than alive, but the fresh air revived him. In the meantime Skillman and his comrades had procured a ladder, thinking that Mount could not possibly get back by the flaming staircase. The ladder was reared against the side of the house, but unfortunately it reached only to the second story. Then they got a hogshead, and on this placed the ladder, which now reached within four feet of the windows of the third story. At this time the flames from the cans of varnish, oil, etc., burst into the street, and the sidewalk appeared to be on fire. When the ladder was reared on the hogshead no one appeared anxious to ascend. Mount said, "I will go," and directed them how to hold the ladder. The flames were now licking the rungs of the ladder, but up the brave fireman went.

The first to make their escape were the two men, who lowered themselves from the window to the top of the ladder. Coward-like, they left the women and children to die. One was the husband of Mrs. Muller. The first time Mount went up, Mrs. Muller handed him one of her children. On his next ascent he received another child. The third time he rescued Mrs. Muller and had great difficulty in doing so. He had to stand on the top rung of the ladder, holding on to the sill with his left hand. The woman clung around his neck. Then he felt for the top rung in making his way down, and slowly descended while the ladder shook as if it would fall. One misstep and death awaited them on the sidewalk. His comrades below held on for dear life. The last woman, Mary Koephe, weighed two hundred and twenty-five pounds. She was in her night dress, and sat on the window sill with her legs out, thoroughly frightened. Mount told her to hold on firmly to him, and she did so. When the gallant man had got down about two-thirds of the ladder, he fainted from over-exertion. His comrades instantly understood the situation, and ran to him; his burden fell into the firemen's arms. The enthusiasm of the spectators found vent in repeated cheers. Mount was taken to Harry Raveno's store, and the doctor found that he was suffering from the inhalation of smoke. When he revived, he vomited, felt better, and went home. His hands were burned, and his clothing, of course, was ruined.

Mr. Mount was also presented with a testimonial by the members of his company. The testimonial was a magnificent gold chronometer watch and chain, valued at two hundred and sixty dollars. The presentation took place at Moss's Hotel, corner of Bowery and Bayard Streets, to which a number of prominent citizens and members of the Fire Department were invited. Mr. W. J. Williams presented the watch in a neat speech. Mr. Mount replied in feeling language. "Words," he said, "are but the sparkling bubbles upon the ocean of feeling; but if you could look down in the lower depth of my inner heart, you would see the pearls and diamonds of a gratitude which I am unable to express." In addition to Mr. Williams the donors were Messrs. Herman Krall, P. H. Cooley, Levy L. Lyons, William Mash, and James L. Clute.

This brave deed of Mount was subsequently the occasion of a fight in the Common Council, the humors of which were given in the daily papers of the period. A committee of the Board of Aldermen reported in favor of appropriating three hundred dollars "to the purchase of some suitable testimonial, to be presented to Mount in recognition of his gallant services." On January 3, 1853, Alderman Wesley Smith (of the Eleventh Ward), who was foreman of Hose Company No. 34, called up the report, moved its adoption, and was seconded by Alderman Bard (of the Fourteenth Ward). Smith was remarkable for his great height. Alderman Sturtevant (of the Third Ward), one of the most pugnacious men in the Board, desired to know "whether Mr. Mount had done anything more than any other man would have done—any one sitting around that Board." "Yes," said Bard, promptly. "Anything more than the gentleman of the Fourteenth himself would have done?" superciliously inquired Sturtevant. Mr. Bard said he was not there. "Then more shame for you. Mr. Mount was there and had the opportunity—" Alderman Sturtevant was going on to say, when he was interrupted by Mr. Smith, who inquired whether the gentleman was speaking for or against the resolution.

Alderman Sturtevant:—"If the gentleman will have a little patience, or exercise what he is not distinguished for, a little civility and politeness, he'll find out what I am talking about. Here is a report before us in favor of awarding three hundred dollars, or three hundred dollars' worth, to Mr. Mount for doing what any true-hearted fireman would be glad to have the opportunity of doing. And I am sure my friend of the Fourteenth, with his fat, cheerful countenance, wishes he had been there and the tall Son of York—"

Here Alderman Smith jumped up to make a point of order. Alderman Sturtevant, he said, was personal, contrary to the rules of the Board. The president ruled against Sturtevant, but that irrepressible alderman continued his remarks in the same strain. Again he was interrupted, other aldermen joined in, and there was quite a hubbub. But Sturtevant managed once more to get the floor, and repeated "the tall Son of York."

"Mr. President," cried Mr. Smith, excitedly, "if this is to be permitted I must ask your leave to throw an inkstand at his head, which I will do, so sure as I sit here, if he repeats those words."

The president interposed. The disorderly city father said: "I mean to do so. But neither the president nor any one else is to tell me what language I am to use, and when I say, without intending any offense, the tall Son of York—" splash went the inkstand, but the other aldermen promptly interfered to prevent hostilities, and the debate was resumed, Sturtevant arguing that they had no right to put their hands in the city treasury for such a purpose. Finally the testimonial was voted. This incident in the Common Council was long remembered. A year or so afterwards, when Brougham produced his burlesque of "Pocahontas" at Wallack's Theater, he referred to it in the following lines which "caught" the house:

"Shut up, dry up, or go to bed,
Or I'll throw an inkstand at your honorable head."

The old volunteer firemen of the city of New York have the honor of being the first to extend the right hand of fellowship to their Southern brethren. In the early part of 1867 the members of "Independence" Hose Company No. 1, of Columbia, S.C., having had all their equipments destroyed during the war, appealed to the Northern firemen for old hose, and such apparatus as they had cast aside, in order to re-establish their old department. Mr. Henry Wilson, who was president of the New York Firemen's Association, immediately called together the members, and steps were at once taken to see what relief could be afforded them. A committee was appointed to raise funds, and in less than one week they realized over five thousand dollars. A new silver-mounted hose carriage, with ten lengths of new hose, was procured, one hundred fire hats, red shirts, belts, trumpets, and white hats for the chief engineer and assistants, were purchased, and shipped early in March of the same year on the steamer *Andalusia*. A committee of fourteen was appointed to proceed to Columbia and make the presentation. At the earnest solicitation of Mr. Ridabock, the committee went by rail, which was no doubt the means of saving some of the lives of the committee, as the steamer *Andalusia* took fire when twenty-four hours out, and with all its valuable cargo was totally destroyed, and twelve lives lost. The committee went by the way of Philadelphia, Baltimore, Fortress Monroe, Norfolk, Wilmington, and Charleston, being received at all these places by the firemen of each city. While at Charleston the mayor, Common Council, Chief Engineer M. A. Nathans, and the whole fire department, as well as the citizens, turned out to greet them. The following morning after their arrival in Charleston, the steamer *Manhattan* came into port with the sad news of the loss of the steamer *Andalusia,* and bringing the rescued passengers. The association had only one thousand dollars insurance on the carriage, the whole having cost over five thousand dollars. The committee were greatly dejected over their loss, and wanted to return home immediately, but the Columbia firemen insisted on their visiting their city, which they did, receiving a most cordial welcome. The committee resolved to duplicate their loss as soon as they got back to New York. On their return home they were the guests of the firemen at Richmond, Washington, Baltimore, and Philadelphia. As soon as they got back to New York they ordered another carriage built, duplicated everything lost on the ill-fated steamer, and in June of the same year shipped it on the steamer *Manhattan*. Messrs. Henry Wilson, William Lamb, Thomas C. Burns, Abraham Clearman, and Lewis J. Parker, being sent to present the same. They reached Columbia in safety, the people turning out in mass to greet them. President Henry Wilson made the presentation in a most impressive speech. Governor Orr, General Barton, Mayor Starke, Hon. S. W. Malton, Chief Engineer McKenzie, and the whole Fire Department being present. Captain Macky, of Hose No. 1 received the gift.

The two carriages with all the equipments cost over ten thousand dollars, and the carriage still stands as a monument to the noble generosity of the old volunteer firemen of New York City.

Between 1855 and 1861 target excursions were a great feature throughout the city of New York. It was not an uncommon thing to see from ten to fifteen pass the *Herald* office every day, while on Thanksgiving and Christmas Day they would exceed one hundred in number. Most all emanated from some one engine, hose, or hook and ladder company. They were well drilled and would put to blush some of the militia companies of the state. Among those that had their origin from the fire department were the Gulick Guards, named after Chief Engineer James Gulick. Oceanus Guards from Engine 11, Peterson Light Guards from Engine 15, Marsh Light Guards from Hose 33 and 40, Baxter Light Guards Hook and Ladder 15, Wildey Guards Engine 11, Washington Guards Engine 20, Union Guards Hook and Ladder 5, Atlantic Light Guards Hose 14, Live Oak Guards Engine 44, Americus Guards Engine 6, Columbia Guards Engine 14, Poole Guards Engine 34, Ringgold Guards Hose 7, Center Market Guards Engine 40, and many others that might be named. The Knickerbocker Guards from the Bowery and Lindsey Blues were also started by firemen.

In 1857 a general parade of all the target companies in the City took place, Fire Commissioner Henry Wilson being commander-in-chief. One hundred and twenty-seven companies turned out, which were divided into two divisions, the first being under command of William Wilson, at one time alderman of the first ward, and, during the war, colonel of the Sixth New York Volunteer Regiment, stationed so long at Santa Rosa Island, and the second under command of John Creighton. Fernando Wood was at that time mayor of the city, and he furnished all the muskets which were delivered to the several companies from the police-station houses by the captains of each ward.

It was on the twenty-third of April, 1857, that the parade took place, over twelve thousand men being under arms. The several companies were neatly equipped. In fact it was one of the most extensive parades ever witnessed in the city prior to the war. Business was suspended, stands erected all along the route or line of march, and the streets were crowded with thousands of people. Many of the companies wore red shirts, some blue overcoats, while others wore uniforms—not the state militia uniform.

The Knights of the Round Table were among the most noted organizations of the old Department. It originated among the members of Lafayette Hook and Ladder Company No. 6, located under Fireman's Hall, Mercer Street. It was organized in the fall of 1848, James P. Decker, Jr., being chosen the first president. The "Knights" convened but once a year—Christmas Eve—and the occasion was one of great enjoyment. Among its members was a large number of the theatrical profession, as well as members of the Fire Department. A grand supper was the principle feature of the gathering. The supper took place at eleven o'clock at night, and was continued until the wee hours of Christmas morning. "Tom and Jerry" was the opening drink for the night's festivities. The tables were loaded down with all the viands of the season.

The feasts were always held in the basement of Fireman's Hall. Wit and humor abounded, intermingled with anecdotes, songs, ballads, and jokes, which kept the whole party in one continual uproar, the Knights of the Cork always endeavoring to outdo one another with all sorts of gags and puns.

Of the many "Liberty Poles" erected in the city the best known was, perhaps, "Tom" Riley's. It stood at the southwest corner of Franklin Street and West Broadway. It was the scene of many a gathering on holidays. These contests took place between rival engines, and these exciting trials attracted numerous spectators, beside members and friends of the Department. Each company was jealous of the reputation of the pumping power of its engine, often challenges were issued to decide the question, and Riley's Liberty Pole was most often selected at which to make the trial. The pole was marked in various places with figures indicating the number of feet high that the several companies had played. Its height has been given as one hundred and thirty-seven feet. Especially on Thanksgiving Day would crowds of enthusiasts gather to see the machines work. The judges sat on the roof of Mr. Riley's hotel and reported the respective heights. Among the trials at Riley's Liberty Pole was a notable one in 1855. The Exempt Engine Company had been organized on November 14 of the preceding year at the house of Mr. H. B. Venn, No. 298 Bowery. The company had procured the abandoned engine of No. 42, which, on account of its great weight, was called the "man killer." On the twenty-fourth of January, while the snow was falling heavily, one hundred and ten exempts marched with the engine to Riley's, and were watched by a big crowd. The trial was a great success, and the company celebrated the event the same evening by a cold collation at Brooks's Rooms in Broome Street.

Riley's pole was first put up in 1834, on Washington's birthday. It was a great day for the Democrats who erected it. There was a feast, there were speeches, and other appropriate exercises. Unfortunately it did not long remain standing. It was struck by lightning in the following year, and so injured that it had to be taken down. Another pole was erected at the expense of the Democrats. It was removed in 1858, and long after "old timers" used to visit the spot where it had stood to talk over the memories of bygone days. Riley's hotel has since been torn down, and a six-story structure for business purposes was built on the site. The old hydrant near it was left standing.

As we have intimated elsewhere, "Old Turk," No. 44, was a famous engine. The most prominent of the old "Forty Fourers," and one whose name even to-day is a household word among all old firemen, was Frank Clark, one of the most remarkable men who ever ran with the "masheen." Clark was born in Paterson, N.J., in 1824, the same year that 44 was organized. He came to New York, and of his school days in Fifth Street he says: "The first day we went to the school the gang tried to pitch the teacher out of the window, but instead got pitched out themselves." Clark was identified with 44 from boyhood. According to himself he "jined" at eleven years of age.

In the early days of 44 the firemen were divided into two classes—regulars and volunteers or runners. While Sam Allen was foreman the volunteers bunked in a house directly opposite the engine house, in Houston Street, between Cannon and Lewis Streets. One night Allen locked the engine house, and going to the bunkers' quarters made an offer of a brand new suit of clothes to the first volunteer who would roll the engine in case of a fire during the night. The volunteers turned into their bunks with their trousers stuck into their boots beside their beds and ready to be jumped into as soon as the alarm sounded. At midnight the Union Market bell "came in" for a fire in the Sixth District. The volunteers jumped into their trousers and rushed across the street only to find the engine already in the street, and Clark on the tongue with neither boots nor trousers on. From that night until his death 44 and Frank Clark were synonymous terms among firemen, not only in New York but in almost every city in the Union. He became a member of 44, and afterwards foreman, a position of honor and power in those days. He led "Old Turk" to Washington to see Pierce inaugurated, and to Philadelphia, where they were received by Bill McMullen's Moyamensing Hose and created a sensation. While foreman of Old Turk Clark married, and on the night of the wedding escorted his bride home from the church. When within a few yards of the bride's house the bell struck six, and Clark left his bride at her door while he rushed to the house, seized his trumpet, and led 44 to the fire in his wedding suit, and for three days never saw his bride. This was at the great Sugar House fire, which lasted three days. When called to account for his conduct he replied:

"What wus a feller goin' to do? Let the injin get passed?"

Volumes might be written about Clark and his exploits. He became prominent in politics, but was not suited for a leader. He was an "Old Line Democrat" of the most pronounced type, and this lost him place time and again. He was not a selfish man, and for forty years he was known to almost every man, woman and child in the Eleventh Ward, and was as much of a boy in his ideas at sixty as he was at twenty. He was "Frank Clark of old 44," and he gloried in his title. The proudest day of his life was when he led 44 on Evacuation Day parade in 1883. Old Turk turned out two hundred strong, and thousands flocked to see her. From far and near the old eastsiders who had moved away years before came back to their old stamping ground. Clark with his red shirt and fire cap, and a silver trumpet covered with flowers, was a prouder man that day than any monarch on earth.

The affection entertained by the people for the men of Old Turk may be gleaned from a letter written to the *Sun* by Mrs. Edward Moynihan, of No. 298 Seventh Street, a few days before the parade. Mrs. Moynihan spoke in glowing terms of old 44 and said:

"They tell me that the old firemen may be short of funds for a band. If that is so, I will freely contribute whatever may be lacking. All I ask is that they march past my window so that I may once more see about all there is left in the Eleventh Ward to remind me of the past." The old lady's wish was gratified. Old 44 marched past her window. As Mrs. Moynihan, bent with age and resting on the arm of her son, appeared at the window, Clark lifted his hat and raised his trumpet, when two hundred of the flower of the old Fire Department raised their helmets and remained uncovered until they passed the old lady's window. It was a memorable day in the Eleventh Ward, and there were few dry eyes among the men of Old Turk. The aged lady had seen old 44 for the last time.

At all demonstrations and at their funerals Clark was a prominent character. Attending a funeral of one of his old comrades he requested that, if he himself should die on Monday, he be kept in until the following Sunday, so that all the old boys might have a chance to go to his funeral. Two weeks from that day his wish was gratified. He died on Monday, May 4, 1884, and his funeral took place on Sunday, May 10. It was the largest demonstration ever witnessed at the funeral of a volunteer fireman not killed in the discharge of his duty, and among the floral tributes was the motto of old 44:

Extinguish one flame and cherish another

Old 44 was also remarkable for her six stalwart Pennys, who were known all over the city as "Old Turk's Big Pennys." Once a foreman of a rival company had a dispute with 44's foreman as to the relative merits of their respective companies, and offered to back his opinion by betting drinks for the two. In those "good old days" good old whiskey could be had for three cents a glass, and the rival foreman banged down six cents on his engine. He had a well-founded conviction that 44's foreman was penniless. Rueful 44 thrust his hands into his empty pockets and looked along the line. His sad eye lighted on one of the Pennys, and a ray of hope entered his thirsty soul. He whispered to this particular stalwart Penny, who whispered to his brothers, and at once each of the six namesakes slapped a penny upon the engine amid a roar of laughter from the spectators. The challenger laughed too and took the whole crowd over to "Johnny" Muldoon's, at Third and Lewis Streets, where they fraternized. As they drank each other's healths Nigger Shee sang the following refrain of the old song:

> I went down town to see my posey,
> Who did I meet but Jim Along Josey.
> Hey, Jim Along, Jim Along Josey,
>   Hey, Jim Along,
>   Jim Along Joe.

John McDermott ("Old Time Enough"), of Excelsior Engine Company No. 2, derived his "nickname" from a peculiarity, the cause of which he tells in this way: "Of course you know that in those days every other man in the Department had a nickname, and if he was at all prominent as a fireman, he was known all over the city by it every bit as well as by his proper name. Indeed many knew him by his nickname who would have been puzzled if asked his right name. As secretary, foreman and in other positions, I always tried to smooth over the little quarrels which were sure to come up. One would present charges against the other for this or that offense, and insist that they be forwarded to headquarters. I knew that a little delay would in every case cause the parties concerned to forget all about them, so my customary reply—indeed it became stereotyped— was, 'Oh, time enough.' Perhaps I may have carried this thing a little too far, but it got me the nickname as my reward, and I suppose I'll bear it to the day of my death.

"Excelsior was known as the Quaker Company, because when I joined it a great many of the boys' fathers were old Broadbrims. Most of the members— among whom I recall Mayor Westervelt's son; Ed. Knight, Librarian of the Supreme Court; ex-Coroner Pat Keenan, ex-Alderman Bryan Reilly, Zophar Mills, and others—belonged to good families, so that we had none of the fighting element with us. It wasn't at all unusual for us to have a forty or fifty-dollar supper after a fire, and in those days forty dollars would buy a great deal of good grub. Some of the wealthier fellows belonged to it, as they did to other companies, to enable them to escape jury duty, and not a few of them would regularly pay as fines every month ten or fifteen dollars. When I joined No. 2 the house was at 21 Henry Street—I believe it is a butcher shop now—but in 1865 we moved to East Broadway, between Catharine and Market Streets.

"In the autumn of '52 a grain-elevator at the foot of Roosevelt Street caught fire on Sunday morning. It was only a few blocks from the house and we happened to be on hand before the alarm was given. Jack Sloper—he was a sort of left-handed Mascot to me always—and I had the pipe down in the hold of the elevator. We heard a noise and happened to back out just in the nick of time, for the machinery had given way. When the ships *Great Republic, White Squall,* and others were burned at the foot of Dover street, the same Sloper and I were on one of the vessels. We had the pipe and were lying on our stomachs between decks, with half hatch on. The gas generating in the hold of the vessel exploded, driving the other half of the hatch up and knocking us heels over head."

Mechanics' Hose No. 47 had a member whose history, though brief, is noteworthy. Daniel Kelly was born in the Eleventh Ward, hailing from the famous old Dry Dock, which has but recently become a thing of the past. Kelly joined No. 47 in 1859. He was a man of great strength, brave as a lion, but very quiet. He became foreman of Mechanics' Hose. About twenty-five years ago, on the Fourth of July, at a fire in Columbia Street, the foreman of a rival of No. 47 attempted to strike Kelly with his trumpet. Kelly simply grabbed the man, threw him across his knee, and spanked him like a schoolboy amid the roars of the crowd. When Kelly had served his time he resigned, and dropped out of sight.

Some years ago a visitor desired to see the monastery at Hoboken, and was referred to Brother Bonaventure. The brother and the visitor were passing through the house when the former suddenly turned and pressed the hand of the visitor, exclaiming "How do you do, Joe? Don't you remember me?" Brother Bonaventure was Daniel Kelly, Mechanics' old-time foreman, and "Joe" was one of his former comrades. The monk told his friend that was the only way he could save his soul. Kelly was brought up within the sound of the old Mechanics' bell. Within the monastery was a bell which rang for prayers at midnight. The recluse explained that a special indulgence was granted to the monk who first responded to its peal. Brother Bonaventure's experience and practice in invariably being the first to answer the old fire bell stood him in good stead now, and he gained all the indulgences.

CHAPTER XIII

FIRES OF THE OLDEN TIME

*History of Some of the Great Conflagrations that have Devastated New York.—
The Alleged Incendiary Slave Plots of 1741 and 1796.—The Revolutionary
Struggle and the Attempts to Burn down the City.—Disastrous Fire of 1811.—
A Sailor's Gallant Deed.—The Old Jail Bell and its History.*

The greatest calamities that have befallen New York have been its destructive
fires. Within the comparatively brief space of one hundred years she had
suffered more from the "devouring element" than any city in the world. The
rapidity with which these striking events succeeded each other is remarkable.
The years 1741, 1776, 1778, 1804, 1811, 1835, 1839, and 1845 are in the history
of the city memorable for the ruin and misery occasioned by mighty conflagrations. In the intervals innumerable other fires had occurred, some of them resulting in loss of life and great destruction of property, but those of the years just
mentioned surpass all others in their extent, intensity, and far-reaching effects.
But the frequent recurrence and remarkable destructiveness of these fires are no
reflection upon the zeal and courage of the noble men who had volunteered to
fight the flames. That gallant body had only meager means and unscientific
appliances to help them in their arduous labors. All that brave and watchful men
could do they did, and mortal men could do no more.

With the exception of Constantinople New York has, perhaps, suffered more
frequently from conflagrations than any city in the two worlds. Hamilton said
in his time that one could not be twenty-four hours in New York without
hearing an alarm of fire. This observation was repeated by a writer who published
a small work in 1837, called "A Glance at New York," who added that one
alarm a day would be a small average, and that it would be nearer the truth to
say that the firemen of New York were called out five hundred times a year—a
statement which all familiar with New York at that time have corroborated.
Many of these were undoubtedly false alarms, raised by boys for the pleasure of
running after the engines. The fire of London in 1666 was bigger than anything
this city has seen. Four hundred and thirty-six acres were laid waste, eighty-nine
churches destroyed, with thirteen thousand two hundred houses, leaving two

hundred thousand people temporarily without homes. The fire of Hamburg in 1842 burned sixty-one streets, containing one thousand seven hundred and forty-seven houses. The Chicago fire laid waste over five acres, and left one hundred thousand of her citizens homeless. But if the frequency of fires in the city, the magnitude of some of them, and the amount of property destroyed, be collectively considered, it will be seen that New York, perhaps, has suffered more heavily from this kind of calamity than any other city of modern times. Still these conflagrations have in the end proved of great benefit by causing more spacious and elegant edifices to arise, phoenix-like, out of their ashes.

The first great fire, or rather series of fires, in 1741 was said to be the work of negro slaves. Dr. John Gilmary Shea in 1862 published a paper on the subject, carefully analyzing the evidence for and against the alleged plot. Slavery was almost coeval with the settlement of this city, says Dr. Shea. When the fort was begun in 1625, and colonization properly commenced, the Dutch West India Company immediately promised to each patroon "twelve black men and women out of the prizes in which negroes shall be found." The negroes taken on an enemy's ship were thus sold here as slaves, irrespective of their former condition. Indians were similarly treated. Slaves were also brought in directly from Angola and other parts of Africa, and indirectly through the Dutch West India Islands. Thus the element of negro slavery was introduced and extended during the Dutch rule. Fort Amsterdam itself, that cradle of New York, was finally completed by the labor of negro slaves, whose moral condition was utterly ignored. When the English came they accepted slavery, and gave it the sanction of municipal law.

As time rolled on the laws bore heavily upon the poor negro, and too often the slaves were goaded to commit deeds of violence. Fearful was the retribution. Two slaves of William Hallett—an Indian man and negro woman—of Newtown, Long Island, in 1707 murdered their master, his wife, and their five children, in revenge for being deprived of certain privileges. The woman was burned, the man was suspended in gibbets and placed astride a sharp iron, in which condition he lived some time, and in a state of delirium which ensued, believing himself to be on horseback, would urge forward his supposed animal with the frightful impetuosity of a maniac, while the blood oozing from his lacerated flesh streamed from his feet to the ground.

A conspiracy followed, terrible scenes of bloodshed ensued, and severer laws were enacted. In 1741 the city was in a state of panic. The midnight sky was reddened with the flames of the incendiary, and no man's property seemed safe from the torch of the conspirator. The city contained about eleven thousand inhabitants, and of these about one-fourth were negroes. In those days the governor (Lieutenant-Governor Clarke, an Englishman) resided in Fort George, which stood on an eminence south of Bowling Green. In this fort stood a church, built by Governor Kieft, the king's house, barracks, etc. The church was of stone, but covered with a shingle roof. On the eighteenth of March, about one o'clock in the day, a fire broke out in this roof, and as the wind was high the flames spread rapidly. The fire bell rang out, and thousands flocked to the scene. Just ten years before the new fire engines had been introduced and something like a fire department organized. These slow and unwieldy machines came lumbering to the spot, manned by firemen in civilian costumes as clumsy and uncouth as well could be devised to prevent freedom of limb and muscle. The bucket lines were formed, but not too rapidly, and the contents of the buckets half spilled before reaching the engine. And still the flames mounted high. The ships in the harbor thought the whole city was afire. Soon the church, the king's house, and other buildings in the fort were reduced to ashes. The flames spread beyond the fort, and the rest of the town was menaced, but the further progress of the fire was arrested. A few weeks after four or five other fires occurred in different parts of the city, and then was heard the cry "The negroes are rising!" Everywhere the slaves were hurried to jail, and a wild search was made for suspicious persons. Trials, executions, and bloody laws followed fast till the panic was allayed, and the city became sane and safe again. Four white people were hanged, fourteen negroes burned, eighteen executed, and seventy-one transported to the West Indies and sold.

The next great fire occurred in the stirring times of 1776, and is connected with the battle of Long Island. New York appears to have been a coveted prize for the British, and early in 1776 Howe dispatched General Clinton secretly to attack it. Dr. Benson J. Lossing, in his *History of New York City*, says that General Washington, suspecting New York to be Clinton's destination, sent General Charles Lee thither, and on the evacuation of Boston in March the commander-in-chief marched with nearly the whole of his army to New York, arriving here in the middle of April. He pushed forward the defenses of the city begun by General Lord Stirling. Fort George, on the site of Fort Amsterdam, was strengthened, numerous batteries were constructed on the shores of the Hudson and East Rivers, and lines of fortifications were built across the island from river to river not far from the city. Strong Fort Washington was finally built on the highest land on the island (now Washington Heights) and intrenchments were thrown up on Harlem Heights. In the summer Washington made his headquarters at Richmond Hill, then a country retreat at the (present) junction of Charlton and Varick Streets.

On the 10th of July copies of the Declaration of Independence were received in New York. The army was drawn up in hollow squares by brigades, and in that position the important document was read to each brigade. That night soldiers and citizens joined in pulling down the equestrian statue of King George, which certain tories had caused to be set up in the Bowling Green only six years before. They dragged the leaden image through the streets and broke it in pieces. Some of it was taken to Connecticut and moulded into bullets.

At the close of June, 1776, a British fleet arrived at Sandy Hook with General Howe's army, which was landed on Staten Island. After the landing they were joined by forces under Sir Henry Clinton, who had been repulsed in an attack upon Charleston, S. C. Hessians (foreign mercenaries hired by the British Government) also came, and late in August the British force on Staten Island and on the ships was more than twenty-five thousand in number. On the twenty-fifth of August over ten thousand of these had landed on the western end of Long Island, prepared to attempt the capture of New York. Washington, whose army was then about seventeen thousand strong, had caused fortifications to be constructed at Brooklyn, and he sent over a greater part of his forces to confront the invaders. The battle of Long Island ensued and was disastrous to the Americans. Washington skillfully conducted the remainder (not killed or captured) in a retreat across the East River, under cover of a fog, to New York, and thence to Harlem Heights at the northern end of the island. The British troops followed tardily, crossed the East River at Kip's Bay, and after a sharp battle on Harlem Plains took possession of the city of New York, or what was left of it.

The British had pitched their tents near the city, intending to enter the next morning and were in repose. The whole camp was sunk in sleep, and only the sentinels were awake, pacing their weary rounds. Suddenly, at midnight, arrows of lurid flame shot heavenward from the lower part of the town. The city seemed to be on fire. Afterwards it was asserted that the Americans had formed a scheme to burn down New York rather than let it fall into the hands of the English enemy. At any rate, a conflagration was started, accidently or designedly, at the foot of Broad Street. There were few citizens able or disposed to fight the flames, for most of the inhabitants had fled the town. In the space of a few hours five hundred buildings were destroyed. The soldiers and sailors from the vessels in the river were ordered ashore, and they succeeded in staying the flames before they reached Wall Street. It was General Greene who had simply urged the destruction of the city by fire—a measure afterward so effectively adopted by Count Rostopchin, Governor of Moscow, to arrest the career of Napoleon. General Greene's idea was to deprive the British of the advantage of having their winter quarters established in New York. His reasons for this measure were sound, says W. L. Stone in his *History of New York*, and ought, doubtless, to have been adopted. Washington also was believed to have been of the same opinion, especially as two thirds of the property which it was proposed to destroy belonged to undisguised loyalists. But Congress would not allow the sacrifice, and on the fifteenth of September the city was in full possession of the English.

At this time, according to Hugh Gaine, in his *Universal Register* for 1787, New York contained about four thousand two hundred houses and thirty thousand inhabitants. It would seem as if the idea of firing the city—though given up by Washington and Greene—was still cherished by some of the residents of the city. Scarcely had the British fairly taken possession, when, on the night of the twentieth of September (only six days after they had marched in) a terrific fire broke out which was not subdued until one thousand houses, or about one fourth of the city, were reduced to ashes. Although the value of the property destroyed does not discount that lost sixty years after in the Great Fire of 1835, yet it will be seen that its ravages were of far greater extent. The fire was first discovered in a low dram-shop in Whitehall Slip, called the "Fighting Cocks," tenanted by abandoned men and women. In a few minutes afterward flames were seen to break forth from several other buildings, lying in different directions, at the same instant. For some time previous the weather had been dry, and at the moment a brisk southerly wind prevailing, and the buildings being of wood and covered with shingles, the flames soon caught the neighboring houses and spread with inconceivable rapidity. The fire swept up Broad and Beaver Streets to Broadway and thence onward, consuming all that portion of the town lying on the North River, until the flames were stopped by the grounds of King's (Columbia) College at Mortkill Street, now Barclay. St. Paul's Church was, at one time, in great danger. Fortunately, however, the roof was flat with a balustrade on the eaves. Taking advantage of this circumstance, a number of citizens ascended to the balustrade and extinguished the flakes of fire as they fell on the roof. Trinity Church, with the Lutheran chapel, on the opposite corner of Rector Street, was also destroyed. The Rev. Dr. Inglis was then rector of Trinity, and this sacred edifice, his parsonage and the Charity School (two large buildings) were consumed, entailing a loss of church property to the value of twenty-five thousand pounds. The organ of Trinity alone cost eight hundred and fifty pounds. "The ruins," says Dunlop (who wandered over the scene at the close of the war), "on the southeast side of the town were converted into dwelling places by using the chimneys and parts of walls which were firm, and adding pieces of spars with old canvas from the ships, forming hovels—part hut and part tent." This was called Canvas Town, and there the vilest of the army and Tory refugees congregated.

Captain Joseph Henry, afterward a judge in Pennsylvania, has given, in his "Campaign against Quebec," a vivid description of "the great fire of 1776." He had just returned from Quebec, and was standing on the deck of the ship in the bay when the fire broke out. Captain Henry writes: "A most luminous and beautiful, but baleful, sight, occurred to us—that is, the city of New York on fire. One night (September 21) the watch on deck gave a loud notice of this disaster. Running upon the deck we could perceive a light, which at the distance we were from it (four miles) was apparently of the size of the flame of a candle. This light to me appeared to be the burning of an old and noted tavern called the 'Fighting Cocks' (where ere this I had lodged), to the east of the Battery, and near the wharf. The wind was southerly and blew a fresh gale, the flames at this place, because of the wind, increasing rapidly. In a moment we saw another light at a great distance from the first up the North River. The latter seemed to be an original, distinct, and new formed fire, near a celebrated tavern in the Broadway called 'Whitehall.' When the fire reached the spire of a large steeple, south of the tavern, which was attached to a large church (Trinity Church), the effect upon the eye was astonishingly grand. If we could have divested ourselves of the knowledge that it was the property of our fellow-citizens which was consuming, the view might have been esteemed sublime, if not pleasing. The deck of our ship, for many hours, was lighted as if at noonday. On the commencement of the conflagration we observed many boats putting off from the float, rowing rapidly toward the city. Our boat was of the number. This circumstance repelled the idea that our enemies were the incendiaries, for indeed they professedly went in aid of the inhabitants. The boat returned about daylight, and from the relation of the officer and the crew we clearly discerned that the burning of New York was the act of some madcap Americans. The sailors told us in their blunt manner that they had seen one American hanging by the heels dead, having a bayonet wound through his breast. They named him by his Christian and surname, which they saw on his arm. They averred he was caught in the act of firing the houses. They told us also that they had seen one person who was taken in the act tossed into the fire, and that several who were stealing and suspected as incendiaries were bayonetted. Summary justice is at no time laudable, but in this instance it may have been correct. If the Greeks could have been resisted at Persepolis, every soul of them ought to have been massacred. The testimony we received from the sailors, my own view of the distant beginnings of the fire in various spots, remote from each other, and the manner of its spreading, impressed my mind with the belief that the burning of the city was the doing of the most low and vile persons, for the purposes not only of thieving, but of devastation. This seemed, too, the general sense, not only of the British, but that of the prisoners then aboard the transports. Lying directly south of the city and in a range with the Broadway, we had a fair and full view of the whole process. The persons in the ships nearer to the town than we were uniformly held the same opinion. It was not until some years afterward that a doubt was created, but for the honor of our country and its good name an ascription was made of the firing of the city to accidental circumstances. It may be well that a nation in the heat and turbulence of war should endeavor to promote its interests by propagating reports of its own innocency and prowess, and accusing its enemy of flagrant enormity and dastardliness (as was done in this particular case), but when peace comes let us, in God's name, do justice to them and ourselves."

At this distance of time it is difficult to say whether the fire was or was not the result of incendiarism on the part of the disaffected Americans. Even reliable contemporaneous writers differ widely in their opinion on the subject, some affirming positively that the city was set on fire, and others, again, quite as positively affirming the contrary. Later writers, with all the facts before them and after an impartial survey, are inclined to believe that the fire was the result of a deliberate design; nor, if the newspapers and correspondence of the day can be believed, is there much room left for doubt. According to these authorities one man was seized in the act of setting fire to the College, and he acknowledged to his captors that he had been employed for the purpose. A New England captain, who was seized at the same time with matches in his pocket, also confessed the same. A carpenter, named White, was observed to cut the leather buckets which conveyed the water. "The next day, Saturday," says Steadman, in his *History of the American War*, "a great many cartloads of bundles of pine sticks, dipped in brimstone, were found concealed in cellars of houses to which the incendiaries had not had time to set fire." "The rebels," says the Rev. Charles Inglis, in writing on the same subject a few days after to the Venerable Society for the Propagation of the Gospel in Foreign Parts, "carried off all the bells in the city, partly to convert them into cannon and partly to prevent notice being given speedily of the destruction they meditated against the city by fire when it began. . . . Several rebels secreted themselves in the houses to execute the diabolical purpose of destroying the city." Notwithstanding, however, this seeming mass of testimony, it was found impossible to obtain legal proof sufficient to fasten the act upon any particular individual—for all who had been caught at the time with matches, etc., had been killed on the spot by the soldiery—and the result was that several of the citizens, who had been arrested and imprisoned on the charge of being the incendiaries, were acquitted.

Two years after this event, on August 3, an hour after midnight, a fire broke out in the store of Mr. Jones, ship-chandler, on Cruger's Wharf. Sixty-four dwelling-houses, besides stores, were consumed, and two small vessels were burned. On this occasion the firemen were assisted by the military, with Colonel Coburn and the other officers of the Thirty-fifth Regiment.

On December 9, 1796, a great conflagration, known as the "Coffee House Slip Fire," took place. It began between one and two A.M., in Robinson & Hartshorne's store on Murray Wharf (now the eastern end of Wall Street), and extended to Maiden Lane, consuming a part of the old Fly Market and rendering necessary the pulling down of another part of it. So rapid was the spread of the flames that all the buildings below Front Street, from Murray Wharf to the Fly Market, over fifty in number—many of them large and well-stocked stores— were in ashes in about four hours, and one of the engines (believed to be No. 18) was thrown into the river to save it from being burned. In this year, as in

1741, the negroes were accused of forming plots to burn down the city. In the previous year seven hundred and thirty-two persons had died from yellow fever, and the people were still nervous and excitable after that dreadful scourge. In the month of December, 1796, the Fish Market was torn down for the purpose of arresting a very destructive fire. The *Minerva* of December 9, then edited by Noah Webster, and a few years afterwards by Zachariah Lewis, when its name was changed to the *New York Commercial Advertiser*, thus notices this conflagration: "About one o'clock this morning a fire broke out in one of the stores on Murray's Wharf, Coffee House Slip. The number of buildings consumed may be from fifty to seventy—a whole block between the above slip, Front Street, and the Fish Market. The progress of the fire was finally arrested by cutting down the Fish Market."

So many fires occurring about the same time led many of the citizens to believe that the slaves were again conspiring to destroy the city. Great excitement was caused and much preparation made to guard against such a calamity. The same paper of the fourteenth instant following says: "*Serious Cause of Alarm.*— Citizens of New York, you are once more called upon to attend to your duty. It is no longer a doubt, it is a fact, that there is a combination of incendiaries in this city aiming to wrap the whole of it in flames! The house of Mr. Lewis Ogden, in Pearl Street, has been twice set on fire—the evidence of malicious intent is indubitable—and he has sent his *black man*, suspected, to prison. Last night an attempt was made to set fire to Mr. Lindsay's house in Greenwich Street. The combustibles left for the purpose are preserved as evidence of the fact. Another attempt, we learn, was made last night in Beekman Street. A bed was set on fire under a child, and his cries alarmed his family. Rouse, fellow-citizens and magistrates! Your lives and property are at stake. Double your night-watch and confine your servants."

The Common Council on the fifteenth of December, 1796, passed resolutions, offering five hundred dollars reward for the conviction of offenders, and recommended that good citizens in the several wards should arrange themselves into companies or classes, "to consist of such numbers as shall be necessary for the purpose of keeping such watch for the safety of the city." A citizen of that day, in writing to a friend, also says: "The yellow fever produced not such extraordinary commotion. The present alarm—as it is contagious—may be called the *fire fever*." The "fever," however, soon died out, as the precautions taken had the desired effect, even if there had not been any actual design or conspiracy.

In connection with the Coffee House Slip fire is an interesting story told by Mr. Philip W. Engs, who was president of the Association of Exempt Firemen in 1857: "On this occasion one of the stores was found to contain several kegs of powder, when an individual by the name of Richardson Underhill entered the store, took the powder from thence, and, placing it in an open boat, rowed off into the stream, and remained there with it until the fire was extinguished. This same person, when in the year 1798 New York was so terribly visited with yellow fever, at the hazard of his life nursed the sick and cared for the dead, and yet to the disgrace of human nature, and because in his business matters he had been guilty of improprieties, was suffered to die and be buried from our then miserably-kept almshouse (in Chambers Street). 'Ingratitude, thou marble-hearted fiend!' "

On January 17, 1800, the city was again alarmed in consequence of the occurrence of several fires. One was P. Dunstan's house in the neighborhood of the New Banks, in the northern part of the city. The second was on board the ship *Admiral Duncan* at Salter, Son & Co.'s wharf, near Old Slip. It was impossible to save the vessel, which was cut loose from the wharf. The *Admiral Duncan* drifted among the shipping, setting fire to some, bobbed about among the wharves, and was finally consumed off the Battery.

Mr. Engs again writes of a fire on May 22, 1803, at No. 37 Vesey Street, known as the New York Bread Company's Bakery. "This building," he says, "was remarkable for its thickness of walls and general strength, and had been erected by a stock company for the purpose of putting down the price of bread, in which the people were at that time much imposed upon, as well as in the quality. The general interest felt in the success of this enterprise caused great excitement when it was known the building was on fire, and strenuous exertions were made to save it. A very remarkable incident occurred at this fire. A ladder being raised to the cornice in the rear was, from the necessity of getting all the elevation possible, placed too nearly erect. Two firemen had reached its top, when the cry below was, 'The wall is falling!' One of the men slipped down by the rungs. The other, being higher up, and the cornice above him on fire, gave a sudden jerk to the ladder which threw it with great force across the yard, precipitating him through a glass window in the second story of a house, and landing him on the floor without any very serious bruises. It was supposed that the preservation of his life was owing in a great degree to his having on a fire cap, without which he could not have passed through a glass window without dangerous gashes in the head. As it was he was tolerably well scratched, but yet able to get up and go home. There is so much romance connected with this leap that it might be set down among the doubtful, were it not for the statement being confirmed by our former chief engineer, Mr. Uzziah Wenman, who, at that time a young lad, lived with his father in a house fronting on Partition (now Fulton) Street, in the rear of this fire." Here Mr. Engs makes an "odious comparison" in the following manner: "The walls of this building did not fall, and the premises were repaired, and subsequently occupied as a warehouse. I occupied it in later years, and considered it a model as to thickness of wall, by which our laws in relation to building might have been properly guided. Within two or three years that building was taken down to give place to one of those elegant warehouses which are now ornamenting that part of our city, but not one among which would bear such a heat as the Old Bakery walls endured without tumbling to the ground."

This interesting old fireman continues: "It was during this year (1803) that the Lumber Yard Fire, on the premises of Mr. Bonsel, took place, the flakes from which, when in a blaze, were blown on to St. Paul's Church steeple, at a great height from the ground, causing it to take fire, and threatening the destruction of that part of the city, the wind being very high. Despair was in every countenance, but a gallant sailor volunteered his services to climb the lightning rod, taking with him a cord, which he made fast at one end, and then let it down to the ground. A bucket was then tied to it, and, being filled with water and a tin cup placed in it, was hoisted up to the noble fellow, who, holding on to a column with one hand, used the tin pot with the other to cast on water, and extinguished the fire kindling on another column in the highest part of the steeple, thus preventing immense destruction, and doing the city a great service, which, it is gratifying to say, was not forgotten, but met with proper notice and reward." The hero's name, however, seemed of no consequence.

On the eighteenth of December, 1804, the progress of the city was again impeded for a short time by a disastrous fire, which began at two o'clock in the morning in a grocery on Front Street. The air was cold, and a high wind blowing, and the engines late in their appearance. The buildings from the west side of Coffee House Slip, on Water Street, to Gouverneur's Lane, and thence down to the East River, were swept away, and crossing Wall Street, the houses upon the east side of the slip were burned. Among them was the old Tontine Coffee House, so celebrated in its day, and which had a narrow escape in the great fire of 1835. Most of the buildings being of wood, their destruction caused new and fire-proof brick edifices to be built in their places. About forty stores and dwellings were consumed—fifteen on Wall Street, seventeen on Front, and eight on Water Street—the value of the property destroyed amounting to two million dollars. The fire was supposed to have been the work of eleven incendiaries, from anonymous letters sent to a merchant previous to the event. A reward of five hundred dollars was accordingly offered by the mayor for the apprehension of the guilty parties, but no one was arrested.

On August 25, 1808, a general alarm of fire was given at 1 A.M. It began at the soap and candle factory of Edward Watkeys, in Nassau Street. The factory was surrounded by several large wooden buildings, which soon were all in flames. The Department struggled for at least two hours, and the fire was not subdued till six buildings were destroyed. The loss of life, however, was great, for four persons perished in the flames.

The War of 1812 was a period of darkness and depression for New York, but the city's resources were additionally crippled by the terrible conflagration of May 19, of the preceding year (1811). The fire broke out on Sunday morning in Lawrence's coach factory in Chatham Street, near Duane, and raged furiously for several hours. Mr. John W. Degrauw was then a small boy in a store in the Bowery with his uncle. Passing by at the outbreak of the disaster he ran down Chatham Street crying "Fire!" and soon got the old jail bell near the City Hall ringing. A brisk northeast wind was blowing at the moment, and the flames, spreading with great rapidity, for some time baffled all the exertions of the fire-men and citizens. Between eighty and one hundred buildings on both sides of Chatham Street were consumed in a few hours. Mr. G. P. Disosway was then a Sabbath-school boy and a teacher in a public school room near by, at the corner of Tryon Row. The school was dismissed, and, as usual, proceeded to old John Street Church, while thick showers of light, burning shingles and cinders were falling all over the streets. That was the day of shingle roofs. When the teachers and scholars, their number very large, reached the church the venerable Bishop McKendall occupied the pulpit, and seeing the immense clouds of dark smoke and burning embers enveloping that section of the city, he advised the men "to go to the fire and help in its extinguishment and he would preach to the women and children." This advice was followed.

By this time the scene had become very exciting, impressive, even fearful. The wind had increased to a gale, and far and wide and high flew the flakes in whirling eddies, throwing burning destruction wherever they lit or fell. The lofty spires near by of the Brick Meeting Church, St. Paul's, and St. George's Chapel, enveloped in the flying embers, soon became the special objects of watchfulness and anxiety. Thousands of uplifted eyes were directed to these holy places, threat-ened with destruction. But there was no cause for fear. Near the ball at the top of the Brick Church a blazing spot was seen outside, and apparently not larger than a man's hand. Instantly a thrill of fear evidently ran through the bosoms of the thousands crowding the park and the wide area of Chatham Street. "They feared the safety of an old and loved temple of the Lord," says an old chronicler, "and they feared also, if the spire was once in flames, with the increasing gale, what would be the terrible consequences in the lower part of the city."

"What can we do?" was the universal question. "What in the world can be done?" was the query in everybody's mouth. The kindling spot could not be reached from the inside of the tall steeple, nor by ladders outside, neither could the most powerful fire-engine of the day force the water to that lofty height. With the deepest anxiety, fear and trembling all faces were turned in that direc-tion. At this moment of alarm and dread a sailor appeared on the roof of the church, and very soon he was seen climbing up the steeple, hand over hand, by the lightning rod, a rusty, slender piece of iron. The excitement became intense, and the perilous undertaking of the daring man was watched every moment, as he slowly, grasp by grasp, foot by foot, literally crawled upwards by means of this slim conductor. Many fears were expressed among the immense crowd, watching every inch of his ascent, for there was no resting place for hands or feet and he must hold on or fall and perish. Should he succeed in reaching the burning spot how could he possibly extinguish it, as no water, neither by hose nor bucket, could be sent to his assistance? At last he reached the kindling spot, and, firmly grasping the lightning rod with one hand, with the other he removed his tarpaulin hat from his head and by blow after blow beat out the fire. Shouts of joy and thanks greeted the noble fellow as he slowly and safely descended to the earth again. Who was the hero? He was the father of the Rev. Dr. Hague, pastor of the Baptist Church at the corner of Thirty-first Street and Madison Avenue, who died about 1871. The "Old Brick" was thus preserved from the great conflagration of that Sunday morning. The gallant sailor quickly disappeared in the crowd, and, it was said, immediately sailed abroad, with the favorable wind then blowing. A reward was offered for the generous act, but it was said an impostor succeeded in obtaining it.

The cupola of the Old Jail which stood on the spot now occupied by the Hall of Records also took fire. This was extinguished through the exertions of a prisoner "on the limits." This was the famous institution where unfortunate debtors were confined and deprived of liberty, and without tools, book, paper, or pen were expected to pay their debts. It was a kind of Calcutta Black Hole, and the inmates, having no yard, had to use the top of the building to take exercise. Here they might be seen every hour of the day. Generally discovering fires in the city, they gave the first alarm by ringing the jail bell. This became a sure signal of a conflagration, and on this occasion they saved the legal pest-house from quick destruction. The Corporation rewarded the debtor who had extinguished the blaze in the cupola. If the building had been destroyed, and its inmates saved, there would not have been much public regret at the loss, for it had been a veritable dungeon to American prisoners of war during the Revolution. After General Washington's success, in the year 1777, in New Jersey, a portion of these poor prisoners were exchanged, but many of them, exhausted by their confinement, before reaching the vessels for their embarkation home, fell dead in the streets. These are some of the historical reminiscences of the "Old Debtors'-Prison" which so narrowly escaped burning in the fire of May, 1811.

"The dependence for water at this fire," says Mr. Engs, "was entirely upon street pumps, private cisterns, and the Manhattan Works. These were plied with all the then existing means, and even the assistance of numerous females was volunteered to pass the buckets. The short supply of water and the strong wind baffled all exertions, and resort was had to pulling down some houses before the progress of the flames could be arrested. In two hours and a half 102 houses were destroyed. Scudder's Museum, situated in Chatham Street, opposite Tryon Row, prevented it spreading farther in that direction, and the open space in Tryon Row arrested its progress there. . . . The flakes had caught in forty-three places quite away from the great scene of the conflagration, and this may be accounted for, to a great extent, from the fact that the buildings were nearly all of wood, filling the air with sparks and cinders, which the heavy wind sped on to mischief. In the opinion of the engineers a stop could not be put to this conflagration without applying the hooks and razing the houses in Tryon Row and elsewhere to the ground. The Recorder, Mr. Van Wyck, had the power by law and forbade it, threatening the commanding engineer with expulsion if he gave such orders. It was no time to hesitate, and Engineer Roome, indignant at the interference, cried out, 'Come on, Hook and Ladder! and you, Pierre Van Wyck, stand on one side, or we will bury you in the ruins!' "

This fire was long remembered in the Department on account of a fatal accident. William Peterson, foreman of Engine Company No. 15, was one of the bravest and most devoted of firemen, and had often signalized himself by his exhibition of courage and zeal. While the Chatham Street fire was at its height Foreman Peterson was suddenly stricken down, overcome by his too great exertion and by exposure to the heat. He was carried home in an almost lifeless condition, and within a few hours he died. The last solemn rites were attended by the whole Department, and the chiselled marble at Greenwood tells to posterity the story of his worth. There was another accident also at this fire. Chief Engineer Thomas Franklin while attempting to pass from one street to another, both sides of which were swept by flames, was overcome by the heat, and his clothes took fire. At once he was drenched with water from the engines, and in an exhausted state was taken home. He soon recovered from his injuries.

On August 3, 1813, an accident occurred at a fire in Ross's buildings in Fulton Street (then called Fair Street), near Broadway, which for long after gave work for the lawyers. Jeremiah B. Taylor, who had no connection with the Department, and, it is said, was not a citizen, was looking on at the burning building, standing near the pipe of Engine Company No. 21. Suddenly a wall fell upon him, burying him and killing him, and cutting off a length of hose. The pipe man escaped without injury, but Foreman Howe suffered from a severe blow on the head from a falling brick. The generous-hearted firemen at once set on foot a subscription to relieve Taylor's family, and raised between seven and eight hundred dollars. His funeral was attended by the whole Department, and the expenses paid by the men. Subsequent discoveries, however, showed that the firemen's charity was misplaced, and the fund was then held for their own benevolent purposes. Taylor's heirs, however, began suit, and for years the litigation dragged its slow length along, and finally became a dead letter.

The next few years have a record of accidents. On August 31, 1815, William

Meekleworth, our old chronicler P. W. Engs and A. Lent were knocked down by the fall of the cornice of Zion Church in Mott Street, and Meekleworth was very much hurt. On December 3, 1816, George Herrick fell from the loft of Mr. Allen's store in Water Street, while on duty at a fire, was buried under some fallen bricks, and had his leg broken. On June 22, 1820, Charles W. Abrams, of Engine Company No. 18, died in consequence of injuries sustained at a fire in Broadway, and was buried in Trinity Church yard. The fatal fire in Broadway began at Cram's distillery, and thirty-six houses were burned. Early in the present century turpentine distilleries were allowed to be erected on and about the old Collect, between Orange and Rynders Streets, considered in 1820 to be the upper part of the city. These distilleries would burn out two or three times a year, calling for machines to be drawn to them from the distant parts of the city without being able to do any good, as it was impossible to arrest the flames by water, and there were no houses so near as to be much in danger. The nuisance became so great that firemen and other citizens applied to the authorities to forbid their location within the "lamp and watch district," and the distilleries were finally driven out. On January 24, 1821, at three A.M., an alarming fire broke out in a house in Front Street, near Crane's Wharf, which destroyed twenty-four buildings and did much injury to seven others. A number of vessels at the wharf were also injured. The weather was so cold that the hose was with difficulty kept from freezing.

The Department suffered a loss at a fire at a ship-yard on March 24, 1824. It occurred in the yard of Adam & Noah Brown, bounded by Stanton Street, Houston Street, Goerck Street, and the East River. There were two steamboats and two ships on the stocks, under cover of the ship-house. Early as was the hour, half the city seemed aroused and hastened to the scene of the conflagration. The firemen rapidly put their engines to work, but their enemy had got a good way ahead of them. The steamboats on the stocks were nearly finished, and Mr. Adam Brown, who was present, determined to make an attempt to launch them. A strong force of workmen and citizens was got together, and the effort was made. They were aided by the firemen, especially by Engine No. 33, under Foreman James P. Allaire and Assistant Foreman Ebenezer Worship, who endeavored to check the flames at that point. But in vain; the conflagration spread so rapidly that the workmen were driven from the vicinity of the stocks, and the attempt had to be abandoned. Engine No. 33 stood her ground bravely; but, unfortunately, was in a moment almost surrounded by fire. "Jump for your lives!" cried hundreds of spectators who saw the peril of the men. Some of the firemen were able to get away, but Charles Forrester, Philander Webb, Jeremiah Bruce and Harry Esler had to jump into the river to escape the flames. They were quickly rescued, but their engine was destroyed, nothing remaining of it but a blackened scrap-heap. The fire now raged furiously and unchecked, and in the space of an hour every vessel and all the property in the yard were burned.

A still sadder event occurred on March 8, 1827, when two firemen were killed. It was during a fire at Bowen & Co.'s store in Maiden Lane. A ladder had been placed against the building to enable the firemen to get their hose to play into the interior. David W. Raymer, of No. 40 Engine, stood at the top, Assistant Foreman Francis Joseph, of No. 1 Engine, under him, and just below a third man. The smoke and flame that poured out of the windows obscured the top of the building so that no one perceived the wooden cornice was tottering. Without the slightest warning down it crushingly came, smashing the ladder and burying three men. There was a simultaneous rush of firemen to the spot to extricate their unfortunate comrades. Quicker than it takes to write the words, the blazing cornice was removed, flung aside, and the wounded men lifted tenderly out. It was found that Raymer and Joseph were very severely injured, but that the third man had escaped with trifling hurts. Raymer and Joseph were conveyed to hospital, but the former survived only an hour, and the latter died before morning. There was universal mourning for those brave men, for they were well known and liked for many estimable qualities. The two were buried on the same day, the Fire Department attending the joint funeral in a body. The Department collected a handsome sum of money for Raymer's destitute widow and orphans. Fifty years afterwards Mr. Charles Forrester, of No. 33 Engine, which was destroyed in 1824, was giving reminiscences of the old days, and remarked that firemen were more reckless in those times than in later years. "They didn't care so much for their lives," said Mr. Forrester, "they ran up slate roofs, for instance, in a most careless fashion."

In reference to the deaths of Raymer and Joseph the *Commercial Advertiser* of that date had the following pertinent remarks: "Thus we have lost two valuable members of the Society by the careless manner in which buildings are suffered to be erected in this city, and until we have a law clearly defining the manner in which houses should be constructed the lives of our firemen will be endangered not only by overhanging wooden gutters and cornices, but in many other respects. One of the morning papers speaking of the melancholy accident of yesterday suggests the propriety of the more general use of copper gutters which are secured in such a manner to the building as to prevent their falling in case of fire."

In May, 1828, many fires had occurred in the upper part of the town, and it was supposed they were the work of incendiaries. The greatest of them occurred on the twenty-sixth, when the Bowery Theater was destroyed. A colored man was apprehended on suspicion, and he confessed to having been hired to set fire to the building. The fire originally broke out in Chambers & Underhill's livery stable in Bayard Street, about a quarter before six o'clock in the evening. The wind blew freshly from the southwest, and in a few minutes six or seven wooden buildings in the vicinity were enveloped in flames. The firemen could not prevent their progress, the buildings being full of combustible materials. The fire soon communicated to the Bowery Theater, both in front and in the rear in Elizabeth Street. The flames were driven by the wind full upon the play-house, whose side wall was fire proof, with iron shutters to the windows. At length the wooden cornice took fire. The flames singeing the ends of the rafters were driven violently into the interior of the building. A pyramid of flame rose from the burning roof to an immense height with a dazzling intensity of brightness and heat that drove back the bystanders, and shed over the city a light like that of day. The roof, chimneys, and the west wall shortly after fell, and the fire raged inside about three hours. But when the cornice fell it brought down death with it. John Bradshaw, of Engine Company No. 21, was at work beneath it and was crushed to death. It was impossible to rescue the body, and it was not until weeks after that the mangled remains could be dug out. A young man, Benjamin Gifford, Jr., who lived at No. 139 Madison Street, and who used to run with the engines, was also supposed to have perished in the ruins. Bradshaw's funeral, at No. 2 Liberty Street, was attended by his company. The Rev. Mr. Feltus officiated and delivered a very appropriate and feeling address to the fireman.

The buildings beyond the theater were also consumed with much rapidity, being full of ardent spirits and other inflammable articles. At one period of the conflagration the gas in the pipes which supplied the theater became ignited, and the effect which its instantaneous combustion produced on the distant spectators was like that of lightning. Others supposed it was the explosion of gunpowder. An individual was on the roof of the theater when the flames began to envelop it. He escaped with great hazard from his peril by letting himself drop from the eaves about twenty feet to the roof of an adjacent building. Part of the rear wall fell during the night and the remainder fell in the morning.

When the fire first broke out, there was great difficulty experienced in getting a supply of water, and it was not until a line of engines was formed, extending from the scene of the conflagration to the East River at Catherine Slip, and another line from the corporation supply engine at the corner of Leonard and Elm Streets, that the fury of the flames could be arrested. The engine from Yorkville was brought down by three horses, and the firemen of Brooklyn assisted with promptness and activity. It was not until eleven o'clock that the fire was subdued. All the properties of the Bowery Theater were destroyed, and some persons escaped from it with difficulty. Mrs. Gilfert, the wife of the manager, was to have had a benefit, and as a full house was expected, it was a fortunate circumstance that the fire broke out before the hour of admission. The roof of the building was sheeted with lead, which soon melted from the intensity of the heat. Sixty thousand dollars insurance had been effected which did not cover the whole loss. Five horses and several carriages and gigs were destroyed in the livery stable. The Shakespeare Tavern, kept by D. Scribner in the Bowery, was burned.

The *Commercial Advertiser* of May 28 (ten days after the fire) said:

It is very much to be regretted that the police, with the mayor at the head of it, should not be prompt and efficient on such occasions. The watch was not seen on Monday when the first fire broke out, and very few constables made their appearance on the ground. The consequence was that an idle crowd, with a whole gang of thieves and pickpockets, interrupted the operations of the firemen, and prevented property from being saved if they did not actually assist in its destruction. When the mayor was compelled to preside as a judge in the sessions, half the year round, we well recollect that the duties of the office, as related to the Police Department, were faithfully attended to by Messrs. Clinton and Colden, and that all the officers were required to attend on occasions of fire. Such was also the case with Mr. Hone after the judicial functions of the office were removed. He was indefatigable as a police officer, and generally among the first on the ground at a fire. The presence of the mayor is not only necessary to control the spectators, who can do no good, but to inspirit the firemen, to whose laudable exertions he should be a witness.

The *Morning Courier* of the day of the fire had the following notice:

BOWERY THEATER.—A CARD. —Mrs. Gilfert's Benefit. Mrs. Gilfert respectfully announces to her friends and the public that, having recovered from her recent severe indisposition, her benefit, which in consequence of that event was postponed, will take place this evening, the 26th inst. Upon this occasion will be performed the TRAGEDY OF THIRTY YEARS; or, the Life of a Gambler—heretofore received with the most distinguished approbation. The part of Georgette, for this night only, will be personated by Miss Sophia Gilfert, being her first appearance. THE HUNDRED POUND NOTE will also be presented, the part of Billy Black by Messrs, Roberts and Chapman. Mdme. Labassee will dance her favorite *pas seul*, "I've been roaming." Mons. Barbere and Mad'slle Celeste will appear in a grand *pas de deux*. Seiltanzer Herr Cline will perform on the elastic cord, displaying many novel and highly effective evolutions. ☞Seats may be secured at the box office.

The large number of fires previous and subsequent to the burning of the Bowery Theater caused the various insurance companies to offer a reward of one thousand dollars for the apprehension and conviction of any incendiary.

The year 1829 was prolific of misfortunes to the Department. There were many fires, but though not serious in themselves they proved disastrous to the firemen. At a fire in a dwelling house in Broome Street, near Sheriff, on April 23, a ladder had been raised to facilitate the efforts of the hosemen. On the ladder were Messrs. Conklin, Titus and Chappell, of No. 14 Engine, and William Stoutenburgh, of No. 5 Engine. Without any sign of warning the front of the building suddenly fell outwards, breaking the ladder in two and burying the men in the ruins. Their escape from death was miraculous. In a few seconds the firemen were extricated, and, strange to say, only one was found to have sustained any serious injury. This was Titus, who soon recovered. Much the same kind of accident happened on July 9 to members of Hook and Ladder Company No. 1. At a fire in a four-story store, No. 28 South Street, some of the men were injured by the falling of a ladder, and several other firemen were buried in the ruins of the fallen gable end of the building. They were all saved from death, but some of them were so severely injured that at first it was thought they would die. Happily they recovered. A tremendous storm struck the city some few weeks after, on August 15, and at half-past three in the morning the lightning set fire to a house at the corner of Mulberry and Hester Streets. The Secretary of No. 21 Engine makes a satirical remark at the end of his report of this occurrence: "The engine was dragged to the fire," he says, "through one of the most severe storms of thunder and rain experienced for many years, the flashes of lightning following each other almost instantaneously, and the rain pouring down in torrents. It was also slyly reported (how true I know not) that some of the members—rather short, to be sure—had to put their swimming powers in operation to reach the fire."

Three fatal accidents occurred in 1832. On July 5, Cornelius Garrison, a member of Engine Company No. 32, was killed at a fire, and on September 25, Nathaniel Brown and James Hedges, members of Engine Company No. 42, met the same fate.

The City Hotel was burned on April 24, 1833. This vast structure occupied the whole block west of Broadway, between Cedar and Thames Streets. It was about one hundred feet in length by sixty feet in breadth. It was owned by John Jacob Astor, who purchased it about 1830 at a cost, including the land, of more than one hundred and twenty thousand dollars. It was one of the most exciting fires of the period, from the narrow escapes attending it and for the gallantry of ex-Chief Engineer U. Wenman. About ten in the morning smoke was seen issuing from the roof of the hotel, south end, rear side. At first a barrel of water would have extinguished it, but the great height of the building rendered it inaccessible to the firemen, and the consequence was that in a short time the southern half of the roof was in a blaze, sending its immense volumes to the skies, and in half an hour the northern part of the roof had shared the fate of the rest. As soon as the fire had descended within reach of the firemen's powers, they poured in upon it a flood of water from every direction, and finally subdued the flames, leaving the three lower stories uninjured, except by water. The upper story, as well as the attics of the roof, was destroyed, except the walls. In the attempt to check the progress of the fire, eleven persons ascended the upper story, immediately under the roof. Among them Mr. Jennings, the keeper of the hotel, Mr. Uzziah Wenman, who the year before was chief engineer, Mr. Charles Baldwin, lawyer, Mr. Thomas Austin, a city auctioneer, Mr. A. S. Fraser, a clerk of Mr. Aaron Clark, and Mr. James Thompson. Absorbed in their work of trying to save the building, they did not notice the progress of the flames. The greater part of the ceiling of the upper story fell, and the fire then rushed up the scuttle and cut off their retreat by the staircase. The structure was so high that no ladder could be raised to relieve them, nor even near enough to throw a rope by which they might descend. In this perilous situation, on the verge of the roof, and the raging element making frightful advances toward them, they had for some time a melancholy prospect of being crushed by the fall of the burning timbers around them. One or two exclaimed, "We are lost!" Long ladders were spliced, but for some moments all efforts to reach them were in vain. Calmness was recommended in this dreadful emergency. The ex-chief with an axe which he had brought with him cut away the skylight. Samuel Maverick, an exempt fireman, was in the story beneath, and, by extraordinary effort, with the assistance of a flag-staff, sent up the end of a drag rope. Providentially it stuck fast. Assistant Alderman Day, of the Eighth Ward, took this drag rope, which was very heavy, and about one hundred and fifty feet in length. Nevertheless, he made several coils, and ran with it along the gutter, where a slight inclination or false step would have dashed him to the ground. Mr. Wenman seized the rope and fastened it to the dormer casement. He then began lowering his companions, beginning with Charley Baldwin, who was much larger than himself. The situation was watched with great anxiety. Broadway was lined with people from Rector Street to the Park, and the adjoining roofs, windows and balconies were filled with spectators. The work of destruction proceeded rapidly, and the flames burst through the roofing with such violence as to throw the tiles off in masses, which tumbled down upon the pavement below, to the imminent danger of the firemen and others beneath.

When all his companions had been relieved, a ladder was brought to the interior of the fourth story, which reached to the attic, and on that Mr. Wenman was enabled to descend. His hands had been much cut by holding to the rope while he was letting down the other men. One of these imperilled persons had given up all hope, but he manifested a great degree of coolness. He waved his hands to his friends below, bidding them, as he believed, a last farewell. For a long time the rumbling of scarcely a cart or carriage was to be heard in that part of the city. Business seemed to pause while the work of destruction was going on.

There were some casualties, but not of any moment. One of the hook and ladder men of No. 2 was somewhat severely cut in the face by the falling of a tile from the roof. He had his wound dressed, and then manfully returned to his duty. Another man was badly scalded by the molten lead falling on him. Although the destruction of property was immense, yet it was calculated that, by the excellent supply of water from the hydrants, one hundred and fifty thousand dollars' worth of property was saved. The damage to the building was about ten thousand dollars; insured. The occupant, Chester Jennings, was also insured to a much greater amount than his loss. The hotel was crowded with guests, and for days before applicants had been refused.

The first trouble of any account between the firemen of the city of New York and the authorities was the "Bailey trouble," which occurred in 1828. John P. Bailey, who was the foreman of United States Engine Company before John Ryker, Jr., and who was a manager in the old Sugar House at the corner of Church and Leonard streets, was in command of his company at a fire, and refused to allow Thomas Shephard, the Assistant Alderman of the Fifth Ward, to go through the fire lines. Shephard left threatening vengeance, and on August 11, 1828, had Bailey dismissed. The firemen thought this unjust, and at the next fire, which proved to be at the Vauxhall Garden, which then ran through from the Bowery to Broadway, after they had done their duty and put out the fire, they turned their caps and dragged the engines home by the tail ropes, and gave other evidences of their feeling in the matter. The affair created great excitement at the time, and Bailey was finally reinstated in his command.

CHAPTER XIV

OTHER DESTRUCTIVE CONFLAGRATIONS

Accidents to Firemen.—Two Hundred Families Rendered Homeless.—The Calamity at Niblo's Old Theater and Burning of the New.—The Bowery Theater in Flames Three Times.—An Old Play Bill.—Revolt of the Firemen on Account of Chief Gulick.—Introduction of Politics.—Destruction of the Old National Theater.—A Scene of Magnificence and Splendor.—A Million Dollar Conflagration in Water Street.

On April 30, 1833, at eleven o'clock at night, a destructive fire began in the large stable of Kipp & Brown, corner of Hudson and Bank Streets, in that part of the city then called Greenwich Village, and which old newspapers describe as being two miles from Wall Street. The contents of the stables were very combustible, and large flakes of fire and burning shingles fell upon the buildings adjoining which caught almost immediately. The wind was from the eastward, and its strength helped to spread the flames. In the stables were forty-seven horses, and their agonizing cries were dreadful to hear. It was impossible to save them, they were all burned, and next morning they were found lying in rows, side by side, just as they had stood in their stalls. The population in that part of the city was very dense, very many were foreigners, and few were above comfortable circumstances. The houses were generally two stories, many of them with brick fronts. In less than twenty minutes the block bounded by Hudson, Bank, Greenwich, and Hammond Streets, and containing sixty or seventy dwellings, was destroyed. One hundred and fifty or two hundred families were rendered homeless. The scene of confusion and consternation was almost indescribable. A hundred or more families who had removed their furniture to places supposed by them to be secure were seen flying in every direction before the fury of the all-devouring element. In many instances furniture, after being removed, was destroyed by fire. Through the dense cloud of smoke and burning cinders children half naked were to be seen running to and fro, crying for their parents, and parents in despair shrieking the names of their children. Among those who exerted themselves to arrest the progress of the flames were Aldermen Murray, Whiting, Robinson, and Peters, who remained on the ground till morning. The fire was said to have been caused by a woman to revenge herself on a man who had slighted her. The loss was about one hundred and fifty thousand dollars.

On September 5, 1833, on the way to a fire, Engine No. 41 and Engine No. 37 were running a race with the characteristic emulation of the day. It was almost a neck-and-neck affair, and along the route hundreds of persons ran cheering the contestants. No. 41 was just about passing its rival, when a horse and wagon ran into the head of the rope. It was at a corner around which the wagon was coming. The men, taken unaware, let go their hold of the rope, and several were thrown down, and among them Mr. Sutton. Mr. Sutton was struck by the king-bolt of the engine and dragged some distance. This put a stop to the race, and that gentleman was picked up much injured. A more serious event happened on March 7, 1834. A fire broke out in the store of Maitland, Kennedy & Co., at Front and Depeyster Streets, at which Mr. John Knapp, of Engine No. 32, was killed. The firemen were doing good work, and though it was seen that the building would be gutted, the men had the satisfaction of knowing that they were confining the fire to that building. Mr. Knapp was standing in the doorway playing on the flames with the pipe which he held. His comrades suddenly noticed the front wall bulging and gave the alarm. Knapp dropped the pipe to effect his escape, but before he had got a few steps from the building he was overwhelmed by the falling torrent of bricks. Bruised, mutilated, disfigured, Mr. Knapp was taken from under the mass, but life was extinct. The dismay among the men of No. 32 was inexpressible. Placing their dead comrade upon their engine, they detached their hose and sorrowfully bore the body home.

A few months subsequent to this, on July 1, another calamity occurred. We quote the details from the minutes of Engine Company No. 13: "This morning, about a quarter before three A.M., a fire was discovered in the store of Haydock, Clay & Co., 273 Pearl Street. The entire stock of goods was destroyed and also the building. Toward the latter part of the fire an accident happened which cast a gloom over the happiness of a large and highly respectable body of young men belonging to the Fire Department—the death of Messrs. Eugene Underhill and F. A. Ward, both members of this company. They died in the honorable and fearless discharge of their duty. What made their sudden death more deeply felt was that there seemed an unusual flow of spirits among the company who were almost to a man witnesses of the scene and standing near the building when the wall fell, and many of them had been in the building during the fire and almost by a miracle escaped. On Wednesday, second instant, they were followed to the grave by a large concourse of citizens. The procession started from Broadway down Beekman Street to Pearl Street, when the procession halted to receive the remains of Mr. Ward, then moved up Madison to Market, up Market to Henry Street, where the procession then halted again to receive the remains of Mr. Underhill.

Order of Procession.

First,

The Head of Fire Department.

With the Fire Department Banner, then Members of the New York and Brooklyn Fire Departments with Banners placed at Equal Distance in the procession. Then the Hearse containing the Body of Mr. Ward.

Supported by Eight Pall Bearers in the following order:

KNAPP,		FITZGERALD,
MILLER,		FRANKLIN,
GLARHAM,	WARD.	C. MILLER,
SHARP,		MITCHELL.

The Friends and Relations of the Deceased.

J.T. MOORE,		TOMPKINS,
MICHALETTI,		MACY,
SILLECK,	E. UNDERHILL.	VARIAN,
GRAHAM,		PHILLIPS.

The Friends and Relatives of Mr. Underhill, then the Members and Volunteers of our Company Followed by the Members of No. 10.

"The procession moved up Henry Street to Gouverneur Street, through Gouverneur Street to Grand, down Grand to Broadway, up Broadway to Houston Street, through Houston to Varick Street to the burying-ground. The procession then opened from the front so as to let the left of the line countermarch into the yard.

"They were buried as they were found, *Side by Side*. One Monument will Cover the Remains of those two Young Men who were Cut off in the prime of life—the Dawn of Manhood. Peace to their ashes."

And now we come to one of the most memorable years in the fire history of New York—1835. To that great conflagration, so sweeping and so dire in its results, we feel it necessary to devote special chapters which follow this one. It was a year in which a fire fiend seemed to have taken possession of the city. We will mention here only one or two fires which, though large, were yet dwarfed by the terrible calamity of December 16. On June 8 no less than two hundred families (as in 1833) were rendered homeless by a fire that broke out in the rear of 209 Elizabeth Street. It was a fearful night for that thickly populated district. Every building on the block bounded by Prince, Mott, Elizabeth, and Houston Streets was swept away by the flames. Women and children fled screaming from the roaring element, and considering the little army that had been housed in the burning buildings, it was marvelous how any escaped with their lives. The firemen behaved splendidly in getting these people safely away.

On September 17 Niblo's Garden had a narrow escape. For a neighbor it had a fireworks manufactory. About one o'clock in the afternoon the spontaneous combustion of some articles took place. Three or four explosions in rapid succession alarmed every one in the locality, and the firemen were called. Before they reached the scene, however, the fire had spread to Niblo's Garden, damaging it to the extent of fifteen thousand dollars. But a fatality was a still sadder result of the conflagration. The persons employed in the theater, and who were preparing for the evening performance, had barely time to escape before the building was enveloped in flames. A colored boy named Isaac Freeman was slow in getting out. In the upper part of the building two firemen were fighting the conflagration. One was Fire Warden Purdy, Jr., of the Tenth Ward (a son of Alderman Purdy), and the other W. Harris, of No. 2 Company. Volumes of thick black smoke accompanied by tongues of fire suddenly rolled around them. The firemen called to Freeman to get on his knees and crawl along with them. But Freeman was almost instantly suffocated, and Purdy and Harris then made a dash through the flames and with difficulty got through a window. They crawled along the gutters, and at last, amid the congratulatory shouts of the crowd, succeeded in reaching a ladder. Purdy's left hand was badly burned and his hair and face scorched. Harris escaped without injury. The fire did not prevent a concert taking place next night as announced. It was Mons. Gillaud's Benefit Concert, at which Signorina Albina Stella, Mrs. Franklin, Signor Montressor, and other well-known artists of the day assisted. The loss was about fifteen thousand dollars.

In early years a circus called the "Stadium" was established on the northeasterly corner of Broadway and Prince Street. These premises were purchased when Bayard's farm was sold off in lots by Mr. Van Rensselaer, and occupied the site of the Metropolitan Hotel and Niblo's Garden. Shortly after the War of 1812 the enclosure was used as a place for drilling militia officers who were cited to appear at the "Stadium" for drill. The circus edifice was surrounded by a high fence, the entrance being on Prince Street. Afterwards two brick buildings were erected on Broadway, one of which was for some time occupied by James Fenimore Cooper, the novelist. William Niblo, previously proprietor of the Bank Coffee House in Pine Street, removed to this locality in the year 1828, and established a restaurant and public garden. In the center of the garden was still remaining the old circus building, which was devoted by Mr. Niblo to exhibitions of theatrical performances of a gay and attractive character, which soon attained such popularity as to induce him to erect a building of more pretensions as a theater. This edifice was constructed even with a line of Broadway, but having a blank face on that street, the entrance being from within the garden. The latter was approached from Broadway. The interior of the garden was spacious and adorned with shrubbery, and walks lighted up with festoons of lamps.

Five days afterward the famous Bowery Theater was burned. This unfortunate playhouse has had many such experiences. One of the first was on November 20, 1826, and was in consequence of a flaw in a gas pipe. The 1828 fire is already described. The accident of 1826 occurred about 5 P.M. The gas must have been escaping some time, as the moment a lamp was lighted the flames ran up to the gallery. They burned through the gallery in the saloon, but fortunately no great damage was done. The fire was extinguished by buckets only, without the aid of the engines. On September 22, 1835, however, it was entirely destroyed. The fire began, singularly enough, about the same hour, 5 P.M. In a short time, notwithstanding the efforts of the Fire Department, the edifice was a total loss. Engine Company No. 26 was indefatigable amid the falling timbers. One of its members, George Mills, had his leg crushed by a falling beam, and it was feared that he would lose the limb. Mr. T. J. Parsons, in the employ of Messrs. Benedict & Benedict, of Wall Street, was also injured by a beam which fell on his head. An inventive genius of the time, Matthew Carey (at that date a very old man), had suggested the plan of covering adjacent buildings, while a fire was in progress, with wet carpets, blankets, etc., a plan which was the forerunner of the present method of the Fire Insurance Patrol. His scheme was tested at this fire, and, it was said, proved eminently successful in saving property. Forty-five minutes after the outbreak the roof and part of the rear wall fell in. Half an hour afterward the front wall came down, injuring the persons named above and several others. One hundred and fifty thousand dollars were swallowed up. The building and lot were owned by Hamblin, Hamilton & Gouverneur. Hamblin was the sole owner of the scenery, properties, wardrobe, etc. Miss Medinas, one of the actresses, lost twenty thousand dollars, which included manuscript copies of "Norman Leslie," "Rienzi," "Pompeii" and "Lafitte." Mr. Gates, an actor, lost five hundred dollars. On the previous evening, Miss Waring, an actress, had met with a very serious accident. During the performance one of her legs was fractured. Nevertheless, it was declared that this fire was a fortunate occurrence for the city. The theater had stood in the way of opening Canal Street, and it was thought that the destruction of the large and expensive edifice would permit the proposed plan to go into execution. The theater was rebuilt on an enlarged scale—indeed, made the largest edifice in the city, but it met the same fate in the following year, and the occurrence is described further on.

The city had only a brief respite before it experienced another series of memorable fires. A notable circumstance occurred on February 18, 1836. The extensive printing and book manufacturing establishment in Mulberry Street, widely known as the Methodist Book Concern, was burned. Nothing of value could be rescued except the account books of the *Christian Advocate and Journal*. In the morning fragments of burnt books were found on Long Island. As in 1835, the night was intensely cold, and the hydrants frozen, so that it was impossible to procure water. The singular circumstance was that one of the fragments found on Long Island was a charred leaf of the Bible, containing the sixty-fourth chapter of Isaiah. Very little of the leaf was legible, except the eleventh verse of that chapter, which reads: "Our holy and our beautiful house, where our fathers praised thee, is *burned up with fire*, and all our pleasant things are laid waste." This discovery occasioned much comment at the time. More than two hundred persons were thrown out of employment. The loss of this establishment and its valuable presses and stereotype plates was severely felt by the Methodist Episcopal denomination, the accumulation being the result of forty years of persevering industry, and the calamity occurring at a most unfavorable time, the Great Fire of '35 having rendered bankrupt many of the insurance offices.

In this year (1836) we strike upon a portion of the history of the old Fire Department, where its members allowed their personal predilections to overcome their sense of public duty. The trouble originated in the famous fire of the preceding year. The citizens, as well as the press, on the day after the December conflagration of 1835, laid great stress on Chief Engineer Gulick's ability as a fireman, many claiming that it was his fault that the fire had gained such headway and that so much property was destroyed. They never gave it a thought that the firemen had been up two nights before, or the lack of water. Gulick was a very determined, independent, outspoken man, and when his pride was piqued, especially as to his qualifications as a fireman, he was up in a jiffy. He stood six feet two inches, was stout, and said to have been the finest looking man in the Department. The result of the many rumors caused the Common Council, who in those days had control of the Department, to order an investigation to be made. The discussion continued until May, 1836, when the Fire and Water Committee held a special meeting, at which Alderman Paul, of the Fourth Ward, made a long speech in denunciation of Gulick, charging him with having done certain things at the fire that was the means of aiding its extension in place of arresting its progress. Gulick was standing in the lobby at the time, while the room was crowded with citizens and firemen, all deeply interested in the proceedings. Gulick became quite excited over what old Paul stated, and he gave the alderman the lie, and left the room. At the conclusion of the meeting the committee went into secret session, and unanimously agreed to report in favor of removing Gulick at the next meeting of the Board, which was to be held on the following day.

About the time they were to convene (May 4, 1836) a fire broke out in Union Market, at the junction of Houston and Second Streets. Gulick was not aware at that hour what decision the Fire and Water Committee, had arrived at, but while at work at the above fire, which consisted of two small brick buildings, Charles G. Hubbs, of Engine Company No. 13, whom it seemed had learned the secret intention of the Fire and Water Committee, came up to Gulick and told him what he had heard. Gulick would not believe it at first, but when assured by Hubbs that it was so, Gulick went away from the fire, turning his cap as he did so. The men saw at a glance that something was wrong. Several ran after him, and soon learned that he was to be their chief no longer. The fire had been nearly subdued, when the firemen started for home. About an hour afterward it broke out anew, when all the firemen came on the ground with their apparatus, and their hats turned. They refused to go to work, when Charles H. Haswell, foreman of Engine Company No. 10, mounted the box of his engine and made a long speech to the men, contending that the removal of Gulick was an insult to the Department, and that his command should not go to work, let the consequences be what they might. So the firemen all agreed to side with Haswell. At this stage of the proceedings Carlisle Norwood, President of the Lorillard Insurance Company in 1875, came on the ground, and, seeing the state of affairs (the fire still raging at the time), went to Haswell and appealed to him not to create discord among the men. Haswell was unrelenting, and while Norwood stood conversing with him, John Coger, foreman of Engine No. 8, afterward assistant engineer, came up. Norwood appealed to Coger to get his company to work, as there was no knowing where the fire would terminate unless some efforts were made to arrest its progress. Coger consented to put his men on the brakes, but had no sooner brought a stream to bear on the fire than his hose was cut in several places. Several of the leading firemen, with Mr. Norwood, now consulted together as to what was best to be done; it was finally decided that the only hope lay in getting Gulick to return to the fire, and for him to get the men to go to work. Thereupon Benj. H. Guion, one of the Fire Wardens, went in search of Gulick, and succeeded, after repeated entreaties, in getting him to resume command of the Department until the fire was extinguished. As Gulick hove in sight cheer after cheer rent the air from the members of the Department. He marched down among the men, with Carlisle Norwood on the one side, and Mr. Guion on the other, and exclaimed to the members of the Department: "Now, boys, let's all go to work and put out this fire, and we will attend to the Fire and Water Committee afterward." And so they did with a will, and the fire was soon after extinguished.

Just previous, however, to Gulick's reaching the fire the last time, word had been sent down to Mayor Lawrence of the demoralized condition of the firemen, and the great destruction of property that was sure to follow. The mayor started post haste to the scene, and undertook to direct the firemen, but they paid no attention to his orders. They hooted at him, and cheered incessantly for Gulick.

The result was that the mayor was finally compelled to leave, and started for his office swearing vengeance on Gulick for the insults offered him by the firemen. On reaching the City Hall he found the Common Council in session; he at once made known to them the state of affairs at the fire, and urged the removal of Gulick at once. The result was that his wishes were complied with. The news spread like wildfire throughout the city—the Common Council having appointed, as chief, John Riker. When the firemen learned that Gulick had been decapitated, they called special meetings and passed resolutions that Gulick must be reinstated, or they would abandon their engines. Efforts were made to induce Riker to resign, but without avail. The several companies kept on doing duty, but all the while urging the reinstating of Gulick. When they found that the Common Council would not accede to their requests, they marched up to the City Hall in a body and tendered their resignations. The course thus pursued by the men was in no way aided by Gulick, as he remonstrated against their withdrawing from the Department on his account.

Many of the old exempt firemen and citizens seeing that the city was now without a department, tendered their services, and took command of the several companies. The old members then organized themselves into what was known as the "Resigned Firemen's Association." Wm. Corp, foreman of Engine Company No. 4, and in after years paying teller of the Bank of New York, was chosen president. So matters jogged along until autumn, Riker remaining chief, when the firemen got together and nominated Gulick for Register. They then appointed a committee to wait on the Tammany Hall Convention, to request them to endorse Gulick, nearly all the firemen being Democrats in those days. As Tammany would not agree to their demands, they waited on the Whig party, the latter having always been in the minority, and they were very willing to take up Gulick. The result was that he was elected by over seven thousand majority.

The following spring the firemen dovetailed with the Whigs again, and for the first time the Whigs got the control of the Common Council, each candidate, however, on the Whig ticket being pledged to remove Riker, if elected. As soon as they got in power they gave the chief engineership to Mr. Corp, President of the "Resigned Firemen's Association," but he declined the honor, so they made Cornelius V. Anderson chief. Then all the old members went back into the Department. During 1836 the Common Council passed an ordinance that the Board of Foremen and Assistants should elect the chief, this being the first concession made to the firemen.

To bring this subject to a close we must skip three years and come to 1839, when the Democrats again got control of the city; they at once determined to remove Anderson. In order, therefore, to obtain a majority in the Board of Foremen and Assistants they got together twenty prominent men of their party, among whom were Oliver Charlick and Superintendent of Police John A. Kennedy. Each of the twenty got ten men and formed twenty hose companies, which the Common Council agreed to confirm as firemen, thus sending forty new votes into the Board of Foremen. The meeting at which these twenty companies were legalized was not held until near midnight, the object being to get certain members to go home before the "job" was rushed through. David Graham, a well-known lawyer, then Assistant Alderman of the Fifteenth Ward, smelt a mouse, tarried and soon learned what was going on. As the members of the Council took their seats, just fifteen minutes before twelve, Graham arose from his chair, and, in his loud, stentorian voice, exclaimed: "At this dead hour of the night you are going to do the darkest deed ever perpetrated by human being." He then took his hat and left the chamber. The "job" was, however, put through, and Edward Hoffmire, the Ring candidate for chief, was, by the addition of these forty votes, elected over Anderson by nine majority. None of these new companies had ever any location or apparatus. When Charlick used to be asked what company he belonged to he would reply: "I belong to one of these things that spins around in the middle (meaning a reel), but I have never been able to find out where she lays."

The day following Hoffmire's election the papers came out with long articles denouncing the action of the Common Council, while many of the leaders of the Democratic party saw that the successful scheme would eventually be a detriment to them politically, and, moreover, they found they were doing themselves no good by fighting the firemen; the result was that Hoffmire was never confirmed as chief engineer. Soon after the firemen passed a resolution at Fireman's Hall that no member could vote who had not been an active fireman three months, and thus killed the new hose cart members—the "June Buggs," as they were called—not over half a dozen companies ever becoming permanently organized. Anderson remained chief until relieved by Alfred Carson. Gulick was for many years in the crockery business. After serving three years as Register, he ran for a second term, but was defeated. His salary was from eighteen to twenty thousand per annum, but he lent and spent to such an extent that all he had soon vanished. He finally got down in the world, losing all ambition; in fact, he seemed humiliated at his defeat, and thought every friend had failed him, and he finally sank so low in life that he died in the most extreme poverty, and without a friend near at hand to administer to his wants.

Very many unimportant fires happened while the firemen were in this state of "passive resistance." Everybody took a hand in the discussion. In the daily papers of the period the fire engine companies published "cards" almost every morning, invariably beginning satirically thus: "Whereas the Common Council, *in their wisdom*," and ending by telling the public they, the firemen, had resigned because of the bad treatment by the aldermen of Chief Engineer Gulick. The

Morning Courier and New York Enquirer of September 24, 1836, had the following paragraph:

> This morning, at about three o'clock, a fire was discovered in the small wooden Church of the Nativity in Avenue D, one door from Fourth Street, which was entirely destroyed, and a brick building adjoining. The flames also extended to a number of small tenements in Fourth Street, which were burning when we went to press. We are sorry to add that a great number of the Fire Department were inactive lookers-on at the conflagration.

In reference to this celebrated fight the *Morning Courier and New York Enquirer* of September 26, 1836, has a long leading article, which we here reproduce in a condensed form:

> A difference has arisen between most of the fire companies of this city and the Corporation, in consequence of which many of the former at the fire which took place on Saturday morning early remained inactive spectators of the conflagration and have resigned. . . . Our intention is to avail ourselves of this opportunity to point out the necessity that exists for the introduction here of a totally new system for the extinguishment of fires. In this respect, too, it is very evident that we have not kept pace with the vast increase of the population and extent of the city. . . . When fire companies were formed, the members composing them were known to the whole community. . . . But the case is now materially altered. The firemen are still generally, it is true, held to be a very meritorious body of men, but the individuals composing it are little known or cared for. How, under this state of things, they have remained efficient so long as they have is a matter of astonishment. . . . Of late years, however, a system of pecuniary rewards to a small extent has grown up; the Chief Engineer and six assistants have had salaries allotted to them, and now the firemen generally work for nothing, though as there were loaves and fishes to be distributed they ought to have something to say in the distribution. . . .
>
> We are evidently at present arrived at that state of things that the best interests of the city imperiously require that a system for the extinguishment of fires should be introduced here commensurate with its increased extent. . . . In casting about as to what that system ought to be, the cities of the continent of Europe will afford us no guide. There fires are so very rare, and fire insurance so little resorted to, that the cases are not at all similar. In London it is different. There fires are frequent—though not as frequent as here—and insurance against fires is generally resorted to. Now we find in London that the measures adopted for the extinguishment of

fires are under the control of the Fire Insurance Companies, and indeed that they cheerfully defray the greatest part of the expense. . . . It is their duty and interest to investigate the causes of fire. . . . The fire engines in London are chiefly built at the expense of the fire companies—they too pay the firemen. These firemen are ticket-porters, watermen, mechanics, etc., who can readily quit their occupations when a fire occurs.

After describing the emulation of the London firemen and their rewards, the *Courier* continues:

We are not prepared to say that it would be desirable to introduce a system of pay here at once, but that it will eventually be necessary we have no doubt. A gradual adoption of it would probably work best. Pay to the head engineer and to one or two men employed in taking care of the engine—by which the crowds of boys we now see about our engine houses would be avoided—is perhaps now all required. Horses should assuredly be immediately used for conveying the engines to a fire. We learn that in London the fire engine is placed ready for use in a vehicle, to which horses standing in a stable close by are immediately attached on an alarm of fire, and it is strange that so obvious an advantage should not have been introduced here. The necessity for it becomes daily more apparent as the city increases.

On May 26, 1836, Richard S. Ritchie, a member of Engine Company No. 6, was killed at a fire.

About four o'clock on the morning of July 19, 1836, a fire was discovered in the large four-story brick building, 117 Nassau Street, belonging to the American Bible Society, and used as their printing establishment by Daniel Fanshaw. There were nineteen power presses in the building, together with type, which were destroyed with the building. Loss, one hundred and forty thousand dollars.

Once more, in 1836, was the Old Bowery Theater burned down. On September 22 at 4 A.M. smoke was seen to issue from the center of the roof, and in a very few minutes the whole building was completely enveloped in flames. So sudden and so rapid was the conflagration that it was impossible to save the building when the firemen arrived at the spot. The wardrobes, the valuable properties, in fact everything was swept away, except the clock, a piano, and the large mirror of the greenroom. A man, named Frederick, who was employed as a sort of janitor, slept in the building, and had a narrow escape of his life. He managed to get, but in his night clothes, safely out into the street. The upper portion of the side walls fell on Nos. 40 and 44 Bowery, and crushed in the roofs. Mr. Hamblin, the lessee, estimated his loss at from seventy-five thousand to one hundred thousand dollars, not a cent of which was insured, the policy having expired three days before, and the negotiations for the new one had not been completed. The loss to the members of the company was very great.

At ten o'clock in the morning several people were standing in the portico of the ruins when one of the burned beams fell from aloft, striking Frederick Parsons, of No. 26 Reade Street, on the head, and injuring him severely. A boy, named Thomas Butler, living at the Bull's Head, was also struck on the shoulder, which was dislocated.

The following was the advertised programme for the performance at the Bowery Theater:

> Fourth night of the New Drama entitled "Lafitte, the Pirate of the Gulf," by Miss Louisa H. Medina, authoress of "Last Days of Pompeii," "Norman Leslie," Rienzi," and a number of other pieces.
> THIS EVENING, September 22, will be presented the Drama of LAFITTE, THE PIRATE OF THE GULF.
> Lafitte.............. Mr. Hamblin.   Theordore .... Miss Waring.
> Alphonso .... Harrison.   Constanza...........Mrs. Harrison.
> Gen. Jackson............Woodhull.   Oula.................Mrs. Herring.

Seven days after this event fire was discovered in a brick building in the rear of Guppy's large sugar house on Duane Street, at about three o'clock in the morning. The flames communicated to the sugar house, which, with its contents, was entirely destroyed. Loss, one hundred and fifty thousand dollars. The adjoining buildings were touched by the flames, but the firemen saved them. At this fire several old citizens, who for years had been on the exempt list, manned the engines, and among them was the venerable ex-alderman of the Second Ward. Soon after the fire began one or two interlopers, when they saw ex-Chief Engineer Gulick come along, attempted to raise a groan. They were immediately ordered into custody.

In the following year there was another melancholy occurrence. Fire was discovered about 4 A.M. at No. 109 Washington Street, and before the engines got to the spot the building was doomed. Hose Company No. 13 was nearest to the burning building, and the alarm was given that the walls were tottering. Thomas Horton, of No. 13, was the last to run, and was caught in the fall of the north gable end of the wall and instantly killed. He had been only a week a member of the company, and in the minute book the entry of his election was next to the record of his death. His funeral took place from No. 34 First Street, and a large number of firemen, including Chief Engineer Anderson, attended. Most of the companies carried banners draped in mourning, and on the banner borne by his own company was the inscription, "His death was occasioned in the discharge of his duty." Again, on February 6, 1838, a gallant fireman fell. At a fire in a row of buildings in Laurens Street (now South Fifth Avenue), between Broome and Spring Streets, occupied by Peter Lorillard, tobacconist, the rear wall of one of the buildings fell. John Buckloh, of Engine Company No. 19, who at the time was standing on a short ladder against the wall holding the pipe, was buried beneath the rubbish. He had a grand funeral, the mayor, the Common Council and a large body of citizens attending the obsequies.

It was at the fire in the stable in Laurens Street that a most thrilling incident occurred. The men were working away bravely and were standing on some well-filled bags. "Give them another wetting, boys," said Chief Anderson, as he was about leaving the scene. The men subsequently discovered that they had been standing over what might have been their graves—the innocent looking bags contained powder. They had been left there by a cartman, who had brought them from a packet ship late one afternoon, and, knowing that the store where they were to be deposited was closed, had taken them to his stable, intending to leave them there until morning. For some time after the firemen looked out for bags when they were called to a conflagration.

February 18, 1838, saw the ill-fated Bowery Theater destroyed for the third time. As on other occasions it occurred, fortunately, at a time when there was no performance. It began about two o'clock on Sunday morning in a carpenter shop on the third story, and in a little while the large and handsome edifice fell. The iron safe, containing money and all the books and papers of the establishment, was saved. The wardrobes, valued at seven or eight thousand dollars, were lost, and the scenery, machinery, and stage property, estimated at fifty-two thousand dollars, were also destroyed. There was no insurance on the wardrobes, scenery and other properties. Insurance to the amount of thirty-five thousand dollars had been effected upon the building, which, it was supposed, would not cover one-half of the whole actual loss. Very few of the actors had any property in the theater. Of the origin of the fire there was but one opinion—it was the work of an incendiary.

Fire broke out in the soap factory of Baurmeister & Scheplin, situated in the rear of No. 160 Hammond Street, on August 1, 1838. Before the progress of the flames could be checked large portions of the block of buildings bounded by Hammond, Washington, Perry, and West Streets were destroyed. A very large number of families were by the calamity deprived of their homes and turned out upon the world with but little more property in their possession than they carried upon their backs. By this fire fifty buildings were destroyed, the loss aggregating many thousands of dollars. On July 25, 1839, a fire broke out in the paint shop attached to a wheelwright's shop on Sixteenth Street, between Ninth and Tenth

Avenues, owned and occupied by Mr. Martin, which with the contents was entirely destroyed. The fire communicated to the next building on Sixteenth Street, and to the rear of a range of buildings on Tenth Avenue between Sixteenth and Seventeenth Streets, all of which were burned. The loss was thirty thousand dollars.

One of the most destructive fires since that of 1835 broke out on Monday afternoon, September 23, 1839. The volumes of smoke rolling over the city and the general alarm created soon spread the news of its locality—the National Theater, corner of Leonard and Church Streets. The great combustibility of the material in the building explains the rapidity with which the fire marched in its destructive course. Three fine churches shared the fate of the theater. Some of the persons employed in the latter discovered fire in the vicinity of the gas-room, which they endeavored to extinguish with a small force-pump, but in a few minutes they were compelled to beat a hasty retreat. Before six o'clock, or a little after the outburst of the flames from the roof of the theater, the fire had communicated to the French Episcopal Church, corner of Franklin and Church Streets, and to the African Church opposite, on the corner of Leonard and Church Streets. The rear gable end and a part of one of the side walls of the playhouse fell, burning the rear part of the two story brick front dwelling No. 14 Leonard Street. The Dutch Reformed Church in Franklin Street, between Chapel and Church Streets, the inside of which, together with the roof of the two story schoolhouse next adjoining, and belonging to the church, was also destroyed. It was a scene of great magnificence and splendor, and also a peculiar one. In the neighborhood of the churches were houses of ill-repute, and the unfortunate inmates of these dwellings rushed frantically out in the attire in which the alarm found them, to add to the terrific grotesqueness of the picture. Thousands of persons congregated in the vicinity, pushing and struggling from one point to another, shouting and cursing and swearing. Odd-looking stage properties were thrown from the theater, sacred vestments and furniture hurled from the churches, and flaunting finery dragged from the temporary homes of the unfortunate. Carts and wagons were pushed here and there, the excited owners of property striving to save all they could. It was a scene worthy of a painter's pencil. The clamor of trumpets and voices, the steady working of the engines, the moving masses, the screaming of women, and the helter-skelter passage of every sort of furniture borne off or heaped upon the streets; Bibles, prayer books, altar ornaments, and the sacred chalice, mixed up with gorgeous theatric costumes and tomes of Shakespeare, and librettos and scores of Rossini, Bellini, and Auber, and wardrobes and gewgaws of a more ambiguous character, thrown from houses of ill-fame on fire or threatened in the vicinity; the troops of actors, orchestral performers, the retinue of supernumeraries and scene shifters running to and fro, mingled with the cries of the colored people, of French citizens, looking unutterable despair on the combined havoc of all that was dear to them as the source of their livelihood, or upon the temple where they worshipped—all these scenes—fearful realities—defy description. The whole spectacle, in fact, the blending of things sacred and profane below, heightened by the sea of flame and smoke above, presented a lively tableau—a serio-grotesque picture. Through it all the firemen worked calmly, persistently, and successfully. But notwithstanding their efforts four hundred thousand dollars were swallowed up that evening.

In connection with this fire we meet with the name of Mr. James Wallack, the father of the famous actor, Mr. Lester Wallack. His loss was estimated at twenty-five thousand dollars—no insurance. The theater was owned by Messrs. Ayman & Co. and O. Mauran, and was leased to Mr. Wallack. The building was valued at sixty thousand dollars and insured for thirty thousand dollars. The French church was a splendid edifice of white marble, the portico in front supported by very large granite pillars. It was erected in 1822, and cost about eighty thousand dollars. The fine organ and most of the furniture were saved, but very much damaged. There was an insurance of twenty-four thousand dollars. Of the Dutch Reformed Church, the Rev. J. Harkness, pastor, only the walls remained. It was insured for ten thousand dollars. The Zion African Methodist Episcopal Church was built in 1820, and cost eighteen thousand dollars. It was insured to the full amount of its value. Numerous other buildings, dwelling houses, etc., were more or less injured—some nearly destroyed.

The above fire was destructive enough, but the next one in the month of October was a million dollar calamity. On October 5, at 11:45 P.M., the secretary of an engine company writes: "Fire corner of Eldridge and Broome; engine did not roll owing to her being out of order." An hour and a quarter after, a fire that assumed alarming proportions broke out in the fur store of Halsey & Co., in Water Street, near Fulton. The wind was blowing fresh at the time, and the flames swept through Water Street and Burling Slip, Pearl and Fletcher Streets. The United States Hotel (which previous to that time had been called Holt's) was in imminent danger. It was saved by placing wet blankets in each window fronting the fire. It was a terrible night for the Department, whose energies were taxed to the utmost. Whole blocks were swept away, and the destruction of property was enormous. For eight hours the fire lasted, illuminating the whole city. This great conflagration was considered to be second only to that of 1835. Two-thirds of the block bounded by Water Street, Burling Slip and Front Street, together with several new stores in Water Street, between Burling Slip and Fletcher Street, and two or three buildings in Fletcher Street, one of which was occupied by John T. Hall, a member of a fire company, were consumed.

The night of January 30, 1840, was an extremely busy one for the firemen. From seven o'clock in the evening until the dawn of the following morning they had scarcely any respite from their labors, one alarm succeeding another with remarkable rapidity. For the few months preceding fires had been singularly numerous, and the sound of the fire bell had fallen with regular and mournful cadence upon the tired ears of the firemen. It seemed as though the destroying angel had been sent abroad. On this night the first conflagration broke out at 7:15 P.M. in Front Street, near Broad Street, destroying a grocery. Then a fire half consumed Forker & Co.'s ship-chandlery store in South, near Dover Street. There were other alarms besides. The South Street fire had not been entirely subdued, and at three o'clock in the morning it broke out afresh. The flames communicated to the immense tea-store of Thomas H. Smith and to five other stores. Smith's was occupied as a public store. One of the five stores was the extensive one of J. J. Hix. They were all destroyed. The public store covered an area fifty by two hundred feet. The total loss was estimated at over one million dollars.

The tenderest expressions of sympathy from firemen were called forth by the death of two of their comrades on April 15, 1840. Assistant Engineer James S. Wells and James Glasgow, a member of Hose Company No. 15, were killed by the falling of a wall at a fire in Eldridge Street. A meeting of engineers, foremen and assistants was held at Firemen's Hall on the sixteenth, upon the call of Chief Engineer Anderson. Mr. Anderson proposed a funeral programme, which was approved, and on the motion of Mr. Kane, Colonel Thomas F. Peers was appointed marshal for the occasion, with the following aids: Owen W. Brennan, John Carland, John T. Rollins, George F. Ramppen, and Joseph W. Long. On motion of Mr. Suydam, Daniel R. Suydam, Carlisle Norwood and Edward Brown were appointed a committee to draft resolutions of sympathy, and reported the following:

Resolved: That in the dispensation of an all-ruling Providence by which Messrs. James S. Wells and James Glasgow have met with a sudden death, we have to deplore the loss of two valuable members of the Department— men whose private virtues and strict integrity had endeared them to all, and whose decease has left a blank in their families which cannot be filled.

Resolved: That this Department do sympathize deeply with the relatives of the deceased on this mournful event, and that they will testify the regret which they feel by attending in a body the funeral to-morrow (Thursday) afternoon, and by wearing crape on the left arm for thirty days.

Resolved: That a copy of the foregoing resolutions be forwarded to the families of the deceased, signed by the officers of the meeting and published.

May the same all-wise and beneficent Providence sustain the widow and fatherless in their affliction.

The Fire Departments of Brooklyn and Williamsburg were invited to attend the funeral. On the following day the various companies met in Canal Street. The line was formed on the north side of the street, the right resting on Hudson Street. Engine, Hook and Ladder, Hose, and Hydrant Companies No. 1 together constituted the base or right of the line; Engine, Hook and Ladder, Hose, and Hydrant Companies No. 2 were next, and in the same order to the left; Engine Company No. 49 was on the extreme left.

In May, 1841, there were several extensive fires. On the seventh five five-story warehouses were destroyed in Pearl and Water Streets. On the nineteenth four hundred thousand dollars' worth of property was destroyed in buildings whose site had been swept by the fire of 1835.

But on the twenty-ninth a still more notable fire occurred. The new National Theater had been in existence only two years since its first destruction in 1839, when it again went down before the devouring element—its destruction this time being the work of incendiaries. The manager was Mr. Burton, his stage manager Mr. Wemyss. When these gentlemen entered the house about five o'clock (it was Saturday), they were met by one of the company, Mr. Okie, who said that he thought he smelt fire. Investigation proved the accuracy of his surmise. In the prompter's box fire was found in three places, and in the pit ticket office a quantity of spirits of turpentine was discovered to have been thrown into a box of loose rubbish, and the office on fire in two places. The bottom of the rear door of the office was also found burning. These were scarcely extinguished when Mr. Russell, the treasurer, and his assistant, Mr. Glessig, found that a fire had been started under the staircase leading from the rear of the box-office to the suite of apartments above, occupied by Mr. Russell and his family. It was only with the greatest difficulty that this conflagration was extinguished. But this was not all. In a room in the second story adjacent to Mr. Russell's rooms two other fires were found burning; spirits of turpentine had been strewn over a pile of theater tickets, and in another part of the room manuscript music and other papers were on fire. These fires having been extinguished a roll of paper thrown from an upper story window into Leonard Street was found to contain a quantity of friction matches. Below was the Turkish Saloon, where a box of matches of a like kind was found. It was clear that an attempt had been made to fire the saloon also, and that there was more than one incendiary. Notwithstanding his alarming discovery Mr. Burton decided to let the performance go on.

At the close a thorough search was made of the premises, and nothing suspicious was found. At 3:30 A.M. Mr. Russell went to bed. He could not sleep, however, and at six o'clock arose, went to the stage door in the rear, and stood talking to the private watchman. In a few minutes, to the treasurer's astonishment, flames burst from different parts of the building, and with amazing rapidity they spread. Indeed Mrs. Russell had a narrow escape of her life. Her husband dashed to her room, rolled her up in the bed clothes, and with difficulty got her out of the burning building. The walls of the theater proved to be of the flimsiest, and in a short time the rear wall and the side wall on Franklin Street both gave way. It was a miracle that numbers were not crushed to death in the adjoining houses. Engineer John T. Rollins, who lived close by the theater, was on the spot in a few moments. He went inside, and found the stage blazing, and it was his opinion that the fire had been started half an hour before. Chief Engineer Cornelius V. Anderson said that within fifteen minutes of its discovery he saw the fire bursting through, at the back of the theater. He warned all the people living in the rear to clear out, for he noticed the miserable walls, unable to bear the weight of the roof, bulging and cracking everywhere. But the chief engineer's warning was too late in one instance. In Franklin Street was a notorious house, kept by Julia Brown, a woman remarkable for her good looks. She escaped, but one of her unfortunate boarders, a woman, was killed by the falling wall. Next day her body was discovered by Zophar Mills. Mr. Burton had, but a few days before, brought his valuable wardrobe from Philadelphia, and it was lost. Miss Cushman, the celebrated tragedienne, who was playing here, and Messrs. Shaw and Howard also lost heavily. Among the adjoining edifices injured or partly burned were the French Protestant Episcopal Church, the Dutch Reformed Church in Franklin Street, and the African Church on the corner of Leonard and Church Streets, opposite the playhouse. The work of destruction lasted only one hour.

On March 31, 1842, there were three fires—one of great magnitude. The whole of two large blocks of dwellings, including at least one hundred houses, was laid in ruins. At least two hundred and fifty families were rendered homeless. The fire originated in a two-story house, occupied as a grocery and dwelling. At least forty or fifty of the houses were worth from three thousand to four thousand dollars each, the aggregate being about three hundred thousand dollars, and the furniture destroyed being worth twenty or thirty thousand dollars. On May 31 J. Harker & Bros., Nos. 80 and 82 Cliff Street, publishers, lost one hundred thousand dollars in a fire.

CHAPTER XV

OLD VOLUNTEERS FIGHTING FIRE

More Fires of the Olden Time.—A Terrible Snow Storm and Burning of the Tribune Building.—The Bowery Theater Destroyed for the Fourth Time.— The Awful Fire of 1845.—Thrilling Incidents.—Niblo's Garden in Flames.— The Fearful Hague Street Disaster.—The Harpers' Fire.— The Park Street Theater.

A terrible snow storm swept over New York on February 4, 1845, and the cold was intense. At four o'clock on the morning of February 5 the office of the *New York Tribune*, occupying the corner lots Nos. 158 and 160 Nassau Street, was destroyed by fire. A boy had lighted a stove, and in half an hour the apartment was in a blaze. The fire engines were at a disadvantage in this great storm. The streets were almost impassable; some of the machines could not get out of their stations at all, and those that did could scarcely be dragged through the streets. Some of the engines were pulled a few rods, and then the task had to be given up. The hydrants were found to be frozen and had to be broken open with axes. Hence it was no wonder the *Tribune* building and the adjoining structure on the corner of Spruce and Nassau were entirely destroyed in a short time. There were some narrow escapes. One of the proprietors, Mr. Graham, and a clerk were asleep in the second story, and when aroused found the door and stairway afire and egress that way cut off. They saved themselves only by jumping from the window. The compositors in the fifth story and the pressmen in the basement got out with great difficulty. Tammany Hall was at one time in imminent danger. The rear part, connecting with the *Tribune* building, caught fire, but the firemen succeeded, by hard work, in extinguishing the flames. The publishers, Greeley & McElrath, publicly thanked the fire laddies for their labors. The office was temporarily located at No. 30 Ann Street (formerly the *New World*).

A few months after the *Tribune* fire came a greater conflagration—the total destruction, for the fourth time, of the ill-fated Bowery Theater. Indeed, this year (1845) is very remarkable for the number of disastrous fires which occurred in the city. The "new historical drama" of "Robin Hood, the Outlaw," was to have been played that evening (Friday, April 25), and Mr. Davenport, a popular actor of the period, was to have taken his benefit. As on previous occasions, the calamity was the work of a diabolical incendiary. The supposition is proved by the fact that the flames first proceeded from a vault filled with shavings under the carpenter's shop, to which there was access by a trap door. The carpenter's shop was on the south side of the theater, from which it was separated by an iron fire-proof door. It was about six o'clock when the flames were discovered, and before the fire-proof door could be closed they caught the scenery, and, like a flash, the whole house was ablaze. When the engines arrived the theater was already doomed. The carpenters and actors had manfully struggled, but in vain, to save the wardrobes. Dense volumes of smoke drove them back. The firemen mainly directed their efforts to saving the block of three-story houses opposite, and succeeded after great exertions. At first, however, there was great danger of a wide-spreading conflagration. One of the greatest calamities feared was lest the gas-house next to the theater should take fire and explode. Happily, however, the flames did not touch it. When the fire burst through the roof and windows of the playhouse the scene became one of mingled grandeur and terror. The roaring of the flames, the breaking of glass, the cracking of the burning rafters, the continuous thud, thud, of the well-manned engines, and the hoarse voices of the foremen as they gave the necessary directions, all combined to increase the excitement. In about half an hour the fire was at its height, blazing with fearful intensity. The glowing heat was almost unbearable, affecting the houses opposite; it was so intense, indeed, that those buildings were often concealed under a dense cloud of steam from the constant streams of water thrown on them by three engines. Soon the roof fell in and the fiery furnace sent forth a cloud of ignited particles, which spread to a great distance and endangered the surrounding property. About a quarter before seven the peak of the rear wall on Elizabeth Street fell outward with a fearful crash, and several persons narrowly escaped death. About ten minutes later the north half of the end wall also fell, and five minutes later the remaining half. The wind being from the northeast the heat and main body of the flame were felt most on Elizabeth Street. As the flames burst forth from the front windows and caught the heavy cornice the whole interior was revealed to those on the roofs of the opposite houses, and the furniture of the saloon, the pictures, glasses, sofas, etc., could be distinctly seen as each became a prey to the spreading flames. When the heavy cornice in front fell many persons were standing on the steps and narrowly escaped death, but some were slightly bruised. The houses on either side several times caught fire, and the roofs of some of them were destroyed. The inmates threw their furniture out of the windows, and the scene became one of disaster and confusion. The house of Mr. Cox, on the north side of the theater in Elizabeth Street, was much injured. Several small tenements in this street were nearly a total wreck, and some of the inmates escaped with difficulty. One poor woman had barely time to snatch up her two children before her room was in a blaze. She forced her way through the flames and smoke into the street. The children were uninjured, but the mother was burned in several places.

Among the buildings very considerably damaged were the Bowery Hotel (Nos. 50 and 52), Shaw's Hotel, south of the theater in the Bowery, and the store of Mr. Cort, plumber. The loss of T. S. Hamblin and James R. Whiting was very heavy. Mr. Hamblin's loss in stock, stage appointments and wardrobe was about one hundred thousand dollars, and no insurance. The veteran manager was at his home in Franklin Street when his acting manager, Mr. Davenport, rushed into the house with the news of the conflagration.

"There go the labors of seven years!" said Mr. Hamblin, sadly, as he reflected upon the previous misfortunes that had befallen him. Then he brightened up in his characteristic, enterprising way, and exclaimed: "But we are not dead yet, boys!"

In the next month the city was again startled by a destructive conflagration. Fire was discovered on May 31 in the stables of Peters & Palmer in Eighteenth Street, which were entirely consumed, with twenty horses. From thence the fire spread to a range of twelve two-story houses on Eighteenth Street to Sixth Avenue, and with the exception of two or three two-story brick houses on the corner of Sixth Avenue, crossing into Nineteenth Street, destroyed about a dozen dwellings on the south side and five or six on the north side, besides the roofs of six or eight brick dwellings; thence through to Twentieth Street the flames destroyed a large number of dwellings, nearly the whole of which were occupied by poor families, and some of whom had lost their all. The number of persons who were burned out was not less than four hundred. One hundred buildings in all were destroyed, and the loss was one hundred thousand dollars.

Not since 1835 had there been so calamitous a fire in the city as in the month of July of this year (1845). Perhaps it would be more accurate to say that it was the most fearfully destructive fire in the annals of the Department, for thirty lives were sacrificed on that terrible morning of July 19, and many persons were injured. Over three hundred buildings were burned down, and more than ten million dollars' worth of property laid waste. The event is still fresh in the memory of many of our old citizens and firemen, and they still recollect the mourning that long characterized the city over the loss of so many estimable men and the injury to so many others. The fire broke out about 3 A.M. in the sperm oil establishment of J. L. Van Doren, No. 34 New Street, and soon spread to a chair factory adjoining. Chief Engineer Anderson and the Department were quickly at work, but in spite of their efforts the fire traveled with great rapidity, extending to Exchange Place, Broad Street, and finally to the large storage house of Crooker & Warren, on the latter street. This building, it seems, was stored with saltpeter; it had hardly been on fire ten minutes when it blew up, the shock breaking over a million panes of glass throughout the whole city, even up as high as Canal Street. Not a vestige of the edifice was left except the bricks, while six or seven of the adjoining buildings were partly demolished.

The explosion shook the city like an earthquake. It was felt in Jersey City and Brooklyn, while the report was plainly heard away out to Sandy Hook. Engine Company No. 22 was stationed directly in front of the ill-fated building, and had one stream on the fourth story. Garret B. Lane was then foreman. Soon after he had got his engine to work he discovered a heavy black smoke rolling up the stairway, which at once struck him that the lower portion of the building was on fire. He ordered his men to back out, which they did with much difficulty, as the smoke was so dense that they were nearly suffocated. All got out in safety except Francis Hart, Jr. Hart remained to let down the hose, and when he tried to descend the flames and smoke were so great as to prevent him, and he went on the roof of the chair factory. He clambered from that building to the corner of Broad and Exchange Streets, breaking each skylight as he proceeded over the roofs, but found no stairs leading from any. Finding himself thus on the third building from the chair factory, without any means of getting down, Hart sat in the scuttle. "I did not then consider myself in any danger," he subsequently reported to an investigating committee. "I had been there about five minutes when I heard the first explosion—a species of rumbling sound—followed by a succession of others of the same kind. The gable of the house next to this corner shook with the first and successive explosions, so that I had prepared myself, if it threatened to fall, to jump through the scuttle of the corner house. After the small explosion the great explosion took place, the noise of which seemed to be principally below me. I perceived the flames shooting across the street. I felt the building falling under me, and the roof moved around so that a corner of it caught on the opposite side of Exchange Street and was thrown off into that street. As far as I could judge the whole roof that I was on moved in one piece, and the walls under it crumbled down beneath it. I think there were some fifteen or eighteen small explosions. I could see one engine from the roof I was on."

How Hart finally escaped death reads like a page in a romance, such as Jules Verne might imagine. Just as the members of No. 22, of which Mr. Waters was foreman, had got about twenty feet away from the building, it blew up. The engine of No. 22 was blown clear across the street, and buried beneath the ruins, where it was finally consumed by fire. Hart, who had managed to reach the roof, had passed to the roof of the adjoining building when the explosion took place. He was carried on the top of the roof upon which he was standing, clear up into the air, and landed in safety on a building on the opposite side of the way, the only injury that he received being the dislocation of one of his ankles.

Augustus L. Cowdrey, a young and promising lawyer, a member of No. 42, was in company with Dave Van Winkle, of Engine No. 5, holding a pipe in another building, when another explosion took place, and that was the last ever seen of young Cowdrey. Van Winkle was blown clear out into the street, and escaped with slight injuries.

Some of the fire engines near the building were shivered to atoms. The explosions were accompanied by shocks resembling earthquakes, and so powerful as to shatter windows within the circuit of a mile. The doors of the American Exchange Bank, in Wall Street, were burst open with a loud crash. The City Bank doors were also burst through. Massive iron doors and window shutters were bent and twisted in every direction. The explosion not only carried away three buildings and shattered doors and windows, but it hurled flames and burning timbers into adjoining warehouses. The buildings which stood on New Street, from Wall to Exchange Place and thence to Beaver Street, were laid in ashes. A famous place of resort on Beaver Street known as the Adelphi Hotel was destroyed. Thirty or forty valuable stores with their contents were consumed. The splendid hotel known as the Waverly House on Broadway, with twelve warehouses on Broad Street, on both sides from Wall Street to Exchange Place, and thence to Beaver Street; Exchange Place, from Broadway to Broad Street, and from Broad to William Street, and silk warehouses and dry goods stores were destroyed—forty buildings in all. The loss by this fire was greater than all the fires since 1835.

The extent of the conflagration was quickly known on the other side of the East River, and among the companies that came from Brooklyn was Jackson Engine Company No. 11, who performed such efficient duty that they were tendered a fine collation by the citizens at Brown & Hall's on Bridge Street. No. 7 of Williamsburg and Nos. 3, 4, and 5 of Newark did noble duty. The Croton Hotel, the Philadelphia Hotel, the Pearl Street House, the City Hotel, and the Broad Street Hotel were open for three days free to all the poor people that were burnt out.

During the fire Engine Company No. 38 was stationed on Bridge Street, No. 25 at the Bowling Green, and No. 13 at the corner of Morris and Greenwich Streets. Among the prominent persons encouraging the firemen were Mayor W. F. Havemeyer, George W. Matsell, then a justice of the peace, afterwards president of the Police Board; ex-Chief Engineers Gulick, Wenman, and Riker, the three last rendering valuable service. Lafayette Hook and Ladder Company No. 6 were the hardest-working truck company at the fire. They, with Hose Company No. 22, were feasted at the Astor House, by invitation of Coleman & Stetson. James M. Murray was then foreman of Hook and Ladder Company No. 6, and Richard H. Welch foreman of Hose Company No. 22. The Delmonico brothers had a very narrow escape. They kept the bon-ton restaurant in those days, but their property was saved through the efforts of Engine Companies

Nos. 30 and 40 of this city, and No. 7 of Williamsburg. The Delmonicos gave them a splendid repast before they started for home, and one of the brothers afterwards joined the Department.

The calamities at this fire were so unprecedented that a special committee of the Common Council was appointed to investigate the cause of the occurrence, and report upon the proceedings at that conflagration. The committee consisted of Messrs. Emanuel B. Hart, B. J. Meserole, James C. Stoneall, Geo. H. Purser, Archibald Macclay, Jr., and Joseph C. Albertson. In the course of their report the committee said: "If the person who had charge of the public bell on the City Hall had struck it, as was his duty, the fire would have done very little damage, not extending beyond the building in which it originated. But Mr. Henry J. Ockerhausen, one of the engineers, who resided in Rose Street, states that a fireman, attached to No. 5, came from Fulton Street to his (Mr. Ockerhausen's) house, to inform him of the alarm. Mr. Ockerhausen dressed himself, and had only run as far as Nassau Street, when he distinctly saw the smoke issue from the fire. He heard no bell sounded until he had reached Fulton Street. There he perceived the blaze of the fire, and heard an alarm from the bell on the Post-office Building; but, although he listened attentively for the sound of the City Hall bell, he swears that it was not struck before he reached the fire."

Among the incidents of the fire was the destruction of an old bell which hung in the cupola of the old jail during the Revolution. When the jail was remodeled into the present Hall of Records the bell was taken down, and placed on the Bridewell as a fire alarm bell. Among the old firemen it was cherished as a dear friend of bygone years, and during the chieftainship of John Lamb and "Tommy" (who was dubbed "Pleasant-faced Tommy") it was the principal means of giving notice of a fire. On the destruction of the Bridewell the old bell was placed in a cupola on the house of Naiad Hose Company, in Beaver Street, a house longer devoted to its ancient uses than any other. But this disastrous fire silenced forever the brazen tongue that had for a century given forth its warning notes. Its old enemy at last prevailed, and one decisive victory compensated the fire fiend for many a defeat of yore.

On September 18, 1846, Niblo's Garden was burned again at four o'clock on a Friday morning, the whole building being consumed in two hours. The next evening Gabriel Ravel, of the famous Ravel family of tightrope dancers, was to have had a benefit. The fire originated in the greenroom. One of the firemen, Thomas Boesé, while holding a pipe went so near the flames that his clothing caught fire. Another pipeman, thinking he was doing well, turned a stream of water on him, but the suddenness of the transition from heat to cold paralyzed Boesé. Mr. Boesé afterwards became clerk in the Register's Office. The old passion, however, was strong within him, and whenever the City Bell sounded an alarm, he would drop his pen, blotting his book, and rush in the direction of the fire. In 1872 he was appointed clerk of the Superior Court. The theater was rebuilt, and opened July 3, 1849, under the management of Chippendale & Sefton, with the Ravels, and with a dramatic company that included Mr. Charles Burke. This famous playhouse was originally established by Mr. William Niblo (from whom it took its name) when Jackson was president. It was a house and garden of entertainment, and quickly sprang into popularity, becoming at last the house of the most distinguished artists. In 1837 Mrs. Watson, Mrs. Bailey, Mrs. Knight, Mr. Plumer, and Mr. T. Bishop appeared there in concert. Joseph Jefferson—father of the present renowned comedian of "Rip Van Winkle" fame—produced musical farces there. Other noted players were Mrs. Maeder and Clara Fisher. Burton was the reigning star at Niblo's in 1839, and that year witnessed the first production of the Ravel pantomime "The Green Monster," which kept the stage for many years. In the fall of that year Mr. Wallack leased the house—his National Theater having been burned—and brought forward the renowned Miss Vandenhoff. In 1842 Tom Placide acted there. Next year saw the debut of E. L. Davenport, who on August 9 played Frederick Fitzallen in "He's not Amiss." On the fifteenth of September the opera of "Lucia" was first given there, and in the company were Signoras Majocchi, Thamesi, and Miss Coad, and Signori Valtelina, Antognini, Albertazzi, and Maggiori. Mr. W. Corbyn brought out John Brougham in the autumn of 1844. The features of the season of 1846 (the year of its destruction) were H. Placide's Haversack in the "Old Guard," Hackett's Falstaff, George Holland's Mr. Golightly, and a series of impersonations by Burton.

A fire that broke out in the Duane Street sugar house on the night of April 2, 1848, caused the death of three gallant firemen and severe injuries to two others. The front wall of the building suddenly fell into the street, burying George Kerr, assistant engineer, and Henry Fargis, assistant foreman of Engine Company No. 38. Mr. Jennings, of Hose Company No. 28, Mr. Robert Roulston, of Hose Company No. 38, and Mr. Charles J. Durant, of Hose Company No. 35, were severely injured by the falling bricks and timber. Mr. Durant was so severely hurt that he died a few days after. Mr. Kerr had charge of the Department on that occasion, and the owners of the structure, in defending the stability of their building afterward, claimed that Kerr and Fargis had rashly exposed their lives and those of their men. But it was proved that the edifice was of the flimsiest description. Chief Engineer Anderson, in a letter to the Common Council on this event, says: "As an evidence of the insecurity of the wall, I would call attention to the fact that when it fell outward there was not the least appearance of fire in that story. * * * Mr. Kerr, so far from being rash or imprudent, was one of the coolest, most experienced, and judicious engineers that the Department has ever had. * * * Mr. Fargis was a young man of high promise in and out of the Department, and had won the confidence and esteem of all who knew him. ★ ★ ★ The death of two such men is a public calamity, and if by care and proper precaution such melancholy accidents can be prevented hereafter, I have the fullest confidence that your honorable body will take every step to insure the consummation of an end so desirable."

The joint funeral of these unfortunate firemen was the greatest public demonstration the city had ever seen. Fully fifty thousand persons witnessed the obsequies. The funeral service was held on April 4 in Dr. Ferris's Church, in Market Street. Mr. Zophar Mills was marshal of the immense procession, the order of which was as follows: Exempt Firemen; the Fire Department in the order of companies; body of George Kerr; assistant engineers as pall bearers; relatives and friends; chief engineer; body of Henry Fargis; members of Engine Company No. 38 as pall bearers; officers of Fire Department; Common Council; chief of police and aids; jewelers and silversmiths; citizens.

The engine house of Engine Company No. 11 was injured by fire on April 18, 1848, which broke out in Wooster Street, near Spring, and destroyed twelve buildings, causing a loss of one hundred and seventy-five thousand dollars. A few weeks afterward, on May 26, a dreadful event happened. The large stables of Kipp & Brown, on the corner of Ninth Avenue and Twenty-sixth Street, were burned, when twenty-seven stages, one hundred and thirty horses, a large number of swine, three thousand four hundred bushels of grain, and forty tons of hay, were destroyed. Messrs. Kipp & Brown were old members of Engine Company No. 10, their names were household words in the city, and consequently much sympathy was expressed for them.

As great a calamity occurred on November 18 of the same year, when another stable, that of Messrs. Murphy, at the corner of Third Avenue and Twenty-seventh Street, was burned down. Indeed, a continuous series of fires spread dismay everywhere. All night, and till the dawn of morning, the warning bells rang incessantly. From the reflection of the fires every street in New York was filled with lurid light. The hearts of the citizens sickened at the sight of the whole city wrapped in the light of conflagration and with a high wind blowing. In Messrs. Murphy's stables were one hundred and seventy-five horses. They stood to their halters while the flames gathered around them. Firemen and citizens had rescued about twenty-five of the poor brutes, when portions of the roof began to fall, and then no one dared venture again into the stables. It was an awful picture to look upon. The horses, held by their halters, reared and sent forth terrific shrieks and groans, but one by one they fell and perished in the flames. One animal broke loose and rushed out of the burning building, but before it could be secured it neighed in a frenzied sort of way and then rushed back into the flames. The fearful sounds emitted from the stables would have melted a heart of stone. But not alone was there solicitude for these poor brutes. The flames had communicated to several small wooden buildings in the rear of

Twenty-eighth Street, occupied by needy families. Women were running in every direction, seeking their children, and children seeking their parents. One of the most gallant rescues on record happened on this awful night. One woman, supposing that her child was still in her burning dwelling, with the frenzy of despair rushed into the house and ascended the stairs to the second story, but the heat was so great she was forced to return. But a noble fireman had been before her, and he soon appeared, bearing in his arms the object of the distracted mother's love. In a moment more the baby was in her arms, and, shrieking with joy and in an ecstasy of delight, she fell upon her knees and called down the blessings of heaven on the deliverer of her infant. It is such acts as these that endear the firemen to the citizens. Even amid that scene of confusion stern men were deeply affected by the sight they witnessed.

In the center aisle of the stable thirty-three stages were arranged and only seven were saved. In the rear of the building thirty very beautiful sleighs were destroyed. Behind the building the St. Barnabas Protestant Episcopal Church caught fire some time after and went down before the flames. Then the Rose Hill Methodist Church with its parsonage ignited and was barely saved. Next the Public Schoolhouse No. 15 adjoining was enveloped and was soon a pile of ashes.

Ding, dong, ding, dong, tolled the bells. Another fire at the corner of the Bowery and Broome Street. Here several buildings were laid in ashes, and the Baptist Church, No. 350 Broome Street, was much damaged. In this locality, Mr. Thomas Cochran, of Hose Company No. 9, was seriously hurt by falling from the roof of a back building. While these fires were raging, still another large stable at the corner of Thirty-fifth Street and Eighth Avenue, with two wooden buildings, were razed through a conflagration. And as the gray dawn was breaking, still one more stable was ablaze in the rear of No. 103 West Seventeenth Street, and here four valuable horses were burned to death.

Mme. Adele Montplaisir, the celebrated ballet dancer, was to have taken a benefit on December 16, 1848, at the Park Theater—then the most fashionable resort in the city. At 6:15 P.M., one hour before the doors were to have been opened, while some members of the ballet were in the dressing room, smoke was seen issuing from the rear window in Theater Alley. One of the young ladies had carelessly pushed a gas jet near some playbills. The result was that, for the second time, the theater was burned down. The building was owned by Messrs. Astor & Beekman, and was valued at thirty thousand dollars. It was the first fire at which Mr. Alfred Carson officiated as chief engineer.

The Park Theater was commenced in 1795 by Lewis Hallam and John Hodgkinson and others, all professional actors. The theater was situated in the center of the block, the entrance being on the north side of John Street, midway between Nassau Street and Broadway. The new theater was finished about the year

1798, at a cost of one hundred and seventy-nine thousand dollars. The exterior of the building was plain, but the interior was fitted up with much elegance. On the night of May 24, 1820, it was consumed by fire. The theater was rebuilt in April, 1821. It was not again rebuilt after the 1848 fire.

Abraham Brown, a fireman, effected a gallant rescue at a fire in the house of Mr. Ward, in Catharine Street on April 11, 1849. In the confusion Mrs. Ward had left behind one of her children, a two year old girl. Brown heard the distracted mother bemoaning the loss of her child, ascended a ladder, and effected an entrance through the front window. He found the baby in a back room lying on a bed. He picked her up, and though flames and smoke barred his way he dashed through them and brought the child into the street at the risk of his life. Unhappily, the babe was dead.

On a bright, pleasant, wintry morning, the fourth of February, 1850, at twenty minutes after eight o'clock, the citizens of the Fourth Ward and vicinity were startled by a loud explosion which rent the air, and caused many buildings in Pearl and Frankfort Streets to shake from their very foundations, and shattered many hundreds of panes of glass, the fragments of which were hurled in every direction on the pedestrians who were wending their way to their places of business. A few moments, and the sad news spread like wildfire that a fearful explosion had taken place at Nos. 5 and 7 Hague Street, that both buildings had been blown into atoms, and that one hundred human beings were buried beneath the ruins. The report proved too true, for it was soon discovered that the two hundred horse-power boiler in the extensive press room and machine shop of A. B. Taylor & Co. had exploded; that at the time over one hundred people employed by Taylor & Co., and St. John, Burr & Co., hatters, were at work on the premises. It was claimed by those that witnessed the terrible explosion that the building was lifted full six feet from its foundation, and then fell a mass of ruins. Instantly flames burst out in every direction, and here and there could have been seen legs and arms sticking out from the ruins, while the most piercing shrieks could be heard from those buried in their living tomb.

The firemen were not long in reaching the scene of disaster, with Chief Engineer Alfred Carson at their head. A general alarm having been sounded, nobly did the members of the Department turn their untiring efforts toward rescuing those still alive. They soon controlled the flames, and then body after body was carried out, some mangled and bruised beyond recognition. Among those early on the spot was Engine 21; while among the companies who mounted the hot bricks were Engines 4, 5, 13, 14, 22, and Hook and Ladder 1 and 4. All the down-town companies lent a helping hand. Wm. Story, of No. 4, at the risk of his own life, rescued many, among them a little boy named Freddie Tieman. Story had to crawl down into a hole seven feet before he could get to where the little fellow lay. He was alive, and the first word he said was,

"Mr. Fireman, that fire is close to my feet." Story gave him his fire cap and told him to put it over his face to keep the steam off, and he would put a stream on the fire. The lad did as he was told, and waited for the hour of deliverance. While he lay thus wedged in between two heavy beams he heard others beneath him giving way to the agony of despair. His words to those were: "What's the use of giving up? The firemen are hard at work; they will get us out if anybody can."

They finally sawed away a large timber, Zophar Mills superintending the whole affair, and the little hero was saved. Away down near the bottom lay another brave little fellow, whose name is still stamped upon the heart of many an old fireman, one Samuel Tindale, fifteen years old, and by him one of his comrades, Thomas Vanderbilt, nineteen years old. Around them were burning timbers and hissing bricks. Tindale soon made known his whereabouts, and the firemen worked like beavers to rescue him. His brother was quickly by his side, and when the boy heard him he said: "Go tell mother I am still living; not to worry; that I hope soon to get out." At the same time he told the firemen he was up to his neck in water, and said: "You must stop that water or I shall drown; there is a stick across my leg, and I cannot move."

The firemen kept carting away basket after basket of rubbish, and finally worked their way down to an old side door, where they made considerable headway, when young Tindale hallooed to them that he was scorching. Finally they got near enough to hand him a blanket. As he took it he said there was a dead man lying alongside of him. All day long he remained in the same position. It seemed a miracle how he ever survived; but his brother remained by him, encouraging him and furnishing him with stimulants. About nine o'clock at night it was found that a heavy iron bar held him fast. About eleven o'clock he said he thought they could not save him, and exclaimed: "I shall be the third one who has been killed by this affair." He had no idea how many had fallen victims in this deplorable disaster. At one o'clock the iron bar was lifted, when it was discovered that another bar still held him a prisoner. As soon as the poor boy heard this he exclaimed: "Pull me out, whether you draw my legs off or not!" On worked the firemen, never faltering for a moment, and at four o'clock in the morning, amid the shouts of all, the noble youth was lifted out and borne to Dr. Traphagen's drug store, No. 308 Pearl Street, where he died shortly after. He had been twenty hours in the ruins.

Sixty-four persons were killed, the greater portion of whom were young men and boys, while about seventy were injured. Among the latter was John Vanderpool of Engine 15. He succeeded in rescuing a young lad named George West, William Merritt of Hose 13, and Henry A. Burr. The Common Council, headed by Mayor Westervelt, did all they could to aid the sufferings of the wounded and the families of the dead. No fire ever occurred in this city that was attended with a greater loss of life.

On December 10, 1853, Franklin Square was the scene of one of the most disastrous of conflagrations. Several buildings were within a few hours transformed from gigantic warehouses, into smouldering ruins, and hundreds of artisans and workmen engaged in comfortable occupations were within the same time robbed of employment and thrown destitute upon the world. The fire began a little after one o'clock in the afternoon in the extensive publication establishment of Harper Brothers just after the employees had returned from dinner. It was said that a boy had dropped a lamp into the camphene in the engine room, which would account for the rapid spread of the flames. The building being filled with paper and matter of a light and combustible nature, the ignition from roof to basement was almost like the flashing of powder. By two o'clock nothing was standing of the immense warehouse except the outside walls, and within those the angry flames were sporting like infant demons. At this hour the apprehension was very great. There was no reason to doubt the destruction of many blocks in the vicinity. The wind was very high, and huge coals of fire were carried off to the distance of Beekman Street, and even there fell thick and fast upon the roofs of buildings and the heads of spectators. From Harper's buildings the flames ignited the opposite side of Pearl Street, although very wide at this spot, and for a time there was every appearance that this block would be licked by the increasing fire. Soon after the fire a heavy cloud of smoke hung over the city, filling many of the down-town streets to a burdensome degree. There were many narrow escapes. One young woman jumped out of a window and fortunately escaped injury. Another young woman had her dress take fire and saved herself by stripping it off. Policeman Masterson took her to the chief's office.

As soon as the fire had extended across Pearl Street the efforts of the firemen were divided. The first building which caught on this side of the street was the Walton House, of Revolutionary memory. This was No. 326 Pearl Street, and every effort of the hard-worked firemen to preserve it on account of its historical associations was of no avail. In a few moments it was completely gutted. The Walton House was a large three-story edifice built in the English baronial style of the last century. It was erected about 1754 by an aristocratic gentleman from whom it took its name. Finally it was turned into a boarding house. Adjoining the Walton House was the Franklin Square Hotel, which shared the fate of its neighbor. Next to this hotel was the extensive bakery of ex-Alderman James Kelly, No. 330 Pearl Street. For a long time it was feared this would go with the rest, but Mr. Kelly being an old favorite of the Fire Department, and an ex-member himself, every nerve was strained to save his dwelling. Wet blankets were hung out of the windows, and his roof was kept well-flooded. A hole was burned through his roof, but the house sustained very little other injury. As evening advanced the fire had a terrific beauty of its own. Harper was one mass of rubbish, comprising six houses on Cliff Street, running through to Pearl and taking in the same number of houses on that street. On the opposite side of Cliff Street the buildings Nos. 81 and 83, also occupied by Harper, were much scorched. Adjoining Harper's buildings, next to Ferry Street, was the large publishing house of George F. Coolidge & Brother, which also fell before the fiery blast. The fire was stopped on the side toward Ferry Street at No. 319, the drug store of W. W. Thayer, which was somewhat damaged by water. On the other side the fire was arrested at a new building which the Harpers were erecting, in addition to three other buildings. There the flames met with nothing but a shell of a house of stone, and had it not been for this the work of destruction would probably have extended much farther. In all sixteen buildings were burned, and four or five more or less injured.

The energy of the firemen on this occasion was said to be very noticeable. For a long time before there had not been so large a turnout of the Department. Almost every engine in the city was on the ground, and even the Harlem engine was on hand. The bells rang a general alarm, which had not been done for months before. There were present four of the Brooklyn companies, Nos. 1, 4, 5, and 7. The Brooklynites formed a line through Peck Slip and took their suction from the dock. Of our firemen the *New York Herald* of that date said:

We cannot again refrain from speaking of the noble conduct of our firemen. At the time the fire broke out there were some six hundred human beings in the establishment of Messrs. Harper, men, women, and children, and immediately upon giving the report of the fire the greatest consternation prevailed—every window was filled with frantic souls crying for help. We are told there was abundance of time for every one to come down safely, but in the terror of the moment all rushed for the windows. The firemen immediately mounted their ladders, and brought all down in safety to the ground, perilling their own lives in doing so. * * * Amid crackling timber and hissing flames they forced their way, regardless of every peril in their efforts to roll back the billows of fire. Some idea can be formed of the degree of heat, considering the fact that it was difficult at times to bear it even in the upper part of Franklin Square. Yet amid all this for three long hours the heroic firemen worked at their engines, and yielded not till they were masters of the angry element.

Hook and Ladder Company No. 1 (Mutual) was the second apparatus on the ground, and by means of their ladders several girls made their escape. Some of the members of the company directed their efforts to rescue the safes. They got out the larger seven feet high one, and Mr. James Harper requested them to rescue the smaller, but it was impossible. Hook and Ladder Company No. 6 had the task of throwing down the walls on the Pearl Street side; on the Cliff Street side No. 11 did the same work; Nos. 2, 3, 4, 5, and 8 were at work in different parts. All the ladders of No. 1 were broken by the fall of a portion of the Cliff Street wall.

The loss to the Harpers was eight hundred thousand dollars; Coolidge & Bros., two hundred thousand dollars; and taking the other firms and houses altogether nearly one million five hundred thousand dollars. Ten years before on June 1, 1842, the firm lost one hundred thousand dollars through a fire.

In the newspapers of December 12, 1853, under the heading "The Firemen," we find the following advertisements:

A CARD. —Oceanus Fire Engine No. 11 return their sincere thanks to Mr. Joseph Carlisle, of Centre and Leonard Streets, for the bountiful supply of refreshments furnished them after their return from the fire in Pearl Street.

By order.   DAVID BAKER, *Foreman.*

WM. J. LEWIS, *Secretary.*

A CARD. —At a special meeting of Hook and Ladder Company No. 4, held at the truck house after the return from the fire in Pearl Street, it was unanimously

Resolved, That the thanks of the company be tendered to Mr. and Mrs. John Baulch for the bountiful supply of refreshments furnished us after the above fire.

JOHN CORNWELL, *Chairman.*

JOHN SLOWY, *Secretary.*

On December 14 Foreman Chas. F. Meyons and Secretary Martin Wise published a similar card in reference to Mr. James Kelly.

A fire that broke out on December 26, 1853, in a store in Front Street, spread to the shipping in the docks. Among the vessels burned was the big ship *Great Republic* (three hundred and twenty-five feet long and four thousand five hundred and fifty-five tons burden). The total loss was six hundred thousand dollars.

The gallantry of the firemen was conspicuous at the burning of Tripler Hall and the Lafarge House on Broadway, nearly opposite Bond Street, on June 8, 1854. T. F. Goodwin, foreman, and Hugh Curry, both of Hose Company No. 35, particularly distinguished themselves by their courage. The fire caught from one of the hotel furnaces under the orchestra box of the concert room, and in one hour the buildings were in ruins. Tripler Hall was built by Mr. Tripler, and first opened to the public on the fourteenth of October, 1850, and could seat four thousand persons. It was a concert room in the Lafarge House. The Lafarge House cost three hundred thousand dollars, and was leased to Wright, Laniers & Co., for fifty-four thousand dollars a year. It was elegantly furnished. Among the first of the brilliant stars who occupied the boards of the Lafarge House was Jenny Lind, who was hailed as the "Gifted Swede," and welcomed as "Sweet Warbler," in a motto at Castle Garden. Indeed, Tripler Hall was built especially to accommodate the large audiences which evening after evening flocked to hear the Swedish Nightingale. It was costly and magnificent beyond anything at that time in the city, and cost one hundred thousand dollars. It was the largest music hall in the world, except the opera houses of London, Milan, and Havana. But the first voice heard within its walls was that of the sweet singer Madam Anna Bishop. Then followed Jenny Lind. Here also Miss Catherine Hayes entertained crowded and distinguished audiences; here Alboni and Madame Sontag sang; and here the monster Jullien concerts drew immense houses night after night. The name of the concert room had been changed to Metropolitan Hall, and the last announcement previous to its destruction in 1854 was for Wednesday evening, January 18, when the ballroom of the Lafarge House, communicating with the concert room, was to have been thrown open for ladies and gentlemen patronizing Jullien's Grand Ball Paré, to obtain admission to which full evening dress was indispensable. The hall was also used for political and other meetings. There were heard the ringing tones of Thomas D'Arcy McGee, the Irish patriot of 1848, who had to fly from his country. Other well-known names in its history are those of Lucy Stone, Lloyd Garrison, and Wendell Phillips.

The work of rebuilding the hotel and theater was at once begun, and on the eighteenth of September the "Great Metropolitan Theater and New York Opera House" was opened with a poem spoken by Harry Eytinge, the song of "The Star Spangled Banner," and Bulwer's play of "The Lady of Lyons." Brief, however, was the second period of the brilliant career of the Metropolitan. Toward the close of 1854 the famous Italian priest Gavazzi, who had abandoned the Catholic Church, made his appearance in this country on a crusade against his ancient faith. He was a man of keen intellect, and his eloquence was forceful and earnest. Everywhere he went the Catholic part of the population, especially the foreign element, opposed him most strenuously. His life was threatened, and vengeance was vowed against him if he persisted in his attacks. Saturday night, November 8, Gavazzi lectured at the Metropolitan. Although threats had been made to tear down the building should the apostate priest speak there, it was not thought that any serious results would follow. He had spoken there before and had not been interfered with. On this occasion Father Gavazzi lectured to five thousand persons, and the meeting passed over tranquilly. A few hours after its close, however, the building was in flames, and the efforts of the firemen could not save it from destruction.

CHAPTER XVI

FINAL FIRES OF THE OLD DEPARTMENT

Great Loss of Life at the Jennings Fire.—Charity's Compassionate Hand.—
"Andy" Schenck's Marriage and Untimely Death.—The Crystal Palace
Conflagration and Destruction of Engines.—Joseph Skillman's Death.—Fires
Through the Draft Riots, and Heroism of the Firemen.—Exciting and Perilous
Times.—Alleged Southern Plot to Burn Hotels in 1864.

About 3 A.M. on September 3, 1849, the noble packet ship *Henry Clay*, lying at the foot of Fletcher Street, was discovered to be on fire amidships. The alarm was given by the Fulton Market bell, which struck as the first glare of light shone up, and although the firemen were promptly on the spot some delay occurred in starting the various hydrant streams. Hose Companies 1, 2, 3, 8, 10, 15, 18, 21, 25 and 28 were on hand and furnished water to Engines Nos. 5 (which was first to work), 20, 38, 14, 2, 13 and 21. No. 13 was obliged at first to use suction in consequence of the small number of hydrant lines.

A fearful loss of life in the Fire Department occurred on Tuesday night, April 25, 1854. It broke out at eight o'clock in the clothing store of William T. Jennings & Co., No. 231 Broadway, and defied all the efforts of the firemen. On the south of the building stood the American Hotel, and on the north the establishments of Meade Bros., photographers, and of Mr. Batchelor, hairdresser. John A. Cregier was standing on the roof of Meade's building in company with another engineer, Noah L. Farnham. They let down to the street the halyards of the flagstaff, and with great difficulty succeeded in drawing up one end of a length of hose. Scarcely had they begun to play on the fire when the rear wall of Jennings' buildings suddenly toppled over backward upon the extension, letting the upper floors fall upon thirteen or fourteen firemen who were in the second story of the burning store. There was, it seems, a huge iron safe in the upper story, and this dashed through the several floors to the basement, instantly killing two firemen. The scene around that fire, when it was known that over twenty firemen were buried beneath the ruins, beggars description. It required but a moment's thought, and then the members of the Department rushed into the building, regardless of their own lives, to rescue those of their comrades. Cregier directed the pipe of his hose toward a part of the burning roof that hung over the spot where the men were buried, and which seemed about to cave in.

"Stop that water!" called a voice from below, "it is scalding the men"—not the buried men only, but the gallant fellows who were trying to extricate them.

More perilous, however, than the scalding water were the heavy rafters on the eve of falling, and Cregier cried out in stentorian tones, while still flooding the place with water:

"It can't be done; the roof will go;" and by his decision he saved many lives.

All night long they worked, braving danger at every turn, and not until they had taken out the lifeless remains of eleven of their comrades, with some twenty bodily injured, did they retreat from the ruins. Of those who fell in the discharge of their duty were John O'Donnell, of Engine 42, a son of Coroner O'Donnell. He was in the ruins over eight hours, and conversed with his friends until res-cued. He died in the New York Hospital the same night. James McNulty, of Engine 20, Andrew C. Schenck, of Hook and Ladder 1, John A. Keyser, of Hose 8, two brothers, Daniel and Alexander McKay, of Engine 21, a boy named Michael Flynn, a runner of Hose 53, James E. Deegan, of Hose 18, an old man named Wilson, a runner of 21 Engine, and one John Reinhardt. Some of the ruins having been reached by cutting holes through the basement walls of Meade's building, "Andy" Schenck was seen to be dead, and young O'Donnell so bruised that the top of his head, as an old fireman expressed it, was "as big as a stove and just about as black." Dr. O'Donnell had been anxiously pacing in front of the ruins waiting for his son to be brought out. Hugh Gallagher, of Engine Company No. 23, was found pinned against a wall by a heavy safe, which had fallen from the floor above.

Of poor Andy Schenck it is related that when the alarm for the fire sounded that night he was calling at the house of the young lady to whom he was engaged to be married, and who earnestly urged him to stay. "No," said he, after some hesitation, "I'll go to this fire, and this is the last fire I will go to." It was indeed his last, for there he found his grave.

When the sad news was announced in the journals of the following day, thousands upon thousands congregated around the ruins and at the dead-house in the hospital yard to view the mangled remains of those brave but unfortunate men. The firemen of Brooklyn, Jersey City and Newark held meetings of sym-pathy, while in the Common Council Alderman Blunt presented a series of resolutions upon the death of the firemen, and one thousand five hundred dollars was appropriated to defray their funeral expenses. The Board of Foremen and Engineers met and passed resolutions, presented by Timothy L. West, and it was agreed that the Department turn out in a body to pay the last tribute of respect to their deceased brethren.

The citizens also came forward with donations to the families of the deceased. The funeral procession being one of the most solemn ever witnessed in this city.

Engine Company No. 40 carried the Department banner, and the whole Fire Department, and the City Council, headed by Mayor Westervelt, turned out. The line of march was up Chatham to the Bowery, then through Astor Place to Broadway, and down Broadway to the South Ferry. Alexander McKay was killed while endeavoring to rescue his brother Daniel, and McNulty died soon after being conveyed into Rushton's drug store, under the Astor House. It seems that there was an iron arch in the rear of the building extending from one side of the edifice to the other which supported the rear wall; this became red hot, and the effect of the water from the pipe of Engine Company No. 22 cracked it, thus letting down the whole rear wall. A coroner's jury was impaneled, with John N. Genin, the well-known hatter, as foreman, and it was decided that the place was set on fire by thieves, three of whom were afterward sent to State Prison. The loss at this fire was estimated at seventy-five thousand dollars, and to this day the old "vets" talk of that lamentable event.

Harry Howard, then Assistant Engineer, testified as follows before the coroner's jury: "At half-past eight o'clock the two upper stories were on fire. I think there were then about fifty persons in the store, firemen and others. Engine Company No. 21's pipe was throwing a good stream of water towards the staircase into the third story. I then discovered a skylight, and ordered the men to get out on the roof of the extension [in the rear of the building] and play water into the front building, * * * but I had no conception of the building falling at this time. If the men had reached the point where I ordered them they would have been saved. Some of them did as I ordered them, and they were not killed; others had not time." The jury censured the builders for the flimsy character of a portion of the structure.

At noon on July 1, 1854, a fire broke out in a furniture store, No. 371 Grand Street, at which Mr. John W. Garside, a member of Columbia Hose Company No. 9, rescued three persons—two women and a boy fourteen years old. Mr. Garside climbed up the gutter, being helped up by one of his associates, and, hanging on to the window, succeeded in passing them in safety to the adjoining building. As the last one was being taken out, the window sash, which was held by a button, fell on his arm, and the glass cut his hand severely, and while he was having it dressed at a drug store opposite, the building from which the people were rescued fell in with a crash, not standing five minutes after they had been taken out. Mr. Garside carries an elegant extra jewelled Liverpool gold watch and chain which was presented to him with a box containing two hundred and fifty dollars in gold at a dinner which was given to him at Odd Fellows Hall shortly afterwards. Soon thereafter the Common Council adopted a resolution appropriating one hundred and fifty dollars for a gold medal to be presented to Mr. Garside as a token of reward for his heroic conduct. Mayor Fernando Wood in March, 1855, was deputed to present Mr. Garside with the gold medal. A number of Mr. Garside's friends were present to witness the presentation. His honor the mayor, in his address, highly complimented the gallant fellow on being the recipient of such a well deserved tribute.

The Latting Observatory on Forty-third Street, between Fifth and Sixth Avenues, two hundred and eighty feet high, was destroyed on August 30, 1856. A few months afterwards at a fire in Sixth Street, between Avenues B and C, Engine Company No. 44 and Hook and Ladder Company No. 13 rescued twelve persons, and among the bravest of the rescuers was Joseph L. Perley, who subsequently became President of the Board of Fire Commissioners. The laying of the Atlantic cable was commemorated on August 17, 1858, by an exhibition of fireworks at the City Hall. At midnight the roof was found to be on fire, and the cupola, with its clock, was finally destroyed.

The Crystal Palace in Reservoir Square was burned on the fifth of October, 1858. It was opened on July 14, 1853, for the exhibition of the industry of all nations, and was located in the vicinity of the aqueduct at Forty-second Street. "The fairy-like Greek cross of glass, bound together with withes of iron," says a writer of the period, "with its graceful dome, its arched naves, and its broad aisles and galleries, filled with choice productions of art and manufactures, gathered from the most distant parts of the earth, quaint old armor from the Tower of London, gossamer fabrics from the looms of Cashmere, Sevres china, Gobelin tapestry, Indian curiosities, stuffs, jewelry, musical instruments, carriages, and machinery of home and foreign manufacture, Marochetti's colossal statue of Washington, Kiss's Amazon, Thorwaldsen's Christ and the Apostles, Powers's Greek Slave, and a host of other works of art beside, will long be remembered as the most tasteful ornament that ever graced the metropolis." Beautiful, however, as was this fairy-like palace it vanished in smoke in the short space of half an hour, and fell, burying the rich collection of the American Institute, then on exhibition within its walls, in a molten mass of ruins. The Crystal Palace contained one thousand two hundred and fifty tons of iron, and thirty-nine thousand square feet of glass. A grand concert, which fully ten thousand persons were expected to attend, had been arranged for the evening. The total loss was estimated at two million dollars.

About five o'clock smoke was seen issuing from a large room in the north nave, and in front of the entrance on Forty-second Street. The flames spread with incredible rapidity in every direction. There were about two thousand persons scattered about the edifice at the time, all of whom, the moment the alarm of "fire!" was raised, made a rush for the Sixth Avenue entrance, the doors of which were thrown open. The entrance on Fortieth Street was closed. Under the direction of ex-Captain Maynard, of the police, and several of the directors the crowd was conducted safely to the street. Mr. Smith, an employee in charge of the jewelry deparament, saw the fire and ran back to his case of jewelry. He dragged the case from its fastenings along the gallery, down a flight of stairs, and into the street. He was almost the last person out, and had a narrow escape of his life. The view from the street and neighborhood was very grand, and thousands of persons flocked to the conflagration. The firemen of the district were soon on the spot, and twenty or thirty streams were thrown into the building, but without having any visible effect. Many firemen rushed into the edifice, hoping to save the apparatus that were on exhibition, but they were compelled to retreat on account of the smoke. Again and again they gallantly rushed into the palace, and eventually succeeded in saving the carriage belonging to No. 40 Hose Company (Empire), and the carriage of No. 36 Hose Company (Oceanic). However, the carriages of No. 1 Hose Company (Eagle), and No. 6 Hose Company (Croton), engine of No. 16 (Gotham), Hook and Ladder No. 1 (Mutual), and engine No. 28 (Pacific) were destroyed.

Mr. Frederick W. Geissenhainer, chairman of the Board of Managers of the American Institute, was standing in the south nave when the fire broke out. He ran to the Forty-second Street entrance, where he discovered a quantity of wooden patterns of the ironwork used in the construction of the palace enveloped in flames. The pitch-pine floors only invited the flames, which licked over the planking, rolling up dense clouds of smoke, nearly suffocating those in the north nave. After despatching a man to turn off the gas, Mr. Geissenhainer ran to a hydrant with hose attached, near the north nave, and caused the water to be turned on. Owing, however, to the lowness of the water in the reservoir it was of no avail. There was no hope of saving the building, and the employees and officers turned their attention to all the nooks and retired spots they could get at in order to drive out any lingering persons.

The flames ascended to the second floor and seemingly rolled along the surface of the woodwork like molten iron, at a speed as rapid as the ordinary pace of a pedestrian in the street. After going through two of the galleries Mr. Geissenhainer proceeded to the picture gallery. He went behind the panorama, thinking that the men who were engaged in winding it for the evening exhibition might still be there. When he returned he found both stairways in a blaze. He ran to one of the towers, and finding one board displaced in the floor he easily removed another and slid down the iron pipe leading from the water tank to the floor below, and a moment after escaped from the building. The last person had scarcely left when the dome fell in with a terrible crash, just twelve minutes after the fire was discovered. One old gentleman was found senseless at the foot of one of the stairways, having failed to escape. He was rescued just before the dome fell.

It was said that the fire was the work of incendiaries who ignited papers in the lumber room. The amount of property destroyed was over five hundred thousand dollars. Among the property destroyed were several valuable steam engines, and some fine pictures belonging to Mr. Furis, of the "Root Gallery," corner of Broadway and Franklin Street.

Next day thousands visited the ruins. Eight of the turrets and a portion of the iron framework of one of the galleries were left standing. The whole area to the depth of three or four feet was covered with broken pillars and columns, melted glass, and disordered machinery. Wandering among the rubbish were many exhibitors searching for any of their property that might be worth saving. A large heap of coal, about fifty tons, continued to burn all day, and all attempts to extinguish it were unavailing. Comptroller Flagg, when the palace fell into the hands of the city, had the concern insured for fifty thousand dollars in ten companies—five thousand dollars in each.

On October 8, three days after the fire, the chief engineer issued a call for a mass meeting of the Department at Firemen's Hall, to consider the best means of replacing the apparatus destroyed. Mr. Howard occupied the chair, and James F. Wenman officiated as secretary. The chief engineer stated that it was useless to petition the Common Council to replace the engines and hose carriages burned, as there was no appropriation for the purpose, and it might require years to get them to act on the matter. A resolution was offered to appoint a committee of thirty to solicit subscriptions toward rebuilding the machines. This was strenuously objected to on the part of many of the foremen, who held that it was the duty of the Common Council to make good the loss of corporation property, and at all events they contended that only officers of the Department were entitled to meet in that hall. But the resolution prevailed.

For several years from 1858 there was an absence of great fires, but still there were many lively and many sad nights of conflagration for the Department. No. 5 engine was buried by the fall of a wall, and some of the men injured, on December 29, 1859. Daniel Scully, of Engine Company No. 40, with members of his company, rescued six persons at a fire in Elm Street on February 2, 1860. He climbed to the third story by means of the leader, and handed the tenants down to men at the windows, one after the other. The Common Council presented him with a gold medal. James R. Mount, at that time foreman of Hose Company No. 15, distinguished himself on this occasion by saving two persons. About twenty persons were suffocated or burned to death. This calamitous fire led to the Common Council passing an ordinance compelling the placing of fire escapes on all tenements. For the first time their attention was turned to this necessary adjunct of such buildings. Hook and Ladder Company No. 4 saved several persons at another fire in Doyers Street. July 26, the same year, Thomas Cox, of Hose Company No. 50, was killed at a fire in Broad Street. On December 3 several persons were saved by firemen in No. 203 Division Street. Fifteen days later the new steamship *John P. King* was burned at Pier No. 4, North River. Several members of No. 38 Engine were playing on the flames in the engine room. The vessel was cut loose and towed out into the stream, to the astonishment of the firemen. Two or three jumped from the blazing steamer and were picked up by boats. Thomas R. Smith, who was rescued by the police boat, was much less concerned at the danger to which he had been exposed than at the loss of a new length of rubber hose and a brass pipe belonging to his engine. He almost wept over the loss.

Very disastrous was the fire that broke out in the lower part of the city on December 29, 1859. About five o'clock in the morning the Second Ward police were alarmed by observing smoke issuing from Black, Gramm & Co.'s store, No. 53 Beekman Street. In the meantime the flames spread rapidly, and in the course of half an hour extended to No. 61, only one door from the police station, and occupied by several parties. The large paper warehouses of Bulkley & Co., and Cyrus W. Field were adjoining, and caught fire. Admirable efforts were made to stay the fire, but in vain, and it reached the other side of Ann Street, catching Nos. 90 and 92, and sweeping onward until it reached Nos. 83 and 85 Fulton Street. A wall unexpectedly fell into the street, burying No. 5 engine, and some of its members were injured, but not seriously.

Joseph Skillman, of Hook and Ladder Company No. 15, was killed at a fire in Fulton Street on February 8, 1861. The cold was intense. The members of No. 38 protected their engine from the cold wind by building around it a thick wall formed of bundles of wrapping paper. A number of small fires occurred in 1861 and 1862.

A very destructive fire occurred on January 1, 1863, in Fulton, Gold and Beekman Streets. The cracker bakery of John T. Wilson & Co., and other business and manufacturing establishments at Nos. 66 to 79 Fulton Street, Nos. 56 to 60 Gold Street, and Nos. 69 to 79 Beekman Street, were damaged or destroyed. The firemen had not experienced such a fearful conflagration for some time previously. In a building adjoining the bakery there lay the body of a man who had died the day before. Some of the members of Pearl Hose Company No. 28 went in and found the body laid out on a board, near a window in the second story. Strange to say, above the chamber of death there were signs of jollity—a table was set for New Year's callers.

At another cracker bakery fire (Goodwin's, No. 209 Cherry Street) on February 3, 1863, loss of life occurred. Three firemen—John Slowey and George W. Badger, of Engine Company No. 19, and Thomas Sweeney, of Engine Company No. 6, were buried by a falling wall. Slowey and Badger died of their injuries. Every company passed resolutions of sympathy and sorrow. Hose Company No. 36 eulogized Mr. Badger for his "correct, manly deportment and many sterling qualities which have endeared him to all." His funeral took place from the Stanton Street Baptist Church, the services being conducted by the Rev. Dr. Hiscox and the Rev. Dr. Armitage. The Fire Department, with its banner (carried by Phoenix Hose Company No. 22), escorted the hearse to Fulton Ferry on its way to Greenwood. The Board of Foremen acted as a guard of honor. Mr. Slowey entered the Department in 1849 as a member of Engine Company No. 15. He afterwards joined Engine Company No. 19, when it had but seven members, and became its foreman. His friends raised six thousand dollars for the benefit of his widow and three orphans. At the firing of the Colored Orphan Asylum, at Forty-third Street and Fifth Avenue, during the Draft Riots, July, 1861, the chief engineer, with his own hands extinguished the burning brands. The desperate ruffians threatened to kill him if he persisted in thwarting their diabolical purpose. Standing upon the steps of the building the bold fire chief appealed to the infuriated crowd of two thousand half drunken wretches. The mob again set fire to the building, and Decker and his gallant little band extinguished the flames. This thoroughly exasperated the shameless crew, and the scoundrels advanced upon the chief engineer. His men determinedly closed around him, and the cowards were afraid to carry out their intent to injure the chief. But they eventually succeeded in burning down the asylum. Some twenty of the poor little orphans were seized by the mob. A young Irishman, Paddy McCaffrey, with four stage drivers of the Forty-second Street line and Engine Company No. 18, dashed in upon the fiends and rescued the children from their grasp. They struck right and left, and in triumph bore the little ones off to the Thirty-fifth Precinct station house.

The heroism of the New York firemen in these days of danger was the theme of the public press and of all well-disposed citizens. While some buildings were burning at Fourteenth Street and Avenue C, Assistant Engineer Elisha Kingsland tried to remove a wagon in the street to make room for the approach of a carriage.

"If you touch that wagon I'll blow your brains out," cried a ruffian, who was backed by hundreds of his kind.

The engineer got upon the wagon and shouted, "If this fire continues, it will cross the street and burn the houses of your friends."

"Get down from there! Shoot him! Mangle them!" were the responses.

Nevertheless, Mr. Kingsland gained his point. Again, at the corner of Twenty-ninth Street and Broadway, Chief Engineer Decker, Assistant Engineers William Lamb and Elisha Kingsland had a hand-to-hand fight with a big crowd. Lamb was knocked down, but his comrades set him on his feet, and they finally succeeded in arresting three of the ringleaders who were stealing bales of silk.

The *New York Tribune*, of July 20, 1863, says: "During the progress of the fire on the corner of Second Avenue and Twenty-first Street, on Monday afternoon [July 13] Lafayette Engine Company No. 19 were threatened by the mob that if they attempted to extinguish the fire, or in any way endeavored to save the building, they would be instantly stoned. Nothing daunted, the brave and energetic foreman, Mr. James G. W. Brinkman, urged his men to instantly stretch their hose and make preparations to save the building. Thereupon the mob cut the hose and endeavored to break the engine; but being assailed and driven off by the company with the assistance of the police, they carried out their destructive propensities in other directions. At the burning of the lumber yard, corner of Avenue C and Fourteenth Street, on Wednesday morning, pretty much the same scenes above described were enacted. The company worked at the fire for six hours and succeeded in saving a considerable amount of property. The police of the Seventeenth Precinct speak in great praise of the members of this company, who, led by their foreman and Assistant Engineer Kingsland, assisted, in conjunction with the members of the precinct, in dispersing mobs and saving the dwellings and property of the residents of the ward. . . . In the absence of the police of this precinct (they being stationed in the more riotous parts of the city), these firemen actually patrolled the ward day and night, and thus rendered a service which will not be soon forgotten."

In some portions of the city the firemen organized themselves into patrols for the protection of their respective neighborhoods. The firemen in the Seventh Ward placed themselves under the command of Captain Rynders and John McDermott, foreman of Engine Company No. 2. The members of Engine Company No. 20 and Hose Companies Nos. 8, 18 and 49, organized a First Ward patrol. Hose Companies Nos. 26 and 31, Engine Companies Nos. 7 and 12 and Hook and Ladder Company No. 10 are mentioned as conspicuous in this service. Escaping and terrified negroes found protection in the engine houses of Engine Company No. 13, in Duane Street, and Engine Company No. 2, in Henry Street.

Some idea of what the firemen had to contend with may be gathered from the following estimate, made by Fire Marshal Baker:

Monday, July 13, 1863.

11:05 A.M.—No. 677 Third Avenue, brick building, Provost Marshal Jenkins's enrolling office; three buildings destroyed. Total value about twenty-five thousand dollars.

3:05 P.M.—Lexington Avenue, between Forty-fourth and Forty-fifth Streets, two brownstone dwelling houses and their contents, valued at seventy-eight thousand dollars, totally destroyed.

4:35 P.M.—Forty-fourth Street, between Fourth and Fifth Avenues, Bull's Head Hotel, brick building, owned by Mr. Allerton, destroyed with its contents. Loss about seventy thousand dollars.

4:50 P.M.—A five-story brick building, northeast corner of Twenty-first Street and Second Avenue, used for manufacturing firearms by Marston &

Co., completely destroyed, together with contents. Loss about seventy-five thousand dollars.

5:15 P.M.—No. 1140 Broadway, Provost Marshal B. F. Manierre's enrolling office, twelve brick buildings destroyed, the whole block on Broadway, from Twenty-eighth to Twenty-ninth Street, and buildings on Twenty-eighth and Twenty-ninth Streets. Total value, including their contents, one hundred and twenty-five thousand dollars.

6:50 P.M.—Fifth Avenue, between Forty-third and Forty-fourth Streets, Colored Orphan Asylum, brick building, totally destroyed. Loss about thirty-five thousand dollars.

8:18 P.M.—No. 429 Grand Street, enrolling office and dwelling of Provost Marshal Captain John Duffy, brick building, sacked and burned. Loss, including contents, about ten thousand dollars.

9:20 P.M.—No. 62 Roosevelt Street, frame dwelling, occupied by colored people. Damage about one hundred dollars.

9:27 P.M.—Eighty-seventh Street, residence of Postmaster Abram Wakeman, totally destroyed. Loss twenty-five thousand dollars. The Twenty-third Precinct Police Station, directly in the rear, on Eighty-sixth Street, caught fire from sparks and was also destroyed. Loss about fifteen thousand dollars.

Tuesday, July 14.

3:30 A.M.—One Hundred and Twenty-ninth Street, corner of Third Avenue, six frame buildings were burned. Total value about twenty-two thousand dollars.

12:22 P.M.—Eleventh Avenue and Forty-first Street, hotel owned by Mr. Allerton, brick building destroyed. Loss about fifteen thousand dollars.

3:04 P.M.—Weehawken Ferry-house, frame, foot of Forty-second Street, North River. Loss six thousand dollars.

5:03 P.M.—Nos. 73 and 75 Roosevelt Street, brick front, two dwelling houses, occupied by colored families, totally destroyed. Loss three thousand dollars.

11 P.M.—No. 163 East Twenty-second Street, Eighteenth Precinct Station House, brick building; also the fire alarm bell tower, and No. 51 Engine House, all destroyed. Loss about twenty thousand dollars.

11:45 P.M.—No. 24 East Thirty-third Street, dwelling house of Mr. Jared W. Peck, port warden, brick building; a library, valued at five thousand dollars, destroyed; the building fired. Loss by the fire about one thousand dollars.

Wednesday, July 15.

2:40 A.M.—Avenue C, corner of Fourteenth Street, lumber yard of Ogden & Co. Damage about two thousand dollars.

10:50 A.M.—No. 91 West Thirty-second Street, three brick tenement houses, occupied by colored people, all destroyed. Loss about fifteen thousand dollars.

The total amount is estimated at three hundred and sixty thousand one hundred dollars.

At a fire in Twenty-ninth Street, on December 2, 1863, John Brown, assistant foreman of Hose Company No. 30, rescued some persons from the flames, and for his gallantry received a silver trumpet from the Common Council. Eight hundred and sixty-seven thousand three hundred and thirty-four dollars was lost in the destruction of Auffmordt & Hessenburg's extensive establishment in Duane Street on January 16, 1864. John Fitzpatrick, of No. 34 Engine, had just emerged from the building with two children, when the wall fell and he narrowly escaped. Not so, however, George W. Burridge, an honorary member of No. 42 Engine, who was caught under the wall and instantly killed.

Between one and two o'clock on Sunday morning, May 29, 1864, a fire broke out in the second-hand furniture store No. 75 Division Street, owned by Bernard Heller, who also occupied the upper part of the building as a dwelling. When the doors were broken open the fire was seen burning in the center of the store. The flames immediately rushed out at the door, and extended up the front of the building, which was of wood, and two stories and an attic in height. The occupants of the premises were aroused, but too late to escape by the stairs, which were at the rear part of the store. Engine No. 31 and Hook and Ladder Company No. 11 were quickly on the spot, and it was through their exertions that Mr. Heller and his wife and four children were taken from the second floor, through the windows. Mr. Heller had fallen on the floor, where he was found by the firemen nearly exhausted. He was very badly burned about the face and hands, and his wife was also much injured about the breast, face, hands, and arms. The youngest child, a boy ten months old, was severely burned. Three girls, five, seven and eight years old respectively, were rescued uninjured. The firemen carried the baby and one of the girls to the hospital. Frank Mahedy, foreman of No. 31, whose untimely end while chief of battalion in the new Department is recorded in another chapter, distinguished himself in rescuing the family. So, too, did Thomas McGrath, of the same company. In a short time the entire building was enveloped in flames, when the front wall bulged. Assistant Engineer Perley ordered the firemen out of the building, but the order being misunderstood was not obeyed. Shortly afterwards the chimney fell, which carried down the floors, and several firemen were buried beneath the timbers. They were soon extricated, however, from their perilous position. Mahedy was very badly bruised, but had no bones broken. He was taken to the engine house and his hurts attended to by a surgeon. Messrs. John Armstrong and Eberhardt, of the same company, were also much bruised, as were also Roundsman Witcomb, of the Seventh Precinct, and several others. Jacob Deitschburger, a cigarmaker, who occupied a room in the attic, jumped from the roof to the awning, escaping with only a few bruises. A child named Batti, three years old, was burned to death in the building, without the knowledge of the firemen.

July 11, 1864, at 1 o'clock A.M., the steamboat *John Potter* was destroyed by fire at Pier No. 1, North River. Several companies were on the dock with their apparatus and while busy at work were surrounded by the fire. Southwark Engine Company No. 38 had to abandon the big old white hand engine belonging to Fulton Engine Company No. 21, temporarily placed in their charge. The small jumper of City Hose Company No. 8 was also abandoned. The truck of Mutual Hook and Ladder Company No. 1 was dragged off the dock in time to save it from destruction. A large number of firemen had to jump overboard and were picked up by small boats, or had to climb out as best they could. No lives were lost.

The Lafayette Theater, in Laurens Street, with several adjacent buildings, was entirely destroyed by fire on Thursday, April 10, 1829. The loss was two hundred thousand dollars. Henry Yates owned the theater, and had not a cent insured.

On July 13 a famous place of amusement was destroyed—Barnum's Museum, which then stood at the corner of Ann Street and Broadway. It was about noon when the fire broke out, and at that hour there were few persons in the building, so that no human lives were lost, but half a million dollars' worth of property was destroyed. It was a unique scene, and afforded opportunity for a great deal of graphic and humorous writing in the press. The firemen had much fun with the monkeys, the whale, the bear, and the "Happy Family." The Fat Lady and the Giantess were handed out in safety with the tenderest solicitude for their welfare. Several of the laddies said they were completely smitten with the woolly-headed Albino woman. The enterprising Barnum soon erected another and a more splendid edifice, the burning of which gave occasion for similar gallantry on the part of the new Department in 1868.

But a serious and almost tragic affair took place about the same time in Forty-fourth Street, west of Eighth Avenue. This was the site of the old village of Bloomingdale, where vegetable markets abounded. Several houses were on fire, and at an upper window of one of them a woman appeared with a child in her arms. The fire at Barnum's left this locality short of its complement of engines, and no hook and ladder company was at hand. But the members of Equitable Engine Company No. 36 were equal to the occasion, and adopted an ingenious mode of saving life. One of the men climbed up the front of the building by the windows until he reached the room in which the woman stood. A comrade stood in the window below. Two others stationed themselves in the window on the lower floor. Others held a bed beneath, and then, first the child and afterwards the woman were lowered from story to story, and dropped on the bed. The spectators hailed this daring act with cheer upon cheer.

In Trinity Church yard, facing Broadway, is a memorial shaft and tablet, commemorative of the death and burial of a number of firemen.

The last hour of the gallant old volunteers was at hand, and their last duty was marked by disaster to themselves. On August 21, 1865, several of these brave and devoted citizens were injured by the falling of a wall at Nos. 203 and 205 South Street. A fire extended from No. 204 South Street to the bonded warehouse of J. J. Hicks at No. 401 Water Street, and the loss amounted to three hundred thousand dollars. The beloved engines had thrown their last streams, the noble men who had risked their lives for their fellow citizens stood silent and mournful in the station houses. The ties that had bound them together were broken, and they made way for the new organization, which is perpetuating their glory, their daring, and their historic self-sacrifice. The deeds of the old volunteers have gone into history and will live forever.

CHAPTER XVII

THE GREAT
CONFLAGRATION OF 1835

*A Night of Destruction and Terror.—Seventeen Degrees below Zero.—Frozen
Rivers and Frozen Engines.—Twenty Million Dollars' Worth of Property
Swept Away.—A Mountain of Flame Lighting up the Bay.—Despair of the
Citizens.—Gallant Struggles of the Firemen.—Alexander Hamilton's Views.*

The most destructive fire that has visited New York, the third greatest on
this continent, needs at least a chapter to itself. The great conflagration of
1835, though of world-wide fame, has never been fully told with all its incidents
and all its consequences. It was a terrible day for the first city of the land. The
destruction was fearful, and so were the results. In a few months the United
States banks suspended payment; then followed the commercial distress of 1837,
and for a time business seemed paralyzed. Next came bankruptcy after bankruptcy in quick succession, and soon the banks of the state stopped payment for
one year. The legislature legalized this necessary public act. The gloomiest fore-
bodings prevailed, and well they might, considering the terrible reverses which
the Empire City experienced from this memorable fire. But if the destruction
was so great, the rebuilding and the recovery were no less marvelous. New York
quickly arose from her ashes, and acres of splendid granite, marble, brown stone,
and brick stores filled the entire space that had been swept by the flames.

Three years before the terrible conflagration of December, 1835, there was a
visitation of Asiatic cholera, which had recurred season after season, carrying off
numbers of the population, and spreading consternation throughout the city. In
the summer of 1835 the epidemic seemed to have exhausted itself, and the
harassed people were congratulating themselves upon a bright and happy future
when another cloud spread over them to dash their spirits, and misfortune once
more drove them almost to despair. The fearfulness of the night was intensified
by the depth of the snow, the tempestuousness of the weather, and the extreme
bitterness of the cold, for the thermometer was far below zero. And yet our
bold, self-sacrificing firemen did their whole duty—did it, too, under the most
adverse circumstances. Two nights previous to this disastrous event the men had
been on duty at two heavy fires, one at Christie and Delancey Streets, at which

some half a dozen buildings were consumed, and the other on Water Street. The latter broke out in a spike and nail establishment belonging to Fullerton & Peckerings, No. 173, which was totally destroyed. When the fire was at its height the side walls fell out, crushing in No. 171, the latter taking fire almost instantly, and was the means of communicating to several others. Seven buildings and two carpenter shops were destroyed. Consequently the firemen came to this biggest of fires almost fagged out.

The flames raged from sixteen to twenty-four hours, swept away six hundred and seventy-four buildings, covering seventeen blocks, and fifty acres of ground, in the very heart of the city. It destroyed the section which contained the banks, the Stock Exchange, the Post Office, two churches, the dry goods warehouses, and some of the finest buildings in the city. The losses were estimated at twenty million dollars, which, in proportion to the size and wealth of the New York of to-day, is equivalent to what two hundred million dollars would represent now. The great fire of 1835 had never had an equal in any English speaking country since the destructive fire of London in 1666.

On Wednesday night, the sixteenth of December, the brazen tongue of the old jail bell, near the City Hall, and other fire bells, rang out their dreadful alarm upon the frosty air. The gusty wind blew the warning sounds east, west, north, and south. Out tumbled the gallant fire laddies, and through the snow-covered streets, assisted by the excited citizens, dragged their engines. A private watchman, Peter A. Holmes, while patrolling his beat, had discovered smoke issuing from the five-story building, No. 25 Merchant Street, which extended through to Pearl Street, and was occupied on the first floor by Comstock & Andrews, fancy dry goods merchants, and the upper part by Henry Barbaud, a French importer. In twenty minutes the flames spread to Exchange Place, then to Water Street, taking both sides of Old Slip and Coenties Slip, then to Beaver, to Jones' Place, to Front and South Streets. The breeze from the N.N.W. amounted almost to a gale. The rivers were frozen solid; so thick indeed was the ice that the firemen had to cut through it to clear the ends of the pier before they could strike water. Several of the engines were lowered down on the ice and there worked by the men. Every cistern and well was frozen in like manner. As the water from the rivers was pumped into the hose it froze in part and choked the flow. The firemen worked hard, stamping upon the hose to break the ice, and laboring at the pumps. The streams that were thrown by hydrants and engines were blown back in the faces of the toilers, falling congealed at the feet of the firemen. These efforts seemed to add only to the fury of the elements.

Many of the buildings were new storehouses with iron shutters and copper roofs, and so intense was the heat that the metal was melted and ran off the roof in streams. The harbor was lighted up brilliantly, the water looking like a sea of blood. Every spar and every rope in the ships was distinctly visible. Clouds of smoke, like dark mountains suddenly rising into the air, were succeeded by long banners of flame, reaching to the zenith and roaring for their prey. Street after street caught the terrible torrent, until acre after acre was booming an ocean of flame. The Tontine Building (Hudson's News Room), which had a shingle roof, caught fire, and dark smoke in huge masses tinged with flickering flashes of bright flame, burst from all the upper windows. The Tontine was on the north side of Wall Street, and had the flames consumed this building, nothing would have saved the upper part of the city. The old Tontine Coffee House was the exchange of the city, and Buyden, its keeper, is described as a rough but pleasant old fellow. It is related of him that when the first anthracite coal was offered for sale in New York, he tried it in the hall of the Tontine. He pronounced the new article worse than nothing, for he had put one scuttle into the grate and then another, and after they were consumed he took up two scuttlefuls of stones. Two solitary engines, with what little water they managed to obtain, were throwing their feeble and useless streams upon the flaming stores opposite, when Mr. Oliver Hull, calling their attention to the burning cornice of the Tontine, promised to donate one hundred dollars to the Firemen's Fund "if they would extinguish that blaze." In the vicinity was No. 13 Engine, of which Mr. Zophar Mills (who is still living) was foreman. Seeing the danger and knowing that in the ordinary way the hose would not convey the water to the top of the Tontine, Foreman Mills directed his men to get a counter which had been taken out of one of the stores, and to place on the top a gin or brandy puncheon and hold the nozzle so that the water could be thrown on the shingles of the building. By this means the fire was kept under at this point, and the upper part of the city was saved. This was at about four o'clock in the morning, and the cold was so penetrating that it was almost next to impossible to hold the nozzle of the hose in position. Thousands of citizens had flocked to the scene, and their aid was welcome to the tired firemen.

Subsequently there was a controversy as to what company was entitled to the reward for, and honor of, extinguishing the blazing cornice. The dispute was referred to Mr. Hull, the gentleman who offered the reward, who wrote a letter to Mr. Zophar Mills in which he says:

"Other firemen came in to assist from various directions; but the company to whom I spoke, and who piled up the packages on the counter, are, in my estimation, mostly, if not entirely, entitled to the honor of extinguishing the fire. I stood at the corner of Water Street, and observed the whole transaction. Several firemen afterwards called at my store, and stated that they had assisted in preventing the fire from crossing Wall Street at various places, and all of them appeared very much to rejoice in their success in arresting the fire, and seemed desirous to share in the honors. I do not remember which company I paid the money to, but remember that there was some controversy between 8 and 13 as to which was entitled to receive it. But, as it went into the Charitable Fund of the Fire Department, that was not deemed of much consequence. I make this statement with much pleasure, as I consider that we were indebted to the great exertions of our brave fellow citizens the firemen, on that disastrous night, in preventing the fire from crossing Wall Street, thus saving millions of property, and our beautiful city from probably entire ruin."

It was clearly proven at the time that the counter referred to was placed by Engine Company No. 13 upon the sidewalk and an empty liquor cask placed thereon. On the erection thus made Wm. Fitz Randolph held the pipe of Engine No. 13, while Alfred Willis was engaged in raising the hose. The pipe was held at as great an elevation as possible, and by the united force of the company applied to the engine, an unusually strong stream was forced upon the burning cornice. The following certificate was drawn up and signed by witnesses of the action:

We, the undersigned, do hereby certify and declare that we were present at the great fire on the night of the sixteenth of December, 1835, and that we saw the stream of water from the pipe of Fire Engine No. 13 reach and extinguish the fire on the cornice of the Tontine Building which was then in a blaze and burning rapidly.

Onward, still onward, swept the fiery besom of destruction. The hydrants were exhausted—the engines had long been frozen up with their hose. Westward, the South Dutch Church, which had been made the hasty depository of stores of precious goods, was in flames, which threatened to extend to Broad Street throughout. At this supreme moment a man was caught setting fire to the house at the corner of Stone and Broad Streets. Was he a maniac or maddened by liquor? The excited citizens paused not to inquire, but seizing this fiend in human shape lynched him on the spot. On the south a desperate struggle was made at Hanover Square. The firemen had turned their energies to saving property. In that large space was piled an immense amount of goods, thought to be perfectly safe in that spot. There was accumulated the stock of all the French stores, a mass of silks, satins, laces, cartons of dresses, capes, cashmere shawls, and the richest kind of fancy articles, forming a little mountain sixty feet wide by twenty-five feet in height, or nearly one hundred feet square. The large East India warehouse of Peter Remsen & Co., situated on the northeast corner of Hanover Square, was at this moment an object of absorbing interest. It was filled with a full stock of valuable goods. Before the fire reached it goods were cast out of the windows in the upper stories into the street, and merchandise from the lower floors were piled up with the rest of the large mass in the square. But the warring flames came swiftly on. Just as the goods were stacked a gust of flame, like a streak of lightning, came from the Remsen building, and shooting across the square, blown by the strong wind, set fire to the entire mass. In a few minutes the costly pile was reduced to cinders, it disappeared like figures in a dissolving view, and then the fire was communicated to the houses opposite. Notwithstanding the presence of this mighty furnace, the cold was so intense that the firemen were compelled to take the fine blankets saved, and, cutting a hole through them, convert them into temporary cloaks. In this attire they were seen at daylight dragging home their engines, many of the men so exhausted by fatigue that they were asleep as they walked. One entire company, thus accoutred, had artificial wreaths and bunches of artificial flowers of the richest kind in their caps, taken from the wreck of matter, and presenting a very singular contrast with their begrimed faces and jaded appearance.

It is said the illumination was so great that it was observed at places a hundred miles distant. At one time turpentine which took fire on the wharf ran down into the water and floated off, making a blazing sea many hundred yards square. The shipping in the docks of the East River was endangered, and saved only by strenuous exertions and its removal into the stream. The brig *Powhattan*, lying between Murray's Wharf and Coenties Slip, caught fire, but the flames were soon extinguished. No. 33 Engine was run upon the deck of a brig, in order to take the water with her suction, and played into No. 2, which gave her water to No. 13. This last engine (Mr. Zophar Mills's), as already stated, played in the fire at Wall Street. The members of No. 33 Engine, according to Mr. Charles Forrester, "had their own fun on the deck of the brig. The cook on the vessel made a fire in the galley, and six men would get in there and shut the doors, and when they got thawed out a member outside would place his fire cap over the pipe and smoke them out; then a new set would go in, and so it was kept up through the night. The engine did not cease working until daylight, when she stopped for a few seconds, and upon the orders to start again she was found so frozen that they could get no water through her. The company was then ordered home to thaw out."

To depict the scenes of that awful night would require a volume in itself. The surging crowds, the struggle of the police to restrain them, the thousand and one pieces of property rescued from the burning or endangered buildings, and carried hither and thither, the innumerable thefts, the shouts of the assembled thousands, the fights ending in bloodshed, the roar of the flames, and the hoarse creaking of the laboring engines no pen can do adequate justice to. It was a saturnalia for the lawless of the populace. Men, and women too, seized on the cases of wine and barrels of liquor that were thrown about anywhere and everywhere. It is supposed that a thousand baskets of champagne were broken and destroyed, the tops being unceremoniously knocked off, and the contents drunk by the maddened throngs surrounding the fire. An immense quantity of baskets of champagne were seen floating in the docks, and cheese and provisions were scattered there and about the slips. It was soon seen that to save the rest of the city several buildings must be blown up to check the progress of the fire. James Gulick, the hero of the "June Bugs," who was then chief engineer, decided to blow up the houses that were immediately threatened. Chief Engineer Gulick sent for some kegs of gunpowder, but a sufficiency could not be obtained in the city—not being allowed as an article of merchandise. Other messengers were sent in hot haste to the fort on Governor's Island, but in vain. Though a most bitter night, a navy barge was despatched, against a head tide, to the magazine at Red Hook, a distance probably of four or five miles from the Yard for a supply of powder.

Then when the first faint streaks of dawn were struggling with the unnatural redness in the sky, a corps of marines arrived with some powder, and the demolition of the buildings began, but it was not till noon of Thursday that the necessary break was made at Coenties Slip. It was truly remarkable, the characteristic sangfroid with which the sailors of Captain Mix's party carried about, wrapped up in a blanket or a pea-jacket, as it might happen, kegs and barrels of gunpowder, amid a constant shower of fire, as they followed their officers to the various buildings indicated for destruction. On the north side the extraordinary strength of the Wall Street buildings—many of them resisting firmly the assaults of the destroyer, and none of the walls crumbling and falling into the street, as is too generally the case—did more for the safety of that part of the city than anything within the power of human effort. For hours it was doubtful whether the flames could be resisted here, and, if not, there was little hope that they could be before reaching Maiden Lane.

The advent of the marines and sailors from the Navy Yard had a beneficial effect upon the crowds. The marines, eighty in number, under command of Captain Walker, formed a complete chain of sentinels along South Street, from the Fulton Ferry to Wall Street, and up Wall to the Exchange. They kept their posts all night, and thus afforded great protection to the property exposed. Great prices were offered and given for help in removing goods. One merchant is said to have purchased a horse and cart on the spot for five hundred dollars with which he succeeded in saving his stock. Leary, the hatter, in the midst of the fire gave away hats to any fellow who would help him remove a bundle. To one fellow he gave a hat who handed it back. "What's the matter?" "It doesn't fit," was the saucy reply. "Give me one to fit, if you are giving away hats." Many of the merchants, in the excitement of removing their goods, gave away blankets or anything to poor people who aided them. One poor man had removed several valuable packages to a place of safety. "Here's a coat, a pair of pantaloons, and a blanket for you," said the merchant, handing over the articles.

The violence of the gale continued all night. Burning embers were carried across the East River to Brooklyn, and set fire to the roof of a house, which, however, was speedily extinguished. Mr. John A. Meyers, of One Hundred and Fourth Street, near Ninth Avenue, who celebrated his golden wedding with four generations on February 8, 1886, was then living in a farmhouse on the site of the present Joralemon Street, Brooklyn, said that on the following morning he found the space around his dwelling black with embers flown over from the great fire. The grandest and most inspiring views were from Brooklyn, Weehawken, and Staten Island. Thence the whole city seemed in one awful sheet of flame. The merchants, aided by the firemen and the well-disposed citizens, devoted themselves to removing to places of supposed safety such property as could in their haste be got together. With this intent an immense quantity of goods was placed in the Merchants' Exchange in Wall Street and in the Reformed Dutch Church in Garden Street, where it was presumed they would be secure. But in a short time these buildings with their contents were reduced to ashes. The Exchange was one of the largest edifices in the city, situated on the south side of Wall Street, and embracing one hundred and fifteen feet of the front between William and Hanover Streets. It was three stories high, exclusive of the basement, which was considerably elevated. Its southwest front was one hundred and fourteen feet on Exchange Street. The front on Wall Street was of Westchester marble. The first and second stories of the Ionic order, from the Temple of Minerva Pallas, at Prigue, in Iona; a recessed elliptical portico of forty feet wide introduced in front. A screen of four columns and two antæ, each thirty feet and three feet four inches in diameter above the base, composed of a single block of marble, extended across the foot of the portico, supporting an entablature of six feet in height, on which rested the third story, making a height of sixty feet from the ground. The principal entrance to the rotunda and exchange room was by a flight of ten marble steps, with a pedestal at each end. On ascending to the portico three doors opened to offices. The vestibule was of the Ionic order, from the little Ionic Temple of Illysus. The exchange room, which was the rotunda, was seventy-five feet long, fifty-five feet wide, and forty-five feet high, to which were attached four principal rooms, and in the rear of the rotunda another, used for the auction sales of real estate, shipping, and stocks. The building was begun on the first of April, 1825, and occupied twenty-seven months in its erection, having first been occupied in July, 1827. The plan was that of the architect, Mr. E. Thompson.

This structure long resisted the flames. It did not catch until 2 o'clock on Thursday morning. The end in which the spire pointed to heaven, in the background, was the spot where it was fired. It extended from that point to the cupola and dome. In the centre of the rotunda was erected, by the liberality of the merchants of the city, a statue of General Alexander Hamilton, sculptured by Ball Hughes. The statue was about 15 feet high, including the base on which it was elevated, and chiselled from the whitest marble. The figure represented him holding a scroll in the left hand, resting on the thigh, and a scarf partly covering the body. For a long time this splendid statue was seen towering brightly amidst the sea of flames that dashed against its crackling base, seeming to cast a mournful glance on the terrific scene. About four o'clock the magnificent dome caved in with an awful crash, one lurid glare ascended to heaven, and then the marble effigy of Hamilton fell nobly, perishing under the crush of the edifice of which it had been, as it were, the tutelary genius. But one gallant effort had been made to save it by a young officer from the Navy Yard with a party of four or five blue jackets. They had actually succeeded in partly removing it from the pedestal when the warning cry was uttered that the roof was about to fall, and they had to seek safety in flight.

Another fine sight was the handsome church of the Rev. Dr. Matthews, in Garden Street. For a long while it withstood the mass of flames in their course towards Broad Street. The church possessed a famous organ. Many and many a solemn dirge had been played upon it at the burial of the dead, and now, the holy temple being on fire, some one commenced performing upon that organ its own funeral dirge and continued it till the lofty ceiling was in a blaze. The music ceased, and in a short time the beautiful edifice, with its noble instrument and immense quantities of goods stored inside and out, were all irrecoverably gone, nothing escaping save the long-sleeping dust and bones of the buried dead. Above the church the bright gold ball and star on the highest point of the spire gleamed brilliantly, and still, while they were both shining on the deep blue concave with an intensity of splendor which attracted general remark, gave one surge and fell in all their glory into the heap of chaos beneath them.

On the following day the heart of the city seemed to have ceased to beat. Of business there was none; New York was stricken as with paralysis. From five to ten thousand persons had been thrown out of employment, and universal sorrow prevailed. The people gathered in their thousands around the smoking ruins and sadly thought of the many families whose daily bread was gone. Swiftly flew the news to other cities, and sympathy of a practical kind was the response. The same locomotive that early on Thursday morning carried the tidings of the fire to Newark brought to the city within an hour afterwards the New Jersey engines, which at once went to work. The conduct of the Philadelphia firemen was noble. Immediately on the receipt of the intelligence from New York four hundred of them organized themselves and started to come on. Unfortunately, by the breaking down of one of the cars on the railroad, a large number of them were obliged to go back, but some arrived early on Saturday morning, and the remainder followed with as little delay as possible. Stations were assigned them amid the ruins, and they went to work with great spirit and excellent results. On the succeeding nights, patrol duty was done by the Third and Ninth Regiments and the light infantry companies. Civic patrols were also formed in several wards, and thus property to a great amount was saved from depredation. Large quantities of merchandise, carried off in boats on Wednesday night were secreted on the Long Island and Jersey shores and in the upper wards of the city.

The scene at Police Headquarters was indeed heartrending. The squalid misery of a greater part of those taken with the goods in their possession, the lies and prevarications to which they resorted to induce the magistrates not to commit them to prison, their screeching and wailing when they found they must relinquish the splendid prizes they had made during the raging of the fire, and the numbers in which they were brought by the police and military, exceeded any scene of a similar kind on record. For the previous three days and nights every place capable of detention was crammed with these miserable objects—sometimes as many as one hundred being in confinement at the same moment. Hundreds were discharged without detention or other punishment than merely taking from them their plunder; and but very few of the whole number, even those who had stolen hundreds of dollars' worth, could be convicted, in consequence of the impossibility of the identification of the property stolen.

Mr. James Gordon Bennett, the elder, was then, by his characteristic enterprise and liberality, building up his paper, the *Herald*. In his issue of December 18 he gives the following graphic description of his visit to the ruins on the morning following the fire:

"At nine o'clock yesterday morning I went to see the awful scene. It was heartrending in the extreme. I walked down William Street. Crowds of people of both sexes were wandering in the same direction. It was piercing cold, and every other person had a woollen comforter wrapped around his neck. On approaching the corner of Wall and William Streets the smoking ruins were awful. The whole of the southern side of Wall Street was nearly down. The front walls of the Exchange were in part remaining, covered with smoke and exhibiting the effects of the fire. The splendid marble columns were cracked in several parts. The street was full of people, the sidewalks encumbered with boxes, bales, bundles, desks, safes and loose articles. There was no possibility of then proceeding further down William Street. Both sides were burned down and the streets were filled up with hot bricks, burning goods and heaps of rubbish. United States soldiers were stationed here and there to protect the goods, yet the boys, men and women, of all colors, were stealing and pilfering as fast as they could. From this spot I proceeded down Wall Street in the center. I saw the *Journal of Commerce* sign—all the rest gone. The various brokers' offices to the right were a heap of ruins. The Josephs, the Allens, the Livingstons and various others, all in ruins. From the Exchange down to the river, one side of Wall Street is a heap of ruins.

"On going down Wall Street I found it difficult to get through the crowd.

The hose of the fire engines was run along the street and frozen. The front blocks of houses between Exchange Place and Pearl Street, on Wall, were standing, behind which were all ruin and desolation. At the corner of Wall and Pearl, on looking southwardly, I saw a single ruin standing about half way to Hanover Square. I proceeded, climbing over the hot bricks, on the site, as I thought, of Pearl Street—but of that I am not sure—till I got to the single, solitary wall that reared its head as if it was in mockery of the elemental war. On approaching I read on the mutilated granite wall, "Arth—Tap—n, 122 Pe—1 Street." These were all the characters I could distinguish on the column. Two stories of this great wall were standing—the rest entirely in ruins. It was the only portion of a wall standing from the corner of Wall Street to Hanover Square; for beyond that there are nothing but smoke and fire and dust.

"Proceeding along on the ruins, sometimes on Pearl Street, sometimes out of it, I found several groups of boys and men digging among the hot dust and bricks. 'What are they doing?' 'Damn them,' said he, 'they are looking for money. Some of them have found gold pieces and others franc pieces.' 'Hillo?' cried a dirty looking little fellow, 'I have got something.' In several other places there were small groups of pilferers and thieves. In the center of Hanover Square I found a variety of goods and merchandise burning. Several men and boys were warming themselves at a fire made of fine French calicoes and Irish linens. Here the smoke was intense. From Hanover Square I could neither proceed south, east nor west. William Street, Pearl and down to the wharf were all impassable. The smoke was suffocating. The whole of the space between the corner of William and Pearl up to the Exchange, with all the streets, stores, etc., I saw to be a sad heap of utter ruins. 'Good God!' said a man to me, 'what a sight!' 'What a sight, truly!' said I. From this spot, near the *Gazette* office which was entirely burned down, I returned the way I came, climbing over burning bricks, knocking against boys, encountering bales and boxes, till I again reached a firm footing in Wall Street. I then proceeded down the northern side of Wall Street to the wharf below. The crowd of spectators was greater here than ever. The street was full of boxes and goods. I felt quite cold. I saw a large group of men stirring up a fire in the center of Wall Street, between Water and Front, which is here wide. On going near to warm myself I found the fire was made out of the richest merchandise and fine furniture from some of the elegant counting rooms.

"I proceeded to Hudson's News Room, which escaped, having been on the windward side of Wall Street. I could not find an entrance. It was full of goods and bales of merchandise. I proceeded to the corner of Wall and Front Streets. Here I saw a horrible scene of desolation. Looking down South Street toward the south nothing could be seen but awful ruins. People were standing shaking their heads and stamping their feet—still quite cold—and uttering melancholy exclamations. A small boy at the corner was caught by an honest black porter stealing some goods. 'What are you going to do with that?' asked the porter. 'Nothing,' said the boy. 'Then lay it where you found it and go to the watch house with me.' The rascal attempted to escape. He cried out. 'Let the scoundrel go!' said a gentleman, and straightway the honest black man gave him a kick and let him run.

"From the corner of Wall Street I proceeded southwardly, for I cannot now talk of streets; all their sites are buried in ruins and smoking bricks. No vessels lay here at the wharves; all were gone. I went down the wharf; the basin was floating with calicoes, silks, teas, packing cases, and other valuable merchandise. Piles of coarse linen and sacking encumbered the street. The carts were busy driving the mutilated goods away. Going a little further south, on what was formerly Front Street, I encountered a cloud of smoke that burst from a smoking pile of stores. I was almost suffocated. Emerging from this sirocco I found myself near a group of boys and ragged men huddling round a fire made of some curious species of fuel. All around appeared to be large heaps of small dust. The fragrance was fine. I asked one of the boys, 'What is that?' 'Tea, sir,' said he, with perfect nonchalance; 'fine Hyson tea; doesn't it make a fine fire? Come, Jack, throw in a little more of that fuel,' and sure enough he did. A fire was hissing away, made out of tea boxes and fine Hyson tea itself. Several little dirty girls were here gathering up Hyson tea and putting it away in baskets. Proceeding further, I encountered hogsheads of raw sugar, half emptied, and their contents strewed, like the Hyson tea, over the pavements and bricks. Boys and girls were eating it as fast as they could.

"I could not get further than a short distance down Front from the corner of Wall. The smoke, ruin, hot bricks, and all were too horrible to get over or through. Retracing my steps, I returned up Wall Street. The same scenes presented themselves to me. The crowds were immense. Carts, porters, merchants, brokers, bankers, women, children crowded from Front to the bottom of Wall Street. I passed the solitary columns of the Exchange, I under the corner of Broad Street, and attempted in that direction to reach the southwest part of the scene of conflagration. All Broad Street was crowded with goods, merchandise, carts, porters, and crowds. I attempted several times to thread my way down to the wharf at the foot of Broad Street. I could not do it. From the center of this street, looking to the left over the buildings in the direction of William, I saw nothing but flames ascending to heaven, and prodigious clouds of smoke curling after it as if from a volcano. Emerging from Broad Street I went up by a narrow street to the Bowling Green. Here was deposited on the sidewalks half a million of fine goods. The whole street was lined. Clerks were standing around the several piles watching them. I went down Whitehall Slip. It was equally crowded with rich merchandise. One whole end of the Battery was covered with the richest silks, sarsnets, brocades, and woollen cloths. The plunderers were here quite busy. Several were caught, and sent to the watch house. I turned the corner at the southern end of South Street, and wended my way along the wharves in the direction of Coenties Slip. I found all the merchants in Front Street busy removing their goods.

"On reaching the corner of Front Street and Coenties Slip the most awful scenes burst upon my eyes. I beheld the several blocks of seven story stores, full of rich merchandise, on the northern side of the slip, in one bright, burning, horrible flame. About forty buildings were on fire at one moment. The front on the slip was piled up with goods. 'What nonsense!' said the people, 'the goods will burn up also.' Here the crowd was immense. All the upper part of the slip on the northern and eastern side was burning or burned up. At the southern corner of Pearl and Coenties Slip it was just passable. All to the right was on fire, and every store back to Broad Street it was feared would go. Pushing through the crowd, I attempted to get back to Broad Street through Pearl. It was hardly possible, so much was the street encumbered with goods, crowds, and carts.

"From this point I retreated up Broad Street through an immense crowd to the Custom House, to which the Post-office had retreated. Here I found a few of the Post-office clerks in an apartment leading from Pine Street, all in an awful state of confusion. They scarcely knew what they had lost or saved, and could not tell when the mails would be ready. On falling in with several of our most respectable citizens, I said, 'Awful! horrible!' 'Truly, truly,' said they, 'we are all ruined; I have two sons gone; each of their stores is burned down. The insurance companies will not be able to pay five shillings in the pound. New York is bankrupt. New York is put twenty years back. Philadelphia and Boston will now start ahead of us.' 'What shall be done?' asked I. 'Shall we not go to war with France?' 'Tush! tush!' said he. 'The surplus revenue ought to pay for this night's work. We paid it to the government—let them give it back to us; we are ruined and bankrupt.'

"There were five hundred stores destroyed. Many of them were worth three hundred thousand dollars. Put them at forty thousand dollars each average, and we have a loss of twenty million dollars—the probable truth. To cover this loss there are twenty-six insurance companies in operation with a capital of nine million four hundred and fifty thousand dollars. Probably two-thirds of this is good for the losses—say six millions. Add two millions insured in Boston and elsewhere, makes eight millions of insurance, which, all paid, leaves a dead loss of twelve millions of dollars to individual merchants and owners of real estate. Some of the oldest families in the city are ruined."

Of the six large morning newspapers only two escaped the general wreck— the *Mercantile* and the *Courier and Enquirer*. The *Daily Advertiser, Journal of Commerce*, and *Gazette* were burned out of both printing and publication offices; the

Times of printing office only. The *American* among the evening papers was entirely destroyed. All Mr. Minor's periodicals, *Railroad Journal, Mechanics' Magazine*, etc., were included in the wreck. The printers of the *Knickerbocker* also. The following were the number of buildings destroyed on each street:

Water	41	Old Slip	83
South	37	Jones' Lane	10
Front	80	Gouverneur Lane	20
William	44	Exchange Place	62
Beaver	23	Exchange Street	31
Stone	60	Guyless Alley	20
Mill	38	Hanover Square	3
Pearl	70	Merchant Street	25
Hanover	10		
Coenties Slip	10	Total	674

Arthur Tappan & Co., escaped the absolute ruin in which so many were involved. Their store being of stone, and having window shutters of thick boiler iron (put on after the mobs of 1834), withstood the flames for nearly an hour, while all was in a blaze around it, so that the books and papers, and a very large amount of goods, probably one hundred thousand dollars' worth, were carried out, and after two removes placed beyond the spread of fire. The energy and daring with which the colored people pressed to save these goods greatly impressed the bystanders. It was with difficulty they were restrained from rushing in after the flames had burst out at the door.

Arthur Tappan had an insurance effected on his store and goods to the amount of three hundred thousand dollars at one of the Boston offices. No office in New York City would insure him because he was an abolitionist.

On the second night after the conflagration a couple of gentlemen observed a stout woman making up Pearl Street, near the corner of Wall Street, with a large bundle under her cloak. When she saw the gentlemen looking at her, she immediately commenced singing "Hush-a-by, baby," etc. The gentlemen, thinking that the poor baby was quite worrisome, offered their aid to quiet its infant restlessness. "Oh, bless your honors, she's asleep now." The gentlemen still persisted in having a peep at the blooming little cherub. She resisted, but in vain. On opening the cloak, they found that the dear little creature, in the terror of the moment, had actually changed into an armful of the richest silk and satin goods, slightly burnt at the ends. The affectionate mother was immediately secured.

During the fire a store was burnt in which was contained eight hundred thousand pounds of lead, belonging to a merchant in Philadelphia. After the fire was over, and the rubbish removed, it was found that the lead had melted into large masses, so that the owner was obliged to *quarry* it out.

The quantity of French goods destroyed was very great. Out of twenty-seven French importing merchants, twenty-three had been completely burned out. There were only four left in the city, and of these, but one of any magnitude— H. Boerdam & Co. French goods advanced twelve per cent. About twelve hundred packages of Manchester print goods were alone destroyed in Exchange Place, commonly called Calico Row. Of linens, also, a large quantity had been destroyed. Stephen Whitney lost $500,000 in houses and real estate; John Suydam, probably $200,000 in stores and insurance stocks. Out of $200,000 in insurance stocks, Dr. Hasack, who died four days after, only saved $20,000. About ten crockery stores were completely destroyed, and also nine or ten hardware. The McNeals, of Salem, were the losers of the great cargo of tea in the store of Osborne & Young. On Tuesday, the day before the fire, they were offered $60,000 profit on the whole cargo. They said to their supercargo, "Shall we take it?" "I would advise you not," said he. "You can, by keeping it a month, make $200,000." They did so, and lost the whole. After the fire the supercargo recalled the conversation and regretted it. "No," said they, "it is all for the best. Providence knows better than you do. It might have been bought by some one that could not bear the loss so well as we can." Noble fellows! Probably about four thousand boxes of sugar of all kinds had been destroyed, and at least forty thousand bags of coffee. On Old Slip there were piled up at least five thousand bags.

Gabriel P. Disosway, of the firm of Disosway & Brothers, 180 Pearl Street, near Maiden Lane, writing some years after the occurence, has given one of the best accounts of the fire. "I then resided in that pleasant Quaker neighborhood, Vandewater Street," said he, "and, hearing an alarm of fire, hastened to the front door. I put on an old warm overcoat and an old hat for active service on my own hook. Years afterwards these articles, preserved as curiosities, bore marks of the heat, sparks and exposure of that fearful time . . . My own course that night was to obtain voluntary aid, and, entering the stores of personal friends, remove, if possible, books and papers . . . It is impossible to imagine the fervent heat created by the increasing flames. Many of the stores were new, with iron shutters, doors and copper roofs and gutters, 'fireproof' of first-class, and I carefully watched the beginning and the progress of their destruction. The heat alone at times melted the copper roofing, and the burning liquid ran off in great drops. At one store, near Arthur Tappan & Co.'s, I warned some firemen of their danger from this unexpected source. Along here, the buildings were of the first-class, and one after another ignited under the roof, from the next edifice. Downward from floor to floor went the devouring element. As the different stories caught, the iron closed shutters shone with glowing redness, until at last forced open by the uncontrollable enemy. Within, they presented the appearance of immense iron furnaces in full blast. The tin and copper bound roofs often seemed struggling to maintain their fast hold, gently rising and falling and moving until, their rafters giving way, they mingled in the blazing crater below of goods, beams, floors and walls.

"On the north side of Hanover Square stood the fine storehouse of Peter Remsen & Co., one of the largest East India firms, with a valuable stock. Here we assisted, and many light bales of goods were thrown from the upper windows, together with a large amount of other merchandise, all heaped in the midst of the square, then thought to be a perfectly secure place. . . . Water Street, too, was on fire, and we hastened to the old firm of S. B. Harper & Sons, grocers in Front Street, opposite Gouverneur Lane, where there appeared to be no immediate danger. The father and sons had arrived, and we succeeded in removing their valuables. As we left the store after the last load a terrible explosion occured near by with the noise of a cannon. The earth shook. We ran for safety, not knowing what might follow, and took refuge on the corner of Gouverneur Lane, nearly opposite. Waiting for a few minutes a second explosion took place, then another and another. During the space perhaps of half an hour shock after shock followed in rapid succession, accompanied with the darkest, thickest clouds of smoke imaginable. The explosions came from a store on Front Street, near Old Slip, where large quantities of saltpeter in bags had been stored. Suddenly the whole ignited, and out leaped the flaming streams of these neutral salts, in their own peculiar colors, from every door and window. Some might have called them fireworks. . . . One of the most grand and frightful scenes of the whole night was the burning of a large oil store at the corner of Old Slip and South Street. It was four or more stories high, and filled with windows on both sides without any shutters. This was before the days of petroleum and kerosene, and the building was full of sperm and other oils. These fired hogshead after hogshead, and over the spacious edifice resembled a vast bonfire or giant beacon, casting its bright beams far and wide on the river and surrounding region, but finally the confined inflammable mass from eaves to cellar shot out with tremendous force through every window and opening, and soon all disappeared except the cracked, tottering, and falling walls. . . . I sought the premises of Burns, Halliburton & Co., one of the most popular firms of that day. They were the agents of the Merrimac and other works, and had an immense valuable stock of calicoes, muslins, and flannels. In one of the upper lofts I met a member of the firm, Mr. Burns, one of nature's noblemen, since dead, with his other partners, and he was weeping. 'Too hard,' said he, 'after all the toil of years, to see property thus suddenly destroyed!' 'Cheer up,' we replied, 'the world is still wide enough for success and fortune,' and so it proved to him and many other sufferers.

"From Maiden Lane to Coenties Slip, and from William Street to the East

River, the whole immense area, embracing some 13 acres, all in a raging un-controllable blaze! To what can we compare it? An ocean of fire, as it were, with roaring, rolling, burning waves, surging onward and upward, and spreading certain universal destruction; tottering walls and falling chimneys, with black smoke, hissing, clashing sounds on every side. Something like this, for we cannot describe it, was the fearful prospect, and soon satisfied with the alarming, fearful view, we retreated from our high lookout.

"Not long after we left our high standpoint it was enveloped in the universal blaze, and soon the Garden Street Church, with its spire, organ, and heaps of goods stored within and out side, was consumed. There, too, was lost the ven-erable bell which had been removed at an early period in New York history from the old St. Nicholas Church within the present Battery. 'What more can be done to stop the progress of the flames?' became the anxious and general inquiry. Mr. Cornelius W. Lawrence, the Mayor, appeared with his officers, and, after consultation, it was determined to blow up some buildings, and the east corner of Coenties Slip and Coenties Lane (a narrow street) was selected as the proper place to begin the necessary work. On the opposite was the store of William Van Antwerp & Co., hardware dealers and relatives of the writer, who, engaged at this point in saving goods, could see the necessary preparations for the blast. The building to be blown up, I think, was occupied by Wyncoop & Co., grocers. It was large and of brick. Colonel Smith soon arrived with the powder, and a gang of officers and sailors from the Navy Yard, and none else were permitted to interfere. They commenced mining in the cellar, and, placing heavy timbers upon the powder kegs and against beams of the floors, everything was soon ready for the explosion. A friend near by said to an old tar, 'Be careful or you will be blown up!' 'Blow and be——!' was the careless and characteristic reply to the warning; but, all having been admirably and safely arranged, the crowd retreated. The torch was applied, and in an instant the report followed; then the immense mass heaved up as if by magic, and losing its fastenings, from the cellar to the roof, tottered, shook and fell. A shout went up from the gazing spectators, and at this point the common danger was evidently arrested, thanks to Colonel Swift, Lieutenant Reynolds, and Captain Mix of the Navy and their noble, brave sailors. Heroism can be as much displayed at a terrible catastrophe of this kind as on the bloody field of battle, and it was to-night. This party of miners arrived about 2 o'clock in the morning, when their important work commenced. They continued it successfully in another direction; indeed, it was believed that the conflagration was at last checked by this blowing up of the buildings.

"Wearied with watching, labor and anxiety, thousands wished for the return of day, and at length a dim, increasing light in the east, but enshrouded with dull, heavy clouds of smoke, foretold the coming morning. And what an un-

expected, melancholy spectacle to thousands did New York present! The generous firemen from Philadelphia soon after made their appearance, but the fire
had been checked. The immense remains continued to blaze and burn for many
days. We could now travel around the bounds of the night's destruction, but no
living being could venture through them. Many a merchant living in the upper
section of the city went quietly to bed that night, and strange as it may seem,
when he came down town the next morning, literally could not find his store,
not enough of his stock remaining to cover his head—every yard, ell, pound,
gone! There were official statements of several stores, in each of which a quarter
of a million dollars in goods was consumed, with books, notes, and accounts.
New York the next day sat, as it were, in sackcloth and ashes, and real sorrow
began to appear on men's faces as the losses and ruin were discovered by the
light of day.

"During the conflagration, then under full headway toward Broad Street, the
presence of mind of one man saved much property. This was Downing, the
oyster king, of Broad Street fame. Water was out of the question, and at this
emergency he thought of his supplies of vinegar, which were large, and with
careful application by pailful after pailful a large amount of property was saved
in that direction from the general destruction.

"In the estimated thirteen acres of the burned district only one store escaped
entire. This was occupied by the well-known John A. Moore of this day in the
iron trade on Water Street, near Old Slip. Watched inside, and fire proof, in
their wildest career the rapid flames seemed, as it were, to overleap the building,
destroying all others. There it stood solitary and alone amidst surrounding entire
destruction, as a sad monument stands alone amid the general ruin."

Among those who were deeply affected by this calamitous fire was the celebrated Colonel Alexander Hamilton. Colonel Hamilton wrote the following
letter in reference to the fire to the *Mercantile Advertiser and New York Advocate:*

In the anxious state of the public mind will you permit me to suggest a
few reflections, which appear to me not unworthy of the attention of those
who hold important stations controlling the destinies of the community. In
the first place, it is not necessary to magnify the distressful consequences of
the disastrous conflagration, in which we have all, rich and poor, a most
painful subject of contemplation. The evil is not without its remedy, and
in such a community as ours it cannot be of long endurance. The common
inquiries are everywhere heard, "What is to be done?" "Where is the mischief to end?" "From what quarter are we to look for assistance?" To all
which interrogations the answer is readily suggested, by a recurrence to the
immense pecuniary ability of the country, which, if wisely administered,
cannot fail to afford immediate relief. In the onset, it is important that our

insurance companies and our banking institutions should, in their respective capacities, create conservative committees to ascertain the losses which they have actually sustained, and their means of meeting them. These are certainly necessary preliminary steps, and essentially important. This being determined on, it will then be advisable that application should be made to Congress to place at the disposal of our State government whatever amount of money it may judge proper to employ in order to administer to the urgent wants of this crisis. The necessity of some legislative interference cannot be questioned, and if promptly given when the legislature meets in January, the benignant influence of confidence will be generally felt. In order to extend assistance the State Treasury should be authorized to loan on all the good securities, bonds and mortgages, etc., in the possession of the insurance companies, to afford them an immediate opportunity to pay the amount of their indebtedness on their policies of insurance, without which they will have to depend on the dilatory course of law, and, in the operation, necessarily increase the distress by extending the embarrassment to others, and thus, independent of the procrastination, defeat the very object in contemplation. In the panic of 1832 the Bank of England advanced on title deeds, bonds and mortgages, etc., with a promptness and vigor at once honorable to that noble institution and to the government which sanctioned the assumption of such a responsibility. These negotiations were made on the character of the applicants, free from all petty cavilling, which saved Great Britain from bankruptcy. It was a measure full of patriotism, intelligence, and worthy the occasion. If, then, the Governor of the State of New York will promptly enter into a correspondence with the United States Treasury to produce an immediate action on the part of Congress, suggesting that in his annual message he will recommend to the Legislature to interpose its credit for the general relief of the public, there can be no doubt that an appropriation will be immediately made. The commercial community will instantly recommence business, the fiscal operations of the country will assume their wonted activity, and the whole community will soon feel the invigorating influence of restoring order and system in place of alarm and chaos.

Is it to be credited that a country which has realized hundreds of millions within the last three years, with its public credit undoubted, should relapse from its high state of prosperity by the deduction of less than twenty million dollars' worth of property? That this will be found the maximum of the loss, I entertain no doubt. The stock of goods in store at this season of the year is well known to be small, and it is equally a fact that a very limited amount of the spring orders have as yet been executed. The open policies of insurance on goods will be found on investigation to attach to valid claims disproportioned to the general apprehension. To make this investigation the more complete, a general insurance committee should be organized, of active, intelligent merchants, of sufficient numbers to appoint adequate sub-committees to make strict inquiries to enable them to compare evidences.

It is necessary that promptness of action should be pursued; every delay but increases the embarrassment, and renders the palliative more difficult of application.

At the public meeting which takes place this evening let the Mayor be requested to address the executive of this State, asking him immediately to enter into a correspondence with our representatives, desiring them to bring this interesting subject, important to the United States, instantly before the National Government, and to solicit him to recommend to the legislature to interpose its credit to procure the only prompt relief which the nature of the case will admit. In the meantime, there can be no doubt as to the course proper for our banks to pursue, which the intelligent gentlemen comprising their direction well know how to apply. In short, a discreet forbearance on the part of the banks, and the prompt action of the Government, will save many of the individuals implicated, relieve the community from further distress, and eventually give new vigor to our commercial enterprise, the vital spirit of our national prosperity.

Alexander Hamilton.

CHAPTER XVIII

GUNPOWDER CHECKS THE FLAMES

Ravages of the Great Fire.—Graphic Description by Eye-Witnesses.—
Insurance Companies Bankrupted.—Terror and Dismay.—The Fairest Portion
of the City in Ruins.—Action of the Authorities.—Arrival of
Philadelphia Firemen.

A public meeting, to express sympathy, took place in the City Hall at noon on December 19. The assemblage was called to order by Judge Irving, upon whose motion the mayor took the chair. The meeting was addressed by Samuel L. Stone, Prosper M. Wetmore and several other prominent citizens, after which the following resolutions were, on motion of James G. King, unanimously adopted:

> *Resolved*, That while the citizens of New York lament over the ruin which has left desolate the most valuable part of this city, and deeply sympathize with the numerous sufferers, it becomes them not to repine, but to unite in a vigorous exertion to repair the loss, that the extent of her commerce, wealth, and enterprise of her citizens justify, under the blessing of Divine Providence, a primary reliance upon her own resources.
>
> *Resolved*, That we consider it the duty of our citizens and moneyed institutions, who stand in the relation of creditors to those who have directly or indirectly suffered by the late fire, to extend to them the utmost forbearance and lenity.

On motion of Dudley Selden, it was further

> *Resolved*, That a committee of the Mayor and one hundred and fifty citizens be appointed to ascertain the extent and probable value of the property destroyed, and how far the sufferers are protected by insurance. Also with power to make application to Congress for relief by an extension of credit for debts due to the United States, and a return of remission of duties on goods destroyed, and also to ask such other aid from the general

state and city governments as may be deemed expedient. Also to ascertain the origin and cause of the fire, and what change, if any, should be made either in the regulating of streets, the erection of buildings, or the arrangements of the Fire Department, to prevent a recurrence of similar calamities, and take such other measures as the emergency may demand.

Resolved, That the committee to be appointed take the earliest and most effectual measures to ascertain and relieve the necessities of those who have been reduced to want by the recent unfortunate event.

On motion of Colonel Murray, it was also

Resolved, That the thanks of this meeting be and they are hereby tendered to the citizens of Philadelphia and Newark for the spontaneous expression of their sympathy in our misfortunes, and that they be especially tendered to the firemen of those cities who, with a promptitude and kindness unexampled, have left their homes at this inclement season to offer their services, and which they are now tendering at the scene of the calamity.

On motion of Prosper M. Wetmore it was finally resolved that the member, of the two Boards of the Common Council be *ex officio* members of the committee to be appointed. The committee, the names of whose members are well-known to-day, was then announced.

Scarcely had this committee been appointed, when a communication was received from the president of the Board of Trade announcing the names of a committee from that body to co-operate in the objects of the meeting.

An investigation was commenced on December 23 (Wednesday) and carried on in the grand jury room on Monday, before Col. Murray, the Chairman of the Committee of Citizens, aided by Justice Lownds, and Messrs. Ward and Jordan, of the Fire Committee of the Board of Assistant Aldermen, relative to the origin and cause of the fire. From a mass of testimony received from numerous merchants, clerks and others, under oath, it appeared to be incontrovertibly established that the fire originated in the store at No. 25 Merchant Street, and that it was seen simultaneously in the first and fourth stories of that building, occupied by Messrs. Comstock & Andrews, the two intermediate stories occupied on the Pearl Street side by Mr. Henry Barbaud, that a report like an explosion of a gas pipe was heard in No. 25 to proceed from No. 28, and soon after the flames seemed to have been enkindled on the first floor, and shot up with the rapidity of lightning through the scuttles in the several floors to the upper story and through the roof. It was the opinion of the committee that it must have been produced by the bursting of a gas pipe, and the distribution of the gas, until it came in contact with the coal in the stove or grate, by which it was ignited. The store No. 25 had been closed a little after five o'clock, and the fires well secured to guard against any accident or injury therefrom. This was the result of a long and critical investigation, and proved that no blame attached to any one.

The Board of Assistant Aldermen held a meeting on the seventeenth of December, 1835. The President, James R. Whitney, being absent, on motion of Mr. Townsend, Mr. Ingraham was called to the chair. The following message was received from his honor the mayor:

Mayor's Office, New York, December 17, 1835. Gentlemen of the Common Council: I have requested your meeting this afternoon for the purpose of taking such measures as you may deem necessary for the protection of the immense amount of property exposed to the dreadful conflagration of last night. I propose that the watch be doubled, which will give about three hundred additional guard, and that the mayor accept the volunteer aid of one thousand citizens, together amounting to thirteen hundred. I deem it essential that the property now exposed should be protected as far as practicable. So large a number of citizens in the streets would be likely to notice any appearance of fire, and would doubtless in case of need, be prepared to aid the firemen in the discharge of their arduous duties.

I need not refer to the occurrences of last night, and to the valuable services rendered by our citizens, but I feel it my duty to acknowledge the aid furnished by Commodore Ridgely and the active personal services of Captain Mix, Lieutenant Nicholas, and the officers, seamen and marines under their command. Our acknowledgments are also due to Lieutenant Temple, of the United States Artillery, and to Geo. Swift.

In conclusion I would suggest to your consideration the propriety of inviting a meeting of the citizens to consider the emergency in which our business community is placed, and to devise such measures as may be proper for remedying, as far as possible, the effects of the serious calamity by which our city has been visited. If it be the desire of the Common Council, I will, under your authority, invite the citizens to meet at such time and place as may appear to be expedient.

C. W. Lawrence

After reading the above message, the chairman offered the following resolutions, which were unanimously adopted, and sent to the Board of Aldermen for concurrence:

By Mr. Ingraham—*Resolved*, That during the present emergency his honor the Mayor be invested with full power to employ such additional aid, either to the police watch, or firemen, as in his judgment shall be necessary, and that this Common Council will recognize all engagements which he may think proper to make for the protection of the city from fires, and guarding the property of the citizens, and that the Comptroller pay the necessary expenses that may be incurred thereby.

Resolved, That his honor the Mayor be requested to call a meeting of the citizens at such time and place as to him may appear expedient, to devise such measures as may be proper for remedying the effects of the serious calamity with which this city has been visited, and from preventing any further extension of the same.

Mr. Cleaveland offered the following resolution:

Resolved, (If the Board of Aldermen concur) That a special committee of five members from each board be appointed to institute an inquiry into the cause or causes originating the destructive conflagration in the First Ward, on the night of the sixteenth instant, with power to conduct such inquiry in any manner which to said committee shall seem judicious, and to report the result of their investigations to the Common Council Committee on the part of the Board of Assistants, and that Assistant Aldermen Cleaveland, Jordan, Clark, Stewart, and Townsend, be the committee on the part of this board. The resolution was sent to the Board of Aldermen for concurrence.

Mr. Brady offered the following resolution:

Resolved, (If the Board of Aldermen concur) That suitable apartments in the City Hall, or other public buildings, be offered to the postmaster of this city, for the accommodation of the post-office, until the general government shall make arrangements therefore. Adopted unanimously and sent to the other Board for concurrence.

Mr. Clark offered the following resolution:

Resolved, (If the Board of Aldermen concur herein) That the Mayor of this city be requested to apply forthwith to the proper department of the Government of the United States, and respectfully request said government to extend every possible facility to all the banks in this city, and especially by loaning to said banks a large portion of the surplus revenue of the United States, and affording relief to the citizens who have sustained loss by the late fire in this city.

At the suggestion of the chairman, the above resolution was amended by adding, after the word "requested," the words "in connection with the presidents of the Board of Trade and Chamber of Commerce." The resolution thus amended was adopted unanimously, and sent to the Board of Aldermen for concurrence.

The resolutions of Mr. Ingraham were sent back from the Board of Aldermen with an amendment, by adding the word "military" to the other classes of citizens whom it was proposed to invest his honor the mayor with authority to employ, and the amendment was concurred in.

The resolution of Mr. Brady was received from the Board of Aldermen with the following additional resolution, which was concurred in:

> *Resolved,* That a committee of three be appointed on the part of this Board with power to carry the above resolution into effect.

Aldermen Delamater, Banks, and Stilwell were appointed the committee. The resolution of Mr. Cleaveland was received from the Board of Aldermen, that Board having concurred in said resolution, and appointed Aldermen Benson, Taylor, Nixon, and Lovett as their part of the committee.

Mr. Curtis offered the following resolution, which was adopted unanimously:

> *Resolved,* That the northwestern chamber of the City Hall, known as the Superior Court Room, be placed at the disposal of the merchants of the city for their use as a Merchants' Exchange Room.

Laid on the table.

Mr. Whiting offered the following resolution:

> *Resolved,* That a committee of two from each Board be appointed to act conjointly with the chief engineer, and that they give him all the aid in their power, and that they have power to destroy any buildings they may think proper to prevent any farther extension of the fire.

Adopted; and Messrs. Whiting and Jordan were appointed to wait on the Board of Aldermen with a copy of the resolution.

Mr. Whiting, on behalf of the committee, reported that they had presented the resolution with which they were intrusted to the Board of Aldermen, and that said Board had laid the resolution on the table.

The Board of Assistants met on the eighteenth of December. There were present: James R. Whiting, Esq., President; Messrs. Townsend, Brady, Paulding,

Greenfield, Ingraham, Stewart, Power and Ward. Mr. Ingraham offered the following resolution, which was adopted.

> *Whereas,* The Franklin Market, at the Old Slip, has been destroyed at the late fire, and the butchers having stands therein have been deprived of the same, therefore, *Resolved,* that the Superintendent of Buildings, under the direction of the Market Committee, cause a temporary shed to be erected in Old Slip or Broad Street for the accommodation of the butchers and others having stalls in the late Franklin Market, until other provision shall be made therefore.

The president offered the following resolution, which was adopted:

> *Whereas,* The late conflagration should admonish us of the absolute necessity of establishing a more perfect and proper organization of the Fire Department, and of the necessity and propriety of being better prepared to resist the ravages of fire; therefore,
> *Resolved,* If the Board of Aldermen concur, that a committee of three from each Board be appointed to devise, with his honor the mayor and chief engineer, some plan and system of operations to be pursued in case this city should again be visited with a fire threatening to be calamitous. Adopted, and the Fire and Water Committee, with the President of this Board, appointed.

Mr. Ingraham offered the following resolution:

> *Whereas,* The late extensive conflagration on the night of the sixteenth of December, instant, was increased to a very great extent by the narrow streets and high stores on each side thereof, and the total destruction of all the buildings in that section of the city, renders it expedient and advisable to alter the route and width of the streets through the same; therefore,
> *Resolved,* That the Common Council recommend to the owners of the lots in that section of the city to meet together on Wednesday next at twelve o'clock, in the Superior Court Room of the City Hall, and take the necessary measures for the adoption of a suitable plan for altering the same before commencing any building thereon. Adopted unanimously.

There are many well-known citizens still living who worked at or witnessed the Great Fire, and the reminiscences of these veterans we here reproduce:
"The thermometer was seventeen degrees below zero," said Mr. Mills not

long ago, who, with Mr. Wheeler, was discussing this memorable night, "and the fire broke out at about nine o'clock in the evening. The wind was northwest and blowing a gale. The hydrants would not furnish half enough water for one engine, and as the wind made the tide very low there was a great scarcity of water, eh, George?"

"Yes, yes; oh, yes," responded Mr. Wheeler, rubbing his silk hat the wrong way.

"Hence the suctions of the engines could not reach the water in the river, and they had to be lowered in the dark and cold down on to the boats and the decks of vessels. Everything seemed to conspire to cause the greatest conflagration that ever afflicted this city, and cause terror and despair in the hearts of those who witnessed it—what, George?"

"Oh, yes; yes, yes," said Mr. Wheeler, arousing himself from a reclining position for just a moment.

"Hundreds of buildings were burned that did not have a drop of water thrown upon them. I was foreman of Eagle Fire Engine Company No. 13, which was located in Dover Street, near Pearl. When the City Hall bell struck the alarm we rolled out—"

"There wasn't any City Hall bell then," interrupted Mr. Wheeler, as he adjusted his stock and high turn over collar.

"You're right, George" (with a brotherly lingering upon the name of George). "It was the bell on the old jail that used to be between the City Hall and Broadway. Well, with a fast run, we were the first company at the fire, which was in Merchant Street, near Wall, a very narrow street. Hanover Street is where Merchant Street was, and it's twice as wide. Two four story stores were blazing from bottom to top, like a carpenter's shop on fire. The fire had already crossed Merchant Street toward Pearl. An engineer ordered me to take my hose into Pearl Street, and, if possible, stop the fire from crossing that street. Five or six stores were then blazing in Pearl Street. Our one stream of water seemed almost useless to contend with such a conflagration. There were no iron shutters there then, and in a few minutes twenty windows of the upper stories of the high buildings on the east side of Pearl Street were in a blaze. Although Chief Gulick and every man under him did everything possible to stop the fire, my heart sank within me to notice the awful destruction of property. After the fire crossed Pearl Street it rushed to the river and south to Coenties Slip with little opposition. Over six hundred buildings and property worth twenty million dollars were destroyed. The Merchants' Exchange stood where the Custom House now stands, corner of Wall and Hanover Streets. It was a large white marble building. Chief Gulick ordered me to take my engine to the front. The building was high, and I was ordered away to keep the fire from crossing Hanover Street, and we stopped the fire then and there, to our great joy. We thus saved all of the buildings on that side of Wall Street, from Hanover to Pearl, the only buildings saved on that side of Wall Street from William Street to the East River. Am I right, George?"

"Yes, yes," echoed Mr. Wheeler, and, taking a musty book from his pocket, he straightened up, and said: "Don't you want to know the enjines that formed our line? No. 33 was at the river. She gave water to 26, and 26 gave water to 41. Do you remember the pipe of brandy we had to put in the engine to keep it from freezing?"

"Oh, of course," said Mr. Mills, "I had to put some of the brandy in my boots to thaw my stockings loose. By the way I made an inquiry some time ago about the members of my company. I found that eighteen are dead, five are living, and three I could find out nothing about. In those days each fire engine was allowed twenty-six men only. The living members are John T. Hall, of Brooklyn; Cornelius T. Nostrand, of Connecticut; Josiah G. Macy, of Nantucket; and Zophar Mills, of New York. Chief Gulick is dead. Do you remember, George, that the Common Council blamed him for not stopping the fire, and how we turned that Common Council out of office, and elected Gulick register?"

Chief Justice Charles P. Daly has still a vivid recollection of that night. Speaking about it on its anniversary in 1885, Chief Justice Daly observed: "I was nineteen years of age at that time, and I remember on the night of the fire I was attending a lecture at Clinton Hall. When the alarm came I went down-town to see what the fire was. When I got there of course, like other young gentlemen who had been attracted to the scene in the same way that I had, I set to work to save property. We did secure a great deal, although it was not saved. We piled it up in Hanover Square, thinking, of course, that the fire would never reach that locality. But it did, and all the goods that we had been so zealous about were destroyed.

"On the call of the mayor a meeting was held at the Shakespeare Hotel, then the principal hotel of the city, which was situated at the corner of Fulton and Nassau Streets, to take measures for the protection of property, for, of course, the police were utterly insufficient for such an emergency, and I, with others, formed an insurance patrol. I captured, I remember, a negro who was stealing some silks. I was a very active and athletic young man, and I know I had about as much as I could do to secure him, but I did, and he was locked up. I think the fact that it was a remarkably cold night is what impresses itself the most upon my memory. The patrol I spoke of was continued for several days. There was a public meeting to take measures for assisting those who had been made destitute by the fire, and for the organization of plans by which the business firms who were sufferers could continue their business. Many, of course, were ruined, but some went on again. I attended that meeting, and if the records say that I spoke and moved a resolution, I probably did, but I had no impression that I was in public life so early. I was not then studying for the law, but was engaged in some mechanical occupation."

The eagle-like eye of Harry Howard, ex-chief of the Volunteer Fire Department, sparkles yet, and when spoken to about the great conflagration, he sighed, and wondered how old the people imagined him to be. "I was only a 'chippy' then," said he. "I was about thirteen years old, and not being of sufficient age to join the Department, was one of the lads known as runners. The runners used to do lots of good work, such as pulling on the ropes and working on the brakes. I used to run with Peterson Engine No. 15, of Christie and Bayard Streets. I recollect it was in the evening, and that it was a big fire, and that I couldn't stay at it as long as I wanted to because my boss always made me come home at ten o'clock. I was an indentured boy for eleven years—apprenticed to Abijah Matthews, a cabinetmaker, in Catharine Street. He's dead now. He used to live in *bon ton* style over on East Broadway. All the big bugs lived over there then, especially the Quakers, who were also scattered through Madison, Rutgers and Henry Streets. I was disappointed at having to leave the fire, because I gloried in a big blaze, and the greater the havoc the better I was pleased. I recollect that when the fire broke out the old bell on the Dutch Church, corner of Fulton and William Streets, rang as I had never heard it ring. The engine I used to run with was out of service, laid up for repairs, and I ran to the fire with Phoenix Engine No. 22, of Hester Street, between Eldridge and Allen Streets. The fire was around Wall Street and Exchange Place, and spreading fast. There was great excitement. Yes, there were lots of stories about the fire, such as a house being saved in the middle of the burned district, and of a man being thrown over five or six blocks and coming down safe. To be respectful you have to listen to these yarns, but you ain't obliged to believe 'em."

"There can be no topic more interesting than this to an old New Yorker," said Mr. George Wilson, of the Chamber of Commerce, "and I have gleaned many interesting particulars relative to it from the survivors of that day. The Chamber lost its charter in that fire. It was an immense document, with seals and ribbons, and had been given to us by George III a few years before the Revolutionary War. It has not yet been found, but I am confident that it exists. These two portraits," he continued, pointing to the full lengths which graced either end of the room, "are of Cadwallader Colden and Alexander Hamilton, painted for us, and are almost all that we saved from the wreck, except the books. They were carried out of the Merchants' Exchange by patriotic citizens at the risk of their lives. This building—the Merchants' Exchange—which was the finest one destroyed, was one of the largest in the city. The loss of this edifice was a most serious inconvenience to the mercantile community, particularly at such a time of disorder. In it were included not only the rooms I have mentioned, but also those used by the Chamber of Commerce and Board of Brokers; the Post-office; the Ship Letter Office and News Room; the Ship Telegraph Office, several newspaper offices and extensive refreshment rooms.

"The Garden Street or Exchange Place Church, another prominent building destroyed, was erected in 1807. It was a plain, substantial house, of stone, thirty-six by sixty-six feet, with a gallery. The pastor was the Rev. James M. Matthews. It had in it the bell which was originally brought from Holland, but which was destroyed by the fire. A schoolroom adjoined, and there were in the yard a number of ancient tombstones. This building and its grounds were used as a place of refuge, but without avail. The whole was destroyed. In digging the foundation for the extension to the Mills Building some of the bones of those buried here were found. The Post-office, which was among the places burned, was then very small in comparison with its later proportions. Only one of the clerks of that day still lives, and he has been in bad health for some time. Immediately after the fire the Postmaster, Samuel L. Gouverneur, removed it to the Rotunda in the City Hall Park, but not without receiving many indications of dissatisfaction from business men, who complained that it was too far up town!

"Among the well-known business houses which have continued down town to the present time, but were then burned out, were Halsted, Haines, & Co., Howland & Aspinwall, James Bleecker & Son, and Delmonico's. There are many others, but the firm names have so much changed that they cannot be recognized readily. Howland & Aspinwall, B. Aymar & Co., and S. V. S. Wilder, three of the largest mercantile houses, gave notice promptly after the fire that they would cash all paper of theirs which was out in the hands of the sufferers, and their example was followed by many others. Three thousand clerks, porters, and carmen, were thrown out of employment, many of them having families to support. Very heavy losses were inflicted upon French commerce. Only three French importers escaped. One cargo alone, which had arrived and was destroyed before distribution, was estimated to be worth two hundred thousand dollars. There was little English insurance capital here, owing to restrictive laws against foreign companies, and the loss fell almost entirely upon American companies, many of which were ruined.

"The naval storehouses in Brooklyn, lying directly across the river, caught fire several times, but the flames were promptly subdued. The sails of the schooner *Alonzo*, lying at the wharf at Brooklyn, were burned. The passengers on the Hudson River boats saw the flames from the Highlands forty-five miles distant, and the light, so says an old chronicler, was also distinctly seen in New Jersey as far as Cranberry. Assistant Postmaster Gaylor, then a boy, recollects seeing it from the court house at White Plains, and others saw it from Morristown, N.J.

"Shanties or sheds were erected near the ruins in South Street, into which the damaged merchandise was removed, and Castle Garden was taken as a depot for the reception of goods which were unclaimed and of which the owners were unknown.

"The *Journal of Commerce* building, which was in the rear of Dr. Matthews's church, was saved by the application of vinegar. Several hogsheads were in the rear of the lot and were unheaded, parts of the fluid being thrown on the roof and other exposed places. Downing saved his restaurant in the same manner.

"The losses of Stephen Whitney, the merchant, and next to John Jacob Astor the richest man in New York, were reported to be immense—in the neighborhood of half a million dollars. Great complaints were made of the defective architecture of the buildings which were burned. Most of the bricks which were lying in heaps through the streets looked as clean as if mortar had never touched them. In the old buildings, the newspapers of the day said, the mortar was harder than the bricks themselves. The great extent of the fire was ascribed to pernicious inventions to save money. Wooden gutters, cornices and window frames were common. Copper gutters and iron window frames and shutters would have saved the Exchange. The new and lofty building at the corner of Wall and William Streets was on fire at the cornice several times, and with difficulty saved.

"One building was saved in the burned district in Water Street. It was built by Carman for Herman Thorne. He was told that the structure must be fireproof, and declared that it should be so. Although the building stood surrounded by a sea of flames it redeemed his promise and remained uninjured with its goods safe within it.

"While the fire was going on, Louis F. Wilkins, a midshipman, then recently returned from a voyage to the Pacific, heard the agonizing cries of a woman, whose child was left in a building already in flames. He immediately forced his way up stairs, in spite of the warnings of the firemen that he would certainly perish, and rescued the child, which was not in the least frightened, but was, on the contrary, pleased with the brilliancy of the light. He restored it to its distracted mother, who with frantic joy threw her arms about him and exclaimed, 'My God! my God! Thou hast not forsaken me.' Persons were reported to be killed by the fire, but the rumors did not seem to be authenticated. John Lang, of the New York *Gazette*, died shortly after from the excitement and worry the fire occasioned. Among other things noted was that there was danger from melted lead, and that the saltpeter in warehouses in Front Street, near Old Slip, exploded, with a loud noise."

Mr. William Callender, who is now in his seventy-ninth year, and yet looks and feels as hale and active as a man of fifty, has a vivid recollection of old New York. He was not connected with the Fire Department, but, like all New Yorkers in the olden time, he took a lively interest in all that concerned it, and as often as circumstances permitted personally attended most of the conflagrations with which the city was visited from time to time. His remembrance of events which occurred more than fifty years ago is most reliable. Of the Great Fire of 1835 he says:

"The destruction of that night and the suffering that followed were terrible. If you will suppose that to-night all that portion of the city below Canal Street was absolutely and completely swept away, you can form some idea of the extent of that fire. I was chief clerk of the Police Department from 1834 to 1836, and I had to take statements of the losses sustained in that fire. As well as I can remember they footed up over twenty-two million dollars. Insurance companies were wiped out, and millions of the losses were never made good. The night was bitterly cold—seventeen degrees below zero—and the wind blew a hurricane. I stood at the corner of Wall and Pearl Streets, where there is an open space like a funnel. The fire in great sheets of flame leaped across that space, cavorting around in maddening fury. Bales of goods and merchandise that were thrown from the windows were caught up by the wind and whirled about as though they were but flecks of chaff. Rolls of light goods that became untied in their descent from the windows were swept up by the wind and carried off to long distances, and fragments of goods, books, and papers were actually found the next morning on the Jersey meadows. The water supply was had from the reservoir at Thirteenth Street, and from the river, because the hydrants were frozen solid. The tide on the river was so low that it required six engines on a line to bring one stream to play on the fire. Remember these were only hand engines. Of course such means were utterly inadequate to stem the course of the fire.

"The fire broke out in Hanover Street (then called Merchant Street) in the dry goods store of Comstock & Andrews. It spread with great rapidity, the illuminating gas not long before introduced in the city and then in general use in the stores serving to help the conflagration and increase the danger. The Dutch Reformed Church in Garden Street, about two blocks away from the outbreak of the fire, was opened, and valuable goods were taken there and stored, in the belief that they would be safe. The sacred edifice looked in a brief time like a warehouse. The open space at Hanover Square was also piled up with goods from the threatened and burning buildings. Along the slips on South Street were other heaps of valuable merchandise. But the flames continued to increase in fury and these supposed houses of safety with their contents were one after another consumed. The old church building was completely obliterated, and so was the synagogue on Mill Street near South William Street. The Fire Department was powerless to stem the current of destruction."

The action of the gallant Philadelphia firemen on the occasion of this great conflagration needs to be told in detail, and is best related in the words of Mr. J. B. Harrison, of Summitville, Tenn., who, in 1835, was a member of the

Franklin Fire Company of Philadelphia. Mr. Harrison, who is a well-preserved gentleman of sixty-nine years, says:

"In the year 1835, December 16, the great fire in New York City broke out. Friday, the eighteenth, the mayor of New York sent for the firemen of Philadelphia to come and help put it out. As quick as the boys of the Ben Franklin heard it twenty-three of us manned the rope and started for the Walnut Street wharf to get on the boat to cross to Camden and take the railroad. The river was so full of heavy floating ice the boat could not cross. There were other firemen there who, when they found they could not cross the river, returned home. We concluded to go to Kensington Road and get on there. When we got to the road we found the ice so thick on the rails that the cars could not run; it was raining and freezing as fast as it fell. We then concluded to go afoot. It was then four o'clock. The word was given. 'Man the rope, boys, we will go to the Trenton bridge and cross the Delaware.' We got to Trenton at twelve o'clock that night, and went to the tavern. When we entered the room we found a large stove red hot. The ice was about an inch thick on our coats and hats. In a short time the ice melted, and the floor was full of water. After we warmed a little, we got up on the seats the best we could to get out of the water and to rest. It was not long, however, till we got cold, and concluded that we had better start on our journey. The word was given, and away we went for the Sand Hills. It was then Saturday morning about four o'clock, and some of our boys were getting weak. On the way we hired a man with a horse to help us along to Sand Hills.

"About five miles from Sand Hills there was a large house, and some of our boys proposed to stop and get some supper, it being nearly night. We halted and asked them for supper; they would not let us have any, although we offered to pay them well for it. We were forty miles from home, and had not stopped to eat a meal. Some of the boys had given out, and some said they could not go much further. While we were talking to the man of the house, one of our boys stepped to the back part of the house to get a drink of water, and, seeing through the window a large table filled, he called all the boys to come and look. A large table loaded with everything good to eat that a man could wish for was more than our hungry boys could resist, and so we filed in at one door as a large company of guests entered at another. We sat down and ate a hearty supper. The other crowd had to take a stand against the wall until we got through. No one helped us, but we helped ourselves, as it was all before us. When we got through we were polite enough to thank them for supper, and then rolled on to Sand Hills.

"The next day, Tuesday, Fire Company No. 1 came to visit us and offering their services as our escort. We went to see the ruins of the fire, which had been checked by blowing up buildings in advance of it with powder. While we were there we got an invitation to go to a theater, which we accepted, taking Company No. 1 with us. When we got to the theater we told them No. 1 was our escort, and we wanted them to go in with us. They refused, and we told them we would go back to our hotel and spend the evening. We had not gone far until we were halted by a messenger from another theater: 'Franklin boys, come with me; I will take you to a theater where you can go in and take whom you wish.'

"On Wednesday I thought I would go and see an uncle in the upper part of the city. Walking along on the sidewalk I was stopped by a cabman, who asked: 'Fireman, where are you going?' I told him. He said that it was too far for me to walk, and took me in his cab. We could not step out anywhere but we were halted by some one wanting to do a kind act for us. We could not spend any money in New York. I bought a few things and laid down the money to pay for them, which was refused. The merchants said: 'You are welcome to anything you want, your money I will not take.'

"When we got ready to go home the New York firemen pulled our engine to the wharf, the mayor appointed a committee to escort us home, and after that the firemen got to visiting from one city to the other."

The following are personal recollections of the great fire by Mrs. Mary LeRoy Satterlee:

"The evening of the great fire in New York City was intensely cold. The bells began to ring an alarm about eight o'clock P.M., and my husband started at the sound which told him of danger to the large warehouses in Pearl Street, one of which his firm occupied. It seemed as if all the bells were ringing their loudest. Mr. Satterlee left our house in Chambers Street, accompanied by his cousin, who was a clerk in the establishment. As the alarm continued, his nephew, a boy of fourteen years, could no longer be restrained, and followed, leaving me very anxious and alone. About ten o'clock the boy returned, saying that the cold was intense, and it was almost impossible to work the engines, and the fire was still raging. He had narrowly escaped being struck by a falling wall. 'Is the store in danger?' I asked. 'No; the wind is driving the flames in an opposite direction, but all hands are helping those whose property is in danger.'

"Eleven o'clock came, then midnight, to find us sitting shivering, dreading to hear, yet most anxious to see, those who had gone to the scene of the calamity. Suddenly our cousin entered, his arms full of books. Icicles clung to his clothing and stiffened his hair. Entirely exhausted by emotion and fatigue, it was some moments before he could relate how the wind suddenly changed and blew as strongly in the other direction and delivering whole blocks to the seemingly uncontrollable flames. I asked for my husband. He had sent up his books and was working with others to get the most valuable part of their stock of silk goods under the roof of the South Dutch Church, never thinking that it could be destroyed before the fire was under control. At three o'clock in the morning—such a very long night—I heard wheels, and my husband returned safe in a carriage piled up with goods. After paying the driver a fabulous sum—for every vehicle was in demand—the goods were tumbled, the wet with the dry, into the hall.

"Next day the fire demon was subdued, but the ruins smoldered sullenly in the best business part of our fair city. The insurance offices were closed, and ruin to some and great loss to many made every heart sad. While the fire was at its height, my sister, who lived in the lower part of the city and was watching the lurid sky and the burning buildings, was told by one of the firemen that she had better pack up all valuables, as, if the fire was not mastered before it reached a certain corner near by, several buildings would be blown up, her house among the rest. She was always calm, but energetic, and seeing that the firemen were terribly exhausted, she summoned her servants, and putting all the tea and coffee they had into large boilers, they got together all the provisions in the house, baked the buckwheat meal into griddle cakes, hailed an early milk cart, and were enabled to feed and refresh every fireman around by calling them into the kitchen ten or twelve at a time. They were almost perished with cold and prostrated by their severe labor."

CHAPTER XIX

THE FIRE ZOUAVES

(Eleventh N. Y. S. V.)—Brave Deeds that have Gone into History.—The Firemen Gallantly Respond to President Lincoln's Appeal for Men.—Formation of the First Regiment of Fire Zouaves.—On to Washington.—Death of Colonel Ellsworth.—Colonel Farnham Taken from the Field in a Dying Condition.—Captain Jack Wildey.—Colonel Leoser.—Lieutenant Divver.—The Second Regiment of Fire Zouaves.—Their Valiant Services in the Field.

When the gun was trailed on Sumter from which was fired the shot that, in no very metaphorical sense, may be said to have been "heard around the world," like that which woke the echoes of Bunker Hill when the "embattled farmers" stood in array for the defense of their rights, no class of our citizens more quickly rose to the level of the great occasion, or more heartily responded to President Lincoln's appeal for men, than did the volunteer firemen of New York City. Nor was there anything in their subsequent record that indicated, at any period of the war, the slightest diminution in the earnest patriotism which inspired them at the beginning of the struggle. Although early deprived of their especial military organization, they were ever ready, around whatever regimental flag they may have rallied, to use their best efforts towards the suppression of the rebellion. Thus, as will be seen, the record of the volunteer firemen of New York, wherever made, and led by whatever officers they may have enlisted under, was one which both they and their fellow-citizens may contemplate with unmixed satisfaction. The First Fire Zouaves, officially known as the Eleventh New York, was recruited amid a tempest of enthusiasm, and with a celerity that will hardly be credited in less heroic days, a quarter of a century after the event. Colonel Ellsworth seemed to have infused some of his own restless energy into the firemen of that time, and every engine house was turned into a recruiting station. In some cases as many as eighteen and twenty men volunteered out of a single company, and the question was not who were to go, but who were to be so unfortunate as to be left behind. It thus took but a few days to rally the eleven hundred men that pushed on to Annapolis, but it was not the number so much as the extraordinary spirit and dash of its members that characterized this representative regiment. Colonel Ellsworth, breaking through the red-tape regulations that would have retained him in the vicinity of New York until a more convenient season, and having obtained the necessary arms directly from Washington instead of through the state officials, ignoring all obstacles, marched his men to the defense of the national capital in advance of its other defenders. Arrived in Washington, the first duty to which the regiment was assigned was the extinguishing of a fire in that well-known hostelry, Willard's Hotel. They went into camp on the Maryland side of the Potomac, and captured Alexandria May 24, where the gallant Ellsworth met his glorious fate. On the twenty-ninth the regiment moved to Shooter's Hill. About June 5, a picket-guard was detailed for duty at McCloud's Mills, when one man was killed and one wounded. This was the first loss in the field.

These were the officers in command of the First Regiment of First Fire Zouaves (Eleventh Regiment, N. Y. S. V.):

Elmer E. Ellsworth, Colonel,
Noah L. Farnham, Lieutenant-Colonel, Assistant Engineer Hook and
Ladder Company No. 1.
John A. Cregier, Major, Assistant Engineer Hose No. 40.
Charles McK. Leoser, Adjutant.

Company A,	John Coyle,	–	–	–	–	Hose 22
"	B, Edward Byrnes,	–	–	–		Engine 16
"	C, Michael C. Murphy,	–	–	–		Hose 41
"	D, John Downey,	–	–	–	–	Engine 34
"	E, John B. Leverich,	–	–	–		Hose 7
"	F, William H. Burns,	–	–	–	–	Engine 6
"	G, Michael Teagen,	–	–	–		Engine 13
"	H, William Hackett,	–	Assistant Engineer			Engine 20
"	I, John Wildey,	–	–	–	–	Engine 11
"	K, Andrew D. Purtell,	–	–	–		Engine 14

When the First Zouaves left the city they left it as a "three months' regiment" (sworn in April 20, 1861). On the seventh of May they were sworn in to serve during the war. The Zouaves performed picket duty in the vicinity of the Mills until July 16, when orders were given to march on to Bull Run. The command, on the death of Colonel Ellsworth, had devolved upon the brave Farnham, who was serving as lieutenant-colonel, and who at the time of enlisting was one of the engineers of the New York Fire Department. On the night of the seventeenth the regiment encamped at Fairfax Station, and in a brisk encounter with the enemy captured a sergeant and several men belonging to a South Carolina regiment, together with the first Rebel flag that came into its possession. On the morning of the eighteenth orders came to push forward to Centreville, and when within five miles of that place the men were ordered, at double-quick, to the support of the Sixty-ninth, Seventy-ninth, and Twelfth New York, then in action. In this brush only three or four men were wounded, and none killed. On the morning of the twenty-first another start was made for Bull Run. Colonel Farnham had been in hospital, but left his sick bed to assume command. During the battle that ensued he was shot behind the left ear and taken to Washington, where he died. The record of the regiment in this, its first engagement of any consequence, was a noble one: from seventy-five to one hundred killed, two hundred wounded, and one hundred and twenty-five taken prisoners. But this was not all. Before falling back on Centreville, the well-known Captain Jack Wildey and a few men performed one of the most gallant deeds of the war. Reckless of his own fate, Captain Wildey threw himself upon a party of the Confederates, and recaptured from them the colors of the Sixty-ninth New York, which he restored to their owners.

The next encampment of the regiment was at Shooter's Hill (Fort Ellsworth). Two weeks later, orders were given to return to New York, that the depleted ranks might be filled up to their original strength. While there, the regiment was stationed at Scarsdale, Bedloe's Island, and the Battery. In September, being again ready for duty, and now under command of Colonel Leoser, the Zouaves were ordered to Newport News. In the meantime the regiment had been largely reofficered: Major John A. Cregier, assistant engineer of the Fire Department and the first major of the regiment, had resigned on reaching New York, Captain McFarland, of Company H, being promoted to be major in his stead. He was a Seventh Regiment man, as were the majority of the new officers. After reaching Newport News the regiment was engaged in several skirmishes, among them one near Young's Mills while on a foraging expedition, when twelve of the Zouaves were taken prisoners, among them Corporal Richard Gleason, of Company A, who was afterwards shot dead by a sentry at Libby Prison for looking out of a window.

Colonel Leoser now asked permission for the regiment to join the expedition to Norfolk, but the request was denied. This seemed to throw a damper upon the entire organization, as it was evidently the intention of the authorities to keep the men engaged in garrison duty, while all the fighting was to be done, all the chances of promotion taken, by the more fortunate members of other commands. The result of such a policy, when the spirit of patriotism and adventure which characterized the First Fire Zouaves is taken into consideration, may be readily imagined. Colonel Leoser and a majority of the officers resigned, and numbers of the men when mustered out enlisted in other regiments, many going with Banks to New Orleans.

While on the Peninsula, however, the men were not allowed to be idle. The regiment participated in a couple of skirmishes at Newmarket and Big Bethel, while encamped at Newport News. During the famous engagement, March 8, 1862, between the *Merrimac* and the *Monitor* and the *Cumberland,* the regiment occupied rifle pits on shore with a view to repel any force the enemy might attempt to land. One company, under command of Colonel Leoser, had charge of a 12 lb. rifled gun, which he himself sighted and fired from the bluff.

The First Zouaves were soon sent home, and mustered out of the service, June 2, 1862, at Fort Columbus, New York Harbor, by order of the War Department. Lieutenant-colonel McFarland (one of the Seventh Regiment officers), after Colonel Leoser resigned his command and joined the regular service, took command of the regiment at Newport News, and came home with them to be mustered out at Governor's Island.

Having thus no longer any regimental organization, the identity of the First Fire Zouaves became merged, in the persons of its original members, with that of other corps during the remainder of the war. As soldiers serving under other colors, the New York "fire laddies" never failed to give a good account of themselves, and wherever the fighting was hottest, the danger greatest, they were sure to be found; thus proving how great a mistake the authorities of the War Department had made when they mustered out of service a body of men like the First Zouaves and condemned them to the monotony of doing garrison duty. On the other hand, had the matter been decided by those possessing ordinary discernment and common sense, and had not adverse influences been at work, a regiment composed of such material would have been pushed to the front, given work worthy of it to do, and afforded an opportunity to reflect credit upon the organization that under such circumstances would have been so dear to them. Among those who cast in their lot with other regiments, when they found the opportunity for promotion denied them in their own, may be mentioned, Thomas Riley, who served as an adjutant in General Spinola's brigade, and was killed at the Battle of the Black Water. Captains Coyle and Murphy enlisted in the Irish Legion, and served until the end of the war. Captain Byrne joined the Eighteenth New York Cavalry and came home a brigadier-general, Captain Murphy returning as colonel. Sergeant Garvey, Company A, went out as lieutenant and returned as captain in the Fourth New York. He was wounded in the last engagement of the war at Appomattox Courthouse. Lieutenant Powers, originally of Company A, and afterwards transferred to Company I, served throughout the war. Corporal Donnelly, Company A, enlisted in the Seventy-second New York, and was killed in the Battle of the Wilderness, in which Private Meek, who had joined the same regiment, also lost his life. Corporal Ebling, of Company A, was among the killed at the first battle of Bull Run. Private Kane, of Company G, also went out in the Eighteenth New York Cavalry, and returned as first lieutenant.

Of those who fought through the war and are to-day still doing yeoman work in the Fire Department, must be mentioned Private O. O'Rorke, who volunteered in the Eighty-fourth New York, and returned in 1864. Sergeant-Major Goodwin went out in another regiment and came home captain. William Kennedy and Thomas Curtis returned respectively captain and lieutenant of the One Hundred and Sixty-second New York Volunteers.

Many of the old firemen of twenty-five years ago are to-day buried in the soldiers' cemeteries at Gettysburg and Antietam. After the glorious fever of that time "they sleep well;" scarcely a battle ground of the old Army of the Potomac but is reddened with the life blood of some of them, who in spite of the obstacles placed in the way of their patriotic efforts to serve their country, at last achieved the renown that must ever attach to those who have fought and died for "God and native land."

In fact, not over two hundred of the old regiment that left New York on the twenty-ninth of April, 1861, are still living. Many of the survivors have been reunited in the Farnham Post of the Grand Army of the Republic, which was organized, with the approval of Col. Leoser, by Private O'Rorke mentioned above. It counts today two hundred and twenty-five members in good standing, with Col. Leoser in command.

Among the prominent members are Gen. Newton, Brig.-Gen. Fitzgerald, now commanding the First Brigade, Police Superintendent Murray, Order of Arrest Clerk Martin, Alderman Cowie, of the present board, and Chief Engineer George W. Magee, now on duty in the Brooklyn Navy Yard, Colonel Clark, Seventh Regiment, Colonel Gilon, tax assessor, General Ferrero, Colonel Farnham's two brothers, etc. The rosters of but few regiments can make a better showing of its old members who have achieved distinction in civil life.

Of the First Fire Zouaves as a whole, nothing worse could be said when they took the lead in that grand military advance on Washington—the first fruits of one of the most remarkable national uprisings known to history—than that, in the words of one of their number, they were "a reckless harum-skarum lot." Although mostly very young men, they were thoroughly imbued with the esprit de corps that distinguished the Old Fire Department of New York to an extraordinary degree. If they were good for service of any kind, it was to be pushed to the very front of the fighting as soon as they had been accustomed to the routine of army life and their duties as soldiers. To select such a regiment, composed of elements so peculiar and so thoroughly permeated with the spirit of intrepid bravery—a spirit that regards the most heroic deeds in the light of everyday achievements—for the dull routine of permanent garrison duty, was a blunder as great, in the opposite direction, as that which was responsible for the famous, but fatal charge at Balaklava.

In referring to the Zouaves, Col. Leoser said recently that were he called upon to recruit a regiment to-morrow, he would prefer, had he his choice of material, to recruit it from the old firemen of New York. It was also his opinion that if they made any failures during their brief regimental existence, it was due to the mistakes of the officers and not to any lack of bravery on the part of the rank and file. Col. Leoser's relations to the regiment were of the most agreeable character, and he was both esteemed and beloved by his men.

Frank E. Brownell, who so gallantly avenged the killing of the heroic Ellsworth, has given this account of the tragedy:

"It was on the night of the twenty-third of May, about ten o'clock, that Colonel Ellsworth called the regiment out, and he said: 'Boys, I heard this morning that a movement was to be made on Alexandria. I went to General Mansfield and told him that, as we were the first volunteer regiment mustered into the service for the war, we would consider it a deep affront if we were not allowed the right of the line. Prepare yourselves for a night ride, with perhaps a skirmish at the end of it. When we arrive in Alexandria, I want you to act like men, and show the enemy that we are gentlemen as well as soldiers. Not a shot must be fired without orders.'

"We were camped at Giesboro Point, and between two and three o'clock next morning the boats to convey us to Alexandria arrived. As we approached Alexandria, we found the gunboat *Pawnee* lying off the town, and as our steamers moved up to the wharf, a boat put off from the *Pawnee* with a white flag flying. Upon the landing, the officer in command of this boat had a consultation with Colonel Ellsworth, and I have always understood, informed him that the city had been placed under a flag of truce, or at least been given a certain time to surrender. At all events, the town was under a flag of truce from the officer commanding the *Pawnee*, and for that reason it was not deemed imprudent for Colonel Ellsworth to leave his regiment and go up into the city. We landed at the foot of Cameron Street, and as the regiment disembarked, Colonel Ellsworth started up into the town accompanied by our chaplain and the correspondents of the New York *Times* and *Tribune*. As he passed the right of the regiment it was suggested by some one that he take a guard with him. He called for the first group on the right of the first company to follow him, which was made up of a sergeant, two corporals and two privates. As we turned into King Street, the first thing that met our gaze was the Rebel flag floating over the Marshall House. When he saw the Rebel flag, Colonel Ellsworth turned to the sergeant and told him to hurry back to Captain Coyle, who commanded Company A, and tell him to hurry up there with his men as soon as possible. We were on the opposite side of the street from the hotel; and after passing the house, however, the colonel stopped for a moment or two, and then turned across the street and entered the building. There was a man behind the office counter, and Colonel Ellsworth asked him if he was the proprietor. He replied that he was not. Colonel Ellsworth then started up the stairway for the roof followed by the whole of our party. We pulled down the flag and started back. I was in advance, and as I made the turn between the third and second stories, I saw Jackson standing at the head of the flight wing to the next story. I jumped towards him, and with my musket struck down his gun. As my weapon slid off his, I sprang backward and lost my footing, and just at that moment Colonel Ellsworth appeared around the turn of the stairs coming down. Jackson raised his gun and turned to give me the other barrel. I had recovered my feet, however, and fired upon him first, immediately following up my shot with the bayonet, my thrust pushing him down the stairs, the other barrel of his gun going off as he fell."

"What do you think prompted Colonel Ellsworth to undertake to pull down that flag himself?"

"I have always been under the impression that he did it to prevent any outbreak, and that he was afraid to allow the regiment to see it."

"Do you know anything regarding Colonel Ellsworth's personal character?"

"I don't believe, if history were searched through to find a life to hold up for the emulation of the youth of our country, that you would find one that better illustrates the character of a true patriot and gentleman than that of Colonel Ellsworth. I have a number of his letters, and what is perhaps the best evidence of his character, his private diary."

Captain Brownell produced a small book bound in red leather. Turning over the leaves, which were filled with neat round handwriting of the dead hero, he read numerous extracts. It was a concise history of the daily life of the young soldier when he was a law student in Chicago, struggling for an honorable position among men, living upon bread and water, and sleeping upon the bare floor of his employer's office. Pages were filled with affectionate allusions to his aged parents and his fond hopes for a future that would shed happiness and comfort over their declining years.

This is an extract from a letter written by President Lincoln to the bereaved mother of Colonel Ellsworth:

"My acquaintance with him began less than two years ago, yet through the latter half of the intervening period it was as intimate as the disparity of our ages and my engrossing engagements would permit. To me he appeared to have no indulgences or pastimes, and I never heard him utter a profane or intemperate word. The honors he labored for so laudably, and in the sad end so gallantly gave his life, he meant for them no less than himself. In the hope that it may be no intrusion upon the sacredness of your sorrow, I have ventured to address this tribute to the memory of my young friend, and your brave and early fallen child. May God give you the consolation which is beyond earthly power.

Sincerely your friend in a common affliction,

A. Lincoln."

THE FIRE ZOUAVES AT THE BATTLE OF MANASSAS

John Wildey, an active fireman from 1844 until the dissolution of the volunteer Department, was foreman of 11 Engine at the outbreak of the Rebellion. He assisted in organizing the Eleventh Regiment, Fire Zouaves, and went to the front as captain in that command.

Captain Wildey says that while the regiment was forming in line on King Street, news came that Ellsworth was killed. The regiment then marched through the city to the railway station. The captain went to the Marshall House and took charge of Ellsworth's remains, and held possession of the Rebel flag and the double-barreled shotgun used by Jackson. These trophies were sent North with the colonel's body.

Wildey was with his regiment at Shooter's Hill (where a fort was constructed, and named after Ellsworth) when the order to advance on Manassas was received. For weeks previous to this advance the regiment had been constantly drilled and disciplined by competent officers. Colonel Noah L. Farnham, who succeeded Ellsworth, had been a member of the Seventh N.Y. Regiment, and Adjutant Leoser was a graduate of West Point. In fact, when the regiment started out for Bull Run, it was in a high degree of efficiency, considering its short service; it was easily manœuvered, thoroughly equipped, and possessed of an esprit de corps that would have proved irresistible in any ordinary combat.

In the engagement at Manassas the regiment held the extreme right of the line in the brigade of General Wilcox, and first came under the fire of a Rebel battery and a corps of sharpshooters concealed in rifle pits. On hearing the first "whizz" of bullets, Wildey says he experienced a sensation similar to that felt years before when going into an old-time firemen's fight in front of the Astor House. The Zouaves charged under a murderous fire, drove the enemy out of the rifle pits, and cleared the field in front of them. Their loss, however, was severe. Among the fatally wounded was Colonel Farnham, who received a shot in the head above the ear. Captains Wildey and Purtell carried his body to the rear. He was sent to the hospital, where he died two weeks afterwards. Wildey returned to the front in time to see a body of cavalrymen coming swiftly down towards the right of the line, shouting and waving an American flag. At first it was thought the cavalrymen were friends, but an order rang out to "lie down and prepare to receive cavalry." The Zouaves instantly dropped to the ground, and the Rebel cavalry, waving captured flags, and yelling like demons, came down at a charge. Suddenly Rickett's Union Battery, in rear of the Zouaves, opened on the mounted Rebels, killing many men and horses, and throwing them into confusion. Wildey fired his revolver at the leader of the Confederates, and saw him fall. He was Colonel Ashby, of the famous "Black Horse Cavalry." As the Rebels turned to flee, the Zouaves jumped to their feet, and charged furiously into the midst of them. One of the Rebels bore aloft the green flag of the Sixty-ninth Regiment, captured a short time before. His horse was shot and tumbled. As the Rebel sprang off, Captain Wildey was upon him with his sword, and snatched the glorious flag away. This was one of the most brilliant individual exploits of the great battle. The flag was returned to the Sixty-ninth, and is still proudly held by that organization.

Wildey says that after the dispersion of the "Black Horse Cavalry," the Zouaves were elated with their victory, and thinking the battle was over, some of them began picking up trophies from the field to send to their friends at the North. But they were suddenly called into the ranks again upon the approach of a fresh force of the enemy. It proved to be General Joe Johnston's command, just arrived by rail from Winchester, where General Patterson had been vainly sent to detain him. These fresh troops resumed the battle, and turned the tide of victory. Our men were now thoroughly exhausted with long marching, excessively hot weather, and severe fighting. Their canteens were empty, and rations wasted or consumed; for they had not yet acquired the foresight of veterans in carefully husbanding supplies of food and water. All were suffering from thirst. Besides these great disadvantages, the moral effect upon young soldiers in discovering that their hard fought victory was not a victory at all, but only the prelude to another mighty encounter, could not fail to be disastrous. Considerable confusion ensued upon the renewed onset of the Confederates, but Wildey avers that, so far as the Zouaves were concerned, there was no breaking of ranks, as reported at the time. The regiment, or what was left of it after losing two hundred and eighty men in killed, wounded, and prisoners, retired in good order, maintaining its company formation, firing and retreating slowly. The Zouaves, in fact, formed the rear guard of the whole Union army in its retrograde movement as far as Centreville, where they slept that night, retiring the following day to Fairfax Court-house.

Shortly after this battle Captain Wildey was ordered to New York, on recruiting service. While so engaged, he was nominated for coroner on the Union ticket, and elected. This closed his army career. He served as coroner six years.

Noah Lane Farnham, eldest son of George W. and Caroline (Thompson) Farnham, was born at New Haven, Connecticut, on the first day of March, 1829. When he was about two years old his parents removed to the City of New York. When about eight years of age he was sent back to New Haven to one of its best schools, now the celebrated Collegiate and Commercial Institute of that city. After spending three years at that institution, he was sent to the Episcopal Academy at Cheshire, Connecticut, then, as now, one of the best church schools in the country. At the age of fourteen he was taken from there and placed in the then well-known dry goods commission house of Clapp, Kent & Beckley, of New York.

At the age of eighteen he joined the City Guards, a well-known and popular military organization of the time. Shortly after the celebrated Astor Place riot took place, and his company, having been called upon to take part in suppressing it, he participated with them in the duties and dangers of the hour. The alternation of drill and festivities which characterized the "crack" companies of the day did not suit his restless and energetic spirit, so that as soon as he came of age he joined Empire Engine Company No. 42, in which he served for about two years, when he resigned and joined Mutual Hook and Ladder No. 1, located in the same house now occupied by the company of the same number in the present department. His merit soon promoted him to the command of the company, from which position he was afterwards elected to be one of the assistant engineers of the department, serving as such under Chiefs Carson and Howard. While in the hook and ladder company he was associated with ex-Mayor Wickham, Andrew C. Schenck (killed at the Jennings' fire), and others who did concurrent duty in the Seventh Regiment, and his military tastes reasserting themselves towards the close of his term of service in the department, he was elected a member of the second company of the Seventh Regiment. From the ranks he was promoted to second sergeant, and from that office to those of second and first lieutenant in rapid succession.

At the breaking out of the Rebellion he held the last-named position, under Captain (now Colonel) Emmons Clark. On the memorable nineteenth of April, 1861, he marched down Broadway for the last time, in command of a platoon of his company, arm-in-arm with Colonel Ellsworth, whom he was so soon, by the fatal fortunes of war, to succeed. The history of the Seventh's campaign is familiar to the world, and need not be repeated here, but it may be noted that Lieutenant Farnham commanded the first detail of skilled skirmishers which was ever displayed in the war of the Rebellion. While in camp with his regiment at Washington, his commission as lieutenant-colonel of the Fire Zouaves was sent him from Albany, which he immediately accepted, and bade farewell to his comrades of the Seventh, reporting without delay to Colonel Ellsworth. Immediately upon the tragic death of that gallant officer Colonel Farnham assumed command. The history of those trying hours is told elsewhere in this book. Some weeks after his promotion he was prostrated with typhoid fever, and had hardly passed the crisis of the disease when the advance which resulted in the Bull Run disaster was ordered. Weak, ill, and physically unfit, he insisted on accompanying his regiment, and against the remonstrances of his surgeons and officers, was lifted on his horse, and led his men into the battle, where he received his death wound. He was taken to the Washington Infirmary, where he lingered under faithful treatment until the fourteenth day of August, 1861, when he died peacefully and without a struggle. His brothers, who were present at his deathbed, caused the remains to be taken to his father's house in New York City. Funeral services were held on Saturday, the seventeenth, at Christ Church on Fifth Avenue. The remains were taken to New Haven, which was a city of mourning on that day, with stores closed and buildings draped. A long procession of the military, local Fire Department and delegations from the Seventh Regiment and Fire Department of New York, followed the remains to the grave in the family plot in the Old Grove Street cemetery, where the committal services were read by the rector of Trinity Church, the church of his fathers.

Colonel Farnham was a man of great force and energy of character. Descended from a long line of New England ancestors, fighters in all the wars from the colonial Indian battles, on through the French War and wars of the Revolution and of 1812, he inherited an abiding love of country, and of liberty for every man of whatever race or color. He was the soul of honor, pure in heart and life, unselfish to a fault, and in all respects a model for the young men of America to admire and imitate.

Colonel Charles McKnight Leoser was born in Reading, PA, in 1839, and graduated at West Point in May, 1861. He was at once commissioned in the Second United States Cavalry and was ordered to drill the First Fire Zouaves (Eleventh New York Volunteers) in July. On the death of Colonel Noah L. Farnham he was chosen to serve in his stead. He remained in command of the regiment until April 18, 1862, when he resigned and rejoined his own regiment, with which he remained until the end of the war. Colonel Leoser's record with his own command was an exceedingly brilliant one, he having taken part in over forty engagements. Among them may be mentioned those at Spottsylvania Court-house, Hanover Court-house, Fair Oaks, White Oaks Swamp, and Cold Harbor. He was with Sheridan in his raid to Haxall's Landing, and was present at Beaver Dam, Yellow Tavern and Hawes shop, his command having had nineteen distinct encounters with the enemy in seventeen days. At Trevillian Station, June 11, 1864, Colonel Leoser was wounded and captured. He remained a prisoner about three months, and so did not take part with his regiment in the battle of Gettysburg. He resigned from the army in October, 1865, since which time he has been engaged in business in this city.

He is now president of the Wine and Spirit Traders' Society, first vice-president of the American Institute, and a member of the Chamber of Commerce. Colonel Leoser is an ideal cavalry officer, bold, dashing, and as fearless as a lion. Of all the contests in which he engaged during the war he is of opinion that his experience at Bull Run brought him into closest quarters with death, the Zouaves having been for some time on that disastrous day exposed to a cross fire, and that the officers escaped alive is considered little less than a miracle. Whoever is responsible for the untoward result of that engagement, it is certainly neither the Fire Zouaves nor their gallant colonel.

Lieutenant Daniel Divver, of Company G, Eleventh New York Volunteers (First Fire Zouaves), was born in Ireland in 1839, came to this country when he was a child, and resided in the Fourth Ward with his parents. He attended the public schools and learned his trade of tanner in the "Swamp," where he was well-known and popular. At the breaking out of the war of the Rebellion he was, and had been for two years previously, an active member of Eagle Engine Company No. 13, his record as a fireman being unexcelled. When Colonel Ellsworth called for recruits from our old Volunteer Fire Department, Lieutenant Divver was among the first to subscribe to the roll of membership of Company G, in which command he was unanimously elected second lieutenant.

In camp, before the regiment crossed the Potomac to take Alexandria, he became endeared to all his comrades by his genial disposition and his untiring efforts for the comfort of the rank and file. With his fellow-officers he was a great favorite.

On the march to the battlefield of Bull Run he divested himself of all superfluous garments, entering the field with his gallant comrades in his shirt sleeves, and they rolled above the elbows, sword in hand, and, with the familiar yell of the old engine company, "Get down, Old Hague!" he rushed forward to his death. When the excitement of the charge (the Rebels being driven back into the woods) was over, Lieutenant Divver was found on the field, his life blood ebbing away from over a dozen fatal wounds. He was carried off by some of his faithful comrades and was taken into a wheelwright shop by Paul Chappell and others by direction of Surgeon Gray of the regiment, where he expired almost immediately. The Rebels, being reinforced, made another sally, and all those in and around the wheelwright shop who were able to do so, were off to resist the charge. Those who were left behind were eventually taken prisoners. Lieutenant Divver's body was never recovered, though many efforts were made by his family. He met the death of a gallant soldier at the head of his men, and lies in an unmarked grave with his fallen comrades. Lieutenant Daniel Divver was the brother of Alderman Patrick Divver.

THE SECOND FIRE ZOUAVES

Of all the regiments which the Empire State sent to the front during the Civil War, none made a more honorable record than the Second Fire Zouaves. It was organized May 3, 1861, and consisted almost entirely of firemen and runners. At first Governor Morgan declined the services of the regiment, since it was supposed that enough troops to suppress the Rebellion had already been raised. Not until the early part of July did the Zouaves go into "Camp Decker," on Staten Island. The camp was named in honor of Chief Decker, of the Fire Department, who was very active in recruiting the regiment. Even when the boys, eight hundred and fourteen strong, started for the front, August 23, 1861, they had not been recognized by the Albany authorities, and had no State number. Private enterprise had organized and equipped the regiment, which was at first known simply as the Fourth Regiment of the Excelsior Brigade. Fire Commissioner Henry Wilson, Thomas Lawrence, Henry Graham and Judge Dusenbury were among the public-spirited men who aided in the work of Gen. Sickles' Excelsior Brigade. They were mustered into service as United States volunteers.

Colonel James Fairman, who had been organizing a regiment for the Sickles Brigade, agreed to take the companies as they were formed, company by company, and turn over his companies to the other regiments in the same brigade. He eventually did so, and mustered in eight companies of the Second Fire Zouaves at Camp Scott, on Staten Island. The other two companies being mustered in at the camp in Maryland, there was an agreement with the officers of the regiment that they would elect Fairman to the colonelcy, and he started with the regiment. He was, however, relieved of his command on the way to the boat, and Major Moriarty placed in command, which he retained until the regiment was encamped at Mendian Hill, on the outskirts of Washington. The privates of the regiment were in favor of Fairman, and for a time the excitement ran high. When the regiment went into Camp McClellan, in Maryland, just across the river from Washington, the officers held an election for colonel, and William R. Brewster, of Brooklyn, was elected, receiving the votes of all the commissioned officers of the regiment, excepting those of Capt. Daniel Crowley, Company D, formerly member of Engine Company 20; Lt. Wm. Gleeson, Company D, formerly member of Engine Company 3; Lt. John Skelin, Company D, also of Engine Company 20; Lt. J. Hamilton, Company 16, member of Company 14; and Lt. Evans. Col. Brewster proved himself to be an honorable gentleman and a brave soldier, and continued in command of the regiment until the end of the war. The regiment went from Camp McClellan to Point Matthias, and afterwards to Port Tobacco, Md., and from there to join the Army of the Potomac. Below are the names of the other officers: Field and staff—Lieut. Colonel, Louis Benedict; Major, John D. Moriarty; Adjutant, George Le Fort; Surgeon, Henry P. Bostwick; Assistant Surgeon, Frank Ridgeway; Quartermaster, John A. McCosker; Chaplain, Rev. Joseph B. O'Hagen.

Non-Commissioned Staff.
Sergeant-major, Henry H. Lewis.
Quartermaster-sergeant, James T. Brady.

Drum-major, John Ross.
Fife-major, John McIntyre.
Company Commanders.

A,	M. W. Burns,	-	-	-	-	-	Hose 21.
B,	Thomas Smith,	-	-	-	-	-	Hose 56.
C,	A. Gibson,	-	-	-	-	Hook and Ladder 15.
D,	Daniel Crowley,	-	-	-	-	-	Engine 20.
E,	William M. Fisk,	-	-	-	-	-	Engine 32.
F,	Alfred A. Donald,	-	-	-	-	-	Engine 17.
G,	John Feeney,	-	-	-	-	-	Hose 50.
H,	William McCaully,	-	-	-	-	Engine 40.
I,	Charles B. Elliott,	-	-	-	Hose 7, Williamsburg.
K,	Michael D. Purtell,	-	-	-	-	

Among the minor officers may be mentioned: Lieutenants William Gleeson, Engine 3; John J. Glass, Engine 16; Eugene C. Stine, Engine 31; John Phelan, Hose 10; Michael Feeny, Hose 6; Matthew Stewart, Hose 50; John T. Lawrence, Hose 11; Washington Mullen, Hose 22; John P. Skehan, Engine 20.

The State gave the regiment a tardy recognition, and, on November 27, 1861, issued commissions to the officers, and thenceforth the corps was known as the Seventy-third New York Volunteers. But the boys called themselves the Second Fire Zouaves to the end of their service. While they were at Camp McClellan, Good Hope, a delegation of New York firemen, headed by Chief Decker, visited them, and on October 17, 1861, presented them with a handsome stand of colors, the gift of the Department. Early in November the regiment was ordered to Lomer, Maryland, about fifty miles below Washington, and detailed for picket duty on the banks of the Potomac. They crossed the river April 2, 1862, and made a raid on Stafford Court-house, where they destroyed a large amount of Rebel stores. Closely pursued by the enemy, they recrossed the Potomac in good order under cover of their gunboats. Four days after the affair the regiment embarked in the steamer *Vanderbilt* for Yorktown. From Cheeseman's Creek, Virginia, they went to the front, and did picket duty in the trenches until May 4. It was a quiet Sunday morning when a negro clambered over the enemy's breastworks and told the Second Fire Zouaves that the greycoats were evacuating the town. The New York men dashed forward, and entered Yorktown in time to see the enemy retreating. Thomas Madden, of Company H, secured the garrison flag, which the Rebels had forgotten to take away. The trophy was sent to New York, where it remained for many years in the possession of Mr. Henry Jones, foreman of Engine No. 40. It is now the property of the Regimental Veteran Association, having been presented to them by Mr. Jones. In Townsend's "Records" of the First and Last Events of the War is the following:

"The first regiment to enter Yorktown and plant the Stars and Stripes on ramparts of the rebel works was the Seventy-third New York Volunteers, known as the Fourth Excelsior Regiment. Written on the wall of a deserted house in Yorktown was the cheering message, 'Yanks! we evacuate Yorktown to-day by order of our commander, but we will meet you to-morrow at Williamsburg.' Our heroes were on hand in Williamsburg the next day, and lost one hundred and fifty men on the field. Captain Feeney and Lieutenant Glass were among the killed. From that time until Lee's surrender the regiment got its share of every hard knock the Army of the Potomac received. They made a brilliant bayonet charge at Fair Oaks, June 1, which is thus mentioned in General Mc-Clellan's report:

" 'General Sickles, having been ordered to the left, formed line of battle on both sides of the Williamsburg road and advanced under a sharp fire of the enemy deployed in the woods in front of Union. After a brisk countercharge of musketry fire while crossing the open ground, the Excelsior Brigade dashed into the timber with the bayonet, and put the enemy to flight. At Fair Oaks, June 15, the regiment was vigorously attacked during a severe thunderstorm. Company H bore the brunt of the rebel charge, and Captain McCaully was taken prisoner. Ten days later the Zouaves, who were in Hooker's division took part in the action at Oak Grove, which was brought about by the general advance of the Union lines.' "

McClellan's report contains these words: "If we succeed in what we have undertaken, it will be a very important advantage gained. Loss not large for the fighting up to this has been done by General Hooker's division, which has behaved as usual—that is, most splendidly." During the retreat from Richmond the regiment was engaged at Savage Station and Glendale. While the army was in camp at Harrison's Landing, the Zouaves fought under Hooker at Malvern Hill, August 5, 1862. During the night, Hooker, finding himself confronted by a superior force, withdrew. The Zouaves remained at Harrison's Landing until the army left the Peninsula, and on August 21 they embarked at Yorktown for Alexandria. Immediately they were sent to Pope; arrived in time to fight at Bristol Station on August 27. Here a third of the regiment fell. Captain Donalds and Lieutenant John McAllister (Engine No. 1, Williamsburg) were killed. At the second battle of Bull Run, (August 29, 1862), the battered regiment again crossed bayonets with the Rebels. While they were advancing through the woods, the enemy fell upon their left flank and drove them back. The colors would have been taken had not Color-Sergeant George Ramsay torn them from the staff and wrapped them about his body. Many Zouaves were taken prisoners. After the battle of Chantilly, September 1, the regiment went into camp near Alexandria, where several recruits from New York helped to fill the decimated companies. The muster rolls of November 1 show four hundred and eighteen men present for duty. From Alexandria the regiment was ordered to Falmuth, VA. It took part in the slaughter in Fredericksburg, and was stuck in the mud with the rest of Burnside's command during his famous march. Fredericksburg had again thinned the ranks, and at Falmuth on January 20, 1863, the One hundred and Sixty-third New York Volunteers were incorporated with the Fire Zouaves, bringing the strength up to five hundred and sixty-nine, as the muster rolls of March 1 show. On May 2 the fire laddies fought stubbornly at Chancellorsville, holding a position in the wood where Stonewall Jackson received his death-wound. Among the killed was Lieutenant Thomas Dennin (Engine 47).

After the battle the regiment went back to the camp at Falmuth, where it lay until the Pennsylvania campaign. At Gettysburg Colonel Brewster commanded the brigade, which was in the left of the line in Humphrey's division. The One Hundred and Fourteenth Pennsylvania was attacked by the Barksdale, Miss., brigade. Brewster ordered the Zouaves to support the Pennsylvanians at the Peach Orchard. The boys dashed forward into the smoke with a cheer. They went into the combat three hundred and twenty-four strong, and lost fifty-one killed, one hundred and three wounded, and eight prisoners. Captain E. C. Shine and Lieutenant W. L. Herbert, James Marksman and George C. Dennin were killed. July 23, 1863, found the Zouaves at Manassas Gap, where, with the rest of the Excelsior Brigade, under General Spinola, charged Wapping Heights. The regiment was on picket duty in the Rapidan until Lee forced Meade to fall back to Fairfax Court-house. November 7 the boys crossed the Rappahanock, and fought at Kelly's Ford. There they went into winter quarters at Brandy Station, and met the greycoats at Mine Run, November 27. After the action the regiment went back to winter quarters, where it remained until spring. On January, 1864, three hundred and eighteen men were present for duty. Many of them reenlisted, and went on furlough to New York, where their fellow firemen gave them a rousing reception.

The camp at Brandy Station was broken up May 1, 1864, and the regiment crossed the Rapidan. Grant was at the head of the army, and between the Wilderness and Cold Harbor the Zouaves saw plenty of hard fighting. Captains John Phelan, James McDermott, Michael D. Purtell and George L. Fort and Lieutenant B. Leonard were killed during the campaign. On the evening of June 15, the regiment entered the trenches in front of Petersburg, and were hotly engaged the next morning. Patrick Stack, of Engine 53, was the first man to fall. During the siege of Petersburg the regiment was continually on the move, taking part in most all the skirmishes in front of the strong-hold. At Bull Run half of the regiment fell into the hands of the enemy, and the colors would have been taken had not the Color-Sergeant, Patrick Doyle, hidden them under his jacket. While the little band of Zouaves was returning through the mud to camp, the flag slipped unobserved from Doyle's person. He went back after it, and walked two miles without finding either the colors or any one who had picked them up. The cavalry picket refused to let him go further, as the enemy was close at hand. With a heart heavy as lead, Doyle walked towards the camp again. He had not gone five hundred yards, when, to his boundless joy, he found the dear blackened, tattered old flag buried in the mud, where one thousand soldiers had trodden it down.

On March 25, 1865, the regiment captured three officers and one hundred and twenty-four men at Hatcher's Run, while the One Hundred and Twenty-fourth New York and One Hundred and Tenth Pennsylvania and the Zouaves made a night attack April 1 and took many prisoners. They had their last march with the Rebels on the sixth. Three days later came the news of Lee's surrender. On June 29, the regiment, two hundred strong, was mustered out of a service in which it had spent four years, one month and seven days. It had fought gallantly at Stafford Court-house, Yorktown, Williamsburg, Seven Pines, Fair Oaks, Oak Grove, Savage Station, Glendale, Malvern Hill, Bristow Station, Second Bull Run, Chantilly, Fredericksburg, Chancellorsville, Gettysburg, Wapping Heights, Kelly's Ford, Mine Run, Wilderness, Spottsylvania, North Anna, Tolopotomy, Cold Harbor, Petersburg, Strawberry Plains, Deep Bottom and Boylston Road.

William A. Hackett.—At the breaking out of the War of Secession, William A. Hackett was among the first to volunteer his services to the Government as a soldier, was accepted, and assigned to the command of Company H, First Regiment, New York Fire Zouaves (afterwards known as the Eleventh New York Volunteers), under Colonel Elmer E. Ellsworth, which regiment left the city for the seat of war April 29, 1861.

William A. Hackett was born on the corner of Nassau and Liberty Streets, in the City of New York, on March 16, 1834, and became a member of the New York Volunteer Fire Department in 1851, having at that time joined Washington Engine Company No. 20, to which company he was strongly attached from early boyhood, an attachment he ever retained to an enthusiastic degree throughout his entire career as a fireman. His untiring devotion, never-failing attention to duty, and good judgment of fires, soon commanded the admiration of his associates, and he was unanimously elected to the foremanship while yet the youngest man among those on the roll of his company. Fire duty was his all-absorbing study through life, and were it not for his close application to fires, there is little reason to doubt he would have remained among us to this day in some active capacity not far removed from the present department. To enumerate the many noteworthy escapes, accidents, and incidents he experienced during his service would make a volume in itself. At the Jennings' fire on Broadway, where some thirteen firemen were killed by the falling of a heavy safe from one of the upper floors of the burning building, his escape was most miraculous. His labors at Penfold, Parker, and Moore's fire, in Beekman Street, where he was confined within the burning building for several hours, was an exhibition of endurance very few, if any, of his associates could have withstood; and at the explosion during the progress of the fire in the bonded warehouse on Pearl Street, near State, where he received an injury of which he ever after complained, and it is believed was, to a great extent, instrumental in his untimely death. Mr. Hackett was elected in 1859 to the Engineer Board by a very flattering vote, a like honor being extended at every subsequent election up to the close of the volunteer system.

CHAPTER XX

A FAREWELL TO THE VOLUNTEERS

*George Washington An Active Fireman.—His Great Interest in Fire Matters.—
The Growth and Progress of the City.—Some Quaint Fire Ordinances.—Fires
and Fire Bugs.—Life Saving Firemen.—Gallant and Devoted.—Brave Men;
Honest Men.—We May Not Look Upon their Like Again.*

If we have carried the reader along with us thus far he will have noted that
our assertion at the beginning—that the history of the Volunteer Fire Department meant the history of the rise and progress of New York—has been
borne out by the facts we have presented. We have brought to light, among
other important things, one interesting fact that had been forgotten or not generally known—the fact that the Father of his Country had enrolled himself as a
volunteer fireman. George Washington, who was as zealous in the discharge of
his duty as a private citizen as he was eminent and efficient in public life, became
an active fireman in Alexandria, Virginia, about the year 1750. He was then but
eighteen years of age, and resided with his brother Lawrence at Mount Vernon,
several miles from the town, which he visited "on horseback as often as ten times
a week."

As a young man he took an active part in all the affairs of the growing place
until it became an important colonial city. Besides his firmness of character, his
love of active pursuits, his passion for horsemanship and all manly sports made
him a natural leader among the young men of the town. It is related that he was
always one of the foremost to assist in putting out fires, riding even from Mount
Vernon to be present at one. As Alexandria increased in size, the principal citizens
began to organize for protection against fire, and the town record shows that
they each agreed, out of "mutual friendship," to carry to every fire "two leathern
buckets and one great bag of oznaburg or wider linnen." This was the primitive
colonial mode of extinguishing flames.

The watchmen were also enrolled as firemen, and sounded an alarm by sending forth a blast from a huge trumpet which they wore slung about their shoulders. Instead of billies they carried quaint-looking weapons called spontoons,
something between a spear and a halberd. These antique weapons were left

behind in store at Alexandria by General Braddock's troops in 1755, when they marched on their disastrous expedition to the West. The spontoons were appropriated by the municipal authorities, and, strange to say, were still in use by the watchmen when the provost guard of a Michigan regiment in the summer of 1861 relieved these obsolete guardians from further duty.

The Friendship Fire Company of Alexandria, which still survives, was organized in 1774. At that time Washington was a delegate to the Continental Congress in Philadelphia, but the members of the new company evidently remembered his former services as fireman, for at one of their first meetings they unanimously elected him an honorary member, and forwarded him a copy of the minutes. To show his appreciation of the compliment, he at once made a thorough inspection of the different kind of fire engines in use in Philadelphia, and upon his second return there, in 1775, he bought from one Gibbs a small fourth-class engine for eighty pounds and ten shillings, and just before he set out for Boston to become commander-in-chief of the Continental Army, he sent this little engine as a present to the Friendship Fire Company.

The great chieftain did not lose his interest in fire matters through his elevation to position and power. Upon his retirement to Mount Vernon, after his second term as president, and when his fame had spread round the world, he continued to take an active interest in the municipal affairs of Alexandria. It is related that in the last year of his life he was one day riding down King Street, when a fire broke out near the market. He was accompanied by his servant, also on horseback, and noticed that Friendship Company engine was poorly manned, though a crowd of well-dressed idlers stood about. Riding up to the crowd he employed very vigorous language in rebuking their indifference at such a time. He ended by calling out, "It is your business to lead in these matters," and throwing the bridle of his horse to his servant, he leaped off and seized the brakes, followed by a crowd that gave the engine such a "shaking up" as it never knew afterwards.

Washington voted for the last time, in Alexandria, in 1799, a few weeks previous to his death, which occurred just before the dawn of the nineteenth century.

How the old volunteers of New York would have enjoyed the spectacle! The great General pulling on a rope! The survivors must feel a greater pride in their profession, knowing that Washington had been one of their number.

The rapid rise of New York is unprecedented in history. Nearly two centuries and a half ago the island was a wilderness north of the Battery. In 1651, Indians, in canoes, paddled about the waters of the Hudson and the East River. About twenty years before, the whole island had been purchased from the Manhattans for the sum of twenty-four dollars. Think of it, ye rich New Yorkers of to-day, who willingly pay thousands of dollars for a few yards of this same land! Two hundred and fifty years back a fire alarmed the colonists, and because it destroyed much of their property, set them thinking about finding ways and means to prevent such occurrences. Wooden chimneys and thatched roofs were often the cause of fires, and in 1648 an ordinance was passed to abolish this kind of chimney and roof. In those days there was no lack of water for the extinguishment, for all the buildings comprising the city were confined to the neighborhood of the Battery. Proper appliances alone were needed to use the water for putting out the many fires that occurred. Some time elapsed before even the rudest machinery was obtainable for the primitive Fire Department. Naturally, buckets were the first things thought of, and, as we have seen, had very little effect upon a fire.

But as New York extended, the water supply diminished, or, in other words, was inadequate to meet the needs of the people. This was one of the most puzzling problems the inhabitants had to deal with. We have laid before the reader the schemes of individuals and corporations to remedy the evil. No sooner had a system been elaborated and adopted, than the still further growth of the city, in a few years, rendered the new system obsolete. Then another plan had to be devised to satisfy the firemen and the citizens, and when matured, became, like the preceding, in a short time, antiquated and inadequate. This struggle with a difficult question has continued right up to our own day. At last a gigantic project has been undertaken, and when accomplished, will, it is thought, solve the difficulty. The new aqueduct, as it is described in this book from official sources, will, to all appearances, satisfy the mind of the investigator that, at last, the city is furnished with a water supply that will prove ample for all purposes for many and many a year to come. But, if we bear in mind the lessons of the past, we may argue, from what we find in them, that our children will be looking upon the new aqueduct as an old system, unable to furnish the still greater New York with all that it wants for its Fire Department and other purposes. We have seen how New Yorkers have, at various times, prided themselves upon their splendid wells, have rejoiced over the opening of the Erie Canal, celebrated the introduction of the first stream of the crystal Croton, and viewed, with immense satisfaction, the construction of the new aqueduct. Mayhap, some other grand water scheme will, ere the lapse of another half century, occupy the attention of the citizens, and give occasion for another display to honor the event. Who knows? The growth of New York is held to be almost illimitable.

The rise of our city is one of the astonishing facts that strikes the mind of the inquiring foreigner. Nay, there are hundreds and hundreds of old firemen still living, who, though natives, are no less impressed by what they have seen and contemplate. We have men still with us who have known Chambers Street to be the northern limit of the city—men who have wandered among fields and meadows which are now the centers of the busiest neighborhoods in the world.

These veterans are, to the younger generation, objects of veneration. These "old boys" are living links between the generation that ambled buckets of water into what were little better than tubs worked by tanks, and the generation that mans the finest fire machines that modern science can devise. Let the reader turn to the illustrations we have given of those quaint boxes worked by firemen in pig tails, and then take a glance at the magnificent engines of to-day, manned by athletic fellows in neat fitting and appropriate costumes, and he will first be amazed, and then smile, at the thought that those bygone appliances could ever be of the slightest use. We have grown visibly.

Step by step the Volunteer Department became a great institution. Year by year it advanced in public estimation. Its every act was noted and placed on record. As an illustration, in addition to what has already been said on the subject, we give a few quaint extracts from the aldermanic proceedings:

At a meeting of the Common Council held Friday, October 23, 1789, "It being represented to the Board of Aldermen that the law of this corporation to prevent the danger of fire is inadequate, especially with respect to the danger arising from the use of iron stoves in joiners' workshops and other places, be it ordered that the recorder be requested to revise the law in the matter of fires, and to prepare a law with such further provisions as he may deem necessary."

At a meeting of the Common Council held Wednesday, December 5, 1787, a petition of Archibald Kesler was presented on behalf of himself and several of his neighbors in Cherry Street, setting forth that they had purchased a fire engine, which they were willing to appropriate to the use of the public, and to erect a house and purchase a piece of ground for its reception, and they "pray the board to accept it for that purpose, and to appoint the proper number of firemen to take charge of and to work the same." It was ordered that the engineer return the names of ten proper persons to be appointed to said engine.

At a meeting of the Common Council held Friday, November 13, 1789, a petition of the foremen of several of the small fire engines, praying that the number of men to each of said engines may be ten, as formerly, was read and referred to Alderman Stoutenburgh and Messrs. Elsworth and Curtinius, and on reading a petition of the company belonging to Engine No. 13, in favor of Nicholas Brevoort being appointed to their company, it was resolved "that the resolution of this board of August 12, that no person under the age of thirty years be appointed to the office of a fireman of this city, be repealed."

On reading a representation of the company of Engine No. 5 by Frederick Echert, their foreman, that Francis Arden and George Peck, members of that company, "had neglected their duty as firemen, and hoping that this board would order their names to be struck off the list of firemen," it was ordered "that the said Francis Arden and George Peck attend this board at the next meeting to show cause why the request of said company should not be complied with, and that Mr. Echert also attend to support the accusation." The firemen in those days were very particular as to their companions.

The first Fire Department numbered fifty members. In 1865 it had swelled to about four thousand. Year by year its members grew to keep pace with the requirements of the city. When the British took possession of "New Nether-lands," the fire question was agitated. The fire wardens demanded more imple-ments. Ordinances were passed compelling every citizen to furnish one bucket or more. Long after the introduction of fire engines, buckets were in general use. Towards the close of the seventeenth century a night watch was instituted to guard against fires, and a strict supervision of hearths and chimneys was main-tained. Then bells were brought into use for the purpose of giving the alarm, and finally watch towers were erected. When Newsham's engines were brought from London in the beginning of the eighteenth century, the whole city heaved a sigh of relief—now it had really something scientific and effective to protect property from the ravages of fire, so it thought. Now were formed the first fire companies, and now began the fireman's manifestation of his love for the ma-chine—a love which became so conspicuous in after years.

Very soon the Board of Aldermen began to take an active interest in fire matters, as the following facts will show: At a meeting of the Common Council, January 12, 1801, a petition of Thomas Howell, praying for the reasons men-tioned therein, that the board would grant him an additional sum of money towards indemnifying him for his loss on the importation of the new fire engine for Company No. 24 from London, and lately sold to the board, was read, and it was determined that no further sum ought to be granted. He had been allowed five hundred and fifty dollars for the engine, which appears a high price for the old-fashioned engine of those days.

A petition of the firemen for the appointment of a person as chief engineer "in the place of the person now exercising that office," was read and referred to the aldermen of the Sixth Ward, and the assistants of the Second and Fourth Wards, to inquire into the facts stated in the said petition. At a meeting of the Common Council, May 23, 1803, a resolution was passed that "Aldermen Bar-ker, Morris and Stevens be a committee to confer with the engineers and firemen of the respective engines in this city respecting the best mode of keeping the fire engines in good repair from time to time as the same may be required, and also to confer with them and the fire wardens jointly, whether some more effectual means cannot with propriety be adopted than the present rules and order for the government of the Fire Department, and the compulsion of the citizens to assist on such occasions, under proper penalties for neglect or refusal when thereunto required, and the same committee be directed to report with all convenient speed."

A report of the inspector and a letter of Dr. Browne in relation to a big fire in 1804, recommending measures proper for the prevention and extinguishment of fires, was received in Common Council on December 24, De Witt Clinton, mayor, being present. It was ordered, "that such part of the said papers as relates to future improvements in the Fire Department be referred to Aldermen Van Zandt, King, Mr. Bloodgood, Mr. Mott, and Mr. Hopkins. Ordered that the mayor be authorized and requested to issue a proclamation in behalf of this board, and to offer a reward of five hundred dollars for the discovery of any conspiracy to set fire to the city, and a like reward for the discovery of any persons who may have willfully perpetrated the fire on December 18, and also a like reward for the discovery of any person who may have set fire to buildings since that period, and that such reward be paid on the conviction of the offender or offenders respectively." It was likewise ordered "that all officers be vigilant and attentive, as well in the detection of offenders as in preventing the execution of their designs, and that all persons be requested to communicate such information which they may possess in relation to the origin of the late fire, or in regard to future attempts, at the inspector's office. Ordered that the augmentation of the city watch directed by the mayor be continued until the further order of the board, and that the captain of watch of the First District be directed to be particularly attentive to the neighborhood of Burling Slip."

The corporation of the Presbyterian Church, having requested in the latter part of 1805 that the engine house standing on their ground in Nassau Street may be removed, "it is ordered that the engine house in the City Hall Yard be extended so as to admit the deposit of the engine on the said ground belonging to the Presbyterian Church."

In Common Council, March 23, 1807, the chief engineer represented the necessity of moving Engine No. 29 from the house of that number, standing on ground heretofore allotted to that purpose, "but now rented to Mr. Francis De Flyn, who wishes for the removal of said building." It was ordered, "that the alderman and assistant of the Eighth Ward do provide some proper place for Engine No. 29."

The early engines were located in structures little better than sheds. Bye-and-bye the corporation voted sums of money to provide better accommodation, and it was not long before very respectable houses were provided. It was not till about the period of 1840 that regular dwellings were provided for the men who lived at a distance from their engine. At first the expense was borne by the men themselves. Many of the hardy volunteers were content for years with a straw mattress. The "bunking" system enabled the firemen to have a watch all night, and the consequence was that a quicker service was obtained.

Never at any time was there the slightest intimation of a desire for a remuneration. The men gloried in working for nothing. "The voluntary system," wrote ex-Judge Charles P. Daly, "was upon its introduction a most desirable one, and continued to be so for more than three-quarters of a century. For alacrity, intrepidity, skill, and courage, the men who composed it would compare with any body of firemen in the world. At its institution, and for many years, it consisted almost exclusively of the most influential and prominent citizens, who discharged their arduous labors at a great sacrifice of time, and frequently of health, from a high sense of public duty, and the example they set infused into the whole community a zeal and willingness to lend their aid and assistance upon the breaking out of a fire almost without precedent in the history of cities. The effect upon the rising generation was especially marked, and the young were made to feel that to be a fireman was an honorable distinction."

The old engines moved with difficulty, and were cumbrous and rude in construction. They, however, gave place to better machines, and the service improved as the demand upon it grew. The danger of the work was obvious, and a courage and daring which has gone into history began to leave behind it men who were maimed and crippled in the public service, and widows and orphans deprived of their natural protectors and reduced to poverty and want. The firemen themselves were the first to see the growing difficulty, and with characteristic unselfishness sought to provide a remedy.

It took the firemen a long time to find out that their beloved hand engine was not the most perfect machine possible. Really they had done excellent service with it, and no wonder it was hard to wean them from their darling. Steam fire engines were introduced in London in 1832 with a marked increase of efficiency and economy; but it was nearly thirty years afterwards before they were introduced in New York. The influence of the firemen on public officials postponed the adoption of the steam engine long after its practicability had been established. In like manner horses had long been used in London to transport the engines and other fire apparatus more expeditiously. This, too, was regarded as an innovation by the volunteer firemen of this city, who had a strong preference for dragging the engines themselves by hand. But steam and electricity, twin giants, could not long be put down by such puny efforts. They had taken a front place in the van of civilized life, and were soon to revolutionize the world. The Fire Department, it is true, was slow to appreciate these potent facts. Many held that New York was by far more progressive than the Fire Department. It had grown, and was growing apace, while the firemen, seemingly unconscious of this self-evident fact, had stuck to the old-time methods of fire extinguishing in vogue when the city was comparatively a village. "When the city," says ex-Judge Daly, "was embraced within moderate limits, the occasional duty of acting as a fireman was not a very onerous one, but when the city had expanded miles in extent it exacted an amount of time which few were able to give who had their business to attend to, and consequently this class was gradually withdrawn from the department, which was filled by those who could give more time to it. The increasing extension of the city demanded, moreover, a constant augmentation of the force of the department, and as it increased in numbers it degenerated in quality."

A newspaper writer, with a spice of humor, once began his account of the old firemen with the remark: "We don't mean those redoubtable old chaps who had inserted in the by-laws of their company a clause to the effect that it was legitimate for a member, upon arriving at the engine house, after hearing an alarm of fire, to grease his boots at the expense of the corporation before he rolled the machine, or endeavor to catch her if she had rolled." But those "old chaps," nevertheless, were brave as lions. We have given many an instance of the bravery of the volunteer firemen. Saving lives at fires was characteristic of them, and it is to be regretted that more records of their daring acts have not been preserved. Many gallant deeds in the cause of humanity have been forgotten, for no note was made of them at the time. The activity of the firemen in this respect, considering the facilities they possessed as compared with those of to-day, was remarkable. The assistance they rendered operatives and inmates of burning buildings, and the desperate chances they often took to save lives, seem to belong more to the days of knights-errantry than to an era of dollars and cents. In July, 1855, the *Tribune* had the following:

"GALLANT CONDUCT.—About twelve o'clock on Wednesday night, the fourth instant, a fire broke out in the building, No. 138 Prince Street, occupied by J. C. Stone on the first floor as a store for the sale of fancy articles and fireworks and dwelling, upper part as a dwelling by Jas. Nagle and family and Mr. Beebe and family. The fire originated among a quantity of fireworks, and in a short time the building was densely filled with smoke. The flames spread rapidly, and for some time defied the efforts of the firemen, who were promptly on the ground after the alarm was given. A large crowd gathered in the street, among whom the greatest excitement prevailed. The occupants of the building had not yet made their appearance, and it was not known whether or not they had escaped, although it was rumored that they were still in the building. A ladder was soon brought and placed against the second story window, when Thomas O'Brien, Charles Wilson, Levi D. White, of Hose Company No. 56, and Gardner Van Brunt, of Engine Company No. 2, four daring souls, made their way through fire and smoke into the second story. Crawling upon their hands and knees over the floor, they at length found the beds in the different apartments, all of which were occupied. They sought to arouse the occupants, but they were unable to do so, as nearly all of them were about half suffocated and unable to help themselves. No time was to be lost, as the smoke was becoming denser and denser every moment. The gallant fellows seized Mr. Beebe and his wife, and carrying them to the windows, passed them down the ladders to the street. They then returned and brought three young women, Margaret Nagle, Ellen Nagle, and Mary Ann Shannon, a niece of Mr. Nagle, also two sons of Mr. Nagle. Margaret, half crazed by the smoke, leaped from the fireman's arms through the window and fell heavily upon the sidewalk, injuring her back and ankles. Mary Ann was badly burned upon the head and shoulders. Ellen Nagle, while being lowered to the street, had her ankle sprained, and was somewhat burned. Mr. Nagle and his wife were almost gone, and it was only by the kindest attention that they recovered. The sons were also somewhat injured. The parties were conveyed to the Eighth Ward Station House, where they were attended personally by Captain Turnbull and Lieutenants Kohler and Stage, and several physicians. Mr. Stone and his wife escaped by the rear door, first floor. Mrs. Stone, on reaching the door, missed her child, and returned through the smoke to her room, where, recovering her child, she succeeded in escaping without injury."

Indeed, the words courage and fireman were synonomous. The bravery and devotion of the Department amply compensated, in the opinion of the public, for whatever shortcomings it had. The companies had quarrels, to be sure; but they were quarrels arising from a noble rivalry to be the first at a fire or a rescue. In later years the Department was an immense organization. What wonder that evil-disposed persons—big and little—took advantage of it, either to discredit or use it for their own purposes. It was seen that a new era was dawning—that the city wanted a simpler, more effective, and more compact organization. New York was immensely rich. It could afford to pay for this arduous service, and it was resolved to do so. Good citizens generally wished well to the prospect of disbanding the volunteers and establishing a Paid Department. The politicians began to use the Department for their ends, and the people and even the press were afraid to denounce them. The disagreeable duty of abolishing the volunteers was therefore undertaken by the Board of Fire Underwriters.

The work of disbandment went on slowly at first. The new regime was not yet organized, but the transfer of authority was effected with very little friction, all things considered. The disbanded volunteers, by their dignity and forbearance, and their adherence to duty during the last trying hours of their organization, sustained their historic and well-earned reputation as brave men and devoted citizens. The New York *Herald*, editorially, (April 3, 1865), said:

"The conduct of the firemen under the present circumstances—which must be regarded as a great crisis in the history of their organization—is worthy of all admiration. There were many who supposed that upon the passage of the bill abolishing the Volunteer Department, there would have been resistance, and perhaps riotous conduct, on the part of the firemen. So far from that, they have exhibited the finest spirit, submitting cheerfully to the change, and consenting to fulfill their duties to the last in the protection of property and life. Their action proves, what we have always believed to be true, that the Fire Department proper was composed of a gallant, fearless, and honorable body of our citizens. The course which the members of the Department are now pursuing entitles them to the highest praise which is due to law-abiding citizens; and although the Volunteer Firemen's organization is no longer to comprise one of our local institutions, to have been a member of it will be a lasting honor."

On the twenty-ninth of July the work of retiring the volunteers was begun, and by the first of November three thousand eight hundred and ten of their number were stricken from the rolls. That they had "continued faithfully to perform the duties which their obligations imposed," was their crowning glory. Their services could not be entirely dispensed with, however, and the services of the leading officers—engineers and foremen—were retained by the new Board.

At last the hour drew nigh. The volunteers were to be numbered with the past, but their great services were not to be forgotten—they had made history, and they will live in it. Sorrowfully, regretfully, notwithstanding the promise of better things to come, the city said farewell to their old protectors. This book is a tribute—though an insufficient one—to the memory of their gallantry. Take them for all in all, they were brave men, honest men, devoted men—we shall never look upon their like again.

CHAPTER XXI

ORGANIZATION OF THE PAID DEPARTMENT

New York Overtakes the Provinces in 1864.—Paving the Way to a Paid Department.—The only way to Rescue the Volunteers was to Reorganize Them.—The Police, Insurance Men and Citizens Take a Hand to this End.

The establishment of Paid Fire Departments in several cities of the Union, notably Boston, Cincinnati, St. Louis and Baltimore, and their success and advantages had been watched and noted not only as a matter of business by fire insurance underwriters, and citizens whose property was exposed to accident or crime—for near the close of the war arson was resorted to by allies of the South—but by the volunteers and their friends and the general thinking public. The way to the establishment of a Paid Fire Department in New York City had been often paved, but the time for its legalization had not come and the schemes were abandoned when only partially planned. Still it was a striking commentary on New York's pre-eminence in advanced municipal affairs that, in methods of dealing with criminals, the management of the streets, the care of the indigent and criminal classes, etc., she was faithfully copied in every large city of the Union. A few cities, whose population were comparatively a fraction of hers, had looked ahead and provided for the time when buildings should be higher and more numerous, and when little less than a quasi-military organization would be suitable. Citizens had wearied of the noisy enthusiasm of the camp followers of men wedded to an old, slow system, with inadequate apparatus—often so old as to be venerable. It necessitated the services of an average of fifty men to a company, and the firemen, without fee, or hope of other reward than the gratification of a desire for excitement and muscular exercise and the performance of their duties as citizens, did service that well merited substantial recognition in the shape of pay and permanent employment. Volunteer fire duty, it is true, was done as well as possible under the circumstances, all cavil and innuendo to the contrary notwithstanding. It is just to say here that, as a whole, the Paid Department of this city has not, in heroism, intrepidity or disinterestedness, excelled the active volunteers, when all things are taken into consideration. The same company rivalry which, under the old system led to racing and sometimes brawls, still exists, and despite iron-clad rules and public sentiment, crops out now and then, showing that, after all, all firemen are human. The very rivalry which existed between the volunteer companies was in the end an advantage. Had they been apathetic, few apparatuses would have reached a fire in time to prevent serious loss. The racing was based on a point of honor, a test of endurance, skill and strategy. It kept up the esprit de corps, and left laggards in the rear. The anxiety in running to a fire to prevent a rival company from passing was that of an English or American university crew of oarsmen to avoid getting "bumped." The system of competition taught firemen that the shortest distance between two points is a straight line, and that the alert and fleetfooted get to the goal first. So that in these days the company which has the "hitching up" drill well mastered, and leaves the quarters the moment a home signal is ticked off, may reach the station indicated before a less well drilled and not so wide-awake a company much nearer to the rendezvous, and so shame the laggards into better performance of duty another time. The volunteers, once the members of the company assembled and the rope manned, made as good time as bipeds could. Taken as a whole, the active members of the volunteer Fire Department—not the "runners" and hangers-on—were as brave, honest, efficient and earnest, without pay and with antiquated apparatus, as are the active members of the present Department, who are well paid and have the best fire extinguishing appliances that science and mechanical ingenuity can devise or that money can command. Such volunteers, or such of them as would, for proper remuneration, do what they did gratuitously out of a sense of the highest duties and obligations of citizenship, apart from any love of excitement and peril, were worth saving from politicians and the rabble, and the only way to save them, it was asserted, was to destroy the volunteer organization.

This enigmatical assertion is based on facts. Putting aside the question of the injustice of permitting able-bodied men, the majority of them working for their daily bread, to abandon work and risk their lives and expose themselves to the elements and severe toil, to save municipal and private property, and protect the lives and limbs of the community, without substantial reward—the time had come when a line had to be drawn between the volunteers, who were already cursed with political manipulation from their camp followers and the dry rot of expediency which, to serve the purpose of a few intent on using the volunteers as political factors, had discountenanced the introduction of steam fire apparatus and the consequent and inevitable reduction in the number of companies and the working force of such as were retained; the system saddled on the volunteers was virtually at an end with the introduction of the first fire steam engine. This and many which followed were not built as strongly as those of later years, but— taking the complement of a hand engine at fifty men—it pointed a way to relieve six-sevenths of those doing duty with the hand engine, if horses were employed to draw the engine. At the same time, the time required to take an engine from quarters to a fire was so reduced that the necessity of having many companies in each district was obviated, while the employment of an engineer at a salary, although he was elected by the company, insured the strict and interested attention of at least one member of such company to details on which depended the prompt starting of the apparatus from quarters when a signal was struck. The old hand apparatus, made as light as possible to permit quick hand transportation and elegance of construction, had to hug a fire to permit a proper stream being thrown on the flames by ordinary exertion, which, as a rule, was no light work, under extraordinary exertion, and the stimulus of rivalry with the iron-lunged innovation, streams were thrown which equaled, if they did not excel, those thrown by steam power. But it was at once seen that as a rule the steam machine could take a remote hydrant and do as good service as a hand machine, until the men who manned the brakes became exhausted, and then continue to do equally good service as long as fuel lasted. Besides, it was evident that the resources of science and mechanism had not been exhausted in the construction of the first steam fire engines. The horses attached to the engine did away with the rope, and with it the yearning of the rabble to take a hand and "jump her," and the horses did not yell and urge each other to exertion on the way to a fire, but attended strictly to business and left the camp followers who were not the fleetest of foot in the lurch, so that the pranks and depredations of the "sidewalk committees" were done away with. The horses, too, had no fancy for hurrying to rush past a rival company, or halt and fight out a rancorous sentiment, partly jealousy, partly rivalry, while the fire which had started was getting ahead. All New York did not frown at their encounters and jealousies. If the naked truth were told, few outside the Department were gravely anxious about them at all times. To many it appeared that until New York paid for fire service it would be impossible to have such service at all efficient without at least winking at the competition which pitted one company against the other, and resulted generally in a gain in point of speed in reaching a fire. Men who did their utmost to create a Paid Department were members of companies whose reputation for zeal in distancing or vanquishing rivals by feet or hands was the best or worst, as the partisan or critic may determine, and were as eager as their comrades when the apparatus was rolled out and the race began, or when the goal was reached and others were found to have the ground of vantage. How many staid citizens of the volunteer time who yet live will affirm that, even on Sunday, when the races either on genuine or false alarms, were along Broadway or the Bowery, and the ragamuffins ran to see them, and the often consequent unpleasantness between companies, they did not gird up their loins and become interested spectators? And how many, under the pressure of conscience, will fail to admit that at a pinch they vented their preferences, antipathies or interest in a shout or an exclamation, if they did not take a hand in the results of a collision after a war of words? Few citizens but had a tie or an interest of some sort in some engine, hose, or hook and ladder company. Many were impelled to vexation, and so on to exasperation, when their ox was gored, that is to say, when, often for trivial cause, such as a chimney fire or a false alarm, the streets in the neighborhood of their houses or counting rooms were invaded by apparatusses and crowds of excited, wrangling men and the hangers-on at their company quarters, and business and traffic stopped until excited passions were calmed and temper improved. Storekeepers grinned, shouted and lost themselves in excitement in the business avenues until an apparatus cleared the sidewalk, as the malicious practical jokers who followed the regulars upset the goods displayed in front of stores and made havoc of them, if they did not plunder. It is to be doubted if the enemies of the volunteer firemen proper, the active members of companies, were legion, because men of all ranks belonged to it, and persons of all walks in life did duty as "bunkers," "home sleepers" and "Exempts." But those who had dealings with the insurance companies, whose rates were high, were financially interested in any scheme which would put the Fire Department on any footing which would make it independent of those who were beginning to turn it into a political factor, and enable it to squelch the hangers-on or "runners," who were mainly an undesirable class, from the boys to depredators who waited for a fire alarm to run with the apparatus for no good purpose. In this and other ways the volunteers had a bad name with the Paid Police Department, whose members lost no opportunity of exaggerating wrangles or brawls, and making insinuations or flat charges when property was damaged or outrage occurred. The patience of the police, it must be admitted, was often sorely tried. There were few alarms of fire that did not call for action, from especial vigilance to interference, and now and then a policeman got hurt in an encounter, and the blame was always laid on the volunteers, although in the majority of instances the rabble had a hand in the melée, and it was fair to infer would be more likely to surreptitiously injure a policeman than an active fireman. The Hon. Thomas C. Acton and the late John A. Kennedy, superintendent of police, were prepared to encourage any plan to put the volunteers on an independent footing or create a new Department in which volunteers who chose to devote themselves to the service for proper remuneration could be enrolled. The chief engineer of the volunteers in later days was but little better than a creature of the street commissioner, and had to mind his Ps and Qs. The district engineers were in a worse predicament, as had the chief engineer been a martinet, a crank, or a rascal, they could have been harrassed between him and the companies over which they had jurisdiction. The commissioners owed allegiance to the companies because of their suffrages, and the Common Council's supreme influence was baneful.

Proper discipline was out of the question. For excellent political reasons, any black sheep expelled or disciplined could, if he had "a pull," be reinstated, and snap his fingers at discipline.

Such was the condition of affairs in a department whose members had shown what stuff they were made of, and their leaning towards law and order against mob rule and anarchy in the riots of 1863, when it became certain that in the Legislature of 1865 an opportunity to pass a Paid Fire Department measure would be seized upon.

Preparations for the legislative campaign of 1865 were begun early in 1864. On the seventeenth of March of that year the following resolution was passed at a meeting of the Board of Fire Underwriters:

> *Resolved*, That the subject of promoting the greater efficiency of the Fire Department be referred to a special committee to inquire into the same, and report to a subsequent meeting of this Board.

The committee was James M. McLean, president of the Citizens' Fire Insurance Company; Carlisle Norwood, president of the Lorillard; James M. Rankin, secretary of the Fulton; Rudolph Garrigue, Richard A. Reading, T. J. Glover, and T. G. Churchill. With them was associated Le Grand B. Cannon, director of the American. All were men of the greatest experience in fire matters, not only because the majority of them had been members of the Volunteer Department, but because they were experts in insurance business, and had studied European fire extinguishing methods, and the Paid Departments as they were successively established in this country.

Police Commissioner Acton and Superintendent John A. Kennedy furnished the committee with police reasons for a change. The underwriters' committee had for legal advisers Dorman B. Eaton and Abraham R. Lawrence, and much of the legal work was done by Mr. William C. Whitney, Secretary of the Navy under President Cleveland. The police contribution was in the form of affidavits from Captains Helm, Speight, Cameron, Williamson, Jordan, Todd, De Camp, Davis, Mount, Sebring, and others, who told of the disturbances, Sabbath desecration, pilfering, and general nuisances, of which they accused the volunteers and their followers. The underwriters' committee mastered the legal feature of the proposed change, shaped a course from reports from Baltimore, Boston, St. Louis, and Cincinnati, and the first draft of the Paid Fire Department Bill was made by Mr. James M. Rankin, in his house at Second Avenue and One Hundred and Twenty-fourth Street. The late Senator William Laimbeer, who was to father the bill in the Senate, did not trust to theories or reports, but visited the cities in which Paid Departments existed. He was accompanied by the Hon. Hugh Gardner, and profited not a little by that sturdy Scot's shrewdness, com-

mon sense, and practical views. The volunteers got an inkling of what was contemplated, and to offset the iconoclasts, and to put the volunteers in a better
light before the public, and to render them independent of many alliances that
had militated against their prestige and usefulness, concurred—rank and file—in
the drawing up of the ordinance of the thirty-first of December, 1864, which
was intended as an offset to action at Albany. It was entitled "An ordinance for
the better regulation of the Firemen of the City of New York." It provided for
a chief engineer, to be elected every three years by the votes of the members of
the Volunteer Fire Department, the first election to be in February, 1866; but
the election was simply a nomination to the Common Council for "appointment," and the salary was fixed at five thousand dollars per annum. No chief
engineer could serve a second term. Nineteen assistant engineers, two for each
district, except the Ninth, which was to have three, were to be elected in a
precisely similar manner in February, 1865, and to serve three years. Vacancies
were to be filled by ballot within thirty days. The working force of the department was to consist of "such members of fire engine men, hose men, and hook
and ladder men ★ ★ ★ as now are or hereafter may be from time to time appointed
in the manner required by law." Thus the Department was left in the hands of
the voting firemen and the dominant Common Council, and the system that
had been the bane of the volunteers was continued. Apart from these provisions,
the ordinance pursued the best features of the old regimes, and introduced some
new regulations calculated to improve the efficiency of the Department. Discipline and deportment were insisted on. The assistant engineers were to choose
one of their number as senior, and he was to take the place of the chief in the
event of disability or a vacancy. The Board of Engineers and Foremen had the
power to make elections for holding and conducting the elections. The companies chose their own foremen, assistant foremen, and secretaries, by such means
and at such times as they considered proper, but the commissioners of the Fire
Department decided in cases of irregularity and dispute. Stringent rules were in
the ordinances against the admission of persons not members of the Department
entering company quarters, and boys and disorderly characters lounging in their
vicinity, and no boys or improper persons were to be allowed to take hold of
the drag rope. No racing was to be countenanced. The fire commissioners could
reprimand, suspend, or disband any company, and any company could vote for
the expulsion of a member, while the fire commissioners could reverse, modify,
or confirm such act. Sections 37 and 38 provided as follows:

> "Any person who may in future be elected to fill a vacancy to any fire
> company shall present to the Chief Engineer within thirty days thereafter
> a certificate of such election, signed by the foreman and secretary of the
> company in which he has been elected, stating his name, residence, and

business; and said candidate, before the Chief Engineer presents his name to the Commissioners of the Fire Department, shall make affidavit that he is a citizen of the United States, is twenty-one years of age and upwards, that he is physically able, and that it is his intention to perform active and actual duty as a fireman with the company in which his name is enrolled, and that he will promote subordination in the Fire Department and the company to which he belongs, and it shall be the duty of the Chief Engineer to certify on every return whether a vacancy exists in the company. Applicants for appointment as members of the Fire Department must be of good moral character and actually engaged in some lawful business, and must be recommended to the Fire Commissioners as honest, sober, and industrious men, by their employers and three citizens of known respectability, and the Commissioners may confirm or reject any or all such applications."

Proper returns of duty performed were expected from all officers. The chief engineer was given authority to remove any apparatus or corporation property to the Public or Corporation yard. Such removals were to be made if the company was short-handed, was not useful, or became disreputable or riotous. In case of disbandment, facilities were given for members of a company to join another. The Chief Engineer, Presidents of the Department, Board of Trustees, Fire Commissioners, and Board of Commissioners of Appeal were made a Commission of Construction and Repairs of the New York Fire Department, to inquire into applications for changes in locations, for apparatus, or for new companies, or new houses, or for alterations or repairs to houses, or for new apparatus, or for alterations or repairs to apparatus, costing seventy-five dollars or more. The police were required to report any fireman or company violating any law or ordinance of the Fire Department, and it was made their duty to wake up members of the Department who might reside on their beats on a fire alarm being given at night, and the firemen were to supply the police with their names and residences. It was also the duty of the police to form lines at fires and prevent unauthorized persons from invading the territory thus environed. The mayor was empowered to select three bellringers for each signal station at one thousand dollars a year each. Engineers for steam engines were to be appointed by the Board of Engineers on the recommendation of a majority of the members of the company in which the appointee was to serve. Such appointees were to be competent and properly recommended. The uniform of the different members and officers was designated, and the wearing of it insisted on. The following section will be read with interest by the present generation:

"If any of the fire companies shall embellish their apparatus by painting, silver or other plating, polishing or any other embellishment, the chief engineer or other authorities of the City of New York shall not have replaced at the expense of the said city any such embellishment on any fire apparatus which may need rebuilding, alteration, or repairs, but shall only have such apparatus put in good working order without such embellishments, and when any embellishment is placed on any fire apparatus by any person or persons, or fire company, so that the same shall become a fixture to said apparatus, the said person, or persons, or fire company, shall not displace or disfigure said embellishment, and the said embellishment shall belong to the Corporation of the City of New York."

The ordinance embodied such regulations as are now within the province of the Superintendent of Combustibles and the Bureau of Inspection of Buildings. It prescribed the amount of fines for various breaches of discipline and violations of its provisions, and how they should be disposed of.

Chief John Decker, throughout the excitement caused by the legislation at Albany, the testing of the constitutionality of the law, and the merging of the Volunteer System into the Paid System, while he never for an instant swerved from his allegiance to the comrades whose votes placed him at their head, displayed qualities that characterize the law-abiding citizen and conscientious official. The "Ordinance for the better regulation of the Firemen of the City of New York," which became a municipal law on the thirty-first of December, 1864, was prepared at the instance of Commissioner John J. Gorman, with a view of improving the volunteer service. The first steps were taken at Firemen's Hall, on the twenty-seventh of September, 1864, when the Board of Representatives, Fire and Appeal Commissioners, Trustees, Engineers, Foremen, and Assistant Foremen met, discussed the reorganization of the volunteer system, appointed a committee of twenty from all branches of the Department, of which President Gorman was chairman, and left it to devise a plan to meet the requirements of the law, and satisfy the Department and the public. Over his own signature Chief Decker said that this ordinance was all that was necessary for the government of the Department. He went on to say that neither the Department nor its officers were, until the passage of the revised ordinance of December, 1864, responsible for the expenditure of its moneys, and he yet says that Tweed, Cornell, and others, killed the ordinance bill, which was taken to Albany to be passed as a state law. Nearly all the funds charged to the Fire Department, he said, were disbursed lavishly by the Common Council and Street Commissioners' Department, of which he was a subordinate, without consulting any officer of the Fire Department. It was acknowledged by the officers of the Fire Department

322 BIRTH OF THE BRAVEST

that two-thirds of the hose companies could be dispensed with; but until the ordinance of 1864 was passed this could not be done, unless the companies violated a law or ordinance. In five years and a half only three out of fifty-seven hose companies were abolished, but under the new ordinance, in Chief Decker's opinion, more than forty could have been done away with in a year. When the presentation of the Paid Fire Department Bill was announced, Chief Decker did all he could for the volunteers; and he says that the arguments in their favor before the Assembly committee were so powerful, that the Metropolitan Bill would not have been passed had not "some of the insurance companies of this city submitted to a tax on their capital amounting to fifty thousand dollars, and placed it in the hands of a committee who were urging the passage of the Metropolitan Fire Bill, after which arguments were in vain."

The legislation which created a Paid Fire Department was in stirring times. It was while all who could think or read watched the end of the struggle between North and South, and the proceedings at Albany attracted less of general attention than would have been paid to them had they been before the Legislature a year later or a year earlier. Had the measure been introduced in 1864 it is hardly possible to estimate what the result would have been had it become a law. A year later might have seen the innovation put off to another or a still later session by lobbying and influences of various sorts. But the Senate and Assembly were Republican; Reuben E. Fenton was Governor; Thomas G. Alvord, Lieutenant Governor; and G. G. Hoskins, Speaker. James Terwilliger was Clerk of the Senate; and Joseph B. Cushman, Clerk of the Assembly. The Hon. William Laimbeer, on the fourth of January, 1865, gave notice in the Senate of a bill to incorporate a Paid Fire Department for New York City, and in the Assembly a week later Mr. Thomas B. Van Buren gave notice that at an early day he would ask to introduce a similar bill. On the sixteenth of January Senator Laimbeer introduced "An Act to create a Metropolitan Fire District and establish a Fire Department therein," which was read a first time, and referred to the Committee on Cities and Villages, which consisted of Messrs. Laimbeer, Strong, Shafer, White, Dutcher, and Andrews. Mr. Thomas E. Stewart, on January 20, gave notice of the bill in the Assembly. It was introduced there January 23, and read a first time. On the thirty-first of January, on motion of Senator Laimbeer, the Committee on Cities and Villages was empowered to send for persons and papers to aid in considering the bill, but next day an amendment to send for the clerk of the Fire Commissioners and such books, papers, etc., as he might have in charge, prevailed. The Committee heard testimony from all interested persons. On the seventh of February Senator Laimbeer presented a petition for a Paid Fire Department from Exempt Firemen, and two years later the bill was taken from the Senate Committee on Cities and Villages—because of the resignation of six of the members, who were disgusted with Senator Field's eccentricities—

and referred to the following Select Committee: Dennis Strong, G. H. Andrews, William Laimbeer, John B. Dutcher, Ira Shafer, Andrew D. White, and Saxton Smith.

On the fifteenth of February Mr. Andrews reported in favor of the bill, and it was referred to the Committee of the Whole. On the twenty-fourth of February, in the Assembly, Mr. S. C. Reed presented a petition for a Paid Fire Department from residents of Brooklyn. Next day Senator Laimbeer's motion to make the bill the special order for March 2 was adopted. That day Senator Allen reported in favor of passing the bill without amendment. Senator Chrystie's motion to recommit the bill to the Committee on Municipal Affairs, and to strike out the enacting clause, was lost, seven to twenty-one. Senator Cozans moved as a substitute, "An Act for the better regulation of the Firemen of the City of New York," Chief Decker's volunteer measure; rejected, seven to nineteen. After a little more filibustering the bill was ordered to a third reading. Next day Senator Fields moved that the Supervisors of New York assess on the capital stock of the insurance companies (the framers of the Paid Fire Department measure) a sum sufficient to pay the expenses of the Fire Department. This motion was buried, as was a motion from the "Torpedo" to pay each fireman one thousand dollars a year, and each engineer one thousand five hundred dollars a year. Henry C. Murphy moved that at the next general election four Metropolitan Fire Commissioners be elected, but this and several minor and dilatory motions were lost, and the bill was read a third time and passed.

Ayes—Allen, Ames, Andrews, Angel, Beach, Bell, Cole, Cook, Cornell, Dutcher, Folger, Havens, Hayt, Hobbs, Julian, Laimbeer, Low, Mauger, Strong, White, and Williams—21.

Nays—Allaben, Chrystie, Cozans, Fields, Murphy, and Woodruff—6.

On the fourth of March the Assembly received a message from the Senate asking concurrence in the bill, which was read a first time, and sent to the Committee on Cities. A week later the Speaker presented a communication from the General Society of Mechanics and Tradesmen in favor of a Paid Fire Department. On March 15 Assemblyman Perry, of Kings, for the Committee on Cities—J. C. Perry, Kings; T. E. Stewart, New York; W. P. Angel, Cattaraugus; Alexander Ward, New York; G. M. Holles, Otsego; Alexander Robertson, Albany; and J. B. Morey, of Livingston—reported in favor of the measure, which was referred to the Committee of the Whole. March 16, in Senate, the Hon. T. G. Alvord presented the petition of the General Society of Mechanics and Tradesmen as sent to the House. Assemblyman Wood, on the twenty-third of March, presented the report of the minority in the Committee on the Affairs of Cities against the measure. Its conclusions were, in substance:

1st. That the present system is in actual operation with beneficial results.

2d. That the proper mode of legislation on the subject is to improve the present system without making an entire and untried change.

3d. That as a matter of fact, the present system had from time to time adopted such practical reforms as were demanded by the progress of society and special contingencies.

4th. That the abuses alleged to exist were greatly exaggerated in the heat of an oral argument.

5th. That the economy of the present Department is equal to the average of the Paid Departments cited.

6th. That the Metropolitan Fire Department Bill, by its form and terms, was unjust to the people in not providing, either by specific sections or the establishment of any organization for economy or efficiency, or the introduction of any reforms.

The Bill as passed was as follows:

CHAPTER 249.

AN ACT to create a Metropolitan Fire District and establish a Fire Department therein.

Passed March 30, 1865; THREE-FIFTHS BEING PRESENT.

The People of the State of New York, represented in Senate and Assembly, do enact as follows:

SECTION 1. The Cities of New York and Brooklyn shall constitute and they are hereby united into a district to be known as the Metropolitan Fire District of the State of New York.

SEC. 2. The governor shall nominate, and by and with the consent of the Senate, appoint four citizens, residents of the said district, to be "Metropolitan Fire Commissioners" (which office is hereby created with the duties and powers herein contained and imposed), who shall form a Metropolitan Fire Department, to take and have, as provided by this act, control and management of all officers, men, property, measures and action, for the prevention and extinguishment of fires within the said district, to be organized as herein provided, and to be known as the "Metropolitan Fire Department." Said commissioners shall hold the said office respectively for the terms following, to wit: One for two years, one for four years, one for six years, and one for eight years; and at the expiration of each term respectively a successor shall be appointed in the manner above provided, who shall hold said office for the term of eight years. Vacancies in said office shall be filled by temporary appointments by the remaining members of said Department, to hold until the same are filled by the Senate on nomination by the governor. Said commissioners shall be subject to removal by the governor, as is provided by the law applicable to the removals of sheriffs, which are hereby extended so as to relate to each Department, but no removal shall be made until the commissioners contemplated to be removed shall have been served with written specific charges stating the derelictions complained of, and have been afforded an adequate opportunity to publicly answer the same and make his defense thereto.

SEC 3. Immediately after the appointment of such commissioners they shall meet in the office of the Secretary of State and proceed under his direction to determine by lot which of such commissioners shall hold such office for each of the respective terms of two, four, six, and eight years; whereupon they shall take and file with said secretary the oath of office prescribed for State officers, and the Secretary of State shall give to each a certificate of appointment for the respective terms of office so determined as aforesaid.

SEC. 4. Said commissioners, on being qualified, shall meet and organize "The Metropolitan Fire Department," by electing one of said commissioners as president, and appointing a person as secretary, whereupon they shall possess and have all the power and authority conferred upon or possessed by any and all officers of the Fire Department of the City of New York, and to the exclusion of all such officers, and such other powers and duties in said district as are hereinafter conferred. Three of said commissioners shall constitute a quorum for the transaction of business, but the surviving members may at any time fill a vacancy, as provided in the second section of this act.

SEC. 5. The said "Metropolitan Fire Department" is hereby empowered and directed to possess and exercise fully and exclusively all the powers and perform all the duties for the government, management, maintenance, and direction of the Fire Department of the City of New York, and the premises and property thereof which at the time of the organization of said Department are possessed by or under the control of the boards and officers of the Fire Department of said city, or the officers or employees of said city, said powers and duties to be exercised and performed, and said property used in the said city or otherwise, as hereinafter provided, and the said Department shall hereafter have sole and exclusive power and authority to extinguish fires in said City of New York; and all acts conferring upon any other officer and officers any power in relation to the extinguishment of fires in said city are hereby repealed.

SEC. 6. The Board of Commissioners shall have full power to provide in and for the City of New York, supplies, horses, tools, implements, and apparatus of all kinds, (to be used in the extinguishing of fires), and fire telegraphs, to provide suitable locations for the same, and to buy, sell, construct, repair, and have the care of the same, and take any and all such action in the premises as may be reasonably necessary and proper.

SEC. 7. The Department hereby created is hereby empowered and directed to possess and exercise full and exclusive power and discretion for the government, management, maintenance, and direction of the several buildings and premises and property and appurtenances thereto, and all apparatus, hose, implements, and tools of any and all kinds which at the time of the appointment of the commissioners aforesaid were under the charge and control of any and all city officers, or officers of the Fire Department in said city for the use and benefit of the Fire Department of the City of New York; and it shall be the duty of all persons and officers in possession of any property, real and personal, belonging to, or set apart for, or in use by, or for the Fire Department of said city, to deliver the same to the possession and control of said "Metropolitan Fire Department."

Section 8 provided that any commissioner accepting or holding any other political office, or who, holding office as fire commissioner, should be publicly nominated for another elective office without declining the same, should be deemed to have forfeited his office. Section 9 provided for the selection of one of the commissioners as treasurer, on a bond of fifty thousand dollars.

Section 10 provided as follows:

SEC. 10. The "Metropolitan Fire Commissioners" and the comptroller and mayor of the City of New York, convened as a Board of Estimate, five of whom shall form a quorum for business, shall, annually, on or before the first of July, make up a financial estimate of the sums required annually for the payment of salaries, compensation, and rents, for the purchase of supplies, horses, apparatus of any and all kinds, tools, hose, implements, and keeping all of the same in repair; and generally for the purposes of this act, and such general and contingent expenses as may from time to time in the judgment of said Board of Estimate become necessary and proper, with the enumeration thereof. The said estimate shall then be submitted to a Board of Revision, composed of the Board of Supervisors of the County of New York. If the said Board of Revision, on or before the second Monday of October, shall object, in writing, to such estimate, or any portion thereof, and so notify the said Board of Estimate, it shall be the duty of the latter to immediately and carefully revise the same, and consider the said objections. If such Board of Estimate shall adhere to their original action of estimate, or if they shall modify the same without increasing the said estimate, then their final determination shall be binding upon the City of New York.

SEC. 11. The Board of Estimate created by the tenth section shall immediately after the organization of the said "Metropolitan Fire Department" meet, and make an estimate of the probable expenses of the Department in all branches of expenditure which will be required for the year one thousand eight hundred and sixty-five, before money can be realized under the tax levy for that year. They shall specify, as far as may be, to the several objects and purposes of expenditure. This estimate shall be immediately submitted to the Board of Revision, above provided in Section 10, for consideration. Said Board of Revision shall within ten days act upon said estimate, and return the same to the Board of Estimate with their objections, amendments, or approval, and said Board of Estimate shall take final action thereon, in the manner provided in Section 10. Whereupon the amount so estimated shall be levied and collected by the Board of Supervisors of the County of New York, in the same manner as is herein provided in relation to annual estimates for the expenses of the said "Metropolitan Fire Department."

SEC. 12. The comptroller of the City of New York shall have power, and it shall be his duty to borrow on the credit of said city, the amounts of said estimate for the year one thousand eight hundred and sixty-five, in anticipation of the receipt of said sum from the levy, and pay the same to the chamberlain of said city, to be drawn and used by the Metropolitan Fire Commissioners on their requisitions, from time to time, in such sums as they shall deem necessary, and for the purposes specified in this section. The said comptroller shall have the power to issue bonds in the name of the mayor, aldermen, and commonalty of the City of New York, which bonds shall be signed by the said mayor and comptroller, and authenticated by the seal of the corporation of the City of New York.

The remaining sections of the Act provided for officers and employees, a salary of three thousand five hundred dollars a year for the commissioners, the selection of firemen and employees, as far as possible, from the active and exempt members of the Volunteer Fire Department, giving the right of way to fire apparatus over all vehicles except the United States Mail, the raising of money by the Board of Supervisors for the annual expenses of the new Department, the transfer of all apparatus, etc., to the new Department by those having it in charge, the surrender to be to the Mayor, Aldermen and Commonalty of the City of New York, the designation of all real estate occupied by the volunteers and not needed by the new Department, the return of all members of the Volunteer Fire Department to the County Clerk, the same to be honorably discharged as exempt firemen if they continued to do duty until discharged by the new commissioners into whose control they passed by this Act, the guarantee of all benefits from the New York Fire Department Fund to those who up to the time of the passage of the Act were entitled to them, the continuance of the functions of the trustees of the fund, the return by the Clerk of the Common Council of the rolls of the volunteers to the new commissioners, the punishment of those wearing in whole or in part the uniform or insignia of the new Department without authorization, or interfering with its apparatus, the adoption of a common seal, the power to institute and maintain suits in the name of the president for the enforcement of its rights and contracts, and for the possession and maintenance of the property under the control of the department, and the recovery of fines and penalties under Chapter 356 of the Laws of 1862; the transmission of an annual report to the Governor of the State of the condition, management and progress of the Department, setting forth its needs, the selection of uniform and insignia, cooperation in case of need between Brooklyn and New York, and the continuance of the Volunteer Department until the new commissioners organized and entered upon their office.

During the debates in both houses comparatively little acrimony was exhibited. Those in favor of the bill, which was at first a municipal measure and was changed to include Brooklyn to avoid a quibble in regard to its constitutionalty, evinced a disposition to treat the committees fairly, and the understanding that such of them as desired to become members of the new Department could do so, if eligible, was carried out eventually. In making the Senate report, Mr. Andrews said:

"The majority of the members of the New York Fire Department are men whose connection with it is prompted by a laudable devotion to the public interest, stimulated by that love of adventure and fearlessness in the face of danger, which would be accepted as the type of the loftiest heroism."

Senator Andrews also said he had not an unkind word for the New York Fire Department. One of the strong arguments, and in favor of the bill, was the reduction of rates of insurance in Baltimore under a Paid Department from twenty-five to thirty per cent. The opponents of the bill were denounced as prejudiced, and it was represented that the new system would cost but little more than the volunteer system, for which nearly five hundred and fifty thousand dollars were spent in 1864. Some harsh language was indulged in against the laxity of discipline in certain companies of the Volunteer Department, and habitual violation of rules, notably that against persons not members of a company "bunking" in their quarters; and the number of men in the Volunteer Department, four thousand, was ridiculed as excessive. The new measure was called "a dangerous though interesting experiment." Brooklyn was put in the bill to avoid any constitutional objection. One of the opponents of the innovation said it was "a blow to the liberties of the people of New York." The presence of Police Superintendent John A. Kennedy, who favored the bill, in Albany, was a signal for all sorts of comment on the interference of the police with the privileges and traditions of the public. Advocates of a Paid Department said that New York was no longer a village or a town. It had outgrown its former tastes, and its citizens should no longer be disturbed at all hours by "the rush of thousands of excited men and the clangor of bells and apparatus." Senator Andrews' harshest comments were: "It cannot be denied * * * that the luster of its early days has been tarnished by a spirit of insubordination and violence, which has so often led to a breach of the public peace." The advocates of the change were alive to the heroic nature of the measure. One of them admitted, "It is the great change of the times if it becomes a law. Out goes the institution of an age so great that only Mr. Valentine can excavate it out of the dust. It is a revolution." It was "a revolution," in face of the sentiments of Mayor C. G. Gunther, as expressed in his message of January 9, 1865:

"The apparatus of the Fire Department is under the supervision of the street commissioners, together with the numerous houses for its accommodation. No city in the world possesses a more complete fire organization in the number of engines, the effectiveness of the recently-introduced steam machines, the copious supply of water, or the gallant army of volunteers that direct these means, for the preservation of property. No one appreciates more highly than myself the generosity and public spirit of our firemen, and nothing can efface the glorious records of their past history, so full of instances of heroic daring and unselfish toil. Many of its friends are of opinion that the system so admirably adapted to a small city is not suited to a metropolis, and that economy, as well as the new machinery, will compel a change. No one will cling to the old associations more firmly than myself, or surrender them with more reluctance, and nothing but the welfare of the city, and especially of that class whence our firemen are recruited, would reconcile me to the adoption of new ideas."

The last scene in the Assembly was a charge by Mr. Turner that he had been offered five hundred dollars for his vote in favor of the bill, but the accusation was withdrawn, and was without foundation.

It is just as well not to repeat here what was said in the Assembly and Senate when the bill came before the committees. The police gave the strongest testimony. It did not appear fair, as the broadest of the charges made were not properly substantiated. Once, on the fifteenth of March, 1865, in the Assembly, it appeared as if the Paid Bill would be killed, as an adverse report on the Ordinance Bill was laid on the table by a vote of seventy-six to thirty-five.

Twenty-three banks, one hundred and nine insurance companies, and thirteen thousand citizens petitioned in favor of the Paid Bill. Sweeping charges of bribery were made. Most of them were based on such incidents as this: Chief Decker was in Congress Hall bantering James M. Rankin, of the Underwriters' Committee, and said: "See that safe? I've twenty-five thousand dollars in there to beat your bill." "Pshaw," replied Mr. Rankin, "I've two hundred and fifty thousand dollars in my vest pocket to push ours through." How many votes were bought will probably never be known. It is as certain that both sides used money for some purpose, so that no member of any committee profited financially by his efforts, or the provision of a corruption fund.

There were other schemes for a Paid Fire Department. The insurance companies were ready in case of emergency to sustain a fire brigade if they could have its appointment and management, and the police commissioners were prepared to take control of the paid firemen and the Croton Board. A newspaper suggested that the Croton Board, having the water, should enter the list, petition for the empty engines, and with as much justice and consistency as was entrusted them, prevail on the superintendent of the police to have an effective force to work them.

The Police Commissioners, in advocating a Paid Fire Department, said:

"Steam engines with a small force to manage them are the best Fire Department. The voluntary system is unjust, oppressive upon its members, and not entirely trustworthy. The members do good service, perform prodigious labor, and encounter risks and dangers of the gravest character to save life and property from destruction by fire. For this they formerly enjoyed some degree of compensation through exemption from militia service; but even this has ceased, and the public has no right to demand or enjoy their services without pay. They should be paid like other public employees."

Some of the newspapers were very severe. The following savage and intemperate attack, in which not a few truths are buried in abuse, appeared in one of them:

"The Fire Department ought to be reorganized for the following reasons:

"1st. Because, though a voluntary organization, it is unnecessarily expensive, and because the public do not know how expensive it is. Parties who render valuable public service ought not to be expected to render it without compensation, and will not do so for any considerable period without some motive; if the motive is not the compensation, it will be a less laudable one—say the interests of a political party or indirect benefits of an even less reputable character.

"2d. Because being a voluntary organization there can be no penalty imposed greater than dismissal for misconduct. That merely deprives them of the right of serving the public for nothing.

"3d. In effect, the rank and file of the Department appoint all the officers;

therefore the officers have no legal or practical authority. The conduct of the officers must be satisfactory to the men; their tenure of office depends upon that. This is a fatal obstacle to all discipline and subordination. Every legislator should have known that a Fire Department so constituted would become, in time, unmanageable, vicious, and dangerous. It is a wonder that it did not become so much earlier.

"4th. Because associations of young men from the class that supplies volunteer firemen in a great city are removed from the restraints of family and well-ordered society; become proud of vices, and popular with their fellows because they possess them. Being organized and acting under a semblance of command, they feel a degree of strength that impels them too often to defy the law and disturb public order. Their calling as volunteer firemen requires them to turn out at any hour of the day and night, and is incompatible with any steady pursuit of industry, and renders impossible the earning of an honest support by labor. For this reason they are driven by their wants to exercise their wits to supply the deficiency of wages.

"5th. They are four thousand strong; inevitably they will control a political party or a political party will control them. Having sufficient numbers and ample unoccupied time, this body is able to control all the caucuses of the party. There is not a man in that party so strong as to be able to resist them in party nominations. They are therefore able to dictate terms to the city officials who hold the keys of the treasury; and it enables those who stoop low enough to be popular with the firemen to control and override the better members of their party. The effect of this is to reduce the grades of men that hold the public offices of the party. Being, to a large extent, without homes, they are able to vote early and often, without regard to the penalties for fraudulent voting. This may explain why so large a share of firemen are in the Common Council.

"6th. Because it involves an immense waste of time and labor. Four hundred men would be more efficient than four thousand can be. The time of three thousand six hundred men would be saved by a reorganization, and might be, if the men were willing, devoted to valuable productive uses.

"7th. The present system involves the awakening and alarming of a whole city by unnecessary bell ringing, and by the charge and rush of firemen and their ragged followers through the streets; again, the ringing of the fire bells is a signal to every robber in the city that there is an opportunity for him to ply his villainous calling—an opportunity he never omits to improve; all this will be completely remedied when a telegraphic apparatus calls the organized and disciplined firemen to the point of duty.

"8th. Every fire is a mob and a riot under the present system.

"The remedy is in the hands of the Legislature!"

These extracts afford an intelligent insight into the temper of the times. Party passion was running high. The volunteers died hard. They fought to hold their Organization with that tenacity of purpose and grim resolve which so characterized them as firemen.

While the matter was being pushed through at Albany, a newspaper undertook to estimate the cost of the Volunteer Fire Department, and to compare it with other systems, as follows:

"The city furnishes one hundred and twenty-five engine houses at an estimated cost of $10,000 each. This is entirely too low an estimate, but taking it as correct, this is an investment of $1,250,000, on which no interest or taxes are paid to the city, as it cannot tax its own property.

The interest on $1,250,000, and loss of taxes, are a part of the annual expense, say	$150,000
The chief engineer estimates the expense for the present year for new apparatus, repairs, hose, salaries, arrears, etc., at	205,000
New buildings and repairs ordered by the Common Council	142,500
For bells and bell towers	22,000
For bellringers	39,000
Supplies of gas $9,500; wood, etc., $15,000; supplies, $15,000	39,500
	$598,000

"There are a number of smaller items, some arrearages, etc., not reckoned in the above, but which properly belong to the expenses of the department, and the Common Council takes the liberty of ordering our expenditures at its pleasure, whether there be an appropriation or not, so that it is difficult to say what the service will cost in any year. The item of fitting up kitchens, drawing-rooms, etc., in the engine houses, now very fashionable, at $1,000 each, is an example of frequent occurrence.

"Take now the expense of paid Fire Departments in other cities:

In London, with a population four times greater, it cost	$75,000
Cincinnati, with 161,000 population, expense of Fire Department	94,000
Baltimore, with 212,000 in 1864, expense of Fire Department	63,000
Boston, with 178,000 population, expense of Fire Department	105,000
St. Louis, with a population of 160,000, expense of Fire Department	79,000
	$416,000

"All these five great cities, including London, cost less for paid services by nearly $200,000, than this one City of New York, where the firemen work for nothing, and yet the service here is so defective that insurance is double what it is in Boston, Baltimore and Cincinnati, and four times the price of London. We speak, in the above comparison, of the ascertained or publicly vouched for expense of the New York Fire Department. But there are drippings and contributions and stealings, which, if fully accounted for, would, in the judgment of persons who ought to know, swell the total from a million to a million and a half annually.

"Then the enormous waste of human exertion and life is against the voluntary system. We have four thousand regular firemen and six thousand or seven thousand runners and hangers-on, engaged in this exciting and wearying work. Baltimore employs one hundred and twelve officers and men, seven steam engines, and thirty-four horses. Cincinnati, one hundred and fifty-five officers and men, eleven steam engines, and seventy horses. Boston employs thirty-nine men constantly, and two hundred and fifteen who do duty on alarm. St. Louis employs fifty-nine men and seven steam engines. In all these cities less than five hundred and fifty men, while in this city seven thousand or eight thousand men are called out at every serious fire."

Another article, an appeal to the State Legislature, says, "If we except a few decent young men, sturdy and honest workmen, the bulk is composed of rude fellows without any regular calling, lazy clerks, street loungers, bruisers and sportsmen who have their pockets full of money though they never work. ★ ★ ★ There is no actual fire in the City of New York which does not attract at least one thousand two hundred firemen and about as many ex-members with the different companies, the children, the nincompoops and the thieves. ★ ★ ★ We emphatically affirm—because we have seen several fires in both London and Paris, and know how they were disposed of, that the Fire Department of New York is a costly and ridiculous farce."

When the bill was before the Assembly the following comments were made in a prominent newspaper:

"The bill transforming our city's Fire Department into a Paid one, having passed the Senate by a very large majority, is now before the Assembly on its third reading. There is said to be danger that it will be beaten by bribery. We do not credit the imputation, though *without* bribery we are sure it cannot be defeated. And for these reasons:

I.—The insurance companies are necessarily and intimately acquainted with fires and their extinguishment, and know what methods prove effective and what are conducive to needless loss, waste and robbery. And those companies, with scarcely an individual dissenter, are praying for the change proposed. Their officers are of all parties and of none, but on this question they are substantially unanimous. They originated the movement for a Paid Department; we are but deferring to their judgment in the premises.

II.—The precedents and analogies are all in favor of the measure. A village or small city, in which a fire occurs but seldom, adheres naturally and properly to the volunteer system; but wherever fighting fire becomes a business, requiring constant vigilance and the devotion of a large share of the firemen's time, it is simply honest and just that they should be compensated. The very worst way of paying them is to incite them to pay themselves.

III.—Under the present system five times as many firemen are enrolled as are actually needed. They thus secure exemption from onerous public duties, and become members of a powerful organization, which controls nominations and elections, rewards favorites, and takes vengeance on adversaries. The engine houses are dens of political intrigue, wherein primary meetings are rehearsed and regular nominations "fixed"—for a consideration. It is this fact which incites the fierce hostility which the proposed reform encounters. The firemen are the Janizaries, the Prætorian Guard, of our ruling politicians. They make our aldermen and councilmen—a bad lot, but this is owing in good part to the badness of the raw material. To abolish the Volunteer Fire Department is to derange the machinery whereby our city is made to pile up such atrocious copperhead majorities. We do not suppose this will make much difference in the long run, yet the terror and rage of our governing classes argue that the *placer* thus disturbed is a very rich one. But we want no votes for a Paid Fire Department on any other ground than that of its intrinsic right.

IV.—The very men who make the most ado in Albany against it are themselves paid firemen now, and anxious to remain so. The engineers who insist that firemen should not be paid take good care to be well paid themselves. The cost of having our fires put out for nothing, including ground rent, engine houses, engines, trucks, hose, salaries, etc., etc., amounts to several hundred thousand dollars per annum; yet we are asked to consider this an *unpaid* service.

V.—Our firemen now choose their superiors, who of course cannot control them. The chief and assistant engineers are made so by votes cast in the engine houses. This proves fatal to subordination and discipline. If the chief should prove stern, he will be superseded at the next election. Hence lawlessness and crime, which are winked at from interested motives.

VI.—Notoriously, our Fire Department is a nursery of dissipation and vice. Large numbers of the firemen sleep or "bunk" at their respective engine houses. This cuts them off from all home or virtuous female influence, while exposing them to peculiar and urgent temptations. Our city is far more debauched and corrupt than it would be but for the deadly influence which centers in and emanates from our engine houses.

VII.—With a Paid Department we may reduce the number of firemen four-fifths, while the commissioners, being independent of the firemen, could enforce discipline, punish rowdyism, and expose theft. We shall no longer squander on fire extinguishment five times the force actually needed therefor. Vicious boys and rowdies will no longer 'run with the machine' on purpose to steal whatever they can surely hide. We shall save, by the change proposed, time, money, muscle and morals. And, while the whole community is signally benefitted, nobody will be injured, unless it be such as clearly ought to be.

Legislators at Albany! What valid reason, not of the greenback persuasion, can be given for hesitating to pass this bill?"

Mayor C. Godfrey Gunther's sympathies with the volunteers in the legislative crisis were evinced by the following preamble and resolutions prepared by him, which were adopted by firemen at a meeting at Firemen's Hall:

> *Whereas*, the threatened passage of the act now pending before the Legislature of the State, which contemplates the establishment of a Paid Fire Department in lieu of the present Volunteer system, demands at our hands an expression of our sense of the unmerited degradation that is about to be put upon those comprising the present Volunteer system—a system that now is, and from time immemorial has been identified and most intimately connected with the best interests, the development, progress, and prosperity of the City of New York; and
>
> *Whereas*, it is evident, in the opinion of this meeting, not only by the arguments or statements used before the Legislature, by the advocates of the new system, but by the fact that, without any previous intimation of the intention to supersede, violently and suddenly, the present system, without any consultation with its officers as to the best means of improving it, where improvements are needed; without even allowing of an opportunity to test the relative value or efficiency of the two systems, as well as entirely ignoring the opinions or wishes of the people of this city, who are the most directly and the most really interested parties, that it is intended to degrade the present Department, and, through it, the people of this city. Be it therefore
>
> *Resolved*, That we regard the passage of the proposed act as an unmerited rebuke to men who have, on many occasions, voluntarily periled their lives in protecting the lives and property of their fellow citizens; that we regard it as unwise in forcing a new and untried experiment upon the city, when a failure is certain to be followed by consequences that may involve a fearful loss in life and property. We contend that, if intended for the good of the city, and if destined more effectually to guard its property and its interests, a gradual introduction of the new system should be provided for, whereby a test of its advantages over the old one could be made, a decisive com-

parison would be instituted, and the best one of the two be ultimately adopted; we are clearly of the opinion that it is a willful, positive, and direct interference with, and usurpation of, the rights of the people of this city, who, if they desired a change, have the power in their own hands, through their immediate representatives in the city government, to inaugurate a system similar to that now proposed by the State Legislature; and be it further

Resolved, In consideration of the above and many other equally cogent reasons, that we hereby earnestly and fervently yet respectfully remonstrate against the passage of the proposed bill now before the Assembly; more particularly at this time, when the present system was never more efficient, was never better governed or disciplined, and was never in a more advanced state of subordination to duty; and we also fervently and sincerely yet respectfully remonstrate against any change in the present system until it is satisfactorily proven that it cannot be improved in character and efficiency, and until the change shall have been asked for by those who are the most intimately and directly interested—the people of the city—who alone should be consulted and their consent obtained before making the proposed or any other change in any department of their own local government.

The volunteer organs replied sharply to the attacks made on them at Albany and by the press. One article says:

"So long as the opponents of our present Volunteer Fire Department system confined themselves to facts, and admitted the sole intention they had in view was to benefit the existing organization while they did not expect to make any changes, except perhaps to reduce the force, and confine it within certain limits, we let them go on, and remained silent. Since these opponents have taken themselves to argument, and added to argument vituperation and falsehood, we think it is but just for us to say a few words about the matter.

"The insurance men have testified to but little. They make sweeping assertions against the present organization; say that it is cumbersome, expensive, and inefficient, and they believe 'the citizens at large are in favor of a change.' ★ ★ ★ These very insurance men, when steamers were first introduced, were the loudest in praise of the same. Notwithstanding we foresaw the trouble, and protested against the introduction of too many machines of the kind, these same exempt firemen, who had gone into the 'policy' business, expected that as steamers were introduced, fires would decrease, and the losses must consequently be quite light. ★ ★ ★ They wanted steamers—steamers—steamers. They have got them; and what is the result? The damage done by water at fires in New York amounts to more than that caused by flame and smoke. ★ ★ ★ In just the same light we regard some of these insurance men, who, because they cannot be elevated to positions of trust and responsibility in the present Volunteer Fire Department, turn around and villify it. An investigation is demanded we can give these insurance company gentlemen all they ask—and more too.

"A word to the Police Department, who seemed to have joined issue with the insurance companies. It is a well-known fact that Police Commissioner Thomas C. Acton, instead of attending to the business he was appointed to look after, has been bothering his brains over this Paid Fire Department scheme all last summer, and has asserted he can command two hundred and fifty thousand dollars, if necessary, to break up the present organization, and substitute some other plan in its stead. While himself, Superintendent Kennedy, Inspector Carpenter, and 'a number of policemen' are in Albany, lobbying for this Paid Fire Department Bill, the good people of the City of New York who pay those individuals most liberally for what little they do, are almost afraid to walk the streets after dark for fear they may be robbed or murdered. ★ ★ ★ When the violence of the mob was at its height, and not a policeman dared show his face, did not these gentlemen, assisted by certain citizens whom we can name, drive back the mob, so that the different apparatus could get to work? Who patroled the city at night, as a special police, when those paid for the duty could not be seen? Who drove the thieves and rioters out of the stores in the principal streets? Who protected the shipping, the banks, the gas houses, the Croton waterworks, the different factories, and other public buildings, before the National Guard belonging to the city reached home? We answer, the firemen. ★ ★ ★

"So far as reducing the cost and force of the New York Volunteer Fire Department is concerned, of improving it in every shape and way, of making all reasonable and necessary rules and regulations to control the organization, and make every officer and man in it know his proper place, we are with the police commissioners, insurance folk, and everybody else. ★ ★ ★ We admit the mistakes or misdeeds of certain firemen. We stand up as no apologist for them, believing that the time has come when these mistakes can be corrected, and the organization may be improved and perfected. We feel satisfied that the community at large will sustain us in trying to retain the present organization rather than inaugurate an expensive political machine (for such it is intended to be) to gratify a few men who want office and pay.

"As for the doings in Albany, of which too much has already been said, we care nothing. The business there done may be summed up in a few words. Some of the metropolitan police went up (we don't know who paid their expenses) and testified, to what? They thought and believed we had bad men and bad companies in the Fire Department. The clerk of the Board of Fire Commissioners was ordered to read, before the committee, in the case of Engine Companies No. 40 and 53—both wiped out of existence long ago by the fire commissioners—as evidences of rowdyism. Why did they not go back to 1840, when fights among fire companies were of everyday occurrence in New York? ★ ★ ★ Now that a check is placed upon the appropriations, so that hose companies cannot build three-story brown stone houses to contain a reel with eight lengths of hose, and foremen cannot go to this or that alderman and councilman and obtain, through political influence, buildings and machines which are unnecessary, there is a prospect of curtailing expenses and securing economy for the future.

"We have yet to learn who authorized the Police Department, the insurance companies, or the Citizens' Association, to go to Albany and declare war against a body of men who have sacrificed their health and time to save the lives and property of their fellow-citizens. We have yet to learn if the people pay the police for doing such work, or whether the insurance companies expect to reap extra dividends in consequence, or if the Citizens' Association is about to resolve itself into a committee of the whole for the purchase of political patronage. One thing we do know, and that is, the firemen of New York have yet to be heard from." ★ ★ ★

Mr. Philip W. Engs, afterwards a member of the first Paid Fire Department Board, resented the attacks on the volunteers. In a speech at Firemen's Hall, on the fourteenth of February, 1865, before the Board of the New York Fire Department, he said:

"You have been contending with the Legislature of the State regarding the conduct of the firemen of this city. Instead of meeting that issue, we should go before them with this ordinance, which we have passed for the better regulation of the department. They have now become the rules for the government of this department, and we propose by these rules to avoid all the objections that are made against the character of the department. Then all that matter is at an end, no matter what Mr. Acton or anybody else says. It appears to me that we should appear at Albany once more in some shape, and show to these gentlemen that here are the rules under which we propose to act, and under these we can keep the Fire Department together, and still sustain our noble charitable institution, which has such an important bearing upon the proper conduct of the department. I hope that some means will be adopted here to-night by which we shall have this opportunity, and that the chief engineer, the chairman, or some one else, will be authorized to telegraph to Albany, and say that on a certain day we will meet them and see whether we cannot be able to settle this matter. I am very well pleased with the disposition manifested by Mr. Platt, who has appeared before these gentlemen, as did certain gentlemen who went from Washington recently to meet certain other gentlemen from Richmond, not pretending to be clothed with authority, but merely having a friendly conference with them, with the expectation and hope of bringing about some compromise in the affair. I do not see that it can be done here. We want to go to the fountain head at Albany. That is the place where the mischief commences, and this bill will be carried through—for what? To give four certain gentlemen somewhere four places; and I do not see, as I read the bill, but they will have to fix the salaries. It appears to me to be about as improperly prepared a bill, apart from its principles, as I have ever seen. It is not calculated to carry out the object they have in view, and this fact may be made known to these gentlemen if you appear before them. Again, look at its operation upon the jury box, but more particularly upon the militia. It proposes to discharge the whole body of the firemen of the City of New York, if they think best, after they have served but three months, from military service in New York during their lifetime. There is another thing to which I wish to call your attention. Suppose that the firemen of New York, feeling the insult that is put upon them, should say to gentlemen, 'We'll resign to-day; we cannot submit to these charges and slanders upon us,' what would be the feeling of the insurance companies? What would be the feeling of the owners of property in this great city? These appeals ought to be made to them; and so far as concerns the character of the department, I, for one, should be ready to compare the department with the police, taking it from the head down. I would not for a moment stand in the halls of the legislature and hear a man say what was said by Mr. Acton, without bringing the thing home to himself. As an old fireman, I have a good deal of feeling upon this subject, and am quite stirred up about this matter. I desire that we should all stand by our integrity, and show to these gentlemen at Albany that the Fire Department of this city has a character, has integrity, and is equally entitled to honorable mention as any public organization of the kind in this city or elsewhere."

Richmond had fallen, and New York and the entire country were excited over the death struggle of the Confederacy, but the news of the final passage of the bill renewed interest in the fate of the "fire laddies." Much that was harsh and foolish was said and printed. A few hot-headed volunteers said they would not run to fires, but second thought and the proverbial adaptability of the citizens of the metropolis to circumstances prevailed over rash utterances. It was seen that "de masheen" was no more, and the "Mose" element had gone with it. There was much gathering in company quarters and debating, but the sentiment in favor of the new system, provided it was declared constitutional, was over-whelming, and Chief Engineer John Decker, in a communication to the Common Council, asked for instructions. Mayor Gunther sided with law and order in spite of his preferences, and urged the volunteers to turn a deaf ear to "suggestions which may be made by ill-advised or designing individuals, but faithfully to obey the laws of the land and the direction of the officers of the department and others in authority."

The Board of Aldermen passed the following:

> *Whereas*, The Legislature of this State has just passed an act which sub-stitutes the Paid system in place of the present Volunteer organization of the Fire Department in this city; and
>
> *Whereas*, Some time must necessarily elapse ere this new system can be properly or efficiently placed in a position to meet all that would be re-quired therefrom, in respect to the full protection of the lives and property of the citizens; and
>
> *Whereas*, In the interregnum that must exist between the present time and the arranging of said system, in such a way as to be at all equal in efficiency to the present Volunteer organization still continues in active service; therefore,
>
> *Resolved*, That the Common Council of the City of New York would most earnestly urge upon the officers and members of the New York Fire Department the public necessity of their still continuing their former en-ergetic and humane efforts in arresting on all occasions, as heretofore, the progress of the devouring element, thereby not only preventing thousands of helpless women and children from being rendered homeless and desti-tute, but wreathing around the memory of the Volunteer organization of the New York Fire Department a record of fame and usefulness, of which both themselves and their children in after time may well be proud.

John Decker strenuously urged the firemen to continue to do duty, and al-though some company quarters were sarcastically placarded and decorated, a revulsion in feeling occurred so quickly that companies which had been repre-sented to have shown signs of insubordination or resentment, contradicted the reports so that the newspapers began to praise the conduct of the volunteers, and one of them in a laudatory editorial says, very justly:

"This action proves—what we have always believed to be true—that the Fire Department proper was composed of a gallant, fearless, and honorable body of our citizens, and that whatever may have been alleged against the body was the result of the disturbing element which hung upon its flanks in the shape of rowdies and disturbers of the peace, who were to this gallant army of brave, self-sacrificing men, what camp followers and plunderers are to a regular army. The course which the members of the department are now pursuing entitles them to the highest praise which is due to the law-abiding citizens, and although the Volunteer Firemen's organization is no longer to comprise one of our local institutions, to have been a member of it will be a lasting honor."

A newspaper, sketching the social features of the volunteer organization, said:

"What now shall we have in the city to supply the annual balls given by the various companies so numerously that they occupy nearly every dancing night of the winter? What will take the place of the jovial surprise parties continually occurring during the winter at the fire-houses, where the sisters and sweethearts and wives of the laddies enjoyed themselves so genially and hospitably, as there was no opportunity in all other social assemblies of our working classes, and which were to our most aristocratic, richest, and best educated young men an absolute relief from the stately balls and stiff-backed parties of the upper ten? What will become of the excursions, the clam-bakes, the country jaunts, with music and dancing, that the fun-loving firemen indulged in all the summer long? Mayhap there were rough fellows among the fire boys; but they were generous and honest, anyhow, they claimed; and though they had once and awhile a little fight among each other, they were always orderly as a body, they always subserved the good of the city, they were the pride of all great parades, they were the pet institution of the metropolis. The city can never cease to gratefully remember that the draft riots were rendered abortive because of their efforts; that by their exertions, hand in hand with the police, New York was saved from desolation and utter horror, and the mobs were finally quelled. It was certainly not inappropriate to remember these things last night, even though it should be hinted that they might be written in the same spirit as the epitaphs of dead men, in which their faults are consigned to the dust and forgotten for all time.

"Probably the social organization of many of our fire companies will be continued for a long time. There are old companionships, not of the "bunk" and the "run" alone, but of the family, of the ball room, of the festive circle, of the summer excursion company, of the young folks' associations, that cannot be broken up. Most of the companies have on hand private funds of their own, the disposition of which has not been decided, but which it has been proposed to adopt as the fund of social clubs to be established, which may possibly in time—who can tell—rival the "Century" or the "Athenæum." Some of the companies, indeed, have now social organizations comprising their members, though under distinct and separate rules, and these will probably be continued."

Perhaps the best refutation of many charges made against the volunteers is the fact that nearly all the members of the Paid Department were selected from those who were legislated out of honorary, arduous, and unpaid office on March 30, 1865.

While the volunteers acquiesced in the act of the Legislature, Democratic New York in a certain sense took up the cudgels for them, and grumbled at legislative amendment. The manner of appointment of the commissioners was especially offensive to many. "Why not," asked some, "appoint the mayor and Common Council in Albany?" Friends of the volunteers regretted its demise mainly on account of its social features, its balls, enthusiasm, esprit de corps, romance, surprise parties, picnics, and what not. They also remembered how they stemmed the tide of anarchy in the riots of 1863, and were not yet prepared to make room for "a staid, slow-horse, methodical, paid concern." Chief Decker, in a circular, urged all to do their duty *"until such time as the Board of Engineers and Foremen shall determine upon certain matters of interest to the Department in its present condition."*

Governor Fenton acted promptly on the fifth of April, four days before General Lee surrendered. He sent the names of Charles C. Pinckney, Martin B. Brown, Samuel Sloan, and Thomas W. Booth to the Senate for confirmation. Horace Greeley was disappointed in not securing a nomination for his candidate, Harry W. Genet, afterwards known as "Prince Hal."

Mr. Pinckney, a Republican, who is yet in business, and appears to be but little older than he was a score of years ago, was ex-president of the Board of Councilmen, and in the insurance and real estate business. He was a member of the Union League Club, and had done active duty in Phœnix Hose Company No. 22. He was active and adapted to executive business.

Martin B. Brown, also a Republican, the well-known printer, is of course active and rejuvenated, as all good anglers and sportsmen are. He had been a member of United States Engine Company No. 23.

Samuel Sloan, then ex-state senator and president of the Hudson River Railroad, is the present head of the Delaware, Lackawanna, and Western Railroad. At the time of his nomination he had no leaning towards any political faction, but was claimed as a Democrat.

James W. Booth, a Republican, whose death occurred several years ago, was a dyer and contractor. He afterwards was elected state senator.

Clamor was raised in Albany and New York when the names were published, because of the alleged partisan complexion of the board, and on April 11 the New York delegation refused to report on the confirmation of the commissioners. The commissioners were, however, confirmed, but on the thirteenth of April, through trouble between certain senators and Governor Fenton, the Senate rejected the nominations.

The commissioners who were sworn in came to New York with the Secretary of State by the Albany boat, on which they had an informal meeting, and on the afternoon of Thursday, May 4, 1865, held the first meeting of the Metropolitan Fire Department, in the office of the Hanover Fire Insurance Company, of which Mr. Engs was vice-president, at No. 45 Wall Street, after a second informal meeting at Mr. Pinckney's office, No. 8 Pine Street.

Mr. Engs, a Democrat, who was a wine merchant and a member of an old firm, still in business, was a member of Volunteer Engine Company No. 21, Fulton Engine Company in 1813, and assistant engineer of the old Department from 1824 to 1833. He was an officer in various corporations, and a member of the Legislature, and president of the Association of Exempt Firemen. He died on the nineteenth of May, 1875, widely regretted.

Charles E. Gildersleve was born in New York City in 1827, and was a lover of fire duty from his earliest remembrance. As soon as his years would permit he became a member of Oceanus Engine Company No. 11 in 1846; served four years with the old machine, during which time he was secretary and assistant foreman. He resigned in 1850 and joined Mutual Hook and Ladder Company No. 1. This company was in a poor condition, from a fireman's point of view, when Mr. Gildersleve joined. There was no life, no enthusiasm, no push; but in a short time all this was changed, new blood was infused, the roll was filled, and No. 1 became one of the quickest and best truck companies in the city, and an indispensable addition to the down-town working force. Mr. Gildersleve served faithfully with No. 1 as member and officer. When Zophar Mills was foreman of the Exempt Engine, Mr. Gildersleve thought he would try a little more fire duty, and, although he had already passed through sixteen years of service, he joined under the old veteran, and was shortly afterwards made secretary, and then promoted to assistant foreman. At the organization of the new Department Mr. Gildersleve was made clerk to the commissioners, and remained with the Metropolitans from 1865 until 1875. He is still in good condition, looking as if he could stand twenty years more of fire duty.

Commissioners Pinckney, Engs, Booth, and Brown knew that—although the volunteers acquiesced in the public sentiment that nothing illegal should be done—the law would be invoked and the constitutionality of the act of March

BIRTH OF THE BRAVEST

30, 1865, would be tested. So, at the meeting of the fourth of May, they perfected their organization. Mr. Booth presided, Mr. Brown was secretary *pro tem.*,
and after two ballots, Mr. Pinckney was elected president, and Mr. Engs treasurer.
On a second ballot for secretary, Mr. Charles E. Gildersleve was elected. Then
a resolution that Messrs. Pinckney and Brown call on Comptroller Matthew T.
Brennan and Street Commissioner Charles G. Cornell, state their views, and, if
necessary, make a demand for the property of the city belonging to the Fire
Department, was adopted. The volunteers had since the fourth of April been
conferring with the members of the Common Council on the proper steps to
be taken in reference to the "Metropolitan Fire Act."

Next day the commissioners were served with notice of two legal actions
taken by John Cochrane, state attorney general. One was an injunction in the
name of the mayor, aldermen, and Commonalty, and Chief Decker, restraining
the commissioners from taking possession of any real estate then used by the Fire
Department. The other was in the form of *quo warranto* proceedings to compel
the commissioners to show by what warrant they held office. Waldo Hutchins
and Judge Allen were engaged as counsel by the commissioners, and it was argued
that the proceedings before them should be friendly, and on the twelfth of May
judgment against the commissioners was taken *pro forma* before Judge Foster, and
on the twenty-fifth of May Judges Ingraham, Clerke, and Barnard decided "that
the New Department is merely local, and confined to the City of New York,
and in substitution of the former one, and is hence unconstitutional." On this
the case was taken to the Court of Appeals.

On the third of May a special meeting of the Board of Engineers and Foremen
of the Volunteer Department was held at Firemen's Hall. Chief Decker was in
the chair, and Alexander V. Davidson was secretary. The chair announced the
news from Albany, and said that in his opinion the old officers were the only
legal ones, and Commissioners John J. Gorman, president, William M. Tweed,
Thomas Lawrence, Edward Bonnell, and Thomas Flender would go on as if
nothing had been done. The appropriations for the Department had been cut
down one-half to cripple it, but the new fire ordinances of the Common Council
would be carried out. It was time that some action was taken, as there were
signs of insubordination in the Department. On a vote, the following companies
voted to support the old Department:

Engine Companies 1, 2, 3, 4, 7, 8, 9, 11, 13, 14, 16, 17, 19, 20, 21, 22, 23,
24, 25, 26, 27, 29, 30, 31, 32, 36, 39, 42, 44, 46, 47, 48.

Hose Companies 1, 2, 4, 5, 6, 7, 8, 9, 11, 13, 14, 16, 17, 19, 24, 27, 28, 32,
33, 37, 38, 41, 42, 47, 50, 55, 56, 59, 60, 61.

Hook and Ladder Companies 2, 3, 5, 6, 11, 12, 13, 14.

Hose Company No. 21 recorded a vote in favor of the new Department.
Cries of "Put him out," "Disband the company" were raised, and Chief Decker

is reported as saying that if he found any company going back on the old Department he would disband it, and lock up its quarters and apparatus. Others favored allowing any company to vote as it thought fit. A notice was sent to companies not represented to report their choice.

CHAPTER XXII

WORK OF THE NEW COMMISSIONERS

*Enforcing Order and Discipline.—The Metropolitans Getting into Harness.—
Active Co-operation of the Old Companies.—Chief Decker Required to
Continue in the Performance of his Duty.—The Chief Relieved at his own
Request from further Service.—Volunteer Companies Mustered Out.—
Retirement of Engineers.—Introduction of a Uniform.—Regulations for the
Guidance of Firemen.—The Board Acknowledges the Services of the
Volunteers.—Fire, Academy of Music: Tragic Death of Two Brave Firemen.*

The new commissioners, after securing counsel, decided to go on arranging for the organization of the Department, but to keep their proceedings secret. The committee appointed to see Comptroller Brennan reported that he "wanted time for reflection." Street Commissioner Cornell could not comply because of the injunction. Chief Decker, to check an ugly spirit that had manifested itself, issued a circular, in which he said that in his opinion the bill for a Paid Department was unconstitutional, but if the courts decided otherwise the volunteers should and would acquiesce quietly, and surrender their quarters and apparatus. He ordered the force to continue to perform duty under the ordinance of December 31, 1864, and threatened to disband any company guilty of a breach of peace, disobedience of orders, or neglect of duty. The new commissioners requested the clerk of the Common Council, David T. Valentine, to comply with Section 21 of the Metropolitan Act, requiring him to register and return all firemen. Chief Decker was requested to make legal returns to Mr. Valentine. The engineers in charge in Brooklyn reported their force organized and ready for instruction and communication. May 10, at a meeting of volunteer delegates at Firemen's Hall, Engine Companies Nos. 10, 15, 35, 38, 42, and 53; Hose Companies Nos. 21, 25, 36, and 39; and Hook and Ladder Companies Nos. 7 and 8 were recorded as in favor of the new Department. The new commissioners met the same day. There were six or seven hundred applications for appointment as paid firemen, many of them from volunteers, and the following blank was issued:

To the Board of Commissioners of the Metropolitan Fire Department:

The undersigned respectfully solicits an appointment as .... in the Metropolitan Fire Department. Has served as a fireman in the city of .... for the period of ... years in .... Company No. ...

Age...

Occupation ....

Married or single ....

Residence...

(SIGNATURE.)

References...

This settled all doubt of the intention of the new board to appoint volunteers, and had a good effect. The new commissioners were desirous of having the best advice obtainable, and they invited the following gentlemen, who were regarded as thoroughly *au fait* in fire matters, to meet them: Zophar Mills, James M. McLean, Thomas Boese, Peter N. Cornwell, George T. Hope, John A. Cregier, Carlisle Norwood, and James M. McGregor. Messrs. McLean, Hope, Cregier, and McGregor, and J. B. Leverich and James Pinckney met the commissioners a couple of days later and gave their views, and on the nineteenth of May the following estimate of the expenses of the Department for 1865 was prepared, and Mayor Gunther and Comptroller Brennan were invited to meet the board as a Board of Estimate.

FINANCIAL ESTIMATE FOR 1865.

Basis.—30 steamers with tenders attached, 17 hook and ladder trucks with appurtenances complete, 2 hand engines and tenders.

5 new first-class steamers with tenders complete, $25,000; repairing and altering apparatus, viz.: hook and ladder trucks, engines and furnishing tenders, $40,900; building stables, and altering houses, $60,000; horses, 39,000; harness, $99,100; feed for horses, $15,600; horseshoeing, $1,100; new hose, $40,000; fuel, oil, and other supplies, $50,000; repairing apparatus, $30,000; gas and gas fixtures, $7,000. Contingencies—office furniture, stationery, etc., $20,000; telegraph supplies, $9,500. Salaries.—Commissioners, $10,328.80; secretary, clerks, messengers, and yard men, $10,000; telegraph operators, $3,000; bellringers, $9,600; chief engineer, $1,500; 12 assistant engineers, $7,200; 30 engineers for steamers, $13,500; 40 foremen of companies, $16,000; 40 assistant foremen, $15,000; 40 drivers, $14,000; 30 stokers, $10,500; 10 tillermen, $3,500; 280 hose and truckmen, $98,000; 100 men for hand apparatus, $5,000. Total, $564,228.80.

May 22, Messrs. Engs and Booth were appointed a committee "to examine reports of operations of fire departments of other cities, and collect therefrom such items as may be of interest to the Board, and present a report, with such rules and regulations for the Department as may be necessary," and Commissioner Engs moved "that the subject of communication by telegraph for fires be referred to a special committee of two to report what will be required to be done in addition to the present arrangements in order to secure its entire advantages, and enable the city to dispense with bellringing." The motion was carried, and Messrs. Pinckney and Brown were appointed. Badges, a seal, and uniforms were discussed at this meeting. On the twenty-seventh of May, Edwin Estes, foreman of Hook and Ladder Company No. 7, tendered the services of his company to the new commissioners. June 20 the Court of Appeals reversed the decision of the General Term of the Supreme Court. The opinion was given by Judge Henry E. Davis, and was concurred in by all except Judge John W. Brown.

The commissioners met next day at No. 156 Broadway, and Treasurer Engs presented the draft of an address to the firemen of the City of New York, which was adopted, and ordered to be published, as follows:

NEW YORK, June 21, 1865.

TO THE FIREMEN OF THE CITY OF NEW YORK:

The Act entitled "An Act to create a Metropolitan Fire Department and establish a Fire Department therein," having been decided by the Court of Appeals to be constitutional, the commissioners under said Act deem it to be their duty to apprise you of the fact and to declare their purpose of organizing, without unnecessary delay, the Metropolitan Fire Department.

This incipient step in our official capacity is in advance of all other action in order that your attention may be called to the following extracts from the law under which we act.

SECTION 5.—The Metropolitan Fire Department is empowered and directed to possess and exercise fully and exclusively all the powers, and to perform all the duties for the government, management maintenance, and direction of the Fire Department of the City of New York.

SECTION 19.—All members of the present Fire Department, regularly enrolled at the time of the passage of this Act, shall be retained by the present Chief Engineer under oath to the Clerk of the Common Council of said City of New York, who shall faithfully perform their duties until regularly discharged by said Commissioners, and not otherwise; shall be entitled to all the privileges and exemptions to which exempt firemen are entitled by the laws of this State.

SECTION 20.—Immediately on the organization of said Department, all persons who shall be firemen in the City of New York shall be under the control and government of said Metropolitan Fire Department, and if they shall so remain until they are discharged by said Department, shall be entitled to all the privileges and exemptions allowed by the laws of the State of New York, the same as if they served out the full term as prescribed by the laws of the State of New York, and the said Department shall have full power to discharge by resolution said firemen or any portion of them whenever they may deem proper.

The Act requires that in selecting the appointees of the Metropolitan Fire Department preference shall be given to those applicants who have served in the Volunteer Department, and this shall be most cheerfully complied with, the Board being now ready to receive applications from such of them as may feel disposed to serve in the new organization.

The expressed determination of many of the officers and members of the Volunteer Department to continue their aid until the New Department is in operation demands from us an acknowledgment of this manifestation of public spirit and regard for law and order, and assures our fellow-citizens that the changes which are to take place will be made in a manner to secure public safety.

The commissioners enter upon their duties with some practical knowledge of the various labors which are imposed upon them, but encouraged on their way by the belief that the entire success which has attended the establishment of a Paid Department in other cities cannot fail to be realized here, and that our brother firemen, with whom it has been our happiness to act in the Volunteer Department will, in the end, agree with us that the system, now about to be introduced, is adapted to the best interests of our fellow-citizens. In relation to the Charity Fund of our Old Volunteer Department, it will be both our duty and our pleasure to sustain it by every means in our power, and to give any support to the Trustees of that Fund in continuance of its noble benefits.

C. C. PINCKNEY, P. W. ENGS, JAMES W. BOOTH, M. B. BROWN.

The old companies began to fall into line. G. B. Tunison, foreman of Engine Company No. 52, reported it ready for service, as did Hose Company No. 33. On the twenty-second of June the Fire Commissioners were informed by the Police Commissioners that, if they chose, they could be accommodated at Police Headquarters. D. T. Valentine, clerk of the Common Council, sent in a list of all regularly enrolled firemen on March 30, 1865, and Chief Decker was invited to meet the commissioners. June 23, Hook and Ladder Company No. 8 and Hose Company No. 3 reported for duty. That day the following was sent to Chief Decker:

"JOHN DECKER, Esq., Chief Engineer, etc., etc.

"SIR: The Metropolitan Fire Department desires you to continue in the performance of your duties as chief engineer in the City of New York until further orders. You will therefore require obedience to your authority, and report to this Department any violation thereof.

"By order of the Board,

"C. C. PINCKNEY, *President.*

"CHARLES E. GILDERSLEVE, *Secretary.*"

The commissioners had had an interview with him, and had learned his intention to do his full duty. He was by resolution authorized to procure necessary supplies, if they could not be obtained from the Street Commissioners. June 24, the commissioners first met in Firemen's Hall, and, after selecting the old trustee room for meetings, resolved that it be the headquarters of the board. It was announced at this meeting that the day before the Board of Estimates had resolved, despite the negative votes of Mayor Gunther and Comptroller Brennan, to apply to the Board of Supervisors for six hundred thousand dollars for 1865, and seven hundred and fifty thousand dollars for 1866. Many old companies announced themselves "ready for duty." Dr. J. H. Griscom, through Henry A. Oakley, Esq., secretary of the Howard Insurance Company, set forth the necessity of creating a surgical staff for the department to bar the admission of incompetent persons, and prevent deception by firemen who wanted to get excused from duty on the ground of sickness. The use of Firemen's Hall was given to the Exempt Firemen and Board of Trustees of the Fire Department. The comptroller recognized the new commissioners in the following order:

"CITY OF NEW YORK, DEPARTMENT OF FINANCE,
COMPTROLLER'S OFFICE, JUNE 24, 1865.

"To all persons having charge of the real estate and personal property of the City of New York, now in use and occupation by the Fire Department:

"Permission is hereby granted to the commissioners of the Metropolitan Fire Department, established under an Act passed March 30, 1865, to take possession of the real estate and other property of the city, now occupied and used for the Fire Department, and over which I have any authority or control.

"MATTHEW T. BRENNAN, *Comptroller.*"

Messrs. Pinckney and Brown were, on the twenty-sixth of June, authorized to visit cities where fire engines were constructed, to get information as to the cost and construction of the highest class. June 27, Chief Decker sent in the following communication:

"OFFICE CHIEF ENGINEER, FIRE DEPARTMENT, NEW YORK,
JUNE 27, 1865.

"CHARLES C. PINCKNEY, Esq., President Board of Metropolitan Fire Commissioners.

"SIR: To your note of the twenty-third instant, desiring me to continue in performance of my duties as chief engineer until further notice, I respectfully reply that in accordance with my own feelings I desire to retire from active duty. As I am not an applicant for the position, but in order to act consistently, and to carry out the spirit of the resolution adopted by the Board of Engineers and Foremen of the Volunteer Fire Department, while the controversy relative to the constitutionality of the bill was pending, and while the public mind was fearful that the Old Department would refuse to perform duty, I volunteer my services to the new organization until a reasonable time shall have elapsed sufficient for the new Board of Fire Commissioners to take charge of all matters appertaining to the Department. Very respectfully,

"JOHN DECKER, *Chief Engineer.*"

The same day, on the application of ex-Commissioners William M. Tweed, Edward Bonnoll, Thomas Lawrence, Thomas Flender, and John J. Gorman, Hose Company No. 26 was restored to duty. The pay of bellringers was fixed at eight hundred dollars per annum, and that of engineers at nine hundred dollars per annum. June 30 the engineers and foremen met at Firemen's Hall, and on motion of Assistant Engineer John Hamill, the following resolution was adopted:

Whereas, it was stated at Albany, before the committee, the Volunteer firemen were anxious to get positions in the Paid Department, *Resolved*, that a committee be sent to the new Commissioners that they will perform duty up to the first of August, if the Commissioners will honorably discharge all members of the Volunteer Fire Department. If not, they will cease to perform duty July 10.

This was carried by twenty-nine to twenty-four, but a number of disqualified companies did not vote. July 3 the commissioners tabled the communication, and on the eighth of July notified the firemen and engineers that they were not at present able to comply with the demand. July 17, Assistant Engineers Alexander V. Davidson, William Lamb, John Hamill, Bernard Kenny, and Bartley Donohue gave notice that they ceased to perform duty as assistant engineers on the eleventh of July. That day the Bank of the Manhattan Company was designated as the bank for keeping the funds of the Department, and the following was sent to Chief Decker:

To John Decker, Esq., Chief Engineer.

"Sir: This Board feels that it is due to you and in accordance with your expressed wish, to have a period fixed when we shall be prepared to relieve you from your voluntary services as Chief Engineer of the Metropolitan Fire Department. They would therefore now respectfully inform you that arrangements are in progress by which this can be accomplished on the first day of August next."

The organization of the new Department was watched by the New York Board of Fire Underwriters, and so important was the selection of the chief engineer of the department considered, that a special committee was appointed to place the matter before the underwriters in the form of a report, of which the following are extracts:

★ ★ ★ It is expected of us that we will make such suggestions to the Metropolitan Fire Commissioners as our experience as insurers qualifies us to make, and our deep interest in the efficiency of the Department justifies. Our policies embrace and protect hundreds of millions of property in this city, and we are, therefore, deeply concerned in having the most thoroughly efficient Department possible. ★ ★ ★

The undersigned believe that the realization of the benefits expected to be derived from the new system about to be inaugurated will mainly depend upon the selection of the first executive officer of the Department—the chief engineer. ★ ★ ★

The head of this important arm of the public service is required now to be something more than a "practical fireman," and an expert in extinguishing burning buildings; and we believe the commissioners will make a grave mistake if they do not secure talent and qualifications of a different kind from those which have hitherto been thought to be sufficient for that officer to possess. ★ ★ ★

To place this great emporium in the best state possible with reference to security against fire, is a task requiring the exercise of the highest ability; and the superintendent of the Fire Department, or chief engineer (as the law designates him), being the person whose business it is to take cognizance of existing defects and abuses, to discern danger, to anticipate calamities, and to recommend to the commissioners for their approval such measures as the public interest requires, should be a man of rare acquirements and endowments, and if the office is held by one who will *fill* it, we believe that it will be second to none under the city government in dignity, influence, and usefulness.

The Fire Department of this city should be the most perfect on the Continent. It should be a model not only in the perfectness of its apparatus and the wisdom of its regulations, but the influence of the Department should be felt in elevating the standard of security in warehouses, hotels, places of public assemblage and tenements, and in the buildings of the city generally.

★ ★ ★ The work cannot be divided. It naturally devolves on the chief engineer, and if he proves himself capable, he will not lack for fame and reward. Such a man would not only be the first executive officer of our Fire Department, but he would be in effect the controller and regulator of all the Fire Departments in the country. ★ ★ ★

The assistant engineers should and doubtless will be selected from the most experienced and best qualified firemen of the Old Department. The senior member of the assistants should perform similar duties to those heretofore performed by the chief, and the presence of the superintendent or chief under the New Department would only be necessary when unusual measures are demanded or when circumstances arise calling for the exercise of unusual responsibility.

We do not suppose that it now is or hereafter will be the intention of this board to suggest to the Fire Commissioners the appointment of any particular person to the office of chief engineer, unless they are solicited to do so; but it may not be inappropriate, in view of the difficulty which will probably be encountered in obtaining the services of one possessing the qualifications which the undersigned think indispensable, to suggest to the commissioners (provided the views herein expressed are concurred in by the board), that the proper person could probably be found among the eminent generals of our army, and especially among those whose education as military and civil engineers would qualify them for the important position of chief engineer of the New York Fire Department.

All of which is respectfully submitted,
GEORGE W. SAVAGE, A. B. McDONALD,
HENRY A. OAKLEY.
NEW YORK, July 11, 1865.

This was approved, and a correspondence with the Fire Commissioners resulted, on the fourteenth of July, 1865, in an interview with them, when the report was left with them, it being understood that the commissioners were favorably impressed with the views embraced in it.

July 28, the comptroller was requested to place fifty thousand dollars to the credit of the Fire Department with the city chamberlain, and the "sinews of war" were provided for. The commissioners had been feeling their way to the appointment of the first engine company. A first-class engine, that had been ordered of the Amoskeag Manufacturing Company, to cost four thousand five hundred dollars, and, after several quarters for it had been selected and rejected, it was decided to house it in the building occupied by the Exempt Engine Company, in the northeast corner of the City Hall Park. Commissioner Engs rode on it to its first destination. Foreman John J. Gorman readily complied with a request that the members of the Exempt Engine Company aid the company of the new engine when it was formed. Messrs. Engs and Brown then selected officers and men, and on the thirty-first of July the company was formed. The commissioners appreciated the action of the officers and members of Exempt Engine Company, and on the ninth of August, on a communication from John J. Gorman, foreman of Exempt Engine Company, requesting that the company may be relieved from active duty in connection with Metropolitan Steam Fire Engine Company No. 1, as the Paid Company had been appointed, Commissioner Brown offered the following resolutions, which were adopted:

> *Resolved,* That at their own request, the Exempt Fire Engine Company be relieved from further active duty with Metropolitan Steam Fire Engine Company No. 1.
>
> *Resolved,* That the readiness with which Exempt Engine Company came forward and volunteered to take charge of the new steamer, and the promptness and zeal manifested by that company in the discharge of duty with said steamer, is deserving of special mention and commendation.
>
> *Resolved,* That the thanks of this Board be, and they are hereby, tendered to the Exempt Engine Company for the valuable assistance rendered by them to this Department.
>
> *Resolved,* That the secretary furnish the Exempt Engine Company with a copy of these resolutions.

The organization of the new companies, and the retirement of the volunteers, was effected under the critical observation of the public, who were divided into friends of the old system and the new and the volunteers. It is not necessary to enter into complete details of the action of certain volunteer companies, who, under bad advisement, chose to oppose in various ways the organization of the new Department. There was some exhibition of bad feeling between the volunteers and the new companies. Their allies, the "runners," were responsible for the mischief that was done. Hose were cut at fires, apparatus were retarded in their way to them. The "Mets" were greeted with cries of "Man found dead," etc., and the members of the Fire Insurance Patrol, which was considered to represent the obnoxious insurance interest, fared ill for many months. "Throw the red caps out" was often the cry of "Metropolitans" when, at fires, the insurance patrolmen entered a building to put waterproof covers on property. The detrimental alacrity that distinguished some of the volunteer companies at fires, where slap-dash and reckless activity were very often considered the acme of fire duty, was for a long time continued in the Paid Department. This resulted in unnecessary damage to apparatus and property. Water was used recklessly when a pail or two would have sufficed. Hose costing $1.55 to $1.65 a foot, and which was then of riveted leather—the first step toward better hose was taken a couple of years later—was dashed around or neglected until it became as dry, brittle and unserviceable as bark, and had to be taken to the "yard" to be "slushed" or soaked in vats of grease and other implements of fire fighting. Notably, "butts" were "banged around," to be broken, dented, and in other ways rendered unserviceable. The worst act attributed to the volunteers while the new Department was organizing was the burning of the quarters of Black Joke Engine No. 33, in Fifty-eighth Street, near Broadway, on the twenty-second of November, 1865. The company was then under disability, and its apparatus was removed, and public opinion was divided as to the guilt of a member or members of the company or zealous "runners." The Metropolitans, once under discipline, rarely noticed insult or worse. It was not rare, when paid men came at a fire, for some one to step out of a crowd and vent his displeasure in a blow; but the encounters that took place were petty in comparison with the less serious of the volunteer scrimmages.

John Decker turned over to the new commissioners the following property:

> Thirty-four steam fire engines, thirty-six engine tenders, twenty-five hand engines, forty-nine hose carriages, thirty-nine jumpers, twenty-one crabs, eighteen hook and ladder trucks, one thousand one hundred and ninety-seven lengths of leather hose (59,850 feet), one hundred and fifty-two and a half lengths of rubber hose (7,625 feet), four hundred and twenty-four feet of Croton Hose, eighty-five and a half lengths of suction, ninety-nine brass pipes, two copper pipes, one hundred and fifty-six leather pipes, two thousand two hundred and forty-seven chairs in good order, two hundred and eighteen broken chairs, two hundred and eighty-six lanterns, three hundred pails, two hundred and twenty-six brooms, one hundred and forty-five scrub-brushes, ninety-three Chamois, one hundred and thirty-six axes, two hundred and six hooks in good order, forty broken hooks, forty-two picks, one hundred and twelve ladders, one hundred and fourteen sponges, two hundred and thirty-eight mops, three hundred cans, one hundred and twenty eight hoisting apparatus, seventy-nine tables, five hundred and fourteen wrenches, fifty-six screw wrenches, eighty-seven

loads of wood, twenty-eight and a half tons of coal, two hundred and sixty chandeliers, eight hundred and six brackets, one hundred and thirty-six burners, six hundred and twenty-three globes, thirty-two stoves and pipes, ninety-four hose washers, one hundred and eight jacks, one hundred and twenty-four signals, twenty-seven coal scuttles, eleven monkey wrenches, nineteen crowbars, eight gallons of oil, fifty-one pitchforks, five pipe-holders, two hundred and six straps, two hundred and seventeen ropes, one hundred and ninety-five and a half pendants, fifteen desks, seven hub wrenches, six cap wrenches, one poker, seventy-two side lamps, twelve nozzles, seven reducers, four extra tongues, twenty-four shovels, fourteen benches, five oil feeders, two extra sets of wheels, one length hemp hose, two extra valves, alarm bells, ten striking apparatus, five wash basins, one iron safe, ten field glasses, eleven spy glasses, twelve pounds of cotton waste, one hammer, seven spittoons, one gas stand, seven closets, fifteen dust brushes, twelve clocks, five slates, one book, ten water coolers, one extra lever, eight tool wrenches, five dust pans, fifteen mats, eight tin boilers, three carpets, one lounge, one large closet with pigeon holes, one letter press, two screw chairs, one eyelet puncher, three oilcloths, one mirror slab, three shoemakers' seats, four hundred feet of condemned hose, two hose benches, one platform scale, ten bars of soap, sixteen pairs of hose butts, one windlass and fall, two work tubs.

On the sixth of September, 1865, the organization of the new Department had so far progressed that the commissioners were able to dispense with the services of the assistant engineers of the Volunteer Department. They recognized their services in the following resolution:

> *Resolved,* That the Metropolitan Fire Commissioners are deeply impressed with the obligations they are under to those of the assistant engineers of the Old Volunteer Department who have up to the present time rendered to them and to the city valuable services since the passage of the law creating a New Department, and they respectfully tender to those gentlemen their most sincere thanks for their aid.

The pay of the force was fixed under a construction of the law which created the department as follows:

Chief engineer, $3,000 per annum; assistant to chief, $2,000 per annum; district engineers, $1,200 per annum; foremen, $800 per annum; assistant foremen, $750 per annum; engineers, $900 per annum; ordinary firemen, $700 per annum; suburban engineers, $400 per annum; each suburban company, $1,000 per annum.

The embarrassments of the commissioners were not confined to delay in procuring funds. The resigning of members of all grades when companies were thought to be on an active footing, and the active or passive opposition of the element that at last wrecked the Volunteer system. For many weeks the fire companies that were appointed under the act of the thirtieth of March, 1865, wore such uniforms as they chose. When regular uniforms were discussed in September, 1865, there was instantly opposition from some of the best men in the New Department and a number of like desirable members. At one time it appeared as if a majority of the force would resign rather than wear "livery." The commissioners set a good example by choosing for themselves and wearing the following uniform:

"A blue cloth cap (navy style), a frock-coat made of navy-blue cloth, double-breasted, made to button up close to the neck, with seven department regulation buttons of bronze metal on each breast, three on each skirt behind, and four on each sleeve at the cuff. A single-breasted vest made of the same material as coat, without collar, and eight regulation buttons. Pantaloons made of the same material as coat. Surtout overcoats made of navy-blue pilot cloth, double-breasted, made to button up close to the neck, with seven regulation buttons on each breast, three on each skirt behind, and four on each sleeve at the cuff."

This had the best effect, but many resignations were sent in when the regulations prescribing a uniform for the firemen were promulgated.

The first regulations for the guidance of the paid firemen, gotten up in September, 1865, were as strict as the times permitted. The following were the general rules:

SECTION 13. —The members shall keep the houses and bedding clean and in good order. They shall accompany their apparatus going to or returning from a fire, and when on duty at a fire, when not otherwise directed by the officer in command, shall remain by their apparatus. The foreman shall cause to be kept by the officers and members of the force (serving in rotation as they stand on the roll) a proper and efficient watch day and night, so that at all times two men shall be on patrol in the neighborhood of the engine or hook and ladder house, and one on watch in the house. Members doing such patrol duty shall report at the house hourly until relieved.

SECTION 14. —Racing to or from fires is prohibited; and if the apparatus of the several companies proceed on the same street or avenue to or from a fire, they shall do so in single file.

SECTION 15. —Crossing a line of hose when in use by a steam fire engine is, unless in cases of the most absolute necessity, strictly prohibited.

SECTION 16. —Drivers will be held responsible for any damage caused by them, or carelessness displayed in conveying their apparatus to or from a fire.

SECTION 17. —The officer in command shall precede his apparatus in going to or from a fire.

SECTION 18. —No officer or member of the force shall appear on duty except he be properly clothed in the uniform prescribed for the department; nor shall any officer or member of a fire company appear at a fire without his fire-cap.

SECTION 19. —No spirituous or intoxicating liquors shall be allowed on the premises of any Metropolitan Fire Company, nor shall any game of chance be permitted thereon.

SECTION 20. —No officer or member shall use profane, immoral or indecent language in or about any engine or hook and ladder house, or while at, going to, or returning from a fire; nor shall any officer or member visit places where intoxicating liquors are sold while in the uniform of this department.

SECTION 21. —Officers of companies, after a fire, having hose which do not belong to them, shall return the same to the company to whom it belongs.

SECTION 22. —The driver, engineer and stoker may ride on the engine, and the driver and one man on the tender, in going to or returning from fires, and no more; and the officer in command will be held responsible for a violation of this rule.

As soon as possible after the organization of the Metropolitan Board, a committee was appointed to devise badges, etc., not only for the members of the force, but insurance officers, members of the Fire Patrol, and others having business within the fire lines, to keep out the element that had done so much to bring the volunteers into disrepute. The following rules in regard to badges were adopted:

INSIGNIA AND BADGES

The fire marshal was required to have a fire-cap with "Fire Marshal" on the front or a black patent leather band with same. The superintendent of buildings and his inspectors were required to have on their caps a patent leather band with their title. Reporters were required to wear a badge with the word "Reporter" and the name of their paper. Officers of insurance companies wore an oval silver badge with the name of their company on it. The superintendent of the Fire

Insurance Patrol had a badge with his title on it. The other members of Insurance Patrol had a red fire-cap with their number and initials on it, or a red leather band with "I.P." and number on it in white or gilt letters, or a badge.

Although the commissioners showed no favors to, and disciplined all, rebellious companies and members, both of the Volunteer and Paid Departments, whenever an opportunity occurred to oblige or advantage the retiring force, it was done. In this way the furniture and necessary outfits of many volunteer companies were purchased for the paid force, which took possession of their quarters, and volunteer companies were allowed to take away as relics portions of the apparatus. A pleasant feature of the period between the decision of the Court of Appeals on the constitutionality of the Metropolitan Act and the putting of the paid force into active service, was the readiness which men like John J. Gorman, James Hayes, and many others, who fought the paid system to the end, gave the benefit of their experience, aid and advice, to the new regime. As an illustration of this, take the meeting of engineers and foremen at Fireman's Hall on the first of July, 1865, when Martin J. Keese said in substance that he was going to do his duty as long as the new commissioners desired. He did not care if it was Thomas C. Acton's house that was on fire; he would be one of the first to go and put it out, and when certain organs shortly after announced a terrible riot in the Fifth District between certain companies, Hugh Bonner, W. F. Squires and W. H. Pierpoint lost no time in denouncing the statement as a falsehood gotten up to injure the volunteers. The last meeting of the representatives was held in Firemen's Hall July 24, 1865, and they were addressed by Treasurer John S. Giles.

The appointment of employees on the clerical staff and in the fire telegraph bureau proceeded slowly. Charles L. Chapin was appointed superintendent of telegraph August 4, 1865, vice Charles Robinson, contractor; and John W. Smith, lineman, and S. S. Parker, battery boy, were appointed a few days later. Patrick Dailey, Isaac G. Seixas and Abraham D. Carlock were the first operators. The paid force was then below Eighty-seventh Street, and at first there were only sixty-three signal stations established, and district alarms were sent out above Fourteenth Street. There were no shut boxes, and their establishment was retarded by patent right claims. At one of the first meetings of the Metropolitan Fire Commissioners a plan to stop the ringing of the alarm bells was discussed, but the nuisance was not abated until many years later. August 30, the board received notice from Governor Fenton of the resignation of James W. Booth, and next day Mr. Joshua G. Abbe was appointed commissioner by Messrs. Pinckney, Engs and Brown.

Four days after Mr. Abbe's appointment, a meeting of the board which had been secret was opened to the press and public September 8; Alexander V.

Davidson was retired as chief clerk to the chief engineer, and Garrett B. Tunison was appointed in his stead.

The committees as then appointed were: Appointments and Discipline—Commissioner Abbe. Buildings and Supplies—Commissioner Brown. Apparatus and Hose—Commissioner Engs. Finance and Telegraph—Commissioner Pinckney. Mr. Abbe was able and conscientious, and did his duty as a commissioner as well as circumstances permitted, but the composition of the board was such that the tie votes often thwarted measures of reform, discipline, and improvement, and the result was a lack of efficiency, the rank and file not being slow to take sides indicated by the votes of the commissioners. In spite of this and an increase in the number of fires and losses—which was basely charged to the volunteers—the Paid Department compared favorably with the old system. The records of the mustering out of the volunteers show the number returned as active firemen by the clerk of the Common Council as three thousand eight hundred and ten, but the records of the fire commissioners indicate a less number. These records are known as being far from complete. Several companies did not send in returns, and many firemen did not claim their discharge, while the resolution that no discharge should be granted unless the firemen had done fifty per cent of duty, has since been upset by a decision of the courts. About one hundred and sixty firemen appointed by the old commissioners in April, May, and June were not recognized by the Metropolitan commissioners. Such volunteers as did the duty prescribed were recognized on the sixth of November, 1865, in the following resolution offered by Commissioner Engs:

> *Resolved*, That the Board hereby acknowledges the public services of those members of the Volunteer Fire Department who continued until relieved by resolution, to perform their duty as firemen at the sacrifice of long cherished attachments, thereby exhibiting a striking example of respect for the dignity of Constitutional Law.
>
> *Resolved*, That we tender them individually and officially our sincere thanks for the services thus rendered, and the assurance of our continued regard.

The first step towards creating a fund for the relief of firemen and their families was taken on the twenty-seventh of November, 1865, when Commissioner Engs offered the following:

> *Resolved*, That the Committee on Appointments and Discipline be requested to present to this Board at its next regular meeting a plan for establishing a fund for the care and relief of those members of the Metropolitan Fire Department force who may be injured or become sick

in the performance of their duties, and for the families of those who may die in consequence.

This was legalized by Chapter 756 of the Laws of 1866, creating the Metropolitan Fire Department Relief Fund. Its revenue was derived from all fines and penalties collected by the attorney, fees for permits, etc., all fines of members of the force, donations, and an assessment not to exceed twenty dollars per annum on all persons entitled to its benefits. Section 3 provided that:

"Said fund, as soon as the same shall amount to the sum of ten thousand dollars, shall be liable for the payment of the recipients of relief severally entitled thereto, the sums as follows: To each person permanently disabled while in actual performance of any duty assigned him by said department, the sum of twenty dollars per month for the term of his natural life; to each person who shall become superannuated after a service of ten years in the employment of said department, annually thereafter an annuity of two hundred and fifty dollars, payable quarter-yearly, during the term of his natural life; to the family or relatives of any deceased person who shall be killed while actually engaged in the performance of any duty assigned by said department, or who shall die from any injuries received resulting from the performance of said duties, the sum of two thousand dollars, to be paid in the order following: first to his widow, if any him surviving; second, to his children under fifteen years, if any him surviving, equally, share and share alike; third, to a father living with and dependent on his support for a living; fourth, to a mother living with and dependent on his support for a living.

The first trustees were C. C. Pinckney, president, and P. W. Engs, treasurer, with Mayor John T. Hoffman and James M. McLean, president of the Board of Fire Underwriters, *ex officio* trustees.

The first victims of fire service under the Metropolitan commissioners were Robert Wintringham, of Engine Company No. 1, and George Bell, of Engine Company No. 8. Both died in 1865, the former being run over, and the latter was brought to his grave by exposure.

On the first of November, 1865, the commissioners recognized in complimentary resolutions the services of Assistant Engineers George H. E. Lynch, Michael Halloran, and Abraham Horn; and Halloran, Horn, and John Hart were appointed district engineers in Harlem, Yorkville, Manhattanville, Bloomingdale, and Carmansville. On the same date outrages by the followers of the volunteers had become so frequent that a reward of five hundred dollars was offered by the commissioners for the detection and conviction of any person cutting hose and disabling or impeding engines and firemen.

With the advent of 1866 the commissioners prepared to combat the difficulties which beset them in spite of attacks by the press and a public sentiment that the Metropolitan Department had fallen short of what was expected of it. Early in January Superintendent Chapin had established forty-one special signal stations and one hundred and eighteen ordinary signal stations which were designated, as fires occurred, on the eleven alarm bells. At the end of the year there were one hundred and eighty-seven signal stations. The city above One Hundred and Sixth Street was divided into eight fire districts, viz.:

District No. 1, Ward's Island; District No. 2, Randall's Island; District No. 3, One Hundred and Sixth to One Hundred and Sixteenth Street and Sixth Avenue to the East River; District No. 4, One Hundred and Sixth to One Hundred and Sixteenth Street and Sixth Avenue to the North River; District No. 5, One Hundred and Sixteenth to One Hundred and Twenty-fifth Street and Sixth Avenue to the East River; District No. 6, One Hundred and Sixteenth to One Hundred and Twenty-fifth Street and Sixth Avenue to the North River; District No. 7, north of One Hundred and Twenty-fifth Street and Sixth Avenue to the Harlem River; District No. 8, north of One Hundred and Twenty-fifth Street and Sixth Avenue and from Harlem River to the North River.

The carrying of speaking trumpets, except on parades, was abolished. The care of the one hundred and twenty-four horses in the various quarters necessitated the employment of a superintendent, and William Burns was chosen on the seventeenth of January, 1866. The first hitching-up drill system was ordered at the same time by a resolution offered by Commissioner Abbe.

The public were not backward in recognizing the efficiency of the new Department when its members did good duty, and testimony to this effect was from time to time sent to the commissioners. There was no lack of material wherewith to make firemen; in fact, the applications for appointment accumulated to such an extent that in April a resolution was adopted at the instance of Commissioner Abbe which gave exempt firemen preference over all other applicants, of whom two thousand four hundred had sent in their names. The Legislature at this time slightly increased the salaries of the force. Much anxiety and annoyance were caused by fires which were believed to be incendiary, and that at the Academy of Music, May 21, 1866, led the commissioners to offer a reward for the discovery of the person who set it on fire, and a standing reward of a like sum for six months for any conviction of an incendiary. In June the commissioners required every engine to be supplied with apparatus to keep the water at boiling point, or as near it as possible. Under an act relating to the storage of combustibles, Charles T. Polhemus was appointed attorney to the board at a salary of one thousand two hundred dollars per annum, June 15, 1866.

The cost of the department for 1866 was nine hundred and thirty-six thousand dollars (December 1, 1865, to December 1, 1866), and one hundred and ninety-eight alarms of fire—forty-six of which were for serious outbreaks—were responded to. There were forty-five arrests for incendiarism during the year, and fourteen convictions for arson. Sixteen new first and second-class Amoskeag engines replaced apparatus manned by volunteers. Private Thomas Irwin and Dominick Scott, of Engine Company No. 4, and foreman D. B. Waters and Private P. H. Welsh, of Engine Company No. 5, were killed in the discharge of duty, and their families received each one thousand dollars on policies donated to the members of the force by the New York Accidental Insurance Company.

In their statutory reports to Governor Fenton, the commissioners and chief engineer took occasion to make some laudatory and strong comments. The latter said:

"It cannot be denied that the first attempts to establish this department as an active, reliable force, met with antagonism, not more from the avowed hatred of those who opposed and stood aloof from belonging to it, than from the covert, unsuspected malignity of some who joined its ranks, and, for a while, pretending to be on the side of right, were really plotting its destruction. That day has, however, gone by, and with pleasure do I look upon the body of men now under my command; from time to time there may indeed be causes for the exercise of strict discipline, but they generally will be found to arise more from error of judgment than of heart."

The commissioners' comments were:

"Noise and confusion in our streets on the occasions of alarms of fire have ceased; the sick and dying are no longer disturbed by the yelling of 'runners,' the machinery is drawn quietly to the scene of duty, the inhabitants are left to enjoy their needed rest, and vehicles may pass on unmolested.

"Racing and fighting between companies is unknown, and the city police are relieved from the disagreeable duties which they were formerly called upon to perform by arrests; disputes between companies no more hinder operations at a fire.

"Thieves cannot fully get within the police lines; only the few citizens who have the badge of privilege are permitted to enter. 'Runners' no longer meddle with the duties of our firemen. The loss by theft so commonly added to claims upon insurance companies are rarely alluded to, consequently the saving of property counts by thousands. Beyond these advantages resulting from our present system of fire duty, comes to us the inestimable blessings resulting from the breaking up of the 'runners' organization, and the consequent release of our youth from one of the ways that lead to ruin. We may estimate the loss of wealth, but who can measure the loss of character which befalls the youth so misled, the loss of his services in the walks of life, and an end that puts him beyond the pale of hope. That we have been instrumental in rescuing such from the jaws of destruction, it is to us a gratifying reflection."

Only a few days after this was written the commissioners passed resolutions continuing the reward of one thousand dollars for the conviction of every incendiary, asking the mayor to call the attention of the municipal authorities to the matter, and requesting the co-operation of the Board of Fire Underwriters. The last request led to the appointment of a committee consisting of Messrs. Rankin, Hope and Norwood, by the underwriters, to confer with the fire commissioners. In 1866 the first paid fire-boat, the *John Fuller*, was hired. Blackwell's Island was protected by hand apparatus.

The Academy of Music was destroyed by fire on Monday, May 21, 1866. This fire broke out shortly before midnight; the curtain had scarcely fallen upon the last act of "La Juive"; the audience had just departed, and the artistes had only left their dressing-rooms, when the alarm was given that the Academy of Music was on fire. The gas was not yet extinguished in a portion of the building, and the doors on Fourteenth Street were still open. The first indications were observed in light wreaths of smoke issuing from the upper windows immediately under the roof. The firemen soon arrived and carried their hose into the building, and, as soon as water could be supplied, they poured a stream on the portions of the house where the fire was visible. When the fire first broke out, it was supposed that it could be extinguished by the hydrant streams within the building. Three small lines were promptly attached, but did not reach the flames. On the arrival of Hook and Ladder Company No. 3, lying in East Nineteenth Street and running a tender, they stretched it from a hydrant under direction of Engineer Sullivan, who was in the immediate neighborhood at the time of the occurrence, but the force being insufficient they could accomplish but little. Soon after, Engine Company No. 3 came on the ground, and got a line in on the rear—while Engine Companies 13 and 14 were on duty at the front or main entrance; 13's pipe was stretched nearly to the middle of the parquet, and was manned by John F. Denin and Hugh Kitson, when the gas exploded. Denin was so seriously injured that he had to be conveyed to the New York Hospital for treatment. He was seriously burned, but not fatally so, and finally recovered. Engine No 16, which stood at the corner of Fourteenth Street and Third Avenue, was surrounded by flames, and the members were compelled to abandon it for a time. It was finally drawn away badly injured. Engine Company No. 36, of Harlem, of which Robert C. Brown was foreman, came all the way down to the fire, and worked two hours and a half to save Worcester's piano factory from destruction.

The progress of the fire was checked at daybreak, and immediately afterwards the firemen began the search for their missing brethren. About half-past ten the body of Peter H. Walsh, private of Engine Company No. 5, was discovered below the central portion of the stage, the legs and arms being completely burned off. The remains of David B. Waters, foreman of Engine Company No. 5, were not recovered until about half-past two in the afternoon. They were found lying over one of the heaters near the stage entrance. They were badly burned like his companions. Waters had been a member of 23 Engine in the old Department. Waters and Walsh had started in the building to find their pipe and relieve the men at it, when they unfortunately missed their way and were lost in the smoke and flames. The funerals of the unfortunate men were largely attended, the officers and members of the Department acting as a body guard and as pall bearers.

CHAPTER XXIII

THE NEW DEPARTMENT
SEVERELY CRITICISED

*Resignation of Commissioner Brown.—Appointment of General Shaler,
M. B. Wilson, T. B. Myers, and James Galway.—The Board Exclusively
Republican.—A Manifesto of Much Interest.—Bureau of Combustibles.—A
Reward for the Conviction of Incendiaries.—A Board to Pass on the
Competency of Officers.*

In the year 1867 it was seen that something was amiss with the new Department. In spite of honest endeavors to do better than the volunteers, the Metropolitans were not fortunate at great fires, and insurance rates became higher. Citizens and the press grumbled, and at the assembling of the Legislature it was evident that action would be taken by it. A plea of scarcity of hydrants was ridiculed by some who said that the Volunteers did better with fewer, and the insinuation that the ousted Volunteers were responsible for some of the fires was denounced as infamous. Some of the grumbling was odd. Persons wrote to the papers to complain that the horses attached to the apparatus were driven too fast, and Mr. Henry Bergh addressed a communication to the commissioners on the subject, in which he denounced such driving as reckless, and protested against it. The commissioners tried to stem the tide of public opinion by ordering an investigation of the condition of many of the buildings and warehouses of the city for evidences of their unsafe and improper condition. Steps were taken to organize the suburban companies as paid companies, and the complaint that the discipline of the force was bad was met by a resolution to make trials of delinquents public in order to "contribute largely toward disciplining" them.

But a disastrous fire in Broadway, known as the Chittenden fire, provoked a fresh outbreak of public comment. It was charged that the Metropolitans had there proved their inability to cope with a disaster, and an investigation was ordered by the commissioners, which ended in Messrs. Pinckney, Brown and Engs exonerating the Department, on the twenty-fifth of March. Mr. Abbe dissented. Meanwhile, on the twenty-first of February, 1867, the Assembly insurance committee met at the Metropolitan Hotel "to take into consideration the large loss of property by fire, and inquire into the means of extinguishment." The members were: Messrs. Younglove, Penfield, Frear, Lefevre and Blauvelt.

Mr. George W. Savage, of a committee appointed by the National Board of Fire Underwriters, then in session, first testified. He ascribed the losses, which were unusually heavy, to incendiarism, slowness of firemen to get to work, failure to enforce laws, want of proper inspection of buildings, and accumulation of combustible matter in buildings. He charged that Chief Kingsland was incompetent, and was in favor of a department organized with military precision, with a man of West Point training for engineer. Other witnesses were equally condemnatory. The committee made a report which resulted in several bills being passed with a view of ousting the commissioners. The newspapers which had lauded the new commission turned against it, and one which had spoken very badly of the volunteers had severe things to say of their successors.

Commissioner Brown resigned on the thirtieth of March, 1867, because of the serious illness of his wife, who died shortly after. His act was the subject of unfeeling comment, but Governor Fenton subsequently appointed him Port Warden to emphasize his contradiction of the malicious reports. On the twelfth of April the Assembly passed Chapter 408 of the Laws of 1867, and the Senate passed it five days later. It required the governor to nominate a fifth fire commissioner within a few days of the act becoming a law, said commissioner to hold office for ten years, and the successors of the present commissioners to hold office for ten years. Commissioner Pinckney's term had about expired, and Messrs. Engs and Abbe sent in their resignations. On the eighteenth of April Governor Fenton nominated, and the Senate confirmed, Monmouth B. Wilson, captain of the Thirty-first Precinct, as the fifth commissioner, General Alexander Shaler in place of Mr. Pinckney, Colonel Theodorus Bailey Myers in place of Mr. Engs, James Galway in place of Mr. Brown (who would have been succeeded by Colonel Emmons Clark had he chosen to accept the position), and Mr. Abbe, whose resignation was virtually not accepted.

In 1867, two years after the substitution of the Paid Department system for the volunteer, General Shaler was put at the head of the Fire Department. For three years he remained as president, and until 1873 as a commissioner. The results of the reforms and improvements made under that management were practically manifested by the steady reduction of the losses by fire, from $6,428,000 in 1866 to $2,120,212 in 1870. It was during these three years— 1867–70—that the Department was converted into a well-organized, disciplined, and successful institution, and it is conceded that General Shaler was the controlling master spirit of the commission, and that to him was due the establishment of orderly and systematic methods, as well as the thorough disciplining of the force. During this period the Fire Commissioners had unlimited power over their subordinates, and could dismiss or reduce in grade at will, without the semblance of a trial. This power was, however, not arbitrarily exercised. During this period boards of officers were organized in the Department for the examination of candidates for promotion, and promotions were made for merit only. Candidates for appointment to the corps of firemen were also required to pass a rigid physical examination and to possess the rudiments, at least, of a common school education. These improvements, also suggested by General Shaler, not only stood the test of time, but the principles of good administration underlying the systems thus voluntarily introduced in an important branch of the public service, have since been made the basis of laws for the reform of the entire civil service, national, state and municipal.

General Shaler and his colleagues in the Board of Fire Commissioners during that period also had practically unlimited power in the matter of fixing the amount of the annual appropriations for the Department, the Board of Estimate and Apportionment having then only nominally the authority to determine the amount of the appropriation for the Fire Department. This great power, it is easy to see, could have been much abused by unscrupulous officials. But the expenditures for this period show that no less attention was paid to economy than to the efficiency of the Department. During the period of his presidency, General Shaler organized and taught classes composed of the officers and engineers in their respective duties. His next effort was to rid the Department of the officers who unfortunately could or would not learn. The power of summary dismissal vested in the commissioners was even then not exercised, but all who were deficient were given the further opportunity of passing a board of examination composed of their own officers, which finally decided upon the question of their fitness to remain. To General Shaler is also due the inauguration in 1867 of the admirable property accountability system in the Fire Department so frequently commended then and since in the public press and by public officials.

Until May, 1873, General Shaler remained as one of the commissioners of the Fire Department, continuing, though no longer president, to give all his energies to the performance of his duties.

Theodorus Bailey Mayers, when the Metropolitan Fire Department was created by the Legislature, was appointed by the governor as a member of the Board of Commissioners. Not soliciting the position, and having no claims as an active politician, this was probably due to his successful administration of the affairs of the Sixth Avenue Railway, of which he had been first executive officer, and subsequently president, and aided to restore it to its present prosperity. On the twenty-first of April, 1861, he had left it, on a leave of absence, in the *Baltic*, with the Twelfth Regiment, one of the first that started for the capitol, accepting, without compensation, the temporary position of quartermaster, and in charge of the supplies which had been intended to be thrown into Fort Sumter. After visiting Fortress Monroe, the day after the burning of Norfolk—the Potomac being closed—they proceeded to Annapolis. Finding General Butler, already arrived, in command, on reporting to him and turning over the needed stores, he was, although personally unknown to the general, selected as an *aide de camp*, and assigned to the duty of quartermaster. He visited New York soon after, and raised, under a department order, two hundred and fifty men, without any expense to the government beyond their rations, the use of the Park barracks, and their transportation. With these he proceeded to Baltimore with Colonel Kilpatrick, with the same number of volunteers for his mounted rifles.

When General Wool relieved General Butler, Mr. Myers was placed on his staff—a selection probably due to the circumstance that the general and his father, who had been crippled at Chrystler's Fields, in the Canada campaign, had been captains together in the Thirteenth Regular Infantry in the War of 1812. After much detail duty and some service in reconnaissances, but no regular engagement, he was, in the fall, imperatively recalled to his railroad by a sudden difficulty, which terminated his military service, with less regret because the country had become fully aroused and the material to supply official posts was abundant.

When he became Fire Commissioner, his military experience was found to be invaluable, and he had an able co-laborer in General Shaler. Each company was placed on a basis of efficiency equal to that of a regular section of field artillery. Each man had his place and duty, which he was expected to perform. Rapidity in getting under way on an alarm, and progress to the points of service, system in conveying signals, and all the details for concerted action, first from the nearest post, the putting of an immediate cordon around the burning building to protect property from depredation and exclude unauthorized access; all these were rapidly formulated or improved and enforced. The bill for the storage of combustible materials suggested by the underwriters was one of the measures to which he gave particular attention. He prepared and furthered its passage at Albany. The act giving a half portion of the tax on foreign insurance companies, then held by the old organization, to the Department, was also a subject for his attention. He afterwards represented the Board as its volunteer counsel, for which his profession fitted him, often saving expense.

The board authorized a lyceum, and devoted to its use the large upper hall, in which he collected, by their authority as commissioner in charge, a collection of several thousand volumes, issued to the members as a circulating library, to occupy leisure time at their quarters. In this he also collected examples of old apparatus, emblems, trophies, and curious documents connected with the early history of New York. The librarian was the clerk allowed to him, the first being John R. Thompson, once editor of the *Southern Literary Messenger*, a poet of ability and a gentleman of admirable modesty, who, after serving as a secretary of the Confederate Legation in London and Paris, returned to New York.

Commissioner Myers continued for a time to act as counsel to the Board after his duties had terminated; subsequently he declined a reappointment by Mayor Havemeyer, and has since devoted himself to study and literary pursuits.

This made a Republican Board of able, pushing men, fully aware that to succeed they must, from the start, do away with the causes that made the first commission less efficient and popular than it was expected to be. May 1 they met, and after electing General Shaler president and Mr. Abbe treasurer, provided for the reorganization of the committees, and the revision of the rules and regulations of the force, and the rules of the Board. May 8 the committees were formed as follows: Appointments, Discipline, Supplies, Apparatus, Finance, Telegraph, Buildings and Hose. The clerical force was placed under the direction of the secretary; appointments and promotions were to be under civil service regulations, and foremen, assistant foremen and engineers were to be promoted from the ranks and on grounds of meritorious conduct and qualifications. The system of appointments was first attacked, and a new and better form of application was adopted.

Commissioner Wilson's first act was to condemn the inadequate protection given Blackwell's Island; to suggest better protection for its six thousand inhabitants; to designate it by a fire signal, and to arrange for transportation of fire apparatus to it.

On the first of June the commissioners "declared their intentions" in the following circular to the force. Its ringing tenor drew a line between the present and the past, and no good member of the department misconstrued it:

OFFICE BOARD OF COMMISSIONERS METROPOLITAN FIRE DEPARTMENT,
FIREMEN'S HALL,

NEW YORK, June 1, 1867

To the Officers, Members and Employees of the Metropolitan Fire Department:

It has already been the duty of the Board of Commissioners (sitting as the Committee on Appointments), to pass upon several cases of violations of the rules. These complaints have been disposed of as leniently as possible, in consideration of the fact that the discipline of the Department had been heretofore less vigorously enforced than it will be in future, and that an impression may have resulted that the rules were prepared without an intention to enforce them. This will not, in future, be the case. Members of this Department possess privileges, and receive a compensation from the authorities, far superior to those engaged by any other branch of the public service. ★ ★ ★

For the act of every member the Commissioners are responsible to the public, and it is their duty, when its rules are disregarded, to relieve themselves by promptly bringing the offender to justice. Neglect to do this, from sympathy or any other consideration, would be criminal in them. There can be no middle condition in any organization like this, whether civil or military. ★ ★ ★

There is no lack of material, where a man fails in his duty, to supply his position. Over twenty-three hundred applications already on file, and a daily importunity at Headquarters for appointments, strongly urged by parties whom the Commissioners would be glad to oblige, proves that those who are in the enjoyment of the privilege of membership should do their utmost, by a zealous performance of their duty, to justify the Commissioners, to whom most of them are personally unknown, in adhering to a rule to make no removals except for incompetency or fault. Some of the friends of the old system are hostile to the new organization, have magnified its defects and predicted its failure. This is simply impossible if we do our duty to the public and to each other.

In furtherance of these views, and in anticipation of the publication of all the rules, now in the hands of a committee, the Commissioners consider it proper to call the attention of the officers and employees of this Department to a few general Regulations, which they will expect to see enforced:

1st. That the Assistant Engineers shall be strict and energetic in the performance of the duties laid down for them. That they shall be untiring in their vigilance, as well in the extinguishment of fires as in improving the efficiency and discipline of their several divisions. In case they find any fireman, or other officer or member of the Department, incompetent or unwilling to perform his duties, they shall, without hesitation or favor, see that charges are preferred.

2d. That the foreman or other officer in command of a company shall remember that he occupies a position of great trust, and that upon him the men of his company will naturally look as a model. He should bear in mind that, as an officer, he is not to allow his personal feelings to interfere with the discharge of his duty. All violations of the rules, or factious opposition to their enforcement, must be reported at once. Blank charges for this purpose will be furnished. The omission to make a complaint will be considered as an offense on the part of the officer. While it is desired that the best feeling should exist between officers and men in this Department, it is to be remembered that, to command the respect and obedience of others, self-respect is essential. Too much familiarity between officers and men is not compatible with discipline, nor with the duties that office imposes. When a man occupies a position of rank he acts for the Department, and not for himself. ★ ★ ★ No absence will be allowed, even on leave or lay off, unless reported to the officer in command, and his permission granted.

3d. The quarters of the different companies were left in bad condition by their former occupants, by the removal of their private property, the suspension of repairs, and by changes to accommodate horses. The more pressing emergency to provide for the active usefulness of the Department has caused some delay in repairs, which will be attended with large expense. The Department will place them in condition as rapidly as possible. Every man is naturally attached to his home. To many members of this Department, who are unmarried, their quarters are their only homes, and there is no reason why the same interest in their embellishment and neatness should not be taken by all the members, so far as in their power, as in the case of their own houses. A small company fund, to be voluntarily contributed, would aid much, added to such details as the Department is confined to. The neatness and taste displayed by Hook and Ladder Company No. 5 entitles them to be mentioned in orders, as well as cited as an illustration of what is meant by this suggestion. It is not doubted that a similar spirit will soon be developed by other companies. It has been a matter of surprise to the Commissioners that men should congregate and sit about their apparatus or horses, when they can, in most cases, easily arrange a comfortable sitting-room up-stairs, away from the dampness and fumes of the stable. Lounging about the doors of the house, or congregating on the walk, is constantly complained of by the neighbors and passers-by, and has a very bad appearance. The front doors should be kept open in fine weather, when the company is not absent, as much as practicable, to admit light and air, and in order to allow the public to look in and see the neatness and order prevailing. At least one man should always be on duty on the first floor to guard against trespass or depredation. No visitor not connected with the Department, or having some special business with it, can be allowed to remain for any length of time, beyond an ordinary opportunity to gratify his curiosity, in any of the houses, without a report to the officer in charge, and his consent obtained. Engine houses are places for business, and not for lounging.

4th. The waste of gas, fuel, feed and fodder, is to be avoided. It is to be borne in mind that the expenses of this Department fall upon the people, and the Commissioners are responsible for their application. The waste of gas has become a serious evil. The bill presented each month shows at a glance the waste and economy of each company. Some of the companies who are most extravagant have received notices, which will be followed by a system of personal liability for the waste, if continued. No man is expected to use the property of the Department more economically than he would his own. ★ ★ ★

5th. The officers and men should be neat and cleanly in their appearance.

When on duty at a fire it is not expected that this rule will be enforced, for their first business is to extinguish the fire, without regard to clothing, or even to person, if the emergency require; but after the fire is over, there are no damages which their equipments can suffer, which the use of benzine or French soap on their clothing, of whiting on their buttons and plates, and of blacking on their boots, will not restore. There is an abundance of time for this in the large amount of leisure on their hands. Each company should likewise be *uniformly* clothed on each day (except in case of an alarm, when all considerations of dress, except the fire-cap and overcoat, are to be disregarded); and it is not the meaning of uniform that one man in the same company should be in his shirt, another in his sack, and a third in his overcoat, or one in slippers, another in shoes, another with his boots over his trousers, and yet another with his trousers over his boots. Work to be done about the quarters will call for working dress; when the work is over the regulation dress will be resumed. It is unbecoming the credit of the Department that a few slovenly men should throw it in disrepute, when the means are afforded by their now liberal pay for every member to appear at all times decently and well clad. The accumulation of old and worn citizen's clothing is to be avoided, one serviceable citizen's suit being all that is required to have. It is suggested to the various companies that they purchase new uniforms and caps at the same time of the same cloth, and that if they are furnished by the same person no doubt a saving will be made. This, with the system required as to wearing them, will prevent the variety of color and condition of clothing which is otherwise inevitable. The closets afford ample room for the disposal of clothes not in use, other than the overalls drawn over the fire-boots for instant use. The bathing tubs should be freely used, not only as a sanitary measure, but because cleanliness is essential to public respect. The beds of the companies are to be kept cleanly, and in such condition as to be at all times presentable to visitors without reflecting on their owners or the officers. Want of cleanliness in this will be a subject for charges. It is the intention of the Board to supply each bed with a pillow-case and spread, to be used in the daytime and removed at night, and placed in the closet of its owner, in order to insure uniformity and neatness. In future, as in other branches of the public service, each man will provide his bed-clothes.

6th. When a superior officer, or a visitor accompanied by a superior officer, visits their quarters, it will be apparent that both politeness and discipline require that the officers and men should rise and salute them, showing that degree of discipline and respect for the position which they in turn will require should they attain, as they may if deserving, such promotion as is open to every man in this Department.

7th. The Commissioners have noticed with pleasure the general good condition of the apparatus and of the horses of the Department, and the pride taken by the men in these important elements of usefulness. They desire to encourage this, and also the spirit of honorable emulation. The condition of their brasses, and the sleekness of their horses' coats, strike at once a practiced eye, and give evidence of the good working condition of both. On everything connected with keeping these on an efficient footing, and their prompt use when required in the protection of property and life, too much attention cannot be bestowed. They are like tools of the skillful workman; and the citizens judge from what they see of the condition of the officers and men, and of the cleanliness and order of their apparatus, as to the efficiency of the Department. The reputation of the Department depends on its efficiency, and its perpetuation on its reputation. In both every member has a personal interest.

8th. At a fire each officer and fireman is to remember that his first duty is to extinguish the fire and protect property and life from the flames, and only second to that to prevent the *slightest* pillage or depredation. ★ ★ ★

9th. Some critical member of the Department who seeks to draw his pay without performing his duty, and takes no pride in the service or the buttons he wears, may say to his comrades, in reading the suggestions contained herein, that they dwell on trifles unworthy the attention of the Commissioners or the observance of the men. To such the Commissioners would say that the history of the world shows that everywhere, in every service and in every business, an aggregate of trifles is the basis of discipline; and discipline the guarantee of success. ★ ★ ★

This order will be read to each company in the Department, and placed on file for reference.   By order of the Board,

ALEXANDER SHALER, *President.*

CHARLES E. GILDERSLEVE, *Secretary.*

Chief Kingsland supplemented this by an order calling the attention of the district engineers to their responsibility for the general condition, in all respects, of the companies under their charge, insisting on proper deportment and order, and requiring cognizance and reports of violation of rules.

The aim and intent of this circular was readily understood by all to whom it was addressed. It drew a line between the past and the present, and its date was that of the beginning of the Paid Fire Department on a business basis. The commission was well received by the public and the press. One reform rapidly succeeded another, and the reorganization of the Department was proceeded with briskly and systematically. One of the first measures of importance was the division of the companies among the engineers, as follows, on the tenth of May:

Eli Bates,	Engine Co.'s Nos.	3, 14, 18, 33.	H. & L. Co.'s Nos.	12.
G. J. Orr,	" "	1, 7, 31.	" "	1.
Thomas Sullivan,	" "	5, 35, 28.	" "	3.
M. Shannessy,	" "	2, 19, 23, 34.	" "	4.
John Conley,	" "	4, 6, 10, 29, 32.	" "	10.
B. Sheridan,	" "	9, 12, 15.	" "	6.
W. W. Rhodes,	" "	16, 21, 26.	" "	7.
W. Banham, Jr.,	" "	8, 22.	" "	2.
R. V. Mackey,	" "	11, 17, 20.	" "	9, 11.
W. Brandon,	" "	13, 24, 27, 30.	" "	5, 8.

A system of preferment of charges against delinquent members was adopted, and that of to-day is almost the same, and the results of trials were transmitted to the force with instructive and pertinent comments. The tendency to carelessness and extravagance in the receipt and disposition of supplies was checked by the appointment of Carl Jussen, the present secretary of the board, as storekeeper or property clerk. The volunteers who desired to be honorably discharged had been hurt by an illiberal construction of the law of March 30, 1865, and the following resolution, passed June 5, 1867, on motion of General Shaler, pleased them:

> *Resolved*, That all members of the former Volunteer Department who have faithfully performed their duty, as appears from the records of the company to which they were attached up to the date of being relieved, or who were from good or sufficient reasons prevented from so doing, shall be entitled to receive an honorable discharge from the department.

Civil service reform was recognized on June 19, 1867, in the following, offered by Commissioner Wilson:

> *Resolved*, That the district engineers be, and are hereby, directed to report to the chief engineer the names of privates in their department who have performed meritorious acts since its organization, for the purpose of selecting from the ranks suitable persons to fill vacancies for offices now existing in the different companies.

Commissioner Myers offered the following as a substitute:

Resolved, That the district engineers be directed to report to the chief engineer, for competitive examination, the names of two men from each company possessing, in their opinion, the best qualifications for promotion as assistant foremen. That in making such selection consideration to be given to meritorious conduct in the performance of duty and such characteristics as will command the respect of their subordinates, and without favoritism or personal preference, but solely with a view to the benefit of the department.

The Bureau of Combustibles was organized June 22, 1867, under Chapter 873 of the Laws of 1866, with Commissioner Wilson at its head. Its personnel were: John H. Wilson, clerk, at one thousand five hundred dollars a year; and the following inspectors at five hundred dollars per annum, John A. Cregier, Surveyor Mercantile Fire Insurance Company; A. P. Moore, Surveyor Manhattan Fire Insurance Company; Theodore Keeler, Surveyor of the Lorillard Fire Insurance Company; and John H. Forman, Surveyor of the International Fire Insurance Company. Operations against persons who illegally stored dangerously inflammable articles and explosives were begun immediately. A step toward grading the force was made in the middle of July, when Commissioners Myers and Shaler, in reporting to their colleagues on the estimates for 1868, the increase in expenditures and the necessity of economy, presented the following resolution:

Resolved, That the appointment of firemen hereafter made shall be of acting firemen, at a rate of compensation not exceeding seven hundred dollars per annum, such active firemen to be in the line of promotion, and to have precedence, as candidates for appointments as firemen, whenever the means at the control of the commissioners justify the further increase of that grade, provided that the number of acting firemen shall not at any time exceed six in any company.

Then plans were discussed for the placing in commission of a boat to be used for fires on the river front, and the rules for ringing the alarm bells were amended so that the post-office bell rang for all fires south of Seventy-ninth Street, and the other bells rang five rounds for the first alarm, and seven rounds for a second alarm for signals in the various districts. Rewards were offered for the arrest and conviction of incendiaries, and the public were invited to note suspicious circumstances at fires and communicate information. Violations of law, especially in regard to the proper protection of openings in roofs, having resulted in the death of firemen, and fires having rapidly become uncontrollable because of hatchways being left open, the attorney was directed to frame amendments to existing laws. Stringent regulations for the storage of fireworks were adopted.

On the eighteenth of September a resolution was adopted to improve the intelligence and moral tone of the Department by establishing libraries in the several quarters of companies. The scheme resulted, three months later, in the formation of the Firemen's Lyceum at Fire Headquarters under Commissioner Myers. Charles E. Gildersleve was treasurer, and Charles De F. Burns, now secretary of the Board of Park Commissioners, librarian. The lyceum is now scattered among the battalion headquarters and in several company quarters. The library soon had two thousand five hundred volumes. The Metropolitan Fire Department Mutual Aid Association was started in October, 1867.

A breeze was created in the Board the same month, by a resolution which was offered by Commissioner Wilson, and which was adopted, to the effect that no member of the Department be permitted to be a delegate or representative to any political or nominating convention; and later the Citizens' Association, through Peter Cooper, attacked Mr. Abbe's right to act as a commissioner because he had been nominated for sheriff on the Republican ticket. John H. Martindale, the attorney-general, advised the fire commissioners to appoint another commissioner; but Mr. Abbe, in a communication to his colleagues, denied receiving notice of his nomination, and asserted that he had declined it, so that the other commissioners accepted his statement and declined to act. The first department surgeon, Dr. Charles B. McMillan, was designated at the end of November, 1867. Assistant Chief Engineer Perley was appointed chief of the repair yard in Elizabeth Street, and H. A. Gilbertson, superintendent. Hitherto so little had the volunteer system been changed that few members of companies rode on the apparatus, but ran with the horses. On the fourth of December, 1867, alterations were ordered on all apparatus to enable officers and men to ride. New York, on the first of January, 1868, had no longer companies on a semi-volunteer basis.

The new companies' hosemen were paid three hundred dollars a year each, and the laddermen a like sum. Both were under the rules of the Department, but could follow their avocations when not on fire duty. The changes necessitated others in the assignment of the engineers. Assistant Engineer Perley commanded all the fire organizations north of Twenty-third Street; District Engineer Banham, all the companies above Eightieth Street; Rhodes, all between Twenty-third and Eightieth Streets, east of Sixth Avenue; and Shannessy, all west of Sixth Avenue, between these streets.

The commissioners were eager to acquire knowledge from those who had had experience with Paid and partially Paid Fire Departments, and an examination of the systems in operation; and in November, Messrs. Shaler and Myers visited Boston, Cleveland, Detroit, Chicago, Fort Wayne, Cincinnati, and Baltimore, and made useful and interesting reports. These advocated a semi-paid system for the upper part of the city, and prudence in adopting a new telegraph system. One of the results of offering rewards for the conviction of incendiaries was the sending to prison of two incendiaries, Gaetano Castagnetto and Thomas A. Lambert, and the payment of the rewards offered. Fire Marshal Baker and Policeman Charles Van Duzer, who was pensioned in 1885, shared one reward of one thousand dollars.

The year 1868 saw the commissioners surrounded with interference from Albany, and embarrassed by the gradual increase in the pay of the force. By Chapter 408 of the Laws of 1867, the salaries were: chief engineer, $4,500; assistant engineer, $2,500; district engineers, $1,800; foremen, $1,300; assistant foremen, $1,100; engineers, $1,200; privates, $1,000. The estimate of the year was $893,600, of which sum $716,770 was for salaries. The citizens' association took the Department in hand, and after a conference with the commissioners, and a searching investigation, reported that its workings were marked by the greatest efficiency. The report was signed by William Wood, chairman; William Bloodgood, S. S. Constant, Nathaniel Sands, R. M. Henry and T. J. Powers. But the opponents of the commission, the Paid Department system, and innovations, continued their attacks in the press. One of the organs said:

"At Albany, in the Assembly, after sweeping resolutions of censure and broad charges of corruption and inefficiency, the following committee was appointed to 'investigate' the Fire Department: Alexander Frear, chairman; G. J. Bamler, of Erie; M. C. Murphy, of New York; W. C. Jones, of Kings; Christopher Johnson, of New York; William Bristol, of Wyoming; and Jacob Worth, of Kings. The committee held four sessions, and the testimony adduced was such as to call for the following sarcastic resolutions, which were offered at a meeting of the commissioners by Mr. Myers:

> *Resolved*, That the Board feels gratified for the recent searching investigation by a committee of the Honorable House of Assembly into the system on which its business is conducted, into the efficiency of this Department under their control, into the economy and fidelity with which the public money is disbursed, and into the benefits derived therefrom, directly or indirectly, by individual commissioners, beyond the amount of their salary.
>
> *Resolved*, That without anticipating the report of the said committee, it is matter of pride for this Board to know that this evidence has established the fact that this Department has been so managed as to prove upon such investigation an exception to the theory of many citizens, that to hold public office in New York is necessarily to be incompetent, dishonest, and corrupt.

The committee only reported the testimony taken. The investigation was generally regarded as a political scheme, and the evidence upset the charges of inefficiency, political "dickering," favoritism, extravagance, and corruption. But a bill was sent to the Democratic Assembly to increase the force and its pay, and the Republican Senate asked the commissioners if such were necessary or proper. A code of telegraphic fire signals from Station 2 to Station 727 was adopted. The engineers were redistricted, the rules for sending out alarms were amended, the telegraph system was brought near to that of the present day, and the first inspection of the companies was made in October.

On the twenty-second of October the sign "Firemen's Hall" was taken down at the Mercer Street headquarters, and one bearing "Headquarters Metropolitan Fire Department" put up. November 12, Mr. James M. McLean was appointed to succeed Mr. Abbe.

An order of December 26, 1868, defined the boundaries of the engine districts, organized the battalions and brigades, military fashion, assigned commanding officers, and established the following ranking grades:

Title of Position.	Assimilated Rank.
Chief Engineer	Colonel.
Assistant Engineer	Lieut. Colonel.
District Engineer	Major.
Foreman	Captain.
Assistant Foreman	Lieutenant.
Engineers of Steamers	Sergeant.
Firemen	Private.
Hosemen and Laddermen	Cadet.

In March the various companies were organized for patrol beats in three brigades and eight battalions, and strict rules were made in regard to patrol service and the keeping of the journals of companies.

Chief Kingsland, a Democrat, was not chary of criticism, and some remarks of his in regard to an order of the commissioners which related to the school of instruction, having been reported at headquarters, an inquiry was ordered, which, in the end, brought about his retirement from the service. The investigation was begun in April, and he resigned December 14, 1869. Shortly after, steps were taken to revolutionize the telegraph system. May 12, 1869, Mr. James M. McLean was appointed commissioner, to succeed himself, by his colleagues. In that month fire extinguishers were introduced. May 31 the force was notified of the promotion of C. O. Shay and Christopher H. Reynolds to the rank of district engineers. Preparations to have a well equipped telegraph system went on, and, in June, the treasurer was directed to include in his estimates for 1870 "a sum not exceeding four hundred thousand dollars" for a complete fire alarm telegraph, and on the eleventh of August, C. T. & J. N. Chester's proposal for its construction was accepted.

Captain Eyre M. Shaw, Chief Officer of the Metropolitan Fire Brigade of London, England, visited the United States in July, 1870, and when he was about to start on a tour through the principal cities, he penned a letter to General Alexander Shaler, in which he said: "Before taking my tour through the United States I must trouble you with this short letter, offering my most sincere and heartfelt thanks for all the kindness and attention which I have received from you and your colleagues, and the department generally over which you so ably preside."

This was sixteen years ago, and London is, to-day, almost as antiquated in its methods of fire extinguishing as was New York in 1865, in comparison with the system of 1869.

Captain Eyre Massey Shaw, C. B., is the head of the London Fire Brigade. He was born at Monkstown, County Cork, Ireland, in 1830, being the third son of B. R. Shaw, Esq., of Monkstown and Belvelly, and a cousin of Sir Robert Shaw, Bart., of Bushey Park. He was educated at Dr. Coghlan's well-known academy, Queenstown, and afterwards went to Trinity College, Dublin, where he greatly distinguished himself, taking his B.A. and M.A. degrees. He went to sea for two years, and was a member subsequently of the North Cork Rifles, and for two years was on the staff. After retiring from the army in 1860 he became superintendent of the Borough forces of Belfast, including Police and Fire Brigade, and on the death of Mr. Braidwood, at the great fire in Tooley Street, in 1861 (which burned for a fortnight), was appointed to his present post. He is a deputy-lieutenant in Middlesex, and now a Companion of the Bath. In 1875 he drilled a force in Egypt for the Khedive.

Captain Shaw has been wounded twice very severely in the performance of his duty, and several times less so. In 1865 he visited America for the purpose of inspecting the principal Fire Departments in the country. Originally the London Fire Brigade was appointed by the fire insurance companies, but about twelve years ago the Metropolitan Board of Works took it in hand, and placed Captain Shaw at its head. There are, in the four districts into which he has divided London, fifty fire engine stations, one hundred and nine fire-escape stations, four floating stations, fifty-six telegraph lines, one hundred and four miles of telegraph lines, three floating steam fire engines, one iron barge to carry a land steam fire engine, three large land steam fire engines, twenty-six small land steam fire engines, twelve seven-inch manual fire engines, sixty six-inch manual fire engines, thirty-six under six-inch manual fire engines, seventeen hose carts, one hundred and twenty-five fire-escapes and long scaling ladders, and four hundred and twenty firemen, including the chief officer, the four superintendents, and all ranks.

The Avondale mine disaster, in the autumn of 1869, resulted in an appeal for aid for the families of the sufferers to the members of the Department, and Mr. C. E. Gildersleve, as treasurer of the fund, sent one thousand and twenty-two dollars and twenty-five cents to H. Gaylord, of Plymouth, Pa. On the twenty-fifth of October, 1860, the large death rate having increased the burdens of the Mutual Aid Society, the treasurer was authorized to donate two thousand dollars to it. November 1 a Bureau of Statistics was created, and a few days later, a complete Manual of Instruction for Commanding Officers of Engine and Hook and Ladder Companies in the care and use of their apparatus was issued. November 11 classes of instruction were formed for the instruction of officers of the Department in their duties under the direction of the president. There were three classes—the First, of the engineer officers; the Second, of the company commanders; and the Third, of company officers not in command. The chief engineer, when able, was required to attend the meetings of each class. Chief Kingsland's resignation was accepted, and complimentary resolutions on his administration were passed, when Joseph L. Perley was made his successor. His salary was four thousand five hundred dollars per annum, and that of the "Chiefs of Brigade," two thousand four hundred dollars per annum. The title of chief engineer was changed to "Chief of the Department," and the assistant engineers were made "Chiefs of Battalion," except R. V. Mackey, "Department Inspector," and William Brandon, Eli Bates and W. W. Rhodes, designated respectively as Chiefs of the First, Second and Third Brigades.

The year 1870 found the Legislature at Albany prepared and able to do the bidding of the ring, and it was evident the Fire Department would not be neglected. The commissioners, however, ignored the inevitable, and continued to perfect the system. January 13 an Examining Board was substituted for the Board of Officers. It was composed of the Chief of the Department, the Chiefs of Brigades, the Department Inspector, and the Medical Officer, who were to pass on the conduct and qualifications of the officers of the department. Chief Orr and Lieutenant Eyner, of Engine Company No. 34, were designated as Examiners of Engineers. February 14 two hundred thousand dollars was paid on account of the new telegraph to Chester & Co. In March the ringing of second and third alarms on the tower bells was discontinued, and only three rounds of first alarms was struck on them. March 16 the new telegraph system, with alarm signal boxes, as at present, was completed below Fourteenth Street, for signals 2 to 346, and on the thirty-first of March arrangements were made to connect Blackwell's, Ward's and Randall's Islands with the city by submarine telegraphy. The tower bells were then at the Post-office, Spring Street, Marion Street, Essex Market, Union Market, Jefferson Market, Twenty-fifth Street, Thirty-third Street, Fifty-first Street, Yorkville and Mount Morris.

The "Tweed Charter"—Chapter 137 of the Laws of 1870—was passed April

5, 1870. Henry Close was appointed superintendent of the repair yard, which was moved to Amity Street, now West Third Street, in the place of H. A. Gilbertson, at a salary of two thousand five hundred dollars. July 6, Foreman John L. Cregier, Engine Company No. 12, G. L. Tooker, Engine Company No. 34, A. C. Hull, Hook and Ladder Company No. 6, resigned to follow the fortunes of Commissioner Wilson, who had succeeded John Cornwell as superintendent of the fire insurance patrol. December 15, the committee on telegraph reported in favor of accepting C. T. & J. N. Chester's telegraph line above Fourteenth Street. On the first of January, 1871, alarm-signal boxes 351 to 919 went into service, as well as a complete system of "patrol beats." In March the bell at the Post-office tower ceased to strike, but the tower was used as a lookout station. Charles L. Chapin resigned as superintendent of telegraph, and C. Kinney Smith succeeded him. The office of assistant engineer of steamer, at eleven hundred dollars per annum, was created, and the complement of engine companies south of Twenty-third Street was fixed at one foreman or captain, one assistant foreman or lieutenant, one engineer or sergeant, one assistant engineer or corporal, and eight firemen or privates. North of Twenty-third Street each engine company had six firemen. In other respects the organization was the same. June 7, Charles E. Gildersleve resigned as secretary, and was appointed chief clerk of the Bureau of Combustibles, at a salary of two thousand five hundred dollars, and W. B. White was appointed secretary at the same salary. Dr. Charles McMillan had tendered his resignation, and was succeeded by Dr. Christopher Prince, whose salary was fixed at five thousand dollars per annum. June 28, Foreman Benjamin A. Gicquel, Engine Company No. 5, James H. Monroe, Hook and Ladder Company No. 8, and Walter T. Furlong, Engine Company No. 6, were promoted to the rank of chief of battalion.

The fall of the year 1871 saw the commissioners much embarrassed for want of funds. They had to go around, hat in hand, to procure a loan to pay their men. November 2, the Board met, to learn that the Board of Fire Underwriters had set apart one hundred and eighty-seven thousand dollars to meet the payrolls. Andrew H. Green, Deputy Comptroller, had deposited in the Department bank twenty-seven thousand one hundred and eighty-three dollars and thirty-four cents, the balance of the appropriation for 1871. Thomas F. Jeremiah was instrumental in getting the advance from the underwriters.

The firemen did full and satisfactory duty, nevertheless, and twenty-seven members of it, including Assistant Engineer Rhodes, were in the early morning of the eighth of November, injured to a greater or less degree, by the falling of a wall at No. 479 Sixth Avenue. November 22, at the suggestion of Chief Perley, a system of special telegraph calls and signals was adopted. His Imperial Highness, Alexis, Grand Duke of Russia, on the twenty-eighth of November, witnessed a parade of the Department, composed of three battalions under Chiefs Orr, Shay and Sullivan, and his praise at the appearance and organization of the apparatus and men was as warm as it was unstinted. When news of the condition of the firemen of Chicago, after the great fire there, was received, a subscription was raised for them by the Department, and two thousand six hundred and thirty dollars were collected and sent to Mayor Mason.

On December 20 the title of superintendent of telegraph was changed to chief of telegraph bureau, and the salary was made three thousand five hundred dollars. A week later, on motion of Commissioner Hennessy, the number of assistant engineers was increased to twelve.

The first days of 1872 saw the fire commissioners yet embarrassed for lack of funds to pay the members of the Department and meet obligations. Comptroller Andrew H. Green announced three hundred and fifty-two thousand two hundred and sixty-six dollars and seventeen cents appropriated for the Fire Department from January 1 to April 30, 1872. June 5 Inspectors Moore, Cregier, Forman and Keeler, of the Bureau of Combustibles, were discontinued, and John A. McCosker was appointed inspector at a salary of two thousand dollars per annum. June 22, by an explosion at No. 18 Liberty Street, twenty firemen were injured, and Edward Burke, of Engine Company No. 4, was killed. James Sutton & Co., of *The Aldine*, No. 23 Liberty Street, got up a subscription for the sufferers.

July 17 Assistant Engineer Eli Bates was appointed assistant to Chief Perley. The Post-office tower was finally abandoned September 24, 1872. The commissioners, during the month, again locked horns with the comptroller on a requisition from them for one hundred and twenty-five thousand dollars. Mr. Green held that, under the amended charter of 1870, the Fire Department had no right to a separate treasury and disbursing officer. Proceedings by mandamus were taken against the comptroller by the commissioners, but the Supreme Court denied the motion. The salaries were paid by the comptroller *pendente lite*. In October a system of ambulance calls over the fire wires was adopted.

On the twenty-first of November the commissioners estimated the expenses of the Department for 1873 at one million three hundred and sixty-four thousand nine hundred dollars, of which nine hundred and forty-four thousand four hundred dollars were for salaries; and asked for one hundred thousand dollars more for new buildings.

A detail of firemen of all grades attended the funeral of the Hon. Horace Greeley, on the fourth of December, 1872. On the last day of this year Mr. Alexander T. Stewart sent a contribution of one thousand dollars to the relief fund.

One of the first important acts of the year 1873 was the inspection of theaters and other buildings, with a view of discovering their weak points. January 31, Dr. Charles McMillan came back to the Department as associate medical officer.

April 30, 1873, the Legislature passed the charter of the committee of seventy, known as Chapter 335 of the Laws of 1873. It provided that the mayor—William F. Havemeyer—should nominate, and, by and with the consent of the Board of Aldermen, appoint three fire commissioners—one for two, another for four, and the third for six years, from the first of May, 1873, at a salary of five thousand dollars, except the president, whose salary was fixed at seven thousand dollars.

Although General Shaler framed that part of the act which related to the Fire Department, he was not destined to be a member of the Fire Department of the City of New York. Mayor Havemeyer, without solicitation, sent for Chief Perley, announced his intention of nominating him for commissioner, and he, Mr. Cornelius Van Cott, and Ex-Judge Roswell D. Hatch, were nominated and confirmed, Perley for six years, Hatch for four years, and Van Cott for two years. The Board organized on the nineteenth of May, 1873, by selecting Mr. Perley as president, and Mr. Hatch as treasurer; and the same day Eli Bates was appointed chief of the Department, and Charles Oscar Shay assistant chief. The same day General Shaler issued an address, in which he exhorted the officers and men to be obedient and do their duty under all circumstances.

Joseph L. Perley, born in New York, 1835, was a mechanical engineer. He went to public school (in those days called common school) old No. 5, at Stanton and Sheriff Streets. He learned his trade at Eckfort Iron Works, corner of Cannon and Stanton Streets. Mr. Perley joined the Department in 1856, about the time he came of age, having run as a volunteer for five years previously. He joined Live Oak Engine Company No. 44 in 1856. He was elected an assistant foreman in 1860, and almost immediately after assistant engineer. He served in the latter capacity until 1865. He was appointed under the Paid Department as first assistant engineer, and was assigned to duty in the lower section of the city, south of Canal Street, and at the same time placed in charge of the machinery of the Department and superintendent of the repair shops, all the engines having to be altered to the new system. In 1868 he was relieved from duty in the repair shop and was placed in command of that portion of the city north of Twenty-third Street, for the purpose of organizing the Department in that section. While so serving, in 1869, he was promoted to be chief of the Department, and so served until May, 1873, when Mayor Havemeyer requested him to accept the appointment of commissioner for six years. He was made president, serving for four years, and relieved in 1879.

When Chief Eli Bates retired from the new Department May 1, 1884, he ended a fireman's career which had lasted thirty-eight years and one day. A carpenter by trade, he had not passed his twenty-first birthday, on April 29, 1846, when he received his certificate, and joined Guardian Engine Company No. 29, located at Jefferson Market. His connection with the company lasted until 1862. In 1852 he became assistant foreman, and three years later was promoted to foreman. From 1862 until the volunteer organization was dissolved Mr. Bates performed the duties of assistant engineer, and he joined the Paid Department as district engineer, a rank now designated as chief of battalion. His district lay on the west side of the city, south of Forty-second Street. Later he was transferred to the east side, with Fourteenth Street as the north boundary of his district. In June, 1871, Mr. Bates was made assistant to Chief Perley, whom he succeeded in command of the Department May 19, 1873. For the next eleven years Chief Bates's gray horse and plain buggy were familiar to New Yorkers as they dashed through the streets in answer to alarms. The chief's quarters were with No. 9 Truck in Elizabeth Street, and he attended all fires south of Twenty-third Street. During his term of office there were several fires which caused immense property losses, but none where there was appalling loss of life. Three theaters—the Park, Windsor, and Standard—were burned within a short time, but the first and the last took fire before the time for the performance, while the Windsor began to blaze at midnight on Thanksgiving, 1883. Chief Bates was twice injured in the performance of duty. There was a fire at West and Murray Streets, January 4, 1867, when the ladder on which he was standing slipped, and his right knee was severely injured. Five years ago he entered a burning flour store in South Street, and fell while coming down-stairs. His chest struck heavily upon an iron girder, and his body was bruised over the ribs. In 1869 he was instrumental in saving a family on the fifth story of a house at Cherry and Montgomery Streets.

With other officers of the new Department in 1865 Chief Bates had many difficulties to fight. For the volunteer service—four thousand strong—were substituted five hundred men. The engines were feeble compared with those of the present day, and much of the hose was bad. Friends of the old and enemies of the new organization were ready to spy out defects and errors. There was practically no fire alarm telegraph, but signals were sent by bells and the police wires—two slow and uncertain methods. Except Engine 22, at Third Avenue and Eighty-fifth Street, the "full pay" companies were all south of Fifty-ninth Street. The upper part of the city was defended by volunteer companies, which each received one thousand dollars from the city per year for expenses. "Hosemen" and "laddermen" were paid for work at fires, but went on duty only when alarms sounded. To-day firemen ride to the spot where they are needed; then the machines were too light to carry them, and they had to run. The work was harder and the danger greater than now.

Efforts were made to turn the Robinson system of alarms to account, but they failed. On March 28, 1870, the present telegraph arrangement was ready for service below Fourteenth Street, but the poles were like angels' visits, "few and far between," and often the wires came down, so that there were long delays in getting apparatus at work. Chief Bates attached great importance to a perfect system of alarms. He claimed credit for the invention of the simultaneous call. There had been first, second, and third alarms, and special calls for particular companies, but no signal to bring a large force immediately to grapple with an immense fire. The chief's idea was approved by the commissioners, and an order announcing the new signal to the Department had been drawn up. Before it was officially promulgated, the big fire at No. 444 Broadway broke out, February 8, 1876. Chief Bates sounded his new call, but the telegraph operator at head-quarters refused to recognize it. A second alarm was then sent out from Broadway and Eleventh Street, and as fast as the companies arrived they were sent down to the fire. The order was promulgated without further delay. Although the simultaneous call is rarely heard, it has been used on several occasions when its usefulness was proven beyond question. One other reform Chief Bates instituted: Originally no matter how threatening the fire was, the first, second, and third alarms were sent out in regular order. Now an officer, believing that the circumstances demand it, may send out a third alarm when the fire is discovered.

On two occasions Chief Bates performed fire duty beyond the city limits. Both times the fire was in the Export Lumber Company's yard at Long Island City. The second, and more severe fire, was in the autumn of 1880, when Chief Bates went to the rescue with the fireboat *Havemeyer*. He pushed up the pellucid waters of Newtown Creek, and had to fight the fire from the leeward side. Smoke was blown upon the boat in clouds, and sparks fell upon her in showers. The men demurred, but the chief refused to give up the fight, and held his position until the flames were subdued. Mayor-elect Grace, who had watched the struggle, congratulated the chief upon the success of his pluck. Since his retirement ex-Chief Bates has lived in a pleasant cottage in Harlem.

CHAPTER XXIV

THE DEPARTMENT GAINS
IN EFFICIENCY

*Appointment of a Fire Marshal.—A Corps of Sappers and Miners.—
Steamboats Havemeyer and Mills.—Business Rules and Regulations.—
Superintendent of Buildings.—English and American Fire Services.—
Instructions in Life Saving.—Several Destructive Fires.—The Dry Goods
District.—President Purroy's Water Tank.*

The new Board speedily availed themselves of the sweeping provisions of the law which legislated out of office all but the foremen and members of engine and hook and ladder companies. At about this time peculiar influences which, later on, led to a fearful accident and well-grounded accusations of job-bery and corruption, introduced to the commissioners and Secretary White, Mrs. Mary Belle Scott Uda, a fascinating woman, who procured a patent right for a life-saving and hose-carrying apparatus, known as an aerial ladder, and she was favored in June with tests of her apparatus. William Matthews was made foreman of the machine shops, under Chief of Battalion Orr. Edward Savage was made chief book-keeper at a salary of $2,500 per annum.

The estimate of expenses for 1874 was made at $1,455,011. September 10, the Bureau of Combustibles was moved to Firemen's Hall. Hook and Ladder Company No. 16 was organized on the old Bloomingdale Road, between Ninety-seventh and Ninety-eighth streets, on the 23d of October, 1873.

Under the Act of May 23d, 1873 (afterward amended to Chapter 329 of the Laws of 1873), "to provide for the annexation of the towns of Morrisania, West Farms and Kings Bridge, in the County of Westchester, to the City and County of New York," the Board, on the 21st of November, instructed Superintendent Smith to inspect the territory and report on telegraphic facilities, and Chief Bates was directed to estimate the number of men and apparatus necessary to cover the new district.

Under the Act of the 12th of June, 1873, the corps of sappers and miners was organized. Chief Shay had command of it, and, on the 10th of December, 1873, Julius H. Striedinger was, on the recommendation of Brevet Major General John Newton, United States Engineers, appointed Instructor of the Corps of Sappers and Miners at $2,000 a year. December 24th, J. Elliott Smith, the present

Superintendent of Telegraph, was appointed Assistant Telegraph Operator at a salary of $1,200. The force of the Department in the Twenty-third and Twenty-fourth wards was established at two steam engine companies, four chemical engine companies, and two hook and ladder companies, to be known as the Tenth Battalion, and Engine Companies Nos. 41 and 42, Chemical Engine Companies Nos. 1, 2, 3 and 4, and Hook and Ladder Companies Nos. 17 and 18.

The regulations for these companies provided, among other rules, as follows:

> The hosemen and laddermen herein provided for shall receive pay at the rate of three hundred dollars per annum, sleep in the engine and truck houses, attend all fires, conform to the rules and regulations that are now, or may hereafter be prescribed, attend at the houses of their respective companies on two afternoons in each month, to be designated by the Battalion Commander, for inspection or practice, assist in cleaning the apparatuses and horses after each fire alarm, and in policing the houses when required by the Company Commander, and shall have the privilege of pursuing their avocations at points convenient to the houses of their respective companies. They will also be required to provide themselves with the uniform, which shall consist of a uniform-coat, shirt, fire-cap and fatigue-cap, as prescribed by General Order No. 1, series 1868, office Chief Engineer, and, in addition thereto, dark blue or black cloth trowsers will be worn when on duty.

In December, $1,274 were subscribed by the firemen for the firemen of Memphis, Tenn., who suffered from the scourge of yellow fever.

The first noteworthy event of 1874 was a resolution to propose plans and specifications for a first-class Department fire-boat. At the end of January Assistant Chief Engineer Shay planned the organization of the Corps of Sappers and Miners, and his scheme was approved.

In February certain company quarters were turned into soup kitchens to enable Lorenzo Delmonico to properly dispense the bounty of Mr. James Gordon Bennett, of the *Herald*.

May 15th the revised estimate of expenses of the Fire Department for 1874 was $1,608,654.33. June 24th, Superintendent of Telegraph C. K. Smith resigned, and John H. Emerich succeeded him. William H. Sawyer, Commissioner Hatch's candidate for Superintendent, was made Chief Operator, but he failed to qualify, and, two months later, J. Elliott Smith was given the position. In August, Sharmon Ross rebuilt the Amity Street repair shops, and Wood, Dialogue & Co., of Philadelphia, were awarded the contract for the new steam Fire-boat, their bid being $23,800. In September the estimate of expenses for the Department for 1875 was $1,436,932. In October self-propelling engines were given to Companies 8, 11, 24 and 32. The police boat *Seneca* was equipped for use as a fire-boat. Suitable resolutions were passed December 2d on the death of Mayor William F. Havemeyer, and his memory was officially honored.

During 1874 the Bureau of Combustibles waged war on the dealers in dangerous vinorem, and secured convictions which resulted in driving the stuff out of the market and lessening the number of fires and accidents by it.

In January, 1875, the final estimates of the year were fixed by the Board of Apportionment at $1,316,000. The Committee on Discipline was discontinued, so the Fire Board tried delinquents. January 27, to oust a Chief of Battalion, a resolution was passed directing the Chief Engineer to select ten persons as Chiefs of Battalion from the uniformed force. Monroe was a week later reduced to the rank of Foreman, and sent to Hook and Ladder Company, No. 9, against the wish of President Perley, and E. W. Wilhelm was made Chief of Battalion.

The new steam fire-boat was, on motion of Commissioner Van Cott, named the *William F. Havemeyer.*

Engine Company, No. 39, was organized in March in Sixty-seventh Street, between Third and Lexington Avenues. In April preparations were made to man the *Havemeyer.* Its complement was arranged as follows: One Foreman, one Assistant Foreman, one Engineer, One Pilot and five firemen. Chemical Engine Companies, Nos. 5 and 6, were organized, the former at No. 304 West Forty-seventh Street, and the latter at No. 77 Canal Street, April 17th.

April 28th the *Havemeyer* was reported finished. She was berthed at Pier No. 1, North River.

Vincent C. King was foreman of Hose Company No. 23 from 1853 to 1858. He was also, for four years Commissioner of the Board of Appeal in the Volunteer Fire Department from 1860 to 1864. In 1875 he was appointed Commissioner by Mayor Wickham in the new Paid Fire Department and remained in that position for six years. He was President of the Board for four years when the salary was $7,500 a year, the other commissioners receiving $5,000 a year. The original commissioners of the new Fire Department were Philip W. Engs, Martin B. Brown, James W. Booth and William Hitchman. They had $10,000 a year. But this was cut down subsequently to $5,000 and made the uniform salary for all the commissioners as it is to-day. Altogether in the old and new Fire Departments Mr. King spent over twenty years.

"What was the difference," Mr. King was asked by the writer, "between the old and the new Fire Department?"

"Well," he replied, "they have better engines in the present Department and they have the use of steam to pump and work their supply of water, and they may be able to send a stream of water to a much higher altitude than could be done by the old engines, but the old engines had but one advantage that the present ones have not. There was then a strong and abundant flow of Croton water and it was half the battle in a big fire as it came with a rush from the hydrants. Under the circumstances of the city at the time the Department was equal to every emergency of fire because there were no big buildings then, few higher than three stories and the firemen were able to control them. But there were engines in those days that could throw a stream of water over Reilly's liberty pole, down near Franklin Street and West Broadway, 175 feet high. Reilly (I guess he was the original one) kept a hotel and the boys used to bring their engines down just for the fun of seeing which of them could make the biggest shoot of water. It used to stir up the greatest excitement."

Peter Weir was born in the Sixth Ward about 1840. He joined Fulton Engine Company No. 21 and was elected successively representative, assistant foreman and foreman. In 1865 he was elected assistant engineer and served as such until the Paid Department was organized. He was appointed foreman of Engine Company No. 31. He commanded this company until 1871 when he was transferred to Engine Company No. 25, located in the house formerly occupied by Black Joke Engine Company No. 33. He continued in command of this until his death. Chief Gicquel said: "Peter Weir was a genial, whole-souled man, beloved by everybody. He was one of the hardest worked men in the Department. His name was placed on the roll of merit for gallantry. In appearance he was anything but a dude, but he was every inch a fireman. A better one I don't believe the Department has ever seen. He rarely wore a fire cap at a fire. He seemed to be utterly oblivious of everything, except the fire, when on duty. His death was brought about by over-exertion and exposure."

The collapse of the aerial ladder scheme occurred on the 14th of September, 1875, on the Tweed Plaza, at Canal Street and East Broadway. Several public trials of the invention had been given, and the dangerous character of the apparatus had been commented on. On one occasion, when one of the ladders appeared to be about to topple over, Chief Bates prevented it by slashing a line, which was carried to the top of the ladder. The final experiment was made on the Plaza, in the presence of a vast crowd of spectators and many firemen and others interested in such matters. The ladder was raised in eight sections to a height of ninety-seven feet, and Chief William H. Nash, of the Fourth Battalion, ascended, followed by Fireman Philip J. Maus, of Hook and Ladder Company No. 6; Fireman William Hughes, of Engine Company No. 6, four other firemen and an assistant engineer. Chief Nash had reached the summit of the ladder, when it snapped far below him and dashed Nash, Maus and Hughes, who were above the fracture, to the cobble-stones of the square. Nash and Maus were instantly killed, and Hughes died within an hour. No one else was injured. The accident revived gossip, which charged a corrupt understanding with Mrs. Uda, and the payment of a large portion of the $25,000 she received from the city for her rights, and public indignation ran to an intense pitch. The Fire Commissioners promptly sat down on the aerial business.

September 15th Commissioner King offered a resolution, which was adopted, prohibiting the further use of ladders, as it had been demonstrated that they were useless, and there was good reason to believe that the invention was foisted on the Department at an enormous expense and by corrupt means.

Chief Nash was, during the war, a member of Berdan's Corps of Sharpshooters, and attained the rank of Assistant Adjutant General. He was buried from 149 Clinton Street, and his funeral was attended by six companies formed of details from the various battalions.

The Board had been for six months without a treasurer, when, on the 8th of November, Mr. King having signified his declination of the office, and Mr. Hatch refusing to serve, President Perley took the position. In December the Automatic Signal Company were authorized to make connections for the transmission of fire signals. At midnight, December 31, 1875, the fire bells rang out: "1-7-7-6—1-8-7-6," amid the clang of other bells, firework detonations, cheers and the discharge of fire-arms.

February 8, 1876, saw one of the most destructive fires New York had ever had. It broke out at 6:25 P.M., at No. 444 Broadway, destroyed, or partly destroyed and damaged 22 buildings, occupied by 37 firms, and the loss on an insurance of $3,418,099.97 was $1,750,000. While firemen were keeping a safe in the ruins of No. 444 Broadway cool with a line of hose, a wall fell and killed Foreman David Clute and David Muldrew, of Engine Company No. 30, and so injured Assistant Foreman John H. Bush, of the same company, that he died. Thomas J. Cortissos, also of the same company, was laid up for several months with injuries received.

In May new and complete regulations for the government of the Fire Alarm Telegraph, a revised code of signal stations, and new assignments to duty at them were promulgated, bringing the system up to that of the present day.

June 7, Medical Officer Dr. McMillan resigned, and was succeeded by Dr. A. J. Minor, the vice medical officer. Dr. Frank L. Ives was made vice medical officer. In September the estimate for the expenses of 1877 was made at $1,249,386. On the 22d of December Col. Carl Jussen was made Secretary of the Board.

Colonel Carl Jussen, Secretary to the Board of Fire Commissioners, was born January 2d, 1843, in Julich, Rhenish Prussia. His family emigrated to this country in 1848, and after a sojourn of six months, settled in Columbus, Wisconsin, where his father engaged in business, and five years later removed to Watertown, Wisconsin. He received a common-school education in both places, and was also taught German by his mother, who superintended his education. In 1858 he went to Chicago, and served a two year-apprenticeship to an architect, returning to Watertown in 1860. He read law for a few months in the office of his brother in Madison, Wisconsin, and at the age of nineteen, in 1862, enlisted in the 23d Regiment, Wisconsin Volunteers (Infantry). He was made sergeant of Co. D before leaving the camp of instruction and rendezvous, and was promoted Sergeant-Major in May, 1863, and Adjutant in August, 1863. He was detailed as acting Assistant Adjutant General of the Third Brigade, Second Division, 10th Army Corps, and subsequently as Aide-de-Camp to Brigadier-General Alexander Shaler, then commanding first a brigade of the Reserve Corps of the Mississippi, and last the Third Division Seventh Army Corps, and the geographical district of the White River, Arkansas. He participated in a bloodless campaign in Kentucky to the fall of 1862, then in the attack on Vicksburg from the north at the close of that year, the division resulting in the capture of Arkansas Post on the Arkansas River; the Vicksburg campaign under General Grant in 1863; the Bayou Teche campaign later in the same year; an expedition to Matagorda Bay, Texas, early in 1864; the disastrous Red River campaign in the spring of the same year; the expedition to Mobile Bay in the same year, and numerous small expeditions and raids. When Colonel Jussen was mustered out of service and honorably discharged on July 4th, 1865, he returned to Watertown, Wis., and engaged in business, remaining there until September, 1866, when he removed to this city. He was employed as draughtsman in the office of Renwick & Sands, architects, and was appointed clerk in the Fire Department in 1867. In 1875, was detailed as acting Secretary, and appointed Secretary on January 1, 1877.

Colonel Jussen was married on October 14, 1868, to Camilla J. Shaler, oldest daughter of General Shaler, and has four children. At the same time he was appointed Aide-de Camp by General Shaler, Quartermaster on January 1, 1873, and Division Inspector on October 5, 1874, which latter position he still holds, having also served almost continuously as Acting Assistant Attorney General of the First Division N. G. S. N. Y. in charge of the headquarter's records.

The fire at the Brooklyn Theatre, on the night of the 5th of December, 1876, by which from 250 to 290 persons lost their lives—the number of victims could only be computed, after positive identification of the majority of them, from stray limbs and ashes, and reports of those who met them on the night of the disaster, never to be seen again—awakened a live and earnest interest in the condition of places of assembly in New York. On the 2d of January, 1877, an order was issued directing proper and complete examinations of theatres to discover how the public were protected, and to secure reports of what was needed to prevent such a disaster in this city.

Dr. A. J. Minor, medical officer, resigned in January, 1877, and was succeeded by Vice Medical Officer L. F. Ives, whose position was accepted by Dr. Pierre C. F. Des Landes. The cutting down of the estimates necessitated the creation of the rank of private, at $800 a year for new appointees. March 28th, Mr. C. De F. Burns, Librarian of the Lyceum, was appointed Assistant Secretary. The recommendations to managers of places of public amusement not having been generally complied with, the Board directed the delinquents to procure proper means for extinguishing and preventing fires without delay, by virtue of the power given them in Section 5, Chapter 742, of the Laws of 1871, and persisted until they were obeyed.

John J. Gorman, nominated by Mayor Smith Ely, Jr., was confirmed January 3d to succeed Judge Hatch. Mr. King was elected President, and Gorman Treasurer. Mr. John J. Gorman is a native type of the self-made New Yorker. He was born in this city October 5, 1828, and educated in Public School No. 3, corner of Grove and Hudson Streets. At the age of eighteen he became a member of the Volunteer Fire Department (May 12, 1846), and from that date was a prominent member in several companies. At the disbandment of the Volunteer Fire Department he was foreman of Exempt Fire Engine Company.

Few men now living can point to a record of greater activity and usefulness in Fire Department matters than Mr. Gorman. The highest offices and honors in the Department have been successively bestowed upon him in recognition of his services. He was elected Fire Commissioner in the old Department, May 12, 1859, and held that position until 1862; during the last two years of that period he was President of the Board. In 1865 he was elected a Trustee of the Widows' and Orphans' Fund and elected Secretary thereof, which position he held successively for nineteen years; on the twentieth year he was chosen President of the Fund, which office he still holds. In May, 1877, Mr. Gorman was appointed Fire Commissioner of the Department as now organized, and continued in the Board until November 15, 1883, at which date he resigned, and was appointed one of the Police Magistrates of the city, which position he now occupies. During his terms of Fire Commissioner he introduced numerous improvements, and while President of said Board prepared and introduced a series of invaluable rules and regulations, one of which, regarding the mode for prevention of fire or panic in theaters, was favorably received.

On the organization of the widely known "Free Masons' Club," of this city, he was chosen President, and during its existence devoted considerable time and attention to its interests. In fact, no institution or society has ever been neglected where he was placed in a position of trust and confidence.

Jacob Springsteed, Superintendent of Horses, resigned June 13th, 1877. In July the question of moving the telegraph operators from the first floor of Firemen's Hall to the third floor was considered, and preparations were made to fit up the new quarters. In August, William Terhune, Inspector of Combustibles, was removed and succeeded by Peter Seery, and James Cummings, Property-clerk, was succeeded by Samuel T. Keese. Commissioner Perley voted against these changes as against the removal of several clerks. The estimates for 1878 were made at $1,234,870. September 19th, Dr. Pierre F. C. Des Landes, medical officer, was removed, and Dr. Marion S. Butler was appointed. September 21st, Theodore Elliott, Foreman of Stables, was made Superintendent of Horses. October 23d, arrangements were made to have the gate-house of the Reservoir at Central Park connected with Firemen's Hall by telegraph, to enable the operators to signal for increased pressure of water when a large fire occurred. Pearce & Jones's bids of $7,300 for apparatus for the new telegraph plant, and one of $2,874 for the cabinet and woodwork were accepted in October.

Early in January interest in the cases of several clerks who had been removed, and who sought reinstatement in the courts, centered on the proceedings in Supreme Court, General Term. Ex-Commissioner Roswell D. Hatch appeared for the clerks, and Assistant Corporation Counsel Dean for the commissioners. The clerks who undertook the proceedings were Joseph H. Munday, Michael F. Cummings and David Graham. The clerks removed were called up to say why they should not be ousted because their duties could be better performed by some one else. Judges Davis and Daniels concurred in Judge Brady's decision in favor of the clerks, who were reinstated.

The problem arising from the tendency to high buildings, and an unsatisfactory water supply which prevented operations on the upper floors, was the subject of serious consideration, and on the 28th of January, 1878, John Ericsson, Charles H. Haswell and Julius H. Striedinger, Civil Engineer and Assistant Chief of the Department, C. O. Shay, were created a Board of Survey to test the aerial ladders in the possession of the Department, and report on their safety and efficiency. Mr. Ericsson did not serve. Mr. Haswell simply reported plans to improve the aerial ladders, but they were never carried out. The aerial ladders were never again used, and the one which broke on the Tweed Plaza was broken up at the repair shops. The three others were sold in 1885.

In February, were drawn up and promulgated business-like rules and regulations for the guidance and direction of heads of department superintendents, clerks and employees. March 13th, William Terhune, the reinstated Inspector of Combustibles, was removed, and Peter Seery was appointed. The same month Chief Orr, of the repair shop, was busy with several sets of swinging harness— a California invention now in general use here—which accelerated hitching up in an extraordinary degree. The new telegraph office was ready for occupation on the 26th of March, 1878. In April, in order that the means of communicating alarms of fire be less restricted, the commissioners sanctioned the delivery of keys for street boxes to responsible citizens. The spring and summer of the year were uneventful so far as the history of the growth and progress of the Department are concerned. In August the estimates of the expenses for 1879 were made at $1,291,842.50, which were subsequently cut down to $1,254,970, including

$30,000 for three new quarters for apparatus. In October, President Gorman reported his visit to the National Firemen's Tournament at Chicago, under resolution of the Board of August 7th, and submitted specifications and drawings of the Corps of Pompiers of St. Louis. November 26th, Assistant Fire Marshal Orr was removed for violating rules and causing false reports of official doings to be published, and ex-Trustee William Dodge succeeded him. Early in the autumn a subscription was started in the Department in aid of the Firemen's Charitable Association of New Orleans, to assist those who suffered from the yellow-fever epidemic. Nearly $2,160 was collected, of which $500 went to Memphis; and the firemen of this city sold 1,160 tickets for a concert given at Gilmore's Garden, in aid of the sufferers, by the Firemen's Ball Committee of the Old Volunteer Fire Department. In December, the Firemen's Lyceum was divided into two equal parts, one of which was placed in each of the battalions of the Department as a Battalion Library, and the Assistant Foreman of the battalion quarters was designated as Librarian, and Assistant Secretary Charles De F. Burns was appointed General Librarian. The ringing of the tower bells south of 59th Street was discontinued on the 21st of December.

January, 1879, tested the resources of the Fire Department, and many persons were injured. On the 7th, J. W. Irving of Engine 29 was killed at No. 75 Vesey Street. January 14th, 23 engines and 7 hook and ladder companies were called to a fire which extended from No. 458 to No. 472 Broadway and No. 134 to 136 Grand Street, and caused a loss of $1,321,973.05. Fireman John Reilly, of Engine 17, was killed. January 17th, a fire started at No. 62 and 64 Worth Street, destroyed 4 buildings and damaged 13 others in Worth, Thomas, Duane, Church and Leonard Streets, and 48 firms lost $1,976,735. January 30th, Fireman Edward McGaffney, of Engine 33, had his sight destroyed at a fire at No. 483 and 485 Broadway. The families of the killed and the injured men were relieved by generous subscriptions and the proceeds of an entertainment at Niblo's Garden.

When the Legislature of 1879 met, various schemes to upset the Board of Fire Commissioners were started. Matters went so far that the candidates for four commissionerships to be created were named, but, on May 6th, Mayor Edward Cooper nominated Cornelius Van Cott to succeed Commissioner Perley, whose term of office had expired, and he was confirmed on the 20th of May. Two days later he again sat in the Board as Commissioner.

Cornelius Van Coot, who succeeded Commissioner Perley in the Board of Fire Commissioners, was born in the City of New York, in the Fifteenth Ward, on President Lincoln's birthday, February 12, 1838. He was educated in Public School No. 16, in Thirteenth Street, of which David Patterson was the distinguished principal. He had an early love for books, and chose first the printer's trade, entering the establishment of the old American Tract Society. Subsequently he was apprenticed to Messrs. Dusenbury & Van Dusen, and learned the trade of carriage building. Mr. Van Dusen was foreman of Southwark Engine 38, then located in Ann Street. Young Van Cott quickly got a liking for the fireman's life, and in 1858, when twenty years old, joined Hose Company No. 7. From the very first he was in favor of a paid department. Mr. Van Cott was appointed an Inspector of Customs, a post which he surrendered to engage in the fire insurance business. After he had been elected a director of Ætna Fire Insurance Company (of which Colonel F. A. Conkling was president) he held for several years the office of vice-president of that corporation. He developed into a sound and capable financier, and in time became known as a first-class underwriter. He was also connected with the Hanover Insurance Company, and for a number of years has been a trustee of the West Side Savings Bank.

His education and his training peculiarly fitted him for the office of Fire Commissioner, and in 1873 Mayor Havemeyer appointed him to a seat in the Board. Mr. Van Cott served for six years and was finally elected treasurer. His services were recognized by a graceful testimonial from members of New York's best known merchants and business men. When Mayor Cooper came into power, 1879, Mr. Van Cott was reappointed by him, and his fellow commissioners elected him President of the Board, May 9, 1881. Shortly after he resigned the post of President. It was a great tribute to his integrity and ability that he (a Republican) should have been appointed by a Democratic Mayor and confirmed by a Democratic Board of Aldermen. Subsequently he was re-elected treasurer and again elected President in 1883. His term of office expired in 1885.

Among the acts which distinguished Mr. Van Cott while a Fire Commissioner were the abolition of bell-ringing (which latterly had become a nuisance), the repeal of the law passed for the removal of the Forty-second Street reservoir, the enlarging of the mains in the lower part of the city, the construction of floating steam fire engines, and the appointment of a municipal fire marshal independent of the insurance companies. He was in charge of the repair shops, and his mechanical knowledge was here eminently useful.

Ever punctual, strict as a disciplinarian, having a thorough knowledge of the minutest details of everything connected with the Department, always ready to listen to suggestions for the advancement of the interests of the service and every member connected with it, he had rendered himself by those means one of the most popular of Fire Commissioners.

June 16th, Foreman John McCabe, of Engine Company No. 14, took charge of the repair shops, and Chief Orr was sent to the Tenth Battalion. Serious charges were made against him, but he defeated them, and entirely vindicated himself. At this time Abner Greenleaf's portable water tower had been tested and put into service with a view of buying it. The first public test was in Washington Square, and the advantages of the apparatus were immediately recognized.

In July the position of Chief Operator was abolished, and J. Elliott Smith was appointed Assistant Superintendent of Telegraph. In August the fire-boat *Havemeyer* was sent to her new berth at Pier No. 1, North River. The estimate of expenses for 1880 was made at $1,333,860, including $30,000 for three new company quarters, and $1,307,670 were appropriated. In November Fireman Henry C. Mount was fatally injured at a fire at the Eighth Avenue car stables, Forty-ninth Street and Eighth Avenue, and his family were placed beyond the reach of poverty by subscriptions.

January 28, 1880, Foreman John J. Bresnan, of Engine Company No. 33, and Francis J. Reilly, of Hook and Ladder Company No. 1, were made chiefs of battalion. Preparations were made to give the Blackwell's Island institutions and their inmates additional protection against fire by the construction of quarters for an engine. January 31st J. H. Emerich, Superintendent of Telegraph, was removed, and J. Elliott Smith was promoted to fill the vacancy. A. W. Parmelee was made Assistant Superintendent, and resigned; but two days later the office of Superintendent and Assistant Superintendent were abolished, and those of Chief Operator and Assistant Chief Operator were created for Foreman Thomas Hutchinson and J. Elliott Smith, respectively. In February the officers and men of the Department were permitted to collect subscriptions for the *Herald* Irish Famine Fund, and paid in $3,062.77. February 30th a fierce and uncontrollable fire broke out in the subcellar of Nos. 384 and 386 Broadway, spread to and damaged seven other Broadway buildings, and two in White Street, did $750,000 damage, and called into service 23 engines and 10 hook and ladder companies. By the collapse of the building, due to improper foundations, Firemen Thomas J. Dougherty and John L. Cassidy, of Hook and Ladder Company No. 1, went down with the roof to their death. Subscriptions for their families realized $2,955, Dieckerhoff, Raffloer & Co. subscribing $250. Tefft, Griswold & Co. and other firms were equally generous. The Fire Commissioners ordered an investigation, and, on March 3d, Mr. Van Cott reported that the falling of the floors and roof of Nos. 384 and 386 Broadway were due to the supports of the central girder granite piers in the subcellar and iron columns in the basement, and Chief Bates was directed to report on all buildings similarly perilous in case of fire.

Under the Consolidation Act (Chapter 551 of the Laws of 1880) the Fire Commissioners, on the 3d of June, called on Henry J. Dudley, late Superintendent of Buildings, to turn over to the Board all papers, etc., in his custody, and to give his consent in writing to the transfer of the unexpended balance of the appropriation for the Department of Buildings for 1880 to the Fire Department, and the Board of Estimate and Apportionment was asked for such balance, amounting to $29,315.76. Mr. Dudley got out a writ of prohibition from Judge

Joseph Potter, of the Supreme Court, against the Fire Commissioners. William L. Findley was, on the 4th of June, appointed Attorney to the Fire Department under the Consolidation Act, and on July 1st the position of Chief Operator and Assistant Chief Operator of Fire Alarm Telegraph were abolished, and that of Superintendent of Fire Alarm Telegraph created, and J. Elliott Smith was made Superintendent. At this time Abner Greenleaf introduced the water tower to the notice of the commissioners. It seemed to meet a want of an apparatus to throw a strong stream into the upper floors of buildings, and was taken on test. July 27th, Mr. Dudley submitted gracefully to an adverse decision of Justice Potter, and surrendered his office and records. Assistant Fire Marshal William Dodge was placed in charge of them, at No. 2 Fourth Avenue, and on the 29th of July William P. Esterbrook was made Inspector of Buildings, with a salary of $4,000 per annum, by the votes of Commissioners Van Cott and Gorman. Commissioner King voted for T. H. McAvoy. Edward G. Dumahaut was made Chief Clerk under Mr. Esterbrook, and in a short time the Bureau was further organized, as follows: Wm. H. Clare, Record Clerk; John J. Tindale, Plan Clerk; J. J. Carroll, Charles M. Seibert and Jas J. Giblin, clerks; Charles K. Hyde, Chief Examiner; Andrew Owens, Assistant Chief Examiner, and E. C. Maloy, William Winterbottom, P. B. McGivin, Henry LaForge, John Hughes, Patrick Tallon, John Riley, Robert V. MacKay and John H. Hyatt, Examiners. The Bureau speedily settled down to work. August 9th the Chief of the Department ordered an inspection of buildings to ascertain deficiencies in fire escapes, whether by absence, faulty construction or obstruction, and the Board directed Chief Bates and Assistant Chief Shay to examine all buildings in course of erection, construction or alteration, and report any violation or evasion of law, and officers and members of the Department were required to see that laws in relation to camp-stools and other obstructions in aisles, lobbies and other passages in places of amusement were strictly enforced. In September the estimate of the expenses of the Department were made at $1,568,959, including $60,000 for "a new floating engine," and $36,000 for the Bureau of Inspection of Buildings. In October Theodore Elliot, Superintendent of Horses, was succeeded by Frederick G. Gale.

In November and December Charles Oscar Shay, Assistant Chief of the Department, made, by order of the Board, the most exhaustive tests of the different capacities of several steam fire engines that have ever been made by any Fire Department officer. His reports are regarded to-day as texts for all engineers. They were with the Ahrens Manufacturing Company's engine, from Company 13; the Clapp & Jones engine, from Company 33, and the Manchester Locomotive Works' (Amoskeag) engine, from Company 20. The final results were as follows:

GENERAL AVERAGES.

ENGINES.	STEAM PRESSURE.	WATER PRESSURE.	PRESSURE AT PIPES.
No. 13	120.83	166.70	88.38
No. 20	101.64	143.14	74.54
No. 33	110.83	173.55	93.03

DISTANCE THROWING.

Distance in feet water was thrown, each engine tested three minutes each hour. The last two hours of trial distance not taken.

TIME.	7 to 8	8 to 9	9 to 10	10 to 11	11 to 12	12 to 1	1 to 2	2 to 3
Engine No. 13 ..	205	220	190	240	225	185	210	210
Engine No. 20 ..				205	200	220	180	. . .
Engine No. 33 ..	230	235	230	230	230	235	220	215

AMOUNT OF COAL CONSUMED.

All Engines ....17,028 lbs.

Of which Engine No. 13 consumed ....4,960 lbs. 6 hours' work

Of which Engine No. 20 consumed ....5,692 lbs. 5½ hours' work

Of which Engine No. 33 consumed ....6,694 lbs. 8½ hours' work

AVERAGE PER HOUR.

Engine No. 13 consumed............................... 496 lbs. per hour

Engine No. 20 consumed............................ 993½ lbs. per hour

Engine No. 33 consumed............................ 776⅞ lbs. per hour

During the year "four-way" connections for concentrating water from one to four engines were applied to Hook and Ladder Companies 1, 3, 5, 6, 8, 9, 10 and 12, to reach the tops of high buildings with powerful streams.

In January, 1881, Dr. Samuel M. Johnson was appointed Vice Medical Officer. Charles H. Haswell was directed to prepare plans and specifications for a new floating engine. In March Chief Bates and Assistant Chief Shay were created engineers by the Board for the purposes of Section 3, of Chapter 726, Laws of 1873, giving the "Engineers in command" at a fire authority to raze by explosion any building, or buildings, to arrest the progress of a fire. The city was divided into two medical districts, divided by Broadway, Twenty-third Street and Fourth Avenue to Fordham. March 30th the tests of the water tower had been so sat-

isfactory that the commissioners recommended its purchase for $4,000 to the Common Council. May 9th Cornelius Van Cott was elected President of the Board, and a week after Captain McCabe was made Chief of Battalion. In August Mr. Van Cott resigned as President, and became Treasurer, Mr. John J. Gorman taking the vacant position. September 13th Henry D. Purroy was confirmed as Commissioner, vice Vincent C. King, on a nomination of Mayor William R. Grace, made on the 10th of May, 1880, and laid on the table.

Henry D. Purroy was born in this city on August 27th, 1848. He was the son of the late John B. Purroy, a prominent lawyer many years ago in this city. He was educated in St. John's College, Fordham, and admitted to the bar November, 1869. He was the first representative for the annexed district in the Board of Aldermen, and was President of the Board. Mr. Purroy is a Democrat in politics, and until 1881 was connected with Tammany Hall, having been one of the thirteen Sachems in 1879, 1880 and 1881, and chairman of its Executive Committee during 1880. He joined the County Democracy in 1884, and is now Chairman of its Executive Committee. He was appointed Fire Commissioner in 1881—elected President of the Fire Department in 1885. He introduced many improvements into the Department, among them being the establishment (two years prior to the Civil Service Act) of a School of Probation of applicants for appointment as firemen, the organization of the Life Saving Corps the remodelling of the Department houses, the building of the fire boat, etc., etc.

On the 29th of September the estimate for 1882 was made at $1,498,850, including $134,000 for new quarters. The amount of $1,464,200 was appropriated. October 8th the Examining Board and Examining Board of Engineers were consolidated with Chiefs Shay, Bonner, Rowe, Denman and Reilly as its members. October 10th seventeen engines and six hook and ladder companies battled for 18 hours with a fire that destroyed and damaged the stables of the Fourth Avenue Railroad Company and other of their property, the Morrell storage warehouse and dwellings, and caused a loss estimated at $2,392,691. Foreman D. J. Meagher and Fireman Thos. Carney, of Hook and Ladder Company No. 3, and Private John Flanagan, of Engine Company No. 1, were slightly injured while at work. October 14th Chief of Battalion Gilbert J. Orr was relieved from active service, but retained as a member of the uniformed force at a salary of $1,250 per annum, and Chief of Battalion W. W. Rhodes was retired on a similar pension. Next day Foreman Michael F. Reeves and Francis Mahedy were made Chiefs of Battalion. In November the Board accepted an offer of the Standard Oil Company of the service at fire in New York of the company's boats Standard, F. W. De Voe, Daylight, Brilliant and C. R. Stone. November 9th the rickety buildings, Nos. 53 and 55 Grand street, condemned by the Department fell, killing 9 persons and injuring 5. The commissioners instituted a searching investigation and passed resolutions to take such action official and legislative to prevent such calamities in the future. An investigation resulted in the removal of Chief Examiner Charles K. Hyde, of the Bureau of Inspection of Buildings, for neglect of duty.

In November, Commissioner Purroy reported $2,371.75 collected from the members and employees of the Department for the relief of the sufferers by the forest fires in Michigan.

December 12th, the frightful calamity of the Ring Theatre, at Vienna, prompted the following resolution and subsequent satisfactory action:

> *Resolved,* That an immediate inspection be made of all theatres and places of amusement wherein machinery and scenery are used in the city of New York by the Chiefs of Battalions in their respective districts, with directions to make a detailed report of such inspection in writing to this Board, with an accurate description of each structure, the material of which it is constructed, its size and seating capacity, the location of the dressing-rooms, carpenter and paint shops, the facilities for egress in case of fire or other alarm, stating width of entrances and exits, the method of sending out an alarm, and the exact distance from stage to alarm box, and whether a more direct communication cannot be established between such theatres or places of amusement and the headquarters of this Department; also the location of gas jets or lights of any other description used around the stage or other parts of the building, the protection from ignition, with recommendations, where necessary, from further protection from fire; also the fire appliances on hand and ready for use in case of fire, and whether proper care is taken of each appliances; also any violation of the Combustible or Building Laws; also of what material the proscenium arch is made, its height from the stage, and whether it extends to the roof of the building; the openings that are in it above the stage, and if there are any openings in the roof of the building, with such recommendations as may be deemed necessary for the further protection of life and property in all such places of amusement in the city of New York.

December 24th, all but 6 engines and 2 hook and ladder companies below Thirty-fourth Street were called out to fight four fires that were burning at the same time. One at No. 61 East Twelfth Street did $500 damage; another at No. 359 Broadway—a dry goods warehouse—$195,000 damage; a third at No. 140 Centre Street, slight damage, and the other a tea warehouse, Nos. 71 and 72 South Street, $1,025,800 damage.

One of the last acts of the Board in 1881 was to require the Inspector of Buildings to report within fifteen days all modifications of or additions to the laws relating to buildings or the rules governing the Bureau of Inspection of

Buildings, which, in his opinion, might be necessary to insure the better protection of life and property. Early in February the medical force of the Department was made one Medical Officer and two Vice Medical Officers; and Dr. Robert A. Joyce was appointed to the latter position. January 28th, on the report of Battalion Chief Bresnan, the commissioners adopted a resolution recommending the use of asbestos cloth or other non-inflammable material for stage costumes, and that they be daily inspected.

January 31st, 1882, at 10:12 P.M. a destructive and fatal fire broke out in the Potter or *World* Building, which faced on Park Row, Beekman Street and Nassau Street. It did more than $400,000 damage, and twelve persons were in various ways killed. The fire directed attention to a source of peril to life and property which had before created apprehension, and on the 3d of February Commissioner Purroy offered the following resolution, which was adopted:

> *Whereas*: there have recently been constructed in this city a great number of large flats and business houses, reaching in many cases to a height exceeding one hundred feet; and whereas the extreme height to which it is possible to stretch and manage extension ladders have been probably reached, and does not exceed seventy feet, thus making futile the best efforts of this Department toward rescuing the occupants of the upper stories of the buildings above mentioned whenever such occupants are cut off from escape from below; therefore be it
>
> *Resolved*, That the Chief of Department be and is hereby instructed (keeping in view the increased height of the buildings above mentioned) to report to this Board in writing his views in regard to what improvement in the appliances and complements of the Department, what changes in regard to the erection and construction of fire-escapes, and what regulation as to the construction and maintenance of fire-proof shutters are necessary, together with any suggestions in regard to the better protection of life and property he may deem advisable.

Chief Bates's report favored the providing of each Hook and Ladder Company with scaling-ladders, one of fifteen feet and one of twenty feet, and a life-line, and the principal companies were thus equipped. Commissioner Purroy's foresight was displayed in the resolution which resulted in the "doubling up" of the most important companies.

March 15th Engine Company No. 49 was organized on Blackwell's Island. In the spring a malicious fellow, discharged from the service of the Department, put the Department and the police to much trouble and expense by sending out false alarms. In May Pusey & Jones, of Wilmington, Del., was given the contract for a new floating fire engine, their bid being $45,000, and Clapp & Jones contracted to construct the engines for $11,800. Later on the boat was named the *Zophar Mills* (Engine 51), in honor of an old and distinguished volunteer fireman, and stationed at Pier No. 42, North River. July 14th three fierce fires were burning at the same time in the lower part of the city, namely, in a cotton storage at Nos. 15 to 25 Whitehall Street; the Empire Paint Works, at Nos. 243 and 245 Pearl Street, and at the soap manufactory at Nos. 418 to 424 Washington Street. More than $170,000 damage was done, but the loss was insignificant when the prevention of a conflagration in each case is considered. To these three fires 42 of the 67 fire extinguishing companies in the city were called, with 417 officers and men. July 31st 17 engines and 5 hook and ladder companies were on duty at a fire which started in Hecker's Mills and burned to Water, Monroe and Cherry Streets and Pike Street and Slip, doing $202,000 damage. In September the estimate for 1883 was made at $1,671,905 and $1,551,345 were appropriated. D. G. Gale, Superintendent of Horses, was removed, and James Shea was appointed. The training stables for the green horses of the Department were established at the vacated quarters of Engine Company No. 37, at No. 58 Lawrence Street.

Commissioner Purroy made a report favoring the appointment of an instructor in life-saving, and on January 24th Chris Hoell, of the St. Louis Pompier Corps, was engaged to instruct the Life-Saving Corps, a branch of the School of Instruction, which was located in the quarters of Engine Company No. 47, in their duties. The Corps were instructed and trained in the use of scaling and ordinary ladders and life-lines and other life-saving appliances, at the Old Sugar House, at the foot of West 158th Street. Chief Bonner was at the head of the school and instructor in the practical duties of a fireman, and candidates for appointment had to pass the school, and get a report on the degree of proficiency exhibited and the branch of the service for which they were best qualified.

February 5th Police Inspector Byrnes was thanked for the arrest of the "fire-alarm fiends" and the breaking up of an organized plan of systematic and malicious annoyance to the active members of the Department by sending out false alarms.

During the month, Water Tower No. 1 was placed on test service in the quarters of Engine Company No. 7. In March the District Messenger Companies were required to connect their offices with Fire Headquarters, as several serious fires, and the death of at least one person, were found to be due to a popular belief that the companies had direct communication with the Fire Department.

January 3d, Chief of Battalion Hugh Bonner was made Second Assistant Chief of the Department, and on the 11th Foreman Thomas Gooderson, of Engine Company No. 35, was promoted to the rank of Chief of Battalion. The peril to the city in the event of the destruction of the telegraph apparatus at Headquarters had been considered for several years, and Commissioner Purroy's suggestion that a duplicate set of apparatus be made and put in a fire-proof building is about to be carried out.

The new fire-boat, the *Zophar Mills*, was at this time the subject of much comment and the object of much attention, as it was intended to be the most powerful and useful fire extinguishing auxiliary in the world and worthy of the name of the veteran and famous fireman which had been given it. The boat was known as Engine No. 51, and the tests of her pumps, which were made by the Clapp & Jones Manufacturing Company, of Hudson, N.Y., were made at Pier No. 52, East River, on the 27th of March, 1883. Of it the *Fireman's Journal* said:

"She was taken to the dock at the foot of Montgomery Street and subjected to an eight hours' test, throwing water in a variety of ways. The first test was with eight 1½ inch streams, then the lines were Siamesed into four larger streams, and in every way the most satisfactory results were obtained. With a 3¼ inch hose and a 2½ inch nozzle, a stream was thrown some 280 feet, and but for a cross wind a much greater distance would have been obtained. It was a wet, disagreeable day, with a keen, cutting wind blowing, so that the distance record did not do justice to the work, but the pumps proved satisfactory in every particular."

The official report of Charles Oscar Shay, Assistant Chief, was that the tests were entirely satisfactory. The capacity of the pumps was found to be, with the four pistons, traveling in the aggregate 1,200 feet per minute, and, with the usual percentage deducted for friction, etc., the actual discharge would be about 2,200 U.S. gallons per minute.

In June, keyless street boxes for the transmission of fire-alarms were put up. The first step toward underground telegraphic communication was on the 3d of August, when the Attorney asked what power the Department had to put fire telegraph wires underground, and, if none, what action was necessary to acquire it. Later on, Superintendent J. Elliott Smith was directed to visit Washington and report on a system of underground telegraphic communication there. In September the estimate for the cost of the Department for 1884 was fixed at $1,685,129.20. On the 21st of November Richard Croker, a practical and experienced fireman and engineer, was appointed Commissioner by Mayor Edson, vice John J. Gorman appointed Police Justice.

The question of protecting what is termed the "dry goods district," which may be said to cover the territory bounded by West Broadway, Spring Street, Crosby and Elm Streets and Chambers Street, had become a burning one. Mr. Purroy made a comprehensive and able report which favored a system by which water could be pumped into portable tanks from the rivers to points of vantage by the fire-boats, and taken from the tanks by the land engines. In 1883 double companies were established in the quarters of Engine Companies 12, 13, 16, 31 and 33, and Hook and Ladder Companies 6 and 9. The prominent fires of the year were the Inman Pier fire, February 1; loss, $391,000; and mercantile property, at Nos. 537 and 539 Broadway, September 18th; loss, $435,721.

The "dry goods district" is the richest in the city. In one block of it, bounded by Worth, Thomas, Church Streets and Broadway, the property (including buildings and contents) is worth $25,000,000. From 1877 to 1882 the total losses by fire in the dry-goods districts amounted to $6,490,496; the fire insurance premiums received (less expenses) were $2,345,000; losses over receipts, $4,145,496. No wonder the companies declined to insure fully, and the merchants tried Europe in vain. More water was wanted to induce the insurance men to accept more risks. Chief Bates instanced Ridley's store from Orchard to Allen Streets, and also Lord & Taylor's, each taking in a large space, that were in danger of destruction by fire from a lack of water. "If ever a fire gets hold of these places," said he, "it will burn pretty smartly. In that neighborhood all the pipes are small, and the water pressure is very light. For ordinary uses, it runs well enough, but not for extraordinary fires."

In 1882 there were 2,001 fires in this city, which damaged or destroyed 942 buildings.

Loss on buildings and vessels	978,132
Loss on contents	3,217,828
Total loss	$14,195,900
Estimated insurance on buildings and vessels	9,880,656
Estimated insurance on contents	11,471,745
Total estimated insurance	$21,352,401

"Take the line of Church Street," said Mr. Pollak, then of the North British Mercantile, now of the Niagara, "and you will see buildings from 60 to 100 feet in height full of inflammable material. They contain costly silks, averaging in value in single buildings a million of dollars. Church Street is not over forty feet in width, but there is hardly a warehouse on that line from Vesey Street up that has an iron shutter above the first floor. There is nothing to protect one building from its neighbor opposite in case of fire. In Leonard Street, near Church Street, there is a high building containing enormous wealth. Though it is what we call a brick and stone structure, yet a fire opposite would reach it and cause it to burn down in a very short time. If the wind blew that way, everything would be against the Fire Department. The water in that district is at the very lowest pressure."

"For the better protection of the vast property in the dry goods district," said President Van Cott, of the Fire Commission, "the question of the water supply is a very important one. There is no doubt that it is entirely inadequate on the line of West Broadway. The Fire Commissioners think that stationery cisterns should be placed at all important points in the district, and direct connections made with the Croton water mains. These cisterns could be placed under the sidewalks and properly covered. Then, in the event of a great fire, we could raise the cover and turn on the water to the cistern, into which the suction-pipes of half a dozen engines could be placed at once. Then we would have an abundance of water which cannot be obtained from the hydrants."

"Tanks would be required," said Chief Bates, "at such places as Ridley's in Grand Street, Claflin's, and in Nassau Street. At these points there is danger of a very serious fire. The main water pipes are laid four feet from the surface of the ground, and if the cisterns were put five feet under, they could easily be filled with water. There could be stopcocks to shut off the water from the cistern when full. When an engine has a solid body of water to draw from, she can throw a stream of enormous height and force."

On this subject Lieutenant Kensehan, of Engine No. 31, said: "Some years ago, at the big fire on Grand Street and Broadway, where two of our men were killed, we had about twelve lines on the roof. But there was a fatal lack of water. It would just spurt out and then go back. That was a $3,000,000 fire, destroying five buildings. Some companies get into a main when there is enough water; there are other pipes which won't give any. When these companies get into a main, the best engine gets all the water."

Mr. F. C. Moore, Second Vice-President of the Continental Fire Insurance Company, said: "There are two things which tend to keep alive the apprehension of a great fire in that district which will extend from river to river. One is the fault of the construction of the buildings, many of them being above the height which the Fire Department can reach with their steamers. The other is the lack of water. The great fire in Worth Street in 1876 proved that there were faults in the division walls not known to the underwriters."

The proposed tank system has obtained great favor in all quarters, and may be carried out. When the aqueduct is finished, the Fire Department will have all the water necessary for coping with the greatest of conflagrations.

Mr. Purroy's suggestion in regard to a portable water tank to protect the dry goods district had not been forgotten. Chief John McCabe, in charge of the repair shops carried out the idea, and in February had built a tank on Mr. Purroy's design; on the 25th of February the Board ordered a test of it.

The test was entirely satisfactory, and the tank was put in service on the 15th of March, 1884, under the following general order:

"A portable water-tank to furnish water from the rivers to the land engines, after being supplied therewith by the fire-boats and a four-wheel hose-tender with 600 feet of new rubber 3¼-inch hose, will be put in service on the 17th instant, and pending the preparation of the quarters of Engine Company No. 20, where they are to be permanently located, they will be temporarily placed in the quarters of Engine Company No. 27. The following rules will govern their use:

1. At any fire occurring within the distance of a half mile from the river-fronts where there is either a failure or scarcity of water, the officer will, if in his discretion he deem it advisable, call for the tank, the tender and a fire-boat by means of the special call 18-1, followed first by the number of the station at which the tank is required to be placed, and second, by the number of the station on the river-front nearest to which the fire-boat is required to report as for example; the fire being at Worth Street and West Broadway, the call will be 18-1 (the preliminary signal or notice that the tank, tender and fire-boat will be required), 82 (the station at Washington and Jay Streets, where the tank is to be placed), and 81 (the station at West and Harrison Streets, where the fire-boat is to report).

2. When the special call is sent, the officer in command will at once dispatch a disengaged team of horses from among those at the fire, or elsewhere available, with a detail of two men, to bring the tank to the point designated.

3. Upon the receipt of the special call, the tender designated to co-operate will immediately proceed in advance of the tank to the point indicated for the latter, and stretch its hose by the nearest and best route towards the point on the river-front where the fire-boat lands.

4. The fire-boat at the time designated to respond to alarms from the last station indicated in the call shall at once proceed to the nearest available landing place thereto, and immediately stretch sufficient hose to connect with the hose from the tank.

5. When the officer in command determines upon sending the call he shall at once make all necessary arrangements by detailing officers and men, obtaining additional hose and making such other dispositions as will secure prompt connections between the fire-boat, tank and hand engines, and guard against interference with and damage to the lines of hose.

6. Nothing contained in Section 1 of this order shall be construed to prevent the use of the tank, tender and fire-boat at a greater distance than

a half mile from either line or in any other that may be deemed proper by the officer in command at the fire."

In March, Commissioner Purroy studied, under the authorization of the Board, fire extinguishing methods at Milwaukee, Detroit and other cities, and made a report thereon.

April 23d, 1884, Chief of Battalion, John W. Miller, was retired on a pension of $1,250 a year, and on the 29th came the retirement of Eli Bates, Chief of the Department on $2,350 a year on the report of the medical officers of disability caused or induced by the actual performance of the duties of his position. In May, the office of Superintendent of horses was abolished, and Superintendent Joseph Shay was appointed a foreman with supervision of the Training and Hospital Stables and the selection of horses for the Department. June 10, 1884, the Board offered advancement to any member of the force below the rank of Foreman, and suitable recognition if above that rank, or to a uniformed member who should invent a proper means of casting a life line to the top of a building from a distance of not less than 300 feet within thirty days. October 10th, the estimate of the expenses for 1885 was fixed at $1,774,773. During the year resolutions were adopted that applicants for promotion must have passed through the classes of the school of instruction, and that promotion to the grade of Engineers and Assistant Engineers must be made from men who had attended the repair shops thirty days. It was also provided that men once detailed to one branch of the service should not be transferred to another except in cases of emergency.

In May, the improper and unlooked for uses which persons holding badges put them to caused their recall, and for the use of citizens and the press, officers and members of the uniformed force and the ununiformed officials and subordinates of the Department three badges were designed.

February 4, the Board received the resignation of Mr. William P. Esterbrook, Inspector of Buildings. Mr. Esterbrook's integrity, energy and zeal were conspicuous, but he was independent of office and the severence of his connection with the Department was due to a controversy about the putting of fire escapes on the flats of John H. Sherwood at Forty-fourth Street and Fifth Avenue. The act of resignation was considered hasty and unnecessary. The same month a plan of lightening the labors of the horses and men of the Department by having alarms sent so as to pass by a number of company quarters remote from the fire signalled was suggested, but so far it has not ripened.

February 16th, 1885, Mr. Esterbrook was succeeded as Inspector of Buildings by Mr. Albert F. D'Oench, a practical builder and architect.

Albert Frederick D'Oench, Superintendent of Buildings, was born at St. Louis, Mo., on Christmas Day, 1852. His father, William D'Oench, one of the most prominent of St. Louis' citizens, was of Flemish origin and was born in Silesia, and his mother, whose family were Alsatians, was born in Hamburg. They came to America in 1838 and grew up with St. Louis. Mr. D'Oench studied at Washington University and received the degree of M.E. in 1872 when he went to Stuttgart and took the three years' course of architecture. After traveling in Germany, Austria, Switzerland, France and England he returned to America in the fall of 1875 to become a draughtsman in the office of Mr. Lopold Eidlitz the well known architect and once principally engaged on drawings for the new Capitol at Albany. Afterwards he worked in the office of Messrs. Richard M. Hunt and Edward E. Raht, finishing his course of training in 1881. He established himself as an architect in 1882 and in 1885 on the strongest and most flattering recommendations was appointed Inspector of Buildings to succeed Mr. W. P. Esterbrook by Commissioners Van Cott, Purroy and Croker and under the law was made Superintendent, January 12, 1886. His administration of the affairs of the Bureau of Inspection of Buildings has caused neither his friends nor the public to regret his selection which it is fair to state that in transacting business he departed little from the course laid down by his predecessor.

Belts and snaps were provided for members of the Life Saving Corps to enable them to attach themselves to use their hands and arms freely when secured by the snaps to ladders. Gilbert T. Orr, Chief of Battalion, relieved from duty at fires, died on the 9th of March. March 23d, the following important resolutions were adopted:

> Whereas, frequent and sometimes very serious delays occur in sending alarms after the discovery of fires, notwithstanding the means afforded for that purpose; and
>
> Whereas, the first minutes after the outbreak of fires, if the alarm is properly sent, are of greater value to the householders and owners in the saving of loss, and to the firemen, than subsequent hours of labor and effort to extinguish fires; and
>
> Whereas, the delay in sending alarms for fires generally results from want of information as to the location of the nearest fire-alarm box; therefore
>
> Resolved, That the cards prepared under the direction of this Board, showing the location of the fire-alarm box nearest to each building in this city, giving directions as to the sending of alarms, and suggesting precautions to be taken against fires resulting from some of the most prolific causes, be turned over to the Chief of Department for distribution through the companies in their respective districts, with directions to have one or more carefully and neatly tacked up in each building, above the reach of children, in as conspicuous a position as practicable, and preferably in the various classes of buildings, as follows:

In dwellings of all kinds and office buildings, in the main hallways;

In hotels, factories, warehouses, stables, etc., in the offices or near the front doors;

In schools, churches, etc., in the vestibules or lobbies;

In places of amusement, in or near the ticket office and upon the stages;

In mercantile establishments, etc., in the offices or near the desks; and

Resolved, That the owners and occupants of buildings be requested, by the representatives of this Department detailed to distribute the cards, to permit them to be as conspicuously placed as possible, and that the names and addresses of all persons refusing to receive such cards be reported to the Board.

April 6th, 1884.—The General Term of the Supreme Court having reversed the decision of the Board which dismissed private Robert L. Kent for drunkenness while on duty, and substituted a punishment of suspension from pay and duty for six months, thereby establishing the guilt of the officer and the correctness of the Board's decision, the attorney was directed to appeal the case.

Mr. Elward Smith, a veteran fireman appointed by Mayor Grace to succeed Mr. Cornelius Van Cott, whose term of office had expired, took his seat in the Board on the 9th of May, and Mr. Henry D. Purroy was elected President and Mr. Richard Croker Treasurer.

In April structures put up on the south side of Sixty-second Street, west of Tenth Avenue fell, killing several persons. They were erected by the "jerry" builder Buddensiek, and on the 15th of this month two neglectful examiners of the Bureau of Buildings were removed.

In order to more thoroughly equip the members of the Department for life-saving emergencies, the following resolution was adopted on May 20th:

Whereas, the records of this Department show that since the extension of the life-saving service to all the Hook and Ladder Companies, in August, 1888, the lives of the following persons, viz. : John Hurley, at fire No. 332 East Thirtieth Street, on September 25th, 1888; Louis Castaign, at fire St. George's Flats, on April 7, 1884; Kate Leary, at fire Nos. 16 and 18 South William Street, on February 21st, 1885; a man, woman and boy, named Koernich, and an unknown woman, at fire No. 672 First Avenue, on May 8, 1885, have been saved by means of the scaling-laders and other appliances in the hands of the members of the Life-Saving Corps; and

Whereas, it is believed that the above list of persons saved might have been increased if it had been feasible to extend the life-saving service to the Engine Companies of the Department, for the reason that life is usually lost at fires in the first few moments immediately preceding the alarms, and the Engine Companies, as a rule, arrive ahead of the Hook and Ladder Companies; therefore,

Resolved, That the Foreman in charge of Repair Shops be instructed to fit up, with promptness, the four-wheeled tenders of the Department; in accordance with the suggestions made by the Assistant Chief of Department, so that they will each safely carry at least two of the scaling-ladders and other appliances needed for life saving at fires; and further

Resolved, That with a view of affording some hope to persons who may be forced, as a last chance, to jump from burning buildings, the Assistant Chief of Department be authorized to have made the safest possible jumping-sheet, so that, if adopted, the firemen may be instructed in the use of such sheets, and they may be placed on each Hook and Ladder truck and four-wheeled tender in the Department.

Resolved, That while the air-gun invented by Otto Rigl, and approved by the Assistant Chief, is being approved and perfected, the Board authorize the Chairman of the Committee on Apparatus and Telegraph to purchase six Travis guns with all their attachments, at a cost of $55 each, to be used in firing a life-line to persons in danger on the roofs or in the windows of burning houses.

All these life-saving services are now carried by the truck companies.

June 12th, under the provisions of Chapter 456 of the Laws of 1885, Mr. A. F. D'Oench, Inspector of Buildings, was made Superintendent of Buildings. July 1st, Mr. Charles De F. Burns, Assistant Secretary, resigned to become Secretary of the Department of Public Parks, and the Board recognized his services in very complimentary resolutions. Mr. Enoch Vreeland, Jr., succeeded Mr. Burns as Assistant Secretary on the 19th of August.

In September Chief Charles O. Shay reported the distribution of cards showing the location of alarm boxes, as provided in the resolution of March 22d, as completed. Superintendent D'Oench submitted regulations for the inspection of passenger elevators, and on October 10th they were approved, and Mr. William H. Class was promoted to the supervision of passenger elevators, with M. T. Gaughan and John Crossen as assistants. This action led to a tempest in a teapot. The Board of Examiners, created by the act which reorganized the Bureau of Buildings, who held that the assistants, or "inspectors" or "supervisors," must pass an examination before them, and that they had a right to make rules not only for their government, but for the commissioners. Mr. W. L. Findley, Attorney for the Department; George W. Van Sicklen, the Examiner's lawyer, and

412   BIRTH OF THE BRAVEST

others, spoiled much paper on opinions, and Corporation Counsel Lacombe ended the matter by deciding that the examination was not necessary.

The departmental estimate for 1886 was approved at $1,904,156.10.

In November, 1885, the following rules fixed the stations of hook and ladder men at fires:

I.—Commanding officers of Hook and Ladder companies shall have exclusive control and direction in the raising and placing of all ladders, and shall not permit their use by anyone before they are in proper and safe position; they shall not be used at any time thereafter by any person not a regular or probationary member of the Department, or persons rescued, and by them only under the following restrictions:

1. The number of persons permitted on the various sized ladders simultaneously shall not exceed—

To each 10 to 15 feet ladder, one.

To each 20, 25 or 30 feet ladder, two.

To each ladder more than 30 feet, three.

2. When used for pipe-lines, the pipeman only will be permitted at the pipe, and he will fasten the line to an iron round if conveniently near, or if not, he will hitch it on two wooden rounds, in such manner as to prevent the kinking of the pipe.

3. If it be a 35-feet ladder, the second man shall take position just below the point at which the pressure bends the ladder, where the line will also be fastened, preferably to an iron round, or in lieu thereof, two wooden rounds. With all other ladders, the second man shall take position with feet resting upon the first round above the point where the poles support the ladder, where the line shall be fastened in the manner above prescribed.

4. If a third man is required, he shall take position on the ladder near the butt.

5. While their services are not needed in shifting the line, the second and third man will not be required to maintain the prescribed position.

6. After shifting the line, the second and third man will resume the position prescribed, and fasten it as before indicated.

7. Before shifting a line from a ladder over 25 feet long, it must be cleared of water.

8. Officers and reliefs may use the ladders at any time, but must not pass the second man except at the point above designated for fastening the line.

February, 1886, apprehension was felt along the line of the new aqueduct because of the storage of large quantities of high explosives near the shafts. An explosion at Fordham Landing made decisive action necessary, and Mr. Peter

Seery, Inspector of Combustibles, made such seizures, reports and regulations as to reduce danger to a minimum. March 12th, 1886, Chief Francis Mahedy lost his life from injuries received in a collision while going to a fire.

April 23d Mr. Elward Smith offered a resolution that "Henry D. Purroy be and hereby is appointed a committee to visit England and France for the purpose of examining into the fire departments of London, Paris and other large cities, with reference to their method of appointment, tenure of office, organization, discipline, apparatus and water-supply for fire extinguishing purposes."

Under this Mr. Purroy made a memorable and satisfactory visit to Europe. While he derived but little information or few hints from foreign fire extinguishing methods, his reception everywhere was of the most cordial and gratifying nature. On his return Mr. Purroy published the following:

"A charming and painstaking host in his native country is Colonel A. C. Couston, Chief of the Paris Fire Department or *Regiment des Sapeurs Pompiers de Paris*. This gallant and handsome officer was born in 1834 and entered the French Army when 18. Three years later he was promoted to a Sub-Lieutenancy in the 5th Infantry. He first smelled powder in the Crimean War and was present at the burning of Varna, the battles of Balaclava and Inkerman and in the attack of the Lex on the 2d of May was wounded and was mentioned for conspicuous courage in the orders of the day. He was also at the battle of Tractir, and at the taking of Sebastopol he was again noticed for valor and was made Lieutenant on the 30th of August, 1826. In 1857 he distinguished himself by saving an army captain who was in imminent danger of drowning in the Rhone at Aries and was commissioned as Doctor of Schools and Instructor in Rifle Practice. At the breaking out of the Italian war in 1859 he was assigned as Lieutenant of Voltigeurs and for his conduct on the field was decorated with the ribbon of the order of Military Valor of Sardinia. In 1862 and 1863 he was Staff officer to General de Valazè. Then came the Mexican campaign. He received his commission as captain on the 20th of January, 1864, and was with the Foreign Legion in the expeditionary columns sent to Queretaro, Verde-san-Luis, Tamanlipas, Valle Purissimà and Calorcè. At Rio Feio he was appointed commandant. When in Africa he distinguished himself at the cholera outbreak at Gèryville, with the Arbaouat Column and in the Rasoul and Figuig expeditions. At the outbreak of the Franco-Prussian war he was at South Ovan in Africa. He was registered for active service and went to the field chief of the 7th Battalion. At Coulmiers his first serious encounter with the advancing legions of the Prussians took place. At Juranville he had a horse killed under him and was made an officer of the Legion of Honor of which he became a member in 1855. As commander of the Forty-Second Regiment demarche he was present at the battles of Villersexel, Hèricourt and Cluse and was wounded at the latter engagement, February 1st, 1871. In 1873 he took part in the military manœu-

414   BIRTHOFTHEBRAVEST

vres at St. Quentin as major of the Forty-Fifth, and in 1877 he was promoted Lieutenant Colonel of the Forty-Second Regiment and commanded it at the manœuvres of the Tenth Corps. July 10th, 1881, he was commissioned Colonel of the Eighty-eighth Regiment of Line Infantry. His next service was with the Nineteenth Army Corps at South Ovan and then with the Seventeenth Corps in which he directed the Brigade manœuvres with non-commissioned officers. August 22d, 1881, he was called to the command of the Paris Fire Department. His administration has been a signal success and his fitness has been recognized in very flattering official orders. He traveled in Europe and America to study fire extinguishing service and used the information he acquired in reorganizing that of Paris so that in four years all that was advanced in the systems in vogue in the principal cities of the world and which was possible to apply to the Paris service was adopted even to acquiring engines used in Foreign Departments. Colonel Couston has been an officer of Public Instruction since 1879, and his military and technical knowledge was perfected in travels in Austria, Italy, England, Holland, Belgium and this country. America has no better friend than the accomplished, modest and able Chief of the Sapeurs-Pompiers of the capital of France. Colonel Couston's headquarters are on the Boulevard du Palais. His corps is in the War Department, but the Minister of the Interior has supervision of the expenses and the service at fires is under the Chief of Police."

During his trip he met Chief Benjamin A. Gicquel, of the Seventh Battalion, on leave of absence, who was also the recipient of much appreciated courtesies.

Mr. Purroy returned to New York just in time to act on a painful and embarrassing matter. Ample preparations to protect life and property on the 5th of July, which was on Monday, had been made by Chief Shay. In the evening a fire broke out at No. 2293 Third Avenue, from the ignition of fireworks on a stand, and an alarm was sent out, and Chief of Battalion Francis J. Reilly sent out second and third alarms and special calls for six engines. When Second Assistant Chief John McCabe arrived and took command he found a large fire, but in the judgment of the best men in the Department the engines on the ground were amply sufficient to cope with it, and this opinion is sustained by the fact that they did extinguish it. Chief McCabe was, however, impelled to send out the call known as the "Three Sixes," thus: 6, 6, 6—12—5, 1, 8—767, so that all the companies due on a third alarm at Seventh Avenue and Forty-ninth Street were brought to Third Avenue and 126th Street, so that the city north of Fourteenth Street was entirely unprotected. The engines and trucks summoned by the "Three Sixes" were sent back as they arrived by Chief Shay, but the greater portion of the city was in peril for nearly an hour, despite the prompt action of Assistant Chief Hugh Bonner, who sent apparatus to the district that was deprived of protection by McCabe's action. He was tried by Commissioners Purroy and Smith, after suspension from pay and duty, and was defended by Roswell D. Hatch, E. S. Clark and George B. Mc-Clusky. On July 21st the decision of Messrs. Purroy and Smith dismissed Chief McCabe. The General Term of the Supreme Court ordered his reinstatement, March 2, 1887.

CHAPTER XXV

FIRE DEPARTMENT TELEGRAPH SYSTEM

Its Construction and Development.—Records of the Several Superintendents and their Efforts to Perfect the System.—Superintendent Smith.—A Man with a Creditable Record.—Vigilant, Enterprising, Scientific.—Central Office of the Fire-Alarm Telegraph.

The telegraph in connection with the fire service has become an indispensable adjunct, and as much a necessity in communicating the existence and locality of a fire as the steam and other improved apparatus for extinguishing. Indeed, successful management of fires depends so much upon early and instantaneous information that the telegraphic system is now considered as important as any branch of the department. The old-time method of detecting fires by the aid of look-outs upon high towers situated in different parts of the city, and communicating their existence to the public, and approximating to the locality by striking the tower bells, was kept up until the Fire Alarm Telegraph System was put in operation.

At this time a system of telegraph was in use connecting the various bell towers with each other, which was continued, and the look-outs were maintained at Union Market, Essex Market, Marion Street, Spring Street, Jefferson Market, Twenty-sixth Street, Thirty-third Street, Yorkville and Mount Morris for some time, but they have gradually been abandoned, and the old towers removed, with the exception of the one at Mount Morris and at Morrisania.

The Fire Alarm Telegraph was constructed under the old Gamewell patent, and was put in operation in January, 1871, by the contractors, Messrs. Charles T. and J. N. Chester, and Mr. Charles T. Chapin was appointed Superintendent. The Central Office was located on the second floor of Fireman's Hall, in the room lately occupied by the President of the Board. This system embraced the territory of Manhattan Island, including that of the East River islands, and consisted in its equipment of 2780 poles, 612 miles of wire, divided into 56 circuits, viz., 41 box signal circuits, 3 key and bell circuits, 2 tower circuits, 2 dial circuits, and 1 police circuit, 548 alarm boxes, with 54 alarm gongs and 42 key and bell magnets in the houses of the fire companies, and 16 dial instruments in the quarters of the district engineers or battalion commanders, and the necessary receiving and transmitting apparatus in the Central Office, the alarms from the street boxes and bell towers on receipt at the Central Office being repeated and transmitted to the several companies over the gong circuits, which was the only one source upon which companies depended for receiving alarms. Each company was provided with a key and bell instrument, connected with a talking circuit, for the purpose of informing the Central Office by signal when about to leave quarters, and on their return to quarters after an absence.

Mr. Chapin was succeeded as Superintendent in March, 1871, by Mr. C. K. Smith. The annexation of the Westchester District to the city on January 1st, 1874, made necessary the extension of the lines beyond the Harlem River, and in the early part of that year this was accomplished by cabling the river at Third Avenue and at Macomb's Dam. In this district were located six companies, which were equipped with the regular apparatus as in use throughout the Department. In 1874 the position of Superintendent was vacated by Mr. C. K. Smith, and Chief Operator John H. Emerick was placed in charge until the September following, when Mr. Emerick was made Superintendent and Mr. J. Elliot Smith was made Chief Operator and subsequently appointed Assistant Superintendent. In January, 1880, the position of Superintendent being vacated by Mr. Emerick, Mr. Smith was appointed Superintendent.

J. Elliot Smith, the present head of the Fire Alarm Telegraph System, has been connected with the Department since 1873, at which time he entered the Department as Assistant Operator, was promoted as Operator the following July, and made Chief Operator in September of the same year. In July, 1879, he was promoted to be Assistant Superintendent, the office of Chief Operator being at the same time abolished, and on February 1st, 1880, was appointed Superintendent.

Superintendent Smith was born in Northfield, Vermont, in 1834, received his education in the Select School of the town and at the Vermont Seminary at Newbury.

On the opening of the Boston and Montreal telegraph line under the old Bain system, he learned the art of telegraphy, and was placed in charge of the office at Northfield, then the headquarters of the Vermont Central Railroad, at the age of sixteen, his superintendent being Professor Moses G. Farmer, the original inventor of the Fire Alarm Telegraph System. In this occupation he continued some three or four years, with the exception of an interval of two or three school terms. Engaging then in the transportation office of the Company, going thence to the cashiership of the transportation department of the Boston and Lowell Railroad, which position he left at the breaking out of the war. He joined General Butler's New Orleans expedition. On the arrival of the Federal Army at New Orleans, and the occupation of the city, he was appointed by

General Butler Military Superintendent of Telegraph in the Department of the Gulf, with instructions to take possession and management of all telegraph lines, including those of the Police and Fire Alarm.

As the different lines connecting into New Orleans had been almost completely destroyed by the Confederate authorities as they left the city on the approach of the Union forces, the work of reconstruction was extremely difficult, the more so from lack of the necessary material, and to supply operators it became expedient to draw from the rank and file and establish a school for instruction.

By this method and with the aid of reinforcements imported from the North, the requisite force was provided with which 350 miles of lines were put in operation as fast as reconstructed.

The officials in charge of the Fire Alarm and Police Telegraphs were required by the Commanding General to take the oath of allegiance to the government as necessary to their retention in office. This they refused to do, believing themselves indispensable to the service of the city, consequently secure in their position. Not so, however, with the General, who ordered Superintendent Smith to dispossess the entire force as soon as he could do it with safety. This was done within a few weeks as soon as a relieving force could be organized, and these systems remained under Mr. Smith's management until May, 1864, when they were restored to the civil government. During the twelve years of Mr. Smith's connection with the New York Department, his constant aim and study has been to add every improvement to the telegraph system which would tend to benefit the service. When first entering the Department he saw the importance of reducing the time occupied in the transmission of the alarm signals from the street boxes to the companies, and on his appointment as chief operator he at once directed his energies to the perfecting of the device by which the several companies were enabled to receive alarms from the street boxes direct, and at the same time they are received at the Central Office. For want of space in the operating room at that time the improvement could only be attached to a single circuit, enough, however, to show the immense benefit in gaining of time, and the advantage of an additional means for the transmission of the signals. The importance of this and other suggested improvements so favorably impressed the commissioners, that they provided a liberal appropriation for the purpose, and Mr. Smith was charged with the carrying out of the improvements, the details of which he carefully devised, and which were thoroughly carried to completion under his personal supervision; and at the hour of nine o'clock and twenty minutes P.M., the 25th of March, 1878, the electric life was in a moment transfused from the veins and apparatus of the old office to the new room in the upper story of Fireman's Hall, and to the magnificent and multitudinous paraphernalia prepared for it, and constituting the equipment of the finest arrangement of its kind in existence, and now known as the New York system.

A curious incident connected with the operation was the fact that the first fire signal received and transmitted through the new office was the Headquarter's station, which was received within a few minutes after the transfer had been made, and found to be occasioned by a fire on the same block. On the arrival of the midnight relief force at the old office their astonishment was great to find their former office abandoned and in a state of chaos. The transfer had been a perfect success, not a hitch occurring.

The wires of the New York Fire Alarm Telegraph are carried exclusively on poles, no housetops being used for the purpose. There are now nearly 7,000 poles and 1,050 miles of wire, divided into 78 circuits, all of which are metallic, with two or three exceptions; there are 53 box signal circuits, five of which connect with the public schools, and three connect with theatres, manufactories, hotels and other buildings, and known as special building circuits.

There are four combination circuits connecting with the various company houses throughout the Department which receive the signals at the Central Office from the fire alarm boxes, and convey them direct to the companies. Eight gong circuits carry the alarms to the large gongs in each company's quarters as transmitted upon the repeating instruments, twelve telephone circuits connect with each company, the quarters of the principal officials of the Department, the Gate House in Central Park, the headquarters of the Police Department, and a watchman's circuit connects with the Department repair shops and the hospital stable.

There are 972 signal boxes, 654 of which are attached to poles, 26 are located in city institutions, the property of the city, 131 are located within the public-school buildings, also the property of the city, and 161 are connected with the theatres, hotels, manufactories, and other private buildings.

There are in use in the Department 83 large electro mechanical gongs, 74 combination, alarm, and talking instruments, 92 sets of telephones, forming the equipment of the quarters of the respective companies and the principal officials of the Department.

Among more recent and valuable improvements made is that of placing all the wires centering into headquarters underground in its immediate vicinity, and the introduction of a safety device to prevent damage to the valuable apparatus from the excessive currents from the electrical illuminating wires, which formerly had occasioned much trouble and damage to the apparatus, and on one or more occasions nearly destroying the entire system.

This was caused by the wires of the Department and those of the illuminating companies becoming crossed, whereby the terrific currents of the latter were conducted to the more delicate instruments in the Central Office, burning them up and setting fire to the combustible surroundings. Experiments have been made in the department with underground wires dating back to September, 1884, at which time two six-wire leaden-covered Waring cables were connected along

Eighth Avenue, between Seventy-second and Seventy-third Streets, and the overhead wires removed. Since that time the same kind of cables has been put in service in different parts of the department, and with such good results as to induce Superintendent Smith to recommend that all the wires extending from the Central Office be placed underground for a limited distance, as in case of a serious fire in the immediate locality the entire overhead system would be imperiled. The recommendation was approved, and the work of trenching and laying was commenced on Saturday, the 24th of October, 1885, and as far as the underground work was concerned, was completed the following Tuesday. It is hoped that the success of this initial departure from the hazardous overhead system will result in the speedy placing of every fire alarm wire under ground.

Superintendent Smith's report, made some two months after the completion of this work, is as follows:

"All the wires connecting the Central Office of this department start from the office switch-board in Waring anti-induction cables, and pass to the basement of the building, where they enter a distributing switch for the greater convenience of the circuits in the different streets. From this point the cables, thirty-four in number, and containing one hundred and ninety (190) wires, with an aggregate length of about twenty-eight (28) miles, enter the ground and pass under the streets in different directions to the junction poles. These poles are situated at a distance from one to four blocks away. Here the cables are carried up the poles in wood and iron boxing, where they are joined to the overhead wires through lightning arresters placed in boxes upon the poles. Thirty of the cables contain six conductors each, three have three conductors each, all of the corrugated pattern, and one independent or single wire cables. One of the six-wire cables connects direct to the head-quarters of the Police department and the newspaper press offices in Mulberry Street, and one connects with the conduit of the Western Union Telegraph Company under Broadway. The conduit here mentioned extends south under Broadway to Dey Street and north as far as Fourteenth Street, thence to and up Fifth Avenue to Twenty-third Street. Along this route there are ten street boxes attached to lamp-posts, from each of which extends a Waring cable under the pavement, entering the conduit at a neighboring flush-box or man-hole, and there connecting with the department circuits provided by the Western Union Company, and running the entire length of the conduit, making a circuit of seven miles.

"The work of trenching and laying was begun on Saturday, the 24th of October, 1885, and was practically completed the following Tuesday morning, having caused no interference nor inconvenience to street traffic, although car tracks were crossed at five different points, and one mass of six cables (thirty-three wires) were laid across Broadway, the most crowded thoroughfare in the city. Upon the completion of the work and connecting in this underground system with the aerial lines, not a fault had developod in any of the cables, and all remain perfect up to the present time. In addition to the cables here spoken of are several Waring cables placed in different parts of the city, which were laid in 1884, and all as perfect in their service as when laid.

"While in constant dread of serious disturbances, to which we are liable, from storms, etc., especially in the winter season, it is a satisfaction to feel that, though limited, we have some portion of the system not within its reach, and with a continuance of successful working, a strengthening of the belief that the proper place for the wires of this department, as a measure of economy as well as safety, is under the streets."

The Central Office of the Fire Alarm Telegraph is on the third floor of the Headquarters Building, and located at the east end of a room whose dimensions are 70 by 40 feet. Commencing at the front end of the room is a raised flooring or platform occupying twenty-two feet in width, and extending into the room the same distance, with an extension of three and a half feet, with broad steps leading to it from the main floor. On the two sides of this elevated portion, and the end where it joins the side of the building, elegant and artistic cabinet work of solid mahogany, beautifully carved, and divided into pilasters and paneling to accommodate the electrical apparatus rises ten feet above the platform, the end portion being placed three feet distant from the front wall of headquarters to permit a passage between it and the wall, and leave an opening in the centre six feet in width to correspond to a window directly opposite, the two wings of the cabinet work joining overhead.

On the sides of the windows, within recesses in the wall of the building, are located annunciators connected with lightning arresters and automatic protectors, one hundred upon each side, to which the outside circuits (which here terminate, as before related, in the underground or sub-way cables) are connected. From this apparatus the wires enter the cabinet work at the top and connect at the rheostat switch-board mounted upon an upright marbleized-slate base, and occupying a position in one of the wings, the uses of which are to connect a delicate apparatus for discriminating by a system of measurements the locality of faults on the circuits, etc.

From here the wires extend to the main switches which occupy the central portion of the cabinet on one side of the office, and are mounted upon marbleized-slate bases three feet wide, the aggregate length of which is twenty feet, containing some nine hundred switches, and from which wires radiate to every part of the office, and which have their uses for testing in a variety of ways. Each circuit connecting at the switch-board is provided with a small needle galvanometer, similar to a watch face, and arranged upon a projecting shelf under the switches, and mounted upon marble bases with glass dials. These little instruments show at all times the exact electrical condition of the circuits to which

422   BIRTH OF THE BRAVEST

they belong, and are used in connection with the switches to detect the existence upon the circuits of crosses or leakages, and where such faults are indicated the operator switches in the measuring apparatus at the rheostat switches, and determines the exact locality of the fault. They are also used for determining the condition of the electro-motive force. This consists of a battery of nearly two thousand jars, situated in the basement of the building about two hundred feet distant from the telegraph office.

Two hundred and twenty-five wires, aggregating in length about nine miles, are required to make the connections between the battery-room and the switch-board.

Above the switch-board are placed electric annunciators corresponding in numbers to the engine and hook and ladder companies for informing the operators at a glance the situation of the force—that is what companies are in or out of quarters. This is controlled by a key-board on the desk, in the body of the platform.

When a company leaves its quarters on a still alarm, or for any purpose is temporarily out of service, it signals the Central Office upon the combination circuits, and the annunciator is made to show that such company is out. Likewise on its return to quarters the proper signal is given, and the annunciator is set to show the company "in service." Thus the operators are always informed, when a fire signal is received, just what companies can be depended upon to respond.

The cabinets on the opposite side, facing the switch-board, contain the apparatus for receiving and recording the signals and the system of transmitting to the department simultaneously with their receipt from the street boxes. All the wires entering here are through the main switch-board passing beneath the floor and up into the cabinet. Here under a glass case is a large registering instrument with a capacity of fifty circuits, with an independent ink-recording pen for each box circuit. This instrument is provided with paper ten inches in width, on which the signals are recorded, and which is fed from a roll beneath the instrument passing through and under a glass plate in the counter shelf for a distance of four feet, so that the last signal received is in view, and entering the cabinet is again reeled up. Directly over the register and in the same case is placed the combination switch, consisting of a hard rubber bar about two feet long, sliding in a strip of mahogany placed horizontally and inlaid with numerous metal bearings. Upon each side of the slide, upon the wood are mounted a multitude of flat springs, their ends overlapping and terminating upon the metal bearings in the rubber, by which two or more springs are in electrical contact. To these springs are attached wires connecting with the combination circuits extending to all the department quarters in the city, and to the telephone circuits and local apparatus to which it is desired to give instantaneous connection with a street box circuit. Connected to and extending in a line from the Combination Switch eight feet, on either side, with a covering of plate glass, is a polished steel bar two inches wide and one-fourth of an inch thick, supported on its edge by steel rollers. In the face of this bar at intervals of three inches a slot one-fourth of an inch wide is cut on an angle. Under the bars at corresponding intervals are the circuit switches to work in unison with the combination. They consist of pieces of hard rubber six inches long, three-fourths of an inch wide, inlaid with metal bearings, and slide in perpendicular grooves at right angles to the steel bar. At each side of the slides flat german silver springs having wire connections to the various circuits, etc., are screwed to the wood, and their ends terminating on the metal bearings in the slides. The top end of the slide, which extends above the steel bar, has a friction roller fitting the diagonal slot in the bar. The lower end is connected to a lever with a handle extending outward. By pulling down this handle the bearings of the slide of the circuit switch on which the springs rest are taken from their normal position and placed in contact with others of the springs. The downward movement carrying the friction roller within the slot in the steel bar causes it to move and to carry with it the slide of the Combination Switch, thereby effecting a large number of changes in the circuits by the simple movement of the handle.

All the different pieces of apparatus pertaining to a given circuit connecting with the receiving and automatic transmission are arranged in a line vertically. First the lever switch, etc., then the key, above that the shunt switch, pulling out similarly to an organ stop, for placing in the circuit an increased electro-motive force at will, and shunting the relay to obviate change in its adjustment. Above that, under a glass plate, is the relay, which is connected directly on the circuit, then the local peg switch, which makes connection with the register and the Annunciator over it or with the duplicates in another part of the office, above that being the list of stations on the circuit and the annunciator showing the number of the circuit.

Beside the fifty circuit recording instrument there is a sixteen circuit recorder recently added for the accommodation of new circuits, and a duplicating instrument with fifty-six pieces, whereby in the event of accident any of the circuits can be transferred to the duplicating instrument. There is also an instrument for recording the outgoing alarm signals with an independent pen connecting with each gong circuit through the repeaters, making its records in red ink, and with the combination circuits recording those signals in blue ink, and attached to which is a multipled repeating relay to which the several telephone circuits are connected, and on which all fire signals are repeated; the repeating transmitters through which the alarms are sent on the gong circuits, consist of three, and are located upon pedestals in the middle of the platform. The principal and most important of these is a marvel of mechanism and ingenuity. Two sets of double cylinders connected with a powerful battery, arranged to revolve in unison, and making contact with springs having their connections with the gong circuits so that a single revolution of the cylinder gives one electric pulsation to each circuit. The motive power is a train of numerous wheels, etc., moved by weights. Connecting with this main train or movement is a series of four auxiliary movements, each being independent of the other, and which are brought into action in connection with the main train at the will of the operators. These auxiliary movements consists each of three dials or circular discs, indexed upon their rims with plain figures, the first having 1 to 25, and the other two having 1 to 9, each set moving on one axis. The discs here described control the battery current to the cylinders, and the different figures to which the indices may be set, indicate such number of strokes as are to be transmitted to the instruments in connection with the circuits. If the signal is to be a continuous number of blows with an equal interval of time between them, say a test signal of eleven, the first disc of the series in use will be set to the "11" on the index. The effect will be to supply battery to the cylinder just while eleven revolutions are made, the mechanical arrangement or relationship being such as to cut off the battery supply as soon as the desired number of pulsations have been given, thus feeding to the circuits the eleven pulsations, each of which gives a blow upon the gongs and makes a record on the registers. The capacity for transmitting by any one of the auxiliaries is twenty-five continuous blows or any less number, or any combination up to 999, so that with the four series it is possible to transmit with one setting of the index a continuation of twelve distinct numbers of blows. The available numerals embraced within three digits, or up to 999, having been absorbed, it has become necessary to add the fourth digit for numbering signal stations. If the signal be composed of two numbers in combination like 2–3 the two discs of the same series are used, one being set to 2 and the other at 3, and if another number is to be added to the combination, say 4, then the third disc is set to 4. As soon as the 2 has been given the first disc cuts off the current for an extra interval, then follows the 3, and again an extra interval and the 4 is given, thus the breaking up of the continuity in the nine blows drive them into the combination 2–3–4. To transmit a signal of this class an additional disc of another auxiliary is required, and the full capacity of the two is six numbers or up to 999,999. It is doubtful if the demands of the city, created through its very rapid growth, will ever exceed the possibilities of this instrument for meeting its requirements. Another of the repeaters is provided with contact cylinders, etc., and a case of wheels, one for each station, and to transmit a signal the wheel corresponding to it in number is placed in its position upon a shaft and the machinery is started, the wheel performs the same duty in controlling the battery current as the indexed discs in the other instrument, but its capacity is limited to the regular station signals. The third repeater is much smaller and has but a single dial. It is used for testing and other purposes.

Telephones are affixed to the cabinet-work of the office, and connection is thus maintained with every company house and the principal officials for department business solely. The different apparatus used in the receiving and transmitting of a fire signal having been described, it is only necessary to explain that when a signal box is pulled for a fire the operators on duty are first apprised of it by the dropping of the annunciators, showing the number of the circuit on which the box is located, followed by the number of the box. The handle of the switch and combination is pulled down by the operator, allowing the succeeding signals to be automatically transferred to the companies. Every horse in service is unhitched at the first tap of the instrument. The full signal is struck all through the city upon the instruments of the combination, as well as on the telephone bells, and recorded upon the paper of the register. The assistant operator has meanwhile prepared the transmitting repeater by setting it to the signal number, and the signal then follows over the gong circuits working in the same houses, but over other wires and on different gongs. Except that an imperfection may exist in the combination circuit, such of the force as are assigned to duty at the station indicated rarely ever wait long enough to hear the latter signal, and within thirty seconds from the start of the signal from the box—except, perhaps, in the case of a high number—the companies assigned have left their quarters in response.

The signal boxes which are distributed throughout the city are connected with the Central Office by special circuits—that is, no other use is made of the circuits except for signalling fire alarms. The number of boxes on each circuit is from fifteen to twenty-five, and the arrangement of circuits is such that no two boxes in the same neighborhood are on the same circuit, so that in the event of one of the wires being out of order, there is still a chance for connection by means of the other circuits. Keys for the boxes are placed convenient for access, generally in drug stores and similar public places, and a sign on each box informs the public where the keys are to be found. Every policeman and fireman has keys. They are also provided to reputable citizens who ask for them, it being stipulated that they shall be carried upon their person. A couple of years ago Superintendent Smith began to put the Tooker keyless door, which can be opened by any one by turning a handle, on street boxes. The turning of the handle sounds a bell on the inside of the door, and the sound is continued during the time required to effect the opening and the transmission of an alarm—about a quarter of a minute—ample to attract the attention of the police or other persons in the vicinity, thus rendering it unsafe for persons to tamper with them. Much time is thus saved in important districts in transmitting an alarm, which under other circumstances would necessitate the procuring and use of a key. They proved to be so popular that whenever an opportunity occurs keyless doors are put to boxes, and in the near future few boxes will be closed, and these will be in districts where the funny or malicious adult or child would be able to tamper with a keyless box without great danger of detection. The boxes are arranged with clock-work, and springs furnish power. They are provided with circuit breakers, wheels which are notched, and contact springs which have their ends bearing upon the wheel. On opening the box a hook is seen and a sign "Pull the hook once." The pull operates on the clock-work, and the notches on the wheel passing under the springs *break the circuit once for each notch*, and sending to the tape or record in the Central Office an indication corresponding to the notches on the wheel. The numbers and combination being different in each box, the operators know instantly from what box a signal comes.

The usual method of attaching the boxes to poles has been greatly improved by adopting an invention of Superintendent Smith, whereby iron gas lamp posts are altered into combination lamp and signal posts. The posts are cut off as they stand five feet from their bases, and an ornamental frame-work of iron attached. This has a receptacle for the signal box. The column of the post is connected again at the top of the frame, and on its top is placed the lamp with a red display globe, indicating that a fire signal box is below. The gas supply is through the column and frame. There have been nearly two-score of these combination posts established and connected with the underground cables, for which they were specially designed. They are both practical and ornamental. Another invention of Superintendent Smith recently put in use was the special signal box. They were destined for the schoolhouses of the city, and 130 are now in use. They transmit calls for fire, police, and ambulance service by simply manipulating "pointers" on the boxes and pulling a hook. Then the desired signal is received at the Central Office twice, and the location once. The normal condition of the box is for a fire signal, but when the pointer is used, other boxes are in service which by the use of a key can be made to send four other special signals, among them second and third alarms.

The regular force employed in the operating of the telegraph bureau consists of a superintendent, a chief operator, three operators, five assistant operators, one clerk, two battery men, five linemen, two box inspectors, one instrument-maker, one machinist, and a floating force of climbers and laborers at day wages.

So far this chapter has referred only to the telegraph system and appliances as they existed in the old headquarters in Mercer Street. Arrangements at the present writing are being made to transfer the entire telegraphic paraphernalia to the sixth floor of the new Fire Headquarters, 67th Street, between Third and Lexington Avenues. What changes, if any, this will bring about in the system remains to be seen. It is hardly possible that any considerable improvement can be effected. But the advances in electrical sciences are so rapid and numerous, that it is impossible to prophesy what the near future may bring forth, to revolutionize in a great measure the existing state of affairs.

CHAPTER XXVI

FIRE INSURANCE: ITS BENEFICENCE AND IMPORTANCE

The Great Benevolent Society.—Blest Offspring of Modern Civilization.—The Friend of the Poor, the Guardian of the Helpless, the Protector of Home, the Safeguard of Honorable Competence.

Many volumes each the size of this work would be required to give the history of Fire Insurance and the Board of Fire Underwriters. The united companies virtually control, as mentors and censors, not only the Fire Department of New York, but in a certain sense the men and methods connected with fire extinguishing in the United States, and they are to be regarded as managers of business concerns which profit by the efficiency of a municipal department in the pay of the tax payers. It is not within the scope of this work to present anything like a full history of the Board, but a brief sketch will be necessary and interesting.

One of the best retrospects of combined insurance interests was in an address made in this city on the 26th of April, 1876, to the National Board of Fire Underwriters of the United States, by Henry A. Oakley, Esq., of the Howard Insurance Company, President of the Board. Mr. Oakley regretted that a proposition to erect in the Centennial Grounds, in Philadelphia, a building wherein insurance men could meet, and another building wherein the statistics of fire insurance business in this country during the century should be collected were not carried out. "Fire insurance," he went on to say, "can scarcely claim to have been known in the early part of our nation's history. Philadelphia is entitled to the honor of having established the first fire insurance company in America, for in 1752 the Philadelphia Contributionship, or, as it is sometimes styled, 'Hand in Hand,' was founded, a company still in prosperous existence, and whose chief promoter, and one of whose original directors was Benjamin Franklin. This company celebrated its Centennial nearly a quarter of a century ago, and shows evidence to-day of the wise management which characterized its early career. Differences, however, seem to have arisen among its trustees as to the exposure of property by the trees which at that early date must have been a feature in the

City of Brotherly Love, and from the attraction they presented to lightning, the company ceased to insure property which had trees in front of it. The result was a new organization in 1784, by some of the promoters of the first and other prominent citizens, called the Mutual Insurance Company, which adopted as its seal or mark, a tree in leaf which gave to it the name of the 'Green Tree,' by which it is familiarly known, and its plate bearing this badge is still affixed to houses. In the year 1787 another company bearing the same name—Mutual Assurance Company—was founded in New York, and it still exists with the very appropriate title of the 'Knickerbocker Fire Insurance Company.'

"The next organization was the Insurance Company of North America, of Philadelphia, founded in 1794 on the stock plan, whose representatives are among us to-day as active, earnest promoters of this Board. In 1797 the Massachusetts Fire Company was chartered in Boston, but it long since passed out of existence, and in 1798, in the same city, the Massachusetts Mutual was organized, and after having weathered many storms ceased to exist in 1872, as a result of the great fire. There was established in the town of Boston, in 1724, 'The Sun Fire Office in Boston,' by Joseph Marion, and also about the same period 'The North American Insurance Company,' whose exact date it appears impossible to obtain. Both of these companies are supposed to have been individual enterprises, as no record of their incorporation can be found.

"New York in 1806 organized the Eagle Fire, still extant, and in 1810 Hartford organized its pioneer company, 'The Hartford Fire Insurance Company,' whose importance to us and the public generally we all feel disposed to recognize. Mr. Cornelius Walford, of London, in a paper which I had the pleasure of hearing him read before the Middlesex Archæological Society, made known the fact of the existence of mutual fire associations for two centuries or more before the great fire in London of 1666, while on the continent of Europe individual underwriting was known as far back as the twelfth century. In his curious and interesting article in the Insurance Cyclopædia on 'Fire Insurance,' he has gathered the early history of fire underwriting into a compact form. He states that the first company really formed in England was in 1680, called the Fire Office, afterward the Phœnix; this was followed in 1683 by another, which seems to have been a formidable rival, and was called the Friendly Society. These companies were only organized for the insurance of buildings. The first company chartered to insure merchandise and other personal property was the Lombard in 1704. In 1710 the Sun Fire Office was established, followed in 1714 by the Union, in 1711 by the Hand in Hand, in 1717 by the Westminster, in 1720 by the London Assurance Corporation, and in 1721 by the Royal Exchange. ★ ★ ★ The system of association in boards is as old as the business itself. I was told in London that such an association existed in the latter half of the last century, which has been continued down in various forms to the present day, many of the companies which originated it still being members. As early as 1819 such an association was formed in the city of New York, when only eight companies were in existence, and it continued to make additions to its members until 1827, when it was merged into a regular Board of Underwriters. To show that it was to be proof against disaster either from within or without, it took the euphonious name of the 'Salamander Society.' Its records still exist and are in my possession."

On the 20th of April, 1858, at the First Annual Dinner of the New York Board of Fire Insurance Companies, A. B. McDonald, Esq., of the Royal Insurance Company of Liverpool, in responding to a toast, said that the early history of the Old Association of Fire Insurance Companies was involved in some obscurity, its records having perished in the fire of 1835. Of its original members not one survived, and of those who were members in 1829, when Mr. McDonald joined it, but few survived. "The rapidly increasing population and commerce of this city after the peace of 1815," continued the speaker, "led to the formation of this association about the year 1825 or 1826." Among the companies originally represented in the association, he said, were the Mutual, the first Fire Insurance Company established in this state after the Revolution, a company whose records afford a curious and interesting history of the rise of fire insurance in this city, which has paid in full all just claims upon it since 1787, and still maintains a vigorous existence under its present name of Knickerbocker, the Globe, with a capital of a million dollars, the Eagle, the Washington, the Merchants, with capitals of four hundred thousand dollars each, and many others.

"The rules and regulations of the association," he continued, "were founded on two leading principles, viz.: Uniformity of Rates and Non-payment of Commissions for procuring business. The operation of these principles, which were adhered to with fidelity, elevated the Associated companies to a high position in public estimation; so great was the confidence felt in their stability that, prior to 1835, investments in their shares were made by executors to estates and other trustees in preference to bank stocks. These principles survived the destructive conflagrations of 1835 and 1845, and on the reorganization of the companies after both these calamities they were adopted as the basis of the revived Association. One period in the history of Fire Insurance in this city is so full of instruction and warning as to deserve a notice. About 1843 a large increase of companies, of which a number did not connect themselves with the Association, and were not governed by its rules and regulations, led to a strenuous competition for business. Several members withdrew from the Association and reduced their rates of premium. A reduction of the associated rates followed and was succeeded by reduction after reduction to rates far below a compensation for the losses. The ruin which the companies were thus inflicting on each other was completed by the conflagration of 1845. It may be remarked that the companies which commenced this unfortunate course were hopelessly insolvent, and were never resuscitated."

Other authorities differ with Mr. Oakley. Some writers trace insurance back to the second Punic war, but it appears well established that the first fire insurance was contemplated in 1696, when the "Amicable" Company was established in England.

In 1858, when the "Salamanders," or Old Association of Fire Insurance Companies of the City of New York, was merged in the New York Board of Fire Insurance Companies, interesting majority and minority reports were presented to the association. In one of the reports it was stated that there were at that time doing the business of fire insurance in this city seventy-nine companies which were incorporated by the State of New York, and one incorporated by the State of New Jersey, making a total of eighty companies, employing an aggregate cash capital of sixteen million one hundred and fifty-six thousand dollars; that there were also several mutual companies engaged largely in the same business, but the committee regarded those having cash capitals only, as being more closely allied in interest, and as having a more direct bearing upon the questions under consideration. Of the eighty companies there were forty-three with an aggregate capital of nine million four hundred and four thousand dollars, which were associated for objects of mutual benefit, each company being subject to certain rules and restrictions adopted by such association, the remainder comprising thirty-seven companies, with an aggregate capital of six million seven hundred and fifty-two thousand dollars, had no association in common, but a large majority of them having been organized within the past eight years deemed it necessary, to ensure their success, to act independently of the association, or, in other words, to place their capital in direct competition with that represented in the board. Among other things it was resolved that the agreement to adhere to a standard of rates as signed by the companies not members of the association, be also signed by the members of the Board of Underwriters, that a committee be appointed for the purpose of calling a convention of all the fire insurance companies of New York, Brooklyn, and Jersey City, to devise means for the adoption of a standard of rates, and that to such convention be referred also the subject of paying commission, or modifying the then system of brokerage, or of abolishing the system altogether. The majority report was signed by W. F. Underhill, Robert D. Hart, Horatio Dorr, and John Baker.

In the majority report it was said: "One important fact must not be lost sight of, viz.: that the present standard rates are much higher in this city, taking all things in consideration, than is charged in most, if not all, of the principal cities in the Union. The rates charged in the city of Boston on warehouse risks are from ⅜ to ¾ per cent. In Philadelphia, from 50 to 65 cts. In Baltimore, from 60 to 75 cts; while in this city they range from 65 to 112 cts., averaging about 85 cts. This enhanced rate in New York over the rates prevailing in other cities named, and in cities too that have a large number of home companies, has induced the establishment of numerous agencies in this city, many of the agents being authorized to take risks from 10 to 15 cts. less than the rates charged by this association." Edward Anthony was the signer of this report.

Mr. Underhill was Secretary of the Peoples; Mr. Hart, Secretary of the Astor; Mr. Dorr, Secretary of the Atlantic, of Brooklyn; Mr. Baker, Secretary of the Mercantile, and Mr. Anthony, President of the Lamar.

The Salamander Society, an organization of fire underwriters, which existed between 1819 and 1826, had for several years no standing officers, but at the meeting a president and secretary were elected. At the time of its organization there existed eight fire insurance companies, viz.: Globe, Eagle, Mutual, Franklin, Fulton, Washington, Merchants' and Mechanics', and when it ceased to exist, there were in addition the Ætna, Chatham, Contributionship, Equitable, Firemen's, Farmer's, Greenwich, Howard, Jefferson, Lafayette, Manhattan, North River, Phœnix, Protection, Sun, Trader's, Orange, Tradesmens' and United States. Of the Presidents were Gabriel Furman, Mutual; Swords, Washington; Jackson, Globe; Edward Laight, Eagle, and Henry Rankin, father of James M. Rankin, Globe; of the companies which belonged to the association, the Ætna, Eagle, Equitable, Howard, Manhattan and Mutual, Knickerbocker, survive. At the first meeting held January 29, 1819, it was resolved, on motion of Mr. Henderson, President of the Globe, that buildings of brick or stone covered with slate, tile or metals, and having solid iron doors and window shutters in the rear, and no building in front within 100 feet, be insured as of the first class; by Mr. Henderson, that the risks on ship chandlery be insured at the same premium as groceries.

In May, 1819, rates appeared to have stirred up the Salamanders, for the following was adopted on motion of Mr. Printard, of the Globe: "That a committee of five be appointed to revise the present rates of premium, and the regulations of the Fire Insurance Companies with a view to have the same printed, and the said committee report at the next meeting." The committee consisted of Messrs. Laight, Eagle; Pintard, Mutual; Underhill, Fulton; Harris, Washington; and Lawrence, Merchants'. August 6th, a report on rates and long term policies was made. In it was the following:

Say the premium for one year is $100,

A present payment of 93.45 = $100 payable 1 year hence
A present payment of 87.34 = $100 payable 2 years hence.
A present payment of 81.62 = $100 payable 3 years hence.
A present payment of 76.28 = $100 payable 4 years hence.
A present payment of 71.29 = $100 payable 5 years hence.
A present payment of 66.33 = $100 payable 6 years hence.

By this calculation a person insuring for 7 years, $100 yearly premium, would pay $576.75, whereas by the present rate he pays $600.

The committee therefore recommend that the following discounts should be allowed, which are, fractions excluded, in conformity with the above principle, viz.: for two years, 3½ per cent; three years, 7 per cent; four years, 9½ per cent; five years, 12½ per cent; six years, 15 per cent; 7 years, 17½ per cent.

Insurances made for a shorter term than one year will be charged as follows:

For nine months ⅞ of the annual premium.
For six months ¾ of the annual premium.
For five months ⅔ of the annual premium.
For three months ½ of the annual premium.
For two months ⅖ of the annual premium.
For one month ⅓ of the annual premium.

The classes of hazards and rates of insurance were:

	Addition to rate of house.	Special premium.
Apothecaries	25	
Bakers	37½	
Boat Builders	25	
Booksellers (stocks only)	12½	
Bookbinders	37½	
Brick kilns		75
Brownstone works	25	
Cabinet makers	25	
Carpenters	12½	
Chair makers	12½	
Confectioners	12½	
Chinaware (stock unpacked)	25	
Chocolate makers, with stove	12½	
Colormen (stock only)	12½	
Coopers	25	
Couch makers	25	
Chip and straw hats	12½	

	Addition to rate of house.	Special premium.
Corn in stock		50
Druggists	25	
Dyers	25	
Flax	12½	
Founders	25	
Farmers, viz.:		
Dwelling houses		50
Stables		75
Dead stock therein		75
Live stock therein		50
Stock in stacks		50
Glass, unpacked	25	
Glass, in packages	12½	
Grocers	12½	
Hay in stacks		50
Hemp	12½	
Houses, building or repairing	25	
Looking-glass, in packages	12½	
Looking-glass, unpacked	25	
Malt houses with kiln	50	
Mills, viz.:		
Bark mills		75
Corn and grist mills, no kiln		87½
Corn and grist mills, with kiln		125
Cotton mills		
Flour mills		
Fulling mills		100
Metal mills	12½	
Oil mills, with stove		150
Paper mills, with stove		150
Paper mills, no stove		75
Saw mills		75
Snuff mills		150
Woolen mills		150

N.B.—Distinct sums are to be specified in the insurance of mills under the following heads, viz.:

	Addition to rate of house.	Special premium.
Machinery.		
Movable utensils and stocks.		
Musical instrument sellers (stock only)	12½	
Musical instrument makers	25	
Oil	12½	
Pictures and prints (stock only)	12½	
Pitch	12½	
Sail-makers	12½	
Saltpeter	12½	
Ship chandlers	12½	
Ships and cargoes on board one year		70
Ships and cargoes on board eleven months		65
Ships and cargoes on board ten months		60
Ships and cargoes on board nine months		55
Ships and cargoes on board eight months		50
Ships and cargoes on board seven months		45
Ships and cargoes on board six months		40
Ships and cargoes on board five months		35
Ships and cargoes on board four months		30
Ships and cargoes on board three months		25
Ships and cargoes on board two months		20
Ships and cargoes on board one month		12½
Ship builders	25	
Soap makers	25	
Spirits	12½	
Stables	25	
Stationery (stock only)	12½	
Straw in ricks		50
Sugar refiners	75	
Tallow melters	25	
Tar	12½	
Tavern keepers	12½	
Tile kilns		75
Timber yards, if isolated	50	
Turpentine	12½	
Turpentine manufactories		50

In the case of chocolate makers the policy specified that the company was not responsible for loss of stock in drying. In that of corn in stacks, stock in stacks and hay in stacks the clause was "not responsible for damage in natural heating." Country stores were privileged to keep gunpowder. In the case of mills the several insurance companies were at liberty to fix their own rate of premium. These rates were more or less strictly adhered to, thanks to the prodding of those who were disposed to "cut" by conservative companies. Matters of this sort appear to have been harmonized in February, 1820, by a resolution appointing Messrs. Tibbits, Henderson and Laight a committee "to consider and report at the next meeting of the representatives of the Fire Insurance Companies what penalty ought to be incurred for any willful deviation from the rates of insurance agreed upon by the respective fire insurance offices, which penalty if agreed to shall be referred to the several companies for concurrence, and when concurred in shall be binding on all companies," thus in fact establishing a Tariff Association.

A step similar to that legalized in 1886 was taken in April, 1821, under the following resolution: "That a committee be appointed to examine the policies of the different companies for the purpose of having them uniform." A uniform "Form of Policy" was agreed upon on the 19th of June. It was so clear and distinct in setting forth the interests of the insurer and insured that it was used until recent years as was the "Rent Policy" and "Form of Application" approved of at the same time.

The classes of hazards and rates of annual premiums were set forth in the following table:

CLASSES OF HAZARDS AND RATES OF ANNUAL PREMIUMS.

1st.	2d.	3d.	4th.
Buildings of brick or stone covered with tile, slate, or metal, the doors and windows of solid iron, 22 cents per $100.	Buildings of brick or stone covered with tile, slate, or metal, 25 cents per $100.	Buildings of brick or stone, roofs three-fifths of tile, slate, or metal, the rest shingled, 30 cents per $100.	Buildings of brick or stone covered with wood, 37½ cents per $100.

5th.	6th.	7th.	8th.
Buildings of frame filled in with brick, the front entirely of brick, 50 cents per $100.	Frame buildings filled in with brick, 62½ cents per $100.	Frame buildings, hollow walls with brick front, 70 cents per $100.	Buildings entirely of wood, 75 to 100 cents per $100.

Not Hazardous.—Goods not hazardous are to be insured at the same rates as the buildings in which they are contained, and are such as are usually kept in Dry Goods stores, including also Household Furniture and Linen, Cotton in Bales, Coffee, Flour, Indigo, Potash, Rice, Sugars, Teas, Spices, Paints ground in Oil, and Threshed Grain.

Hazardous.—The following Trades, Goods, Wares, and Merchandise are considered *hazardous*, and are charged with 12½ cents per $100 in addition to the premium above named for each class, viz.: Booksellers' stock, Chair makers, Chocolate makers, Confectioners, China, Glass and Earthenware in Packages, Flax, Hemp, Printers' stock, Milliners, Musical Instrument Sellers' stock, Oil, Pitch, Pictures and Prints, Sail makers, Ship chandlers, Spiritous Liquors, Saltpeter, Tin, Turpentine, Tavern keepers, Tobacco manufacturers, and Watch makers' stock.

Extra Hazardous.—The following Trades and Occupations, Goods, Wares, and Merchandise are deemed *extra hazardous*, and will be charged 25 cents and upward per $100 in addition to the premium above specified for each class, viz.: Aqua fortis, Apothecaries or Druggists, Boat Builders, Coach Makers, Cabinet Makers, Carpenters in their own shops or buildings erecting or repairing, Chemists, China, Glass and Earthenware unpacked and buildings in which the same are packed, Coopers, Dyers, Ether, Founders, Fodder and Grain unthreshed, Hay, Musical Instrument makers, Spirits of Turpentine, Straw, Soap Boilers and Tallow Chandlers, and all manufactories requiring the use of fire heat. Gunpowder is not insurable except by special agreement.

Special.—Mem. Bakeries, Breweries, Bookbinderies, Distilleries, Fulling Mills, Grist Mills, Malt Houses, Paper Mills, Printing Offices, Sugar Refineries, and Saw Mills may be insured at special rates of premium.

Country Houses.—N. B. Country houses standing detached from other buildings, though of the 6th, 7th, and 8th class, will be insured at 50 cents per $100. Barns and stables in the country 75 cents per $100.

☞Ships in port or their Cargoes, and Ship building or repairing may be insured against fire.

The first standing officers of the Salamanders were elected September 8, 1823, when Mr. Jackson of the Globe was chosen Chairman and O. H. Hicks of the Fulton, Secretary. In October Messrs. Tibbitts, Lord, Champlin and Mercein were appointed a committee to draft by-laws for the guidance of the Board. A set was approved of in December. In January, 1826, a new organization, a revision of rates and the consolidation of interests were considered, and among other things it was resolved that a deposit of $500 be made by each company to insure adherence to rules and regulations and that "the funds so deposited by the several companies be placed in charge of a committee of the officers of the same, who are to loan out said funds on the hypothecation of any funded debt of the United States or of this State, or the hypothecation of the stock of any banking institution in this city the value of which said stock when so hypothecated shall be above par, the interest so accruing on said loans to be paid over annually or semi-annually to the respective companies." A meeting was held and the resolutions were agreed to except by the United States, Firemen's and Greenwich Companies, and the outcome was a new association of companies known as the Fire Insurance Association under the presidency of Mr. Jackson. This organization established new tariff rates in 1835, when there was a reorganization due to collapse, in 1842, again in 1844 after the second great fire, and afterward in 1848. The most stable of the associations, the Board of Fire Insurance Companies, was organized in 1850.

We find that prior to 1850 Mr. Edward W. Laight was President of the New York Board of Fire Insurance Companies, and was succeeded in 1850, 1851 and 1852 by Nathaniel Richards, Mr. George T. Hope being secretary. The first call for statements from insurance companies was made from the Comptroller's office, Albany, on Jan. 7, 1829, by Wm. L. Marcy. The Revised Statutes provided that only corporations *thereafter* created should file annual statements, so that it was not until 1864 that all insurance companies, compelled by the new law to do so, sent in their reports. The first New York Fire Insurance Company to file a statement was the New York in 1833, the year after its creation. It was as follows:

The following balance-sheet exhibits a statement of the property and funds of this company January 9, 1833:

Amount of Capital paid in December 18, 1832.............. $200,000.00
Amount of Premiums secured up to January 7–9, 1833......   397.11

Total $200,397.11

By amount of loans on bank stock $156,625.00
By amount of loans in public stocks 15,000.00
By amount of loans on bond and mortgage on real estate ...   7,750.00
By amount of expenses, viz., furniture, books, etc. 771.74
By amount of loans on cash in Merchant's and Trader's
    Bank 20,177.57
By amount of cash in iron chest on hand....................   72.80
                                                          _____
Total $200,897.11

In 1833 Comptroller A. C. Flagg rapped the following New York Stock Fire Insurance Companies over the knuckles, reminding them not only of the financial penalty, but that a failure to report within a month of the receipt of the circular, laid them open to dissolution as insolvent corporations: American, Bowery, Clinton, City, Firemen's, Guardian, Jefferson, Long Island, Mechanics', New York, National, Phoenix, Sun and Union.

The reports to Comptroller Flagg for 1835 had black eyes. "Losses by the late fire in the First Ward of this city" played havoc with the capital. The Stock Companies which made reports from the city were the City, loss, $156,000; Greenwich, $35,182.73; Guardian, $300,000; Bowery, New York, $100,000. In the reports for 1836 we find the City, among its assets, giving a claim for property blown up with gunpowder, $24,244.95. The East River reported its capital swept away by the fire, etc., the commencement of new business with $250,000 of new capital. The Jefferson included in claims against it that of Evans & Carman, whose store was blown up by order of the Corporation of the City amounting to $6,650, and acknowledged the impairment of its capital. The Merchants' took advantage of "An Act for the benefit of certain Insurance Companies in the City of New York" passed 12th of February, 1836. The New York, in its assets, $8,000 due from the United States Bank surplus on an assignment of a bond and mortgage as collateral security for money borrowed to pay wages. The North American speaks of bonds and mortgage coming to it as receivers of the late Phoenix Insurance Company. In the reports for 1845, the great fire of that year is alluded to. In December, 1848, Comptroller Millard Fillmore suggested to the Legislature the taxation of Mutual Insurance Companies. He also addressed a circular to the Mutual Fire Insurance Companies of the State requiring reports, and received a few from suburban companies, one of which was as follows:

Farmers' Mutual Insurance Company of Sherburne, Chenango County. Only loss since the Company was chartered is eleven dollars. N.B.—This company has stopped business in consequence of Mutual Companies having

become of late rather unpopular. Most of the policies run out in 1850.—
December 29, 1848. B. H. Marks, Secretary.

The Act of April 10, 1849, placed Fire Insurance Companies incorporated in
other States, and doing business in the State of New York, virtually on an equal-
ity with the companies of the state, and subjected them to the same restrictions.
They were required, if they did business in New York or King's County, to
have a capital of $150,000. Under the law the following Joint-Stock Fire Insur-
ance Companies filed reports for 1849: Ætna of Hartford, American of Philadelphia, Columbia of Philadelphia, Columbus of Ohio, Delaware Mutual Safety
of Philadelphia, Franklin of Philadelphia, Franklin of Boston, Hartford of Connecticut, State of Pennsylvania, Merchants' of Kentucky, Lexington of Kentucky,
Manufacturers' of Boston, Merchants' of Boston, Nashville of Tennessee, National of Boston, Neptune of Boston, Norwich of Connecticut, North American
of Philadelphia, Protection of Hartford, Protection of New Jersey, Providence
Washington of Rhode Island, and Tennessee of Nashville.

These years marked important events. In them the system of watching for
incendiaries and prosecuting them was perfected by the appointment of a Fire
Marshall, Mr. Alfred Baker. October 15, 1857, it was resolved to in future call
the association the Board of Fire Underwriters, and this preceded the reorganization of April 15, 1868. June 24, 1858, the following resolution in regard to
cutting rates was passed:

> That in case of a deviation from the rates of premium by writing below
> the established rates it shall be the duty of the company making such de-
> viation to pay the amount of premium named on each policy into the
> treasury for the benefit of the Fire Patrol Fund, subject to the decision of
> the Executive Committee.

Anxiety was felt about the water supply at this time, for on the 26th of
October a committee of three was appointed to inquire into the matter.

In December 1861, on a report of a Special Committee on unrefined petroleum, it was declared "positively uninsurable in all buildings in compact portions
of the city, and in all public warehouses, privileged for storage of hazardous, and
extra hazardous merchandise, and such oils are considered insurable only when
in detached and properly ventilated sheds and warehouses, specially adopted by
their construction for that purpose, and devoted exclusively to the storage of
such oils or substances of a similar character, and then only at a special rate, not
less than three per cent." The storage of benzine, benzole, naptha, and refined
petroleum was also restricted.

March 17, 1864, the creation of a Paid Fire Department was foreshadowed by the passing of the following resolution:

> *Resolved*, That the subject of promoting the greater efficiency of the Fire Department be referred to a special committee to inquire into the same, and report to a subsequent meeting of this Board.

November 28th plans had so far advanced that each company was assessed one-tenth of one per cent, of the amount of its capital for the advancement of the scheme, one-half to be handed over to the Citizens' Association and the remainder to the Committee on Paid Fire Department. The same day the Board offered a reward of $3,000 for the conviction of any and all incendiaries in New York, Brooklyn, Jersey City and Hoboken. This was because of the attempt to burn the city by Southern sympathizers, and the mayor had offered a reward of $2,000 for their arrest. The early days of 1865 were passed in discussing the Paid Fire Department Bill presented at Albany. The chief opposition was to including Brooklyn in its operations. February 14th a communication from Mr. Peter Cooper embodied a suggestion which was not carried out until President Henry D. Purroy had his portable tank constructed. Said Mr. Cooper: "In order to stimulate these men and preserve the greatest degree of purity in their body and devotion to the interests of the city I propose that it should be made their pecuniary interest to faithfully perform their duty." He urged the placing of tanks of elevated water held at convenient places in the city so high that the force of water will make all the hydrants equal to fire engines for the purpose of extinguishing fires by simply hoisting a gate so as to let the water press on the mains of the city.

When in April, 1865, the affairs of the Committee on Paid Fire Department were settled it was found that they had spent $21,836.50, more than half of the assessment on the companies, and an additional assessment of one-tenth of one per cent, was ordered. Appropriate action was taken in regard to the victories which marked the close of the war and the death of President Lincoln. On the 17th of April, 1865, the members of the Board met at the Insurance Rooms, No. 156 Broadway, and Messrs. Edward A. Stansbury, Robert O. Glover and James M. McLean passed resolutions regarding the assassination of President Lincoln. One of the resolutions read:

> *Resolved*, That the members of this Board join with the nation and the whole civilized world in execration of the spirit which has prompted this deed, and in profound and personal sorrow for the bereavement which it has inflicted on us.

On January 30th, 1866, a special committee reported a proposed act for the incorporation of the Board. The draft of the bill was not presented until March 5th, 1867, and the Act of Incorporation was passed May 9th, 1867. The first meeting of the new Board was on the 15th of May, when measures were taken to dissolve the association and transfer its property. May 20th Mr. McLean and Mr. Henshaw were re-elected. Shortly after the alarming frequency of fires and the unusual losses therefrom caused an inquiry by the Assembly Committee on Insurance Companies, who met a Committee of the Board. Afterward the Board's Committee made suggestions before a joint meeting of the Senate and Assembly Committees on Insurance. Out of the conference came a bill which created another Fire Commissioner, an act regulating the Storage of Combustible Materials, an act to create a Superintendent of Buildings, and an act to create a Fire Marshal. In November incendiarism had became so common that the Board appropriated $50,000 to be offered in rewards for convictions, not exceeding $5,000 in any one case. The act creating a Fire Marshal was not passed until the spring of 1868, and Captain Charles N. Brackett was appointed.

A leap from 1868 to 1886 is necessitated by want of space to chronicle the minor events of this period against the important events of the last-named year, one of the most important in the annals of underwriting. The only digression permissible is to refer to the important discussions and action of various committees in the Dry Goods District in 1882 and 1883. The district was understood to be that bounded by Chambers, Elm, Crosby, and Spring Streets, South Fifth Avenue, and West Broadway, and the value of the stocks held is estimated at $200,000,000.

The main work of 1886 was the adoption of the standard Fire Insurance Policy of the State of New York, which went into effect on the 20th of October, 1886, under chapter 488 of the Laws.

There was also established the Metropolitan Association of Fire Underwriters under section 19 of the by-laws; who adopted a schedule of minimum rates which with the rates of the New York Tariff Association constituted the rates in the Metropolitan District of the 7th of October, 1886. This was under a compact reported by the committee. The preamble of the compact was as follows:

1. That all risks of every description in the Metropolitan District be equally rated.
2. That no commission be paid in excess of 10 per centum of the premium.
3. That no rebate to the assured be made by the companies from established rates, and that rules be prepared under which the rebating of commissions by brokers shall be effectually prevented.
4. That penalties be fixed for the infraction of any of the rates and rules that may be adopted by the Association.

The New York Board of Fire Underwriters of to-day, whose offices at the Boreel Building, No. 115 Broadway, were first occupied in 1878, is a great institution. The companies having in various ways representation in it have $185,415,352.00 of assets against $10,586,175,402.00 of risks.

President Hall's address to the Board on his election in May, 1886, contained some important statements and figures. The following table gave the assessed valuation of real estate in this city each year since 1866:

1867,	. .	$555,442,062.00	1877, . .	$895,063,933.00
1868,	. . .	623,235,305.00	1878, . . .	900,855,700.00
1869,	. .	684,183,918.00	1879, . .	918,134,380.00
1870,	. . .	742,105,675.00	1880, . . .	942,571,690.00
1871,	. .	769,306,410.00	1881, . .	976,735,199.00
1872,	. . .	797,125,115,00	1882, . .	1,035,203,816.00
1873,	. .	836,691,980.00	1883, . .	1,079,130,669.00
1874,	. . .	881,547,995.00	1884, . .	1,119,761,597.00
1875,	. .	883,643,545.00	1885, . .	1,168,443,137.00
1876,	. . .	892,428,165.00		

The following table showed the premiums reported for fire patrol assessment in the same years, less brokerage:

1867,	. . .	$8,222,845.00	1877, . . .	$5,032,669.00
1868,	. . .	7,369,061.00	1878, . . .	4,008,789.00
1869,	. . .	6,872,885.00	1879, . . .	4,612,948.00
1870,	. . .	6,085,281.00	1880, . . .	4,990,966.00
1871,	. . .	6,606,352.00	1881, . . .	5,103,749.00
1872,	. . .	7,001,802.00	1882, . . .	5,539,049.00
1873,	. . .	8,281,508.00	1883, . . .	5,874,008.00
1874,	. . .	7,879,622.00	1884, . . .	6,089,621.00
1875,	. . .	6,802,331.00	1885, . . .	5,887,577.00
1876,	. . .	5,838,013.00		

He submitted a brief analysis of the business of this city since 1873, selecting this date as it follows the Chicago and Boston fires. The following table gives a comparison of the premiums and their distribution in 1873 and 1885:

		COMPANIES (1873.)		PER CENT.	COMPANIES (1885.)		PER CENT.
Locals,	.	(85)	$5,583,124.00	67	(55)	$2,895,550.00	49
Agency,	.	(77)	1,511,269.00	18	(69)	1,181,224.00	20
Foreign,	.	(11)	1,187,114.00	15	(22)	1,810,803.00	31
			$8,281,507.00	100		$5,887,577.00	100

In the course of his address Mr. Hall said:

"The local companies having decreased in number from fifty-nine to fifty-five, and the foreign companies from twenty-five to twenty-two, the agency companies have increased from fifty-nine to sixty-two, showing that the efforts to secure reform have been, in a measure, thwarted not only by the tariff companies themselves, but by the companies which have ignored the rules of the Tariff Association, many of the latter having most to fear from a failure to correct present abuses."

A history of Fire Insurance and underwriting in New York would be incomplete without a more than passing reference to the friend of Washington Irving, Lewis Gaylord Clark, and many other *literati*, William Pitt Palmer, "the Laureate of the Salamanders." This gentleman, who was the President of the Manhattan Fire Insurance Company, was a native of Massachusetts, and was graduated from Williams College. He came to New York to study law, but he abandoned this profession to study medicine, and just as he had completed his studies he became a clerk in the Manhattan Fire Insurance Company's office. This was in 1834, and he continued in its service until its dissolution. Mr. Palmer had a facile pen in many branches of literature, but it was at the social board that he was conspicuous by his wit and genial conviviality. He was a poet of no mean order, but his forte lay in *jeux de mots*, and some of his rhymes applied to his profession were exceedingly humorous.

CHAPTER XXVII

THE HAND AND STEAM
FIRE-ENGINES

Their Origin, Growth and Development.—Fire Apparatus in Use Before the Christian Era.—The Force Pump.—The Invention of Fire-Engines.— Application of the Air-Chamber.—Introduction of Leather Hose.—Newsham's and Simpkin's Inventions.—Ericsson's Portable Steam Engine, Etc., Etc.

The invention of the fire-engine is of great antiquity and involved somewhat in obscurity. In chronicles relating to the destruction of cities by fire about the commencement of the Christian Era, and particularly concerning the burning of the town of Nicomedia in Bythania, the lack of machines or apparatus proper for extinguishing the flames was mentioned. The word *sipho*, used in said chronicles, being translated and so understood generally as meaning fire engines. Hesychius and Isidorus, who lived in the beginning of the seventh century, prove that in the fourth century at least a fire engine, properly so-called, was understood under the term *sipho*. The question still remains at what time this apparatus for extinguishing fires was introduced at Rome. From the numerous ordinances for preventing accidents by fire, and in regard to extinguishing fire, which occur in the Roman laws, there is reason to conjecture that that capital was not unprovided with those useful implements and machines, of the want of which in a provincial town the historian Pliny complained. In the East engines were employed not only to extinguish but to produce fires. The Greek fire, invented by Callinicus, an architect of Heliopolis, a city afterward named Balbec, in the year 678, the use of which was continued in the East until 1291, and which was certainly liquid, was employed in many different ways; but chiefly on board ship, being thrown from large fire engines on the ships of the enemy. Sometimes this fire was kindled in particular vessels, which might be called fire-ships, and which were introduced among a hostile fleet; sometimes it was put into jars and other vessels which were thrown at the enemy by means of projectile machines, and sometimes it was squirted by the soldiers from hand engines; or, as appears, blown through pipes. But the machines with which this fire was discharged from the fore-part of ships could not have been either hand engines or such blow pipes. They were constructed of copper and iron, and the extremity of them sometimes resembled the open jaws and mouth of a lion or other animal. They were painted and even gilded, and it appears that they were capable of projecting the fire to a great distance. These machines by ancient writers were expressly called spouting-engines. John Cameniata, speaking of the siege of his native city, Thessalonica, which was taken by the Saracens in the year 904, says that the enemy threw fire into the wooden works of the beseiged, which was blown into them by means of tubes and thrown from other vessels. That statement proves that the Greeks in the beginning of the tenth century were no longer the only people acquainted with the art of preparing that fire, the precursor of gunpowder. The emperor Leo (tenth century), in his treatise on the art of war, recommended such engines with a metal covering to be constructed in the fore-part of ships. There is no doubt the use of a force pump for extinguishing fires was long known before the invention of Greek fire. It is uncertain at what time the towns in Germany were first furnished with fire-engines. It is believed that they had regulations in regard to fires much earlier than engines, and the former are not older than the first half of the sixteenth century. The oldest respecting the city of Frankfort-on-the-Main is of the year 1460. The first general ordinance respecting fires in Saxony was issued by Duke George in 1521. The first for the city of Dresden, which extended also to the whole country, was dated 1529. At Augsburg an express regulation in regard to building was drawn up and made publicly known as early as 1447. In turning over old chronicles we find it remarked that great fires began to occur less frequently in the sixteenth century; and this was undoubtedly to be ascribed to the improved mode of building, the precautions enjoined to prevent fires and the introduction of apparatus for extinguishing them. Thus, in the year 1466, straw, thatch, and in 1474, the use of shingles were forbidden at Frankfort.

But by the invention of fire-engines everything in those respects became so much changed that a complete revision of the regulations in regard to the extinguishing of fires was rendered necessary, and therefore the first mention of town fire-engines is to be found in the new fire ordinances of the sixteenth and following century. In the building accounts of the city of Augsburg fire-engines are first mentioned in the year 1518. They are called in those accounts "instrument for fires," "water syringes," useful at fires—which would imply that the machine was then in its infancy. At that time they were made by a goldsmith at Friedberg, named Anthony Blatner, who the same year became a citizen of Augsburg. From the account given as to the construction of the wheels and levers, and the greatness of the expense, there is reason to conclude that these were not small, simple, hand-engines, but large and complex machines.

In the year 1657 the well-known Jesuit father, Casper Schott, was struck with admiration on seeing at Nuremburg a fire-engine which had been made there by John Hautsch. It stood on a sledge, ten feet long and four feet broad. The water cistern was eight feet in length, four feet in height, and two in width. It was moved by twenty-eight men, and forced a stream of water an inch in diameter to the height of eighty feet. The machine was drawn by two horses. Hautsch refused to show the internal construction of it to Schott, who, however, readily conjectured it; and from what Schott has handed down it is easily perceived that the cylinders did not stand in a perpendicular direction, but lay horizontally in a box, so that the pistons moved horizontally and not vertically. Upright cylinders, therefore, belong to the more modern improvements. Schott added that it was not a new invention, as there were such engines in other towns, and he himself forty years before, and consequently in 1617, had seen one, but much smaller, in his native city. Schott was born in 1608 at Königshofen, not far from Würzburg.

The first regulations at Paris respecting fires, as far as is known, were made to restrain incendiaries, who in the fourteenth century, under the name of *Boutefoux*, occasioned great devastation not only in the capital but in the provinces. That city appears to have obtained fire-engines for the first time in the year 1699; at any rate, the king at that period gave an exclusive right to Dumourier Duperrier to construct those machines called *pompes portatives*; and he was engaged at a certain salary to keep in repair seventeen of them purchased for Paris, and to procure and pay the necessary workmen. In the year 1722 the number of these engines was increased to thirty, which were distributed in different quarters of the city. The city, however, besides these thirty royal engines, had a great many others which belonged to the Hotel de Ville, and with which Duperrier had nothing to do.

In the middle of the seventeenth century fire-engines were very imperfect. They had neither an air-chamber nor buckets, and required a great many men to work them. They consisted merely of a sucking-pump and forcing-pump united, which projected the water only in spurts and with continual interruption. Such machines on each movement of the lever experienced a stoppage, during which no water was thrown out; and because the pipe was fixed it could not convey water to remote places, though it might reach a fire at no great distance where there were convenient doors and windows to afford it a passage. At the same time the workmen were exposed to danger from the falling of the houses on fire. Hautsch adapted to his engine a flexible pipe which could be turned to any side; but certainly not an air-chamber, as Schott would have mentioned it. In the time of Belidor there were no other engines in France, and the same kind alone were used in England in 1760. At least that conclusion is induced by the account given by Ferguson, who called Newsham's engine, which threw the water out in a continual stream, a new invention. In Germany the oldest engines were of that kind.

Who first conceived the idea of applying to the fire-engine an air-chamber, in which the included air, by compressing the water, forces it out in a continued stream, is not known.

According to a conjecture of Perrault, Vitruvius seems to speak of a similar construction. But the obscure passage in question might be explained in another way. There can be found no older fire-engine constructed with an air-chamber than that of which Perrault has given a figure and description. He says it was kept in the king's library at Paris, and during fires could project water to a great height; that it had only one cylinder and yet threw out the water in one continued jet. He mentions neither its age nor the inventor; and it can only be added that Perrault's book was printed in 1684. The principle of this machine, however, seems to have been mentioned before by Mariotte, who on this account is by some considered as the inventor.

It is certain that the air-chamber, at least in Germany, came into common use after it was applied by Leupold to fire-engines, a great number of which he manufactured and sold. He gave an account of it in a small work which was published in 1720; but at first he kept the construction a secret. The engines which he sold consisted of a strong copper box closely shut and well soldered. They weighed no more than 16 pounds, occupied little room, had only one cylinder, and a man with one of them could force up the water without interruption to the height of from twenty to thirty feet. About 1725, Du Fay saw one of Leupold's engines at Strasburg, and discovered by conjecture the construction of it, which he made known in the Transactions of the Academy of Sciences at Paris for that year. It is singular that on this occasion Du Fay says nothing of Mariotte or of the engine in the king's library.

Another improvement, no less useful, is the leather hose added to the engine and to which the fire pipe is applied, so that the person who directs the jet of water can approach the fire with less danger. This invention belongs to two Dutchmen named Jan and Nicholas Van der Heide, who were inspectors of the apparatus for extinguishing fires at Amsterdam. The first public experiments made with it took place in 1672, and were attended with so much success that at a fire next year the old fire engines were used for the last time, and the new ones introduced in their stead. In 1677 the inventor obtained an exclusive privilege to make these engines during a period of twenty-five years. In 1682 engines on this construction were distributed in sufficient numbers throughout the whole city, and the old ones were entirely laid aside. In 1695 there were in Amsterdam sixty of these engines, the nearest six of which were to be employed at every fire. In the course of a few years they were common throughout all the towns in the Netherlands.

The employment of flexible hose strong enough to bear a good pressure of water has in no small degree increased the facility and effect with which fires can be controlled by means of water forced through it. The invention of the

Van der Heides, after its introduction into Holland, became common in other parts of the continent, but it did not find its way into England until nearly a hundred years later. The great difficulty with the leather hose was to make it watertight. The seams were sewn like the leg of a boot, and the pressure caused them to open and leak badly, so that much of the water was lost where the hose was carried too far. Notwithstanding this defect, leather was found to be the best material for the purpose on account of its strength and durability, substitutes, such as canvas and seamless woven hose, invariably giving way after short usage. Some sorts of hose were made of canvas covered with a cement or paint to make them watertight; another sort was the seamless hose woven in a tubular form by machines such as has been introduced at a very recent period as a new invention; but leather still continued to be used with such satisfactory results as to prove the truth of the old proverb, that "there is nothing like leather." Until the year 1808 the defective character of the hose seriously impaired its usefulness at fires. In that year Messrs. Sellers & Pennock, of Philadelphia, furnished a most valuable contribution to the means in use for extinguishing fire, by the invention of riveted hose. The substitution of copper rivets for fastening seams removed the last obstacle to its employment, and leather hose has since played a conspicuous part among the instruments for extinguishing fires in America.

Riveted hose, by greatly increasing the effectiveness of engines at a distance from the fire, produced a radical change in the extinguishment of conflagrations. Formerly suction hose was made of short metallic cylinders, placed end in end and covered with canvas or leather. They were easily crushed, however, because they were not sufficiently elastic. Afterward stout spiral wire was substituted and found to answer the purpose. The objections urged against leather hose were the liability to defects—the leather, its tendency to crack, and the constant care necessary to keep it flexible, by the application of grease or oil. Some other materials were invented, among them, besides canvas and linen, india rubber. The india rubber, whether used alone or as a lining for canvas or linen, was held to be superior. This material was first brought out in England in 1827. So well did it stand the severe tests to which it was subjected, that it was soon adopted by the most of the insurance companies. One test was the plugging up the nozzle of a length of india rubber and a length of leather hose attached to a powerful engine well worked. The leather hose blew out or burst in the solid part of the leather, and the india rubber was uninjured and broke down the engine. Many makers preferred this hose when trying engines for range and height, because of the smoothness and evenness of its interior. Moreover, after use and before being rolled up it was only necessary to dry it. At fires it was found necessary to keep hose of this kind away from the heated ruins, and it was recommended that care should be taken in laying out to avoid those parts where damage might arise to it from this cause.

In 1720 hose woven without a seam was made of hemp at Leipsic by Beck, a lace weaver. After this it was made by Erke, a linen weaver of Weimar, and at a later period it was made of linen at Dresden and also in Silesia. In England, Hegner & Ehrliholzer had a manufactory at Bethnal Green, near London, where they made watertight hose without seams.

All the circumstances relating to the Van der Heide invention have been related by the inventor in a particular work which, on account of the excellent engravings it contains, is exceedingly valuable. Of these the first seven represent dangerous conflagrations at which the old engines were used but produced very little effect. One of them is the fire which took place at the Stadt-house of Amsterdam in the year 1652. According to an announced calculation the city of Amsterdam lost by ten fires, when the old apparatus was in use, 1,024,130 florins; but in the following five years after the introduction of the new engines, the loss occasioned by forty fires amounted only to 18,355 florins; so that the yearly saving was ninety-eight per cent. Of the internal construction of these engines no description or plates have been given; nor is there anything to show that they were furnished with an air chamber, though in the patents they were always called "spouting engines," which threw up one continued jet of water. The account given even of the nature of the pipe or hose is short and defective, probably with a view to render it more difficult to be imitated. It is only said that it was made of leather in a particular manner; and that besides being thick it was capable of resisting the force of the water.

The conveyer or bringer was invented also about the same time by these two Dutchmen. This name was also given at a later period to a box which had on one side a sucking pump and on the other a forcing pump. The former served to raise the water from a stream, well, or other reservoir, by means of a stiff leathern pipe screwed to the engine, the end of which widened into a bag, supported near the reservoir, and kept open by means of a frame, while the laborers poured water into it from buckets. A pump, however, to answer this purpose was soon constructed by the Van der Heides, who named it a snake pump. By its means they were able to convey the water from the distance of 1,000 feet, but there is no account of the manner in which it was made. From the figure it is conjectured that they used only one cylinder with a lever. Sometimes also they placed a portable pump in the water, which was thus drawn into a leathern hose connected with it and conveyed to the engine. Every pipe or hose for conveying water in this manner they called a *wasserschlange*, water-snake, and this was not made of leather, like the hose furnished with a force pipe, but of sail cloth. They announced, however, that it required a particular preparation, which consisted in making it watertight by means of a proper cement. The pipe, also, through which the water was drawn up, was stiffened and distended by means of metal rings; otherwise the external air on the first stroke of the pump would compress the pipe so that it could admit no water. Thus it is seen that pipes made of sail cloth are not so new an invention as many have supposed.

From these facts one may readily believe that engines with leathern hose were certainly not invented by Gottfried Fuchs, director of the fire apparatus at Copenhagen in 1697, as was publicly announced in 1717, with the addition that this invention was soon employed both in Holland and at Hamburg. Fuchs seems only to have made known the Dutch invention in Denmark, on the occasion of the great fire which took place on the 19th of April, 1689, at the Opera House at Amalienburg, when the beautiful palace of that name and more than three hundred and fifty persons were consumed. At any rate, in consequence of that calamity an improvement was made in the fire establishment by new regulations issued on July 23, 1689, and that engines on the Dutch construction which had been used more than twelve years at Amsterdam were introduced.

Hose or pipes of this kind for conveying water were, however, not entirely unknown to the ancients. At least the architect Apollodorus says that to convey water to high places, exposed to fiery darts, the gut of an ox having a bag filled with water attached to it might be employed, for on compressing the bag the water would be forced up through the gut to the place of its destination. This was surely a conveyor of the simplest kind.

Newsham's fire-engine was a side-brake, double-cylinder engine, mounted on four wheels, and with an air-chamber, goose-neck and suction pipe. The work on the brakes was assisted by men on the box who threw their weight upon treadles on the pump-levers. Pumps were single-action force-pumps, worked by chains passing over segments on the pump-levers. The engine was perhaps the first successful fire-engine.

The engine which eventually superseded Newsham's was invented by Simpkin, and patented in 1792. The main improvement was in compactness and adaptation to traveling with speed to the spot where its services were needed. The valves were contained in separate chambers, instead of being placed in the cylinders and air-chamber. By this means they were easily reached without the disconnection of the main portions of the pump.

Another form of fire-engine was invented by Bramah in 1793, improved by Rowntree, and eventually by Barton, whose engine was on the vibrating principle.

Steam power for extinguishing fires was in use in manufacturing establishments many years before it was employed on portable machines. Every factory of any pretensions had its steam-driven pump with hose and other attachments calculated to reach every portion of the establishment.

The manufacture of steam fire-engines in England, as a regular branch of industry, is of recent origin. The first steam fire-engine was constructed in 1829 in London by Messrs. Braithwaite & Ericsson. Later on four more were made, and all were eminently successful. So strong, however, was the prejudice against them that from 1832 to 1852 no more were made in that country, and public attention seemed to wane. After a lapse of twenty years, and about twelve years after steam fire-engines had been in use in the United States, the London Fire Engine Establishment altered one of the hand-worked floating engines on the Thames into a steam fire-engine. Until 1860 no further progress was made in the way of encouraging their manufacture. The strongest opponent of the fire-engine in England was Mr. James Braidwood, Superintendent of the London Fire Engine Establishment. In time, however, he changed his opinion. The great objection, strange to say, urged against the new engines from 1829 to 1856 was that they threw too much water. The application of steam power to work a force pump, arranging the engine, boiler, pumps, etc., on wheels, so as to be easily portable, and thus enable it to be readily employed as a fire-engine, was due to Mr. John Braithwaite, civil engineer. In conjunction with Captain Ericsson he constructed an engine of ten horsepower, with two horizontal cylinders and pumps, each steam piston and that of the pump being both attached to one rod. The waste steam from the cylinders was conveyed through the tank containing the feed water by means of two coiled pipes, thus giving the feed water a good temperature previous to its being pumped into the boiler. Its weight complete was 45 cwts., and it threw from 30 to 40 tons of water per hour to a height of 90 feet, having thrown well over a pole that height. In five hours it consumed three bushels of coke. This engine gratuitously rendered signal service at many important fires, saved thousands of pounds' worth of property, and in return the insurance companies presented Mr. Braithwaithe's men with £1 ($5)! The London Fire Brigade antagonized him in every way. In 1831 Mr. Braithwaite constructed his second steam fire-engine, of five horsepower. It had a steam cylinder 7 in. by 18 in., with a pump of 6½ in. by 18 in., giving a proportion of steam cylinder to pump of 1.16 to 1. When working with a steam pressure of 50 lbs. on the inch, and making 40 strokes per minute, it threw 27 cubic feet of water per minute = 15 cwts., through a one-inch nozzle, to a height of 109 feet, and gave 5.6 horsepower. When working with 60 lbs. steam pressure, and making 35 strokes per minute, it threw 23.6 cubic feet of water per minute = 13 cwts. 19 lbs., through a ⅞-inch nozzle, to a height of 108 feet. This engine was worked in France at several towns, with great success, and afterward taken to Russia with similar results.

The third engine built by Mr. Braithwaite had two cylinders, but three pumps, placed horizontally and driven by gearing from the crank shape of the engine, so as to reduce the speed of the pump pistons. The fourth steam fire-engine was the "Comet," of 15 horsepower, built in 1832 for the King of Prussia. Its boiler was similar to the others, and it had two horizontal cylinders, each 12 in. diameter by 14 in. stroke, making 18 strokes per minute, and the two pumps were each 10½ in. diameter by 14 in. stroke. The engine was arranged to work with four sets of hose, together or separately. The total weight was four tons. In from 13 to 20 minutes from lighting the fire the engine was started with 70 lbs. of steam, and with a single nozzle of 1¼ in. diameter the water was thrown from 115 to 120 feet vertically, the engine making 18 strokes per minute, and at this rate the weight of water thrown amounted to 1 ton, 7 cwts. and 13 lbs. per minute. At an angle of 45 to 50 degrees the water was thrown to a distance horizontally of 164 feet. The engine was equal to at least 90 tons of water per hour at the average working rate. The consumption of fuel was about three bushels of coke per hour. The fifth engine was an experimental one, built in 1833.

In 1835 Mr. Braithwaite designed a floating steam fire-engine capable of throwing 187.5 cubic feet of water per minute. In 1850 Mr. P. Clark, the assistant engineer of the West India Docks, arranged one of Downton's pumps in one of their tugs, so that it could be driven by gearing from the engine and the steam engine used in propelling the vessel. This was the first steam-floating fire-engine on the Thames, and it threw 600 gallons of water per minute, 20 feet higher than the highest warehouse in the docks, and with a nozzle of 1½ inch diameter, threw to a distance of from 160 to 180 feet. Until the year 1852 the two most powerful engines of the London Fire Engine Establishment were the two floating engines worked by hand, one stationed at Southwark Bridge and the other, or lower float, at Rotherlithe. Two years later a boat was built and fitted up expressly in a steam-floating fire-engine. It was 130 feet long, built of iron, and cost $15,000. The engines were 80 horsepower. It was said that this engine had thrown 2,000 gallons of water per minute through four separate nozzles at the same time to a distance of 180 feet.

Messrs. G. Rennie & Son in 1836 constructed a portable disc engine and disc pump mounted on wheels for use in the Woolwich Dockyard, either as a steam fire-engine or as a pump for emptying the caissons. The engine had a cylinder 13 inches in diameter and the pump was 9 inches in diameter. It is said that when making 320 revolutions a minute, with 45 lbs. of steam, lifting the water 10 feet and with a pressure of 62 lbs. in the discharge pipe, the water was thrown through a three-inch diameter hose and a nozzle of 13–16 inch diameter to a total height of from 140 to 150 feet.

Messrs. Shand and Mason, the most famous builders in England, constructed their first land steam fire-engine in 1856, and the machine was sent to Russia. The steam cylinder which actuated the pump was inverted and situated near the air vessel of the pump, which was made double-acting, one barrel being placed over the other, and a double-throw crank was placed between them. One or both of the pistons or plungers of the pump was fitted with a valve, and the piston-rod of the steam cylinder was connected directly with the piston of the upper pump barrel, which latter served as a guide to the piston-rod of the steam cylinder. Beneath the seat was placed the hosereel or a box for containing the hose and implements. In 1859 one of Messrs. Shand and Mason's steamers, with an 8½ inch cylinder and 6 inch stroke, was tried at Waterloo Bridge, and in six minutes from lighting, the fire was stated to have had 10 lbs. on the square inch, and in 10½ minutes 30 lbs. with a ⅞ inch nozzle; the height reached was estimated to be 140 feet, and the horizontal distance 161 feet.

Mr. James Shekleton, a Dundalk engineer, constructed in 1860 the first steam fire-engine in Ireland. It weighed 22 cwts., and had a vertical tubular boiler with internal circulating tubes, on the plan of Silsby, Myndorse & Company, of the United States, dry smoke box and an effective heating surface of 40 square feet, the water space around the fire-box being fitted with a circulating plate. The working pressure was 80 lbs. on the square inch, with the engine making 120 strokes per minute.

In July, 1860, a land steam fire-engine was for the first time used by the London Fire Engine Establishment in one of the back streets of Doctor's Commons. The weight of the machine with men, ovals and water, ready to run out, was 84 cwts., and it took three horses to draw it. In the same year a steam floating fire-engine was constructed by the Messrs. Merryweather from the designs of Mr. E. Field, civil engineer, to be placed in a steam tug and used for protecting the warehouses in the Tyne Docks. The water supply, however, was inadequate to the needs of the engine. In 1861 Messrs. Merryweather & Sons constructed, also from the designs of Mr. Field, their first land steam fire-engine, the "Deluge," which was quite a success. It was of 30 horsepower, and threw water through a nozzle 1½ inches in diameter 10 feet over a chimney 140 feet in height, altogether 180 feet, through a 1⅜ inch nozzle to a distance of 202 feet horizontally, and through a 1¼ inch nozzle 215 feet horizontally.

In 1861 Messrs. Shand & Mason manufactured three steam fire-engines on wheels to run on the rails for the London and Northwestern Railway. They had double horizontal cylinders and pumps, and slotted cross heads and fly-wheels. One of them with a nozzle of one and one-quarter inch diameter threw a stream vertically to a height of 170 feet, and horizontally 225 feet. In the next year the firm constructed a steam fire-engine for the town of Sothenbury. In 1861 Messrs. Merryweather & Sons constructed a famous steamer called the "Forrest," which did good service at numerous London fires.

Mr. William Roberts, of Millwall, in 1861, built the first self-propelled steam fire-engine ever made in England or Europe. It was supported on three wheels, one in front being the steering wheel, and arranged so as to be employed in driving machinery. The extreme length was 12 feet 6 inches, extreme breadth 6 feet 4 inches, and its gross weight with ovals, water, hose, ladders and tools complete was a little above 7½ tons. The engine was suspended on springs. The engine power consisted of two vertical cylinders, 6 inch diameter and 12 inch stroke, working the crank shaft, etc., by means of cross heads and side rods. The engine was driven along the public roads at 18 miles per hour. With a nozzle of 1⅜ inches diameter, the stream was thrown over a chimney (140 feet high) and a horizontal distance of 182 feet, exclusive of broken water and spray. The steam pressure varied from 50 lbs. to 160 lbs., with 100 revolutions per minute. On one occasion the engine with 170 lbs. of steam and 112 revolutions per minute, using 1½ inch nozzle, delivered 450 gallons of water per minute. In the same year Mr. William Roberts constructed his second land steam fire-engine, the "Princess of Wales." On the 31st of July, 1863, in twelve minutes from lighting the fire the engine got to work. It accommodated 18 men, with a great quantity of appliances, ladders, etc.

In 1863 Mr. James Shand obtained a patent for improvements in steam fire-engines, in which patent the vertical engines made by Messrs. Shand, Mason & Co., were subsequently substituted. In the same year the change engine "Suth-erland," which gained the first prize of $1,250 at the Crystal Palace trials, with six other engines, English and American, in 1863, was built by Messrs. Merry-weather & Sons. The "Sutherland" discharged ten gallons of water at each rev-olution or stroke, and delivered water through nozzles at the rate of between 800 and 1,000 gallons per minute. It has thrown water through a 1½ inch nozzle to a horizontal distance of 235 measured feet. It was purchased by the govern-ment and placed for service in the Royal Dockyards at Devonport.

In the same year a steam fire-engine for the Imperial Library at St. Peters-burgh, was designed and constructed by Mr. T. W. Cowan, engineer, of Green-wich. The boiler, engines and pumps were carried on a wrought iron framing, 7 inches deep and ¼ inch thick, strengthened with angle iron and mounted on springs, the whole being carried on four wheels. The weight of the engine was four tons, and it was drawn by three horses, when using delivery hose of 2½ inch diameter with a nozzle of 1¼ inches and a steam pressure of 120 lbs., a height of 170 feet and a distance of 210 feet were obtained.

In 1863 Mr. Egestorff, of Hanover, constructed a steam fire-engine for the fire-engine establishment of that city. The cylinder was 8½ inches by 9 inches and the pumps 7 inches; the valves metal of the description known in Hanover as Carretts. In the same year Messrs. Merryweather & Sons constructed a small steam fire-engine for the Alton Volunteer Fire Brigade. The machine had a single steam cylinder and pump, the cylinder being 6⅜ inches by 18 inches stroke, and the pumps 4¾ inches diameter and 18 inches stroke. The weight was 25 cwts. One of these 25 cwt. single cylinder engines was found to have exerted a power equal to 32½ horses, or 1⅓ horsepower for each cwt. of engine. In this year Messrs. Shand, Mason & Co., constructed 17 steam fire-engines, two for the London Fire Brigade, two for Lisbon, three for the Bombay and Barsoda Railway Company, four for Russia, two for New Zealand, one for Austria, one for Poland, one for Denmark and one for Dublin.

In 1865 Mr. William Roberts constructed his third steam fire-engine, the "Excelsior," which was made to order for the Arsenal Rio de Janeiro. With a one inch nozzle the engine threw a stream over a pole 80 feet high and 120 feet from the branch pipe, or a total of 144 feet from the branch to the top of the mast. The vertical lift of the suction at starting was 6 feet and 10 feet when the tide left. In the same year Messrs. Moltrecht, of Hanbury, constructed a small steam fire-engine with a single horizontal cylinder and two horizontal pumps, which was not successful. Also in 1865 Mr. Fland, of Paris, built a steam fire-engine.

In 1865 Messrs. Merryweather & Sons constructed eleven engines: two medium sized cylinder engines for the Spanish Government; one large sized double cylinder for her Majesty's Government for use at Portsmouth Dockyard; one medium sized double cylinder for the Liverpool Corporation; one similar size for the French Government, for Brest Dockyard; one medium single cylinder for the Dutch Government, for the Amsterdam Dockyard; one small sized cylinder for Dublin; one similar size for Manilla: one similar size for Redruth, and one medium sized single cylinder floating engine for the Northeastern Railway, for use at Newcastle. Mr. William Roberts constructed a steam fire-engine for Hong Kong, which was an exact duplicate of the "Excelsior" in all respects, except that brass tubes were used in the boiler in place of iron. In this engine in 45 seconds, the guage started, in 3 minutes and 5 seconds, 5 lbs. of steam, and in 9 minutes and thirty-two seconds the engine was at work with 100 lbs. of steam, throwing through a 1¼ inch nozzle water to the height of full 160 feet.

The following table gives the date when the English firms commenced to build land steam fire-engines, to be drawn by horses, and the total number of such engines made by them in England and Ireland up to 1866:

	Date.	No. Built.
Braithwaite & Ericsson	1820	5
G. Rennie & Sons	1856	1
Shand, Mason & Co	1858	60 of all kinds.
J. Shekleton	1860	1, the first Irish steam fire-engine.
Merryweather & Sons	1861	17 and three floating engines.

	Date.	No. Built.
Wm. Roberts..............................	1862	5, one self-propelled and one floating.
T. W. Cowan............................	1863	1
J. W. Gray & Son........................	1863	1

The Button steam fire-engine has upright tubular boilers, with submerged smoke-box and combustion-chamber. The crane neck frame is employed in the construction of these engines. The pumps are of the best bronze metal, and are so arranged that the water cannot come in contact with any iron, thus preventing the liability to rust, however long they may be out of use.

The Gould steam fire-engine, manufactured by B. S. Nichols & Company, Burlington, Vt., has a vertical tubular boiler with submerged smoke-flues and tapering firebox. The feedwater is heated by passing through the firebox, a circulating valve being placed on the outside between the boiler and heater, so that when the feed-pump is stopped a perfect circulation can be established between the heater and the boiler. The boilers have an uncommonly large heating surface and steam-room in proportion to the work to be done by the engine, consequently they steam very freely, being capable of raising sufficient steam from cold water in from three or four minutes' time, to play through a hundred feet of hose. The engines are vertical, reciprocating; the steam cylinders resting on columns which are attached to the crane-neck frame and to the boiler.

The Jeffer's engine has an upright boiler, steel tubular of peculiar construction, with inverted smoke-box and furnace and copper tubes, which generate steam very rapidly. Steam can be raised in from four and a half to five minutes. The engines are vertical, with steam cylinders resting on independent columns attached to the frame, and have patent cylindrical steam-valves. A straight, wrought-iron frame is employed in the construction of those engines, which is attached to logs on each side of the boiler; the front end sustains the pump, air-vessel and steam-cylinder, while the rear sustains the coal bunker. The discharge-gate is located in front; and in consequence of a patent relief-valve in connection with the pump, and an ingenious cut-off nozzle attached to the hose, the water can be cut off at any time without in any way interfering with the working of the engine, as when the steam is cut off the relief-valve is automatically opened between the discharge and the suction pipes.

The Neafle & Levy engines are horizontal, and stand quite still when working, with the exception of that vibratory motion which is peculiar to all horizontal machines. They are powerful, durable and efficient.

In the Ives' engine the boiler is an upright tubular with conical smokebox, submerged combustion-chamber, and contracted waist. The feed-water is heated before entering the boiler by being passed through a copper coil inside of the smokestack. The engines are horizontal, with the base of their cylinders so formed as to saddle the cylindrical frame to which they are attached by a row of bolts on each side. The valves are so conveniently arranged as to be capable of being cleaned, renewed or repaired at very short notice. Printz's automatic discharge valves are used, by means of which the water can be shut off at the nozzle at any time without stopping the engine.

The firm of Lee & Larned built one or two large self-propelling engines which were very unwieldy and necessarily slow to be brought into service. One of them, the John G. Storms, was placed in charge of the Exempt Fire Company, and located at No. 4 Centre Street, a building which stood in the rear of the Hall of Records. The same firm built a rotary engine of much lighter pattern, weighing about six thousand pounds, and arranged so as to be drawn by hand power. The engine was purchased by the Fire Insurance interests, and presented to Manhattan Engine Company No. 8, and through the exertion of the late Robert C. Brown, proved a success, notwithstanding the great opposition from other companies in the Department. The same year Guardian Engine Company No. 29 received an engine of the same pattern from the same manufacturer, only one size smaller; ex-Chief Eli Bates was foreman. The same year James Smith, builders of fire apparatus in West Broadway, built a piston engine of small size, to be drawn by hand power, and was placed in service and used with great success by Hudson Hose Company No. 21 (after Engine 53). Mr. James Dale, now assistant engineer in the Brooklyn Fire Department, was the engineer of No. 21, who managed to make this style of engine very popular. The company was located in the Erie Building, 304 Washington Street. Dale was mentioned by Mayor Whitney among those deserving honor in 1887 for saving human life. The same year Valley Forge Engine Company No. 46 received from Lee & Larned a rotary engine, same as Engines 8 and 29, and the following year, 1860, New York Engine Company 47 (formerly Hose 5), and Southwark Engine 38, received from same firm a similar engine to that of No. 46.

The Amoskeag Manufacturing Company of Manchester, N. H., in 1860 brought to this city a piston engine which was placed in charge of Paulding Hose Company No. 57, located at 162 West 18th Street, by the authorities, which was afterward bought, and proved to be a valuable auxiliary to the fire service. In the year 1861 Americus Engine 6 and Lexington 7 applied to the Common Council for steam engines and were furnished with rotary engines built by the Silsby, Mynderse & Company, Seneca Falls, N.Y. The same year the Portland Manufacturing Company sold to the city two piston engines. One was placed in charge of Empire Engine Company 42, the other in charge of Jefferson Engine Company 26, and the same year Black Joke Engine 33 and Jackson Engine Company 24 received each one of the Smith pattern. In 1862 Engine Companies 9 and 58 received an engine built by A. B. Taylor & Son, of this city, and Engine Company 11, James Smith's pattern. In 1863

Engine Companies 4, 30 and 51, received engines built by Jos. Banks of this city, and Engine Companies 12, 13, 28 and 31 engines built by Jas. Smith of New York; Engine Company 22 one built by Mr. Jeffers. In 1864 Engine Companies 1, 15 and 37 received engines built by A. Van Ness of this city, and Engine Companies 10 and 20 machines built by Jos. Banks. All these were piston engines.

In the year 1865 the Metropolitan Fire Department was organized, and many of the engines above numerated were altered to be drawn by horses, and were used until larger and more powerful ones were substituted in their places.

The Metropolitan Commissioners in 1865 contracted with the Amoskeag Manufacturing Company, of New Hampshire, to build at once for use twenty (second size engines) of what are called U Tank Single Pump, weight, about seven thousand pounds when equipped for service, with 8-inch steam cylinder, 12-inch stroke and 4½ inch water cylinder, and most of them were in service in January, 1887, being the same style as that used by Paulding Hose Company 57 of the Volunteer Department, an engine which was built in 1860, and at this time still in service.

The engines of more modern pattern are what are called Double Pump Engines, nearly the same as above, only that they are double acting, having two steam and water cylinders with 8-inch stroke. The first engine placed in service under the new system was a large double engine, and known as "Metropolitan No. 1," of which William Corgan was foreman, and was located in the house formerly occupied by Exempt Company No. 4, Centre Street, facing the entrance to the Brooklyn Bridge, at City Hall Park.

During the year 1871, when the horse disease known as the "Epizootic" was raging all over the country, the commission caused to be built five self-propelling engines of large size and placed in service, and assigned to the following companies: Engine Company 20, Foreman, Hugh Bonner, now Assistant Chief; Engine 32, Foreman, Jos. F. McGill, now Batallion Chief; Engine Company 8, Foreman, John Welsh; Engine Company 11, Foreman, Isaac Fisher, and Engine No. 24, Wm. McLaughlin, Foreman. These engines are still in service, and under the able management of the above-mentioned officers rendered good service to the city.

It will be remembered that the large fire in Boston, Mass., occurred at this time, and the want of horses to draw the apparatus was one of the probable causes of delay which gave the fire such a start, which would not have occurred otherwise.

The following clear and interesting explanation of the steam fire-engine is furnished by ex-Chief Engineer Joseph L. Perley:

"The steam fire engine is simple and compact. The engine is attached to the boiler and both are carried on what are called shears. In some cases the water tanks act as such. In large cities the running gear differs according to condition and character of the streets. The boilers differ somewhat as to the interior, the main object being strength and lightness; the outer shell being steel, and the flues or tubes being made of composition, and many of them seamless brass. Some boilers have as many as the space will allow for the purpose of obtaining as much heating surface as possible. The engine is attached to the boiler on one side, so that the steam chest may be as near the steam dome as possible, the cylinder having steam ports at either end, leading directly to the steam chest. The steam before entering, flows from the boiler into the steam chest, then into the cylinder, where it acts upon the piston and produces motion. The steam is admitted from the steam chest to the cylinder through a valve, and when the steam so admitted has performed its work of driving the piston either up or down, another valve opens and permits this steam to escape from the cylinder into a passage for the exhaust. Steam is used in the dome of the boiler, after performing its functions in the steam cylinder to create what is called artificial draft, which adds to the intensity of the fire in the furnace of the boiler. The main water pump is also attached to the boiler, below the steam cylinder, and is connected with the steam cylinder by means of a piston, in the centre of which is what is called a link, which connects with the crank shaft by a link block or journal. The balance wheels are also attached to the shaft, and near the crank is an eccentric which connected by an eccentric rod or strap made of brass, occasions the valves to work the engine when in operation, and to continue so without the aid of any agency other than the revolutions of the engine when in motion. The steam cylinders as a rule are always larger than the water cylinders, sometimes one-half again larger. The stroke generally is from 8 to 12 inches, so that the water pressure can be increased to double that of the steam if necessary. The pumps differ somewhat in form of construction, but perform similar to each other, being double acting receiving and discharging its water at every stroke or revolution. Each pump has a partition separating the water from the receiving and discharging chambers. In that partition there is a valve called a relief valve, which acts to relieve the discharging chamber of the pump, as would the safety valve upon the boiler, and can be adjusted the same so that an overpressure of water can be relieved or returned back to the receiving chamber of the pump. Engines have a steam and water guage placed so the engineer can always see when the engine is in motion. What water is required to feed the boiler and resupply that which has passed out of it in steam, is taken from the main pump when the engine is in motion. Should the boiler require water when the engine is not in motion it can be taken from a tank, which is placed upon the engine for that purpose, which can be done by using the relief valve and allowing the water to circulate in the main pump, without discharging water through the hose. Tanks are connected by supply pipes leading to main pump also to the feed pumps which can be used to inject water into the boiler, on which a check valve is located near the bottom to prevent a greater pressure of steam from forcing it back. These pipes are also protected from frost by a system of small steam pipes which are used to inject steam into, and prevent freezing in extreme cold weather. Engines generally are used to handle the water from hydrants, and to force it to distant points where most required to extinguish fires, also the river water when fires are adjacent to it, for that purpose. Each engine has two large 4½ inch suction pipes, when connected can reach the water from docks or piers. A fuel pan is also arranged in the rear of the boiler and near the furnace door to carry fuel capable of lasting until fuel wagons are brought to the fire. Foreman and engineers of company usually ride on fuel pan in going to and returning from fires. While engine is standing in quarters the boiler is connected to a heating apparatus, which is used in keeping the water in the boiler at the boiling point, that steam may be generated in a short time upon leaving quarters, and the engine be placed in service as soon as proper connections can be made and hose laid to the place where water is required.

Each boiler has a tram pipe attached, with steam whistle and four gauge cocks, to ascertain the quantity of water in the boiler that the engineer may keep it well supplied."

In 1884, at the Annual Convention of the National Association of Fire Engineers held at Chicago, Chief Engineer G. C. Hale, of Kansas, Mo., read a paper on the desirable points of mechanism in steam fire-engines. "A steam fire-engine," said Chief Hale, "to meet the requirements of present engineers, should contain first, a quick-steaming boiler, as time is an element of great importance in combating fires, a delay of a few minutes in a critical case may result in a large conflagration. Especially is this true of fires in large manufacturing establishments filled with combustible material. Delays are dangerous, is an old maxim, and is nowhere more truly demonstrated than in getting up steam in the boiler of a steam fire-engine after an alarm is tapped—other things equal, that engine in which a working steam power is most quickly required is to be preferred. Second, the construction and mounting of the boiler on the engine frame should permit of a satisfactory working on an even ground. It is not always possible to locate a steam fire-engine over the cisterns or other source of supply in such a manner that it will be substantially level from aft and crosswise, and if it was possible, no time can be consumed in levelling it up without serious risk to the burning property. A steam fire-engine boiler should, therefore, be adapted to work equally well whether level or considerably out of plumb. Third, a steam fire-engine, as a whole, should be constructed in such a manner that no reasonable possibility exists of headage or derangement while going to or in use at a fire, and yet it should be provided with facilities for quick and positive repair. Fourth, the general construction of the engine, as a whole, should be especially adapted to rapid and sometimes rough handling in making ready in answering an alarm, and to the severest strains in transit over rough and uneven roads. Fifth, the boiler of a steam fire-engine should be absolutely exempt from the possibility of explosions either while steaming up or at work during a fire. The pumps of a steam fire-engine should be adapted to work without injury with turbid or gritty water, if occasion should require, as it is not always possible to obtain water for fire-engines from clear sources of supply, and engines are frequently compelled to derive water from rivers or other natural water ways, the streams of which carry large quantities of sand or silt in mechanical suspension. Of course such matter must pass through the pumps, and excepting the valves and pistons, are constructed with especial reference to the use of this character of water, they will deteriorate very rapidly, diminishing the efficiency of the engine and demanding frequent repairs."

During the past eighteen or twenty years the improvements in England in steam fire-engines have not been very important. The changes have been improvements in various parts of the working gear.

So far we have touched upon the history of the steam fire-engine in Europe. The first steam fire-engine constructed in the United States was designed and built by Mr. Paul Rapsey Hodge, C. E., in this city in 1840–41. It was a self-propelled engine, the first of the kind ever constructed, with horizontal cylinders and pumps, a locomotive boiler, in some respects like the style introduced by Edward Bury for locomotives; the slab or plate framing to which the cylinder and pumps were attached, afterward used in locomotives, and wrought iron wheels, which were manufactured by the Matteawan Company for Mr. Hodge. It was arranged to be drawn by horses, if required, as well as by hand and its own steam power. The engine was begun on December 12, 1840, and completed April 25, 1841.

Mr. Hodge had induced the several insurance companies to give him a conditional order for a steam fire-engine, his contract being that the engine should be capable of forcing 6,000 lbs. of water per minute to a height of 120 feet. In 1865 Mr. Hodge wrote a letter to an English author stating that he had begun the construction of his engine many months before Captain John Ericsson landed in New York. It had been claimed that Captain Ericsson had built the first American steam fire-engine. Mr. Hodge showed that Captain Ericsson had made a design for one, a copy of which was published in Ewbank's "Hydraulics," but it was never made. It was said to be precisely the same as that built by Mr. John Braithwaite in London in 1829. In the year 1840 Captain Ericsson had obtained the gold medal which was offered by the Mechanics' Institute of New York for the best plan of a steam fire-engine. The difference in the design and in the engine built by Mr. Braithwaite was in the boiler.

The construction of Mr. Hodge's engine was very simple. The surface of the boiler was very great for a boiler of its weight, being only (without water) 1,600 lbs. net. There were two continuous wrought frames on each side of the boiler, on to which the two steam cylinders and two double-acting water pumps were attached. The steam cylinders were 9½ inch diameter and 14 inch stroke. The two pumps were 8¼ inch diameter and 14 inch stroke, the same piston rod working both through engines and pumps direct. In front of the bed plate was an arrangement for a four, three, two or one jet. The larger single jet was through a 2¼ inch nozzle; if two, each through a 1½ inch; if four, each through a 1⅛ inch nozzle. The quantity of water thrown was very much greater than that contracted for. The height of the stream attained 166 feet, and the quantity thrown to that height through a 2⅛ inch nozzle was 10,824 lbs. The engine was drawing the water through four lengths of suction from a depth of 12 feet.

In 1851 Mr. W. L. Lay designed a self-propelled steam fire-engine at Philadelphia, with a rotary pump, and provided with a plan by which carbonic acid gas could be used to propel the engine to the fire whilst steam was being raised. The fire was to be urged by a fan or blower, and when at work the engine was to be raised off the ground so as to allow the driving wheels to act as fly wheels when the engine was pumping, as was done in Mr. Hodge's engine. It was to throw three or four hundred gallons of water per minute, was provided with a hose reel, steering apparatus and the usual accompaniments, and was estimated to weigh 1½ tons.

In 1853 Mr. A. B. Latta, of Cincinnati, constructed a steam fire-engine, a self-propeller, which ran on three wheels. The cylinders were two in number, placed on each side, the pumps being in front of the cylinders, the piston-rods of the steam cylinders were continued to form the rods of the pumps, and the engines were so arranged as to couple to the driving wheels when required when driving-wheels placed behind the firebox. The leading wheel could turn in any direction so as to admit of the easy steering of the engine. It could throw one to six streams of water, and was fitted with a 6½ inch suction hose 24 feet long, and was reckoned to throw 2,000 barrels of water per hour. It would get to work in five minutes, and it required four men and four horses to work it and run it out. On one occasion it threw a stream 291 feet to where the spray fell, the nozzle being 1¾ inch diameter.

In 1855 Abel Shawk, of Cincinnati, built an engine with the following results: Steam was formed in 5 minutes and 15 seconds after the torch was applied, the water being quite cold; in one minute afterward the guage showed 15 lbs., and in 7 minutes 20 seconds after lighting, 50 lbs., and in 8 minutes from lighting the engine was started, the steam quickly rising to 180 lbs. When raising water by the suction from the Delaware against a moderate breeze with a 1¼ inch nozzle, a horizontal distance, excluding spray, 176 feet was reached; with 325 feet of hose and a 1⅛ inch nozzle it threw 120 feet against the wind; with 925 feet of hose and a ¾ inch nozzle the engine threw to a height of 40 feet at 70 feet horizontal distance from the engine, the steam pressure being 96 lbs. on the square inch.

The firm of Messrs. Poole & Hunt, of Baltimore, Md., began building steam fire-engines in 1858, and in 8 years completed seven—one of the first class, four of the second class and two of the third class. Their engines had no screw, bolt or handle, or any other appurtenance more than was necessary. The boilers were upright multitubular, with a square firebox and enlarged steam space. They were fed by a feed or force-pump, and were arranged to take a supply by a connection with the main air vessel. These engines raised sufficient steam for starting in from five to six minutes from the time the fire was lighted, the water being cold in the boiler. The first class engines, with a 1⅜ inch nozzle, threw to a horizontal distance of 257 feet; the second class, with a 1⅛ inch nozzle, to a horizontal distance of 240 feet; the third class, with a 1 inch nozzle, to a horizontal distance of 235 feet.

Messrs. Ettinger & Edmond, engineers and steam fire-engine builders, of Richmond, Va., began the construction of steam fire-engines in 1859. The boilers were vertical with 165 iron tubes of 1½ inches diameter; steam cylinders 9 inches by 15 inches, one in each engine, with two pumps to each placed horizontally, each pump 3½ inches by 15 inches, the contents being equal to the 5 inch pumps. The suction hose was 4½ inches in diameter, and the delivery hose 2½ inches in diameter. The weight of the engine complete, with wood and water ready to run out was 6,600 lbs. These engines would throw water to a horizontal height of 240 feet with a 1⅛ inch nozzle, and to a vertical height of 160 to 180 feet. The average steam pressure used when working at a fire was 60 lbs. on the square inch in 7 minutes from lighting the fire. Two of the first engines were sent to the Fire Department of Richmond Va., the third to St. Petersburg to the order of Messrs. Winans & Harrison.

Toward the close of 1859 trials of steam fire-engines were made at Philadelphia, the engines having been on exhibition at the Fair of the Agricultural Society. The following machines contested:

"Good Intent," built by Reany & Neapie, of Philadelphia—steam cylinder, 8 inches diameter and 12 inches stroke; pump, 4⅜ inches and 12 inches stroke; weight, 5,400 lbs.; 1 inch nozzle, horizontal distance, 169 feet; vertical height, 140 feet.

"Weccacoe," built by Merrick & Sons, Philadelphia—steam cylinder, 8½ inches diameter and 14 inches stroke; pump, 6 inches diameter and 14 inches stroke; 1¼ inch nozzle, horizontal distance, 109 feet, vertical height, 83 feet.

No. 7, "Baltimore," built by Poole & Hunt, Baltimore—steam cylinder, 14 inches diameter and 12 inches stroke; pumps, 6 inches diameter and 12 inches stroke; weight, 5,456 lbs.; 1 inch nozzle, horizontal distance, 196 feet; vertical height, 166 feet.

"Independence," built by Hunsworth, Eakins & Co., at People's Works, Philadelphia—steam cylinder, 10½ inches diameter and 14 inches stroke; pumps, 5½ inches diameter and 14 inches stroke; nozzle, 1¼ inch, horizontal distance, 193 feet; vertical height, 143 feet.

"Washington," built by Poole & Hunt, Baltimore—steam cylinder, 12½ inches diameter and 12 inches stroke; pump, 6⅜ inches diameter and 12 inches stroke; weight, 3,582 lbs; nozzle, 1¼ inches, horizontal distance, 239 feet; vertical height, 178 feet.

"Mechanic," built by Reaney & Neapie, of Philadelphia—steam cylinder, 8 inches diameter and 12 inches stroke; pump 4⅝ inches diameter and 16 inches stroke; weight, 5,760 lbs.; nozzle 1 inch, horizontal distance, 203 feet; vertical height, 167 feet.

"Hibernia," built by Reaney & Neapie, Philadelphia—steam cylinder 1¼ inches diameter and 14 inches stroke; pump, 6½ inches diameter and 14 inches stroke; weight, 8,000 lbs.; nozzle, ¹⁵⁄₁₆ inches; horizontal distance, 254 feet; vertical height, 181 feet.

"Southwark," built by Lee & Larned, New York—steam cylinder. A self-propelling engine; 2 steam cylinders, each 7½ inches diameter and 14 inches stroke; one rotary pump, 17 inches diameter and 10 inches wide; weight, 9,000 lbs.

"Citizen," of Harrisburg (first-class) fully manned, using 10 feet of hose and a nozzle 1 inch in diameter, worked for 2 minutes, reached a horizontal distance of 196 feet.

"Assistance," of Philadelphia (first class), length of hose and diameter of nozzle the same, reached a horizontal distance of 182 feet, 4½ inches.

"Washington" (second class) 50 feet of hose and a ⅞ inch nozzle, reached a horizontal distance of 154 feet.

"Philadelphia" (second class) under the same circumstances, reached a horizontal distance of 188 feet, 3 inches.

"Weccacoe" (second class) as above, a horizontal distance of 154 feet.

"Globe" (second class) as above, a horizontal distance of 150 feet and 5 feet allowance.

"Franklin" (second class) of Frankford, as above, a horizontal distance of 158 feet and 5 feet allowance.

In 1860, Messrs. Ettinger & Edmond, of Richmond, Va., built a steam fire-engine for St. Petersburgh, the machine was placed low down on straight axles, and could not turn over whilst going around corners; complete, the weight was 5,000 pounds. It was the design of Mr. A. M'Causland. It threw a 1⅛ inch stream 220 feet, a 1½ inch stream 143 feet, and a 1⅞ inch stream 183 feet. At a trial in Philadelphia it threw a 1½ inch stream 250 feet. In the same year an engine built by Neapie & Levy, for San Francisco, with a cylinder 8 inches by

12 inches, and pump 4½ inches by 12 inches, threw a 1¼ inch stream at Philadelphia 253 feet horizontally.

In 1860, a small steam fire-engine or model, exhibited at the county fair, Rensselaer, Troy, weighing 2½ lbs., threw a stream about the size of a pin, to a distance of 4 feet 6 inches; the steam cylinder was horizontal, ½ inch diameter, and ¾ inch stroke. At the California State Fair, Henry Rice exhibited a model made by himself; the steam cylinder was ³⁄₁₆ inches diameter, with ⁷⁄₁₆ inch stroke, and ran at the rate of 2,000 revolutions per minute.

Pittsburgh, Pa., had an engine weighing between 4,000 and 5,000 lbs., on the model of the "Southwark," of Philadelphia, which raised steam in 6 minutes and threw a ¾ inch stream over a six-story building.

In September, 1860, the "Huron," a first class double cylinder engine with plunger pumps, at a competition in Troy, threw water in 7 minutes from the lighting of the fire, in 8 minutes reaching 100 feet, in 14 minutes 200 feet, and so on reached 223 feet 9 inches, pumping through 50 feet of 3 inch hose, and using 1⅜ inch nozzle. The "Michigonne," a first class double cylinder engine with rotary pump, played two powerful streams for 4 hours continuously through 1,600 feet of hose, to which two 150 feet lengths with a separate branch on each were attached, making 1,750 altogether, the engine being 75 feet lower than the branches.

In 1860, the "Arba Read" steam fire-engine, a first class single cylinder engine, with double acting plunger pump, threw a single stream through 450 feet of hose, and a 1¼ inch nozzle to a distance of 200 feet horizontally; a 1⅛ inch stream was thrown to a distance of 275 feet through 50 feet of hose. The highest steam pressure used was 240 lbs. on the square inch.

The "Fire-King," a first class double cylinder engine with plunger pumps, belonging to the Fire Department of Manchester, on one occasion reached a distance of 207 feet horizontally with a ⅞ inch jet; then it threw a stream 292 feet with a 1¼ inch nozzle. Another machine that attracted attention was the "J. C. Cary." Its cylinders were 7½ inches diameter with 14 inch stroke, driving a rotary pump. The boiler consisted of 114 pairs of double tubes, each 2½ inches diameter, containing one of 1½ inch diameter inside it, the annular space between the two being occupied by water, whilst the fire is circulated among the larger and within the smaller tubes. The engine weighed 5½ tons, and at a public trial threw 1,100 gallons of water per minute. The height attained with a 1⅝ inch nozzle was 267 feet horizontally; a 2 inch stream reached 232 feet; and a 2½ inch stream through an open butt 196 feet.

In 1862, Messrs. Lee & Larned, of New York, sent to the International Exhibition at London, one of their small sized rotary pump engines, called 5 horse-power, which elicited the greatest approbations from all the engineers who inspected it, both for its beautiful workmanship and satisfactory working. The engine itself, which had neither water tank nor coal bunkers, weighed 1 ton 12 cwt. The cylinder was 7 inches diameter with 8½ inch stroke, and had a pair of light balance wheels to carry it over the centres; the piston rod was 1¼ inch diameter, the crank shaft 1¾ inch bearing, the boiler 4 feet high by 26 inches, outside diameter at steam chest. The boiler had 125 feet of heating surface. A tender at will was attached behind to carry the hose, coals, etc. In the same year the firm built a steam fire-engine in England, weighing 3 tons 2½ cwts; carrying a moderate quantity of coal, several hundred feet of hose, a tool chest and six men.

Many of the engines now in use in this country have conical India rubber disc-valves, held in position by spiral springs, giving sufficient area of opening with very limited lift. Crane neck frames have superseded the straight or parallel, as they admit of the boiler and machinery being placed lower down the frame, and afford great facilities for turning around in narrow streets or contracted situations. The blower pipe, that was at one time so extensively used in the smoke stacks of fire-engines for the purpose of increasing the draught, is now nearly, if not entirely, superseded by the variable exhaust, and nearly if not all fire-engine houses have stationery steam boilers, generally located in the cellar, on which steam is kept up steadily for the purpose of keeping the water in the boiler hot. Steam can now be raised in from 10 to 12 minutes while running to a fire. Now the simplest kind of engine is considered the most durable and efficient. The vertical form of cylinder is held to be the best, as vertical pumps can be attached directly to the boiler, thereby making the working of the engine smoother in consequence of the weight being against the lift. Moreover loss is avoided by carrying steam from the boiler to the cylinder through pipes exposed to the atmosphere. The wear on the rubbing surfaces of vertical engines is also less than horizontal or inclined engines suffer.

The water pistons of steam fire-engines, like those of steam pumps, are almost exclusively made of leather, as that material possesses superior advantages over any other for that purpose, they are either made solid or in the shape of a disc. The difficulty which so materially interfered with the usefulness of the steam fire-engine for many years after its introduction, that of being manufactured at a distance from the place where it was used, is now successfully overcome by the establishment of machine shops in connection with nearly all the Fire Departments of the country, and repairs can be quickly made. Under the Paid Fire Department system all the worn out, complicated or inefficient engines were allowed to fall into disuse, or were sold to country towns and none were retained but those that had a good reputation for efficiency, durability and economy.

Steam engines should be so designed as to be capable of working at either slow or fast speed and to discharge an amount of water proportionate to the speed at which they are worked. The reason why, it has been said, the American system of quick running engines has given more satisfactory results than those of English make, has been that the proportion employed in this country approach very nearly to those used in locomotives, where the suction pipe into the pump is as large as the barrel of the pump itself. This has been considered a common sense proceeding because time, however short, is necessary to enable any operations to be carried out, more especially when its material to be worked on is water, and that as in the steam fire-engine, through all kinds of difficulties in the shape of friction, contracted and awkward passages, small holes or entrances into large spaces, etc. On comparison it has been noted that the engines by American makers have the best proportions: next to these the long-stroked, steady-running English engines; whilst the worst proportions of any are those of the quick-running engines where the direction of motion is changed oftenest in the shortest times, and the area of suction opening is least when compared with the area of pump piston, so that the largest space has to be filled through the smallest hole, and that, too, in the smallest amount of time, the stroke being so short and the direction of motion so rapidly changed in the short period during which the piston moves in any given direction.

The Ahrens' engine is upright and double acting; the steam cylinder resting on columns which are attached to the frame and to the boiler, and forms supports for the crank-shaft bearing. The air-pump is a new and important feature, and is used for keeping the air vessels constantly supplied with air which has the effect of rendering the hose quite steady when the engine is working. These engines are in very general use in the western states.

The Clapp & Jones engine has a vertical boiler with fire and water tubes. The fire tubes extend from the crown sheet of the fire up through the top of the shell. The safety and throttle valves are combined in one piece. The draught can be so regulated by means of variable exhaust nozzles as to maintain a uniform pressure in the boiler. The engines are horizontal, and are known as "piston" engines, and the pumps are double acting. The suction hose is always attached and ready for use. Steam can be raised from cold water in from four to six minutes from the time of lighting the fire.

The Silsby Rotary Engine has a vertical boiler with water tubes passing directly through the fire, which are closed at the bottom, and often at the top, where they pass through a watertight plate and communicate with the water in the boiler. Steam can be generated in from four to six minutes. Salt or sea water can be used without inconvenience. There is an attachment to the boilers by which a portion of the exhaust steam may be turned into the supply tank, for the purpose of heating the water, thus, it is claimed, effecting a great saving in fuel, and relieving the boiler of the evils resulting from unequal expansion and contraction induced by cold feed-water.

The Amoskeag engines are vertical, with steam cylinder and pumps attached to an upright tubular boiler, with inverted smokebox. The pumps are double acting, with receiving screws on each side, and are surrounded by a circular chamber which forms the suction and discharge openings. The discharge and suction chambers of the pumps are connected by a relief valve. The engines are built either single or double self-propelling, or to be drawn by horses, with either straight or crane-neck frames. They can be turned with great ease, within very narrow limits, by means of a set of compound gearing so arranged on the axle that in turning the engine, the two rear wheels are driven at varying speeds.

In General Orders of the New York Fire Department, instructions have been given for the benefit of engineers who have not had much experience in running engines. They are purely technical, and therefore of interest only to professional men. The following are the supplies with which every engine in the Department is furnished:

Twenty feet of suction hose, a suitable brass strained for suction hose, a brass hydrant connection for suction hose, a brass signal whistle, two plated gauges, one to indicate the pressure of water upon the boiler, and the other the pressure of water at the pumps or leading hose, two discharge pipes for leading hose, with a complete set of changeable nozzles from 7½ inch diameter to 1¼ inch diameter inclusive, two brass-bound fireman's hand lanterns, a large brass oil can, a jack-screw for convenience in oiling the axles, an oval shovel and fire poker. A small tool box furnished with such small tools as may be required about the engine in use, such as hammers, wrenches, and the like.

Dimensions of a second-class, double plunge engine, crane-neck frame: Height from floor to top of smokestack, 8 feet 8 inches; length over all, including tongue, 23 feet 2 inches; diameter of boiler, 2 feet 7 inches; diameter of pumps, 4½ inches; stroke of pump, 8 inches; diameter of steam cylinders, 6⅞ inches; number of discharge gates, 2; capacity in gallons per minute, 700; weight, about 5,400 lbs. Second-class double pump crane-neck engine: Diameter of grate surface, 32 inches; size of door, 8 by 12 inches; number of tubes, 258; diameter of tubes (internal), 1⅛ inch; bottom of boiler to bottom of pressure pipe, 20 inches; bottom of pressure pipe to first gauge cock, 12 inches; distance between gauge cocks, 5 inches; number of gallons to third gauge cock, 40 cubic feet; steam room, 3 feet.

A FIREMAN'S LIFE

An engine house now is a very quiet place, except just when an alarm is received and when the company has returned from a fire. When everything has been made clean and trim, the firemen sit around the station house quietly reading, smoking, or chatting. At night the place is still more tranquil. Arranged at equal distances along the sides of a narrow dormitory up-stairs, are ten or a dozen cribs. It is midnight and the cribs are occupied. At the side of each bed is placed a pair of high boots, into which a pair of trousers have been carefully tucked. Everything is in apple-pie order, and the boots and trousers have evidently been arranged with an eye to an emergency.

Below on the ground floor stands a large fire-engine of modern pattern, multiplying the surrounding objects upon its shiny surface. The wheels are painted vermilion, and the paint is without flaw. Every part susceptible of polish is polished. Indeed, the whole thing looks highly ornamental, and the spectator feels that it would be a pity to soil it by a drop of water. When it returns from a fire it is less gay. The furnace is filled with fuel, and a brand soaked in petroleum is ready for lighting; but the steam is already up to a pressure of five pounds, as the tremulous little gauge shows the necessary heat passing into the boiler through a pipe from a stationary furnace in the cellar of the building. The hose carriage, or tender, occupies a place behind the engine, and farther in the rear are three stalls in possession of three fine, large, glossy horses, whose pet names are inscribed in gilt letters over the manger, and whose sleek condition betokens unusual care.

Suddenly the electric current causes a bell to sound, the measured strokes being given in quick and startling succession. The men spring from their beds simultaneously, as if they had been lying awake waiting for this summons. Ten or twelve pairs of legs are at one and the same time thrust into the trousers and boots, and are pulled on with two hitches. The trousers close upon the hips, so that no time is lost with suspenders or belts. There is a terrific racket below. The bell is still sounding, repeating the signal five times over. Down a brass rod in one corner of the room slide the firemen in rapid succession. On the ground floor they find the horses already hitched to the engine, the driver on the box, and the furnace lighted. Each man jumps to his place on the tender, the doors are flung open, and in one minute from the first sound of the alarm the company is on its way to the fire. In fact, it is not unusual for an engine to be out of the house and on its way to a fire within forty seconds of the moment when the bell first strikes. During the first visit of the Grand Duke Alexis to New York, an alarm of fire was sounded at the Clarendon Hotel, in Fourth Avenue near Seventeenth Street, and a stream of water was turned upon the building by an engine within two minutes and thirty-five seconds, the engine having been manned and brought four blocks in the meantime.

The location of the fire is known instantly. Behind the captain's desk is a placard exhibiting the number of every alarm box in town, with the spot where it is placed. While the men are getting ready, the captain glances at the card, and the moment the last stroke of the bell is heard, shouts to the driver the location of the fire. The wild gallops through the streets, the vehement blazing of the furnace, the bright line of sparks following in its wake, the shouts of the spectators, the scurrying of vehicles out of the way, all produce a thrilling effect, even upon the men who have had years of experience. Although an alarm of fire may prove not to have resulted in a dollar's worth of damage, yet the same zeal and celerity are shown as if millions were known to be involved. When the men return to the station, no matter how tired they may be, the engine is restored to its original brilliancy, the horses are groomed, the harness is washed with castile soap, the hose is readjusted on the tender, and soon the company is prepared for another alarm.

Each man has his own place on the tender, where he leaves his hat and coat, donning these articles on the way to the fire. The horses are almost as well trained and as zealous as the men. The moment the alarm sounds they spring out of their stalls and put themselves into the shafts without a word of direction. Up to that moment they have been haltered, but the stroke of the bell releases them by an automatic arrangement of weights, pulleys and shafts. So, too, the pipes connecting the boiler of the engine with a boiler in the cellar of the building, and thus maintaining several pounds of steam in the former, though its furnace is not lighted, are automatic. As the engine leaves the station for a fire, the pipes close themselves, and do not require a moment's attention from the engineer, who has simply to leap with his assistant, on to the platform, and to hold on for dear life. The driver secures himself on the box by straps, without which he could not keep his seat. Alarm or no alarm, the men are always ready and in habitual suspense. The constant watching and waiting take the edge off their capacity for surprise. They are mechanically responsive to the stroke as the weight which releases the halters of the horses. No matter in which quarter of the city a fire is, the alarm is sent to every station house, and at the first stroke of the bell every company is required to prepare for action. The completion of the signal may show that only about one-tenth of the companies in the city are required, but the rest are ready to dash out of the station while the gong is still hammering and vibrating the last note of the signal.

It is because the horses see so little of outdoor life that they display so much activity when an alarm is sounded, and put all their strength into their gait. A foreman of a company was once asked why it was necessary to halter them at all when they were so intelligent in the performance of their duties. "Bless you," he answered, "they'd play tricks on us if we didn't tie 'em up. There's a fellow," he added, pointing to a powerful gray in superb condition that snapped at a visitor who attempted to rub its nose, "that has been steadily at work in the department for over eleven years; knows his business like a man, that horse does; but he's up to many a little game, and would raise brimstone if he'd the chance."

The sitting rooms of the stations are comfortably furnished, decorated with portraits of the past and present worthies of the Department, and supplied with books, dominoes, cards, chess, and other games. In the old days of the volunteers the presence of cards and dominoes would have subjected the owners thereof to fines. The playing of any games of chance would have been considered a dire offense. The following extract from the minutes of Hose Company No. 36 will show how great the difference is between the old and the new Departments on this subject:

November 5, 1851.—*Resolved*, That any member of this company found playing cards or any game of hazard in the house, for the first offense shall be fined one dollar, and for the second offense he shall be expelled from the company, and if not a member of the company, he shall be refused admittance in the house for the future.

Of course, this is not desirable now, as the conditions of the men are changed, and our firemen must have some relaxation, and very little time they get for it. Now, as in olden times, the discussion of politics and the use of profanity are strictly forbidden. "Gentlemen," said a prominent official, once addressing some new appointees, "you have been chosen from among eight hundred applicants, and I expect you all to be sober, industrious, and honest; and I also expect that you will obey all orders with alacrity and willingness. Avoid all discussions with your fellow laborers, and do all your work without grumbling. Politics and religion are subjects which I positively forbid being discussed. Ignore them absolutely. Vote for whom you please, go to any church you choose, but you must not engage in electioneering. Should you become involved in a misunderstanding with a fellow member of the department, come to me and I will arbitrate your difference at once. Be sober, for if you are drunk your brains are out, and you are no longer fit for duty. Drunkenness will certainly not be tolerated. In your whole deportment show yourselves to be gentlemen. I consider you such, and there is no reason why you should not act as gentlemen at all times. Profanity is uncalled for. It is a vile habit, and one which I have always got along without. I never practice it, and hope that you will follow my example. Be polite; and now report at your posts."

The life of a fireman, now as ever, is as adventurous as that of a soldier; nay, it is not too much to say that the former runs far more risk than the latter. The fireman is on duty night and day, facing the enemy that never runs away, but stays to conquer or be conquered. When the alarm rings in the station house no man knows but that it may be the summons to his death. The vehicle that whirls to a fire may be swiftly conveying him to an agonizing end. But of this he never stops to think. The greater the peril the more eager is he to face it. Many and many a time have those soldiers of fire placed themselves in imminent danger and been warned by onlookers to retire. But again and again have these warnings been reiterated ere these gallant men thought of flinching from their posts while a chance remained to check, even in the slightest degree, the ravages of the flames. They mount to the loftiest buildings, from every window of which streams of fire are pouring. Down into suffocating cellars they will go with their hose, while, mayhaps, rivers of molten lead, or avalanches of burning timber are falling around them. Underneath façades swaying to and fro, or tottering walls, half-blinded with smoke, they will toil and toil, while spectators are fearing that every moment will be their last. Into the very jaws of death—a room aflame or filled with volumes of suffocating smoke—they will unhesitatingly rush to rescue women and children.

Acts of heroism, materials for the pages of thrilling romances, are plentiful in the records of the Department. We could fill a volume larger than this with the details of such daring deeds. We can give only a few:

Ten or a dozen years ago, during a fire in Trinity Building on Broadway, a heavy beam fell from the roof on eight firemen in such a way that it prostrated them without crushing them. The wood was on fire from end to end, and did not leave them space to rise in. They lay close to the floor which was smoking and covered with sparks, and the beam continued to burn over them within a few feet of their heads, threatening to roast them to death. One of the pipes had been buried with them, and when they discovered it they turned it against the flames. Steaming to death now threatened them, as the water vaporized in the heat, and filled their crib with scalding white clouds. But the circumstance saved them, by enabling them to abate the fire below until their comrades outside had lifted the beam from over them.

Another building on Broadway was burning in 1877. It was agreed between three hose men, who were stationed on the roof, and one of the officers stationed below, that as soon as the fall of the roof appeared imminent to him he should call to them, and they should leap to the next building, over an intervening alley five or six feet wide. In the meantime they did not distress themselves, but worked steadily with their streams, which were poured down the scuttles. The hiss and lapping of the flames, the fierce pulsations of the engines, the trumpeted orders of the chiefs, and the crash of falling iron and timber were so loud and confusing that a voice might have easily been lost in them. Notwithstanding this fact, the men held to their insecure ground until a gentle rattling indicated that the roof was about to collapse, and they heard the officer below cry, "Leap!" It was a fearful moment. There were hundreds of people watching them. Every spectator held his breath. Then, almost simultaneously, the bold hose men sprang from one parapet to another, and they had barely done so when a dense volume of smoke and sparks shot into the air, and a pit of flame remained where the men had stood before. The pent-up feelings of the crowd were let loose, and a roaring cheer drowned the roaring of the fire and the loud laboring of the engines.

There are many, too many, sad episodes, also to record. A man has been killed by being knocked from a ladder by a misdirected stream of water, or wandering over the roofs of houses, falls down an open scuttle, and is either crippled for life or killed. He runs the risk of his engine or truck colliding with a vehicle, with all the dreadful consequences, and there are a thousand and one other accidents to which he is liable in the service of his calling. Some of these we record in other chapters. The chapter devoted to the Roll of Merit will give an idea of the heroism and dangers of a fireman's life.

There is likewise to be enumerated among the risks run by firemen the probability of coming in contact with contagious diseases. Here is an amusing story from the old Department: "In 1857 a fire occurred in a humble tenement in Baxter Street. Several of the inmates were sick and unable to escape. The men of Hose Company No. 14 dashed in among the flames to the rescue. The last man was carried out by James R. Mount, Cooley, Lyons, and Evans, of No. 14. They were conveying the patient still farther up the street out of the way of the engines, when a woman rushed up and cried, "Thank God, he is saved! But oh! my husband will die, for he has the smallpox bad!" As if their burden was red-hot iron, the affrighted firemen dropped it, and started back aghast. There was a place called Begg's saloon, at No. 71 Mulberry Street, and the firemen made a rush for this to disinfect themselves with as much whiskey as they could carry. They did not care for the fire and the crumbling building, but the smallpox—oh! That was worse than death.

HOW TO BECOME A FIREMAN.

To become a fireman a person must be twenty-one years of age and of good moral character. He goes first to the secretary, and procures from him a blank, which he fills out, and gets four reliable men to sign, certifying that they have known him never to have been indicted or convicted of any crime; that they have known him for a certain number of years. The candidate then returns it to the secretary. He is then sent before the Medical Board and examined as to his physical condition. He is measured, weighed, and the circumference of his chest taken, which must come within the following:

Minimum circumference of chest tolerable in applicants.

STATURE AND WEIGHT.—The stature shall not be below 5 feet 7 inches, nor the weight below that marked as its minimum accompaniment in the subjoined table:

HEIGHT.		CIRCUMFERENCE OF CHEST.	HEIGHT.		MINIMUM WEIGHT.
Feet.	Inches.	Inches.	Feet.	Inches.	Pounds.
5	7	33	5	7	140
5	8	34	5	8	145

HEIGHT.		CIRCUMFERENCE OF CHEST.	HEIGHT.		MINIMUM WEIGHT.
Feet.	Inches.	Inches.	Feet.	Inches.	Pounds.
5	9	34½	5	9	150
5	10	35	5	10	155
5	11	35½	5	11	160
6	—	36	6	—	165
6	1	36½	6	1	170
6	2	37	6	2	175
6	3	37½	6	3	180
6	4	38	6	4	185

He must state whether he is subject to fits, piles, and whether his father or mother are dead? If either or both, what they died of? Whether he has any brothers or sisters dead? What they died of? If this examination is satisfactory, he goes to the gymnasium and his powers of endurance are tested. From there he goes before the Board of Civil Service Examiners. He must have a fair knowledge of the three R's. In the meantime his application has been sent to the Chief of Battalion in whose district he lives, who investigates what he has sworn to in the application. His references are seen and examined. If this is all right, the chief returns it with his approval, presuming that he has passed all the examinations. He is appointed for fifteen days on probation, without pay. Then comes the course of instruction. He reports at the foot of West One Hundred and Fifty-eighth Street every morning at ten o'clock (Sundays and legal holidays excepted); here he is instructed in the use of all the ladders and implements of the life-saving corps. He is taught to hold a pipe, and in fact, everything pertaining to a fireman's career. In the afternoon he goes to the headquarters in Sixty-seventh Street, near Third Avenue. Here a verbal course of instruction is given; when this is over, he is assigned to an engine or truck company, where he sleeps and answers all alarms, and does duty as a fireman. This is the routine which a candidate follows day after day, until his half month of probation has ended. If his company and Batallion commanders report favorably on him, he is appointed, and receives one thousand dollars for the first year, one thousand one hundred dollars for the second, and then becomes a fireman of the first grade with a salary of one thousand two hundred dollars.

THE LIFE SAVING CORPS.

General orders No. 4; issued on June 7, 1888. *Resolved*,
    I. The establishment of a school of instruction, and the rules governing it, are hereby announced to the Department.

II. Second Assistant Chief of Department Bonner is designated as instructor of the school, with power to select two assistants from the uniformed force, to be detailed at his request by the Chief of Department.

III. Until further orders the school will he located in the quarters of Engine Company No. 47, the third floor of which will be suitably arranged and fitted up with all the necessary appliances for the purpose.

IV. The school will be divided into two classes: The first, or "Life Saving Corps," will be devoted to instruction and training in handling and using scaling and ordinary ladders, life lines, etc., and all other life saving appliances now in use or hereafter introduced. The second class to be devoted to general instruction in the practical duties of a fireman in quarters and at fires, and particularly in the handling, care, and use of all implements, tools, etc., employed in extinguishing fires.

V. After passing a satisfactory examination by the medical officer, a candidate applying for appointment to the uniformed force, and volunteering to go to the school of instruction for a term of ten days, on probation and without pay, shall, if appointment is contemplated, be referred to the instructor, by endorsement on his application for appointment, on the direction of either of the commissioners, to determine his qualifications under a course of training in the first class. At the expiration of the term of probation the instructor shall return the application, with his report endorsed thereon, stating the candidate's qualifications. Inability to learn the proper handling of the life saving implements, or indifference to the instruction given, shall be regarded as disqualifying the candidate for membership; and if the instructor shall report a candidate incompetent, from any cause, to become proficient in the first class, he shall be ineligible for appointment. If a candidate is reported suitable and able to become proficient in the first class, and is appointed, he shall at once be assigned to a company, in which he shall perform duty at night, and at other times when his presence is not required in the school of instruction, to which he shall be ordered by the company commander to complete the course of instruction and training, reporting for that purpose to the instructor at the foot of West One Hundred and Fifty-eighth Street, at 10 A.M., on the day after his appointment takes effect, Sundays and legal holidays excepted, and thereafter at such times and places as the instructor may direct. At the close of the training and instruction, the instructor shall return the copy of the order of appointment (transmitted to him at the time of his appointment), with his report endorsed therein, in which shall be stated the degree of proficiency attained, and the branch of the service for which the appointee is best qualified.

VI. Members of the uniformed force volunteering for instruction in the first class, shall be ordered by the Chief of Department to report to the instructor at 10 A.M. on the day after the receipt by him of their application, Sundays and holidays excepted, at the foot of West One Hundred and Fifty-eighth Street, and upon the completion, of the course of instruction, he shall be reported by the instructor as to the degree of proficiency attained.

VII. The instructor shall keep a book of the name, age, height, weight, address or company number, date of entry, and degree of proficiency.

VIII. Each Hook and Ladder Company in the Department shall carry three ladders, three belts, three life lines, and all life saving appliances as may be found necessary.